WEST MIDLAND NETWORK

SHOWING LOCALITIES RECORDED BY EACH FIELDWORKER

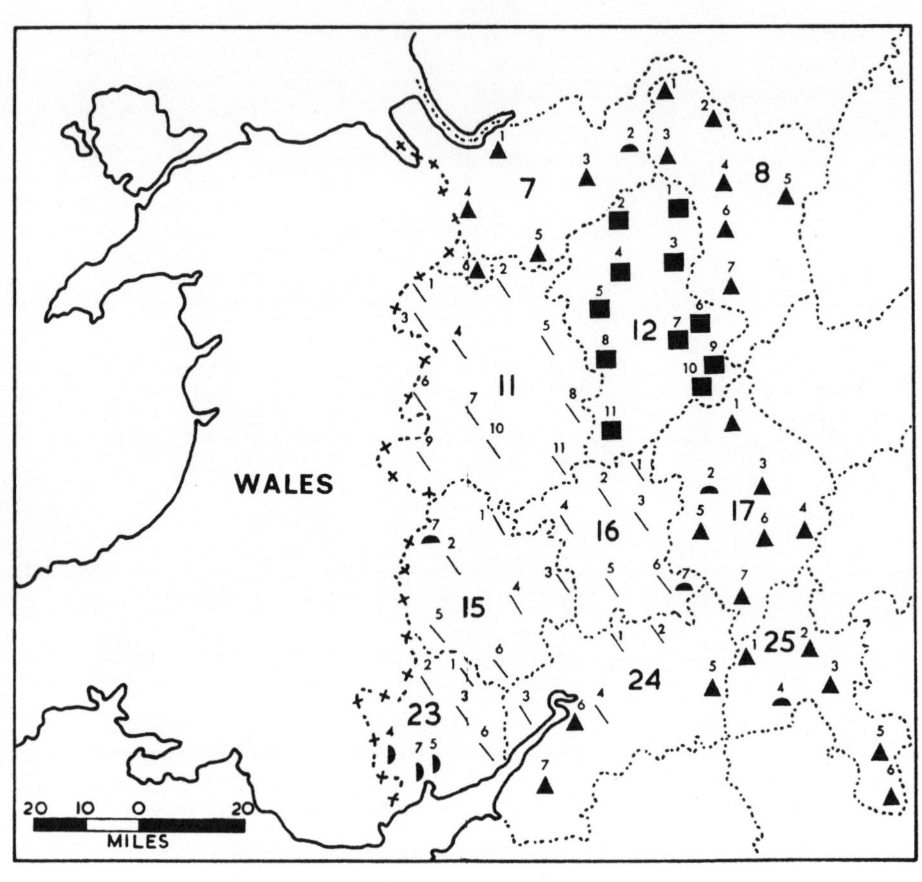

▲ Stanley Ellis ■ Peter H. Gibson ◗ David R. Parry
╲ Donald R. Sykes ◓ Peter Wright

List of Localities in the West Midland Network

The localities are listed below county by county, working in general from north to south, and concurrently from west to east. An attached superior [r] means that at least one informant in the locality concerned was tape-recorded either during the field investigations or subsequently.

7 Ch

1 Kingsley[r]
2 Rainow[r]
3 Swettenham[r]
4 Farndon[r]
5 Audlem[r]
6 Hanmer[r] (Flintshire)

8 Db

1 Charlesworth[r]
2 Bamford[r]
3 Burbage[r]
4 Youlgreave[r]
5 Stonebroom[r]
6 Kniveton[r]
7 Sutton-on-the-Hill[r]

11 Sa

1 Weston Rhyn[r]
2 Prees[r]
3 Llanymynech[r]
4 Montford[r]
5 Kinnersley[r]
6 Chirbury[r]
7 All Stretton[r]
8 Hilton[r]
9 Clun[r]
10 Diddlebury[r]
11 Kinlet[r]

12 St

1 Warslow[r]
2 Mow Cop[r]
3 Alton[r]
4 Barlaston[r]
5 Ellenhall[r]
6 Hoar Cross[r]
7 Mavesyn Ridware[r]
8 Lapley[r]
9 Edingale[r]
10 Wigginton[r]
11 Himley[r]

15 He

1 Brimfield[r]
2 Weobley[r]
3 Cradley[r]
4 Checkley[r]
5 Longtown[r]
6 Whitchurch[r]
7 Lyonshall[r]

16 Wo

1 Romsley[r]
2 Hartlebury[r]
3 Hanbury[r]
4 Clifton-on-Teme[r]
5 Earls Croome[r]
6 Offenham[r]
7 Bretforton[r]

17 Wa

1 Nether Whitacre[r]
2 Hockley Heath[r]
3 Stoneleigh[r]
4 Napton-on-the-Hill[r]
5 Aston Cantlow[r]
6 Lighthorne[r]
7 Shipston-on-Stour[r]

23 Mon

1 Skenfrith[r]
2 Llanellen[r]
3 Raglan[r]
4 Cross Keys[r]
5 Llanfrechfa[r]
6 Shirenewton[r]
7 Newport

24 Gl

1 Deerhurst[r]
2 Gretton[r]
3 Bream[r]
4 Whiteshill[r]
5 Sherborne[r]
6 Slimbridge[r]
7 Latteridge[r]

25 O

1 Kingham[r]
2 Steeple Aston[r]
3 Islip[r]
4 Eynsham[r]
5 Cuxham[r]
6 Binfield Heath[r]

SURVEY OF ENGLISH DIALECTS

(B)

THE BASIC MATERIAL

SURVEY OF ENGLISH DIALECTS

by

HAROLD ORTON

Emeritus Professor in the University of Leeds

and

EUGEN DIETH

(1893–1956)

Sometime Professor of English Language
University of Zürich

SURVEY OF ENGLISH DIALECTS

(B)

THE BASIC MATERIAL

Volume II

THE WEST MIDLAND COUNTIES

edited by

HAROLD ORTON
and
MICHAEL V. BARRY
Lecturer in English, The Queen's University of Belfast
Formerly Assistant Editor of the *Survey of English Dialects*

With the assistance of Mary Lee Al-Azzawi

Part III

London and New York

First published 1971
by E J Arnold & Son Limited

Reprinted 1998
by Routledge
11 New Fetter Lane, London EC4P 4EE

Simultaneously published in the USA and Canada
by Routledge
29 West 35th Street, New York NY 10001

Printed and Bound in Great Britain by
Antony Rowe Ltd., Chippenham, Wiltshire

Publisher's Note

This reprint is taken from an original copy of the book. In many cases the quality of such originals is not perfect, the paper, often handmade, having suffered over time, and the copy from such things as inconsistent printing pressures resulting in faint text, show-through from one side of a leaf to the other, the filling in of some characters, and the break-up of type. The publisher has gone to great lengths to ensure the quality of this reprint, but wishes to point out that certain characteristics of the original copies will, of necessity, be apparent in reprints thereof.

British Library Cataloguing in Publication Data

A catalogue record of this book is available from the British Library

Library of Congress Cataloguing in Publication Data

A catalogue record for this book has been requested

Survey of English Dialects
ISBN 0-415-18514-9
13 Volumes: 0-415-18178-X

FIELDWORKERS

Donald R. Sykes
Stanley Ellis
Peter H. Gibson
Peter Wright
David R. Parry

TABLE OF CONTENTS

PREFACE

This book, the third and final Part of *Volume II* (West Midland Counties) of the *Survey of English Dialects*, contains the informants' responses to Books VII, VIII and IX of the Dieth–Orton *Questionnaire*, together with the relevant incidental and illustrative material from the fieldworkers' recording-books for the West Midland network. The fieldwork was carried out by Mr. Donald R. Sykes, Mr. Stanley Ellis, Mr. Peter H. Gibson, Dr. Peter Wright and Mr. David R. Parry, as explained in the Introduction to *Part I*.

We gratefully acknowledge our indebtedness to our Research Assistants. Mrs. F. H. Al-Azzawi, B.A. (Wayne State University, Detroit, U.S.A.) gave us invaluable aid throughout the whole of the editorial work. Miss H. P. Duncan and Mr. K. R. Lodge both prepared the early drafts of many articles. But the editors themselves are entirely responsible for all of them.

The phonetic transcriptions in the articles were verified from the recording-books by Mrs. Al-Azzawi, Miss Duncan, Mr. Lodge and Mr. Graham Nixon.

The erroneous positions of the symbols for localities 23.5 Mon. Llanfrechna and 23.7 Mon. Newport on the Map of the West Midland Network have now been corrected on the map in this book.

Our printers have again excelled in their handling of such complicated material.

This book could not have appeared but for the considerable financial backing of the University of Leeds, and the substantial grants in aid from the British Academy and The Hamlyn Trust.

H. O.
M. V. B.

Institute of Dialect and Folklife Studies,
University of Leeds.

THE INTERNATIONAL PHONETIC ALPHABET.

(Revised to 1951.)

		Bi-labial	Labio-dental	Dental and Alveolar	Retroflex	Palato-alveolar	Alveolo-palatal	Palatal	Velar	Uvular	Pharyngal	Glottal
CONSONANTS	Plosive	p b		t d	ʈ ɖ			c ɟ	k g	q ɢ		ʔ
	Nasal	m	ɱ	n	ɳ			ɲ	ŋ	ɴ		
	Lateral Fricative			ɬ ɮ								
	Lateral Non-fricative			l	ɭ			ʎ				
	Rolled			r						ʀ		
	Flapped			ɾ	ɽ					ʀ		
	Fricative	ɸ β	f v	θ ð | s z | ɹ	ʂ ʐ	ʃ ʒ	ɕ ʑ	ç j	x ɣ	χ ʁ	ħ ʕ	h ɦ
	Frictionless Continuants and Semi-vowels	w | ɥ	ʋ	ɹ				j (ɥ)	(w)	ʁ		
VOWELS								Front	Central Back			
	Close	(y ʉ u)						i y	ɨ ʉ ɯ u			
	Half-close	(ø o)						e ø	ɤ o			
									ə			
	Half-open	(œ ɔ)						ɛ œ	ʌ ɔ			
								æ	ɐ			
	Open	(ɒ)						a	ɑ ɒ			

(Secondary articulations are shown by symbols in brackets.)

OTHER SOUNDS.—Palatalized consonants: ƫ, ȡ, etc.; palatalized ʃ, ʒ: ʆ, ʓ. Velarized or pharyngalized consonants: ɫ, ᵭ, ᵶ, etc. Ejective consonants (with simultaneous glottal stop): p', t', etc. Implosive voiced consonants: ɓ, ɗ, etc. ɼ fricative trill. σ, ϱ (labialized θ, ð, or s, z). ʅ, ʓ (labialized ʃ, ʒ). ʇ, ʗ, ʖ (clicks, Zulu *c*, *q*, *x*). ɺ (a sound between r and l). ŋ Japanese syllabic nasal. ɧ (combination of x and ʃ). ʍ (voiceless w). ɪ, ʏ, ɷ (lowered varieties of i, y, u). ɜ (a variety of ə). ɵ (a vowel between ø and o).

Affricates are normally represented by groups of two consonants (ts, tʃ, dʒ, etc.), but, when necessary, ligatures are used (ʦ, ʧ, ʤ, etc.), or the marks ͡ or ‿ (t͡s or t‿s, etc.). ͡ ‿ also denote synchronic articulation (m͡ŋ = simultaneous m and ŋ). c, ɟ may occasionally be used in place of tʃ, dʒ, and ʆ, ʓ for ts, dz. Aspirated plosives: ph, th, etc. r-coloured vowels: eɹ, aɹ, ɔɹ, etc., or eʴ, aʴ, ɔʴ, etc., or ɝ, a˞, ɔ˞, etc.; r-coloured ə: əɹ or əʴ or ɹ or ə˞ or ɚ.

LENGTH, STRESS, PITCH.—ː (full length). ˑ (half length). ˈ (stress, placed at beginning of the stressed syllable). ˌ (secondary stress). ¯ (high level pitch); _ (low level); ˊ (high rising); ˏ (low rising); ˋ (high falling); ˎ (low falling); ˆ (rise-fall); ˇ (fall-rise).

MODIFIERS.—˜ nasality. ˳ breath (l̥ = breathed l). ˬ voice (s̬ = z). ʻ slight aspiration following p, t, etc. ̫ labialization (n̫ = labialized n). ̪ dental articulation (t̪ = dental t). ˙ palatalization (ż = ʑ). ̣ specially close vowel (ẹ = a very close e). ̨ specially open vowel (ę = a rather open e). ˔ tongue raised (e˔ or e̝ = ẹ). ˕ tongue lowered (e˕ or e̞ = ę). ˖ tongue advanced (u˖ or u̟ = an advanced u, t̟ = ƫ). ˗ or ˍ tongue retracted (i˗ or i̠ = ɨ˖, t̠ = alveolar t). ˒ lips more rounded. ˓ lips more spread. Central vowels: ï (= ɨ), ü (= ʉ), ë (= ə˔), ö (= ɵ), ɛ̈, ɔ̈. ˌ (e.g. n̩) syllabic consonant. ˘ consonantal vowel. ʃˢ variety of ʃ resembling s, etc.

NOTES ON THE PHONETIC TRANSCRIPTION

The phonetic alphabet used here, and reproduced above, is that approved by the International Phonetic Association in the form revised in 1951. Consistent use has been made of the special symbols (ɩ) and (ɷ), with appropriate modifications to symbolise particular articulations. The plus sign is placed above, and the minus sign below, a vowel symbol to indicate an articulation with respectively an advanced, or a retracted, tongue position. The symbol ¨ has been placed over a vowel to show a greater degree of centralisation. R-colouring of vowels is shown by the appropriate kinds of superior *r* placed to the right of the vowel symbol concerned. A small unfilled superior circle similarly placed denotes that the plosive in question is unexploded.

ABBREVIATIONS

acc.	according to
adj.	adjective
ad loc.	*ad locum* at the place
adv.	adverb(ial)
app.	apparently
approx.	approximately
art.	article
attrib.	attributive
aux.	auxiliary
B.M.	Basic Material
C.	consonant
cf.	*confer* compare
Ch	Cheshire
coll.	collective
conj.	conjunction
cons.	consonant
cont.	continued
cpd.	compound
Db	Derbyshire
def.	definite
dial.	dialectal
distr.	district
D. R. P.	David R. Parry
D. R. S.	Donald R. Sykes
E.	east
Edd.	Editors
EDD	*English Dialect Dictionary*[1]
e.g.	*exempli gratia* for example
el(s).	element(s)
emph.	emphatic
ex(s).	example(s)
exc.	except for
f.n(s).	field-name(s)
foll.	followed, following
fr.	from
freq.	frequently
ft.	feet, foot
f.w(s).	fieldworker(s)
g.	gesticulate
Gl	Gloucestershire
He	Herefordshire
H. O.	Harold Orton
i.	indicate, imitate
i(i).	informant(s)
i.e.	*id est* that is
i.l.	indicate left
i.m.	incidental material
imp.	imperative
in(s).	inch(es)
indef.	indefinite
inf(s).	infinitive(s)
interrog.	interrogative(ly)
intr.	intransitive(ly)
i.r.	indicate right
ir.r(r).	irrelevant response(s)
l.	left
loc(s).	local(ly), locality, -ties
Mon	Monmouthshire
M. V. B.	Michael V. Barry
N.	north
n(n).	noun(s)
n.a.	not asked
n.d.	not defined semantically
n.d.g.	not defined grammatically
neg.	negative
n.f.	not found
n.k.	not known
no.	number
nom.	nominative
nr.	near
n.r.	not recorded
num.	numeral
O	Oxfordshire
OED	*Oxford English Dictionary*
obj(s).	object(s)
obs.	obsolete
obsc.	obscure
obsol.	obsolescent
occ.	occasional(ly)
p.	point to, pressure
p(p).	page(s)
pers. n.	personal name
P. H. G.	Peter H. Gibson
pl.	plural
pl. n(s).	place-name(s)
pos.	positive
poss.	possessive
pp.	strong pressure[2]
p.p. (adj.)	past participle (adjective)
p.pp.	past participles
prec.	preceded, precedes, preceding
pred.	predicative
pref.	preferred
prep.	preposition
pres.	presumably
prob.	probably
pron.	pronoun, pronunciation
pr.p(p).	present participle(s)
pr.pl.	present plural indicative
pr.s(s).	present singular(s) indicative
pr.sg.	present singular indicative
pr. t(t)	present tense(s)
p.t(t).	past tense(s)

1 *The English Dialect Dictionary*, ed. Joseph Wright, Vols. I–VI. Oxford. 1898–1905.

2 If preceding a response; see *Introduction*. p. 25.

p.t.(pl).	past tense (plural)
p.t.s(s).	past tense singular(s)
P. W.	Peter Wright
Q., Qn., q(q.)	question(s)
Qr.	*Questionnaire*[1]
q.v.	*quod vide* which see
r(r).	response(s)
r.b(b).	recording-book(s)
rec(s).	record(s), recorded, recording(s)
ref(s).	reference(s), with ref. to, referring (to)
refl.	reflexive(ly)
rel.	relative
resp.	respectively
rev.	reverse question
S.	south
Sa	Shropshire
S. E.	Stanley Ellis
s.f.	suggested form[2]
sg(s).	singular(s)
St	Staffordshire
St. E.	Standard English
str.	stressed
subj.	subject
s.v.	*sub verbo* under the word
s.w.	suggested word[2]
syll.	syllable, syllabic
trans.	transitive
unstr.	unstressed
u.r(r).	unwanted response(s)
usu.	usual(ly)
V.	vowel
v(v).	verb(s)
vbl.	verbal
viz.	*videlicet* namely
Vol.	volume
W.	west
Wa	Warwickshire
WM	West Midlands
Wo	Worcestershire
yd(s).	yard(s)
yr(s).	year(s)

[1] "A Questionnaire for a Linguistic Atlas of England", by Eugen Dieth and Harold Orton, in *Introduction*, pp. 38–113.

[2] If preceding a response; see *Introduction*, p. 25.

Note on the Special Signs and Symbols Used

superior °	=	excerpted from incidental material
superior □	=	plural form
superior △	=	singular form
superior ¶	=	present participle
superior §	=	unwanted response
+	=	standing before
/	=	alternating with (used in lists of Rr.)
~	=	1) alternating with (used in lists of Rr. with words enclosed within a pair of slants; also indicates relationship between similar forms) 2) identical with preceding form (used in phonetic transcriptions)

Symbols Used in the Questionnaire

□	=	show a picture if necessary
....	=	What do you call, what's your word for
superior *	=	included for phonological importance
superior †	=	included for morphological importance
superior ‡	=	included for syntactical importance

RESPONSES: BOOK VII.

VII.1.1 ONE*

Q. (How many) [*g.*] ?

R. ONE

Note 1—I.m. exs. of ONE in str. positions are reproduced below between square bracket untransliterated.

Note 2—For additional exs. of ONE in str. positions, see VII.8.18; of the numeral ONE, see VII.1.12, VII.2.6 and VII.8.21; and of ONE as a numeral adj. qualifying a n., see IX.8.8. For additional exs. of the pron. ONE, see III.3.7, VIII.8.8, IX.4.13, IX.6.4 and IX.10.3; of the unstr. pronoun ONE after an adj., see V.7.11 (and refs.); and of the unstr. pronoun ONES after an adj., see II.4.5 (and refs.). A ONE occurs at VII.1.17. For exs. of the phrase ONE ANOTHER'S, see III.2.10, III.13.6, and VI.2.8.

7 Ch 1 wɒn, ○wɷn^{4} 2 wən, ○~^{2} [wọn^{1}, wən$^{1(2x),3(4x),4(2x)}$, wɷn^{2,4}] 3 wɒn [wɒn^{3}] 4 wɒn [wɒn$^{1,2(3x)}$] 5 wɷn [wɒn$^{1(2x),3(2x)}$] 6 wɒn [wɒn$^{1,2,3(2x)}$]

8 Db 1 wɒn [wɒn$^{1(2x)}$] 2 wɒn 3 wɒn [wɒn^{3}] 4 wɒn [wɒn$^{2(2x)}$] 5 wɷn ["older"], wɒn ["usu."; wɒn$^{1,2(2x)}$] 6 wɒn [wɒn^{1}] 7 wɷn [wɒn^{1}]

11 Sa 1 wʌn 2 wa:n [wɒn$^{1,2(2x)}$] 3 wʌn 4 wɒ·n 5 wɷn [wɷn$^{2(2x),3}$] 6 wɒn, ○~^{3} [wɒn^{1,3}] 7 wa:n [wɒn$^{1(4x)}$] 8 wɒn [wɒn^{1}] 9 wɒn, ○~$^{1(2x)}$ [wɒn$^{1(2x)}$] 10 wʌn 11 wa:n [wɒn$^{2(2x)}$]

12 St 1 wɒn [wɒn$^{1(2x),2,3(2x)}$, wọn^{2}, wɷn^{2}] 2 wɒn [wɒn^{1,2}] 3 wɷn [wɷn^{2}, wɒn$^{1,2(4x)}$] 4 wọn, ○wɒn^{2} [wɒn$^{2,3(2x)}$] 5 wɒn, ○wɷn^{1} [wɒn$^{2(2x)}$, wọn^{2}, wɷn^{1,2,3}] 6 wɒn, ○~^{1,2} [wɒn$^{1(3x),2}$, ~^{1} V.10.5, ~^{1} VI.13.11, wɷn^{2}] 7 wɒn [wɒn$^{1(4x),3}$, wɷn^{2}] 8 wɒn, ○~^{6} [wɒn$^{1(4x),2,3,5}$] 9 wɒn [wɒn$^{1(4x),2(2x)}$, wɷn$^{1(3x)}$] 10 wɷn [wɷn^{1,4}] 11 wɒn, ○~^{2} [wɒn^{2}, wɷn^{2}]

15 He 1 wʌn [wʌn^{2}] 2 wʌn [wʌn$^{1,2(2x),3}$, ~^{2} IX.9.5] 3 wɷn [wɷn^{1,4}, wɒn^{1}] 4 wən [wʌn$^{1(3x)}$, wɒn^{1}; nəɪntɪwʌn *ninety-o.* VII.1.8] 5 wɷn, ○wʌn$^{1(2x)}$ [wɷn^{1,2}, wʌn^{1}] 6 wɷn [wɷn^{1}] 7 wɒn, ○~^{1} [wɒn$^{1,2,3,4(10x)}$, ~^{2} IX.9.5; ɛvɹɪwɒn^{4} *everyone*]

16 Wo 1 wɷn [wɷn^{1}] 2 wɷn [wɷn$^{1,2(4x)}$] 3 wɷn [wɷn$^{1(3x),2,3(2x),5}$; nɒɪntɪwɷn^{1} *ninety-o.* VII.1.8] 4 wɷn [wɒn^{2} IX.9.5] 5 wɷn [wɷn$^{1(3x)}$] 6 wɷ:n, ○wɷn^{1} [wɷn^{1}] 7 wɷn, ○~^{1}, ○wən^{1} [wɷn$^{1,4(5x)}$, wən$^{1,3(2x),4(4x)}$]

17 Wa 1 wɒn 2 wɷn, ○wən^{1} [wɷn^{3}, wan^{4}, wən$^{1,2(3x),3(3x),4(2x)}$, ~^{1} IX.9.5, ~^{4} VI.3.6] 3 wọn [wɒn^{3}] 4 wɷn 5 wɷn, ○~^{1} [wɷn$^{1(3x)}$] 6 wọn [wɷn^{4}] 7 wɷn

23 Mon 1 wʌn [wʌn[1(2x)]] 2 wɷn, ○wɒn[2] [wɒn[3]] 3 wʌn [wʌn[3]] 4 wʌ̤̈n [wʌ̤̈n[1,3]] 5 wʌ̤̈n, ○~[2] [wʌ̤̈n[2(3x)]] 6 wʌn 7 n.a. [wʌ̤n[1]]

24 Gl 1 wɷ:n [wɷ:n[1,2], wɒn[1,3]] 2 wɷ:n [wɷn[3(2x)]] 3 wœ:n [wœ:n[4(2x)]] 4 wœ:n [wɒn[1]] 5 wɷn 6 wən [wʌn[2]] 7 wən [wən[1]]

25 O 1 wɷn [wɷ̜n[3], wən[1]] 2 wən [wən[1], wʌn[2]] 3 wɷn 4 wɷn, ○~[1] [wɷn[1(6x),3,4], wɒn[3,4(2x)]] 5 wɷn [wʌn[2(2x),3]] 6 wɷn [wɷn[3], wən[3], wʌn[1,3]]

VII.1.2 TWO*

Q. (How many) [*g.*]?

R. TWO

Note—For additional exs. of TWO(–), see I.7.11, III.3.7, III.6.5, VI.10.10, VII.1.19, VII.2.14, VII.3.5, VII.7.5, VII.8.10, VII.8.21 and IX.10.4/5.

7 Ch 1 tᶷu:, ○tʏ:[2] 2 tᶥü:, ○tu:[1,2], ○tü:[3] 3 tɛ̈ɷ 4 tᶷu:, ○tu:[2] 5 tɛ̜ɷ 6 tᶷu:

8 Db 1 tʏ: 2 tᶷu:, ○~[3,4], ○tᶷu[1] 3 tɛ̈ɷ 4 tɛɷ, ○~[1,3] 5 tɛɷ, ○tᶥu:[4] 6 tɛɷ, ○~[1(3x)] 7 tɛɷ, ○tᶥu:[1], ○tɪu[1] [tɛɷtɛɷθt[1] *t.-toothed adj.*]

11 Sa 1 tu: 2 tɪu:, ○tᶥu:[2], ○tʏʉ:[1] 3–4 tu: 5 tɪu:, ○~[2] 6–8 tu: 9 tᶷu: 10–11 tu:

12 St 1 tɛɷ, ○tü[1], ○tü:[4] IX.10.6 2 tɛɷ, ○tü[1], ○tü:[2] 3 tɛɷ, ○~[1(2x),2(2x)], ○~[2] IX.10.6 4 tü: 5 tü:, ○tu:[1] [tu:wɛɪld[1] *t.-wheeled*] 6 tɛɷ 7 tü:, ○~[1], ○~[1] IX.8.6 8 tü:, ○~[1] 9 tɪɷ, ○tɪɷ:[1(2x)], ○tü:[1(3x),2] 10 tü:, ○~[1,2,5], ○~[4] IX.7.2, ○~[4] IX.7.3 11 tü:, ○~[2], ○tu:[2]

15 He 1 tᶥu: 2 tu: 3 tu:, ○~[4] 4 tᶥu:, ○tu:[1] 5 tu:, ○~[1(2x)] 6 tu:, ○~[1] 7 tu:, ○~[1(2x),2(2x),3(3x)]

16 Wo 1 tᵋu:, ○tu:[1] 2 tu:, ○~[1] 3 tᵊu:, ○tu:[4] 4 tu: 5 tu:, ○~[1] [tu:-əɪd[1] *t-eyed adj.* VI.3.1] 6 tu:, ○~[1,2] 7 tu:, ○~[1(5x),3,4]

17 Wa 1 tu:, ○~[1] 2 tu:, ○~[1,3,4(2x)] 3 tᶷu: 4 tü 5 tu:, ○~[1(4x)] 6 tü:, ○~[1], ○tu:[1,3] 7 tu:, ○~[1,2]

23 Mon 1 tᶷu: 2 tu:, ○~[3] 3 tᶥu: 4 tʰu:, ○~[1,3], ○tu[1] 5 tu:, ○~[2(2x)] 6 tu: 7 n.a., ○tu:[1]

24 Gl 1 tu:ᵊ, ○tu:[1] [æɪtɪtu[1] *eighty-t.* VII.1.7] 2 tᶥu 3 tᶷu:, ○~[3] VII.2.12 4 tᶷu: [aɪtɪtᶷu:[2] *eighty-t.* VII.1.7] 5 tu:, ○~[2] 6 tu: 7 tᶷu:

25 O 1 tü:, ○tu:[2(2x)] 2 tu:, ○~[1], ○tü:[2] 3 tᶷu:, ○tu:[2(2x)] 4 tu:, ○~[1(6x),3,4(3x)], ○tɷ[3(2x)] [tɷpəns[4] *twopence*] 5 tü: 6 tu:

VII.1.3 THREE*

Q. (How many) [*g.*]?

R. THREE

Note—For additional exs. of THREE, see VI.10.5/10, VII.1.19, VII.3.5, VII.5.5 and VII.8.21. THREE–LEGGED occurs at III.3.3; THREE–QUARTERED at III.2.7; and THREE–HALFPENCE at VII.7.1.

7 Ch 1 θɹẹ: 2 θɹɩi:, ○~[4], ○θɹi:[1,2] 3 θɹɛɩ, ○θɹi:[2] [twɛntɩθɹɛɩ[3] *twenty-t.* VII.1.12] 4 θɹᵊi: 5 θɹɛɩ 6 θɹᶦi:

8 Db 1 θɹi: 2 θɹi: [θɹi:-ɔ:s bɔ:k[2] *t.-horse baulk*; θɹi-ɔ:s tɩəm[2] *t.-horse team*] 3–5 θɹɛɩ 6 θɹɛɩ [θɹɛɩtɑ̃:ĩnd ak[1] *t.-tined hack* I.7.10] 7 θɹɛɩ

11 Sa 1 θɹi: 2 θɹᶦi: 3–4 θɹi: 5 fɹᶦi: 6–9 θɹi: 10 θɹi:, ○~[2,3] 11 θɹi:

12 St 1 θɹɛɩ 2 θɹɛɩ, ○~[1,2(2x)] [θɹɛɩ-ɒs swɩŋgətɹɛɩ[3] *t.-horse swingle-tree* I.8.4] 3 θɹɛɩ 4 θɹi:, ○~[1] 5 θɹɛɩ, ○~[2(3x)], ○θɹi:[2(2x)] 6 θɹɛɩ, ○~[1,2], ○~[2] VII.8.13 7 θɹəi 8 θɹi:, ○~[3] 9 θɹɛɩ, ○~[2,3], ○θɹi:[1] [θɹi:-ɒs swɩŋgltɹi:[1] *t.-horse swingle-tree* I.8.4] 10–11 θɹi:

15 He 1 θɹi: 2 θɹi:, ○~[2] 3 θɹi:, ○~[1] 4 dɹe: 5–6 dɹi: 7 θɹi:, ○~[3(3x),4(2x)]

16 Wo 1 θɹi: 2 θɹẹ: 3 θɹᵊi: 4 θɹi: 5 θɹi:, ○~[1(2x)] 6 θɹᶦi:, ○θɹi:[2] 7 θɹi:, ○~[1,3(2x),4(2x)] [θɹi:tɔɩnd fɑʳk[1(2x)] *t.-tined fork* I.7.10)]

17 Wa 1 θɹᵉi:, ○θɹᵊɩ[1] 2 θɹi:, ○~[3] 3 θɹᶦi: 4 θɹᶦi:, ○θɹi:[1] 5 θɹᵊį:, ○θɹi:[1] III.3.7 6 θɹᶦi:, ○θɹi:[4(2x)] 7 θɹi: [θɹi: ən twɛntɩ[2] *t. and twenty* VII.1.12]

23 Mon 1 θɹᶦi: 2–3 θɹi: 4 θɹį: 5 θɹi:, ○~[1,2(2x),3] 6 θɹi: 7 n.a., ○θɹi:[1]

24 Gl 1 θɹi:, ○θɹɩ[1] 2 θɹᶦi:, ○~[3] 3 dɹᶦi: 4 dɹᶦi:, ○~[1,2,3] 5 θɹi: 6 dɹi: 7 dɹi:, ○~[1]

25 O 1 θɹi: 2 θɹi:, ○~[1(2x),3] 3 θɹi: 4 θɹi:, ○~[4], ○θɽi:[1(6x),3,5] 5 θɹi:, ○~[2] 6 θɹi:

VII.1.4 FOUR*

Q. (How many) [*g.*]?

R. FOUR

Note 1—I.m. exs. of FOURTEEN and FOURTH are reproduced below between square brackets untransliterated.

Note 2—Exs. of FOUR occ. occur at VI.10.10, VII.1.17 and VII.3.5. For exs. of FOUR–, see I.3.13.

7 Ch 1 foəˢ 2 fɷə, °~[3], °fɔə[1,3] 3 fɛ̈ɷə [fo·əɹ'ʏ:md *f.-roomed* V.2.4] 4 foə 5 fọə 6 fo·ə

8 Db 1 foə·ɹ̠ 2 fo·ə, °foə[2] 3 fo·ᵚwə 4 fo·ə, °~[1] [fo·ətɛɪn[1]] 5–7 fo·ə

11 Sa 1 fɒəʳ· 2 fo:ə, °fo:əʳ[1] 3 fɒəʳ: 4 fɔʳ:əʳ [fɔ:ti:n[2]] 5 fo:əʳ, °~[2] 6 fɔ:ə 7 fo:əʳ 8 fɔ:əʳ 9–10 fo:əʳ 11 fo:əʳ, °fɔ:əʳ[1], °fɔ:ə[2]

12 St 1 fɷə 2 foɷə, °~[1] 3 fɷə, °~[1,2], °fɷ:ə[1(2x)] [foɷθ[1]] 4 fɔ:ə 5 foɷə [fɷətɛɪn[2]] 6 fɷ:ə, °~[2], °foɷə[2] 7–8 fɔ: 9 fɷə, °~[1], °fɷəɹ[1] [+ V.; fɔ:tɛɪn[1]; ən ɔ:l fɷəz[2] *on all fs.*] 10 fɔ: 11 fọ:əɹ

15 He 1–3 fo:əʳ 4 fæɷəʳ [fæɷəʳθ[3]] 5 fo:əʳ [fo:əʳθ[4]] 6 vɒɷəʳ, °fɒɷəʳ[1] 7 fɔ·əɹ, °~[3(2x)], °fɔ·ɹ[3] [fɔ·əɹpnɪ bɪt[4] *fourpenny bit*; fɔ·ɹti:n[3]; fɔ·əɹθ[4]]

16 Wo 1 fɒɷə 2 faɷəʳ 3 fo:əʳ, °foɷəʳ[1] 4 fɒɷəʳ 5 fo:əʳ, °faɷəʳ[1] 6 fɛu:əʳ, °fæɷəʳ[2], °fɒɷəʳ[3] [foɷəʳti:n[2]] 7 fəɷəʳ, °~[4], °fəɷə[1], °fɔ·əʳ[1], °fɔ·əɹ[1] [fəəti:n[4]; faɷəʳθ[1]]

17 Wa 1 fɔ: [fọəlɛgɪd[1] *f.-legged* III.3.3] 2 fəɷə, °~[2], °fɔə[1], °fəɷəɹ [+ V.; nɔɪntɪfəɷə[4] *ninety-f.* VII.1.8] 3 fɔ: 4 foɷə, °fɒɷə[2] 5 fɒɷəʳ, °faɷəɹ [+ V.] III.3.7 6 vɒɷəʳ 7 foɷəʳ, fɒɷəʳ ["rare now, heard in old days"]

23 Mon 1 fo:əʳ, °~[2] 2 fo:əʳ 3 fo:ə [fo:əθ[1]] 4 fo:, °fo[ə1] 5 fọ:, °fou[2], °fɔ:[3] [sɪkstifɔ:[3] *sixty-f.* VII.1.5] 6 fo:əʳ 7 n.a.

24 Gl 1 fæɷəʳ, °~[1,2], °fæɷəʳɽ[2] [+ V.; væɷəʳpɷns[1] *fourpence*] 2 fæɷəʳ, °~[3], °fɒɷəʳ[3] [fæɷəʳθ[3]] 3 vɒɷəʳ [vɒɷəʳθ[3]] 4 vɒɷəʳ 5 faɷəʳ 6 vaɷəʳ 7 vɒɷəʳ [vaɷəɽgɹæɪnd pɪk[2] *f.-grained pick* (i.e. fork)]

25 O 1 fəɷəʳ 2 foəʳ, °fəɷəʳ[1] 3 fɛɷəʳ, °fɔ·ə[1], °fɔ·[ə]ɽ[2], °fɔ·[ə]ɹ[2] [+ V.; fɛɷəʳθ[1]] 4 faɷəɽ, °fɔ·əɽ [faɷəɹti:n[4]; faɷəɽθ[4]] 5 fɔ·əʳ, °fɔəʳ[1] 6 fɔ:əʳ

VII.1.5 SIX*

Q. (How many) [*g.*]?

R. SIX

Note 1—I.m. exs. of SIXTEEN, SIXTY and SIXTH are reproduced below between square brackets untransliterated.

Note 2—Exs. of SIX occ. occur at VI.10.10 and VII.3.5; and of SIXTY at VII.3.5. For exs. of SIXPENCE, see VII.7.4.

7 Ch 1 sɪks 2 sɪks [θət͜ʔɪsɪks[4] *thirty-s.* VII.1.13] 3–6 sɪks

8 Db 1–3 sɪks 4 sɪks, °sɛks[1] 5–7 sɪks

11 Sa 1–2 sɪks 3 sɪks, ○~[3] 4 sɪks 5 sɪks, ○~[3] 6–7 sɪks 8 sɪks [sɪkstɪ[2]] 9–11 sɪks

12 St 1 sɪ̜ks, ○sɪks[1], ○~[2] 2 sɪks 3 sɪ̜ks, ○sɪks[1] [sɪkst[1]] 4 sɪks 5 sɪks, ○~[1] 6 sɪks 7 sɪks [sɛmtɪsɪks[4] *seventy-s.* VII.1.6] 8 sɪks 9 sɪks, ○~[1] 10 sɪks 11 sɪks, ○~[3]

15 He 1 sɪks 2 sɪks, ○~[2] 3 sɪks 4 zɪks, ○sɪks[3(2x)] 5 sɪks, ○~[1] 6 zɪks [zɪkst[1]] 7 sɪks, ○~[2,3(3x),4] [sɪkstɪ:n[3(2x)]; sɪkstɪ[1]; sɪks[4] *sixth*; naɪntɪsɪks[3] *ninety-s.* VII.1.8]

16 Wo 1 sɪks, ○~[3] 2 sɪks 3 sɪks, ○~[1] 4 sɪks 5 sɪks, ○~[1(2x)], 6 sɪks 7 sɪks, ○~[1(2x),3]

17 Wa 1 sɪks, ○~[1] 2 sɪks, ○~[1,4] 3 sɪks, ○~[2] 4 sɪks 5 sɪks, ○~[1] VII.1.11 6 sɪks, ○~[3(2x)] 7 sɪks

23 Mon 1 sɪks 2 səks 3–4 sɪks 5 sɪks [sɪkstifɔ:[3] *sixty-f.* VII.1.4] 6 sɪks 7 n.a.

24 Gl 1 sɪks, ○~[1(2x)] 2 sɪks, ○~[3] 3 zɪks 4 zɪks, ○~[1] 5 sɪks 6 zɪks, ○~[2] 7 zɪks, ○~[1]

25 O 1 sɪks [sɛbmtɪsɪks[1] *seventy-s.* VII.1.6; twɛntɪsɪks[2] *twenty-s.* VII.1.12] 2–3 sɪks 4 sɪks, ○~[5] [sɪkstɪ[4]] 5–6 sɪks

VII.1.6 SEVEN*

Q. (How many) [*g.*]*?*

R. SEVEN

Note 1—I.m. exs. of SEVENTEEN and SEVENTY are reproduced below between square brackets untransliterated.

Note 2—For additional exs. of SEVEN, see VI.10.10, VII.1.17, VII.3.5 and VII.5.4.

7 Ch 1 sɛvn 2 sɛvn, ○sɛvən[2] [sɛvəntɪ[4] VII.3.5] 3 sɪvn 4 sɛvn 5 sɛvən 6 sɛvn

8 Db 1 sɛvən 2–5 sɛvn 6 sɛvən [sɛvnteɪn[1]] 7 sɛvn

11 Sa 1 sɛvn 2 sɛvn, ○~[2,3], ○sɛbm[2] [aɪtɪsɛvn[3] *eighty-s.* VII.1.7] 3–11 sɛvn

12 St 1 sɛvn, ○sɛvən[4] 2–5 sɛvn 6 sɛvn, ○~[1] 7 sɛvən, ○sɛm[4] [sɛmtɪsɪks[4] *seventy-six* VII.1.5] 8 sɛvn 9 sɛvən 10–11 sɛvn

15 He 1 sɛbm, ○~[2] 2 sɛvn 3 sɛvn, ○sɛbm[2] 4 sɛvn 5 sɪvn 6 zɛbm 7 sɛvən

16 Wo 1 sɛbm 2 sɛvɷn 3 sɛvm, ○sɛvn[1] VII.7.5 4 sɛvɷn 5 sɛvɷn, ○sɛvn[1] 6 sɛvn 7 sɛvn [sɛvən[1] *seventh*]

17 Wa 1 sɛbm 2 sɛvn, ○sɛvən[2] 3–6 sɛbm 7 sɛbm, ○~[2]

23 Mon 1–2 sɛvn 3 sɛvən, ○sɛvn[1] 4 sɛvn 5 sɛv^{ə}n 6 sɛbm 7 n.a.

24 Gl 1 sɛbm [sɛvntι[1]] 2 sɛbm 3 zιvɷn 4 zɛvn [zɛvntι[1]] 5 sɛvn, ○zɛvn[2] 6–7 zɛbm

25 O 1 sɛbm [sɛbmtιsιks[1] *seventy-six* VII.1.5] 2 zɛbm[(2x)], ○sɛbm[1] [sɛvntι[2]] 3 sɛbm, ○~[2] 4 sɛvən, ○sɛvn[4] [sɛvəntι-e:t[3] *seventy-eight* VII.1.7] 5 sɛbm 6 sɛbm, ○~[3]

VII.1.7 EIGHT*

Q. (How many) [*g.*]*?*

R. EIGHT

Note 1—I.m. exs. of EIGHTEEN and EIGHTY are reproduced below between square brackets untransliterated.

Note 2—For additional exs. of (-)EIGHT and EIGHTEEN, see VI.10.10, VII.1.17, VII.3.5 and VII.5.6; and of EIGHTH, see VII.2.6.

7 Ch 1 ẹιt 2 ɛιt, ○~[1], ○e:t[2] 3 ɛιt, ○~[3(2x)] 4 ɛιt, ○~[2,3] 5 ɛιt, ○~[1] 6 ẹιt, ○ɛιt[2]

8 Db 1 ɛιt‘, ○ɛιt[2] 2 ɛι^{t}, ○ɛιt[1] 3 ɛιt, ○~[2] 4 ɛιt‘, ○ɛιt[2] 5 e:ˈt 6 ɛιt, ○~[1] 7 ɛιt, ○~[1]

11 Sa 1 ɛιt 2 ɛιt [aιtιsɛvn[3] *eighty-seven* VII.1.6] 3 e:ˈt 4 e:t 5 ɛιt 6–10 e:t 11 aιt [aιtι[2]]

12 St 1 ẹιt, ○ɛιt[4(2x)] [ɛιtɛιn[4]] 2 ẹιt 3 ẹιt, ○ɛιt[1] 4 ɛιt 5 ɛιt [ɛιtι[2]] 6 ɛιt, ○~[1] VI.13.11, ○~[2] 7 ɛιt, ○~[4(2x)] [ɛιtι[1]] 8 ẹιt, ○~[1] 9 ɛ:t 10 ɛιt 11 ẹιt [twɛntι-ɛιt[2] *twenty-e.* VII.1.12]

15 He 1 æιt, ○~[2] 2 æιt 3 æιt, ○~[1,2,4] 4 æιt 5 æιt, ○ɑ:ιt[1] 6 ɒιt 7 eιt, ẹιt ["older"], ○~, ○eιt[4], ○e:t[3]

16 Wo 1 ɛιt 2 aιt 3 e:ιt 4 aιt, ○~[1,2,3] 5 aιt [aιtι[1]] 6 æιt [aιtι[1]] 7 ɛιt, ○~[1]

17 Wa 1 ɛιt 2 ɛιt, ○~[2] [ɛιti:n[2] VII.7.5; ɛιtι[1]; θə:tι-ɛιt *thirty-e.* VII.1.13, VII.3.5] 3 æιt [æ̣ιtι[3]] 4 ɛιt 5 ɛιt, ○~[1] 6 æιt 7 ẹιt, ○ɛιt[1]

23 Mon 1 æιt 2–3 e:t 4–5 eit 6 ɛιt 7 n.a., ○eι̣t[1]

24 Gl 1 æɩᵊt [æɩtɩ[1]; æɩtɩtu:[1] *eighty-two* VII.1.2] 2 æɩt 3 ɒɩt 4 ɒɩt [aɩtˈi:ᵊn[2]; aɩtɩtᵒu:[2] *eighty-two* VII.1.2] 5 æɩt, ○~[2] 6 æɩt, ○~[1] 7 ɛ̧ɩt

25 O 1 æɩt 2 ɛɩt [ɛɩt ən twɛntɩ[3] *e. and twenty* VII.1.12] 3 e:t, ○~[2] [e:tɩ[1]] 4 e:t, ○~[3] [sɛvəntɩ-e:t[3] *seventy-e.* VII.1.6] 5 eˑʔ, ○e:ʔ[2] 6 eɩʔ, ○~[3]

VII.1.8 NINE*

Q. (How many) [*g.*]?

R. NINE

Note—NINE also occurs at VI.10.10 and VII.3.5.

7 Ch 1 nɑɩn, ○~[4] 2 nɑɩn, ○~[2(2x)], ○naɩn[1,3] 3 nɛɩn [nɑɩntɩəθ[3] *ninetieth*] 4–5 nɑɩn 6 naɩn

8 Db 1–3 naɩn 4 nɑɩn, ○~[1] [nɑɩntɛɩn[1] *nineteen*] 5 nɑˑɩn 6 nɑ̃ɩ̃n, ○~[1] 7 nɑ̃:n

11 Sa 1 naɩn 2 naɩᵊn 3–4 nɛɩn 5 nɒɩn, ○~[1] 6–11 naɩn

12 St 1–2 nɒɩn 3 nɒ:ɩn, ○~[1] [nɒ:ɩntɛɩn[1] *nineteen*] 4 nɒɩn 5 nɒ:ɩn 6 nɒ:ɩn, ○~[2] 7–8 nɒɩn 9 nɒɩn [nɒɩntɩ[1] *ninety*] 10 na:ɩn 11 nɑ̊ɩn

15 He 1 næɩn 2 næɩn, ○~[2] 3 nəɩn, ○~[4] 4 nəɩn [nəɩntɩwʌn[1] *ninety-one* VII.1.1; nəɩnθ[2] *ninth*] 5 nəɩn, ○~[3], ○nəɩᵊn[1] 6 nəɩᵊn 7 nӑɩn, ○naɩn[3,4(2x)], ○nạɩn[4] [naɩntɩsɩks[3] *ninety-six* VII.1.5]

16 Wo 1 nɒɩᵊn, ○~[3] 2 nɒɩᵊn 3 nəi:n [nɒɩntɩwɷn[1] *ninety-one* VII.1.1] 4 nəɩn, ○~[3] 5 nəɩᵊn 6 nəi:n, ○nɒɩᵊn[3] 7 nəɩn, ○~[1] [nəɩnɷndəd[3] VII.1.15; nəɩnpəns[3] *ninepence*]

17 Wa 1 nɑɩn 2 nəɩn, ○~[2(2x),4(2x)] [nəɩntɩfəɷə[4] *ninety-four*] 3 nɒˑɩn, ○nəɩn[3] 4 nəɩn, ○~[3] 5 nəɩn, ○~[1] 6–7 nəɩn

23 Mon 1–2 nəɩn 3 næɩn 4 nə̧in 5 nəɩ̣n, ○nəin[1] 6 nəɩn, ○~[1] 7 n.a.

24 Gl 1 nəɩᵊn 2 nɒɩᵊn 3 nəɩᵊn 4 nɒɩᵊn 5 nə̈ɩn 6–7 nʌɩn

25 O 1–2 nə̈ɩn 3 nʌʏn 4 naɩn, ○~[3] VII.7.5 [nəɩ̣nθ[4] *ninth*; nəɩnti:n[4] *nineteen*] 5 nʌʏn 6 nə̈ɩn

VII.1.9 ELEVEN*

Q. How many is this [*write down* 11]*?*

R. ELEVEN

7 Ch 1 ɩlɛvən 2 əlɛvn, ○~[1] VI.10.10 3 ɩlɛvn 4 əlɛvn 5 əlɛvən 6 əlɛvn

8 Db 1 ɩlɛvən 2 ɩlɛvn 3 əlɛvn 4 lɛvn 5 ɩlɛvn 6 əlɛvn, ○ɩlɛvn[1] 7 əlɛvn

11 Sa 1 əlɛvn 2 ɩlɛvn 3 lɛvn 4 ɩlɛvn 5–6 lɛvn 7 ɩlɛvn 8–9 lɛvn 10 ɩlɛvən 11 əlɛvn

12 St 1 lɛvn 2 əlɛvn 3 əlɛvn, ○ɩlɛvn[1] 4 əlɛvn 5 əlɛvn [ɩlɛvnpəns[2] *elevenpence*] 6 əlɛvn 7 lɛvn 8 lɛvn [ɩlɛvnθ[1] *eleventh*] 9 əlɛvn, ○ɩlɛvn[1] 10 lɛvn 11 əlɛvn

15 He 1 lɛbm 2 əlɛvn 3–4 əlɛbm 5 lɛbn 6 lɛbm 7 ɩlɛvn, s.f. lɛvn, ○~[3] [lɛvənzɩz[4] *elevenses* VII.5.11]

16 Wo 1 ɩlɛbm 2 lɛbn 3 əlɛbm 4 lɛbm 5 əlɛbm 6 lɛbm 7 lɛvn, ○əlɛvn[4] VII.3.5

17 Wa 1 əlɛbm 2 əlɛvn 3 ᵊlɛbm, ○lɛbm[3] 4–5 lɛbm 6 əlɛbm 7 lɛbm

23 Mon 1 lɛbm 2 ɩlɛvən 3–5 lɛvn 6 lɛbm 7 n.a.

24 Gl 1 lɛbm, ○əlɛbm[3] 2 lɛbm 3 lɛvn 4 lɛbm 5 əlɛvn 6–7 lɛbm

25 O 1 lɛbm, ○əlɛbm[1] 2–3 lɛbm 4 łɛvn, ○~[2,4(2x)], ○~[5] VII.7.5 [łɛvənzɩz[4] *elevenses* VII.5.11] 5–6 lɛbm

VII.1.10 TWELVE*. DOZEN*

Q. How many is this [*write down 12*]*?*
Or, another name for it when you go to a shop?

Rr. TWELVE
DOZEN

Note 1—The rr. to the two parts of the q. are separated below by a full stop.

Note 2—For additional exs. of TWELVE, see VI.10.10, VII.3.4/5 and VII.5.3; and of DOZEN and TWELVE, see VII.1.17.

7 Ch 1 twɛlv . dɷzn 2 twɛlv, ○~[1]. dɷzn, ○~[2] 3 twɛlv [twɛlvstẹ:ft[1] *t.-staved* I.7.15] . dɷzn 4–5 twɛlv . dɷzn 6 twɛlv . dʌzn

8 Db 1–3 twɛlv . dɷzn 4 twɛlv, ○twalv[2]. dɷzn 5 twɛlv . dɷzn 6 twɛlv, ○~[1]. dɷzn 7 twɛlv . dɷzn

11 Sa 1 twɛlv. dʌzn 2 twɛlv. dɒzən 3 twɛlv. dəzn 4 twɛlv. dʌzn 5 twɛlv. dɒzɪn 6 twɛlv. dʌzn 7 twɛlv. dʌzən 8 θwɛlv [*sic*]. dɒzn 9 twɛlv, ○~[1]. dʌzn 10 twɛlv. dʌzən 11 twɛlv. dɒzn, ○~[(2x)]

12 St 1–4 twɛlv. dɒzn 5 twɛlv. dɒzn, ○~[2] 6 twɛlv. dɒzn, ○~ 7 twɛlv. dɒzn 8 twɛlv. dɒzn, ○~[6] 9 twɛlv. dɒzn 10 twɛlv. dɒzn, ○~[2] IX.8.6 11 twɛlv. dɒ̜zn, ○~[2] IX.8.6

15 He 1–3 twɛɫv. dʌzn 4 twɛɫv. dʌzən 5 twɛɫv. dʌzn 6 twɛɫv. dɒzən 7 twɛlv, ○~[3]. dʌzən, ○~[4]

16 Wo 1 twɛɫv. dɒzən, ○~[3] 2 twɛɫv. dɒzən 3 twəɫv. dɒzn 4 twɛɫv. dɒzn 5 twɛlv. dɒzɒn 6 twɛɫv. dɒzn 7 twɛlv, ○~[1,4(2x)]. dɒzn, ○~[1] VII.1.11, ○~[3]

17 Wa 1–2 twɛlv. dɒzn 3 twɛɫv, ○twɛlv[3]. dɒzn 4 twɛɫv. dɒzn 5–6 twɛɫv. dɒ̜zn 7 twɛɫv. dɒzn

23 Mon 1 twɛɫv. dʌzn 2 twɛɫv. dɒzən 3 twɛɫv. dʌzən 4 tʰwɛlv. dʌ̜̈zn 5 twɛɫv. dʌ̜̈zn, ○~[2], ○□dʌ̜̈zənz[3(2x)] 6 twɛɫv. dʌzn 7 n.a.

24 Gl 1 twɛɫv. dɒzɒn, ○~[1(2x)] 2 twɛɫv. dɒzɒn 3 twɛɫv. dʌzn 4 twɛɫv. dɒzn 5 twɛɫv. dɒ̜zn 6–7 twɛɫv. dəzn, ○də·zn[1]

25 O 1 twæɫv. dʌzn, ○~[2(2x)] 2 twɛɫv. dʌzn 3 twaɫv, ○~[2], ○twɑlv[2]. dʌzn 4 twɛɫv [twɛɫvmɒnθ[1] *twelve-month* (ref. a one-year-old sheep) *n.*]. dɒzn, ○~[4] 5 twæ̜lv. dʌzn, ○□dʌznz[2] 6 twɛəɫv. dɒ̜zn

VII.1.11 THIRTEEN*

Q. *How many is this* [*write down* 13]*?*

We can say, can't we: There were only twelve of us. Now you say it, but make it one more than twelve. There were only . . . . of us.

Note the stress, both when isolated and in the sentence.

R. THIRTEEN

Note 1—The rr. to the two parts of the q. are separated below by a full stop. An attached superior ◇ means that the form concerned occurs in the rr. to both parts. Unfortunately the f.ws. occ. failed to rec. the stresses.

Note 2—Only three i.m. exs. of THIRTEEN occurring in a sentence were rec., namely at 15.7 and 16.7.

7 Ch 1 ◇θəɪːˈtiːn 2 θɔːtin, ○θəʔtiːn[4]. ˈθɔːˈtiːn 3 ◇θəɪːˈtɛɪn 4 θɔːˈtiːən. θɔːtiːn 5 ˈθɔːtɛɪn. θɔˈtɛɪn 6 ◇θəɪ̠ːˈtiːn

8 Db 1 ˈθə̝̞t˳ti:n . θə̝̞t˳ˈti:n 2 θə:ˈti:n . θə:ti:n 3–4 ◇θə:ˈtɛɪn 5 ◇θɒˈti:n
6 ◇θə:ˈtɛɪn 7 ◇θə:ˈti:n, ◇θə:ˈtɛɪn [“older”]

11 Sa 1–4 ˈθəʵ:ʈi:n . θəʵ:ˈʈi:n 5 ˈθəʵ:ʈʻi:n . θəʵ:ˈʈʻi:n 6 θəʵ:ˈʈi:n . ˈθəʵ:ʈi:n
7–11 ˈθəʵ:ʈi:n . θəʵ:ˈʈi:n

12 St 1 ˈθə:tɛɪn . θə:ˈtɛɪn 2 ◇ˈθə:tɛɪn 3 ◇θə:ˈtɛɪn 4 ◇θə:ˈti:n 5 θə:ˈtɛɪn .
ˈθə:tɛɪn 6 ◇θə:ˈtɛɪn 7 ˈθə̊:ti:n . θə:ˈti:n 8 ◇ˈθə:ti:n 9 ˈθə:tɛɪn .
θə:ˈtɛɪn 10 ◇ˈθə:ti:n 11 ˈθə:ɹti:n . θə:ɹˈti:n

15 He 1–2 θəʵ:ˈʈi:n . ˈθəʵ:ʈi:n 3 ˈθəʵ:ʈi:ᵊn . θəʵ:ˈʈi:n 4–5 θəʵ:ʈi:n . θəʵ:ˈʈi:n
6 ˈðəʵ:ʈi:n . ðəʵˈʈi:n 7 θəɹˈti:n, ○ˈθə·ɹti:n[3] . ˈθəɹˈti:n, ○ˈθəɹti:n[3]

16 Wo 1–6 ˈθəʵ:ʈi:n . θəʵ:ˈʈi:n 7 θə:ˈti:n . θə:ˈti:n, ○θə:ti:n[3], ○ˌðə:ˈtɪn[1]

17 Wa 1 ◇θə:ˈtᵉi:n 2–3 ◇θə:ˈti:n 4 ◇θəʵ:ˈʈi:n 5 θəʵ:ˈʈi:n, ○ˈθəʵ:ʈi:n[1] . θəʵ:ˈʈi:n[1]
6–7 ˈθəʵ:ʈi:n . θəʵ:ˈʈi:n

23 Mon 1 ˈθəʵ:ʈʻi:n . θəʵ:ˈʈʻi:n 2 ˈθəʵʈi:n . θəʵˈʈi:n 3 ˈθœ:ti:n . θœ:ˈti:n
4 θœ:t˳ˈi:n . θœˈʈi̞:n 5 ˈθœ̈:ˈʈi:n . ˈθœ̣̈:ˈti:n 6 ˈθəʵ:ʈi:n . θəʵˈʈi:n
7 n.a.

24 Gl 1 ◇θəʵ:ˈʈi:ən 2 ˈθəʵ:ʈi:n . θəʵ:ˈʈi:n 3–4 ˈðəʵ:ʈʻi:n . ðəʵ:ˈʈʻi:n 5
ˈθəʵ:ʈi:n . θəʵ:ˈʈi:n 6 ðəʵ:ˈʈi:n . ðəʵ:ʈi:n 7 ◇ðəʵ:ˈʈi:n

25 O 1 θəʵ:ˈʈi:n . θəʵ:ˈʈin 2 θə̝̞:ˈti:n . ˈθə̝̞:ti:n 3 ˈθəʵ:ʈi:n . θəʵ:ˈʈi:n
4 ˈθəɹˈʔi:n . ˈθəɹˈti:n 5 ˈθəʵʈi:n . θəʵˈʈi:n 6 ◇θəʵ:ˈʈi:n

VII.1.12 TWENTY-ONE*‡

Q. How many is this [*write down* 21]*?*
If your daughter is as old as that today, you'd say she is . . . . today.
Note the order.

Rr. A SCORE AND ONE, ONE AND TWENTY, TWENTY-ONE

ONE AND TWENTY, TWENTY-ONE

Note 1—The rr. to the two parts of the q. are separated below by a full stop. An attached superior ◇ means that the form concerned occurs in the rr. to both parts.

Note 2—I.m. exs. of TWENTY are reproduced below between square brackets untransliterated.

Note 3—TWENTY(–) occurs at VII.3.5 and VII.5.5. For exs. of ONE, see VII.1.1 (and refs.).

7 Ch 1 twɛntɩwɒn, wɒn ən twɛntɩ. twɛntɩwɒn 2 ◇twɛntɩwən. s.w. wən ən twɛntɩ [rare] 3 twɛntɩwɒn. wɒn ən twɛntɩ [twɛntɩθɹɛɩ[3] *t.-three* VII.1.3] 4 twɛntɩwɒn. wɒn ən twɛntɩ 5 twɛntɩwɷn. p. wɷn ən twɛntɩ [old] 6 ◇twɛnɩwɒn

8 Db 1 ◇twɛntɩwɒn 2 twɛntɩwɒn. wɒn ən twɛntɩ 3 twɛntɩwɒn. n.r., ○wɒn ən twɛntɩ 4 twɛntɩwɒn. wɒn ən twɛntɩ [twɛntɩ[3]] 5 twɛntɩwɒn. wɷn ən twɛntɩ 6 ◇twɛntɩwɒn 7 ◇twɛntɩwən

11 Sa 1 ◇twɛntɩwʌn 2 twɛntɩwɑ:n. wɒn ən twɛntɩ [twɛntɩ[3]] 3 ◇twɛntɩwʌn 4 twɛntɩwʌn. wʌn n̩ twɛntɩ 5 twɛntɩwɷn. wɷn ən twɛntɩ 6 ◇twɛntwɒn 7 twɛntɩwɒn. wɒn n̩ twɛntɩ 8 twɛntɩwɒn. wɒn n̩ twɛntɩ [twɛntɩ[2]] 9 twɛntɩwɒn. wɒn n̩ twɛntɩ 10 twɛntɩwʌn. wʌn n̩ twɛntɩ 11 twɛntɩwa:n. wa:n n̩ twɛntɩ

12 St 1 ◇twɛntɩwɒ̣n 2 twɛntɩwɒn. twɛntwɒn 3 ◇twɛntɩwɷn 4 ◇twɛntɩwɷn [twɛntɩ[1]] 5 ◇twɛntɩwɒn, ○twɛntɩwɷn[2] [twɛntɩfəst[2] *t.-first* VII.2.1] 6 ◇twɛntɩwɷn 7–9 ◇twɛntɩwɒn 10 ə skɔ:ɹ ən wɒn. twɛntɩwən 11 ◇twɛntɩwɒn [twɛntɩ-ɛɩt[2] *t.-eight*; twɛntɩ tə tu:[2] *t. to two*]

15 He 1 twɛntɩwʌn. wʌn n̩ twɛntɩ 2 ◇twɛntɩwʌn 3 twɛntɩwɷ:n. wɷn ən twɛntɩ 4 twɛntɩwʌn. wʌn n̩ twɛntɩ 5 ◇twɛntɩwɷn [twɛntɩ[4]] 6 ◇twɛntɩwɷn 7 wɒn ən twɛntɩ. twɛntɩwɒn

16 Wo 1 ◇twɛntɩwɷn 2 twɛntɩwɷn. wɷn n̩ twɛntɩ 3 ◇twɛntɩwɷn 4 twɛntɩwɷ:n. wɷ:n n̩ twɛntɩ [twɛntɩ[2]] 5 twɛntɩwɷn. wɷn n̩ twɛntɩ 6 twɛntɩwɷn, ○~[3]. wɷn n̩ twɛntɩ 7 ◇twɛntɩwɷn [twɛntɩ[4]; twɛntɩmɷn[1] *twenty-man* (the nickname of twenty-first child of a loc. family) VII.1.6; fəɩv ən twɛntɩ[4] *five and t.* VII.1.15]

17 Wa 1 ◇twɛntɩwɒn 2 ◇twɛntɩwən 3 ◇twɛntɩwɒn 4 twɛntɩwɷn. wɷn ən twɛntɩ 5 ◇twɛntɩwɷn 6 twɛntɩwɷn. wɷn ən twɛntɩ 7 twɛntɩwɷn. wɷn ən twɛntɩ [θɹi: ən twɛntɩ *three and t.* (ref. age only)]

23 Mon 1 twɛntɩwʌn. wʌn n̩ twɛntɩ 2 twɛntɩwɷn. wɷn n̩ twɛntɩ 3 twɛntɩwʌn. wʌn n̩ twɛntɩ 4 ◇tʰwɛntʰiwʌ̹n 5 ◇twɛntiwʌ̹n. wʌ̹n ən twɛnti 6 ◇twɛntɩwʌn 7 n.a.

24 Gl 1 ◇twɛntɩwɷ:n [fəɩəv n̩ twɛntɩ[2] *five and t.*] 2 ◇twɛntɩwɷ:n 3–4 twɛntɩwœ:n 5 twɛntɩwɒ̨n. wɒ̨n ən twɛntɩ 6 ◇twɛntɩwən, ◇wən ən twɛntɩ 7 ◇twɛntɩwən

25 O 1 twɛntɩwɒn. wɒn ən twɛntɩ [twɛntɩsɩks[2] *t.-six* VII.1.5] 2 twɛntɩwən. ir.r. [ɛɩt ən twɛntɩ *eight and t.* VII.1.7; twɛnʔɩ[1]] 3 twɛntɩwɒn. wɒn ən twɛntɩ [older] 4 ◇twɛntɩwɒn [fɑɩv ən twɛntɩ[4] *five and t.*] 5 twɛnʔɩwʌn. wʌn ən twɛnʔɩ 6 twɛntɩwɒ̜n. wɒn ən twɛnʔɩ

VII.1.13 THIRTY*

Q. How many is this [*write down* 30]?

R. THIRTY

Note—THIRTY(-) also occurs at VII.3.5.

7 Ch 1 θə:tɩ 2 θə:tɩ [θətʔɩsɩks[4] *t.-six*] 3 θə:tɩ 4 θə:tʰɩ· 5 θə:tɩ 6 θə˞:tɩ

8 Db 1 θə˞ttɩ 2–4 θə:tɩ 5 θətɩ 6 θətɩ 7 θɒtɩ

11 Sa 1–11 θəʳ:ʈɩ

12 St 1 θə:tɩ 2 θəʳ:ʈɩ 3–4 θə:tɩ 5 θə:tɩ, ○~[1] 6–9 θə:tɩ 10 θə:tɩ [skə: ən a:f *score and half* (i.e. thirty)] 11 θə:ɹtɩ

15 He 1–2 θəʳ:ʈɩ 3 θəʳ:ʈi: 4 θəʳ:ʈɩ 5 θəʳ:ɽɩ 6 ðəʳ:ʈɩ 7 θəɹtɩ

16 Wo 1 θəʳ:ʈɩ 2 θɛəʳʈɩ 3 θəʳ:ʈɩ, ○~[2] 4 θəʳ:ʈɩ, ○~[3] 5–6 θəʳ:ʈɩ 7 θəʳʈɩ, ○θə:tɩ[3]

17 Wa 1 θə̝̈:tᵉĭ 2 θə:tɩ [θə:tɩ-ɛɩt[2] *t.-eight* VII.1.7] 3 θə:tɩ 4–7 θəʳ:ʈɩ

23 Mon 1–2 θəʳ:ʈɩ 3 θœ·tɩ, ○θœ:tɩ 4 θœtʰi 5 θœ̝̈:tɩ, ○~[1] 6 θəʳ:ʈɩ 7 n.a.

24 Gl 1–3 θəʳ:ʈɩ 4 ðœ:tɩ 5–7 θəʳ:ʈɩ

25 O 1–3 θəʳ:ʈɩ 4 θəɹtɩ, ○θəɽʈɩ[1] 5–6 θəʳ:ʔɩ

VII.1.14 FORTY*

Q. How many is this [*write down* 40]?

R. FORTY

Note—FORTY occ. occurs at VII.3.5.

7 Ch 1 fɔ:tɩ 2 fɔ:tɩ, ○~[1], ○fɔʔtɩ[1] 3 fɔ:tɩ 4 fɔ:tʰɩ· 5–6 fɔ:tɩ

8 Db 1 fɔ˞:tɩ 2–4 fɔ:tɩ 5 fo:ᵊtɩ 6 fɔ:tɩ 7 fa:tɩ, ○fɔ:tɩ[1]

11 Sa 1 fɔʳ:ʈɩ 2 fɔ:tɩ 3–4 fɔʳ:ʈɩ 5 fo:əʳʈɩ 6 fɔʳ:ʈɩ 7 fo:əʳʈɩ 8 fɔ:tɩ 9 fɔʳ:ʈɩ 10–11 fo:əʳʈɩ

12 St 1 fɔ:tɩ 2–3 foɷtɩ 4 fɔ:tɩ 5 fɔ:tɩ, °~[1] 6 foɷtɩ 7–8 fɔ:tɩ 9 fɔ̜:tɩ 10 fɔ:tɩ 11 fɔ̜:tɩ

15 He 1 fɔ:ʳʈɩ 2 fɔ:tɩ 3–4 fɑʳ:ʈɩ 5 fɑ:tɩ 6 vaʳ:ʈɩ 6 fɒɹtɩ

16 Wo 1 fɒɷətɩ 2 faʳ:ʈɩ 3–4 fɑʳ:ʈɩ 5–6 faʳ:ʈɩ 7 fɑʳʈɩ, °~[3]

17 Wa 1 fɔ:tᵉɪ̈ 2 fɔɷətɩ 3 fɔ:tɩ 4 fɔʳ:ʈʰɩ 5–7 fɔʳ:ʈɩ

23 Mon 1 fɑʳ:ʈɩ 2–3 fɑ:tɩ 4 fɒ̜·tʰi 5 fɔ:tɩ 6 fɑʳ:ʈɩ, °~[1] 7 n.a.

24 Gl 1 faʳ:ʈɩ, °~[1] 2 faʳ:ʈɩ 3–4 vɑʳ:ʈɩ 5 fɑʳ:ʈɩ 6–7 vɔʳ:ʈɩ

25 O 1 faʳ:ʈɩ 2 fɔ:̲:tɩ 3 fɔ·əʳʈɩ 4 fɔɹtɩ 5 fɔʳ:ʔɩ 6 faʳ:ʔɩ ["very old"]

VII.1.15 HUNDRED*

Q. How many is this [write down 100]*?*

R. HUNDRED

Note—I.m. exs. of HUNDREDWEIGHT are reproduced below between square brackets untransliterated.

7 Ch 1 ɷndət 2 ɷndɹət 3 ɷndəd 4–5 ɷndət 6 ɷndə̥d

8 Db 1 ɷndə:̲t 2 ɷndɹəd 3 ɷndəd 4 ɷndəd, °~[1] 5 ɷndɹəd 6 ɷndəd, °hɷndəd[1] 7 ɷndəd

11 Sa 1 ʌndɹɪd 2 ɷndɹəd 3 ʌndəʳ:ɖ 4 hʌndɹɪd 5 ɷndɹɪd 6–7 ʌndɹəd 8 ɷndəʳ:ʈ, °~[2] 9 ʌndɹəʳ:ɖ 10 ʌndəʳ:ʈ 11 ʌndəʳʈ

12 St 1 ɷndɹəd 2 ɷndɹət 3 ɷndət 4 ɷndɹəd 5 ɷndət, °~[2] 6 ɷndɹəd, °~[2] 7 ɷndɹəd, °~[1] 8 ɷndɹəd, °ɷndɹɛd 9 ɷndɹəd [ɷndɹədwɛɪt[1]] 10–11 ɷndɹəd

15 He 1 ʌndɹɪd, °ʌndɹəd[1] 2 ʌndəʳɖ, °~[3] 3 ɷndɹəʳɖ 4 ɷndəd 5 ɷndəʳʈ, °~[1] 6 ɷndəʳɖ 7 ʌndəɹd, °ʌndəd[3], °□ʌndəɹdz[1,3], °□ʌndɹədz[3]

16 Wo 1 ɷndəʳɖ 2 ɷndəʳ:ɖ [ɷndəʳ:ɖ[2] *hundred*(weight)] 3 ɷndɹ̩ɪd 4 ɷndɷd 5 ɷndɷd, °~[1] 6 ɷndɹɪd, ɷndəʳɖ ["older"] 7 ɷndəd, °~[1,3(2x),4(2x)] [ɷndədwɛɪt[3,4]]

17 Wa 1 ɷndɹəd 2 ɷndəd, °~[1] 3 ʌndəd 4 ɷndɹəd 5 ɷndəʳ·ɖ, °□ɷndəʳɖʐ[1] 6–7 ɷndəʳɖ

23 Mon 1 ʌndəd 2 ɷndəʳɖ 3 ʌndɹəd, °ʌndɹəʳɖ[2] 4 ʌ̥̈ndɹʌ̥̈d 5 hʌ̥̈ndɹəd, °ʌ̥̈ndɹəd[3] 6 ʌndɹəd, əndəʳɖ[1] 7 n.a.

24 Gl 1 ɷndəʳɖ, ○□ɷndəʳ:ɖʐ[1], ○□ʌndɹədz[1] 2 ɷndɹɩd, ɷndɷd ["older"] 3 ɷndəʳɖ 4 ɷndɷd 5 ɷndəʳɖ 6 əndəʳ·ɖ 7 həndəʳ:ɖ

25 O 1 ɷndəʳɖ 2 ʌndəʳɖ, ○ʌndəʳ·ɖ[1] [ʌnədwɛɩʔ[1]] 3 ʌnəʳ·ɖ 4 ɷndɹəd, ○ɷndəɽɖ[4] VII.3.5, ○~[4] VI.10.10 5 ɷndəʳɖ 6 ɷndɹəd

VII.1.16 THOUSAND*

Q. How many is this [write down 1000]*?*

R. THOUSAND

7 Ch 1 θaɩznt 2 θæɷzənd 3 θaɩznt 4 θaɷznd, θaɩznd [old] 5 θaɩznd 6 θɛɷznt

8 Db 1 θɛ̧ɷznd 2 θa:znd 3 θɛ̈ɷznd 4 θɛ:znd 5 θɛ̧:ᵊznd 6–7 θɛ:znd

11 Sa 1 θaɷzənt 2 θæɷzn 3 θaɷznd 4 θɛu:znd 5 θɛɷzənt 6 θaɷzən 7 θaɷzn 8 θɛɷznt 9 θaɷzn 10 θaɷznt 11 θaɷzn

12 St 1 θæɷzənd 2–3 θaɩzənd 4–5 θæɷzənd 6 θa:zənd 7 θæ̧ɷznd 8 θæɷznd 9 θaɷzənd 10 θæɷzənd 11 θæɷznd, ○ðæɷznd[2]

15 He 1–2 θæɷzn 3 θəɷzn 4 θəɷzən 5 θʌɷzn 6 ðəɷzən 7 θə̆ųzənd, ○□θaɷzənz[3]

16 Wo 1 θa:zn 2 θɛɷzn 3 θɛu:zn 4 θəɷzn 5 θəɷ:znd 6 θɛu:zn 7 θæɷzən, ○~[1], ○□ðæɷzənz[4]

17 Wa 1 θæɷznd 2 θæɷzənd, ○θæɷzən[1] 3 θɛ̈ɷzn 4 θɛɷ̈zn 5 θɛɷzn 6 θɛ̈ɷzn 7 θɛɷzn

23 Mon 1 θʌɷzn 2–3 θəɷzn 4 θəuzʌ̣̈nd 5 θəuznd, ○~[1] 6 θəɷzn 7 n.a.

24 Gl 1 θəɷ:zɷn 2 θəɷzɷn 3–4 ðəɷzn 5 θʌɷzn 6 ðᵊu:zn 7 θᵊu:zn

25 O 1 θɛ̈ɷzn 2 θɛ̧ɷznd 3 θɛɷzn 4 θa̧ɷzən 5 θɛ̈ɷzn 6 θɛɷzn

VII.1.17 TEN‡

Q. About how many calves does a cow have? About . . . .

Ascertain the occurrence of *a* before the numeral.

This q. was solely intended to ascertain whether or not the indef. art. A(N) was used before a numeral. Therefore any forms of the numerals and of ABOUT rec. here by the f.w. have been reproduced as i.m. in the appropriate articles, e.g. ABOUT at VII.2.8.

R. A

Note—I.m. exs. of *A* + numeral are included below between square brackets.

7 Ch 1–6 no art.

8 Db 1–7 no art.

11 Sa 1–11 no art.

12 St. 1–10 no art. 11 s.f. ə

15 He 1–6 no art. 7 no art. [ə wɒn paɪnt əɹ tu:[3] *a one pint or two*]

16 Wo 1–4 no art. 5 no art. [ɪf ðəʶ wɷz əʶɽ‿ɷn[1] *if there was a one*] 6–7 no art.

17 Wa 1–7 no art.

23 Mon 1–6 no art. 7 n.a.

24 Gl 1–2 no art. 3 no art. [ə sɪks mɷnθs[1] *a six months* VII.3.5] 4–5 no art. 6 no art. [ə dɹi:[1] *a three;* ə vʌɪv[1] *a five*] 7 no art. [ə tᵒu: jəʶ: əgᵒu: *a two year ago* VII.3.5; ə vʌɪv[1] *a five,* ə zɪks[1] *a six*]

25 O 1–6 no art.

VII.1.18 NONE*

Q. If you had two apples and then ate them both, how many would you have left?

Rr. NEVER-A-ONE (ONE), NONE

Note—Comparable material occurs at VII.2.13.

7 Ch 1 nɒn 2 nən 3 nɷn 4–6 nɒn

8 Db 1 nɒn 2 nɷən 3–4 nɒn 5 nɷn 6–7 nɒn

11 Sa 1 nʌn, °nɒn[4] 2 nɷn, °nɒn[2] 3–4 nɒn 5 nọn 6–7 nʌn 8 nɷn 9 nɒn 10 nʌn 11 nɒn

12 St 1 nɒn, °~[3,4] 2 nɒn 3 nɷn 4 nɒn, °~[2], °nɷn[1] 5 nɒn 6 nɒn, °~ 7 nọn 8 nɒn 9 nɷn, °~, °nɒn[1] 10 nɷn 11 nɒn, °~[1]

15 He 1–2 nʌn 3 nɷ:n, °nɷn[2] 4 nʌn 5–6 nɷn 7 nʌn, °~[4], °nɒn[4]

16 Wo 1–3 nɷn 4 nɷ:n 5 nɷn, °nɛɹɷn[1] 6 noɷn, °nɒn[3] 7 nɷ·n

17 Wa 1 nɒn 2 nən 3 nʌn 4 nɷn, °~[3] 5 nɷn 6 nɒn 7 nʌn

23 Mon 1 nʌn 2 nɒn 3 nʌn, ○~[1] 4–5 nạ̈n 6 nʌn 7 n.a.

24 Gl 1 nɒ:ᵊn 2 nɒ:n, nɒɹən [“older”] 3 nœ:n 4 nɒn 5 nʌn 6 nə·n 7 nən

25 O 1 nɒn 2 nɒn, ○nʌn[2(2x)] 3 nʌn 4 nɒn, ○nɒn[1] 5 neəʳɳ wʌn 6 nɒn

VII.1.19 A FEW

Q. You might say to somebody: I'm not going away for long, not even a week, but just for . . . . days.

Rr. A COUPLE OF, §(A) DAY OR TWO, (A) /FEW/TWO OR THREE/ TWO–THREE/

Note 1—In the i.m. below, exs. of TWO (OR) THREE are given only when they mean A FEW. Further exs. occur at VII.3.5.

Note 2—When rec. as foll. FEW in the r., DAYS has been reproduced below.

Note 3—The indef. art. was not rec. before FEW at 7.6, 16.3, 17.6, 23.1/3 and 24.5.

Note 4—The r. (A) DAY OR TWO is here regarded as an u.r. and has been so designated below.

Note 5—For exs. of A FEW and comparable expressions used absolutely, see VII.8.21.

7 Ch 1 §ə de: ə tʏ:, ○ə fjʏ:[2] 2 §ə də: a tɩü, ○ə fjü[3] 3 §ə di: ə tɛɷ 4 §ə dẹ: ə tᶷu:, ə tu: ə θɹɩ dẹ:z, ○tu:θɹɩ[2], ○ə tu:θɹɩ[2] 5 §ə di: ə tɛɷ, ə tɛɷθɹɩ [pref.], ○ə ˈtɷθɹɩ 6 fju:, tu:θɹɩ

8 Db 1 to:θɹɩ 2 ə fu: de:z 3 to:θɹɩ 4 tɛɷθɹɩ 5 tʽu:θɹɩ di:z 6 ə tɛ̃ɷ̃θɹɩ di:z, tɛɷθɹɩ[1] 7 ə tɛɷθɹɩ

11 Sa 1 tu:θɹɩ 2 ə fɩu: dę:ᵊz 3 §ə de: ə tu:, ə fɩu: de:z 4 §de: əʳ tu:, ○ə fɩu:[2] V.8.4 5–6 ə fɩu: 7 ə fju 8 tɷθɹɩ 9 §ə de: ə tu:, ○ə fɩu:[1] 10 ə ˈtɷθɹɩ ˈde:z, ○ə ˈtʌθɹɩ[3] 11 §ə daɩ əʳ tu:, ○ə ˈtu:θɹɩ

12 St 1 ˈtɛɷθɹɩ dɩəz, ○ə ˈtü:θɹɩ[1] 2 ə tɛɷθɹɩ di:z 3 §ə di: ə tɛɷ, ə tɛɷθɹi di:z, ○ə tɛɷθɹɩ[1,2], ○ə tɛ̨ɷθɹi[2] 4 ə fju: dɛɩz 5 §ə di: ə tü:, ə tü:θɹɩ di:z, ə fju: di:z 6 §ə di: ə tɛɷ, ə tü:θɹɩ di:z, ○tu:θɹɩ[2] 7 ə fjü: dɛɩz 8 ə fju: dɛɩz 9 ə tɩɷθɹɩ di:z, ə fɩu:, tüθɹɩ[2] 10 §ə dɛɩ ə tü:, ə fjü: dɛɩz̨ 11 ə fju: dɛɩz, ○ə fju:[2]

15 He 1 ə fjæɷ de:ɩz, ○ə fjæɷ[2] 2 ə fjæɷ 3 ə fjæɷ dɛɩz, ○ə fjæɷ[2] 4–5 ə fjæɷ dæɩz 6 ə vjæɷ dæɩz 7 ə fju: deɩz, ə kʌpəl ə deɩz, ○ə fu: deɩz[4]

16 Wo 1 ə fɩu:, ə tu: ə θɹɩ [“older”], ○ˈtu:θɹɩ[1] 2 ə kɷpl ə daɩz, ○ə fɩaɷ[2] 3 fju: de:ɩz 4 ə fjaɷ daɩz 5 ə fɩaɷ de:z, ○ə fɩaɷ[1], ○ə faɷ[1] 6 ə fju: de:ɩz, ○ə fɩæɷ de:ɩz[2] 7 ə fjɛɷ de:z, ○ə fjɛɷ[1], ○ə fju:[1(2x)], ○ə fjɔɷ[1], ○ə fjɔɷ de:z[4]

17 Wa 1 tɷθɹɩ 2 §ə dæɩ ə tu:, °ə fju:[1,3] [ə gɷd fju: lɛtəz[2] *a good f. letters*] 3–4 ə fju: dɛ̧ɩz 5 tu: ə θɹi: dɛ̧ɩz, ə fjɒɷ dɛɩz 6 fju: 7 tu: ə θɹi: dɛɩz

23 Mon 1 fjæɷ dæɩz 2 ə fju: de:z 3 fju: de:z 4 n.a. 5 ə fjɩu, °ə fju:[2] 6 ˈtu:ˈθɹi: de:z 7 n.a.

24 Gl 1 ə fjæɷ de:ᵊz 2 ə fjæɷ dɛɩz, °ə fjæɷ 3 ə vjæɷ dæɩz 4 ə vjɒɷ daɩz 5 fjɑɷ 6 ə vjaɷ de:z 7 ə vju: de:z

25 O 1 §ə dæɩ əɽ tü: 2 ə fju: 3 ə de: əɽ tᴼu: 4 tu: ə θɹi: de:z, °ə fju: de:z[1,4] 5 tu: ə θɹi: 6 §ə deɩ əɽ tu:

VII.2.1 FIRST*

Q. This is not the sixth (of nine sheep coming through a gate), *nor the fourth, but the* [*p.*] . . . .—April 1953, *at the front* added after *This*.

R. FIRST

Note—I.m. exs. of TWENTY-FIRST are reproduced below between square brackets untransliterated.

7 Ch 1 fəst 2 fə:st, °~[2], °fəst[2] [jɛdfəst[3] *head-f.* VI.1.1] 3 fɒst, °~[2] 4 fɒst, °~[3] 5 fɒst, °~[1] 6 fə:st

8 Db 1 fə̇st 2 fɷst 3–4 fə:st 5 fəst, °fɒst[1] 6 fəst 7 fəst, s.f. fɒst

11 Sa 1 fəʳ:ʂʈ 2 fəʳ:ʂʈ, °fɷst[2] 3 fəʳ:ʂʈ 4 fəʳ:ʂʈ, fʌst, °fəʳ:ʂ[2] 5 fǫst, °~ 6–7 fəʳ:ʂʈ 8 fəʳ:ʂʈ, °fɷst[2] 9 fəʳ:ʂʈ, °~[1(2x)] 10–11 fəʳ:ʂʈ

12 St 1 fə:st 2 fɒst [twɛntɩfɒst[1]] 3 fɒst 4 fə:st [twɛntɩfɒst] 5 fə:st, °fəst[1,2(2x)], °fɷst[2] [twɛntɩfəst[2]] 6 fɷst, °fəst[2(2x)], °fɒst[2] [twɛntɩfɷst[2]] 7 fə:st 8 fə:st, °fɷst[1], °fɛst[6] 9 fə:st, °fɷs[1] 10 fɛst, fɷst, °fəst[5] 11 fə:ɹst, °fɷst[1]

15 He 1 fəʳ:ʂʈ 2 fəʳʂʈ 3 fɷ:st 4 fəst, °fəʳʂʈ[2] 5 fəʳʂʈ 6 vɷst, °fɷst 7 fəɹst, °~[1], °~[3] V.5.10

16 Wo 1 fəst 2 fəʳ:ʂʈ, fɷst ["older"] 3 fəʳ:ʂʈ, °fɷst[1] 4 fɷst, °~[2] 5 fəʳ:ʂʈ, °fɷst[1(2x)] 6 fəʳ:ʂʈ, °~[2(2x)] 7 fɷst, °~[1(2x),4(2x)], °fə:st[4]

17 Wa 1 fə̹:st 2 fə:st, s.f. fɷst, °~[4(2x)], °vəst[4], °föst[3], °fə:st[1] 3 fə:st 4 fəʳ:ʂ, °fəɹəst[2] [*sic*], °fə:s[1] 5 fɷst, °fəʳ:ʂʈ[1] 6 fəʳ:ʂʈ, fɷst ["older"] 7 fɷst, °fəʳ:ʂʈ[2]

23 Mon 1–2 fəʳʂʈ 3–4 fœ:st 5 fœ̹:s, °fʌ̹st[2] 6 fəʳ:ʂʈ 7 n.a.

24 Gl 1 fɒst, °fɷs¹ 2 fɷst, °fəʵ:ʂʈ³, °~³ 3 vɷst, °vɷs¹ 4 vɷst, °~¹,³ 5 fǫst, °fɷst² 6–7 vəst

25 O 1 fʌst 2 fəʵ:ʂʈ, °fəst¹, °fʌst² 3 fʌst, °fəʵ:ʂʈ² 4 fɷst, °fəɽʂʈ¹,⁴ 5 fʌst, °fəʵ:ʂʈ² 6 fəʵ:ʂʈ

VII.2.2 LAST

Q. Which is this (of the nine sheep coming through a gate)*?*—April 1953, *And the one at the back?* replaced *Which is this?*

Rr. HINDERMOST, LAST

Note—For additional exs. of LAST, see V.7.21, VII.2.6 and VII.3.9.

7 Ch 1 last⁽²ˣ⁾ 2 last, °last³, °lɑst¹ 3 last 4 last, °las 5–6 last

8 Db 1 last 2 last, °las⁴ 3–7 last

11 Sa 1 la:st 2 last 3 n.r. 4 laʵ:ʂʈ, °la:st² 5 last 6–7 laʵ:ʂʈ 8 la:st, °~¹ 9 læ:st 10 la:st, °~³ 11 la:st

12 St 1 n.a. 2 last, °las² 3 last, °~¹⁽²ˣ⁾, °las¹ 4 las, °~¹ 5–6 las 7 las, °~⁵ 8 las 9–10 last 11 last, °las²

15 He 1 la:st 2 la:st, °~², la:s³⁽²ˣ⁾ 3 la:st 4 la:st, ɪndəʵməst 5 læst 6 læ·st 7 la:st, °la:s³

16 Wo 1 last 2 la·st, lɑ:st ["older"] 3 la:st 4 læ:st, °~³, °laʵ:ʂʈ² [læsɪz³ *lasts 3 pr.s.*] 5 læ:st 6 la:st 7 lɑ:st, °~³⁽²ˣ⁾

17 Wa 1 last 2 la:st, °la·s¹, °lɑ:st⁴⁽²ˣ⁾ 3 la·st, °~²,³ 4 la:s, °~¹ 5 la:st 6 la:st, °~⁴ 7 la:st, °~²

23 Mon 1 læst 2–3 la:st 4 n.a. 5 la:s, °la·s³ 6 la:s 7 n.a.

24 Gl 1 læ:st, °~² 2 la:st, °læ:st³ 3 læ:st, °~¹ 4–6 la:st 7 la:st, °la:s¹

25 O 1 la:st, °la:s² 2 la:st, °~³ 3 la:st 4 ɫast, °~, °ɫä:st⁴, °ɫɑ:st⁴, °ɫɑ:s⁴ 5 la:st, la:s² 6 la:st, °~³ [la:st² *l. inf.*]

VII.2.3 SECOND*

Q. And this (one of nine sheep coming through a gate) [*p.*]*?*

R. SECOND

Note—For additional exs. of SECOND, see II.9.17.

7 Ch 1 sɛkənt 2 sɛkənd, °~[2] 3 sɛkənd 4 sɛkən 5 sɛkənt 6 sɛkənd

8 Db 1 sɛkənt 2–4 sɛkənd 5 sɛkn 6 sɛkənt 7 sɛkənd, °~ VII.2.6

11 Sa 1 sɛkənt 2 sɛkn 3 sɛkənd 4–6 sɛkənt 7 sɛknd 8–9 sɛknt 10 sɛkənt 11 sɛkn

12 St 1 sɛkənd, °sɛknd[4] 2–8 sɛknd 9 sɛkənd 10 sɛknd 11 sɛkə̣nd

15 He 1 sɛkənd 2 sɛkn 3 sɛkənd 4–5 sɛkənt 6 zɛkənt 7 sɛkənd

16 Wo 1 sɛknd 2 sɛkɷnd 3 sɛkn 4 sɛkɷnd̥ 5 sɛkɷnt 6 sɛkɷnd 7 sɛkɷnd, °sɛkənd[4] III.6.5

17 Wa 1–3 sɛkənd 4 sɛkən 5 sɛkɷnd, °sɛkənd[1] 6 sɛkənd̥ 7 sɛkɷnt

23 Mon 1 sɛkn 2 sɛkənd, °sɛkənt[3] 3 sɛkənd 4 sɛkʰʌ̰n 5 sɛkən 6 sɛkənt 7 n.a.

24 Gl 1 sɛkɷnt, °sɛkənt[3] 2 sɛkɷnd̥ 3 zɛkənt 4 zɛkɷnd 5 sɛkọnt 6 sɛkənt 7 sɛkɷnt

25 O 1 sɛkənt 2 sɛkənd 3 sɛkən 4–5 sɛkənd 6 sɛkənʔ

VII.2.4 THIRD*

Q. And this (one of nine sheep coming through a gate) [*p.*]*?*

R. THIRD

7 Ch 1 θəʴ:d 2 s.w. θə:d, °~[2] 3–5 θə:d 6 θəʴ̠:d, °θə:d[3]

8 Db 1 θəʴ̠:d 2–4 θə:d 5 θɔd 6 θəd 7 θə:d, θɒd

11 Sa 1–11 θəʵ:ɖ

12 St 1–10 θə:d 11 θə:ɹd

15 He 1–5 θəʵ:ɖ 6 ðəʵ:ɖ 7 θəɹd, °~[3(2x)]

16 Wo 1 θə:d 2 θˈəʵ:ɖ 3–6 θəʵ:ɖ 7 θəʵɖ

17 Wa 1 θə̣̈:d 2–3 θə:d 4 θəʵ:ɖ 5 θə:d 6–7 θəʵ:ɖ

23 Mon 1–2 θəʵ:ɖ 3–4 θœ:d 5 θœ̣̈:d 6 θəʵ:ɖ 7 n.a.

24 Gl 1–2 θəʵ:ɖ 3 ðəʵ:ɖ 4 ðœ:d 5 θəʵ:ɖ 6–7 ðəʵ:ɖ

25 O 1 θəʵ:ɖ 2 θəʵ:ɖ, °~[1] 3 θəʵ:ɖ 4 θəɽɖ 5–6 θəʵ:ɖ

VII.2.5 FIFTH†

Q. And this (one of nine sheep coming through a gate) [*p.*]*?*

R. FIFTH

7 Ch 1 fɪfθ 2 fɪft 3–5 fɪfθ 6 fɪft

8 Db 1 fɪft 2–4 fɪfθ 5 fɪft 6–7 fɪfθ

11 Sa 1–4 fɪfθ 5 fɪft 6–10 fɪfθ 11 fɪf

12 St 1–2 fɪfθ 3 fɪft 4–5 fɪfθ 6 fɪft 7–11 fɪfθ

15 He 1 fɪft 2 fɪfθ 3 fɪft 4 fɪfθ 5 fɪf 6 vɪft 7 fɪfθ

16 Wo 1–7 fɪfθ

17 Wa 1–7 fɪfθ

23 Mon 1–2 fɪft 3–6 fɪfθ 7 n.a.

24 Gl 1 fɪft 2 fɪfθ 3 vɪfθ 4 vɪft 5 fɪfθ 6 vɪft 7 vɪfθ

25 O 1–4 fɪfθ 5–6 fɪft

VII.2.6 EIGHTH†. LAST BUT ONE

Q. And this (one of nine sheep coming through a gate) [*p.*]*?*
What else could you call it? Not the last but the . . . .

Rr. EIGHTH

LAST BUT ONE, NEXT (TO) THE LAST, SECOND/ONE FROM THE LAST, THE ONE BEFORE THE LAST

Note 1—The rr. to the two parts of the q. are separated below by a full stop.

Note 2—For additional exs. of LAST, see VII.2.2 (and refs.); and of ONE, see VII.1.1 (and refs.). Exs. of EIGHT, EIGHTEEN and EIGHTY occur at VII.1.7 (and ref.).

7 Ch 1 ɛɪtθ. last bʊt wɒn 2 ɛɪt. p. nɛkst tə‿t last 3 ɛɪtθ. nɛks tə‿t last 4 ɛɪtθ. las bət wɒn 5 ɛɪtθ. last bət wɒn 6 ɛɪt. la:st bət wɒn

8 Db 1 ɛɪtθ. nɛkst tə‿t last 2 ɛɪtθ. las bət wɒn 3 ɛɪtθ. nɛkst tə‿t last 4 ɛɪtθ. last bət wɒn 5 ɛɪtθ. nɛkst tə‿t last 6 ɛɪtθ. las bə wɒn, ○~ 7 ɛɪtθ. sɛkənd fɹəm‿ð last

11 Sa 1 ɛɩtθ. la:st bʌt wʌn 2 ɛɩtθ. last bɷt wɒn 3 e:tθ. wʌn fɹɒm ðə la:st 4 e:ɩθ. nɛkst tə ðə la:st 5 ɛɩtθ. last bɷt wɷn 6 ɛɩθ. nɛkst tə ðə la:st 7 e:tθ. nɛkst tə ðə laᵘ:ʂʈ 8 e:tθ. nɛkst tə ðə la:st 9 e:tθ. læ:st bət wɒn 10 e:tθ. nɛkst tə ðə la:st 11 aɩʔθ. la:st bət wa:n

12 St 1 ɛ̜ɩtθ. nɛkst tə‿t last 2 ɛ̜ɩtθ. nɛkst tə ðə last 3 ɛɩtθ. nɛkst tə‿θ last, las bɩ wɒn 4 ɛɩtθ. las bɷt wɒn 5 ɛɩtθ. las bət wɒn 6 ɛɩtθ. las bɷt wɷn 7 ɛ̜ɩtθ. las bɷt wɒn, °ðə wɒn bɩfɔ: ðə las[4] 8 ɛɩtθ. las bɷt wɒn 9 ɛ̜ɩtθ. las bət wɷn 10 ɛɩtθ. las bət wɷn 11 ɛɩtθ. las bɷt wɒn

15 He 1 æɩtθ. la:s bᵊt wʌn 2 æɩʔθ. la:s bʌt wʌn 3 æɩtθ. la:st bət wɷ:n 4 æɩˀθ. la:s bət wʌn 5 æɩʔθ. nɛks ðə læst 6 ɒɩtθ. læst bɷt wɷn 7 eɩtθ. la:st bət wɒn

16 Wo 1 ɛɩʔθ. last bɷt wɷn 2 ɛɩʔθ. la·st bɷt wɷn 3 ɛɩʔθ. la:st bɷt wɷn 4 aɩʔθ. læ:st bɷt wɷn 5 aɩtθ. læ:s bɷt wɷn 6 e:ɩʔθ. la:s bɷt wɷn 7 ɛɩt. p. la:s bɷt wɷn

17 Wa 1 ɛɩtθ. last bət wɒn 2 æɩt. la:st bət wən 3 ɛ̜ɩtθ. la:st bət wɒ̜n 4 ɛɩtθ. la:s bət wɷn 5 ɛɩtθ. la:s bət wɷn 6 ɛɩtθ. la:s bət wɷn 7 ɛ̜ɩtθ. la:st bət wɷn

23 Mon 1 æɩʔθ. læst bət wʌn 2 e:tθ. lɑ:st bət wɷn 3 e:θ. la:s bᵊt wʌn 4 eitθ, °~[2]. la:s bʌ̹̆t˳ wʌ̹̆n, °~[2] 5 eitθ. la:s bʌ̹̆t wʌ̹̆n 6 ɛɩʔθ. la:s bət wʌn 7 n.a.

24 Gl 1 æɩʔθ. læ:s bət wɷ:n 2 æɩʔθ. la:st bɷt wɷ:n 3 æɩʔθ. læ:s bᵊt wœ:n 4 aɩtθ. nɛkst ðə la:st 5 æɩtθ. la:s bət wɷn 6 æɩtθ. la:s bət wən 7 æɩtθ. la:st bət wə·n

25 O 1 æɩtθ. la:s bət wɷn 2 ɛɩtθ. la:s bət wən 3 e:t. la:st bət wɷn 4 e:tθ. ɫa:st bət wɷn 5 e:tθ. la:s bət wʌn 6 ɛ̜ɩʔ. la:s bət wɒ̜n

VII.2.7 ONCE*

Q. How often a day does the postman come?

R. ONCE

Note—Forms of ONE occur at VII.1.1 (and refs.).

7 Ch 1 wɷns 2 wɷns, °wɷnst[4] 3 wɷns, °wɷnst[2] 4 wɒns, wɷns[(2x)] [older] 5 wɷns 6 wɷnst, °~[2]

8 Db 1–3 wɒns 4—5 wɷnts 6 wɷns 7 wɷns, °~

11 Sa 1 wʌns 2 wɷnst, ○~[2(2x),3] 3–4 wʌns 5 wɷns, ○~[2] 6 wʌns 7 wʌns [at ðə wɒns[1] *at the o.* (i.e. at o.)] 8–9 wɒns 10–11 wʌns

12 St 1–4 wɷns 5 wɷns, ○~[2(2x)] 6–8 wɷns 9 wɷns, ○~[1] 10–11 wɷns

15 He 1 wɒnst, ○~[2] 2 wʌns 3 wɷns 4 wʌns [ət wənst[2] *at o.*] 5 wɒnst, ○~[3,4] 6 wɷns, ○wɒnst[1] 7 wɒns, ○~[3]

16 Wo 1–2 wɷns 3 wɷns, ○~[3] 4 wɷnst, ○~[1,2] 5–6 wɷns 7 wɷns, ○wəns[1]

17 Wa 1 wɷns 2 wɷns, ○~[1(2x)] 3 wɒnts 4 wɷns, ○~[1] 5–6 wɷns 7 wɷns, ○wɷnts[2]

23 Mon 1 wʌns 2 wɷns 3 wʌns 4 wʌ̹̈ns 5 wʌ̹̈ns, ○~[1] 6 wʌns 7 n.a.

24 Gl 1 wɷ:ns 2 wɷns, ○~[3] 3 wœ:ns 4–5 wɷns 6 wəns 7 wənts

25 O 1 wɷns 2 wəns, ○wɒnts[1] 3 wɷnts 4 wɷns, ○~, ○wəns[1], ○wɷns[1(2x)] 5 wɷnts, ○wʌns[1], ○wʌnts[1] 6 wɷnts

VII.2.8 ABOUT*

Q. *And what time, roughly, does he* (viz. the postman) *come? . . . . ten.*

R. ABOUT

Note 1—Since the purpose of this q. is purely phonological, the grammatical function of i.m. exs. of ABOUT has been ignored below.

Note 2—I.m. exs. of ROUND–ABOUT(S) *adv.* are reproduced below between square brackets untransliterated.

Note 3—For additional exs. of ABOUT, see III.1.12.

7 Ch 1 əbɑɪt [ɹaɪndəbaɪt[4]; wɪəɹəbaɪts[2] *where-abouts adv.* IX.9.7] 2 əbæɷt, ○~[2(3x),3], ○~[3(2x)] VIII.6.4, ○əbaɷt[2(2x)], ○bæɷt[2(2x)], ○əba:t[4] 3 əbaɪt, ○~[3] 4 əbaɷt, ○~[2,3] [ɹaɪnd əba:t[3] *round a.*] 5 əbaɪt, ○~[1] 6 bɛ̧ɷt, ○əbæɷt[2]

8 Db 1 əbɛ̧ɷt 2 əba:t, ○~[1(3x),3] 3 əbɛ:t 4 əbɛ:t, ○~[2] 5 əbɛ̧:t, ○əba̧:t[1] 6 əbɛ:t, ○bɛ:t[1] 7 əbɛ:t

11 Sa 1 baɷt 2 əbæɷt, ○~[2] 3 baɷt, ○~[2], ○əbaɷt[2] 4 bɛɷt, ○əbɛɷt[2] 5 bɛɷt 6 əbaɷt, ○~[1,4(3x)] 7 əbaɷt, ○əbu:t[1(3x)] 8 əbɛɷt, ○~[1], ○bɛɷt[1] 9 baɷt, ○əbaɷt[1(3x)] 10 əbaɷt, ○~[2,3] 11 bəu:t, ○əbaɷt[1,2]

12 St 1 əba:t, ○~[2], ○əbaɷt[1] 2 əbaɷt, ○əbaɪt[1,5] [ɹaɪnd əbaɪt[2] *round a.*] 3 əbaɪt, ○~[1(6x)] 4 əbæɷt, ○~[1,3] 5 əbaɷt, ○əbæɷt[1], ○əba:t[2], ○əba̧ɷt[3] 6 əba:t, ○~[1,2(2x)], ○əbæ:t[1,2] 7 əbæɷt, ○əba:t[4] 8 əbæɷt, ○~[5,6] 9 əba:t, ○~[1(3x)], ○əbaɷt[1] 10 əbæ·ɷt, ○əba:t[2,5] 11 əba:t, ○əbæɷt[1,2(2x)], ○əbaɷt[1]

15 He 1 bəɷt 2 bæɷt 3 bəɷt, ○~[1], ○əbəɷt[3] 4 bəɷt 5 bʌɷt, ○~[4], ○əbʌɷt[2], ○bɷt[2] 6 bəɷt, ○əbəɷt[1(2x)] 7 əbə̆ʉ̜t, əbɷt, ○~[4(2x)], ○əbəʉ̜t[1,3(2x),4(4x)], ○bɑɷt[1(2x),3], ○əbəɷt[2(2x)], ○əbaɷt[3], ○əbɑ̆ɷt[4]

16 Wo 1 bɛɷt, ○~[3], ○əbɛɷt[2] 2 əbɛɷt 3 əbɛu:t, ○~[3,5], ○bɛu:t[1] 4 bəɷ:t, ○əbəɷt[2], ○əbəɷ:t[3] 5 bəɷ:t, ○əbəɷ:t[1(2x)] 6 bɛu:t, ○~[3], ○əbɛu:t[3] 7 əbæɷt, ○~[1(3x),2(2x),3(5x),4(5x)], ○bæɷt[1(2x)] [ɹæɷndəbæɷts[1]]

17 Wa 1 əbæɷt, ○əbæ̣ɷt[1] 2 əbæɷt, ○~[1(3x)], ○~[4(5x)] 3 əbɛ̈ɷt 4–5 əbɛɷt 6 əbɛ̈ɷt, ○əbɛɷt 7 əbɛ̈ɷt

23 Mon 1 bʌɷt 2 bəɷt, ○~[3] 3 bəɷt, ○~[1] 4 əbəut˳, ○~[2] 5 əbəut, ○~[1] 6 bəɷt, ○əbəɷt[1] 7 n.a. ○ɹəundəbəut[1] [*round-about n.* V.3.4]

24 Gl 1 bəɷ:ᵊt, ○bəɷt[1], ○əbəɷ:ᵊt[1] 2 bəɷt 3 əbəɷt, ○bəɷt[2] 4 bəɷt 5 əbʌɷt 6 əbᶷu:t 7 bᶷu:t, ○əbᶷu:t[1]

25 O 1 bɛ̈ɷt 2 əbæɷʔ, əbæɷt[1] 3 əbɛɷt 4 əbaɷt, ○~[3,4], ○baɷt[3], ○əbæ̜ɷt[5] 5 əbɛ̈ɷʔ 6 əbɛ̈ɷʔ, ○əbɛɷʔ[3]

VII.2.9 WRAP

Q. By the way, if you want to send something by parcel post, you would first have to [*i.*] *. . . . it up.*

Rr. §BUNDLE/FOLD UP, LAP/§PACK/WRAP (UP)

Note 1—When rec. as separating the two els. of a phrasal v., the pronominal obj. EN/HIM/IT is reproduced below.

Note 2—PACK *v.* occurs at VIII.8.15.

7 Ch 1 lap [“with cloth”], §pak [“with paper”] 2 lap ɩt ɷp 3–4 lap 5 lap ɩm ɷpʻ 6 lap

8 Db 1 ɹap 2 ɹap, s.f. lap, ○¶lapɩn[2] 3 lap, ○~[1] [n.d.g.] 4 lap, ○~[1] *v.* 5 ɹap, lap [“very old”] 6 ɹap 7 lap

11 Sa 1 ɹap 2–3 lap 4 ɹa·p 5 ɹap ɩt ɷ̣p 6 ɹap ɩt ʌp 7 lap, ○lapt[2] *p.p.* 8–9 lap 10 læp, ○~[1], ○læpt [*p.p.*] ʌp[3] 11 lap

12 St 1 lap ɩt ɷp 2 lap, ○lap ɩt ɷp 3–4 lap ɩt ɷp 5 ɹap, lap, ○~[2], ○lapt [*p.t.*] ɩt ɷp[2] 6 §bɷndl ɩm ɷp, lap [“old”] 7 ɹap ɩt ɷp 8 lap ɩt ɷp, ○lap[1] *v.* 9 lap ɩt ɷp, ○laps [*pr.t.*] ɩt ɷp[3] 10 ɹap ɩt ɷp, lap ɩt ɷp [“old”] 11 lap ɩt ɷp

15 He 1 læp ɩt ʌp, ○læp[1] *v.*, ○læps[1] *3 pr.s.* 2 læp ɩt ʌp 3 læp ɩt ɷp 4 læp ɩt ʌp 5 ɹæp ɩt ɷp 6 ɹæp ɩm ɷp 7 ɹap ɩt ʌp

16 Wo 1 ɹap 2 ɹap, lap ["older"] 3 ɹæp ɩt ɷp 4–5 læp ɩt ɷp 6 ɹæp ɩt ɷp 7 foɷld ɩt ɷp, lap ɩt ɷp

17 Wa 1 læp 2 lap ɩt ɷp, °~² *3 pr. pl.* 3 lap 4 ɹap 5 lap, °~¹, °¶lapɩn¹ 6–7 lap

23 Mon 1 ɹæp ɩt ʌp 2 ɹæp ɩt ɷp, °ɹæp² 3 ɹæp ɩt ʌp 4 n.a. 5 §pak ɩt ʌ̹̈p 6 ɹæp ɩt ʌp 7 n.a.

24 Gl 1 ɹæp 2 ɹæp ɩt ɷp 3 ɹæp ɩt ʌp 4 ɹa:p ɩt ɷp 5 lap 6 ɹap n̩ əp 7 ɹap

25 O 1 ɹap 2 lap, °~¹ [n.d.g.] 3 lap 4 ɹap ət ɷp 5–6 ɹap

VII.2.10 BIT OF‡

Q. To do that (viz. wrap up a parcel), *you need not only brown paper, but also a [g.] . . . . string.*

Rr. BIT/LENGTH/LUMP OF, PIECE (OF), §SOME

Note 1—When rec., the indef. art. A is reproduced below. The name of the material used, BAND or STRING, has also been cited when rec. in the r.

Note 2—Cross-refs. have been made in the material below only when the phrase concerned is reproduced in some other article and is not covered by the list of cross-refs. in Note 4 below.

Note 3—At 25.5, the f.w. omitted to note whether or not PIECE was foll. by OF.

Note 4—BIT OF and comparable expressions occur at V.6.11, VI.7.11, VII.5.8 and VII.8.6. For expressions for STRING, see I.7.3 (and refs.).

7 Ch 1 pe̜:s ə [ə bɩt ə dɹe̜:nɩn² *a b. of draining*] 2 ə pi:s ə stɹɩŋg̊, ə bɩt ə bɒnt ["older"], °~¹ [ə bɩt ə gæɷd² *a b. of gold*; ə bɩt ə bɑ:m³ *a b. of barm*; ə bɩt ə bɹa̜ʃ³ *a b. of brash*; ə bɩt ə kɷ:l³ *a b. of coal*; ə bɩt of flæɷə³ *a b. of flour*; ə bɩt ə wa:k³ *a b. of work*; ə bɩt ə kəbləz waks⁴ *a b. of cobbler's wax*] 3 bɩt ə 4 pe̜:s ə stɹɩŋg 5 bɩt ə 6 lɛŋθ ə stɹɩŋg

8 Db 1 bɩt ə 2 bɩt ə, °ə bɩt ə² 3 lɷmp ə bɒnt 4 lɷmp ə stɹɩŋg, °pɛɩs ə stɹɩŋg³ VI.14.17 5 pi:s ə 6 ə lɷmp ə stɹɩŋg 7 pɛɩs ə stɹɩŋg

11 Sa 1 pi:s ə stɹɩŋ 2 pʿi:s ə stɹɩŋg 3 pi:s əv stɹɩŋ 4 bɩt əʳ 5 pʿi:s ə stɹɩŋg 6 §sʌm stɹɩŋ 7 pi:s əv stɹɩŋ 8 pi:s əv [ə bɩt ə ɒbɩ² *a b. of hobby* (i.e. a little fun)] 9 pi:s ə 10 pi:s əv 11 pi:s ə stɹɩŋ

12 St 1 ə pɛɪs ə bɒnt 2 ə lɷmp ə stɹɪŋg, ə pɛɪs ə stɹɪŋg [bɪt ə tʃi:z[5] *b. of cheese*; ə bɪt ə ʃɷgə[5] *a b. of sugar*; ə bɪt əv ə ta:tʊ:[5] *a b. of a tartar* (ref. a clever person)] 3 §sɷm stɹɪŋg, p.p. ə pɛɪs ə stɹɪŋg [bɪts ə tɛɪtə[1] *bs. of potato*; ə bɪt ə bɹɛd[1] *a b. of bread*; ə bɪt kɒsɪn[2] *a b. cursing* (i.e. some cursing)] 4 ə pi:s ə stɹɪŋg 5 §sɷm stɹɪŋg [ə bɪt ə i:[2] *a b. of hay*; bɪt ə fə:taɪl land[4] *b. of fertile land* IV.1.7] 6 ə pɛɪs ə stɹɪŋg, ○~[1] [bɪt əv ə snap[2] *b. of a snap* VII.5.11; pɛɪs ə tʃɛɪz[2] *piece of cheese*; ə bɪt ə ɹɛdɪ[2] *a b. of ready* (cash)] 7 ə bɪt ə stɹɪŋg 8 bɪt ə stɹɪŋg [ə bɪt ə bagmɷk[1] *a b. of bag-muck* (i.e. manure); ə bɪt ə snap[4] *a b. of snap* VII.5.12] 9 ə pɛ̝ɪs ə stɹɪŋg [bɪt əv ə dans[1] *b. of a dance*] 10 pi:s əv stɹɪŋg [ə bɪtəv ə dɒs[4] *a b. of a doss* (i.e. sleep)] 11 ə bɪt ə stɹɪŋg [bɪt ə gɹɷb[2] *b. of grub*; bɪt ə snap[2] *b. of snap*]

15 He 1 bɪt ə stɹɪŋ [ə bɪt ə sʌk[2] *a b. of suck* V.8.4] 2 pi:s ə 3 bɪt ə stɹɪŋg̊ 4 pi:s ə stɹɪŋ [ə bɪt təɪm[1] *a b. time* (i.e. an amount of time)] 5 pi:s ə stɹɪŋ 6 ə pi:s ə stɹɪŋ 7 ə bɪt ə stɹɪŋ [ə bɪt ə bo:θ[1] *a b. of both*; bɪt ə wəɹk[1] *b. of work*; ə bɪt ə beɪt[4] *a b. of bait*; ə bɪt ə ʃɷgɪ[4] *a b. of sugar*; ə bɪt ə tɒmɪ[4] *a b. of tommy* (i.e. food)]

16 Wo 1 pi:s ə stɹɪŋg 2 ə bɪt ə stɹɪŋ 3–4 ə pi:s ə stɹɪŋ 5 pi:s ə stɹɪŋ [ə bɪt əv ə ɹəɪz[1] *a b. of a rise*] 6 bɪt ə stɹɪŋ 7 bɪt ə stɹɪŋ [ə bɪt ə tɷŋwag[1] *a b. of tongue-wag* VIII.3.5; ə bɪt ə snɷf[3] *a b. of snuff*]

17 Wa 1 pᵉi:s ə stɹɪŋg 2 bɪt ə stɹɪŋ [ə bɪt ə flɛɷə[3] *a b. of flour*; ə bɪt ə mɛɪt[3] *a b. of meat*; ə bɪt ə ga:dn̩ɪn[4] *a b. of gardening*] 3 pi:s ə 4 ə bɪt ə [ə bɪt ə slak[1] *a b. of slack*] 5 pi:s ə 6 ə lɷmp ə [ə bɪt ə dəʳ:t[1] *a b. of dirt*] 7 bɪt ə stɹɪŋ

23 Mon 1 pʰi:s stɹɪŋ 2 lɛnθ ə stɹɪŋ 3 bɪt ə stɹɪŋ 4 pi̞:§ ə stɹɪŋ 5 bɪt ə stɹɪŋ [ə bɪtʰ ə bʌ̈tʰə[2] *a b. of butter*] 6 pi:s ə stɹɪŋ 7 n.a.

24 Gl 1 bɪt ə stɹɪŋ 2 pʰi:s ə stɹɪŋ [ə bɪt ə ʃɪps ɷɫ[2] *a b. of sheep's wool*] 3 pʰi:s ə stɹɪŋ 4 bɪt ə stɹɪŋ 5 pi:s ə stɹɪŋ 6 bɪt ə [ə bɪt ə pjɛpəʳ[2] *a b. of paper*; bɪt əv ə zwɪɫ[2] *b. of a swill* (i.e. perfunctory wash)] 7 pi:s ə stɹɪ̞ŋ [ə bɪt ə ɛ̝ɪ[1] *a b. of hay*]

25 O 1 pi:s ə stɹɪŋ [bɪt ə gɹe:s[2] *b. of grease*; bɪt ə kɹa:ft[1] *b. of craft*] 2 bɪt ə 3 pi:s ə 4 bɪt ə stɹɪŋ [ə bɪt əv ə fɽɛnɫɪ gɒsɪp[5] *a b. of a friendly gossip*] 5 §pi:s 6 bɪʔ ə stɹɪŋ

VII.2.11 BOTH*

Q. What will the very greedy boy have, pudding or pie?

Rr. (THE) BOTH

7 Ch 1 bọ:ᵊθ 2 s.w. bɷəθ 3 bọ:θ, ○~³ 4 ðə bʏ:əθ 5 bɛɷəθ 6 bo:ᵊθ

8 Db 1 bʏ·əθ, ○bo:θ¹ 2 bo:θ 3 bü:θ 4 bᵒü:θ 5 bo:ᵒθ 6 bü:θ 7 bᵒü:θ

11 Sa 1 bo:θ 2 bo:θ, ○~² 3 bo:θ 4 bo:ᵊθ 5–8 bo:θ 9 bo:θ, ○~¹ 10–11 bo:θ

12 St 1 bu:θ 2 bụ:θ 3 bɷ:θ 4 boɷθ 5 boɷθ, ○bɷ:θ² 6 bɷ:θ 7 boɷθ 8 boɷθ, ○~¹⁽²ˣ⁾ 9 bɷ:θ, ○~¹˒² 10 boɷθ, ○~¹˒⁴ 11 boɷθ

15 He 1–4 bo:θ 5 bo:θ, ○~² 6 bwəθ 7 bo:θ

16 Wo 1–2 boɷθ 3 boɷθ, ○~² 4 bo:θ, ○~² 5 bwɷθ, ○bo:θ¹ 6 boɷθ, ○~¹ 7 boɷθ, bɷəθ ["older"], ○bᵒuθ⁴, ○bɷθ⁴⁽²ˣ⁾

17 Wa 1 bọɷθ 2 bɔɷθ, bu:θ ["pref."], ○~⁴⁽²ˣ⁾ 3 bọ̈ɷθ 4 bọ:əθ 5 bọɷθ 6 bọɷθ, bɷəθ ["old"] 7 bọɷθ

23 Mon 1 bo:ɷθ 2 bo:θ 3 bo:θ, ○ðə bo:θ² 4 bọ:θ, ○~¹ 5 p. ðə bo:θ 6 bo:θ, ○~¹ 7 n.a.

24 Gl 1 bwəθ, ○bʷɷθ¹ 2 bʷəθ 3 bo:ɷθ 4 bo:əθ 5 bo:θ 6 bwəð, ○~ 7 bwəð

25 O 1 bɔɷθ, ○boɷθ² 2 bɔɷθ 3 bɷəθ, ○~¹ 4 bo:θ, ○~⁴ 5 bɷəθ 6 bɷᵊθ

VII.2.12 WHOLE* OF† IT†

Q. I don't think he'd stop at a third of the pie, or even half of it, he'd want the . . . .

R. WHOLE OF IT

The foll. are clearly u.rr. and have been so designated below:—ALL (/OF IT/THE LOT/), (BLINKING/WHOLE) LOT, (WHOLE) LOT OF IT. WHOLE, too, when rec. in the rr. and not foll. by OF IT, is obviously an u.r., but it has not been so marked because of its phonological importance.

Note 1—When rec. in the rr., the def. art. has been reproduced below.

Note 2—I.m. exs. of WHOLE are reproduced below between square brackets untransliterated. In the transliteration of the i.m. below OF IT is represented by dots. Exs. of the phrase OF HIM meaning *of it* have been included below.

Note 3—Cross-refs. to the pronominal obj. have been made in the material below only when the whole phrase has been reproduced in some other article and is not covered in the list of cross-refs. in Note 4 below. All exs. ref. inanimate objs.

Note 4—WHOLEMEAL occurs at V.6.1. For additional exs. of OF + the 3rd sg. pronominal obj., see VII.2.13, VII.8.7, VIII.7.9, IX.2.5/6/15 and IX.11.5. LOT occurs at VII.8.7.

7 Ch 1 ðə §lɒt, p. o̜:l 2 ʔ‿wɷl ən ɩt [wo:l[1(4x)]; me:d bi:zəmz ən ɩt[1] *made besoms* .... ; bɹɛdθ ən ɩt[2] *breadth* .... ; tɛl əv ɩt[2] *tell* .... ; mɩdlɩn əv ɩt[3] *middling* (i.e. middle) ....] 3 §lɒt, s.w. o:l ɒn‿t [wɷl[3]] 4 §ɔ: ðə §lɒt, s.w. ho:l 5 ðə §lɒt, p.p. ðə wɒl §lɒt 6 ðə §lɒt, p. ð‿o̜:l §lɒt

8 Db 1 §o: ɒn ɩt, p. §o:l [jəɹ:d tɛl əv ɩt[3] *heard tell* ....] 2 o:l ɒn‿t 3 §ɒɷ‿t §lɒt [wɒl[2]; wo:lse:l[1] *wholesale*] 4 §lɒt, §ɒɷ‿t lɒt, pp. §o:l 5 §ɔ: ɒn ɩt, p. o:l 6 §ɔ:‿ð lɒt, s.w. o:ᵒl [ə lɒt ɒn‿t[1] *a lot* .... ; mɛk ti: ɒn‿t[1] *make tea* ....] 7 ð‿wɷl §lɒt

11 Sa 1 o:l §lɒt 2 ðə §lɒt, ðə o:l əv ɩt [ðə ne:m ɒn ɩt[2] *the name* ....] 3 o:l §lɒt 4 ðə ho:l §lɒt 5 ᵒu:l ɒn ɩt [ᵒu:l[1]; kɛtʃt ɛɷt ɒn ɩt[3] *catched* (i.e. caught) *hold* ....] 6 o:l əv ɩt 7 ðə o:l əv ɩt, ðə §lɒt [iəʳɖ ɒn ɩt[1] *heard* ....] 8 ðə o:l ɒn ɩt [plɛntɩ ɒn ɩt[1] *plenty* ....] 9 ðə o:l ɒn ɩt, ðə o:l §lɒt [usu.; me:k ə mɔʳ:k ɒn ɩt[1] *make a mock* ....] 10 ðə o:l ɒn ɩt [θɩŋk ɒn ɩt[1] *think* .... ; bɛst ɒn ɩt[3] *best*, ...] 11 ðə o:l ɒn ɩt, ðə §lɔ:t

12 St 1 t‿§lɒt, ð‿u:l §lɒt [oɷl[1]; ənɷf ɒn ɩt[1] *enough* .... ; lɒt ɒn ɩt[1] *lot* .... ; nɛɩm ɒn ɩt[1] *name* .... ; θɩŋk ɒt ɩt[1] *think at (=of) it*] 2 §oɷ ɒn ɩt, s.w. ðɩ oɷl əv ɩt [oɷ ɒn ɩt[5] *all* .... ; mɷst ɒn ɩt[5] *most* ....] 3 ð‿§lɒt ɒn‿t, s.w. ð‿ɷ:l ɒn‿t [fɒnd ɒn ɩt[1] *fond* .... ; kɛtʃ ɛɷt ɒn ɩt[2] *catch hold* ....] 4 oɷl əv ɩt, ðə §lɒt 5 ðə §lɒt, ɷ:l ɒn ɩt 6 §lɒt, ɷ:l ɒn ɩt [iəd ɒn ɩt[1] *heard* .... ; θɹɛɩ pa:ts ɒn‿t[2] *three parts* ....] 7 ð‿oɷl əv ɩt [spi:k əv ɩt[2] *speak* ....] 8 oɷl əv ɩt [tɛl əv ɩt[1(2x)] *tell* ....] 9 ðə §lɒt, ðɩ ɷ:l ɒv ɩt [ɒɩ θɔ:t ɒn ɩt[3] *I thought* ....] 10 §lɒt 11 ðɩ oɷl §lɒt [ɑ:f ɒn ɩt[2] *half* .... ; θɩŋk ɒn ɩt[2] *think* .... ; mɛɩk ə mɛs əv ɩt[3] *make a mess* ....]

15 He 1 wo:ɫ ɒn ɩt [θɩŋk ɒn ɩt[1(2x),2] *think* ....] 2 ð‿o:ɫ n̩ ɩt 3 ðə wɒɫd ɒn ɩt [fɹəɩtnd ɒn ɩm *frightened* ....] 4 ðə wʌɫ §ɫɒt 5 o:ɫ ɒn ɩt 6 ðə o:ɫ ɒn ɩt [ʃɛɹ ɒn ɩt[1] *share* .... ; tɑ:k ɒn ɩt[1] *talk* ....] 7 ðə §lɒt, p. §ɔ:l ɒn ɩt, p. ðə o:l ɒv ɩt

16 Wo 1 §ɑ:l əv ɩt, ð‿ɒɷl §lɒt [nɛɩm ɒn ɩt‿s ɛɩzl[1] *name .... is hazel*] 2 ðə §la·t, §ɑ:l ɒn ɩt, ðə oɷl §la·t 3 ðə oɷl ɒn ɩt 4 ðə o:ɫ ɒn ɩt, ðə o:ɫ §lɒt 5 ðə o:ɫ §lɒt 6 ðə §la:t, ðə oɷɫ §la:t [ɒn ɩt[1] .... ; ɑ:ɫ ɒn ɩt *all* ....; kɛtʃ ɛu:t ɒn ɩm[2] *catch hold of him*; ɑ:f ɒn ɩm[3] *half of him (=it)*] 7 ðə §blɩŋkɩn §lət, s.w. ðə ɔ:ɫ ən ɩt [ən ɩt[1] ....; tɔ:k ən ɩt[1] *talk* ....; i:ðəɹ əv ɩt[3] *either* ....; θɩŋk əv ɩt[3] *think* ....; fɩəlz ən ɩt[4] *fields* ....; fəðəɹ ən ɩt[4] *fodder* ....; mɛɩk ə kɷpl ə gɹæɷndz ɔ:f ɩt[4] *make a couple of grounds* (i.e. small fields) ....]

17 Wa 1 ðə ϙɷl §lɒt [ðə fɩnɩʃ ɒn ɩt[1] *the finish* . . . .] 2 ðə §lət, §ɔ:l ðə §lət, s.w. ðə ɔ:l ən ɩt [dɹɔ:ɹɩn ən ɩt[2] *drawing* . . . .] 3 p. ϙɷ §lɒt əv ɩt, p. ϙɷl §lɒt əv ɩt [tɔ:k əv ɩt[2] *talk* . . . .] 4 ðə §lɒt, °ð‿ϙɷɫ §lɒt 5 ðə §lɒt, p. ð‿ɒɷ §lɒt, °ðə §lɒt 6 ðə §lɒt, p. ð‿ɒɷl §lɒt 7 oɷɫ ɒn ɩt

23 Mon 1 o:ɷɫ §ɫɒt, °ðə o:ɷɫ §lɒt[2] [θɩŋk ɒn ɩt[1] *think* . . . .] 2 ðə o:ɫ n̩ ɩt [jɛd ɒn ɩt[3] *heard* . . . .; tɑ:k ɒn ɩt[3] *talk* . . . .] 3 o:ɫ n̩ ɩt, ðə §lɑ:t 4 ðə hu:l əv ɩtʰ 5 p. ðə o:ɫ əv ɩt [e:kəz əv ɩt[1] *acres* . . . .; tɔ:k əv ɩt[1] *talk* . . . .] 6 ðə §lɑ:t, o:ɫ n̩ ɩt [ðə ne:m ɒn ɩt[1] *the name* . . . .] 7 n.a.

24 Gl 1 o:ɷᵊɫ n̩ ɩt [fænd ən ɩt[1] *fond* . . . .; tɑ:k n̩ ɩt[1] *talk* . . . .; mɷtʃ ɒn ɩt[3] *much* . . . .] 2 ðə o:ɷɫ ɒn ɩm, §ɑ:ɫ ɒn ɩm [kɛtʃ ɒɷt ɒn ɩt[1] *catch hold* . . . .; θɩŋk ɒn ɩm[3] *think of him* (= *it*)] 3 o:ɷɫ ɒn‿t [tᵂu: ɒn‿t[3] *two* . . . .] 4 o:ɷɫ ɒn‿t [tɷnz ɒn‿t[2] *tons* . . . .] 5 ðə o:l §lɒt [bɛs pəʳ:ʈ ɒn‿t[2] *best part* . . . .] 6 ðə §lɑ·t, p. ðə o: §lɒt 7 ðə §lɒt, pp. ʷɷəl

25 O 1 ð‿ɔɷl ɒn ɩt 2 ɔɷl əv ɩt [gɛt ɹɩd ɒn‿t[1] *get rid* . . . .; tɛɩstɩd ɒn‿t[3] *tasted* . . . .] 3 ɷəl §lɒt 4 ðə §lɒt, ðɩ ɔ:ɫ ɒn‿t, °~ [θɩŋk ɒn ət[5] *think* . . . .] 5 §lɒʔ ɒn ɩʔ 6 ɷ:ᵊɫ §lɒʔ

VII.2.13 EITHER*

Q. A less greedy boy will say: It doesn't matter. I'll have . . . . (pudding or pie).

Rr. EITHER, EVER-A-ONE

Note 1—I.m. exs. of NEITHER are reproduced below between square brackets untransliterated.

Note 2—NEVER-A-ONE occurs at VII.1.18.

7 Ch 1 ẹ:ðə 2 s.w. aɩðə, p. æ̣ðəɹ 3 ɛɩðə, °i:ðə[3] 4 i:ðə 5 ɑɩðə, i:ðə 6 aɩðə

8 Db 1 e:ðəɹ̩· 2 i:ðə, °~[4] 3–4 i:ðə 5 i:ðə, °~[1(2x)], °i:ðəɹ 6–7 i:ðə

11 Sa 1 aɩðəʳ: 2 aɩðə 3 i:ðəʳ: 4–6 aɩðəʳ 7–9 i:ðəʳ 10 i:ðəʳ, °~[2] 11 i:ðəʳ

12 St 1–2 i:ðə 3 ɛɩðəɹ, °i:ðə[2] [nɛɩðə[1]] 4 ɒɩðə 5 ɒ:ɩðə [nɛɩðəɹ[3] (+ V.)] 6 i:ðə [nɒ:ɩdə[1]] 7 ɒɩðə, °~[1], °i:ðə[1] 8–9 ɒɩðə 10 i:ðə 11 a:ɩðə, °i:ðəɹ[1] [+ V.; naɩðə[2]]

15 He 1 i:ðəʳ 2 æɩðəʳ 3 i:ðəʳ 4 əɩðəʳ 5–6 i:ðəʳ 7 aɩðəɹ

16 Wo 1 ɒɩðə 2–4 i:ðəʳ 5 əɩðəʳ 6 i:ðəʳ 7 s.w. əɩðəʳ, °i:ðəɹ[3]

17 Wa 1 i:ðə, °ɑɩðə² 2 əɩðə, s.f. i:ðə ["older"], °~¹ 3 s.w. ẹ:ðə 4 i:ðə, °i:ðəʳ·, °əɩðə² 5 əɩðəʳ, °~, °ɛ:ɹəwɷn¹, °ɛəɹəwɷn¹ 6 əɩðəʳ, æɩðəʳ ["older"] 7 əɩðəʳ

23 Mon 1–2 əɩðəʳ 3 i:ðə, °~¹, °i:ðəɹ¹ [+ V.] 4 əiðə 5 əɩ̜ðə 6 əɩðə̀ʳ 7 n.a.

24 Gl 1 əɩðəʳ 2 ɩi:ðəʳ 3–4 ˈi:ðəʳ 5 i:ðə, °əʳ:ɳ² 6 ʌɩðəʳ 7 i:ðə

25 O 1 i:ðəʳ, °~¹ 2 i:ðə 3 ʌʏðəʳ 4 əɩðəɽ 5 ʌʏðəʳ 6 i:ðəʳ, ə̈ɩðəʳ

VII.2.14 WE TWO‡

Q. In this room there's just you and me, no third person; in other words, just . . . .

Rr. ME AND YOU, (THE) TWO OF US, US BOTH/TWO, WE TWO, YOU AND ME

Note—For additional exs. of TWO, see VII.1.2 (and refs.); and of US, see IX.8.1.

7 Ch 1 ɷs tʏ: 2 tü: ən əz 3 ɷs tɛ̈ɷ 4 ɷz bʏ:əθ 5 ɷs tɛɷ 6 ɷs tɩü̜

8 Db 1 ɷs tʏ: 2 ɷz tᶷu 3 ɷz tɛ̈ɷ 4 ɷz tɛɷ 5 ɷs tɛɷ 6 tɛ̃ɷ̃ ɒn əz 7 ɷz tɛɷ

11 Sa 1 ʌs tu: 2 ɷz tˡu: 3 ʌz tu: 4 ʌs tu: 5 ɷs tᶷu: 6 ʌz tu: 7 ʌs tu: 8 ɷz tu: 9–10 ʌs tu: 11 wi: tu:

12 St 1 uz tɛɷ 2–3 ɷz tɛɷ 4 ɷz tü: 5 wi: tü: 6 ɷz tæɷ 7 wi: tü: 8 ɷz tü: 9 ɷz tɩɷ 10 ɷz tü: 11 ɷz tu:

15 He 1–6 wi: tu: 7 ju: ən mi:, ðə tu: əv ʌs

16 Wo 1–7 wi: tu:

17 Wa 1 ɷz̥ tu: 2 ɷs tu: 3 ʌs tu: 4 ɷz tü: 5 wi: tü: 6 ɷs tu: 7 ɷs tü:

23 Mon 1 wɩi: tᶷu: 2 ɷz tu: 3 ʌs tu: 4 wi· tʰu: 5 mi ən ju: 6 wi: tu: 7 n.a.

24 Gl 1 wi: tu: 2 wˡi: tˡu: 3–4 wˡi: tᶷu̜: 5 ɷz tu: 6 ðə tu: ɒn əz 7 wi: tu:

25 O 1 ʌs tu: 2 ʌs tü: 3 ɷs tᶷu: 4 ðə tu: ɒn əs 5 ʌs tü: 6 wi: tu:

VII.3.1 A WEEK* AGO

Q. If you wanted to tell me that something happened seven days back from now, you'd say: It happened . . . .

Rr. A WEEK AGO/SIN/SINCE

Note 1—The f.w. omitted to rec. AGO at 25.1.

Note 2—I.m. exs. of WEEK(–), AGO and SINCE (=*ago*) are reproduced below between square brackets untransliterated. BACK occurs in the i.m. at 16.4 meaning *ago* and AGONE occurs at 25.4.

Note 3—For additional exs. of WEEK(–), see VI.14.20, VII.3.2 and VIII.4.6/7; and of AGO and SINCE, see VII.3.2/4/5.

7 Ch 1 ə wι̜k sι̜n 2 p. ə wιk sιn [wιk$^{2(2x),3,4}$, wi:k^{3}; sι̜n^{2}] 3 ə wιk sιn [wιk^{2,3}] 4 ə wιk əgω, ○ə wi:k əgọ:^{2} [wιk$^{2(5x)}$, wιk‘^{3}] 5 ə wιk əgo: [wιk^{2,3}; wιkɛnd^{1} *w.-end*] 6 ə wi:k əgọ: [wιk^{3}]

8 Db 1 ə wi:k sιn 2 ə wi:k sιn [wˈi:k$^{4(2x)}$] 3 ə wιk sιnts 4 ə wɛιk sιn [wɛιk^{2}, □wi:k‘^{1}] 5 ə wιk əgω 6 ə wιk sιn 7 ə wιk əg^{ω}u:

11 Sa 1 ə wιk əgo: 2 ə wˈi:k əgo:^{ə} [□wιks^{2}; əgo:^{2,3}] 3 ə wi:k əgo: 4 ə wi:k əgo· 5 ə wιk əgo: [wιk$^{3(2x)}$; əgu:$^{1(2x)}$] 6 ə wi:k əgo· [wi:k^{3}; əgo:^{3}] 7 ə wιk əgo: 8 ə wιk əgo: [wιk^{1,2}] 9 ə wi:k əgo: 10 ə wιk əgo: [wιk^{3}] 11 ə wιk əgo:

12 St 1 ə wιk sɛn [□wιk^{2}, □wi:k^{2}; sιn^{2}] 2–3 ə wιk sιn 4 ə wιk əgoω [wi:ks^{3} *poss. s.*; əgoω$^{1(2x),2(2x)}$] 5 ə wιk əgω: [wιk$^{1(2x),2(4x)}$, □wιks$^{1(2x),2}$; əgω$^{1(2x),2}$; wιkɛnd^{2} *w.-end*] 6 ə wιk əgω: [wιk$^{1(2x)}$, □wιks^{1} VII.3.2] 7 ə wik əgoω [wιk$^{2,4(3x)}$; əgoω^{4}] 8 ə wιk əgoω [wιk^{2}, wιks^{1} *poss. s.*] 9 ə wιk əgω: [wιk$^{2(3x)}$; əgω:^{1}] 10 ə wi:k əgoω [wιk^{2}] 11 ə wi:k əgoω [wi:k^{2}; əgoω$^{2(3x)}$]

15 He 1 ə wιk əgo: [wιk^{2}] 2 ə wιk əgo: [wιk$^{2(2x)}$, □wιks^{3}] 3 ə wιk əgu: [wιk^{3}, □wιks^{1,2}; əgu:^{1}] 4 ə wιk əgu: [wιk^{2}] 5 ə wιk əgo: [wιk^{3}, we:k^{2}; əgo:^{1}] 6 ə wιk əgo: [wιk^{1}] 7 ə wi:k əgoω [wi:k^{3}, □wi:ks^{1,4}; əgoω$^{2,4(3x)}$, əgo:ω^{4}]

16 Wo 1 ə wιk əgu: 2 ə wιk əgu: [□wιks^{2}] 3 ə wιk əgoω [wιk^{1}] 4 ə wιk əgu: [wιk$^{2(2x),3}$, wι:k^{3}; əgu:$^{1(3x)}$; bæk^{2} *back* (=*ago*)] 5 ə wιk əgu: [wιk$^{1(5x)}$; əgu:$^{1(6x)}$] 6 ə wιk əgu: [wιk^{2}; əgoω^{1}, əgu:^{2}] 7 ə wιk əgω: [wιk^{4}, wi:k$^{1,3(3x),4}$; əgω$^{1,3(2x)}$, əgo:^{1}]

17 Wa 1 ə wi:k əgọω [wιk‘^{1}; əgu:^{1}] 2 ə wιk əgω· [wιk$^{1,2(2x),3,4(2x)}$, wi:k$^{2(2x)}$, □wιks^{4}; əgəω$^{1(2x)}$, əgo:^{2}, əgọ:^{2}] 3 ə wi:k əgọ̈ω [wi:k^{2}] 4 ə wιk əgü: [wιk^{1,3}; əgoω^{1}, əgọω^{3}, əgü:^{1}, əgu:^{2}] 5 ə wιk əg^{ω}ü: 6 ə wιk əgu: 7 ə wιk əgü:

23 Mon 1 ə wɩk əgo:ɷ [wɩk[1]; əgo:ɷ[2]] 2 ə wi:k əgo [□wi:k[3]; əgo:[3(4x)]] 3 ə wi:k əgo: [əgo:[2]] 4 ə wį:kʰ əgo: [əgo:[1], əgọ[1]] 5 ə wi:k əgou [əgou[2]] 6 ə wi:k əgo: [wi:k[1]; əgo:[2]] 7 n.a. [wi:k[1]]

24 Gl 1 ə wɩk əgo:ɷ [wɩk[1], □wɩks[2]] 2 ə wɩk əgu: [wɩk[3], □wɩks[3]; əgo:ɷ[2,3], əgᵚu:[3]] 3 ə wɩk əgo:ɷ [□wɩks] 4 ə wɩk əgo:ɷ [wɩk[3]] 5 ə wɩk əgo: [wɩk[1]] 6 ə wɩk əgo: 7 ə wɩk əgᵚu:

25 O 1 ə wɩk [wɩk[1,2(3x)]] 2 ə wɩk əgɔɷ, ə wɩk əgɷ· [wɩk[1,2,3]; əgɷ[3]] 3 ə wi:k əgu: [wɩk[1]] 4 ə wi:k əgo: [wi:k[4]; wi:kɛnz[5] *w.-ends*; əgo:[3,4,5]; əgɒn[4] *agone* (=*ago*)] 5 ə wi:k əgọɷ [wi:k[2(2x)]; əgɷ[2], əgu:[2(2x)]] 6 ə wɩk əgɷ· [əgoɷ[3(2x)]]

VII.3.2 A FORTNIGHT

Q. *And if it* (viz. the event) *was twice that time back?* (You'd say: It happened) . . . . *ago*.

Rr. A COUPLE OF WEEK(S), /COUPLE OF/TWO WEEKS/ AGO, (A) FORTNIGHT (AGO/SIN), TWO WEEKS

Note 1—When rec. in the rr., expressions for AGO are included below. For similar expressions, see VII.3.1 (and refs.).

Note 2—I.m. exs. of FORTNIGHT are reproduced below between square brackets untransliterated.

7 Ch 1 ə fɔ:tnɩt 2 fɔtnɩt 3 fɔ:tni:t 4 fɔ:tni:t, ○~[2] 5 fɔ:tnɩt, ○~[2,3] 6 fɔ:tnɩt

8 Db 1 fɔ̝:tnɩt 2 ə fɔ:tnɩt [fɔ:tnɩt] 3–5 ə fɔ:tnɩt 6 ə fɔ̃:tnɩt sɩn 7 ə fɔ:tnɩt

11 Sa 1 ə fɔʴ:ʈɳaɩt əgo: 2 fa:tnaɩt 3 ə fɔʴ:ʈɳɩt 4–5 ə fɔʴ:ʈɳɩt 6 ə fɔʴ:ʈɳaɩt 7 ə fɔ:tnɩt 8 ə faʴ:ʈɳɩt 9 ə fɔʴ:ʈɳaɩt, fɔʴ:ʈɳɩt 10 ə fɔ:tnaɩt, ə fɔ:tnɩt ["older"] 11 ə fɔʴ:ʈɳɩt

12 St 1 ə fɔ:tnɩt sɩ̞n 2 ə foɷtnɩt sɩn [fɔ:tnɩt[1]] 3 foɷtnɩt sɩn 4 ə fɔ:tnɩt 5 ə fɔ:tnɩt, ○~[2] 6 tɛɷ wɩks əgɷ:, fɔ:tnɩt 7 fɔ:tnɒɩt 8 fɔ:tnɩt əgoɷ 9 ə fɔ:tnɩt 10 fɔ:tna:ɩt, fɔ:tnɩt 11 ə fɔ:tna̠ɩt əgoɷ, ə ○fɔ:tnɩt əgoɷ[2] [fɔ:tnɩt əgoɷ[2]]

15 He 1 kʌpl ə wɩks əgo: 2 tu: wɩks 3 ə faʴ:ʈɳɩt əgu: 4 ə faʴ:ʈɳəɩt əgu: 5 faʴ:ʈɳəɩt 6 vaʴ:ʈɳɩt əgo: 7 ə fɔɹtnaɩt əgoɷ

16 Wo 1 fa:tnɩt 2 ə fa:tnɩt 3 ə faʴ:ʈɳəi:t əgoɷ 4 ə faʴ:ʈɳɩt 5 faʴ:ʈɳɩt 6 ə faʴ:ʈɳɒɩt 7 s.w. ə fɔʴʈɳəɩt əgɷ:

17 Wa 1 ə fɔ:tnɩt 2 ə fɔ:tnɩt əgɷ· 3 ə fɔ:tnɑ̣ɩt 4 fɔ:tnɔɩt 5 fɔʳ:ʈɳɩt 6 fɔʳ:ʈɳət 7 fɔʳ:ʈɳɩt

23 Mon 1 fɑʳ:ʈɳɩt 2 ə kɷpɫ ə wi:k 3 ə kʌpɫ ə wi:ks 4 n.a. 5 fɔ:tnəɩ̣t 6 ə fɑʳ:ʈɳəɩt [fɑʳ:ʈɳɩt[2]] 7 n.a.

24 Gl 1 fɑʳ:ʈɳəɩt, °fɑʳ:ʈɳɩt[1] 2 ə fɑʳ:ʈɳəɩt [fɑʳ:ʈɳəɩt[3]] 3 ə vɑʳ:ʈɳəɩt 4 vɑʳ:ʈɳəɩt 5 ə fɑʳ:ʈɳə̈ɩt 6 ə vəʳ:ʈɳʌɩt 7 ə vɔʳ:ʈɳʌɩt

25 O 1 fɑʳ:ʈɳə̈ɩt 2 fɑ‡:tnə̈ɩt 3 ə fɔʳ:ʈɳʌʏt 4 ə fɒɽʈɳə̣ɩt əgo: 5 fɔ:ʔnə̈ɩʔ 6 ə fɔʳ:ʔnə̈ɩʔ

VII.3.3 APRIL*

Q. *And if* (the event was) *in the month before May?* (You'd say: It happened) *In . . . .*
Note the stress.

R. APRIL

Note 1—The f.ws. occ. omitted to rec. the stress.
Note 2—For additional exs. of APRIL, see VII.4.10.

7 Ch 1 ˈẹ:pɹɪl 2 ˈe:pɹɪl, °~[2], °ˈe:pɩl[2] [*sic*] 3 ˈi:pɹəl 4 ˈẹ:pɹəl 5 ˈe:pɹəl, p. i:pɹəl 6 e:ᵊpɹəl

8 Db 1 ˈe:pɹɪl 2 e:pɹɪl 3–4 ˈe:pɹəl 5 ˈe:pɹɪl 6–7 ˈe:ˌpɹɪl

11 Sa 1 ˈepɹəl 2 ˈẹ:pɹəl 3 ˈe:pɹəl 4 ˈe:pɹɪl 5 ˈẹ:pɹəl 6 ˈe:pɹəl 7–8 ˈe:pɹɪl 9 ˈe:pɹəl 10–11 ˈe:pɹɪl

12 St 1–3 ˈɛɩpɹɪl 4 ˈeipɹəl 5 ˈɛɩpɹɪl 6–7 ˈɛɩpɹəl 8 ɛɩpɹɪl 9 ˈɛ·ɩpɹɪl 10 ˈɛɩpɹəl 11 ˈɛɩpɹɪl

15 He 1–2 ˈe:ɩpɹəɫ 3 ˈæpɹəɫ 4 ˈe:ɩpɹəɫ 5 ˈe:ɩpɹəɫ, °ˈæpɹəɫ 6 ˈɛpɹəɫ 7 ˈeɩpɹəl

16 Wo 1 ˈɛɩpɹəl 2 ˈapɹəl 3–4 ˈe:pɹəɫ 5 ˈe:pɹɪɫ 6 ˈe:pəɹəl 7 ˈapɟɪɫ

17 Wa 1 ˈɛɩpɹəɫ 2 ˈɛ̨ɩpɹəl 3 ˈɛɩpɹɪɫ 4 ˈɛ̣ɩpɹəɫ 5 ˈe:ᵊpɹəɫ 6 ˈe·əpɹəɫ 7 ˈɛɩpɹəɫ

23 Mon 1 ˈe:ɩpɹəɫ 2–3 ˈe:pɹəɫ 4 e:pɹ] 5 ˈe:pɹᵊɫ 6 ˈe:pɹəɫ 7 n.a.

24 Gl 1 ˈe:pɹɷɫ 2 ˈɛɩpɹɷɫ 3 ˈe:ˌpɹəɫ 4 ˈe:pɹəɫ 5 e:pɹəl 6–7 ˈe:pɹəɫ

25 O 1 apɽəɫ ["old, not used"], æɩpɹɪl [pref.] 2 ˈɛɩpɹəɫ 3 e:pɽəɫ 4 ˈe:pɹəɫ 5 ˈe:pɽəɫ 6 eɩpɽəɫ

VII.3.4 A YEAR*

Q. *If* (the event happened) *twelve months back from now?* (You'd say: It happened) . . . . *ago.*

Rr. TWELVE MONTHS, (A) YEAR

Note 1—When rec. in the rr. and i.m., expressions for AGO are reproduced below.

Note 2—I.m. exs. of TWELVEMONTH and YEAR are reproduced below between square brackets untransliterated.

Note 3—Strictly speaking, i.m. exs. of YEARS AGO/BACK/SIN are not synonymous with the wanted expression, but since the q. is a phonological one, these exs. of YEARS have been reproduced immediately following the r. and are marked with the sign of plurality.

Note 4—For additional exs. of YEAR, see VII.3.6/7/18 and VII.4.8. For exs. of YEAR(S) prec. by a numeral, see VII.3.5; and of AGO, see VII.3.1 (and refs.). YEARLING (ref. sheep) occurs at III.6.5.

7 Ch 1 ə jɩə, ○□ɩəz bak[2] 2 s.w. ə jɩəɹ əgɷə, twɛlv mɷnθs əgɷə [ɩə2(3x); □ɩəz2(2x); jɩəlɩn[1] *yearling* III.4.3] 3 ə ɩə [□ɩəz[2]] 4 ə ɩəɹ əgɷ [ɩəz2(3x)] 5 ə ɛɩə 6 ə ɩə [ɩə1,2; □ɩəz2(2x)]

8 Db 1 jə:ɹ̣ 2 ə ɩə [ɩə[4]] 3 ə ɩə [ɩə[1]] 4 ə jɩə 5 ə jɩə [jɩəz[1] *poss.*] 6 ə jɩəɹ əg:ũ 7 ə jɩəɹ əgɷü:

11 Sa 1 ə ɩəʳ [□ɩəz2,3] 2 ə ɩəʳ 3 ə iəʳ 4 ə i:əʳ 5 ə ɩəʳ, ○□ɩəʳʐ̹ əgu:[1], ○□jɩəʳʐ̹ əgu:[2] [□ɩəʳʐ̹[2]] 6 ə ɩəʳ 7 ə ɩəʳ [ɩəʳ2(4x)] 8 ə ɩəʳ [ɩəʳ1(2x); □ɩəʳʐ̹[2]] 9 ə ɩəʳ: 10 ə ɩəʳ· [ɩəʳ[3]] 11 ə ɩəʳ [ɩə1(2x),2]

12 St 1 ə i:ə [i:ə[1], ɩə[2]] 2 ə jɩə sɩn [jɩə[2], ɩə[1], iə[5]] 3 ə jɩə sɩn, ○jɩəɹ əgɷ:[1] [jɩə, □jɩəz[1]] 4 ɔ ɩəɹ əgoɷ 5 twɛlv mɷnθs əgɷ:, ə jɩəɹ əgɷ: [jiə[2]] 6 ə jɩə [jɩə[1]] 7 ɔ ɩəɹ əgoɷ 8 ɩəɹ əgoɷ 9 ə i:ə [jɩə[1]] 10 ə jɩəɹ əgoɷ 11 i:əɹ əgoɷ

15 He 1 ə jɩəʳ 2 jɩəʳ [ɩəʳ[3]; □ɩəʳʐ̹[3]] 3 ə jəʳ:ɽ əgu:, ○□jəʳ:ʐ̹ əgu:[4] [jəʳ:[4]] 4 ə jəʳ:ɽ əgu:, ○□jəʳ:ʐ̹ əgu:[3] 5 ə jəʳ, ○~[3] 6 ə jəʳ: 7 ə jɩəɹ əgoɷ [jɩəɹ[1] + pause)]

16 Wo 1 ə ɩə, ○□ɩəʳʐ̹ əgu:[2] [ɩəʳ[1]; ɩəʳlɩn kɑ:f[1] *yearling calf*] 2 ə ɩəʳ [□jəʳ:ʐ̹[1]] 3 ə jəʳ:ɽ əgoɷ 4 ə jəʳ:ɽ əgu: [ɩəʳ[2], jəʳ:[3]] 5 ə ɩəʳ [jəʳ:[1]; □jəʳ:ʐ̹1(2x)] 6 ə ɩəɽ əgu: [□ɩəʳ:ʐ̹[1], □jəʳ:ʐ̹[1]] 7 ə jəʳ· əgọ:, ə ɩəɽ əgɷ: [pref.], ○□ɩəz əgoɷ[1] [jəʳ1,2, jəʳ·2,3, ɩəʳ[1]; □jə:z1,3(2x),4, □jəʳʐ̹1(2x),4]

17 Wa 1 ə jə̹̣:ɹ əgọɷ 2 ə ɩə əgɷ, ○□ɩəz əgəɷ[1] [ɩə4(2x)] 3 ə jɩə bæk, ○□jɩəz əgọ:[2] [jɩə[2]] 4 ɔ ɩə 5 ə ɩəʳ əgü: [ɩəʳ1(2x)] 6 ɩ jɩəʳ [ɩə[4]] 7 ə jɩəɹ əgü: [ɩəʳ[1]]

23 Mon 1 jəʳ [jəʳɽ[2] (+ V.)] 2 ə jəʳ: 3–4 ə jœ:ɹ əgo: 5 ə jœ̹̣:ɹ əgo: 6 ə jəʳ: 7 n.a.

24 Gl 1 ə jəʳ: [jəʳ:[3(2x)]] 2 ə jəʳ: [jəʳ:; □jəʳ:ʐ[1,2]] 3 jɩəʳ, ○□ɩəʳʐ əgᵒu:[4] [ɩəʳʐ[4]] 4 ɔɩəʳ [□ɩəʳ:ʐ[3], □ɩəʳʐ[3]] 5 ə jəʳ əgo:, ○□jəʳ:ʐ əgo:[2(2x)] 6 ə jəʳ: 7 ə jəʳ:ɽ əgᵒu [jəʳ:[1]]

25 O 1 ə jəʳ: 2 ə jɩəɹ əgɔɷ 3 ə jɩəʳ əgu: [ɩəʳ[1]] 4 ə jəɽ əgo: [twɛɫvmɷnθ[1]; jəɽɭɩn[1(2x)] *yearling n.*] 5 ə jɩə 6 jɩəʳ

VII.3.5 TWO YEARS†

Q. *And if* (the event happened) *twice that time* (viz. one year) *back* (from now)*?* (You'd say: It happened) . . . . *ago.*

Rr. A COUPLE OF YEAR(S), TWO YEAR(S)

Note 1—When rec. in the rr., expressions for AGO are included below.

Note 2—I.m. exs. of YEAR(S) and comparable expressions of time prec. by a numeral other than ONE are reproduced below between square brackets.

Note 3—Exs. of an uninflected n. prec. by a numeral also occur at VI.10.10, VII.7.8 and VII.8.2. For additional exs. of TWO(-), see VII.1.2 (and refs.); of YEARS, see VII.3.4; and of AGO, see VII.3.1 (and refs.).

7 Ch 1 tʏ: ɩə sɩn 2 tü: jɩəɹ əgɷə [fɔʔtɩ ɩə[1], fɔ:tɩ ɩə[1] *forty y.*; tu: ᵊθɹi: de:z[1] *two or three days*; sɩkstɩ mɩnɩts[2] *sixty minutes*; θɹi: jɩə sɛn[2] *three y. sin*; sɩksti:n wɩk[4] *sixteen week*; twɛlv mɷnθs əgɷə *twelve months ago* VII.3.4] 3 tɛ̈ɷ ɩə sɩn 4 ə kɷpl ᵊ ɩə [sɛvn ɩə[3] *seven y.*] 5 tᶦʏ: ɛɩə 6 tᵒu: ɩə [tɛn ɩəz[1] *ten ys.*; sɛvn dẹ:z[2] *seven days*; sɩks mɷnθ[2] *six month*]

8 Db 1 tʏ: jəᶦ [θɹi: mɷnθ ɔ:f[1] *three month off*] 2 tᵒu: ɩə, ○~[1] [tɛn ɩə sɩn[1] *ten y. sin*; θɹi: ɩəɹ[4] (+ V.) *three y.*] 3 tü: ɩə 4 tɛɷ jɩə sɩn [θɹɛɩ wi:k[1] *three week*] 5 tɛɷ jɩə 6 tɛɷ jɩə sɩn 7 tɛɷ jɩəz

11 Sa 1 tu: ɩəʳ 2 tɩu: ɩəʳʐ 3 tu: i:əʳ: 4 tu: i:əʳ 5 tɩu: ɩəʳʐ [tɛn mɪ̣nɪ̣ts[1] *ten minutes*; faʳ:ɽɩ jɩəʳʐ[2] *forty ys.*] 6 tu: ɩəʳ [fɩfti:n ɩəʳ o:ld[4] *fifteen y. old*] 7 tu ɩəʳ [θɹi: de:z[1] *three days*] 8 tu: ɩəʳ [fɔ:tɩ ɩəʳʐ[1] *forty ys.*; twɛntɩ ɩəʳɽ əgo:[2] *twenty y. ago*] 9 tu: ɩəʳ: 10–11 tu: ɩəʳ

12 St 1 tɛɷ i:ə sɩn 2 tɛɷ jɩə sɩn [foɷəɹ ɩə[5] *four y.*; θɹɛɩ mɷnθ[2] *three month*] 3 tɛɷ iəz əgɷ: [sɩks di:z[1] *six days*; twɛlv mɷnθ sɩn[1] *twelve month sin*] 4 tü: iəz [fɔ:ɹ iəz əgoɷ[1] *four ys. ago*] 5 tü: iə [θɹɛɩ wɩks[1] *three weeks*] 6 ə kɷpl ə jɩə 7 tü: ɩəz, ○~[1] [θə:tɩ ɩə[1] *thirty y.*] 8 tü: ɩəɹ əgoɷ [fɔ:ə ɪ̣əz[1] *four ys.*; twɛlv mɷnθs[1] *twelve months*] 9 tɩɷ i·əz əgɷ [fɷəmɷnθæɷd[1] *four-month-old adj.*; nɒɩn mɷnθs[1] *nine months*; sɛvn ɔɹ ɛɩt iəɹ oɷld[1] *seven or eight y. old*; θɹi: dɛɩz[2] *three days*] 10 tü: jɩəɹ əgoɷ 11 tu: ɩəɹ əgoɷ [θɹi: ɔ fɔ: iəz[1] *three or four ys.*; twɛlv mɷnθs[1] *twelve months*; foɷəɹ iəz[2] *four ys.*]

15 He 1 tu: jɩəʳ [twɛntɩ jəʳ:ʐ bæk[1] *twenty ys. back* (=*ago*)] 2 tu: jɩəʳɽ əgo: [ˈfɔ:ˈjəʳˈɽo:łd[2] *four y. old*; fɩftɩ ɩəʳ əgo:[3] *fifty y. ago*; fəɩv ɩəʳ[3] *five y.*; θɹi: wɩks[3] *three weeks*] 3 tu: jəʳ:ɽ əgu: [sɛvn jəʳ:[1] *seven y.*; ɛɩt jəʳ[2] *eight y.*] 4 tu: jəʳ: 5 tu: jəʳ:ʐ 6 tu: jəʳ: 7 tu: jɩəɹ əgoɷ, °ə kʌpəl əv ɩəɹz əgoɷ, °tu: jɩəɹz əgoɷ[4], °tu: ɩəɹz əgoɷ[4] [sɩks wi:ks[1] *six weeks*; tu:jəɹo:ld[1] *two-yr.-old adj.*; e:ti:n jəɹz[2] *eighteen ys.*; sɛvənti:n əɹ eɩti:n jɩəɹ[3] *seventeen or eighteen y.*; θəɹti:n jə·ɹz[3] *thirteen ys.*; tu: əɹ θɹi: jəɹ o:ld[3] *two or three y. old*; fɩftɩ jəɹz əgo:ɷ[4] *fifty ys. ago*; θɹi: jɩəɹz əgoɷ[3] *three ys. ago*; twɛntɩ jə·ɹz[4] *twenty ys.*]

16 Wo 1 tu: ɩə [tu: ə θɹi: dɛɩz[2] *two or three days*] 2 tu: ɩəʳ [θɹi: jəʳ:[2] *three y.*] 3 tu: jəʳ:ʐ 4 tu: jəʳ:ɽ əgu:, °tu: ɩəʳ[3] [sɛvn daɩz[2] *seven days*; tu: jəʳ:ɽ aɷd[2] *two y. old*] 5 tu ɩəʳʐ əgu: [aɩtɩ jəʳ:ʐ[1] *eighty ys.*; tu: wɩks[1] *two weeks*] 6 tu: ɩəʳʐ 7 tu: jəʳʐ əgǫ:, tu ɩəʳʐ əgɷ [pref.], °tu: jə:z[3] [fəəti:n ə fɩfti:n deɩz[1] *fourteen or fifteen days*; θɹi: ə fɔɷə jəʳ·ʐ[1] *three or four ys.*; θə:tɩ jə:z[3] *thirty ys.*; twɛlv mɷnθs əgɷ[3] *twelve months ago*; ɷndəd jə:z[3] *hundred ys.*; əlɛvn jəʳʐ[4] *eleven ys.*]

17 Wa 1 tu: jə̣:z 2 tu: ɩəz əgɷ [θə:tɩ-ɛɩt jɩə[2] *thirty-eight y.*; sɩks wɩks[4] *six weeks*; θə:tɩ jɩə[4] *thirty y.*] 3 tu: jɩəz bæk 4 tü ɩəɹ əgü: 5 tu: ɩəʳʐ əgü:, °tu: ɩəʳ·ʐ[1] 6 tü: ɩəʳɽ əgu: 7 tü: jɩəɹ əgü:

23 Mon 1 tᵚu: jəʳɽ əgo:ɷ 2 ə kɷpł ə jəʳ:ʐ 3 tu: jœ:z [tɛn jœ:ɹ o:łd[2] *ten y. old*] 4 tʰu· jəz 5 tu: jœ̣:z əgo: [sɩkstifɔ: jˈœ̣:z[3] *sixty-four* (VII.1.4/5) *ys.*] 6 tu: jəʳ:ʐ əgo: 7 n.a. [fo: mʌ̣nθs[1] *four months*; sɩks mʌ̣nθs[1] *six months*]

24 Gl 1 tu jəʳ:ʐ [θɹi: ə fæɷəʳ dæɩəz[2] *three or four days*; θɹi: wɩks[2] *three weeks*] 2 tˈu: jəʳ:ʐ, °tu: jəʳ:ʐ əgo:ɷ[3] [sɩks wɩks əgᵚu:[3] *six weeks ago*] 3 tᵚu: jɩəʳ [ə sɩks mɷnθs[1] *a six* (VII.1.17) *months*] 4 tᵚu: ɩəʳ 5 tu: jəɹ əgo: 6 tu: jəʳ:ɽ əgo: 7 ə tᵚu: jəʳ:ɽ əgᵚu:

25 O 1 tu: jəʳ:ʐ 2 tu: ɩəʳ 3 tᵚu: jɩəʳ əgu: [sɛbm əɽ e:t ɩəʳʐ[2] *seven or eight ys.*] 4 tu: jəɽʐ əgo: [twɛlvmɷnθo:łd[1] *twelve-month-old adj.*; ə kɷpł ɷndəɽɖ jəɽʐ[4] *a couple* (of) *hundred ys.*; faɩv jəɽʐ[3] *five ys.*; sɩkstɩ jəɽʐ əgo:[3] *sixty ys. ago*; fəɩv ə sɩks, jəʳ əgɒn[4] *five or six y. agone* (=*ago*); fɩftɩ jəɽʐ[5] *fifty ys.*] 5 tu: ɩəʳ [tu: ɛɷəʳʐ[2] *two hours* VII.5.7; sɛbm deɩz[2] *seven days*] 6 tu: ɩəʳʐ [sɛbm deɩz[3] *seven days*]

VII.3.6 SPRING

Q. *If* (the event happened) *in the season after winter?* (You'd say: It happened) *In* . . . .

Rr. RISE, (THE) SPRING (OF THE YEAR)

7 Ch 1 spɹɪŋ 2 spɹɪŋg, °spɹɪŋ ə‿tð‿ɪə[2] 3 spɹɛŋg 4–5 spɹɪŋ 6 spɹɪŋ, °~

8 Db 1 spɹɪŋg 2 spɹɪŋ, °~[4] 3 spɹɪŋg 4 spɹɪŋ 5–7 spɹɪŋg

11 Sa 1–4 spɹɪŋ 5 spɹɪŋg 6 spɹɪŋ 7 ðə spɹɪŋ ə ðə ɪəʳ, °~ 8 spɹɪŋ 9 ðə spɹɪŋ 10 ðə spɹɪŋ ə ðə ɪəʳ 11 spɹɪŋ

12 St 1 spɹɪŋ 2 spɹɪŋg 3 spɹɪŋg, °~[1] 4–6 spɹɪŋg 7 spɹɪŋg, °~[1] (2x) 8 spɹɪŋg, °~[1] 9–11 spɹɪŋg

15 He 1 ðə spɹɪŋ 2–6 spɹɪŋ 7 ðə spɹɪŋ, °spɹɪŋ[1]

16 Wo 1 spɹɪŋg 2 spɹɪ̹ŋ 3 spɹɪŋg̊, °ðə spɹɪŋg ə ðə jəʳ:[5] 4–5 spɹɪŋ 6 spɹɪŋ, °~[3] 7 spɹɪŋ

17 Wa 1 ðə spɹɪŋg 2–4 spɹɪŋ 5 ðə spɹɪŋ 6 spɹɪŋ 7 ðə spɹɪŋ

23 Mon 1 spɹɪŋ ə ðə jəʳ 2–3 spɹɪŋ 4 n.a. 5–6 spɹɪŋ 7 n.a.

24 Gl 1 spɹɪŋ 2 spɹɪŋ, ɹəɪz [rec. in «ðə ɹəɪz n̩ fɑ:ɫ ə ðə jəʳ:» *the rise* (i.e. spring) *and fall* (i.e. autumn) *of the year*)] 3–6 spɹɪŋ 7 ðə spɹɪŋ

25 O 1–2 spɹɪŋ 3–4 spɹɪŋ 5 spɹɪŋ 6 ðə spɹɪŋ

VII.3.7 AUTUMN

Q. *If* (the event happened) *in the season after summer?* (You'd say: It happened) *In* . . . .

Rr. (THE) /AUTUMN/BACK–END/FALL/, /BACK–END/THE FALL/ OF THE YEAR

Note—Very likely the absence of the def. art. from a r. is not significant.

7 Ch 1 bakˈɛnd 2 bakɛ̧nd ə‿tð‿ɪə (2x) 3 bakɛnd 4 bakˈɛnd, °ðə ˈbakˈɛnd, °ˈbakˈɛnd[1] 5 bakˈɛnd 6 bakɛnd, °~[3]

8 Db 1 bakˈɛnd 2–7 bakɛnd

11 Sa 1 ˈbakˈɛnd 2 ɔ:təm, ˈbakɛn 3 ˈbakɛnd 4 ˈba·kɛn 5 a:tɷm 6 ɔʳ:ʈəm 7 ˈbækˈɛnd, ɔ:təm 8 aʳ:ʈəm, ˈbakɛnd 9 ɔʳ:ʈəm 10 ɔ:tʌm 11 ɔ:təm, ðə ˈbakɛn

12 St 1 aɷtɷm, ˈbakɛnd 2 oɷtəm, ˈbakˈɛnd, °~[1,2] 3 oɷtəm, ˈbakɛnd, °~[1,2] 4 ɔ:tɷm, bakɛnd ["old"] 5 ð‿ɔ:təm, ˈbakɛnd 6 oɷtəm 7–8 ɔ:təm 9 ɔ:təm, ˈbakɛnd ["old"] 10 ɔ:təm 11 ɔ:tɷm

15 He 1 ɔ:təm, ðə ˈbækˈɛnd ["usu."], °ɔ:təm[1] 2 ɔ:təm 3 ɑʳ:ʈɷ:m 4–5 ɑ:təm 6 ɑ:tɷm 7 ðə ɔ̜:təm, ðə ˈbḁkɛnd [i.e. "late a."]

16 Wo 1 ɑ:tɷm, °~[3] 2 ɒtəm, °~[2] 3 ɑ:təm 4 ɑʳ:ʈɷm 5 ɑ:tɷm 6 ɑʳ:ʈɷm 7 ɔ:təm, s.w. bakɛnd [i.e. "late a."]

17 Wa 1 ðɩ ɔ:tɷm 2 ɔ:təm, s.w. bakɛnd [pref.], °~ 3 ɔ:ᵊtɷm, s.w. fɔ:l, °ðə fɔ:l ə ðə jɩə 4 ɔ:tɷm, s.w. bakɛnd [rare] 5 ðᵊ ɔ:tɷm, °ð‿ɔ:tɷm[1], °ðə ɔ:tɷm[1] 6–7 ɔ:tɷm

23 Mon 1 fɑ:ɫ 2 fɑ:ɫ ["usu."], ɑ:təm 3 fɑ:ɫ 4 n.a. 5 ɔ:tʌ̤̈m 6 ɑ:təm 7 n.a.

24 Gl 1 ɑʳ:ʈɷm 2 ɑ:tɷm, fɑ:ɫ [rec. in «ðə ɹəɩs n̩ fɑ:ɫ ə ðə jəʳ:» *the rise* (=*spring*) *and fall* (=*autumn*) *of the year*] 3 ɑʳ:ʈəm 4 ðə vɑ:ɫ ə ðə ɩəʳ 5 ɔ:tɷm 6 ɔ:təm 7 ðə fɔ:ɫ ə ðə jəʳ:

25 O 1 ɔ:təm 2 a:təm, °~[3] 3 ɔ:təm 4 ɔ:təm, °~[4] 5 ɔ:ʔəm 6 ðə ɔ:təm, s.w. fɔ:l ["formerly used"]

VII.3.8 YESTERDAY*

Q. If (the event happened) *not today, but 24 hours ago?* (You'd say: It happened)

R. YESTERDAY

7 Ch 1 jɩ̜stədẹ: 2 s.w. jɩstədɩ 3 jəstədi: 4 jəstədẹ: 5 jəstədi:, °~[2] 6 jɛstədɩ

8 Db 1 jɩstəde: 2 jɛstəde: 3 jəstəde:, °jɛstəde:[1] 4 jɩstədi: 5 jɩstədɩ 6 jɩstədi: 7 n.a.

11 Sa 1 jɛstəde: 2 jɛstədɩ 3 jɛstəʳɖe· 4–6 jɛstədɩ 7 jɛstəʳ·ɖe: 8 jɛstədɩ 9 jɛstəʳ·ɖe: 10 jɛstəʳɖe: 11 jɛstəʳɖɩ

12 St 1–3 jɛstədi: 4–5 jɛstədɩ 6 jɛstədi:, °~[2] 7–8 jɛstədɩ 9 jɛstədi: 10–11 jɛstədɛɩ

15 He 1 jɛstəʳɖɩ 2 jɩstəʳɖɩ, °ɛstəʳɖɩ[2] 3 jɛstəʳɖi: 4 ɩstəʳɖɩ 5 ɛstəʳɖɩ 6 jɩstəʳɖɩ 7 jɛstəɹdɩ

16 Wo 1 jɛstədɩ 2 ɩstədɩ, °~[2] 3 jɛstəʳɖɩ̥ 4 jɛstəʳɖɩ 5 jɷstəʳɖɩ 6 jɛstəʳɖɩ 7 ɩstəʳɖɩ, °jɛstdɩ[3]

17 Wa 1 jɛstədɛɩ 2 jɩstədɩ, °jɛstdɩ[1] 3 jɛstəʳɖɩ 4 ɩstədɩ 5 jɩstəʳɖɩ 6 jɩstədɩ 7 jɛstədɩ

23 Mon 1 jɛstəʳɖɩ 2–3 jɛstədɩ 4 jɛstʰədi 5 jɛstədi 6 jɛstədɩ 7 n.a.

24 Gl 1–2 jɛstəʳɖɩ 3 ɩstəʳɖɩ 4 jɛstəʳɖɩ 5 ɩstəde: 6 jəstədɩ 7 ɩstəʳɖɩ

25 O 1 jɩstədeɩ 2 ɩstədɩ 3 ɩstəʳɖɩ 4 jɩstədɩ 5 ɩstəʳɖɩ 6 jɛstəʳɖɩ

VII.3.9 LAST NIGHT

Q. *If* (the event happened) *yesterday, but about* 9 *p.m. or so?* (You'd say: It happened)

R. LAST NIGHT

Note—For additional exs. of LAST, see VII.2.2 (and refs.); and of NIGHT, see VII.3.11/12.

7 Ch 1 las nɛɩt 2 s.w. last ni:t, ○~[4] 3 last nɛɩt, ○las nɛɩt[3] 4 las ni̞:tʻ 5 las nɛɩt 6 la:s naɩt

8 Db 1 la:s ni:t 2 las ni:t 3 las ni:t 4 las nɛɩtʻ 5 las nɛɩt, ○~[4] 6–7 las nɛɩt

11 Sa 1 la:st naɩt 2 last næɩt 3 la:s naɩt 4 la:s nɛɩt 5 las nˡi:t 6–8 la:s naɩt 9 læst naɩt 10–11 la:s naɩt

12 St 1 las naɩt 2–3 las nɛɩt 4 las nɒɩt 5–6 las nɛɩt 7 las nɒɩt 8 las ni:t 9 las nɛ̨ɩt 10 las nɒ̨ɩt 11 las na̱ɩt

15 He 1 la:s nəɩt 2 n.a. 3–4 la:s nəɩt 5 læs nəɩt 6 læ:s nəɩt 7 la:s naɩt

16 Wo 1 las nɒɩt 2 la·st nˡi:t 3 la:st nəi:t, ○la:s nəi:t[2] 4 læ:s nəɩt 5 læ:s nəɩᵊt 6 la:s nɒɩt 7 lɑ:s nəɩt, ○lɑ:st nəɩt[1,4]

17 Wa 1 las nɑɩt 2 s.w. lɑ:s nəɩt, ○~[4] 3–7 la:s nəɩt

23 Mon 1 læs nəɩt 2–3 la:s nəɩt 4 n.a. 5 la:s nəɩ̨t 6 la:s nəɩt 7 n.a.

24 Gl 1 læ:s nəɩt 2 la:s nəɩt 3 læ:s nəɩt, ○~[4] 4 la:s nəɩt 5 la:s nö̆ɩt 6–7 la:s nʌɩt

25 O 1–2 la:s nö̆ɩt 3 la:s nʌʏt 4 ɫɑ̈:s nəɩt 5 las nö̆ɩʔ 6 la:s nö̆ɩt

VII.3.10 THIS MORNING

Q. *If* (the event happened) *in the early part of today?* (You'd say: It happened)

Rr. §AFORE NOON, IN THE MORNING, THIS MORN/MORNING

Note—For additional exs. of THIS MORNING, see VII.3.5; of MORNING, see VII.3.11 (and refs.); and of THIS, see VII.3.14/18 and IX.10.2/7. FORENOON meaning *morning* occurs at VII.3.11/15.

7 Ch 1 ðɩs mɔ:nɩn 2 ɩ‿t mɔ:nɩn, °ðɩs mɔ:nɩn[2] 3 ðɩs mɔ:nɩn 4 ðəs mɔ:nɩn 5–6 ðɩs mɔ:nɩn

8 Db 1 ðɩs mɔʴ:n 2–4 ðɩs mɔ:nɩn 5 ðɩs mɔ:nɩn, °~[1] 6–7 ðɩs mɔ:nɩn

11 Sa 1 ðɩs mɔʵ:ɳɩn 2 ðɩs mɔ:nɩn 3 ðɩs mɔʵ:ɳɩn 4 ðɩs mɔ:nɩn 5 ðɩs mɔʵ:ɳɩn 6 ðɩs mɔʵ:ɳɩn, °~[4] 7 ðɩs mɔʵ:ɳɩn 8 θɩs [*sic*] ma:nɩn 9 ðɩs mɔʵ:ɳɩn 10 ðɩs mɔ:nɩn 11 ðɩs mɔʵ:ɳɩn

12 St 1 əfoɷə nɛɷn, ðɩs mɔ:nɩn 2–3 ðɩs moɷnɩn 4–7 ðɩs mɔ:nɩn 8 ðɩs mɔ:nɩŋg 9 ðɩs mọ:nɩn 10–11 ðɩs mɔ:nɩn

15 He 1 ðɩs mɔʵ:ɳɩn 2 ðɩs mɔ:nɩn 3–6 ðɩs mɑʵ:ɳɩn 7 ðɩs mɔɹnɩn, °~[3,4]

16 Wo 1 ðɩs mɑ:nɩn 2 ðəs mɑ:nɩn 3–4 ðɩs mɑʵ:ɳɩn 5 ðɩs mɑʵ:ɳɩn 6 ðɩs mɑʵɳɩn 7 ðɩs mɑʵɳɩn, °ðɩs mɔʵɳɩn[3], °ðɩs mɑ:nɩn[4(2x)]

17 Wa 1 ðɩs mɔ:nɩn 2 ɩn ðə mɔ:nɩn, s.w. °ðɩs mɔ:nɩn, °~[4] 3 ðəs mɔ:nɩn 4 ðəs mɔ:nɩn, °ðɩs mɔ:nɩn[3] 5 s‿mɔʵ:ɳɩn 6 ðɩs mɔʵ:ɳɩn 7 ðɩs mɔʵ:ɳɩn, °~[1(2x),2]

23 Mon 1 ðɩs mɑʵ:ɳɩn 2–3 ðɩs mɑ:nɩn 4 n.a. 5 ðɩs mɔ:nɩn, °~[2(2x)] 6 ðɩs mɑ:nɩn 7 n.a.

24 Gl 1 ðɩs mɑʵ:ɳɩn, °~[1] 2–5 ðɩs mɑʵ:ɳɩn 6 ðɩs mɔʵ:ɳɩn, °s‿mɔʵ:ɳɩn[2], s‿mɑʵ:ɳən[1] 7 ðɩs mɔʵ:ɳɩn

25 O 1 ðɩs mɔʵ:ɳɩn 2 s‿mɔʴ:nən, s‿mɑʴ:nən[3] 3 ðəs mɑʵ:ɳɩn 4 ðəs‿mɔ̃ɽɳɩn, °ðəs‿mɔɽɳɩn[3,4] 5 ðɩs mɔʵ:ɳən 6 s‿mɔʵ:ɳɩn

VII.3.11 MORNING*, AFTERNOON*, EVENING, NIGHT*

Q. *What do you call the various parts of the day?*
Confirm the existence of evening.

Rr. FORENOON, MORNING
AFTERNOON
EVENING
NIGHT

Note 1—The rr. to the four parts of the q. are separated below by full stops. A superior ◇ attached to NIGHT means that the f.w. expressly stated that EVENING was not used.

Note 2—I.m. exs. of AFTER are included between square brackets below, untransliterated, foll. AFTERNOON.

Note 3—For additional exs. of MORNING, see VII.3.10/13/15; of FORENOON, see VII.3.15; of AFTERNOON, see VII.3.14; of AFTER, see III.3.7 and VIII.1.9/23; and of (-)NIGHT, see VII.3.9/12. AFTERINGS =*strippings* occurs at III.3.4.

7 Ch 1 mɔ:nɪn. aftənʏ:n. ◇nɛɪt [gɷd nɛɪt *good n.*] 2 mɔ:nɪn, fɷənü:n, s.f. fɷ̜ənü:n, ○mɔ:nɪn[2(2x)], ○mɔ̜:nɪn[3], ○mɔənɪn, ○foənü:n. aftənü:n [aftə[1,2(2x)], əˈtaftə[1(2x),4] *at-after* (=*afterwards*)]. ◇ni:t, ○~[2(2x),3(2x)], ○nɑɪt[1] I.4.2, ○~[1] 3 mɔ:nɪn. aftənʏ:n [aftə[3(2x)]]. ◇nɛɪt 4 mɔ:nɪn. aftənu:n. ◇ni̜:t 5 mɔ:nɪn, ○~[2]. aftənʏ:n. ɛɪvnɪn. nɛɪt, ○ni:t[3] 6 mɔ:nɪn. aftənᶷu:n. i:vnɪn. naɪt

8 Db 1 mɔʳ:ɳɪn. aftənʏ:n. ◇ni:t 2 mɔ:nɪn. aftənu:n. ◇ni:t, ○~[3,4] 3 mɔ:nɪn, ○~[2]. aftənü:n. ◇ni:tʻ, ○nɛɪt[1,3], ○ni:t[1,3] 4 mɔ:nɪn. aftənɛɷn. ◇nɛɪt, ○ni:t[2] 5 mɔ:nɪn. aftənˡu:n. ni:t, ○~[3] 6 mɔ:nɪn. aftənɛɷn. nɛɪt, ○~[1(3x)] 7 mɔ:nɪn, fo·ᵊnɛɷn. aftənɛɷn. ◇nɛɪt

11 Sa 1 mɔʳ:ɳɪn. aftəʳɳɪu:n. i:vnɪn. ni:t 2 mɔ:nɪn, ○mɔ:nɪŋg[3]. aftənˡu:n. i:vnɪn, ○i:vnɪŋg[3]. naɪt 3 mɔʳ:ɳɪn. aʳ:ftəʳɳu:n. i:vnɪn [i:vnɪn e:pəʳ:ɳ[2] *e. apron* V.11.2]. nɛɪt 4 mɔʳ:ɳɪn. a:ftəʳɳu:n, i:vnɪn. naɪt 5 mɔʳ:ɳɪn. aftəʳɳᶷu:n. ◇nˡi:t 6 mɔʳ:ɳɪn. a:ftəʳɳu:n. ivnɪn. naɪt 7 mɔʳ:ɳɪn. a:ftənu:n [aftəʳ[1]]. i:vnɪn. naɪt 8 ma:nɪn. aftənu:n. i:vnɪn. naɪt, ○~[2] 9 mɔʳ:ɳɪn. æftəʳɳu:n [æ:ftəʳ[1]]. i:vnɪn. naɪt 10 mɔʳ:ɳɪn. æftəʳɳu:n. i:vnɪn [rare]. naɪt 11 mɔʳ:ɳɪn. atəʳɳu:n. i:vnɪn. naɪt

12 St 1 mɔ:nɪn. aftənu:n. i:vnɪn. nɒɪt, nɛɪt 2 moɷnɪn, ○~[1(2x)], ○moɷnn̩[5]. aftnɛɷn [aftə[1,5]]. ◇nɛɪt 3 moɷnɪn. aftənɛɷn [aftə[2], aftəɹ[1,2] (+ V.), aftɹ[2] (+ V.)]. ◇nɛɪt 4 mɔ:nɪn. aftənu:n. i:vnɪŋg. nɒɪt 5 mɔ:nɪn[(2x)]. aftənü:n [aftə[2(3x)], aftɹ[2] (+ V.)]. ◇nɛɪt, ○nɒ:ɪt[3] 6 mɔ:nɪn. aftənɛɷn [aftə[1,2], aftəɹ[1] (+ V.)]. ◇nɛɪt 7 mɔ:nɪn. n.r., ○aftənu:n[1]. i:vnɪn. nɒɪt[(2x)] 8 mɔ:nɪŋg. n.r. [aftə[2,6]]. i:vnɪŋg. ni:t 9 mɔ̜:nɪn. ○mɔ:nɪn[1]. aftənɛɷn. i:vnɪn [rare]. ◇nɛ̜ɪt[(2x)] 10 mɔ:nɪn. aftənü:n, ○~[4]. i:vnɪŋ, ○i:vnɪn[4]. na:ɪt 11 mɔ:nɪŋg, ○~[2], ○mɔ:nɪn[2]. aftənu:n [aftəklaps[2] *after-claps* (i.e. consequences)]. i:vnɪŋg. nɑ:ɪt

15 He 1 mɔʳ:ɳɪn. æftəʳɳu:n. i:vnɪn. næɪt 2 mɔ:nɪn. ætəʳɳu:n, ○~ [æftəʳ[1]]. i:vnɪn. næɪt 3 mɑʳ:ɳɪn, ○~[1(2x),3]. ætəʳɳu:n [ætəʳ[1(2x)], a:ftəʳ[4]]. i:vnɪn. nəɪt 4–5 mɑʳ:ɳɪn. æftəʳɳu:n. i:vnɪn. nəɪt 6 mɑʳ:ɳɪn. ætəʳɳu:n, ○~[1], ○ætəʳɳɷn[1]. i:vnɪn. nəɪt 7 mɔ·ɹnɪn, ○mɔ̜·ɹnɪn[3]. a:ftəɹnu:n [æ:ftəɹ[2] (+ V.), a:ftəɹ[4], ɑ:ftəɹ[4] (+ V.), aftəɹ[4]]. i:vnɪn, ○~[3]. naɪt, ○~[3], ○nạɪt[4], ○□naɪts[3,4]

16 Wo 1 mɑ:nɪn. aftənu:n [aftəɹ[2]]. i:vnɪn. nɒɪt 2 mɑ:nɪn. atəʳɳu:n [a·ftəʳ[2]; a:ftə:wəʳ·ɖʐ[2] *afterwards*]. i:vnɪn. nˈi:t 3 mɑʳ:ɳɪn. aftəʳɳu:n, ○~[1] [æftəʳɽ[1] (+ V.), ætəʳɽ[2] (+ V.)]. i:vnɪn. nəi:t, ○~[2(2x)] 4 mɑʳ:ɳɪn, ○~[3], mˈɑʳ:ɳɪn[1,2]. ætəʳɳu:n [ætəɹ[1(2x),2,3]]. i:vnɪn. nəɪt, ○~[2] 5 maʳ:ɳɪn, ○məʳ:ɳɪn[1]. ætəʳɳɷn [ætəʳ[1], æ·təʳ[1], æ:təʳ[1], ætəʳɽ[1] (+ V.)]. i:vnɪn. nəɪt [mɪdłnəɪt[1] *middle-n.*] 6 mɑʳ:ɳɪn, ○mɑ:nɪn[2]. ætəʳɳu:n, ○a:ftəʳɳɷnz[1] [æ:təʳ[2(3x),3]]. i:vnɪn. nɒɪ[ə]t, ○nɒɪt[1] 7 mɑʳɳɪn, ○~[1(2x),3(2x)], ○mɔ:nɪn[1], ○mɔənɪn[3] [mɔ·ʳɳ[1] *morn*]. ɑ:ftəʳɳu:n [ɑ:ftəʳ[1,4], ~[4] III.13.18, ɑ:ftəɹ[1], ɑ:təʳ[1,4], ɑ:tə[3,4]]. ◇nəɪt, ○~[1,3], ○□nəɪts[1]

17 Wa 1 mɔ̜:nɪn. aftənu:n. ◇nɑɪt 2 mɔ:nɪn, fɔ:nu:n, ○mɔənɪn[2]. aftənu:n[1,2] [ɑ:ftəɹ[1,3] (+ V.), ɑ:təɹ[4] (+ V.)]. ◇nəɪt 3 mɔ:nɪn. äf:tənu:n [a:ftə[1], aʳ:ʈəɹ[2] (+ V.)]. i:vnɪn. nəɪtʻ 4 mɔ:nɪn. aʳ:ʈnü:n, ○~[2]. ◇nəɪt, ○~[1] 5 mɔʳ:ɳɪn. aʳ:ʈənɷn, ○~[1] [aʳ:ʈəʳ[1], aʳ:ʈə[1(2x)]]. nəɪt[1(2x)] 6 mɔʳ:ɳɪn. aʳ:ʈənɷn [a:təʳ[3]]· ◇nəɪt, ○~[3] 7 mɔʳ:ɳɪn. aʳ:ʈəʳɳɷn. ["*evening* a polite word"]. nəɪt

23 Mon 1 mɑʳ:ɳɪn, ○~[1]. n.f. ˈi:vnɪn. nəɪt 2 mɑ:nɪn. a:ftəʳɳu:n [a:ftəʳ[2]]. i:vnɪn. nəɪt, ○~[1] 3 mɑ:nɪn, ○~[2]. æftənu:n [æftəʳ[2], a:ftə[3]]. i:vnɪn, ○~[3]. nəɪt 4 mɔ:nɪn. aftʰənɷn. ɨ:vnɪn. nəitʰ 5mɔ:nn̩. a:ftənu:n. i:vnɪn. nəɪ̞t, ○nəit[1] [nəɪ̞tʃeid[1] (deadly) *n.-shade*] 6 mɑ:nɪn, ○~[2] V.4.2. a:ftəʳɳu:n [a:ftəʳ[1(2x)]]. i:vnɪn. nəɪt, ○~[1] 7 n.r.

24 Gl 1 mɑʳ:ɳɪn. æ:fnu:n, ○æ:ftəʳɳɷn[3] [æftəʳ[1], æ:təʳ[2(2x)]]. i:vnɪn. nəɪt 2 mɑʳ:ɳɪn. æ:təʳɳu:n. ◇nəɪt 3 mɑʳ:ɳɪn. æ:ftəʳɳᶱu:n. ˈi:vnɪn [ˈi:vnɪn klo:ɷz[1] *e. clothes*]. nəɪt 4 mɑʳ:ɳɪn. a:ftəʳɳᶱu:n, ○atəʳɳɷn[3(2x)] [atəʳ[1]]. ˈi:vnɪn, ○e:vnɪn[3]. nəɪt 5 mɑʳɳɪn, ○~[2(2x)]. aʳ:ʈəʳɳɷn [aʳ:ʈə[2]]. [*evening* polite acc. i.]. ◇nöɪt 6 mɔʳ:ɳɪn, ○~[1]. aʳ:ʈənɷn [aʳ:ʈə[1]]. ◇nʌɪt 7 mɔʳ:ɳɪn. aʳ:ʔənɷn. nʌɪtʻ

25 O 1 mɔʳ:ɳɪn, ○mɔʳ:ɳɪn[2]. aʳ:ʈənɷn [aʳ:ʈəʳ[1], aʳ:ʔəʳ[1]]. ◇nöɪt, ○~[1(2x)] 2 mɔɹ̝:nən. aɹ̝:tənɷn, ○~[1] [aɹ̝:təɹ̝[1(3x),3], aɹ̝:ʔəɹ̝[1]]. ◇nöɪt, ○~[3] 3 mɑʳ:ɳɪn. æʳ:ʈənɷn [a:ftə[1], aʳ:ʈə[2]]. e:vnɪn, ○~[1] VII.3.12. nʌʏt 4 mɔ̃ɽɳɪn, ○mɔɽɳɪn[4,5] [mɔɽɳɪn[5] *m.* (=*Good m.*!)]. a:ɖəɽɳu:n, ○a:ftəɽɳü:n[4] VII.4.1, ○~[4] [a:təɽ[1(2x)]]. ◇nəɪt, ○nə̜ɪt[1], ○nɑɪt[3] 5 mɔʳ:ɳən. aʳ:ʈənɷn, ○aʳʔənɷn[2],

°aᵀ:ʔənɒn² [aɪ̞:ʔəɪ̞², aɪ̞ʔəɪ̞²]. ◇nʌʏt, °~² 6 məᵀ:ɳɪn. aᵀ:ʈəᵀɳɒn [old; rare], °a:ftəᵀɳɒn³, °a:ftənɒn³ [a:ftəᵀ³]. i:vnɪn [old, rare]. nöɪt

VII.3.12 TONIGHT*‡

Q. *You will see him again, not this morning, not this afternoon, but . . . .*

R. TONIGHT

Note—For additional exs. of –NIGHT, see VII.3.11 (and ref.).

7 Ch 1–2 təni:t 3 tənɛɪt 4 tənḭ:t‘ 5 tənɛɪt 6 tənɛ̞ɪt

8 Db 1–3 təni:t 4 tənɛɪt 5 təni:t, °~, °tənɛɪt 6–7 tənɛɪt

11 Sa 1 təni:t 2 tənæɪt 3–4 tənaɪt 5 tənꜞi:t, °~¹, °tənɛɪt¹ 6–11 tənaɪt

12 St 1–2 tənɛɪt 3 tənɛɪt, °~¹,² 4 tənɒɪt 5 tənɛɪt, °~ 6 tənɛɪt 7–8 tənɒɪt 9 tənɛ̞ɪt 10 təna:ɪt 11 tənȧɪt

15 He 1–2 tənæɪt 3 tənəɪt, °~³ 4–6 tənəɪt 7 tənă̞ɪt, °tənaɪt⁴

16 Wo 1 tənɒɪt 2 tənꜞi:t 3 tənəi:t 4–5 tənəɪt 6 tənɒɪt 7 tənəɪt

17 Wa 1 tənɑɪt 2 tənəɪt 3 tənəɪt‘, °tənəɪt² 4 tənəɪt 5 tənəɪt, °~¹ 6–7 tənəɪt

23 Mon 1 tənəɪt 2 tənəɪt, °~³ 3 tənəɪt 4 tʰɔ̜̈nəitʰ 5 tənəɪ̞t 6 tənəɪt, °~¹ 7 n.a.

24 Gl 1 tənəɪt, °~¹ 2–3 tənəɪt 4 tənəɪt, °~³ 5 tənöɪt 6–7 tənʌɪt

25 O 1–2 tənöɪt 3 təni:t 4 tənəɪt, °~³ 5 ʔənʌʏʔ 6 tənöɪt

VII.3.13 TOMORROW MORNING

Q. (You will see him again) *Not tonight, but just after you have got up, so . . . .*

Confirm this means before mid-day.

Rr. IN THE MORN, (/EARLY/FIRST THING/) IN THE MORNING, MORROW MORNING, TOMORROW (FORENOON/MORNING)

Note—For additional exs. of TOMORROW, see VII.4.1; and of MORNING, see VII.3.11 (and refs.).

7 Ch 1 təmɒɹə mɔ:nɪn 2 ɔ:lɪ ɪ‿t mɔənɪn 3 təməɹə mɔ:nɪn 4–6 təmɒɹə mɔ:nɪn

8 Db 1 təmɒɹə mɔ˗:nɪn, ɪ‿t mɔ˗:n [pref.] 2 ɪn‿t mɔ:nɪn 3 təmɒɹə mɔ:nɪn 4 ɪ‿t mɔ:nɪn 5 ɪn‿t mɔ:nɪn 6 ɪn‿ð mɔ:nɪn, təmɒɹə mɔ:nɪn 7 fəst θɪŋg ɪ‿ð mɔ:nɪn, p. təmɒɹə mɔ:nɪn [rare]

11 Sa 1 təmɒɹə mɔ˞:ɳɪn 2 təmɒɹə mɔ:nɪn 3 təmɒɹə mɔ˞:ɳɪn 4 təməɹə˞ mɔ˞:ɳɪn 5 təmɒɹə mɔ˞:ɳɪn 6 təmɒɹə mɔ:nɪn 7 təmɒɹə mɔ˞:ɳɪn 8 təmɒɹə˞ ma:nɪn 9 təmɒɹə mɔ˞:ɳɪn 10 təmɒɹə˞ mɔ˞:ɳɪn 11 təmɒɹə mɔ˞:ɳɪn

12 St 1 təmɒɹə mɔ:nɪn 2 təməɹə moɷnɪn 3 təmɒɹə moɷnɪn 4 təmɒɹə mɔ:nɪn 5 təmɒɹə mɔ:nɪn 6 fɒst θɪŋ ɪ‿t mɔ:nɪn, təmɒɹə mọ:nɪn 7–8 təmɒɹə mɔ:nɪn 9 təmɒɹə mọ:nɪn 10 ɪn ðə mɔ:nɪn, təmɒɹə 11 ɪn ðə mɔ:nɪn, təmɒɹə mɔ:nɪn

15 He 1 təmɒɹə˞ mɔ˞:ɳɪn 2 təmɒɹə˞ mɔ:nɪn 3–4 təmɒɹə˞ mɑ˞:ɳɪn 5 təmɒɹə mɔ:nɪn 6 təmɒɹə˞ mɑ˞:ɳɪn 7 fəɹst θɪŋ ɪn ðə mɔ·ɹnɪn

16 Wo 1–2 təmɒɹə mɑ:nɪn 3 təmɒɹə mɑ˞:ɳɪn 4 təmɒɹə˞ mɑ˞:ɳɪn 5 təmɒɹə˞ mɑ˞:ɳɪn 6 təmɒɹə˞ mɑ˞:ɳɪn 7 ɪn ðə mɑ˞ɳɪn

17 Wa 1 ɪn ðə mọ:nɪn 2 təməɹə mɔ:nɪn, °təməɹə fɔ:nu:n 3 təmɑɹ[ə] mɔ:nɪn 4 ɪn ðə mɔ:nɪn, təmɒɹə mɔ:nɪn 5–7 təmɒɹə mɔ:nɪn

23 Mon 1 təmɒɹə˞ mɑ˞:ɳɪn 2–3 təmɒɹə mɑ:nɪn 4 n.a. 5 təmɸ̣·ɹə mɔ:nɪn 6 təmɒɹə mɑ:nɪn 7 n.a.

24 Gl 1 təmɒɹə mɑ˞:ɳɪn 2–4 təmɒɹə mɑ˞:ɳɪn 5 təmɒɹə mɑ˞:ɳɪn 6 təmɒɹə mɔ˞:ɳɪn 7 təmɑɹə mɔ˞:ɳɪn

25 O 1 ʔəməɹə mɔ˞:ɳɪn 2 təmɑɹə mɑ˗:nən 3 mɒɽə mɑ˞:ɳɪn 4 mɒɽə mɔɽɳɪn, 5 ɪn ðə mɔ˞ənɪn 6 təmɒɽə mɔ:˞ɳɪn

VII.3.14 THIS AFTERNOON*

Q. (You will see him again, not this morning, but) *Today, between 2 and 4 p.m., so . . . .*

Rr. /IN THE/THIS/ AFTERNOON, THIS EVENING

Note—For additional exs. of THIS, see VII.3.10/15/18 and IX.10.2/7; and of AFTER(NOON), see VII.3.11 (and refs.).

7 Ch 1 ðɪs aftənʏ:n 2 ɪ‿t aftənü:n 3 ðɪs aftənʏ:n 4 ðəs aftənu:n 5 s‿aftənʏ:n 6 ðɪs aftən[ʊ]u:n

8 Db 1 ðɩs aftənʏ:n 2 ðɩs aftənu:n 3 ðɩs aftənü:n 4 ðɩs aftənɛɷn 5 ðɩs aftənˈu:n 6 s‿aftənɛɷn 7 ðɩs ɛftənɛɷn

11 Sa 1 ðɩs a:ftəʳɳu:n 2 ðɩs aftənʏʉ:n 3 ðɩs aʳ:ftəʳɳu:n 4 ðɩs a:ftəʳɳu:n 5 ðɩs aftəʳɳᴼu:n 6 ðɩs a:ftəʳɳu:n 7–8 ðɩs aftənu:n 9 ðɩs æ:ftəʳɳu:n 10 ðɩs æftəʳɳu:n 11 ðɩs atəʳɳu:n

12 St 1–3 ðɩs aftənɛɷn 4 ðɩs aftənu:n 5 ðɩs aftənü:n 6 ðɩs aftənɛɷn 7–8 ðɩs aftənu:n 9 ðɩs aftənɛɷn 10–11 ðɩs aftənu:n

15 He 1 ðɩs æftəʳɳu:n 2–4 ðɩs ætəʳɳu:n 5 ðɩs æftəʳɳu:n 6 ðɩs ætəʳɳu:n 7 ðɩs ạ:ftəɹnu:n

16 Wo 1 ðɩs aftənu:n 2 ðɩs a·təʳɳu:n 3 ðɩs a:ftəʳɳu:n 4 ðɩs ætəʳɳu:n 5 ðɩs ætəʳɳɷn 6 ðɩs ætəʳɳu:n 7 s.w. ðɩs ɑ:ftəʳɳu:n

17 Wa 1 s‿aftənu:n 2 ðɩs ɑ:ftənu:n 3 ðəs a:ftənu:n 4 ðɩs aʳ:ʈɳü:n 5–6 ðɩs aʳ:ʈənɒn 7 ðɩs aʳ:ʈɳɷn

23 Mon 1 ðɩs ˈi:vnɩn 2 ðɩs a:ftəʳɳu:n 3 ðɩs æftənu:n 4 ðɩ§ aftʰənɒn 5 ðɩs i:vnɩn 6 ðɩs a:ftəʳɳu:n 7 n.a.

24 Gl 1 ðɩs æ:fnu:n 2 ðɩs æ:təʳɳu:n 3 ðɩs æ:ftəʳɳᴼu:n 4 ðɩs a:ftəʳɳᴼu:n 5 ðɩs aʳ:ʈəʳɳɷn 6 ðɩs aʳ:ʈənɒn 7 s‿aʳ:ʔənɒn

25 O 1 s‿aʳ:ʈənɒn 2 ðɩs aʴ:ʈənɒ́n 3 ðɩs æʳ:ʈənɒn 4 ðəˡs‿a:fəʈɳü:n 5 ðɩs aʳ:ʔənɒn 6 ðɩs aʳ:ʈəʳɳɒn

VII.3.15 THIS FORENOON

Q. (You will see him again, not this afternoon, but) *Today, between 9 and 12 noon, so* . . . .

Rr. AFORE DINNER, BEFORE NOON, (/IN THE/THIS/) FORENOON, (THE/THIS) MORNING, THIS MORN

Note—For comparable material, see VII.3.10. For additional exs. of THIS, see VII.3.10/14/18 and IX.10.2/7; and of FORENOON and MORNING, see VII.3.11 (and refs.).

7 Ch 1 ðɩs fo:ᵊnʏ:n 2 əfɷə dɩnə, s.f. ɩ‿t fɷənü:n 3 ðɩs fọ·ənʏ:n 4–6 ðɩs mɔ:nɩn

8 Db 1 ðɩs mɔʴ:n 2 ðɩs fɒnᴼu:n 3 ðɩs mɔ:nɩn 4 ðɩs fo·ənɛɷn 5 ðɩs mɔ:nɩn, ðɩs fɔ:nˈu:n 6 ðɩs mɔ:nɩn 7 ðɩs fo·ənɛɷn

11 Sa 1 ðɩs məʳ:ɳɩn 2 ðɩs mɔ:nɩn 3 ðɩs fəʳ:ɳu:n 4–7 ðɩs məʳ:ɳɩn 8 ðɩs ma:nɩn 9 ðɩs fəʳ:ɳu:n 10 ðɩs məʳ:ɳɩn 11 ðɩs fo:əʳɳu:n

12 St 1 ðɩs foɷənɛɷn 2 bɩfoɷə nɛɷn 3 ðɩs moɷnɩn, s.w. ðɩs fɔ:nɛɷn 4 ðɩs fɔ:nu:n 5 ðɩs mɔ:nɩn, s.w. ðɩs fɔ:nü:n 6 mɔ:nɩn 7 bɩfɔ: nu:n 8 fɔ:nu:n 9 ðɩs fɔ:nɛɷn 10 ðɩs mɔ:nɩn 11 ðɩs fɔ̣:nu:n

15 He 1 ðɩs məʳ:ɳɩn 2 ðɩs mɔ:nɩn 3–6 ðɩs maʳ:ɳɩn 7 ðɩs mɔ·ɹnɩn

16 Wo 1–2 ðɩs ma:nɩn 3–4 ðɩs maʳ:ɳɩn 5 ðɩs maʳ:ɳɩn 6 ðɩs maʳ:ɳɩn 7 s‿maʳɳɩn

17 Wa 1 s‿mɔ:nɩn 2 ðɩs fɔ:nu:n 3 ðəs mɔ:nɩn 4 ðɩs mɔ:nɩn 5 ðɩs məʳɳɩn 6–7 ðɩs məʳ:ɳɩn

23 Mon 1 ðɩs maʳ:ɳɩn 2–3 ðɩs ma:nɩn 4 n.a. 5 ðɩs mɔ:nɩn 6 ðɩs ma:nɩn 7 n.a.

24 Gl 1 ðɩs maʳ:ɳɩn 2 ðɩs maʳ:ɳɩn 3 ðɩs‿maʳ:ɳɩn 4–5 ðɩs maʳ:ɳɩn 6 ðɩs məʳ:ɳɩn 7 s‿məʳ:ɳɩn

25 O 1 s‿məʳ:ɳɩn 2 s‿maɹ̣:nən 3 ðɩs maʳ:ɳɩn 4 ðəs‿məʈɳɩn 5 ðə məʳənən 6 ðɩs fɷəʳɳɷn

VII.3.16 ANY* TIME

Q. If you don't mind when you see him, you say, not come some time, but come ....

R. ANY TIME

Note 1—Unfortunately the f.w. at 11.6/9, 16.6, 23.4 and 25.5 omitted to rec. TIME.

Note 2—I.m. exs. of ANY, ANYBODY, and ANYWHERE(S) are reproduced below between square brackets untransliterated.

Note 3—For additional exs. of ANY(–), see V.8.16; and of TIME, see VII.5.1.

7 Ch 1 ɛnɩ taɩm 2 p. ɛnɩ taɩm [ɛnɩ[2,3]; ɛnɩbədɩ[1(2x)]] 3 ɛnɩ ta:m [ɛ̣nɩ[2]; ɛnɩbɒdɩ[2]] 4 ɛnɩ taɩm [ɛnɩ[2(2x)]] 5 ɛnɩ ta:m 6 ɛnɩ tɛɩm

8 Db 1 ɒnɩ taɩm 2 ɛnɩ ta:m 3 ɛnɩ taɩm 4 ɛnɩ taɩm [ɛnɩ[2,3]] 5 ɒnɩ taɩm 6 ɛnɩ tã:m, °ɛnɩ taɩm 7 ɒnɩ tã:m

11 Sa 1 ɛnɩ tɛɩm 2 ɛnɩ tæɩᵊm 3 ɛnɩ tɛɩm 4–5 ɛnɩ taɩm 6 ɛnɩ 7 ɛnɩ taɩm 8 ɛnɩ taɩm [ɛnɩwɩəʳʐ[2]] 9 ɛnɩ [ɛnɩ[1]] 10 ɛnɩ taɩm [ɛnɩ[2]] 11 ɛnɩ taɩm [ɛnɩ[2]]

12 St 1 ɒnι tɒιm [ɛnι[1,2]; anιwɛ:[3]] 2 ɛnι tɒιm [ɛnι[5]] 3 ɒnι tɒ:ιm [ɒnι[1(3x)]; ɒnιwιə[2]] 4 ɛnι tɒιm [ɛnι[2,4]; ɛnιbɒdι[2]] 5 anι tɒ:ιm [ɒnιbɒdι[2]] 6 ɒnι tɒ:ιm [ɒnι[1], ɛnι[2]; ɒnιbɒdι[1]; ɛnιwιə[1]] 7–8 ɛnι tɒιm [ɛnι[1]] 9 ɛnι tɒιm, ɒnι tɒιm ["older"; ɒnι[3(3x)], ɛnι[1]; ɒnιbɒdι[3]; ɒnιwiə[2,3]] 10 ɛnι ta̠:ιm [ɛnι[5]] 11 ɛnι ta̠:ιm [ɛnι[2(2x)]; ɛnιbɒdι[2]]

15 He 1 ɛnι tæιm [ɛnι[1]] 2 ɛnι tæιm 3–5 ɛnι təιm 6 ɛnι təιm [ɛnι[1]] 7 ɛnι taιm [ɛnι[2], ɛnιwə:ɹ[4]]

16 Wo 1 ɛnι tɒιᵊm [ɛnιwιəᶦ[2]] 2 ɛnι təιm, ○~[2] 3 ɛni: təi:m [ɛnι[3(2x)]] 4 ɛnι təιm [ɛnι[1,2]] 5 ɛnι təιᵊm 6 ɛnι 7 s.w. ɛnι təιm [ɛnι[1,3(2x),4]]

17 Wa 1 ɛnι tαιm [ɛnι[1]] 2 s.w. ɛnι təιm [○ɛnι[1], ○ɛnιbədι[4]] 3 ɛnι təιm [ɛnι[1]] 4 ɛnι təιm 5 ɛnι təιm [ɛnι[1]] 6 ɛnι təιm [ɛnι[1,3]] 7 ɛnι tʌιm

23 Mon 1–3 ɛnι təιm 4 ɛni 5 ɛni təι̜m 6 ɛnι təιm 7 n.a. [ɛni[1]]

24 Gl 1 ɛnι təιᵊm 2 ɛnι təιᵊm [ɛnιwəᶦ[1]] 3 ɛnι təιm 4 ɛnι təιᵊm 5 ɛnι tə̈ιm 6–7 ɛnι tʌιm

25 O 1–2 ɛnι tə̈ιm 3 ɛnι tʌʏm [ɛnιbɒdι[2]] 4 ɛnι təι̜m [ɛnι[1(5x),3,5]; ɛnιbɒdι[5]; ɛnιwɛəɽ[5]] 5 ɛnι 6 ɛnι tə̈ιm

VII.3.17 ALWAYS*

Q. A man who is never idle is a man that's busy, not just now and again, but . . . .

Rr. ALWAYS, REGULAR

Note—Exs. of ALWAYS occ. occur at VIII.9.1.

7 Ch 1 ɔ:ləs 2 n.a. ○ɔ:ləz[1], ○ɔ:ləs[1(2x),2(2x),3] 3 ɔ:lιz, ○ɔ:lιs[2] 4 ɔ:lwιz, ○ɔ:lwəz[2] 5 ɔ:wιz 6 ɔ:lwəz

8 Db 1 ɔ:ləs 2 ɔ:ləz, ○ɔ:ləs 3 ɔ:lιz, ○~ 4 ɔ:lιz, ○ɔ:lιs[1] 5 ɔ:lιs 6 ɒlιs, ○ɔ:ləs[1] 7 ɔ:lιs, ○ɔ:ləs[2]

11 Sa 1 ɔᶦ:ɭwιz 2 ɔ:lwιz, ○~[1], ○ɔ:lwιn[1] [rec. in «ιts ˈɔ:lwιn ˈdɷn[1]» *it's always done*] 3–5 ɔ:lwιz 6 ɔᶦ:ɭwιz, ○ɔ:lwιz[3], ○ɔ:lιs[4] 7 ɔᶦ:ɭwιz, ○ɹɛgləᶦ 8 ɔ:lwιz 9 ɔ:lwιz, ○~[1(5x)], ○ɔᶦ:ɭwιz[1] 10 ɔᶦ:ɭwιz 11 ɔ:lwιz, ○~[1(2x),2], ○ɔ:lιz[2], ○ɔ:lιs[2]

12 St 1 aɷlwιz, ○ɔ:lιz[2] 2 oɷlwιz 3 ɹɛgjələ, ɔ:lιz, ○ɔ:lιs[2], ○ɒ:lιs[1] 4 ɔ:lwιz, ○ɔ:lιs[1,3], ○ɔ:lιz[1] 5 ɔ:lιz, ○ɔ:lιs[1(3x),2] 6 ɔ:lιs, ○~[1(3x),2(2x)], ○ɔ:lwιz[1] 7 ɔ:lwιz, ○ɔ:lιs[1,2,4] 8 ɔ:lwɛιz, ○ɔ:lιz[1(2x),5], ○ɔ:lιs[1(2x),5] 9 ɔ:lwιz, ○ɔ:lιz[1,2], ○ɔ:lιs[1(2x)] 10 ɔ:lιz, ○ɔ:lιs[6] 11 ɔ:lwɛιz, ɔ:lιz, ○ɔ:lιs[2(3x)]

15 He 1 ɔ:lwɪz 2 ɔ:ɫɪz 3 ɑ:lɪs, °ɑlɪz, °ɑ:ɫɪz[4] 4 ɑ:ɫɪz 5 ɑ:ɫwɪz, °ɹɛgləʴ 6 ɑ:ɫwe:ˈz 7 ɔ:lwɪz, °~[4(2x)], °ɔ:ləs[3(2x)], °ɔ:ləz[3(2x)]

16 Wo 1 ɑ:lɪs, °~[1,3] 2 ɑ:lɪz, °ɔ:lwɪz[1], °ɑ:lwɪz[2], °ɒʊɪs[2] 3 ɑ:ɫwɪz 4 ɑ:lwɪs, °ɑ:ɫɪs[1,2], °ɑ:lɪs[1] 5 ɑʴ:l̩ɪz, °ɑ:ɫɪz[1], °ɑ:ɫwɪz[1], °ɑ:lɪz[1] 6 ɹɛgləʴ, ɑ:ɫwɪz, °~[1] 7 ɔ:lwəs, °ə:ləs [*sic*], °ɔ:ləs[1(4x),3(2x),4(4x)], °ɔ:ləz[1(2x),2,3(2x)]

17 Wa 1 ɔ:lwɪz, °ɔ:ləz[1] 2 p. ɔ:ləz, °~, °~[4], °ɔ:ləs[1,4] 3 ɔ:ɫwəz, °ɔ:lwɪz[3(2x)] 4 ɔ:lɪs 5 ɔ:ɫwɪz, °ɔ:lɪs[1(4x)] 6 ɔ:lɪs 7 ɔ:ləs

23 Mon 1–2 ɑ:ɫwɪz 3 ɑ:ɫwɪz, °ɑ:ɫɪs[1] 4 ɒ̟̣·lwəz, °ɒ̟̣·lʌ̣̈z[1], °ɒ̟̣·ləz[1] 5 ɒ̟̣·lwəz, °~[2], °ɒ̟̣·ləz̥[2] 6 ɑ:ɫwɪz 7 n.a., °ɔ:lwəz[1]

24 Gl 1 ɑ:ɫwɪz, °~[3] 2 ɑ:ɫʊs, °~[1], °ɑ:ɫɪz[3] 3 ɑ:ɫwɪz, °~[1] 4 ɑ:ɫwɪz 5 ɔ:ləs 6 ɔ:lwɪz 7 ɔ:ɫwɪz

25 O 1 ɒləs, ɹɛgləʴ, °ɒləs[2], °ɔ:ləst[2], °ɹɛgləʴ 2 ɔ:ɫwɪz 3 ɔ:lɪs, °ɔ:lə[1], °ɔ:lwez[1], °ɔ:lwəz[2] 4 ɔ̣:ɫwəz, °ɔ:ɫwɪz[1,5] 5 ɒləs, °ɔ:lwɪz[1,2,3], °ɔ:lwəz[3], °ɔ:ləz[3] 6 ɔ:ɫwɪz

VII.3.18 THIS YEAR*

Q. There's last year, there's next year and what do you call the one between?—Christmas 1957, *then* added after *and*, and *we're in now* replaced *in between.*

R. THIS YEAR

Note—For additional exs. of THIS, see VII.3.10/14/15 and IX.10.2/7; and of YEAR, see VII.3.4 (and refs.).

7 Ch 1–4 ðɪs ɪə 5 ðɪs ɛɪə 6 ðɪs ɪə

8 Db 1 ðɪs jə̝̍: 2–3 ðɪs ɪə 4–7 ðɪs jɪə

11 Sa 1 ðɪs ɪəʴ 2 ðɪs jə: 3 ðɪs i:əʴ· 4 ðɪs i:əʴ 5 ðɪs ɪəʴ 6 ðɪs ɪəʴ· 7–8 ðɪs ɪəʴ 9 ðɪs ɪəʴ· 10–11 ðɪs ɪəʴ

12 St 1 ðɪs ji:ə 2 ðɪs jɪə 3–4 ðɪs ɪə 5 ðɪs iə 6 ðɪs jɪə 7 ðɪs ɪ̣ə 8 ðɪs i·ə 9 ðɪs iə 10 ðɪs jiə 11 ðɪs i:ə

15 He 1 ðɪs ɪəʴ 2–4 ðɪs jəʴ: 5 ðɪs jəʴ, °ðɪʃ jəʴ[1] 6 ðɪʃ jəʴ 7 ðɪs jˈə·ɹ, ðɪs jə·ɹ

16 Wo 1 ðɪs ɪə 2 ðɪs ɪəʴ 3 ðɪs jəʴ: 4 ðɪs ɪəʴ 5 ðɪʃ jəʴ: 6 ðɪs ɪəʴ 7 ðɪs jəʴ, ðɪs ɪəʴ [pref.]

17 Wa 1 ðɪs jə̣: 2 θɪs jɪə, s.f. θɪs ɪə [pref.] 3 ðɪs jɪə 4–7 ðɪs ɪəʳ

23 Mon 1 ðɪs jəʳ 2 ðɪs jəʳ: 3 ðɪs jœ: 4 ðɪs jə 5 ðɪs jɐ: 6 ðɪs jəʳ: 7 n.a.

24 Gl 1 ðɪʃ jəʳ: 2 ðɪs jəʳ: 3 ðɪʃ jɪəʳ 4 ðɪʃ ɪəʳ 5 ðɪs jəʳ: 6 ðɪs jə: 7 ðɪs jəʳ:

25 O 1 ðɪs jəʳ: 2 ðɪs ɪə˗ 3 s.f. ðɪs ɪəʳ 4 ðɪs jəɽ 5–6 ðɪs ɪəʳ

VII.4.1 TOMORROW

Q. There's yesterday, there's today, and the 24 hours after today you call . . . .

Rr. (TO)MORROW, TOMORN

Note—For additional exs. of (TO)MORROW, see VII.3.13.

7 Ch 1 təmɒɹɪ 2 təmɒɹə 3 təməɹə 4 təmɒɹə 5 təmɒɹə, ○~[1] 6 təmɒɹə

8 Db 1 təmɔ˗:n 2 təmɒɹə, s.f. təmɔ:n [old] 3 təmɒɹə, ○~[2] 4 təmɒɹɪ, ○təmɒɹə[3] 5–7 təmɒɹə

11 Sa 1 təmɒɹəʳ 2 təmɒɹə 3 təmɒɹəʳ· 4–5 təmɒɹə 6 təmɒɹo· 7–8 təmɒɹəʳ 9 təmɒɹo: 10 təmɒɹə 11 təmɒɹəʳ, ○~[2]

12 St 1 təmɒɹə 2 təməɹə 3–5 təmɒɹə 6 təmɒɹə, ○~[(2x)] 7 təmɒɹə 8 təmɒɹoɷ 9–10 təmɒɹə 11 təmɒɹọɷ

15 He 1–3 təmɒɹəʳ 4 təmɒɹo· 5 təmɒɹəʳ: 6 təmɒɹəʳ 7 təmɒɹə

16 Wo 1 təmɒɹə 2 təmɑɹə 3 təmɒɹoɷ 4–6 təmɒɹəʳ 7 təməɹə, ○~[4]

17 Wa 1 təmɒɹə 2 təməɹə 3 təmɑɹə 4 təmɒɹə 5 təmɒɹə, ○təmɒɹɪ[1] 6 təmɒɹə, ○~[1] 7 təmɒɹə

23 Mon 1 təmɒɹə, ○təmɒɹəʳ[1] 2 təmɒɹəʳ 3 təmɒɹo· 4 tʰɷmɒ̣·ɹə 5 təmɒ̣·ɹə 6 təmɒɹəʳ 7 n.a.

24 Gl 1–3 təmɒɹəʳ 4–6 təmɒɹə 7 təmɑɹə

25 O 1–2 təmɒɹə 3 təmɒɽə 4 təmɒɽə, ○mɒɽə[4] [rec. in «mɒɽə a:ftəɽɳün» *m. afternoon*] 5 təmɒɹə 6 ʔəmɒɽə

VII.4.2 MONDAY*, TUESDAY*, WEDNESDAY*

Q. What do you call the days at the beginning of the week?

Rr. MONDAY
TUESDAY
WEDNESDAY

Note 1—The rr. to the three parts of the q. are separated below by full stops.
Note 2—For exs. of WHITMONDAY, see VII.4.8.

7 Ch 1 mɷndɩ. tʃu:zdɩ. wɛnzdɩ 2 mɷndɩ, ○~[2]. tjü:zdɩ. wɛnzdɩ, ○~[3(4x)] 3 mɷndɩ, ○~[3]. tʃʏ:zdɩ. wɛnzdɩ, ○~[3] 4 mɷndɩ. tʃu:zdɩ. wɛnzdɩ 5 mɷndɩ. tʃʏ:zdɩ. wɛnzdɩ 6 mɷndɩ. tʃu:zdɩ. wɛnzdɩ

8 Db 1 mɷndɩ. tʃʏ:zdɩ. wɛnzdɩ 2 mɷndɩ. tɩu:zdɩ. wɛdnzdɩ 3 mɷndɩ tʃu:zdɩ, ○tü:zdɩ[2]. wɛnzdɩ 4 mɷndɩ. t[ɷ]üzdɩ. wɛnzdɩ 5 mɷndɩ. tɛɷzdɩ. wɛnzdɩ 6 mɷndɩ. tü:zdɩ. wɛnzdɩ 7 mɷndɩ. t[ɷ]ü:zdɩ. wɛnzdɩ

11 Sa 1 mʌndɩ. tʻuzde:. wɛnzdɩ 2 mɷndɩ. tʻu:zdɩ. wɛnzdɩ 3 mʌndɩ. tu:zdɩ. wɛnzdɩ 4 mʌndɩ. tɩu:zdɩ. wɛnzdɩ 5 mɷndɩ. tɩuz:dɩ. wɛnzdɩ 6 mʌndɩ. tɩu:zdɩ. wɛnzdɩ 7 mɷndɩ. tu:zdɩ. wɛnzdɩ 8 mɷndɩ. tju:zdɩ. wɛnzdɩ 9 mʌnde:. tu:zde:. wɛnzde: 10–11 mʌndɩ. tju:zdɩ. wɛnzdɩ

12 St 1 mɷndɩ. tju:zdɩ. wɛnzdɩ 2 mɷndɩ. tʃu:zdɩ. wɛnzdɩ 3 mɷndɩ. tü:zdɩ, tɛɷzdɩ. wɛnzdɩ 4 mɷndɩ. tʃü:zdɩ. wɛnzdɩ 5 mɷndɩ. tü:zdɩ. wɛnzdɩ 6 mɷndɩ. tü:zdɩ, ○tu:zdɩ. wɛnzdɩ 7 mɷndɩ. tü:zdɩ. wɛnzdɩ 8 mɷndɩ, ○mɷnd[6] [+ «aftə» *after*]. tʃu:zdɩ. wɛnzdɩ 9 mɷndɩ. tɛɷzdɩ. wɛnzdɩ 10 mɷndɩ. tjü:zdɩ. wɛnzdɩ 11 mɷndɩ. tʃu:zdɩ, ○~[2]. wɛnzdɩ

15 He 1 mʌndɩ. tju:zdɩ. wɛnzdɩ 2 mʌndɩ. tu:zdɩ. wɛnzdɩ 3 mɷndɩ. tju:zdɩ. wɛnzdɩ 4 mʌndɩ. tju:zdɩ. wɛnzdɩ 5 mɷndɩ. tju:zdɩ. wɛnzdɩ 6 mɷndɩ. tʃu:zdɩ. wɛn[ə]zdɩ 7 mʌndɩ. tju:zdɩ. wɛnzdɩ

16 Wo 1 mɷndɩ. tɩu:zdɩ. wɛnzdɩ 2 mɷndɩ. tu:zdɩ. wɛnzdɩ 3 mɷndi:. tju:zdi:. wɛnzdi: 4 mɷndɩ. tju:zdɩ. wɛnzdɩ, ○~[3] 5 mɷndɩ. tʃu:zdɩ. wɛnzdɩ 6 mɷndɩ. tju:zdɩ. wɛnzdɩ 7 mɷndɩ, ○~[1]. tju:zdɩ. wɛnzdɩ

17 Wa 1 mɷndï. tu:zdï. wɛnzdï 2 mɷndɩ. tju:zdɩ. wɛnzdɩ 3 mɷndɩ. tu:zdɩ. wɛnzdɩ 4 mɷndɩ. tü:zdɩ. wɛnzdɩ 5–6 mɷndɩ. tʃu:zdɩ. wɛnzdɩ 7 mɷndɩ. tü:zdɩ. wɛnzdɩ

23 Mon 1 mʌndι . tjᶷu:zdι . wənzdι 2 mɷndι . tju:zdι . wɛnzdι 3 mʌndι . tju:zdι . wɛnzdι 4 mḁ̈ndi . tʰιu·zdi . wɛnzdi 5 mḁ̈ndi . tju:zdi . wɛnzdi 6 mʌndι . tju:zdι . wɛnzdι, ○~[1] 7 n.a.

24 Gl 1 mɷndι . tʃu:zdə . wɛnzdι 2 mɷndι . tʃu:zdι . wɛnzdι 3 mʌndι . tʃᶷu:zdι . wɛnzdι 4 mɷndι . tjɷu:zdι . wɛnzdι 5 mɷndι . tʃu:zdι . wɛnzdι 6 məndι . tʃu:zdι . wɛnzdι 7 məndι . tju:zdι . wɛnzdι

25 O 1 mɷndι . tʃu:zdι . wɛnzdι 2 mʌndι . tu:zdι . wɛnzdι 3 mɷndι . tju:zdι . wɛnzdι 4 mɷndι . tju:zdι . wɛdnzdι 5 mʌndι . tˡu:zdι . wɛnzdι 6 mɷndι . tu:zdι . wιnzdι

VII.4.3 THURSDAY*

Q. *And* (what do you call) *the day after Wednesday?*

R. THURSDAY

7 Ch 1–2 θə:zdι 3 θəʴ:zdι, ○θə:zdι[3] 4–5 θə:zdι 6 θəʴ̠:zdι

8 Db 1 θəʴ̠:zdι 2–4 θə:zdι 5 θɔzdι 6 θəzdι 7 θɒzdι

11 Sa 1 θəʳ:ʐɖι 2 θə:zdι 3–8 θəʳ:ʐɖι 9 θəʳ:ʐɖe: 10 ðəʳʐɖι 11 θəʳ:ʐɖι, ○~[1]

12 St 1 θə:zdι 2 θəʴ:zdι 3–7 θə:zdι 8 θɛ̠:zdι 9 θə:zdι 10 θɛ:zdι 11 θə:ɹzdι

15 He 1–2 θəʳ:ʐɖι 3 ðəʳ:ʐɖι 4–5 θəɽʐɖι 6 ðəʳʐɖι 7 θəɹdι [*sic*]

16 Wo 1–6 θəʳ:ʐɖι 7 θəʳʐɖι

17 Wa 1 θə̣̑:zdï 2 θɑ:zdι 3 θə:zdï 4 θəʳ:ʐɖι 5 θɷzdι 6 θəʳ:ʐɖι 7 θɷzdι

23 Mon 1 ðəʳʐɖι 2 θəʳʐɖι, ○θəʳ:ʐɖι[3] 3 θœ:zdι 4 θœ:zdi 5 θœ̣̈:zdi 6 θəʳ:ʐɖι 7 n.a.

24 Gl 1–2 θəʳ:ʐɖι 3 ðəʳ:ʐɖι 4 ðœ:zdι 5 θəʳ:ʐɖι 6–7 ðəʳ:ʐɖι

25 O 1 θəzdι 2 θɔzdι 3 θəʳ:ʐɖι 4 θəɽʐɖι 5–6 θəʳ:ʐɖι

VII.4.4 FRIDAY*

Q. *And* (what do you call the day) *after Thursday?*

R. FRIDAY

Note—For additional exs. of FRIDAY, see VII.4.7.

7 Ch 1–2 fɹɑɩdɩ 3 fɹɑ:dɩ, °fɹɑɩdɩ 4–5 fɹɑɩdɩ 6 fɹaɩdɩ, °fɹɛ̝ɩdɩ

8 Db 1 fɹaɩddɩ 2 fɹɑɩdɩ 3 fɹaɩdɩ 4 fɹaɩddɩ 5–6 fɹɑɩdɩ 7 fɹɑ̃·ĩdɩ

11 Sa 1–3 fɹaɩdɩ 4 fɹɛɩdɩ 5–7 fɹaɩdɩ 8 fɹɒɩdɩ 9 fɹaɩde: 10–11 fɹaɩdɩ

12 St 1–2 fɹɒɩdɩ 3 fɹɒ:ɩdɩ, °~[1] 4 fɹɒɩdɩ 5 fɹɒ:ɩdɩ 6 fɹɒ̝:ɩdɩ 7 fɹɒɩdɩ, °~[4] 8 fɹɒɩdɩ 9 fɹɒ·ɩdɩ 10 fɹɔ̝ɩdɩ 11 fɹa̠:ɩdɩ

15 He 1–2 fɹæɩdɩ 3–4 vɹəɩdɩ 5 fɹəɩdɩ 6 vɹəɩdɩ 7 fɹaɩdɩ

16 Wo 1–2 fɹɒɩdɩ 3 fɹəi:di: 4–5 fɹəɩdɩ 6 fɹəi:dɩ 7 fɹəɩdɩ, °~[1]

17 Wa 1 fɹɑɩdĭ 2–4 fɹəɩdɩ 5 fɹʌɩdɩ 6–7 fɹəɩdɩ

23 Mon 1–3 fɹəɩdɩ 4 fɹəidi 5 fɹəi̩di 6 fɹəɩdɩ, °~[1] 7 n.a.

24 Gl 1–2 fɹəɩdɩ 3–4 vɹəɩdɩ 5 fɹə̈ɩdɩ 6–7 vɹʌɩdɩ

25 O 1–3 fɹə̈ɩdɩ 4 fɽəɩdɩ 5–6 fɹə̈ɩdɩ

VII.4.5 SATURDAY*

Q. And (what do you call the day) *after Friday?*

R. SATURDAY

7 Ch 1 sɛtədɩ, °sɛtdɩ[2] 2 sɛʔtdɩ, °~[1] 3 saʔdɩ 4 satədɩ 5 sɛtdɩ, °sɛtədɩ 6 satədɩ

8 Db 1 sɛtdɩ 2 satdɩ, °sɛtdɩ[2] 3 sɛtədɩ, °sɛtdɩ[1,3] 4 satdɩ 5 sɛtdɩ 6 sɛtədɩ 7 sɛtədɩ, °sɛtdɩ[1]

11 Sa 1 satəɽ:ɖɩ 2 satədɩ 3 satəʳ:ɖɩ 4–7 satəɽɖɩ 8 satdɩ, °~ 9 sætəʳɖe: 10 sætəɽɖɩ 11 satəɽɖɩ

12 St 1 sɒtdɩ, °satədɩ[3] 2 sɛtdɩ, °~[5] 3 satədɩ 4 satdɩ 5 satdɩ, °satədɩ[3] 6 sætdɩ 7 satədɩ 8 satədɛɩ 9 satdɩ, °~[2] 10 saʔdɩ, °satədɩ[4] 11 satədɩ, °~[2]

15 He 1–2 sætəʳɖɩ 3 sætəʳɖɩ, °~[1] 4 sætəʳɖɩ 5 sætəʳɖɩ, °zætəʳɖɩ[3] 6 zætəɽɖɩ 7 satəɹdɩ, °satədɩ[4]

16 Wo 1–2 satədɩ 3 sætəʳ:ɖi:, °sætəʳɖi·[2] 4 sætəʳɖɩ 5 sætəʳɖɩ, °sætɷdɩ[1] 6 sætəɽɖɩ 7 satəʳɖɩ, s.f. sɛtəɽɖɩ [pref.]

17 Wa 1 satədĭ 2–3 satədɩ 4 sad̥ədɩ 5–6 satədɩ 7 satəɽɖɩ

23 Mon 1–2 sætəɽɖɩ 3 sætədɩ 4 satᵊdi 5 satədi 6 sætəɽɖɩ 7 n.a.

24 Gl 1 sætəɽdɩ 2 sætəɽdɩ, °~[3] 3 zætəɽdɩ 4 zatəɽdɩ 5 satəɽdɩ 6 zadədɩ 7 zad̥əɽdɩ, °zatəɽdɩ[1]

25 O 1 saʔədɩ 2 sad̥ədɩ 3 sadədɩ 4 sätəɽdɩ, °sadəɽdɩ[4(2x)] 5–6 saʔəɽdɩ

VII.4.6 WORKDAYS

Q. What do you call all the days of the week together except Sunday?

Rr. /WEEK/WORK/WORK–A/WORKING/WORKY/–DAYS

Note—Expressions comparable with some of those listed above also occur as adjs. at VI.14.20. For additional exs. of WEEK, see VII.3.1 (and refs.); and of WORK, see VIII.4.8 (and refs.).

7 Ch 1 wɩkde:z 2 wə:kɩnde:z 3 wəᶦ:kdi:z 4 wə:kɩnde:z 5 wə:kɩndi:z 6 wəᶦ:kɩndẹ:z

8 Db 1 wəᶦkde:z 2 wə:kɩnde:z 3 wə:kde:z 4 wə:kdi:z 5 wəkɩnde:ˈz 6 wə:kɩndi:z 7 wə:kədi:z

11 Sa 1 wi:kde:z 2 wə:kɩndẹ:ᵊz 3–4 wəɽ:kɩnde:z 5 wəɽ:kɩndẹ:z 6 wi:kde:z 7–9 wəʳ:kɩnde:z 10 wɩkdɩz 11 wəɽ:kɩnde:z

12 St 1 wɩkdɛɩz 2 wɩkdi:z 3 wə:kɩndi:z 4 wə:kdɛɩz 5 wɩkdi:z 6 wɒkdi:z 7 wə:kɩndɛɩz 8 wɩkdɛɩz 9 wə:kɩndɛɩz 10 wi:kdɛɩz, wɩkdɛɩz 11 wi:kdɛɩz

15 He 1–2 wəʳ:kɩnde:ɩz 3 wəʳ:kɩndæɩᵊz 4 wəʳ:kɩndæɩz 5 wəʳkɩnde:ɩz 6 wɩkdæɩz 7 wəɹkɩndeɩz

16 Wo 1 wɩkdɛɩz 2 wɩkde·z 3 wəʳ:kde:ɩz 4 wəʳ:kɩndaɩz 5 wəʳ:kɩnde:z 6 wəʳ:kɩnde:ɩz 7 wɩkdeɩz [pref.], s.w. wəʳkɩndeɩz

17 Wa 1 wi:kdɛɩz, °wə̹:kdɛɩz 2 wə:kɩndɛɩz 3 wəɽ:kdɛɩz 4 wə:kdẹɩz 5 wəʳ:kɩndɛɩz 6 wəʳ:kdɛɩz 7 wəʳ:kɩndɛɩz

23 Mon 1 wɩkdæɩz 2 wəʳ:kɩnde:z 3 wi:kde:z 4 n.a. 5 wœ̣̈:kɩndeiz 6 wəʳ:kɩnde:z 7 n.a.

24 Gl 1 wəʳ:kɩndæɩz 2 wəʳ:kɩndɛɩz 3 wɩkdæɩz 4 wœ:kɩndaɩz 5 wə:kɩde:z 6–7 wəʳ:kɩnde:z

25 O 1 wəʳ:kɩndeɩz 2 wəᶦ:kədɛɩz 3 wəʳ:kɩnde:z 4 wi:kde:z 5 wəʳkɩnde:z, wəʳkɩde:z ["older"] 6 wəʳ:kɩndeɩz

VII.4.7 ON‡ FRIDAY WEEK

Q. When you know that a week after this Friday you'll be back here again, you could say: I'll be back again . . . .

Rr. A WEEK (NEXT) FRIDAY, A WEEK ON §MONDAY, (ON) FRIDAY WEEK, §MONDAY/§THURSDAY/§SATURDAY WEEK, NEXT FRIDAY (WEEK), (A) WEEK COME/ON FRIDAY

Note—For additional exs. of FRIDAY, see VII.4.4; and of WEEK, see VII.3.1 (and refs.).

7 Ch 1 ə wɪk ə fɹɑɪdɪ 2 nɛks fɹɑɪdɪ, °nɛks fɹaɪdɪ 3 ə wɪk ɒn fɹɑɪdɪ 4 ə wɪk nɛkst fɹɑɪdɪ 5 ə fɹɑɪdɪ wɪk 6 ɒn fɹɛɪdɪ wi:k‘

8 Db 1 ə wɪk nɛks fɹaɪddɪ 2 ə wi:k nɛks fɹɑɪdɪ 3 ə wɪk nɛks fɹaɪddɪ 4 ə wɛɪk ə fɹɑɪddɪ 5 ə wɪk kɷm fɹɑɪdɪ 6 ə wɪk ə fɹɑɪdɪ 7 ə wɪk ə fɹɑ̃·ɪ̃dɪ

11 Sa 1 ə wi:k ən fɹaɪdɪ 2 ə wi:k nɛkst fɹæɪdɪ 3 ə wi:k ə fɹaɪdɪ 4 fɹɛɪdɪ wi:k 5 ə wi:k ə fɹaɪdɪ 6 n.r. 7 ə wi:k ə fɹaɪdɪ 8 fɹɒɪdɪ wɪk 9 wi:k kʌm fɹaɪdɪ 10 ə wɪk ə fɹaɪdɪ 11 ə wi:k ə fɹaɪdɪ

12 St 1–2 ə wɪk ə fɹɑɪdɪ 3 fɹɒ:ɪdɪ wɪk 4 ə wɪk ɒn fɹɒɪdɪ 5 wɪk ɒn fɹɒ:ɪdɪ 6 ə wɪk ə fɹɒ:ɪdɪ 7 ə wi:k ɒn fɹɒɪdɪ 8 fɹɒɪdɪ wɪk 9 ɒn fɹɒ·ɪdɪ wɪk 10 ə wi:k ə fɹɔ̣ɪdɪ 11 fɹaɪdɪ wi:k

15 He 1 ə wɪk ə fɹæɪdɪ 2 ə wɪk kʌm fɹæɪdɪ 3 ə wɪk kɷm vɹəɪdɪ 4 ə wɪk nɛks fɹəɪdɪ 5 §sætəʳɖɪ wi:k 6 ə wɪk kɷm vɹəɪdɪ 7 fɹaɪdɪ wi:k, ə wi:k fɹaɪdɪ, °ə wɪk fɹaɪdɪ [from i.'s wife, nat.]

16 Wo 1–2 ə wɪk ə fɹɒɪdɪ 3 ə wɪk ə fɹəi:dɪ 4 §mɷndɪ wɪk 5 fɹəɪdɪ wɪk 6 ə wɪk ə §mɷndɪ 7 ə wɪk ə fɹɔɪdɪ

17 Wa 1 fɹɑɪdɪ wi:k 2 fɹɔɪdɪ wi:k 3 ə wi:k nɛks fɹɔɪdɪ 4 ə wɪk ə fɹɔɪdɪ 5 nɛks fɹʌɪdɪ wɪk 6 ɒn fɹɔɪdɪ wɪk‘ 7 ə wɪk kɷm fɹɔɪdɪ

23 Mon 1 fɹəɪdɪ wɪk 2 §θəʳ:ẓɖɪ wi:k 3 fɹəɪdɪ wi:k 4 ə wi:k nɛks fɹəidi 5 fɹəɪ̣di wi:k 6 fɹəɪdɪ wi:k 7 n.a.

24 Gl 1 ə wɪk ə fɹəɪdɪ 2 fɹəɪdɪ wɪk 3–4 vɹəɪdɪ wɪk 5 ə wɪk ə fɹə̈ɪdɪ 6 ə wɪk kəm vɹʌɪdɪ 7 nɛks vɹʌɪdɪ wɪk‘

25 O 1 ə wi:k ə fɹə̈ɪdɪ 2 ə fɹə̈ɪdɪ wɪk 3 ə wɪk nɛks fɽʌʏdɪ 4 ə wi:k fɽɔɪdɪ 5 ə wi:k nɛks fɹʌʏdɪ 6 ə wi:k ə fɹə̈ɪdɪ

VII.4.8 EASTER, WHITSUNDAY*, CHRISTMAS*, CHRISTMAS EVE, NEW YEAR'S DAY

Q. What specially important days are there during the year?

Rr. EASTER (§MONDAY/SUNDAY)
WHITSUNDAY, WHITSUN (SUNDAY)
CHRISTMAS (DAY)
CHRISTMAS EVE
NEW YEAR({'S} DAY)

Note 1—The rr. to the five parts of the q. are separated below by full stops.
Note 2—For additional exs. of EASTER, see VII.4.9.

7 Ch 1 ẹ:stə. wɩtsɷndɩ. kɹɩsməs. kɹɩsməs ẹ:v. nju: ɩəz dẹ: 2 e:stə, °~. s.w. wɩtsɷndɩ. kɹẹsməs, °kɹɩ̹sməs[1], °kɹəsməs[2]. kɹẹsməs i:v. nü: jɩəz de:, °nü: ɩə 3 ɛɩstə. wɩsn sɷndɩ. kɹɩsməs. kɹɩsməs ɛɩv. njʏ: ɩəz di: 4 i:stə. wɩtsɷndɩ. kɹɩsmɷs. kɹɩsmɷs i:v. nju: ɩəz de: 5 ɛɩstə. wɩtsɷndɩ ["older"], wɩtsn sɷndɩ. kɹɩsməs. kɹɩsməs ɛɩv. nju: ɛɩəz di: 6 i:stə. wɩtsɷndɩ. kɹəsməs. kɹəsməs i:v. nju: ɩəz de:

8 Db 1 e:stə. wɩsndɩ. kɹɩsməs. kɹɩsməs i:v. njʏ: ɩəᶦz de: ["very old"] 2 i:stə. wɩtsɷndɩ, s.f. wɩsndɩ ["rare"]. kɹɩsməs. kɹɩsməs i:v. nju: ɩə de: 3 ɛɩstə. wɩtsɷndɩ. kɹɩsməs(2x). n.r. njü: ɩəz di: 4 i:stə. wɩsndɩ. kɹɩsməs di:. kɹɩsməs ɛɩv. n°u: jɩəz di: 5 ɛɩstə, °i:stə[4]. wɩsndɩ [wɩsntaɩd[4] *W.-tide*]. kɹɩsməs. kɹɩsməs ɛɩv. nˈu: jɩəz de:ˈ 6 e:ˈstə. wɩtsɷndɩ. kɹɩsməs. kɹɩsməs ɛɩv. njü: jɩəz di: 7 i:stə. wɩsn sɷndɩ. kɹɩsməs di:. kɹɩsməs ɛɩv. n°ü: jɩəz di:

11 Sa 1 i:stə. wɩtsʌndɩ. kɹɩsməs. kɹɩsməs i:v. nɩu jəʳ: de: 2 i:stə. wɩtsɷndɩ. kɹɩsməs. kɹɩsməs i:v. nɩu: jəz de: 3–4 i:stəʳ. wɩtsʌndɩ. kɹɩsməs. kɹɩsməs i:v. nɩu: jəz de: 5 ˈi:stəʳ. wɩtsəndɩ. kɹɩsməs. kɹɩsməs ˈi:v. nˈu: jəʳz̹ dẹ: 6 i:stəʳ. wɩtsʌndɩ. kɹɩsməs. kɹɩsməs i:v. nɩu: jəz de: 7 i:stə. wɩtsʌndɩ. kɹɩsməs. kɹɩsməs i:v. nju: jəz de: 8 i:stəʳ. wɩtsəndɩ. kɹɩsməs. kɹɩsməs i:v. nju: jəz de: 9 i:stəʳ. wɩtsəndɩ. kɹəsməs. kɹɩsməs i:v. nju: jəz de: 10 i:stəʳ. wɩtsʌndɩ. kɹɩsməs. kɹɩsməs i:v. nɩu: jəz de: 11 i:stəʳ. wɩtsəndɩ. kɹɩsməs. kɹɩsməs i:v. nju: jəz de:

12 St 1 i:stə. wɩtsɷndɩ. kɹɩsməs dɩə. kɹɩsməs ɛɩv. nju: ɩəz di: 2 i:stə. wɩtsɷnd [*sic*]. kɹɩsməs. kɹɩsməs ɛ̹ɩv. nju: ɩəz di: 3 ɛɩstə. wɩtsɷndɩ. kɹɩsməs di:. kɹɩsməs ɛɩv. nju: jɩəz di: 4 i:stə. wɩtsɷndɩ. kɹɩsməs,

○~[1]. kɹɪsməs i:v. njü: ɪəz dɛɪ 5 i:stə. wɪtsɒndɪ. kɹɪsməs di:, ○kɹɪsməs[2]. kɹɪsməs ɛɪv. nju ɪəz di: 6 ɛɪstə. wɪtsɒndɪ. kɹɪsməs di:. kɹɪsməs ɛɪv. nju jɪəz di: 7 i:stə. wɪtsɒndɪ. kɹɪsməs. kɹɪsməs i:v. nju: ɪəz dɛɪ 8 i:stə sɒndɪ. wɪtsɒndɪ [wɪtmɒndɪ[6] *W.-monday*]. kɹɪsməs dɛɪ, ○kɹɪsməs[6]. kɹɪsməs i:v. nju: ɪəz dɛɪ 9 i:stə. wɪtsɒndɪ. kɹɪsməs di:, ○kɹɪsməs[1]. kɹɪsməs i:v. nju: iəz di: 10 i:stə §mɒndɪ. wɪtsɒndɪ [wɪtmɒndɪ *W.-monday*]. kɹɪsməs. kɹɪsməs i:v. njü: jɪəz dɛɪ 11 i:stəɹ. wɪtsɒndɛɪ. kɹɪsmǫs dɛɪ. kɹɪsməs i:v. nju: ɪəz dɛɪ

15 He 1 i:stəʳ. wɪtsndɪ. kɹɪsməs. kɹɪsməs i:v. nju: jəz de:ɪ 2 i:stəʳ. wɪtsndɪ. kɹɪsməs. kɹɪsməs i:v. nju jəʳz̧ de:ɪ 3 i:stəʳ. wɪtsəndɪ. kɹɪsməs. kɹɪsməs i:ᵊv. nju: jəʳ:z̧ dæɪ 4 i:stəʳ. wɪtsʌndɪ. kɹɪsməs. kɹɪsməs i:v. nju: jəʳz̧ dæɪ 5 i:stəʳ. wɪtsəndɪ. kɹɪsməs. kɹɪsməs i:v. nju: jəʳ:z̧ de:ɪ 6 i:stəʳ. wɪtsəndɪ. kɹɪsmɒs. kɹɪsmɒs i:v. nju jəʳz̧ dæɪ 7 i:stəɹ. wɪtsʌndɪ [wɪtsəntaɪd *W.-tide*; wɪtwɪk *W.-week*]. kɹɪsməs. n.r. nu: jəɹz deɪ

16 Wo 1 i:stə. wɪ̧tsəndɪ. kɹɪsməs. kɹɪsməs i:v. nɪu: jəz dɛɪ 2 i:stəʳ. wɪtsɒndɪ. kɹɪsmɒs. kɹɪsməs i:v. nju: jəʳz̧ de: 3 i:stəʳ. wɪtsəndɪ. kɹɪsmɒs. kɹɪsmɒs i:v. nju: jəʳ:z̧ de:ɪ 4 i:stəʳ. wɪtsɒndɪ. kɹɪsmɒs. kɹɪsmɒs i:v. nju: jəʳ:z̧ daɪ 5 i:stəʳ. wɪtsɒndɪ. kɹɪsmɒs. kɹɪsmɒs i:v. nju: jəʳ:z̧ de: 6 i:stəʳ. wɪtsəndɪ. kɹɪsmɒs. kɹɪsmɒs i:v. nju: jəz de:ɪ 7 i:stəʳ, s.f. ɛɪstəʳ [pref., "older"]. wɪtsɒndɪ. kɹɪsmɒs, ○~[1], ○kɹɪsməs[4] [¶əkɹɪsməsɪn[1] *a-Christmasing* (i.e. singing carols)]. n.r. nu: ɪəʳz̧ de:, ○nu: jəʳ[1]

17 Wa 1 i:stəɹ. wɪtsɒndï. kɹɪsməs. kɹɪsməs i:v. nu: jə̧̂:z dɛɪ 2 i:stə, p. ɛɪstə ["older"]. n.r. kɹɪsməs. kɹɪsməs i:v. nu: jɪəz dɛɪ, s.f. nu: ɪəz dɛ̧ɪ 3 i:stə. wɪtsɒndʳɪ [wɪsntəɪd *W.-suntide*]. kɹɪsməs. kɹɪsməs i:v. nju: jɪəz dæ̧ɪ 4 i:stəʳ. wɪsn sɒndɪ. kɹɪsmɒs. kɹɪsmɒs i:v. nᶦü: ɪəʳz̧ dɛɪ 5 i:stə. wɪtsɒndɪ. kɹɪsmɒs. kɹɪsmɒs i:v. nju: ɪəʳz̧ dɛɪ 6 i:stəʳ. wɪtsɒndɪ [wɪtsn *W.-sun*]. kɹɪsmɒs. kɹɪsmɒs i:v. nju: ɪəʳz̧ dɛɪ 7 i:stəʳ. wɪsn sɒndɪ. kɹɪsməs. kɹɪsməs ɛɪv. nu: ɪəʳz̧ dɛɪ

23 Mon 1 ᶦi:stəʳ. wɪtsʌndɪ. kɹɪsməs. kɹɪsməs ɪi:v. nj°u: jəʳz̧ dæɪ 2 i:stəʳ. wɪtsəndɪ. kɹɪsməs. kɹɪsməs i:v. nju: jəʳz̧ de: 3 i:stə. wɪtsəndɪ. kɹɪsməs. kɹɪsməs i:v. nju jœ:z de: 4 n.r. wɪtsndei. kɹɪsmʌ̧̈s. n.r. n.r. 5 ɨ:stə. wɪtsn. kɹɪsmʌ̧̈s. kɹɪsmʌ̧̈s i:ᵊv. nju· jœ̧̂:z dei 6 i:stəʳ. wɪtsəndɪ. kɹɪsməs. kɹɪsməs i:v. nju: jəʳz̧ de: 7 n.r.

24 Gl 1 i:stəʳ. wɩtsəndɩ. kɹɩsmɷs. kɹɩsməs i:ᵊv. nju: jəʳ:ʐ dæɩ 2 ɩi:stəʳ. wɩtsɷndɩ. kɹɩsmɷs. kɹɩsmɷs ɩi:v. nju: jəʳ:ʐ dɛɩ 3 ɩi:stəʳ. wɩtsəndɩ. kɹɩsmɷs. kɹɩsməs ˈi:v. njᴼu: jəz dæɩ 4 ɩi:stəʳ. wɩtsəndɩ. kɹɩsməs. kɹɩsməs ɩi:v. njᴼu: jəʳ:ʐ daɩ 5 e:stəʳ. wɩtsɷndɩ. kɹɩsmɷs. kɹɩsməs i:v. nju: jəʳʐ de: 6 e:stəʳ. wɩtzəndɩ. kɹəsməs. kɹəsməs i:v. nju: jəʳ:ʐ de: 7 i:stəʳ. wɩtzəndɩ. kɹɩsməs. kɹɩsməs i:v. nju: jəʳ:ʐ de:

25 O 1 i:stəʳ. wɩtsɷndɩ. kɹɩsməs. kɹɩsməs i:v. nju: jəʳ:ʐ dɛə 2 eˈstəʳ. wɩtsʌndɩ. kɹɩsməs dɛɩ. kɹɩsməs i:v. nu: ɩəʳ 3 e:stɽ. wɩtsɷndɩ. kɹɩsməs. kɹɩsməs i:v. nju: ɩəʳ 4 i:stəɽ. wɩtsɷndɩ [wɩtsəntəɩd[4] *W.-tide*]. kɽəsməs, kɽɩsməs, ᴼ~[1]. kɽəsməs i:v, kɽɩsməs i:v. nju: jəɽʐ de: [nju: jəɽʐ i:v[4] *New Year's Eve*] 5 i:stəʳ. wɩtsʌndɩ. kɽɩsməs. kɽɩsməs i:v. nju: ɩəʳʐ deˑ 6 i:stəʳ. wɩtsʌndɩ. kɹɩsməs. kɹɩsməs i:v. nu: ɩəʳ

VII.4.9 EASTER EGGS

Q. During one of these (local) *festivals* (viz. Easter) *children, especially, eat hard-boiled eggs. What do you call them?*

Rr. EASTER/PACE EGGS

Note —For additional exs. of EASTER, see VII.4.8; and of EGGS, see IV.6.4.

7 Ch 1 ẹ:stɹ‿ɛgz 2 s.w. e:stəɹ ɛgz 3 ɛɩstəɹ ɛgz 4 ẹ:stəɹ ɛgz 5 ɛɩstəɹ ɛgz 6 i:stəɹ ɛgz

8 Db 1 pe:s ɛgz 2 ɩəstəɹ ɛgz [pi:s ɛg ple: *Pace Egg Play*] 3 ɛɩstəɹ ɛgz 4 i:stɹ‿ɛgzᵊ 5 ɛɩstə ɛgz 6 e:ˈstəɹ ɛgz 7 n.k.

11 Sa 1 i:stəʳɽ ɛgz 2 i:stəɹ ɛgz 3 i:stəʳ: ɛgz 4 i:stəʳɽ ɛgz 5 ˈi:stəʳɽ ɛgz 6–11 i:stəʳɽ ɛgz

12 St 1–2 i:stəɹ ɛgz 3 ɛɩstəɹ ɛgz 4–5 i:stəɹ ɛgz 6 ɛɩstəɹ ɛgz 7–11 i:stəɹ ɛgz

15 He 1–7 i:stəʳɽ ɛgz

16 Wo 1 i:stəɹ ɛgz 2–6 i:stəʳɽ ɛgz 7 ɛɩstəʳ ɛgz

17 Wa 1 i:stəɹ ɛgz 2 ɛɩstə ɛgz 3 i:stəɹ ɛgz 4 n.k. 5–7 i:stəɹ ɛgz

23 Mon 1 ˈi:stəʳɽ ɛgz 2 i:stəʳɽ ɛgz 3 i:stəɹ ɛgz 4 n.a. 5 ɨ:stəɹ ɛgz 6 i:stəʳɽ ɛgz 7 n.a.

24 Gl 1 i:stəʳɽ ɛgz 2–4 ɩi:stəʳɽ ɛgz 5–6 n.k. 7 i:stəʳɽ ɛgz

25 O 1 i:stəɽ ɛgz 2 eˈ:stəɹ ɛgz 3 e:stɽ ɛgz 4 i:stəɽ ɛgz 5 i:stə^{ɽ} ɛgz 6 i:stə^{ɽ}ɽ ɛgz

VII.4.10 AN† APRIL FOOL

Q. On the 1st of April you like to make a person . . . .

Rr. (A/AN) APRIL FOOL, A TOM-FOOL, (/A/AN OLD/) FOOL

Note 1—Since the f.ws. were always on the look-out for the inclusion of the indef. art. in the r., its omission below means that it was undetected in the rr. concerned.

Note 2—I.m. exs. of FOOL are reproduced below between square brackets untransliterated.

Note 3—For additional exs. of APRIL, see VII.3.3; and of FOOL, see VIII.9.7.

7 Ch 1 ȩ:pɹɪl fʏ: 2 ə e:pɹɪl fu: [fu:^{2}] 3 ə ȩ:pɹəl fʏ: 4 ȩ:pɹəl fų̈: 5 i:pɹəl fʏ: [fˈʏ:^{1}] 6 ən e:pɹəl fü:

8 Db 1 ən e:pɹɪl fʏ: 2 e:pɹəl fu:l 3 ə e:pɹəl fɛ̈ɷl [fɛ̈ɷl^{2}] 4 ə e:pɹɪl fɛɷl 5 e:ˈpɹɪl fˈu:l 6 ə e:ˈpɹɪl fɛɷl [fɛɷl^{1}] 7 e:ˈpɹɪl fɛɷl [fȩɷl^{2}]

11 Sa 1 ə e:pɹəl fu:l 2 ə e:pɹɪl fˈu:l 3–4 ə e:pɹɪl fu:l 5 ȩ:pɹəl fɪu:l 6–7 ə e:pɹəl fu:l 8 ə je:pɹɪl fu:l 9 ə e:pɹəl fu:l 10 ə e:pɹɪl fu:l 11 ə e:pɹəl fu:l

12 St 1 ɛɪpɹɪl faɷl 2 ə ɛɪpɹɪl fɛɷ [fɛɷ^{1}] 3 ə ɛɪpɹɪl fɛɷ 4 ɛɪpɹəl fu:l 5 ɛɪpɹɪl fü:l [fu:l^{1} VI.1.5, fu:l^{1} VIII.9.3] 6 fȩɷl [fü:l^{1}] 7–8 ɛɪpɹəl fu:l 9 ɛɪpɹɪl fɛɷl [fu:l^{1}; ɔ:l fɛɷls di: *All Fools' Day*; wɛt ɛg^{2} *wet egg* (i.e. "silly fool")] 10 ən ɛɪpɹəl fü:l 11 ɛɪpɹəl fu:l

15 He 1–2 ə e:ɪpɹəɫ fu:ɫ 3 ə æpɹəɫ fu:ɫ 4–5 ə e:ɪpɹəɫ fu:ɫ 6 ə ɛpɹəɫ fu:ɫ 7 ən eɪpɹəl fu:l [y̥uɷl^{4}]

16 Wo 1 ən ɛɪpɹəl fu:l 2 ən‿apɹɪl fu:l 3 ə e:ɪpɹəɫ fu:ɫ 4 ə e:pɹɷɫ fu:ɫ 5 ə e:pɹɪl fu:ɫ 6 ə e:ɪpɹɪɫ fu:ɫ 7 ən ɔɷl fu:ɫ, ə eɪpɹəl fu:ɫ [fu:ɫ$^{1(2x)}$, fu:l$^{1(2x)}$, □fu:ɫz$^{1(2x)}$; ɔɷl fu:ɫz de: *Old Fool's Day* (i.e. April Fool's Day)]

17 Wa 1 ən ɛɪpɹəɫ fu:ɫ 2 eɪpɹəl fu:l [fu:l$^{4(4x)}$, □fu:lz^{4}] 3 ^{ə} ɛɪpɹɪɫ fɷɫ 4 ə ɛɪpɹəɫ fu:^{ə}ɫ 5–7 ə ɛɪpɹəɫ fu:ɫ

23 Mon 1 ə e:ɪpɹəɫ f^{ɷ}u:ɫ 2–3 ə e:pɹəɫ fu:ɫ 4 ə e:pɹɭ fu:l, ○∼^{3} 5 e:pɹəɫ fų̈:l 6 ə e:pɹɪɫ fu:ɫ 7 n.a.

24 Gl 1 ə ɑ:ɫ fu:^{ə}ɫ 2 ə ɑ:ɫ fu:^{ə}ɫ [fu:ɫ^{3}] 3 ə e:ˈpɹəɫ f^{ɷ}u:^{ə}ɫ 4 ə e:pɹəɫ v^{ɷ}u:^{ə}ɫ 5 e:pɹəɫ fu:^{ə}ɫ 6 ən e:pɹəɫ fu:ɫ 7 ə e:pɹəɫ fu:^{ə}ɫ

25 O 1 ə tɒmfu:ɫ 2 ɛɪpɹəɫ fu:ɫ 3 ə e:pɹəɫ fu:ɫ 4 ə e:pɽə fu:ɫ 5 e:^{ə}pɹə fu:ɫ 6 eɪp‿ʔɹəl fɷɫ

VII.4.11 FESTIVAL

Q. What do you call your local festival or holiday?

Describe it.

Rr. BARNABY, CLUB (FETE/WALK), CLUB'S WALKING, (/DEAD MAN'S/HORSE/JUNE/MAY/ST. GILES'S/WOOL/) FAIR, FEAST, FETE, FLOWER SHOW, FORESTERS' DINNER/FEAST, HARVEST FESTIVAL, /MAY/OAK-APPLE/ DAY, MOP, ODD-FELLOWS' CLUB (DAY), ROAST, ROUT, §SPORTS, STATUTES, WAKE(S), WAKES SUNDAY, WALK, WELL-DRESSING

Note 1—The name of the loc. itself, or of some neighbouring place, was often included in the rr. All the names in question have been transliterated below.

Note 2—In order to indicate the kind of activity involved or the nature of the occasion, the foll. superior signs have been prefixed to the expression for FESTIVAL:— ɑ = sale of cattle; ᴅ = sale of horses; × = sale of sheep; ‖ = dinner; ʙ = band; ᴄ = church service or religious festival; ᴇ = fairground entertainment; ꜰ = sponsored by local Friendly Society; ɢ = games; ʜ = hirings; ᴘ = procession; ʀ = races; ꜱ = sports; ᴡ = dancing; and ◇ denotes obs.

Note 3—The 1st r. at 7.1, the 3rd r. at 17.4 and the 3rd r. at 17.7 were unfortunately recorded only orthographically. They have, nevertheless, been included in the list above.

7 Ch 1 Kingsley ^{EFP}Club, ○kɩŋzlɩ ◇wẹ:ks [acc. tradition, with bear-baiting], ○wẹ:ks [in some nearby village, but not loc.] 2 ^{C}bɔ:nəbɩ [i.e. St. Barnabus, June 11th, when the loc. mills were closed], maklsfɩld [=*Macclesfield*, 2½ SSE.] we:ks [Oct. 1st–3rd] 3 swɛtnəm [=*Swettenham*] ‖ꜰᴘꜱwɔ:k, ma:tn [=*Marton*, 2½ ENE.] ^{E}we:ks 4 ◇ꜰLadies Club Day [3rd Wednesday in June], ◇ꜰMen's Friendly Society Day [Whitmonday] 5 ɔ:ləm [=*Audlem*] ◇ᴇwi:ks [Whitsuntide] 6 anmə [=*Hanmer*] we:ks [fig pie; Sunday after March 2nd]

8 Db 1 tʃo:zəθ [=*Charlesworth*] ^{E}we:ks 2 bamfəd [=*Bamford*] ^{W}we:ks [celebrations finished at Hathersage (2 SSE.) Fair; 2nd Friday after Oct. 11th] 3 ^{FP}local societies [Whitsunday], bɷkstən [=*Buxton*, 1 ENE.] wɛldɹɛsɩn [June] 4 jo:lgɹɩ [=*Youlgreave*] ◇ꜰfi:st [All Saints' Day] 5 ◇we:ˈks, ○◇~¹ [1st week in July] 6 nɛɩtn [=*Kniveton*] ◇ᴇwe:ˈks [1st Sunday after 11th Oct.; now replaced by Chapel Harvest Festival, with a fair on the foll. Monday; farm-labourers have holiday] 7 sɷtn [=Sutton] ^{F}tlɷb, sɷtn ^{C}fɛɩt, s.w. ◇we·ɩks ["very old"]

11 Sa 1 ^{EF}klʌbs ["festival and fair organised by loc. "Druids" (a Friendly Society); in summer"] 2 pɹi:s [=*Prees*] ^{EFRW}klɷbs [held on a Saturday at end of June], gɔ:bɩ [pres. Gorby in Shrewsbury, 15 SSW.] ^{H}fe:ə 3 n.f. 4 gɔʳ:bɩ

[=*Gorby*] fɛəʳ [in Shrewsbury, 4 ESE.; May 1st] 5 n.k. 6 ^FP^fɒɹəstəʳ:ʐ fi:st [free beer; 1st Wednesday after June 18th] 7 ^D^əʳ:ʂ fe:əʳ [May], wɷl fe:əʳ [when wool was paid for; June], dɛd manz fe:əʳ [Nov.] 8 ^BCW^klɷb [Monday nearest June 24th] 9 ^E^me: fɛəʳ [May 11th] 10 ^W^klʌbz [coconut shying; anytime in summer], ^E^me: fə:-əʳ [at Craven Arms, 3⅞ SW.; May 24th] 11 ^BCFPSW^klʌb [Monday nearest June 24th]

12 St 1 wɔ:zlə [=*Warslow*] wɛɩks [2nd Sunday in Aug.], ^○FP^klɷb wɔ:ks 2 mɛɷ [=*Mow* (i.e. Mow Cop)] ^R^wɛɩks [coconut shying; July] 3 oɷtn [=*Alton*] wi:ks [June], ^‖P^klɷbz woɷkɩn 4 ba:ləstən [=*Barlaston*] wɛɩks [roundabouts and swings; July] 5 ^EP^ɛklʃəl [=*Eccleshall*, 2 NNW.] we:ks [Trinity Sunday], ^EP^klɷbz 6 ^F^æɷdfɛləz klɷb di: [oɷkbɔ:lɩn *oak-balling* (i.e. chasing children who have no oak apple and stinging them with nettles); May 29th] 7 ɹɩdwə [=*Ridware*] ^E^wɛɩks [Sept. 5th–11th] 8 wi:tn astən [=*Wheaton Aston*, 1⅛ WSW.] ^S^spǫ:ts [Monday after Whitmonday] 9 ɛdɩŋl [=*Edingale*] ^HW^wę:k 10 wɩgɩntən [=*Wigginton*] ^E^wɛɩks [end of Oct.], ^○E^~[4], ^○^taməθ [=*Tamworth*, 2¼ S.] statʃɩts[4] [pres. hirings, Edd.] 11 ^‖BE^ɹɷt [ate Banbury cakes; Whitmonday], ^○^ɩmlɩ [=*Himley*] ɹɷt

15 He 1 ^BFS^klʌb wɔ:k [in an orchard; June] 2 wɛblɩ [=*Weobley*] ^EW^fe:əʳ [May 8th] 3 lɛdbɹɩ [=*Ledbury*, 6¼ SSE.] ^EH^fɛəʳ: [2nd Tuesday in Oct.] 4 maʳ:ɖɩfəʳɖ [=*Mordiford*, 1 NW.] ^‖ERW^klʌb [June] 5 klɷdəks[=*Clodock's* (*poss. sg.*), 1½ SSE.] ^‖BW^fi:st [Nov. 7th] 6 wɩtʃəʳ:tʃ [=*Whitchurch*] ^‖BW^fɛəʳ [May 29th] 7 fɛəɹ, ^○^kɩŋtən [(=*Kington*), 2¼ WNW.] meɩ fɛəɹ, ^○^pɛmbɹɩdʒ [=*Pembridge*, 4 NNE.] ^H^meɩ fɛəɹ

16 Wo 1 ^‖EW^fɒɹəstəz dɩnə [Summer] 2 ^CEFSW^oɷkapɫ de: [May 29th] 3 ænbɹi: [=*Hanbury*] ^H^mɒp [open market; Midsummer Day] 4 klɩftɷn [=*Clifton*] ^RW^mɒp [garden fetes and show; Aug.] 5 bɑ:tɷn [=*Baughton*, ½ ESE.] ^RW^we:k [shooting; May 29th] 6 ɒfnɷm [=*Offenham*] ^ERW^we:ɩk [May 29th] 7 ^E^mɔp [Stratford-on-Avon and Evesham; Oct. 11th], ^○^wɩləzɩ [=*Willersley*, 2½ SSE.] węɩk[4]

17 Wa 1 ^EFP^ɒdfɛləz klɷb [1st Saturday after June 17th] 2 ^E^mɔp [oxen roasted, Stratford, 11 SE.], ^E^węɩk [smaller], ^○^taməθ [=*Tamworth*, 19 N.E.] we:k; ^○EF^klɷb [small] 3 wɛɩk, aʃə [=*Ashow*, 2¼ SSW.] wɛɩk [now a celebration on bonfire night on village green when loc. nobility would talk with tenants], ^○◇F^stoɷnlɩ [=*Stoneleigh*] wɛɩks, ^○◇E^wɛɩk 4 naptən [=*Napton*] ^ES^wɛɩks [stalls and roundabouts], sɛɷθəm [=*Southam*, 3 WNW.] ^H^mɒp, ^◇^Wakes Sunday [3-day holiday; 1st Sunday after August 21st] 5 a:sn [=*Aston* (i.e. Aston Cantlow)] ^EW^we:ᵊk [crockery stall, cheapjacks, bowling for a

pig; 2nd Saturday in July] 6 lɔɩtən [=*Lighthorne*] we:ᵊk [Monday after Aug. 21st], ◇Fklɷb wɔ:k ["bigger" celebration, Whit Tuesday] 7 DEdʒu:n fɛ·ə, ɹoɷst [beast roasted in Main Street; 1st Tuesday after Oct. 10th], FGRClub Fete [Whitmonday]

23 Mon 1 Eme:ɩ fɛəʴ [in Abergavenny, 10½ SSW.], FRWklʌb wɑ:k [greased pig chased] 2 RWme: fɛəʴ [May 1st] 3 tu:ɩn [=*Twyn*, 2½ WNW.] Efɛə [Trinity Monday] 4 n.a., ○a:vïs fɛstïvəl³, ○mei dei³ 5 n.k. [Whitsun treat and Chapel anniversaries] 6 RWn.r. [Whitsunday] 7 n.a.

24 Gl 1 tʃɷksbɹɩ [=*Tewkesbury*, 2½ NNE.] Efæɩəʴ [October 10th] 2 gɹɛʔn [=*Gretton*] we:ək, GWMay Day [maypole] 3 En.r. [miners' demonstration, at Speech House in centre of the Forest of Dean; 3rd Saturday in July] 4 n.k. 5 ʃɛʴ:bən [=*Sherborne*] Ewe:k [rent day; Michaelmas] 6 slɩmbɹɩdʒ [=*Slimbridge*] flʌɷə ʃɑɷ [fruit, flower and vegetable show, and garden competition] 7 akn [=*Acton* (i.e. Iron Acton), 2 SSE.] ◫×Evɛɩəʴ [April 25th and Sept. 13th], sɒdbɹɩ [=*Sodbury* (pres. *Chipping S.*, Edd.) 4½ SE.] ◇Hmɑp

25 O 1 ‖Hmɒp [Chipping Norton, 4 ENE.], ‖Fklʌb, ○Hmɒp² 2 CEFn.r. [July 4th] 3 ‖CFGn.r. 4 ɛnsəm [=*Eynsham*] fɛ̹əɽ [Sept.], wɩtnɩ [=*Whitney*, 5 WNW.] fi:st [Sept.], snt dʒɑɩɫzɩz fɛ̹əɽ [Oxford, 5 ESE.; Sept.], kasɩntən [=*Cassington*, 1¼ ENE.] fi:st [Sept.] 5 bɹʌʔl [=*Brightwell* (i.e. Brightwell Baldwin), ½ WSW.] ◇EGWfi:st 6 Fn.r.

VII.5.1 WHAT TIME IS IT‡?

Q. Suppose your watch has stopped and you want to know whether it is 5 or 6, what would you ask someone?

Rr. WHAT TIME /BEES'T/BE IT/(OF DAY) IS IT/?, WHAT'S THE (RIGHT) TIME?

The following, since they do not include IS IT, are, strictly speaking, u.rr.:—CAN YOU TELL /ME THE TIME/US WHAT TIME IT IS/?, CANST THEE GIVE US THE TIME?, COULD YOU TELL ME /THE TIME/WHAT TIME IT IS/?, DOST KNOW THE TIME OF DAY?, DOST THEE KNOW THE TIME? GOT THE TIME ON YOU? HAST GOT (THE) TIME ON THEE? HAST THEE (GOT) THE TIME (ON THEE)?, HOW'S THE CLOCK GOING?, HOW'S THE TIME (/GOING {ON}/LOOKING/)?, TELL US THE TIME, WHAT'S /ABOUT THE TIME/THE TIME OF DAY/?, WHAT'S THE

CLOCK SAY?, WHAT TIME /DOST CALL IT/DOST MAKE IT/ DO YOU CALL IT/HAST THOU/?

Note—I.m. exs. of TIME are included below between square brackets untransliterated Exs. of WHAT occur at VII.8.16/17; of TIME, at VII.3.16; and of -TIME, at V.8.4 and VII.5.19.

7 Ch 1 wat taım ız ıt [taım²] 2 kən jə tɛl mı‿ʔᵗ taım 3 wɒt taım a‿t [=*hast thou*] 4 wɒt taım ız ıt [tɑːˈm¹, taım²] 5 ast gɒt taım ɒn ðı [taım³] 6 wɒts ðə taım

8 Db 1 ɛɷz‿ʔ taım [taım¹] 2 wɒt taım ız ıt 3 ast gɛt‿ʔ taım ɒn ðı 4 wɒt taım ız ıt [taım¹, □taımz¹] 5 wat taım ız ıt 6 wɒts ð‿ɹɛıt taım, wɒt taım ıs‿t [□tɑ̃ːmz¹] 7 wɒt tɑ̃·ĩm ız ıt [taım¹]

11 Sa 1 aɷz ðə taım 2 kɷd jə tɛl mı wɒt tæım ıt ız 3 wɒt taım ız ıt 4 wɒt tɒım ız ıt [tɛım²] 5 wɒt taım ız ıt 6 wɒt taım də jə kɔːl ıt 7 aɷz ðə taım 8 aɷz ðə klɒk goːın, aɷz ðə taım əgoːın 9 tɛl əz ðə taım 10 as θiː ðə taım 11 wɒts ðə taım əv daːı

12 St 1 wɒt tɒım ɛs‿t 2 wɒt tɒım ız ıt, ○wɒt tɒım dɷst mak ıt 3 wɒt tɒːım ıs‿t 4 wɒt tɒım ız ıt 5–6 wɒt tɒːım ız ıt [tɒːım²] 6 wɒt tɒːım ız ıt 7–8 wɒt tɒım ız ıt 9 a·ɷz ðə tɒım gɷː-ın ɒn, wɒt tɒım ız ıt 10 kɷd jə tɛl mı ðə taːım, wɒt taım ız ıt 11 wɒt taːım ız ıt

15 He 1–2 wɒt tæım ız ıt 3 wɒt təım ız ıt 4 əz ðiː gɒt ðə taım ɒn θə 5 wɒts ðə təım [təım¹⁽²ˣ⁾] 6 wɒt təım ız ıt 7 wɒts ðə taım, wɒts ðə klɒk seı, wɒts əbəʉt ðə taım

16 Wo 1 wɒt tɒıᵊm ız ıt [tɒım³] 2 wɒt tɒım ə deː ız ıt [təım¹⁽²ˣ⁾] 3 wɒts ðə təiːᵊm 4 wɒts ðə təım 5 wɒt təım bıst 6 wɒts ðə tɒım 7 dɷz noɷ ðə təım ə deı

17 Wa 1 wɒt taım ız ıt 2 wəts əbæɷt ðə təım 3 wɒt təım ız ıt 4 wɒt təım ız ıt 5 wɒts ðə təım 6 kan jə tɛl əs wɒt təım ıt ız 7 ɛ̈ɷz ðə təım

23 Mon 1 wɒts ðə təım 2 ʌɷz ðə təım goː-ın 3 wɒts ðə təım 4 wɒ̣·t tʰəim ız ıtʰ 5 wɒ̣·t təım ız ıt 6 əɷz ðə təım lɷkın 7 n.a.

24 Gl 1 wɒ təıᵊm biː ıt 2 dɷs ðiː næɷ ðə təım 3 əɷz ðə təım əgɒɷın 4 əɷz ðə təım əgɒɷın 5 wɒt tö̈ım ız ıt 6 kəst ðiː gı əs ðə tʌım 7 wɒt tʌım‿st kɔː‿t

25 O 1 wɒt töım ız ıʔ 2 wɒts ðə töım 3 gɒt ðə tʌʏm ɒn jə 4 wɒts ðə töım 5 wɒt tʌʏm ız ıʔ 6 wɒts ðə tʌʏm

VII.5.2 I DON'T KNOW

Q. Suppose he hadn't his watch with him (when you asked him the time), *he would say: . . . .*

Rr. I CAN'T SAY, I CAN'T TELL (YOU), I CAN'T TELL YOU THE TIME, I COULDN'T TELL YOU, (I) DON'T KNOW, I'VE NO IDEA

The foll. are u.rr.:—I CAN'T SAY, I HAVEN'T GOT /A TIME–PIECE/MY WATCH (WITH ME)/NO WATCH/THE TIME/, I HAVEN'T THE TIME WITH ME

Note 1—In the lists of rr. above CAN'T subsumes CANNA, DON'T subsumes DUNNA; HAVEN'T subsumes HAVENA; and YOU subsumes THEE.

Note 2—I.m. exs. of KNOW are reproduced below between square brackets untransliterated. 3 pr.pls. have either an attached superior +, indicating that the form was prec. by a n.pl., or ×, indicating that it was preceded by THEY.

Note 3—For additional exs. of CAN'T, see IX.4.16; and of DON'T, see IX.4.10 and 1X.5.2. KNEW occurs at VI.5.17.

7 Ch 1 ə kɒnə tɛl ðι, a dɷnə no: [$^{\times}$nọ:n^{2} *3 pr. pl.*] 2 ɑ: kɒnə tɛl jə‿ʔ^{t} taιm, °a du:nt nu:^{2}, °a dɷ: nɷ:^{3}, °a dɷnə nọ:^{3} [nɔ:^{1,3} *inf.*; nɔ:^{2}, nɔ^{3} *1 pr.s.*; nɔ̄:z^{2} *1 pr. pl.*; nɔ:n$^{1(2x),4(2x)}$ *2 pr. pl.*; nɔ:d^{2} 1 *p.t.s.*; nọ:z^{1} *pr.t.*] 3 a dɷnə nọ: 4 a dɷnə nọ: [¶no:ιn^{3}] 5 a dɷnə no: 6 dɷnə no:

8 Db 1 a dɷnə no:, a kɒnə tɛl ðι 2 a do:nt no: [no:n^{2,4} *2 pr. pl.*] 3 a dɷnə no:, °~^{1} [a kɷdnə tɛl ðι *I couldn't tell thee*] 4 a dɷnə no: [nɔ:^{1} *inf.*] 5 a: kanə tɛl jə, a: dɷnə no:^{ɷ} [nɔ:z^{1} *2 pr.s.*] 6 a dɷnə no:^{ɷ} 7 a dɷnə no·ɷ, °~^{1,2}

11 Sa 1 aι dʌn no 2 aι dɷnə no:, °~^{1}, °aι ˈdɷ ˈno:^{1}, °aι do: no:^{2} 3 aι ˈdo: ˈno:, °aι dɷnə no:^{2} 4 a kɒnə tɛl jə 5 aι dɷnə no: [no:^{1,3} *inf.*] 6 aι dɷnə no:, °~^{3} [no:$^{3(2x)}$ *inf.*; ~^{4} *2 pr.s.*; $^{\times}$~^{4} *3 pr.pl.*] 7 aι dʌnə no:, °aι da:n no^{1} 8 aι dɷnə no: [$^{\times}$dɷnə (*3 pr.pl.*) no:^{2}; no:^{1} *1 pr.s.*; ~^{2} *1 pr.pl.*] 9 aι dʌnə no: [no:^{1} *inf.*; ~$^{1(2x)}$ *1 pr.s.*] 10 aι dʌnə no: 11 aι dɷnə no:, °~^{2} [no:^{1,2} *inf.*; ~^{1,2}, no:z^{1,2} *1 pr.s.*]

12 St 1 §aι anə gɛt mι wɒtʃ, °a dɷnə noɷ^{2} [noɷ^{1} *inf.*; ~^{3} *1 pr.s.*; ~^{1} *2 pr.pl.*] 2 a dɷnə noɷ, a kɒnə si:, °a kɒnə tɛl ðι [noɷ$^{1,2(2x)}$ *inf.*; nɛɷ^{4}, nɷ:st *2 pr.s.*] 3 §ɒ:ι anə gɒtn noɷ wɒtʃ, a kɒnə tɛl ðι, °a dɷnə noɷ^{1,2} [nɷ:^{1} *inf.*] 4 a kɒnə tɛl jə [noɷz^{2} *3 pr.s.*] 5 a kɷdnt tɛl jə, °a dɷnə nɷ:^{2,3} [no:^{2,3} *inf.*; nɷ:^{3} *v.*; noɷ^{2} *1 pr.s.*] 6 ɒ:ι dɷnə noɷ, °a dɷnə noɷ^{2} [noɷ^{1} *inf.*] 7 a doɷnt noɷ [noɷ$^{1(3x)}$ *inf.*; ~^{2,3} *1 pr.s.*; ~^{3} *2 pr.pl.*] 8 §aι avnt ðə tɒιm wιð mι, °ɒι doɷ noɷ^{2} [noɷ^{1} *inf.*; noɷz^{1} *3 pr.s.*] 9 ɒι dɷnə noɷ, °~^{3}, °a dɷnə noɷ^{3} [noɷ^{1} *inf.*; nɷ:z^{2} *3 pr.s.*] 10 a:v noɷ a:ιdιə 11 a doɷn noɷ [noɷ$^{1,2(2x)}$ *1 pr.s.*; noɷz^{2} *pr.t.*]

15 He 1 ˈæɪ ˈdɑː ˈnoː [næɷz[1] *1 pr.s.*] 2 ˈæɪ ˈdɔː ˈnoː, §æɪ ænə gɒt noː wætʃ 3 æɪ dɷnə noɷ, ○ˈəɪ ˈdoː ˈnɒɷ[4], ○ˈɒɪ ˈdɑː ˈnoː[3] [nɒɷ *1 pr.pl.*; ~[2,4], næɷ[3] *2 pr.pl.*] 4 əɪ doːnt næɷ, ○ˈəɪ ˈdoː ˈnoː[1] [nɒɷz[2] *1 pr.s.*] 5 əɪ ˈdoː ˈnoː, ○əɪ ˈdoː ˈnæɷ[1(2x)], ○əɪ ˈdɑː ˈnɑː[4] 6 ə dʒɷnt nɒɷ, ○əɪ də nɒɷ[1] [nɒɷ[1(2x)] *inf.*] 7 aɪ dɷ̃ɷ̃nt nɷ̃ɷ̃, §aɪ anə gɒt ðə taɪm, §aɪ anə gɒt ə taɪmpiːs, ○ɔɪ də noɷ[3], ○ɔɪ də ˈnoː[4] [noɷ[1] *inf.*; noː[2(2x)], noːz[1], noɷz[4] *1 pr.s.*; ×~[3] *3 pr.pl.*]

16 Wo 1 ɒɪ dɒɷnt nɒɷ, ○ɒɪ dɒɷn nɒɷ[3] 2 ɒɪ kanə tɛl [noɷ[2] *inf.*; noɷz[1] *1 pr.s.*; noɷ[2] *2 pr.pl.*] 3 ɒɪ ˈdoɷ noɷ [noɷz[2] *1 pr.s.*] 4 ɒɪ dɷ ˈnaɷ, ○ˈɒɪ dɷ ˈnoː[1] [naɷ[1] *2 pr.pl.*] 5 ˈɒɪ ˈdɑː ˈnaɷ [naɷz[1] *1 pr.s.*; ×~[1] *3 pr.pl.*; naɷ[1(2x)] *2 pr.pl.*] 6 ɒɪ ˈdoɷ ˈnoɷ [noɷ[1] *inf.*; næuː[2] *2 pr.pl.*] 7 s.w. ɔɪ doɷnt noɷ, ○əɪ dɷ nəɷ[3], ○əɪ də nəɷ[3], ○əɪ dəɷnt nəɷ[4] [×doɷnt (*3 pr.pl.*) noɷ[1]; ~[4] *pr.t.*; noɷ[1] *inf.* VII.5.1; nəɷz[1,2] *1 pr.s.*; ~[4] noɷz[4] *2 pr.pl.*]

17 Wa 1 a dǫɷnt nǫɷ, ○a dɷ no[1] 2 ɔɪ kaːnt tɛl jə, s.w. ɔɪ dəɷnt nəɷ, ○ɔɪ dəɷ nə[1] [nəɷ[1,2,4] *inf.*; ~[1,3,4(4x)] *1 pr.s.*; ~[4] *2 pr.pl.* 3 a dǫɷnt nǫɷ 4 ɔɪ doɷ noɷ 5 ɔɪ doːnʔ nɒɷ [nɒɷ[1] *2 pr.s.*] 6 ɔɪ dǫɷnt nǫɷ 7 ɔɪ doɷnt nǫɷ

23 Mon 1 əɪ ˈdoːɷ noːɷ: [nɒɷ[1] *inf.*] 2 əɪ ˈdoː noː, ○əɪ doː noː[3] [noː[3] *inf.*] 3 əɪ ˈdoː ˈnːoː, ○~[1] [noː[1,2,3], nɒɷ[3] *inf.*] 4 n.a., ○ə̧i dǫːn nǫː[○1] 5 əɪ̧ doun nou 6 əɪ ˈdoː noː, ○əɪ ˈdoː ˈnoː[1] 7 n.a. [noː[1] *inf.*]

24 Gl 1 əɪ ˈdoː næɷ, ○əɪ ˈdoː ˈnæɷ[1] [næɷ[2] *inf.*; ~[1] *1 pr.s.*] 2 ə doːɷnt næɷ [nɒɷz[3(2x)] *1 pr.s.*; næɷ[3] *2 pr.s.* VII.5.1] 3 ə doːɷ noːɷ 4 ə ˈdoː ˈnoːɷ [naɷ[1], nɒɷ[1,3] *inf.*] 5 ə̈ɪ doːnt nɑɷ 6 ʌɪ doːnt nɑɷ 7 ʌɪ kɷdn tɛl ðə [noː[1] *inf.*]

25 O 1 ə̈i‿d nǫɷ [nəɷ[1] *inf.*] 2 dɷənt nəɷ [nəɷ[2] *inf.*; +nəɷz[2] *3 pr.pl.*] 3 §ʌʏ aʳːɳʈ gət mʌʏ wətʃ wɪ mɪ, ʌʏ dǫɷnt nǫɷ, ○ʌʏ dʌ noɷ[2] 4 ɔɪ doːn noː[○], ○əɪ də noː[3(2x),4(3x)] [də nə[3] *2 pr.pl.*; nǫː[1,2], nəː[5] *1 pr.s.*; noːz[1] *2 pr.pl.*] 5 ʌʏ dəːnʔ noː [nəɷz[2] *2 pr.pl.*] 6 ɔɪ dɷ noɷ

VII.5.3 A QUARTER TO‡

Q. □ *What time is this? .... twelve.*

Rr. A QUARTER, (A) QUARTER TO

Note 1—When rec. in the r., TWELVE is reproduced below.

Note 2—The final *-er* of QUARTER has occ. been assimilated to the prep. TO QUARTER TWELVE at 11.8 and 16.6 pres. represents QUARTER TO TWELVE.

Note 3—I.m. exs. of QUARTER are reproduced between square brackets untransliterated.

Note 4—QUARTER TO also occurs at VI.10.5. QUARTER meaning *teat* occurs at III.2.7; ref. moon, at VII.6.5; and ref. direction, at VII.6.26. For exs. of QUART, see VII.8.1. TWELVE occurs at VII.1.10 (and refs.). Comparable exs. of TO occur at VII.5.6.

7 Ch 1 ə kwa:ʔə tʏ: 2 ə kwa:tə tə twɛlv [kwa:təɹ[2] (+ V.) VII.8.2] 3–4 ə kwa:tə tə 5 ə kwa:tə 6 ə kwɔ:tə tə

8 Db 1 ə kwaˡ:tə tə 2 ə kwa:tə tə [kwa:tə tə foə *q. to four*] 3 kwɔ:tə 4–5 ə kwa:tə tə 6 kwɔ:t tə 7 ə kwɔ:tə

11 Sa 1 kwɔ:t tə twɛlv 2 kwɔ:tə tə twɛlv 3 ə kwɔʳʈə tə 4 kwɔ:tə tə twɛlv 5 ə kwɔ:tə tə 6 kwɔʳ:ʈ tə twɛlv 7 kwɔ:tə tə twɛlv 8 ˈkwɔ:tə ˈtwɛlv 9 kwɔʳ:ʈə tə twɛlv 10 kwɔ:ʔ tə twɛlv 11 kwɔ:tə tə twɛlv

12 St 1 kwɔ:tə tə twɛlv 2 kwoɷtə tə twɛlv 3 kwoɷtə tə twɛlv [kwoɷtəɹ[1] (+ V.); kwɔ:təɹ ɩlɛvn[1] *q.* (to) *eleven*] 4 kwɔ:t tə twɛlv 5 ə kwɔ:tə tə twɛlv 6 kwɛɷtə tə twɛlv 7 kwɔ:tə tə twɛlv 8 kwɔ:tə tə twɛlv [kwɔ:tə t‿ɛ̧ɩt[1] *q. to eight*] 9 ə kwɔ:tə tə twɛlv [kwɔ:tə[2] V.6.9] 10 kwɔ:tə tə 11 kwɔ:tə tə twɛlv

15 He 1 kwɔ:tə tə twɛɫv 2 kwɔ:təʳ tə twɛɫv 3 ə kwaʳ:ʈəʳ tə twɛɫv 4 kwaʳ:ʈəʳ tə twɛɫv 5 kwaʳ:ʈə tə twɛɫv 6 kwa:təʳ tə twɛɫv [kwaʳ:ʈəʳ[1]] 7 kwɔ·ɹtəɹ tə twɛ̈lv [kwɔɹtəɹ[4], kwɔ:təɹ[4] (+ V.)]

16 Wo 1 kwa:tə tə 2 ə kwa:təʳ tə 3–4 ə kwaʳ:ʈəʳ tə twɛɫv 5 kwa:təʳ tə twɛlv 6 kwaʳ:ʈəʳ twɛɫv 7 kwaʳʈəʳ tə twəlv [kwɔʳʈəʳ tə wɷn[1] *q. to one*; □kwɔ:təz[3], □kwaʳʈəʳʐ[3]]

17 Wa 1 ə kwɔ:tə tu: 2 kwɔ:tə tə twɛlv [ə kwɔ:t tə fɔɷə[2] *a q. to four*] 3 ə kwɔ:t tə twɛɫv 4 ə kwɔ:tə tə 5 ə kwɔʳ:ʈə tə [kwɔ:təɹ[1] (+ V.)] 6 ə kwɔ:d̥ə tə 7 kwɔ:tə tə

23 Mon 1 kwaʳ:ʈə tə 2 kwa:təʳ tə 3 kwa:tə tə 4 kwɔ:tʰə tʰö̜ 5 kwɔ:tə tö̜ twɛlv 6 kwaʳ:ʈəʳ tə 7 n.a.

24 Gl 1 kwaʳ:ʈəʳ tə twɛɫv 2 ə kwaʳ:ʈə tə twɛɫv 3 ə kwaʳ:ʈəʳ tə twɛɫv 4 kwaʳ:ʈə tə 5 ə kwaʳ:ʈə tə 6 kwɔ:ʔə tə twɛɫv 7 kwɔʳ:ɽə tə twɛɫv

25 O 1 ə kwɔʳ:ʔə tə twæɫv 2 ə kwaʳ:ʈəʳ tə 3 ə kwɔʳ:ʈə tə 4 kwɔ·ɽd̥əɽ tə twɛɫv [kwɔ·ɽʈəɽ[4] VII.8.4] 5 ə kwɔ:ʔəʳ tə [kwɔʳɽʔəʳ[2]] 6 kwɔ:ʔəʳɽ ə twɛɫv

VII.5.4 HALF* PAST SEVEN*

Q. ☐ *And* (what time is) *this?*

Rr. HALF AFTER/PAST SEVEN

Note 1—I.m. exs. of HALF are reproduced below between square brackets untransliterated.

Note 2—The various numerals, included as parts of phrases in square brackets below, also appear in the relevant articles where the numeral is the keyword.

Note 3—For additional exs. of HALF(–), see VII.7.1/6 and IX.8.8. For additional exs. of SEVEN, see VII.1.6 (and refs.).

7 Ch 1 ẹ:f pas sɛvn 2 e:f pas sɛvən [e:f$^{2(4x),3,4}$] 3 e:f past sɛvn [e:f$^{3(3x)}$] 4 i:f pas sɛvn [ẹ:f$^{2(3x)}$] 5 i:f pas sɛvn [i:f^{2}, e:f^{2} VII.6.5] 6 e:f pa:s sɛvn

8 Db 1 e:f pas sɛvn 2 e:f pas sɛvn [e:f$^{3,4(2x)}$] 3 e:f pas sɛvn [e:f^{1}] 4 e:f pas sɛvn 5 e:f pas sɛvn [e:f^{4}] 6 e:ˈf pas sɛvn [e:f^{1}] 7 e·ɪf pas sɛvn [e·ɪf^{1}]

11 Sa 1 e:f pa·st sɛvn 2 e:f past sɛvn [a:f$^{1(2x)}$] 3 a:f pa:st sɛvn 4 a:f pa:s sɛvn 5 ẹ:f past sɛvn 6–7 e:f pa:st sɛvn 8 e:f pa:s sɛvn 9 e:f pæst sɛvn [e:f^{1}] 10 e:f pa:s sɛvn [ᵒɔ:vz^{2}] 11 ɔ:f past sɛvn [ɔ:f$^{2(2x)}$]

12 St 1 ɛɪf pas sɛvən 2 ɛɪ pas sɛvn 3 oɷf past sɛvn [ɔ:f^{1}, ɛɪf$^{1(2x)}$] 4 a:f pas sɛvn [a:f^{2}] 5 a:f past sɛvn, ɛɪf past sɛvn 6 ɛɪf pas sɛvn [ɛɪf$^{1,2(3x)}$] 7 a:f pas sɛvn, ᵒɑ: pas sɛm^{4} [a:f^{1}] 8 ɑ̊:f pas sɛvn 9 ɛɪf pas sɛvn [a:f$^{1(2x)}$] 10 a:f pas sɛvn 11 ɑ̊: past sɛm [ɑ̊:f$^{1,2(2x)}$, ɑ:f^{2}, a:f^{3}]

15 He 1 a: pa:s sɛbm 2 i: pa:st sɛvn [e:f pa:st tɛn^{1} *h. p. ten*; a:f^{3}] 3 a: pa:st sɛbm [a:f^{1}] 4 e:f pa:st sɛbm 5 æ pæs sɛbm 6 æ pæ:s sɛbm 7 a: pa:s sɛvən [eɪ pạ:s nạɪn^{4} *h. p. nine*; a: pas sɪks^{3} *h. p. six*; a: pas θɹi:^{4} *h. p. three*; a: pas twɛlv^{3} *h. p. twelve*; a: pas tu:^{3} *h. p. two*; a:f$^{1,3(2x),4}$, ạ:f^{4}, æ:f$^{3(2x)}$, æ̹:f^{3}]

16 Wo 1 af past sɛbm 2 ɑ:f pɑ:st sɛbm [a:f^{2}] 3 a:f pɑ:s sɛbm [a:f^{1,4}] 4 aʳ:f pæst sɛbm 5 a: pæ:st sɛbm [a:f^{1}] 6 ɑ:f pæ:s sɛvn [ɑ:f^{3}] 7 ɑ: pɑ:s sɛvn [ɑ:f pa:st ɛɪt^{1} *h. p. eight*; a:f$^{1,3(2x),4}$]

17 Wa 1 a:f past sɛbm [a:f^{1}] 2 a·f pa:s sɛvn [a:f$^{1(2x),4(5x)}$, ä:f^{4}, ɔ:f^{1,4}] 3 a: pa:s sɛbm 4 a:f pa:s sɛbm 5 a: pa:s sɛbm [a: pa:s^{1}; a:f^{1}] 6 a: pa:s sɛbm 7 a: pa:s sɛbm [a:f^{2}]

23 Mon 1 a: pæs sɛbm 2 a: pa:s sɛvən [a:f^{1}] 3 a:f pa:st sɛvn 4 a·f pʰastʰ sɛvn [a:f^{1}] 5 a: pa:s sɛvᵊn [a: pa:s θɹi:^{1}; a: pa:s fəiv^{2}; a:f^{2}] 6 a: pa:s sɛbm [a: pa:s^{1}; a:f^{1}] 7 n.a. [ha:f^{1}]

24 Gl 1 æ: pæ:s sɛbm [æ: pæ:s sɪks[1] *h. p. six*; æ:f[1(2x),2]; æ:fmu:ᵊn[1] *h.-moon* VII.6.3] 2 a: pa:st sɛbm [a:f[2], æ:f[3]] 3 æ:f pæ:s sɛvn [æ:f[2]] 4 a: pa:st sɛbm [a:f[3]] 5 a: pa:s sɛbm 6 a: pa:s zɛbm [a:f[2] IX.2.7] 7 a: pa:s sɛbm [a:fpɪtʃɪnpɪk[1] *h.-pitching-pick* I.7.11]

25 O 1 a: pa:s sɛbm 2 a:f aʳ:ʈəʳ sɛbm [a: pa:s tɛn[1] *h. p. ten*; a:f[3]] 3 a: pa:s sɛbm 4 a:f pa:s sɛvn [a:f[1(2x),3,4(2x)]] 5 a:f pa:s sɛbm [a:f[2]] 6 a: pa:s sɛbm

VII.5.5 TWENTY-FIVE‡ TO‡ THREE*

Q. □ *And* (what time is) *this?*

Rr. FIVE AND TWENTY (MINUTES) TO THREE, TWENTY-FIVE (MINUTES) TO THREE

Note 1—The f.w. omitted to rec. THREE at 7.6 and 17.5, and TO THREE at 23.1.

Note 2—For additional exs. of TWENTY(-), see VII.1.12 (and ref.); of FIVE, see VII.5.6 (and refs.); and of THREE, see VII.1.3 (and refs.).

7 Ch 1 twɛntɪfaɪv tə θɹẹ: 2 twɛntɪfaɪv mɪnɪts tə θɹi:, p. faɪv ə twɛntɪ tə θɹɪi· [pref.] 3 twɛntɪfa:v mɪnɪts tə θɹɛɪ 4 faɪv ən twɛntɪ mɪnɪts tə θɹᵊi̞:, faɪv ən twɛntɪ tə θɹᵊi̞: 5 faɪv ən twɛntɪ mɪnɪts tə θɹɛɪ 6 twɛntɪfaɪv mɪnɪts tə

8 Db 1 twɛntɪfaɪv tə θɹi: 2 twɛntɪfaɪv tə θɹi: 3 faɪv ən twɛntɪ mɪnɪts tə θɹɛɪ 4 twɛntɪfaɪv tə θɹɛɪ 5 faɪv ən twɛntɪ tə θɹi: 6 faɪv ən twɛntɪ tə θɹɛɪ 7 fɑ̃·ɪ̃v ən twɛntɪ tə θɹɛɪ

11 Sa 1 faɪv ən twɛntɪ tə θɹi: 2 faɪv n̩ twɛntɪ tə θɹi: 3 twɛntɪfaɪv tə θɹi: 4 faɪv n̩ twɛntɪ tə θɹi: 5 faɪv n̩ twɛntɪ tə θɹˈɪ: 6–7 faɪv n̩ twɛntɪ tə θɹi: 8 fɒɪv n̩ twɛntɪ tə θɹi: 9 twɛntɪfaɪv mɪnɪts tə θɹi: 10–11 faɪv n̩ twɛntɪ tə θɹi:

12 St 1 twɛntɪfɒɪv tə θɹɛɪ 2 fɒɪv ən twɛntɪ tə θɹɛɪ 3 twɛntɪfɒ:ˈv mɪnɪts t‿θɹɛɪ 4–5 fɒɪv ən twɛntɪ mɪnɪts tə θɹi: 6 twɛntɪfɒ:ɪv tə θɹɛɪ 7–8 fɒɪv ən twɛntɪ mɪnɪts tə θɹi: 9 fɒɪv ən twɛntɪ tə θɹɛɪ [twɛntɪfɒɪv[1] *twenty-five*] 10–11 fa:ɪv ən twɛntɪ tə θɹi:

15 He 1–2 fæɪv n̩ twɛntɪ tə θɹi: 3 fəɪv n̩ twɛntɪ tə θɹi: 4 fəɪv n̩ twɛntɪ tə dɹe: 5 twɛntɪfəɪv mɪnɪts tə dɹi: 6 fəɪv n̩ twɛntɪ tə dɹi: 7 faɪv ən twɛntɪ tə θɹi:

16 Wo 1 fɒɪv n̩ twɛnti: tə θɹi: 2 fɒɪv n̩ twɛntɪ tə θɹi: 3 twɛntɪfəi:v tə θɹi: 4 fəɪv n̩ twɛntɪ tə θɹi: 5 twɛntɪfəɪᵊv tə θɹi: 6 fɒɪv n̩ twɛntɪ tə θɹi: 7 twɛntɪfəɪv tə θɹi:

17 Wa 1 twɛntɪfaɪv mɪnɪts tə θɹ^{e}i: 2 twɛntɪfəɪv tə θɹi:, s.w. fəɪv ən twɛntɪ tə θɹi: ["older"] 3 fəɪv ən twɛntɪ tə θɹ^{ə}ɪ 4 twɛntɪfəɪv tə θɹi: 5 fəɪv ən twɛnɪ tə 6–7 fəɪv ən twɛntɪ tə θɹi:

23 Mon 1 fəɪv n̩ twɛntɪ [twɛntɪfɪft^{2} *twenty-fifth*] 2 fəɪv n̩ twɛntɪ tə ðɹi: 3 fəɪv n̩ twɛntɪ tə θɹi: 4 fəiv ən t^{h}wɛnt^{h}i tɷ θɹi: 5 fəɪv ən twɛnti tɷ̜ θɹi: 6 twɛntɪfəɪv tə θɹi: 7 n.a.

24 Gl 1 fəɪv n̩ twɛntɪ tə θɹi: 2 fəɪv n̩ twɛntɪ tə θɹ'i: 3 vəɪv n̩ twɛntɪ tə dɹ'i: 4 vəɪv n̩ twɛntɪ tə dɹ'i: 5 fə̈ɪv ən twɛntɪ tə θɹi: 6 twɛnɪvʌɪv mɪnɪts tə dɹi: 7 vʌɪv ən twɛntɪ tə dɹi:

25 O 1 fə̈ɪv ən twɛntɪ mɪnɪts tə θɹi: 2 fə̈ɪv ən twɛntɪ tə θɹi: 3 twɛntɪfʌʏv mɪnɪts tə θɹi: 4 fəɪv ən twɛntɪ mɪnɪts tə θɹi: 5 fʌʏv ən twɛnʔɪ mɪnɪʔs tə θɹi: 6 twɛnʔɪfə̈ɪv mɪnɪts tə θɹi:

VII.5.6 FIVE* TO‡ EIGHT*

Q. And (what time is) *this?*

Rr. FIVE (MINUTES) TO EIGHT

Note 1—I.m. exs. of FIVE are reproduced below between square brackets untransliterated. The uninflected MINUTE at 25.5 is striking.

Note 2—TO EIGHT was unfortunately omitted at 17.4.

Note 3—For additional exs. of (-)FIVE, see VI.10.10, VII.1.17 and VII.5.5; and of EIGHT(-), see VII.1.7 (and refs.).

7 Ch 1 fɑɪv t‿ɛɪt 2 faɪv mɪnɪts tɷ ɛɪt [faɪv^{1,2}, fɑɪv^{2}] 3 fɑ:v mɪnɪts tə ɛɪt 4–5 fɑɪv mɪnɪts t‿ɛɪt 6 faɪv mɪnɪts t‿ɛɪt

8 Db 1 faɪv t‿ɛɪt 2 fɑɪv tə ɛɪt 3 faɪv mɪnɪts tə ɛɪt 4 fɑɪv mɪnɪts t‿ɛɪt 5 fɑɪv mɪnɪts t‿e:'t 6 fɑɪv mɪnɪts t‿ɛɪt 7 fɑ̃·ɪ̃v mɪnɪts tə ɛɪt

11 Sa 1 faɪv mɪnɪts tə e:t 2 faɪv tɪ ɛɪt 3 faɪv mɪnɪts tə e:t 4 faɪv tə e:t 5 faɪv tə ɛɪt 6–7 faɪv tə e:t 8 faɪv tə e:t [fɒɪv^{1}] 9 faɪv mɪnɪts tə e:t 10 faɪt tə e:t 11 faɪv tə aɪt

12 St 1 fɒɪv t‿ɛɪt 2 fɒɪv t‿ɛɪt [fɒɪv^{5}] 3 fɒ:ɪv mɪnɪts t‿ɛɪt 4 fɒɪv mɪnɪts tü: ɛɪt [f̆aɪv^{1}] 5 fɒɪv mɪnɪts t‿ɛɪt 6 fɒ:ɪv t‿ɛɪt 7 fɒɪv t‿ɛɪt 8 fɒɪv mɪnɪts tü: ɛɪt 9 fɒɪv mɪnɪts t‿ɛɪt [fɒɪv$^{1(2x),2}$; fɒɪvə^{1} *fiver* (i.e. period of five minutes) VII.5.8] 10 faɪv mɪnɪts tü: ɛɪt, fa:ɪv mɪnɪts tü: ɛɪt [prec. by «ɪʔ wɒnts» *it wants*; fa:ɪv$^{2(2x)}$, faɪv^{2}] 11 fa:ɪv mɪnɪts tɷ ɛɪt

15 He 1 fæɪv tə æɪt 2 fæɪv tə æɪt [fəɪv^{3}] 3 fəɪv tə æɪt [nəɪntɪfəɪv^{1} *ninety-five* VII.1.8] 4 fəɪv tə æɪt 5 fəɪv tə æɪt [fəɪ^{ə}v^{4}] 6 vəɪv tə ɒɪt [vəɪv^{1}] 7 faɪv tɷ eɪt, faɪv t^{ə} eɪt [fr. i.'s son; faɪv$^{3(3x)}$, fă̜ɪv^{3,4}]

16 Wo 1 fɒɪv tə ɛɪt [fɒɪv²] 2 fɒɪv tə aɪt [fəɪᵊv²] 3 fəi:v mɪnɪts tə e:ɪt [fəi:v¹, fɒɪᵊv⁵] 4 fəɪv tə aɪt 5 fəɪv mɪnɪts tə aɪt [fəɪᵊv¹] 6 fɒɪv mɪnɪts tə e:ɪt [fɒɪv³] 7 fəɪv mɪnɪts tʊ ɛɪt [fəɪv^3,4(4x)]

17 Wa 1 fɑɪv mɪnɪts t‿ɛɪt 2 fəɪv mɪnɪts tʊ ɛɪt [fəɪv^1(2x),2] 3 fəɪv mɪnɪts t‿ɛɪt [fəɪv²] 4 fəɪv mɪnɪts 5 fəɪv mɪnɪts t‿ɛɪt [fʌɪv¹, fəɪv¹] 6 fəɪv t‿e:ᵊt [fəɪv³; e:ᵊt *eight* ("very old")] 7 fəɪv tə ɛɪtʻ

23 Mon 1 fəɪv tə æɪt [fəɪv¹] 2 fəɪv tə e:t [fəɪv³] 3 fəɪv tə e:t [fəɪv¹] 4 fəiv tʰu· eitʰ 5 fəɪ̞v tu eit [fəiv² VII.5.5] 6 fəɪv tə ɛɪt [fəɪv¹] 7 n.a. [fəɪ̞v¹]

24 Gl 1 fəɪᵊv tə æɪᵊt [fəɪᵊv n̩ twɛntɪ²; vəɪᵊv¹] 2 fəɪv tə æɪt [fəɪᵊv^3(2x)] 3 vəɪv tə æɪt [vəɪᵊv³] 4 vəɪv tə aɪt [vəɪv³, vəɪᵊv³] 5 fə̈ɪv mɪnɪts tə æɪt 6 vʌɪv tə æɪt [fʌɪv¹, vʌɪv²; ə vʌɪv¹ *a f.*] 7 vʌɪv mɪnɪts tə hɛ̞ɪt [vʌɪv; ə vəɪv *a f.*]

25 O 1 fə̈ɪv mɪnɪts t‿æɪt 2 fə̈ɪv t‿ɛɪt 3 fʌʏv mɪnɪts te he:t [vɪftʻi:ᵊn³ *fifteen*] 4 fəɪv mɪnɪts tə e:t [fəɪ̞v¹, fɑɪv^3,4, fəɪv⁴] 5 fʌʏv mɪnɪʔ [*sic*] t‿e:ʔ, °fʌʏv mɪnɪʔs t‿e:ʔ 6 fə̈ɪv mɪnɪts t‿eɪʔ

VII.5.7 HOUR*

Q. Sixty seconds make a minute, sixty minutes make one . . . .

R. HOUR

7 Ch 1 aʊəɹ 2 æʊə, °æʊəɹ³ [+ V.] 3–4 aʊə 5 ɛʊə 6 aʊə

8 Db 1 ɛ̞ʊəɹ 2 aʊə 3 ɛ̈ʊə 4 n.a. 5 aʊə, ɛ̞:ə ["older"] 6–7 ɛʊə

11 Sa 1 aʊə 2 aʊwə 3–4 aʊəʳ 5 ɛʊəʳ 6–11 aʊəʳ

12 St 1–3 aʊə 4 æʊə 5–6 aʊə 7 æʊə 8 aʊə 9 a·ʊə, °aʊə¹ 10 æʊwə 11 æʊəɹ

15 He 1–2 æʊəʳ 3 ɛʊəʳ 4 əʊəʳ 5 ʌʊəʳ 6 əʊəʳ 7 aʊəɹ, °ɑwəɹ¹, °ɑ̆ʊəɹ³

16 Wo 1 aʊə 2 ɛʊəʳ 3 ɛu:əʳ 4–5 əʊ:əʳ 6 ɛu:əʳ 7 æʊəʳ⁽²ˣ⁾, °æʊəɹ¹ [+ V.]

17 Wa 1–2 æʊə 3 ɛʊə 4–7 ɛʊəʳ

23 Mon 1 ʌʊəʳ 2 ʌʊəʳ, °~³ 3 əʊə 4 əu-ə 5 əu-ə, °əu-əɹ¹ [+ V.] 6 əʊəʳ, °~¹ 7 n.a., °əu-ə¹

24 Gl 1–2 əʊ:əʳ 3–4 əʊəʳ 5 ʌʊəʳ 6–7 °u:əʳ

25 O 1 ɛʊəʳ 2 æʊəʳ 3 ɛʊə 4 æ̞ʊəɽ 5 ɛʊəʳ, °□ɛʊəʳʐ² 6 ɛ̈ʊəʳ, °~³

VII.5.8 LET ME HAVE A TURN

Q. What do you say to a workmate when you want him to stop working for a time, while you take his place?

Rr. COME OUT /AND LET ME HAVE A DO/SIRRAH AND I'LL DO THEE A BIT/, GET OUT /AND LET ME COME IN/FOR A BIT/, §HALF A MO A MINUTE, HAVE BLOWINGS, HERE LET ME HAVE A GO, HOLD ON A BIT AND I'LL CARRY ON, I'LL COME AND GIVE THEE A HAND IN HALF A MO, I'LL DO /A BIT WHILE THOU RESTS THEE/THE WORK/, I'LL GIVE /THEE A REST/YOU A SPELL/, I'LL HAVE A GO (NOW), I'LL TAKE /IT ON NOW A BIT/ON NOW/THEE OUT NOW/YOU OFF FOR A BIT/ YOUR PLACE/, KNOCK OFF FOR A BIT, LET I HAVE A GO (AT IT YOU), LET ME /COME (IN)/HAVE A BIT OF A DO AT IT WHILE YOU HAVE A REST/HAVE A DO/HAVE A GO (AT THAT)/ HAVE A GO NOW/SPELL YOU A BIT/TAKE YOU OUT A BIT/, LET'S /HAVE A GO~ON/TAKE IT OUT A BIT/, THEE GET OUT THE ROAD WHILE I HAVE A GO, THEE STAND /BACK AND I'LL DO A BIT/TO ONE SIDE/, THOU HAD BETTER /REST THEE FOR A BIT/STOP OFF A BIT I'M GOING TO DO THY WORK/, WE'D BETTER SWOP JOBS, YOU BETTER HAVE A REST WHILE I DO A BIT, YOU HAVE /A BLOW WHILE I HAS A GO/A REST AND I'LL TAKE ON/, YOU'N BETTER HAVE A FIVER

Note 1—In the list above, the rr. are given, as usual, without punctuation, but the appropriate pauses are self-evident.

Note 2—Although the 1st word of the r. at 12.9 app. represents YOU'N, the syntax is questionable. Similarly, the imp. at 24.7 seems to represent LET'S.

7 Ch 1 lɛt mi: kɷm ɩn 2 ða‿d bɛtə stɔp ɔf ə bɩ̢t ɑɩm gɷɩn‿t du: ðɩ wə:k, ða‿d bɛtə ɹɛst ðɩ fəɹ ə bɩt, al du: ə bɩt wɑɩl ðə rɛsɩs ðɩ 3 al tak ðɩ a:t naɩ 4 al gɩv jə spɛl 5 ðɩ stand bak ən ɑ:l dʏ: ə bɩt 6 lɛt mi: av ə go:

8 Db 1 lɛ mi: av ə dʏ: 2 lɛ mi: av ə go: 3 lɛt mɛɩ av ə dü: 4 n.a. 5 lɛt mi: ɛ ə gɷ 6 kɷm ɛ:t ən lɛt mɛɩ av ə dɛɷ 7 gɛɹ ɛ:t ŋ̩ lɛt mɛɩ kɷm ɩn

11 Sa 1 lɛt‿s av ə go: 2 lɛt mi: av ə go: 3 lɛ mi: av ə go: 4 lɛt mi: av ə du: 5 lɛt‿mɩ av ə go: 6–7 lɛt mi: av ə go: 8 aɩl av ə gu: naɷ 9 lɛt mi: av ə go: 10 lɛt mi: æv ə go: 11 lɛts av ə ɒn

12 St 1 lɛt mɩ tak ðɩ aɷt ə bɩt 2 lɛts tɛk ɩt aɷt ə bɩt 3 kɷm aɩt səɹɩ ən ɒ:ɩl dɛɷ ðɩ ə bɩt 4 lɛt mɩ tɛk jəɹ æɷt ə bɩt 5 nɒk ɒf fəɹ ə bɩt, gɛt aɷt fəɹ ə bɩt, lɛt mɩ kɷm 6 lɛt‿s ɛɩ ə gɷ: 7 lɛt mi: av ə bɩt əv ə dü: at ɩt wɒɩl ju: av ə ɹɛst 8 §ɑ:f ə moɷ ə mɩnɩt [*sic*] 9 ju:n bɛtəɹ av ə fɒɩvə [i.e. five-minute break], ɒɩl tɛk jəɹ ɒf fəɹ ə bɩt 10 aɩl av ə goɷ 11 lɛʔ mi: av ə goɷ əʔ ðat, jə bɛtəɹ av ə ɹɛst wɑ:ɩl aɩ du: ə bɩt

15 He 1–3 lɛt‿s æv ə go: 4 lɛt mi: æv ə gu: 5–6 lɛt‿s æv ə go: 7 ɩəɹ lɛt mi: av ə goɷ, ju: av ə bloɷ waɩl aɩ az ə goɷ

16 Wo 1 lɛt mi: av ə gɒɷ 2 lɛt mi: av ə goɷ 3 lɛt mi: æv ə goɷ nɛu: 4–5 lɛt mi: æv ə go: 6 lɛt mi: æv ə gu:, °æv blæɷɩnz 7 ɔ:l kɷm ən gɩv ðɩ ə and ɩn a:f ə moɷ

17 Wa 1 ɑɩl tɛk ɩt ɒn næɷ ə bɩt 2 wɩ‿d bẹtə swəp dʒəbz, əɩl tẹɩk jə plẹɩs 3 ɒɷld ɑn ə bɩt ən əɩł kaɹɩ ɑn 4 lɛt mi: av ə goɷ 5 lɛt mi: av ə gu: 6 ał tɛk ju·əʳɽ plɛɩs 7 lɛt mi: av ə go: at ɩt

23 Mon 1 lɛt mʲi: æv ə go:ɷ 2 lɛt mi: spɛł ju: ə bɩt 3 lɛt mi: æv ə go: 4 n.a. 5 əɥl tẹ:k ɒ̣·n nəu 6 lɛt mi: æv ə go: 7 n.a.

24 Gl 1 lɛt mi: æv ə go:ɷ 2–3 lɛts æv ə go:ɷ 4 lɛt əɩ av ə go:ɷ 5 ði: gɛɹ ʌɷt ðə ɹo:d wöɩl öɩ av ə go: 6 al gɩ ði: ə ɹɛst, ði: stand tə wən zʌɩd 7 lɛs ʌɩ av ə go: at ɩt ju:

25 O 1 lɛt mi: av ə go: 2 lɛt mi: ɛv ə gəɷ 3 lɛt mi: av ə gu̦: 4 łɛt mi: av ə go: 5 ju: av ə ɽɛst ən al te:k ɒn 6 öɩl du: ðə wəʳ:k

VII.5.9 STOPPING TIME

Q. What do you call the time when you stop work for the day?

Rr. BLOW–UP, CHUCK/PACKING–UP–TIME, FINISH, FINISHING TIME, GIVING–OUT/OVER–TIME, JACKING/KNOCK/ KNOCKING/LEAVE/LEAVING–OFF–TIME, KNOCK–OFF, LOOSE–ALL, LOOSE–IT, ? ir.r. MY TIME, TIME (TO GIVE OUT)

Note 1—For additional exs. of TIME, see VII.3.16 and VII.5.1. Expressions comparable with some of those listed above also occur at VIII.6.2.

7 Ch 1 nɒkɩnɔ:ftɑɩm 2 gɩvɩnoɷətɑʲm, gɩvɩnəɷətɑʲm 3 nɒkɩnɒftɑɩm 4 nɒkɩnɔ:ftɑɩm 5 nɒfɩnɒftɑ:m [*sic*, ? error for «nɒkɩn-», Edd.] 6 le:vɩnɔ:ftɑɩm, °nɒkɩnɔ:ftɑɩm[3]

8 Db 1 fɩnɩʃ 2–3 nɒkɩnɒftɑɩm 4 nɒkɩnɒftɑɩm 5 nɒkɒf 6–7 nɒkɩnɒftɑ̃·ɪ̃m

11 Sa 1 nɒkɪnɒftaɪm 2 nɒkɪnɔ:ftæɪm 3 nɒkɪnɔ:ftaɪm 4 nɒkɪnɔ:ftɛɪm 5 nɒkɒftaɪm 6 nɒkɪnɔ˞:ftaɪm 7 tʃʌkʌptaɪm, nɒkɪnɔ:ftaɪm 8 nɒkɪnɔ:ftaɪm 9 pækɪnʌptaɪm 10 nɒkɪnɔ:ftaɪm 11 nɒkɔ:f

12 St 1 fɪnɪʃɪntɒɪm, nɒkɪnɒftɒɪm 2 lu:sɪt [toʊdz lu:sɪt *towards l.*] 3 nɒkɪnɒftɒ:ɪm 4 nɒkɪnɒftɒɪm 5 nɒkɪnɒftɒ:ɪm 6 bloʊ-ʊp [in a brewery], nɒkɪnɒftɒ:ɪm 7–9 nɒkɪnɒftɒɪm 10 lü:sɔ:l, nɒkɪnɒfta:ɪm, nɒkɒf 11 nɒkɪnɒftɑ̊:ɪm

15 He 1 li:vɪnɔ:ftæɪm 2 nɒkɪnɔ:ftæɪm 3 nɒkɪnɔ:ftəɪm 4 nɒkɪnɑ:ftəɪm 5 nɒkɪnɒftəɪm 6 nɒkɪnɑ:ftəɪm 7 nɒkɪnɒftə̆ɪm

16 Wo 1 nɒkɪnɒftɒɪᵊm 2 nɒkɪnɑ:ftəɪm 3 nɒkɪnɑ:ftəi:m 4 nɒkɪnɑ˞:ftəɪm 5 nɒkɪnɑ:ftəɪm 6 nɒkɪnɑ:ftɒɪm 7 nəkɪnɔ:ftəɪm

17 Wa 1 ? ir.r. mɑɪ tɑɪm 2 nəkɪnɔ:ftəɪm 3 təɪm 4 li:vɪnɔ:ftəɪm 5 təɪm, nɒkɪnɔ:ftəɪm, ○~1 6 nɒkɪnɔ:ftəɪm 7 nɒkɪnɔ:ftəɪm, təɪm tə gɪv ɛʊt

23 Mon 1–3 nɒkɪnɑ:ftəɪm 4 n.a. 5 nɒ̝˂kɪnɔ:ftə̜ɪm 6 nɒkɪnɑ:ftəɪm 7 n.a.

24 Gl 1 nɒkɪnɑ:ftəɪᵊm 2 nɒkɪnɑ:ftəɪm 3 fɪnɪʃɪntəɪm 4 nɒkɪnɑ:ftəɪᵊm 5 fɪnɪfɪntə̈ɪm 6 nɒkɪnɔ:ftʌɪm 7 tʌɪm

25 O 1–2 nɒkɪnɔ:ftə̈ɪm 3 dʒakɪnɔ:ftʌʏm 4 nɒkɪnɒftəɪm, ○~4 5 gɪvɪnɛ̈ʊʔtʌʏm 6 li:vɔ:ftə̈ɪm

VII.5.10 BREAKFAST*

Q. What's your word for the first meal of the day?

R. BREAKFAST

7 Ch 1 bɹɛkfʊst 2 bɹɛkfəst(2x), ○~2 3 n.a. 4 bɹɛkfʊst 5–6 bɹɛkfəst

8 Db 1 bɹɛkfəst 2 n.a. 3 bɹɛkfɛst [*sic*] 4–7 bɹɛkfəst

11 Sa 1–6 bɹɛkfəst 7 bɹɛfəst 8–11 bɹɛkfəst

12 St 1 bɹɛkfəst 2 bɹɛ̜kfəs 3 bɹɛkfəst 4 bɹɛkfʊst 5–7 bɹɛkfəst 8 bɹɛkfʊst 9–11 bɹɛkfəst

15 He 1–2 bɹɛkfəst 3 bɹɛkfʊst 4–5 bɹɛkfəst 6 bɹɛkfʊst 7 bɹɛkfəst

16 Wo 1–4 bɹɛkfʊst 5 bɹɛkfʊst, ○~1 6 bɹɛkfʊst 7 bɹɛkfʊst, ○~4

17 Wa 1–3 bɹɛkfəst 4–5 bɹɛkfʊst 6 bɹɛfəst 7 bɹɛkfʊst

23 Mon 1 bɹɛkfʌst 2–3 bɹɛkfəst 4 bɹɛkfʌ̥̈stʰ 5 bɹɛkfʌ̥̈st 6 bɹɛkfəst 7 n.a.

24 Gl 1 bɹɛkfɷs, °bɹɛkfɷst[1] 2–5 bɹɛkfɷst 6 bɹɛkfəs 7 bɹɛkfəst

25 O 1–2 bɹɛkfəst 3–4 bɽɛkfəst 5–6 bɹɛkfəs

VII.5.11 SNACK

Q. Tell me, do you have anything to eat between meals?

State what and when.

Rr. BAGGING(S), BAIT, BEAVER, BIT OF A SNAP, CLOCKING, DRUM-UP, ELEVENSES, JAWER, (A LITTLE) LUNCH, NUNCHING, SNACK(-BIT), SNAP, TEN-O'CLOCK, TOMMY

Note 1—In the rr. below, an attached superior ◇ indicates that the snack was ascertained to have been taken between breakfast and the mid-day meal. Where the contents of the snack were rec., bread was always the major constituent. In addition, an attached superior × indicates a butter-. B a bacon-, C a cheese-constituent and S an unspecified component.

Note 2—Some of the rr. listed above also occur at VII.5.12. BAIT also occurs at III.5.2/3.

7 Ch 1 bagɩn, °~[4] 2 ◇dɹɷmɷp 3 ◇Cbagɩnz [also taken at 4 p.m.] 4 ◇Slɷnʃ 5 ◇×lɷnʃ, ◇×bagɩn [pref.] 6 Clɷnʃ

8 Db 1 Ssnap‘ 2 ◇Cbagɩn, ◇Csnap 3 lɷntʃ 4 ◇Csnap 5 Bsnap 6 ◇Ssnapɩn [+ pastry] 7 ◇Ctlɒkɩn

11 Sa 1 ◇Clʌnʃ 2 ◇Clɷnʃ 3 ◇Clʌnʃ 4 Clʌnʃ 5 ◇Cbe̹:t 6 ◇Clʌnʃ 7 ◇CBbe:t 8 snakbɩt, snapɩn 9 ◇Cbe:t 10 ◇Clʌnʃ 11 ◇Csnak [or bacon]

12 St 1 Cklɒkɩn, Cbagɩn 2 Cbagɩn 3 ◇Csnak [+ cake] 4 ◇Ctɛnəklɒk 5 ◇lɷnʃ 6 Cbɩt əv ə snap 7 snak 8 ◇Slɷnʃ 9 ◇snak 10 ◇snap [rec. in «snaptə̹ɩm» *snap-time*] 11 ə lɩtl lɷnʃ, snap [usu.], °lɷnʃ[2] [snapɩntɑ:ɩm[2] *snapping-time*]

15 He 1–4 ◇Cbæɩt 5 ◇Cbe:ɩt 6 ◇Cbæɩt 7 ◇Cbeɩt, °~[4], °tɒmɩ, °◇lɛvənzɩz[4] [modern; beɩtɩntaɩm[4] *baiting-time*; tɒmɩbag[4] *tommy-bag*]

16 Wo 1 ◇Cbɛɩt 2 ◇Cbe:ˈt 3 Clɷnʃ 4–5 ◇Cbaɩt 6 ◇Clɷ:nʃ 7 s.w. beɩt, lɷnʃ

17 Wa 1 n.f. 2 ◇Clɷnʃ, p. snak [pref.] 3 ◇Clɷnʃ 4 lɷnʃ [only bread] 5 ◇Clɷntʃ, °◇~[1] 6 Csnak [+ onion], °bɛɩvə [rec. in «bɛɩvətəɩm» *beaver-time* (during hay-making or harvest)] 7 Cnɷnʃɩn

23 Mon 1 ◇Cbæɩt 2 Cbe:t 3 ◇Cbe:t 4 n.a. 5 Ctɒ̹·mɩ [or biscuits], Csnak [or biscuits] 6 ◇Cbe:t 7 n.a.

24 Gl 1 ◇ᶜbæɪᵊt [+ onion] 2 ◇ᶜbæɪt 3 snæp 4 ᶜbɛɪt 5 lɷntʃ, ᶜdʒɑɷəʳ [+ meat; older, pref.] 6 ᶜbæɪt 7 ◇ᶜbɛ̞ɪt

25 O 1–3 lɷntʃ 4 ◇ᶜbi:vəɽ [rec. in «bi:vəɽtəɪm» *beaver-time*], ◇ᶜɫɛvənzɪz ["modern"] 5 lʌnʃ 6 lɷntʃ

VII.5.12 MEAL OUT

Q. What do you call the food you take to work with you as a meal?

Rr. BAGGING, BAIT, BREAKFAST, DINNER, GRUB, LUNCH, MEAT, SNAP, SNAPPING, TOMMY, VICTUAL

The foll. are obviously u.rr.:—BOILED BEEF, BREAD AND CHEESE

Note 1—MEAT at 7.2 pres. means *food.*

Note 2—Some of the rr. listed above also occur at VII.5.11. BAIT also occurs at III.5.2/3.

7 Ch 1 dɪnəɹ 2 bɹɛkfəst, dɪnə, me:t 3 snapɪn 4 dɪnə 5 snapɪn 6 dɪ̞nə

8 Db 1 tɒmɪ 2–4 dɪnə 5 snap 6 gɹɷb 7 dɪnə

11 Sa 1 snapɪn 2 bagɪn 3 dɪnəʳ 4 be:t 5 lɷnʃ 6 be:t 7 lʌnʃ 8 be:t 9 lʌnʃ 10–11 be:t

12 St 1–3 snapɪn 4 bɪˈgan [*sic*; ? error for «bagɪn» *bagging*, H.O.] 5 bagɪn ["usu."], snapɪn 6 snap 7 snapɪn(2x), tɒmɪ 8 snap 9 snap 10 snap 11 gɹɷb, snap

15 He 1 tɒmɪ [tɒmɪbag *t.-bag*] 2 tɒmɪ 3 tɒmɪ(2x) 4 tɒmɪ 5 lɷnʃ 6 tɒmɪ 7 dɪnəɹ

16 Wo 1 gɹɷb 2 fɪtɫ, ○~² 3–6 dɪnəʳ 7 §bɹɛd ən tʃi:z [rare]

17 Wa 1 lɷnʃ 2 §bɹɛd ən tʃi:z, §bəɪld bi:f 3 dɪnə 4–5 dɪnəʳ 6 dɪnəʳ, tɒmɪ 7 dɪnəʳ

23 Mon 1 lʌnʃ 2–3 tɒmɪ 4 n.a. 5 tɒ̣·mi, bẹ:t 6 tɒmɪ 7 n.a.

24 Gl 1 tæmɪ 2–4 tɒmɪ 5 dɪnəʳ 6 gɹəb, dɪnəʳ 7 dɪnəʳ

25 O 1–3 dɪnəʳ 4 dɪnəɽ 5–6 dɪnəʳ

VII.6.1 SKY*

Q. What can you see up there?

Ascertain the existence of *lift*.

R. SKY

7 Ch 1 skɑɩ 2 skaɩ 3–5 skɑɩ 6 skaɩ

8 Db 1 skaɩ 2 skɑɩ 3 skaɩ 4 skɑɩ 5 skɑ·ɩ 6–7 skɑ̃·ɩ̃

11 Sa 1–4 skaɩ 5 skɒɩ 6–11 skaɩ

12 St 1–2 skɒɩ 3 skɒ:ɩ 4 skɒɩ 5 skɒ:ɩ 6 skɒ:ɩ, skɛɩ 7–8 skɒɩ 9 skɒ·ɩ 10 ska:ɩ 11 skɒ·ɩ

15 He 1–2 skæɩ 3–6 skəɩ 7 skaɩ

16 Wo 1–2 skɒɩ 3 skəi: 4–5 skəɩ 6 skəi: 7 skəɩ

17 Wa 1 skɒɩ 2–7 skəɩ

23 Mon 1–3 skəɩ 4 skəi 5 skəɩ̹ 6 skəɩ 7 n.a.

24 Gl 1 skəɩ 2 skɒɩ 3 skəɩ 4 skɒɩ 5 skə̈ɩ 6–7 skʌɩ

25 O 1 skə̈ɩ 2 skəɩ 3 skʌʏ 4 skəɩ 5 skʌʏ 6 skə̈ɩ, ○~[3]

VII.6.2 CLOUDS*†

Q. When you can't see the blue sky, then it must be covered with . . . .

Rr. CLOUD(S)

Note—I.m. exs. of CLOUDY *adj.* are reproduced below between square brackets untransliterated.

7 Ch 1 klaɩdz 2 klæɷdz 3 tlaɩdz 4 tlaɷdz 5 tlɛɷdz 6 tlœɷdz

8 Db 1 tlɛ̧ɷdz 2 kla:dz 3 tlɛ̈ɷdz 4 klɛ:dz 5 tlɛ̧:ᵊdz 6 klɛ:dz 7 tlɛ:dz

11 Sa 1 klɷu:dz 2 klæɷdz 3 klaɷdz 4 klɛudz 5 klɛɷdz 6 tlaɷdz 7–10 klaɷdz 11 kləɷdz

12 St 1 klæɷdz 2–3 klaɷdz 4 klæɷdz 5 klạɷdz 6 kla:dz 7 klæɷdz 8 klaɷdz 9–11 klæɷdz

15 He 1–2 klæɷdz 3–4 kləɷdz 5 klʌɷdz 6 kləɷdz 7 klə̆ɷdz [gɹʌbɩ[4] *grubby* (=*cloudy*) *adj.*]

16 Wo 1 klaɷdz 2 klɛɷdz 3 klɛu:dz [klɛu:di:[5]] 4–5 kləɷ:dz 6 klɛu:z [*sic*] 7 △klæɷd, ○klæɷdz[1] [klæɷdɩ]

17 Wa 1 klæɷdz 2 klæɷdz, ○~ [ɹɛɩnklæɷd *rain-c.*] 3 klɛɷdz 4 tlɛɷdz [dɷstlɛɷdz[3] *dust-cs.*] 5 klɛɷdz 6 klɛɷd 7 klɛ̈ɷdz

23 Mon 1–2 klʌɷdz 3 kləɷdz 4–5 kləud 6 kləɷdz 7 n.a.

24 Gl 1 kləɷᵊdz 2 kləɷ:dz 3 kləɷdz 4 kɫəɷdz 5 klʌɷdz 6 klᵒu:dz 7 klᵒu:dz [klᵒu:dɩ]

25 O 1 klɛ̈ɷdz 2 klɛ̨ɷd 3 klɛɷdz 4 kɫæɷdz [kɫæɷdɩ[4]] 5–6 klɛ̈ɷdz

VII.6.3 STARS*, MOON*

Q. What can you see in the sky on a clear night?

Ascertain the existence of *stern.*

Rr. STARN, STARS

MOON

Note 1—The rr. to the two parts of the q. are separated below by a full stop.

Note 2—MOON occurs at VII.6.5.

7 Ch 1 sta:z. mʏ:n, ○~[4] 2 sta:z. mü:n, 3 sta:z. mʏ:n, ○~[1] 4 sta:z. mu:n 5 sta:z. mᶦʏ:n 6 sta:z. mʉ̨:n

8 Db 1 sta:ˡ:z. mʏ:n 2 sta:z. mᵒu:n, mɷɩn [old; mu:npɛnɩ[3] *m.-penny* (ref. a sort of daisy)] 3 sta:z. mü:n 4 sta:z. mɛɷn 5 sta:z. mᶦu:n 6–7 sta:z. mɛɷn

11 Sa 1 staʳ:z̨. mu:n 2 sta:z. mᶦu:n 3–4 staʳ:z̨. mu:n 5 staʳ:z̨. mɩu:m [*sic*] 6–8 staʳ:z̨. mu:n 9 staʳ:z̨. mᵒu:n 10–11 staʳ:z̨. mu:n

12 St 1 sta·z. mu:n, ○maɷn[4] 2–3 sta:z. mɛɷn 4 sta:z. mü:n 5 sta:z. mü:n, ○~[2] 6 sta:z. mɛɷn, ○~[1] 7 sta:z. mu:n, ○~[1] 8 stɑ:z. mu:n, ○~[6] 9 sta:z. mü:n 10 sta:z. mu:n 11 stɑ̇:z. mʉ̨:n

15 He 1 sta:z. mu:n 2–6 staʳ:z̨. mu:n 7 stäɹz. mu:n

16 Wo 1 stɑ:z. mᵒu:n 2–5 staʳ:z̨. mʉ:n 6 stəʳ:z̨. mu:n 7 stɑʳz̨. mu:n

17 Wa 1 sta:z. mu:n 2 stɑ̈:z. mu:n, ○~[1] 3 stą:z. mᵊü:n 4 sta:z, ○~[3]. mü:n, ○~[1] 5–6 sta:z. mu:n 7 staʳ:z̨. mü:n

23 Mon 1 staʵ:ʐ. mᵚu:n 2–4 sta:z. mu:n 5 sta:-a:z [*sic*]. mu:n 6 staʵ:ʐ. mu:n 7 n.a.

24 Gl 1 staʵ:ʐ. mu:ᵊn 2 staʵ:ʐ. mu:n 3–4 staʵ:ʐ. mᵚu:n 5 stəʵ:ʐ. mu:n 6 staʵ:ʐ. mu:n 7 staʵ:ʐ. mᵚu:n

25 O 1 stəʵ:ʐ. mɷn 2 staʵ:ɳ [old]. mɷn 3 staʵ:ʐ. mu:n 4 stɑ·ɽʐ. mu:n, ○~4(2x) 5 stæʵ:ʐ. mü:n 6 staʵ:ʐ. mu:n

VII.6.4 HALO

Q. What can you sometimes see round the moon?

Rr. CIRCLE, HALO, MIST, RING, WEATHER

Note—For additional exs. of RING, see I.3.5.

7 Ch 1 ɹɪŋ 2 wɛðə [rec. in «wɛðə ɹæɷnd‿t mu:n» *weather round the moon*] 3 ɹɛŋ, wɛðə [pref.], ○~ [rec. in «ð‿wɛðə ɹaɪnd‿ð mʏ:n» *the weather round the moon*] 4 sə:kl, ɹɪŋg ["older"] 5 sə:kl 6 səɹ̵:kl

8 Db 1 ɹɪŋg, səɹ̵tl 2 a:lo, sə:kl 3 ɹɪŋg 4 ɹɪŋg, sə:kl 5 ɹɪŋ 6 ɹɪŋg 7 sə:kl

11 Sa 1 ɹɪŋ 2 sə:kl 3–4 səʵ:kl 5 ɹɪŋg 6 səʵ:kl 7 e:lo: 8–11 səʵ:kl

12 St 1–3 sə:kl 4 ɹɪŋg 5 sə:kl 6 ɹɪŋg 7–8 ɹɪŋg 9 sə:kl 10 ɛɪloɷ 11 sə:ɹkl

15 He 1 səʵ:kɫ 2 səʵkɫ 3 ɹɪŋ 4 æɫo 5 səʵkɫ 6 səʵ·kɫ 7 ɹɪŋ

16 Wo 1 səʵ:kl 2–4 səʵ:kɫ 5 səʵ:kɷɫ 6 səʵ:kɫ 7 sə:kɫ, ○~1

17 Wa 1 p. sə:kl 2 sə:kl 3 sə:kɫ 4 səʵ:kɫ 5 ɹɪŋ 6–7 səʵ:kɫ

23 Mon 1 səʵ:kɫ 2 səʵ:kəɫ 3 sœ:kəɫ 4 n.a. 5 ɹɪŋ 6 səʵ:kɫ 7 n.a.

24 Gl 1 səʵ:kɷɫ 2 ɹɪŋ 3 mɪst [i.e. "a halo or circle"] 4 sœ:kɫ 5 səʵ:kɫ 6 səʵ:kl 7 ɹẹŋ

25 O 1–3 səʵ:kɫ 4 e:ɫɔ:, s.w. ɽɪŋ 5–6 səʵ:kɫ

VII.6.5 To WAX. To WANE

Q. The moon is always changing its size. How do you speak of that?

Rr. Wax:—COME (UP {TO THE FULL}), FULL, GET /BIGGER/FOR FULL/UP/, GO /FOR THE FULL/UP/, GROW, RISE, WAX

The following rr. contain a 3 pr.s.:—COMES AFRESH, GETS BIGGER, HE'S /MAKING HIMSELF/FULLING/ON THE GROW/, IT'S GETTING TO THE FULL

Wane:—BE ON THE WANE, DIE (DOWN), FADE, FALL, GET SMALLER, GO AWAY/BACK/DOWN/LESS, LOSE (SIZE), PASS (AWAY), SET, SINK, WANE/WASTE (AWAY), WEAR

The following contain or presuppose a 3 pr.s.:—DIES AWAY, FADES, IT'S /ON THE WANE/PAST ITS FULL/, HE /BEGINS TO WANE/ WASTES AWAY/, HE'S WANING AWAY, ON THE WANE/WEAR

Note 1—The rr. to the two parts of the q. are separated below by a full stop.

Note 2—Often the f.w. rec. an expression ref. a state of the moon. These and comparable expressions have been included below between square brackets following the r. to the second part of the q.

7 Ch 1 ɹɑɪzɪn. fɔːɪn 2 ɪts gɛtɪn tə‿t fɷl, kɷmz əfɹɛʃ. diːz əweᵊ, feːdz [t‿müːnz ət fɷl *the moon's at full*; kwaːt ə‿t müːn *quarter of the moon*] 3 n.k.. güːɪn bak 4 gɛtɪn bɪgə. gɷɪn lɛs [fɒst kwaːtə *first quarter*] 5 n.k.. gɷɪn bak [eːf mʸʏːn *half moon*] 6 n.k. gɷ bak

8 Db 1 n.k. gʏː bak 2 n.k. weːn 3 n.k. gɷ bak' 4 n.k. gᴼuː bak 5 gɛt bɪgə. gɷ bak 6 güːɪn fə‿θ fɷl. güːɪn bak 7 gɹo·ɷ. fɔːl

11 Sa 1 n.k. 2 kɷm ɷp. goː dæɷn 3 kʌm ʌp. goː daɷn 4 gɛt ʌp. goː dɛun 5 kɷm ɷp. goː dɛɷn 6 n.k. weːn 7 kʌm ʌp. goː daɷn [wɛn ɪts kʌmɪn fɹɒm ə babɪ tuː a fɷl muːn *when it's coming from a baby to a full moon*] 8 kɷm ɷp. guː əweː 9 gɹoː. sɪŋk 10 kʌm ʌp. goː daɷn 11 kʌm ʌp. biː ɒn ðə weːn

12 St 1 n.r. [tʃɛɪndʒ ə‿t maɷn *change of the moon*] 2–3 n.k. 4 gɹoɷɪn. wɛɪnɪn 5 n.r., °weːnɪn² [ðə tʃɛɪndʒ ə ðə müːn *the change of the moon*; ɪnkɹiːs ə ðə müːn *increase of the m.*] 6 n.r. [fəst kwoɷtə *first quarter*; ɛɪf ə mɛɷn *half a moon*] 7 n.r. [ðə tʃɛɪndʒɪn əv ðə muːn *the changing of the moon*] 8 waks. wɛɪn [fəːst kwǫːtə *first quarter*] 9 n.r. [fəst kwɔːtə *first quarter*; fɷl mɪɷn *full moon*] 10 waks. wɛɪn 11 n.r. [ðə tʃɛɪndʒ ə ðə muːn *the change of the moon*]

15 He 1 gɛtɪn ʌp. gwɛɪn dæɷn 2 gɹɒɷɪn. goːɪn dæɷn 3 kɷmɪn ɷp tə ðə fɷɫ. ɒn ðə weːɪn 4 gɹæɷ. ɪts paːst ɪts fɷɫ 5 gɹoː, °ɪz ɒn ðə gɹoː. wɛəʳ 6 ɹəɪzɪn. go·ɪn dəɷn 7 n.k. [ðə muːn ɪz nɪəɹ ðə fɷl *the moon is near the full*]. ɪts ɒn ðə weɪn, weɪnɪn

16 Wo 1 kɷm ɷp . gɒɷ bak 2 kɷm ɷp . goɷ dɛɷn 3 əkɷmɪn ɷp . əgoɷɪn dɛu:n 4 əɹəɪzɪn . əsɛtɪn 5 əɹəɪzɪn . əlu:zɪn səɪz 6 i:z əme:ɪkɪn ɪmsɛɫf . i: we:ɪsɪz əwe:ɪ 7 s.w. waksɪn . i: bɪgɪnz tə wein, i:z weɪ·nɪn əweɪ, ən ðə weɪn

17 Wa 1 n.k. 2 p. gɹəɪ-ɪn . wɛɪnɪn [fə:st kwɔ:tə *first quarter*] 3 n.k. wɛ̜ɪnɪn 4 n.k. wɛ̜ən 5 n.k. fɛɪd 6 gɷ ɷp . wɛɪn 7 n.k. wɛɪn

23 Mon 1 gɹo:ɷ . we:ɪst 2 gɹo: . ɒn ðə wɛəʳ 3 kʌm ʌp . go: dəɷn 4 n.a. 5 dəɪ̞-ɪn 6 gɹo:ɪn . go:ɪn əwe: 7 n.a.

24 Gl 1 gɛt bɪgəʳ . we:s əwæɪ, °ɪ we:sɪz əwæɪ [æ:f mu:ᵊn[1] *half moon*] 2 fɷɫ, °ɪz fɷɫɪn . we:ˈst 3 gɹæɷ . we:ˈst [vɷɫ m°u:n *full moon*] 4 ɹəɪz . gɛt smɑ:ɫəʳ 5 gɹo:ɪn . we:st 6 p. gɹɑɷ . we:st 7 gɹo: . we:n əwæ̣ɪ

25 O 1 kʌmɪn . pas əwæɪ 2 ɹɔ̈ɪzɪn . dɔ̈ɪ dæɷn 3 gɛts bɪgəɽ . we:nz 4 n.k. we:nɪn 5 gɛʔɪn fəʳ fɷɫ . we:nɪn 6 ɹɔ̈ɪz . lu:z

VII.6.6 HOAR-FROST

Q. When in spring or autumn it has been cold at night, what may you see on the ground next morning?

Rr. (/HOAR{Y}/RIMY/WHITE{-HOAR}/-)FROST, HIME, (WHITE-)RIME

7 Ch 1 fɹɒst 2 wɑɪtfɹəst 3 wɛɪtfɹɒst 4 wɑɪtfɹɒst, ja:ɹɪfɹɒst ["older"] 5 wɑɪtfɹɒst, wɛɪtfɹɒst [pref.; fɹɒst[2] *f.*] 6 wɛ̜ɪtfɹə:st

8 Db 1 fɹə:st 2 o·əfɹɒst, aɪm ["older"] 3 fɹɒst, °~ 4 ɹɑɪmɪfɹast 5 o·əfɹɒst 6 wɑ̃ĩtfɹɒst 7 ɹɑ̃·ĩm

11 Sa 1–3 fɹɒst 4 fɹə:st 5 fɹɒst 6–7 fɹə:st 8 fɹə:st, ɹɒɪm ["older"] 9–11 fɹə:st

12 St 1–3 fɹɒst 4 wɒɪtfɹɒst [fɹɒstbɒɪt[2] *frost-bite* VI.10.6] 5 fɹɒst, °ɹɒ:ɪm, °□ɹɒ:ɪmɪfɹɒsɪz 6–7 fɹɒst 8 ɹɒɪm 9 fɹɒst 10 fɹɒst [fɹɒstɪ[6] *frosty*] 11 fɹɒst

15 He 1 fɹə:st 2–3 fɹɒst 4–6 fɹɑ:st 7 ɹạɪm, °ɹaɪmɪfɹɒst

16 Wo 1 fɹɒst 2 ɹɒɪmɪfɹɑ:st 3 fɹɒ:st [fɹa:st[1] *f.*] 4 fɹɑʳ:ʂɽ 5 fɹɑ:st [fɹɑʳ:ʂɽɪ[1] *frosty adj.*] 6 fɹɑ:st [fɹɑ:st[1] *f.*] 7 fɹə:st[(2x)], p. ɹəɪmɪfɹə:st, s.w. ɹəɪm [fɹəst[3] *f.*]

17 Wa 1 ɹaɪmɪfɹɒst 2 wɔɪtfɹɔ:st, ɹɔɪm [pref.], ɹɔɪmɪfɹɔ:st [blɑ·kfɹɔ:st *black-f.*] 3 fɹɔ:st 4 wɔɪtfɹɔ:s [blakfɹɔ:st *black-f.*] 5 wʌɪtfɹɔ:st [fɹɔ:st[1] *f.*] 6 wɔɪtəʳ:fɹɔ:st 7 ɔʳ:fɹɔ:st'

23 Mon 1–2 fɹɑ:st 3 fɹɒst 4 n.a. 5 fɹɒ̞·st [fɹɒ̞·sbɪt∘n[2] *frost-bitten adj.*] 6 fɹɑ:st 7 n.a.

24 Gl 1 fɹɑ:s [fɹɑ:sɪz[1] *fs.*] 2 fɹɑ:st 3 vɹɑ:st 4 fɹɑ:st, vɹɑ:st 5 wɔ̈ɪtfɹɔ:st 6–7 wʌɪtvɹɔ:st

25 O 1 ɹɔ̈ɪmɪfɹɔ:st 2 wɔ̈ɪtfɹɔ:st 3 ɹʌʏmɪfɹɔ:st 4 fɽɒst 5 wʌʏtfɹɔ:st, wɔɪtɹʌʏm 6 wɔ̈ɪʔfɹɔ:st

VII.6.7 DEW*

Q. On other days, especially in late summer, the grass in the early morning is very wet. What has there been during the night?

Rr. DEW, FLOP

7 Ch 1 djʏ: 2 djü: 3 dʒʏ: 4 dju: 5 dʒʏ:(2x) 6 dʒṳ̈:

8 Db 1 dʒʏ: 2 dɪu: 3 dɪü: 4 d°u: 5 dˡu: 6 dü: 7 dˡu:

11 Sa 1 dʒɪu: 2–4 dʒu: 5 dju: 6 dɪu: 7 dʒu: 8 dʒ°u: 9 dɪu: 10 dʒu: 11 dɪu, dʒu: [older]

12 St 1 dɪü: 2 djɛɷ 3–4 dju: 5 djü: 6 dɛɷ 7–8 dju: 9 dɛɷ, °~ 10 djü: 11 dju:

15 He 1 dʒˡu: 2–3 dʒu: 4 dju: 5 djʌɷ 6 dʒu: 7 dju:

16 Wo 1 dɪu: 2 dʒu:, °~[2] 3 dʒˡu: 4 dʒu: 5 dju: 6 dʒu: 7 dju: [dʒu:bɛɹɪ[4] *d.-berry* IV.11.3]

17 Wa 1 dɛ̈u: 2 dju: [dju·ɪ *dewy adj.*] 3–4 dˡü: 5 dʒu: 6 dju:, p. du: [dju:pɒnd[3] *d.-pond* IV.1.5] 7 dʒu:, flɒp [usu.], °flɒp

23 Mon 1 dj°u: 2 du: 3–4 dju: 5 djˡu 6 dju: 7 n.a.

24 Gl 1 dʒu: 2 dʒæɷ [dʒæɷbɛɹɪz[3] *d.-berries* IV.11.3] 3–4 dʒ°u: 5 dʒu:, °dʒɒɷ[2] 6 dʒu: 7 dju: [fɒgdju:[1] *fog-d.* VII.6.9]

25 O 1 dʒu: 2 flɒp ["older"], dɪu 3 dju: 4 dju: [dju·ɪ[4] *dewy*] 5 du: 6 dü:

VII.6.8 MIST

Q. In patches of low-lying ground near rivers, what do you sometimes see, especially in the early morning or the evening?

Rr. FOG, HAZE, MISK~MIST, STEAM

Note—For additional exs. of FOG, see VII.6.9.

7 Ch 1 mɪst [ẹ:zɪ² *hazy*] 2 mɪ̣st [ɹaɪmɪ *rimy* (=*misty*)] 3 e:z 4 mɪ̣st 5–6 mɪst

8 Db 1–7 mɪst

11 Sa 1–11 mɪst

12 St 1–2 mɪst 3 fɒg, mɪst 4–5 fɒg 6 mɪst, fɒg ["pref."] 7–8 mɪst 9 fɒg, mɪst 10–11 mɪst

15 He 1–6 mɪst 7 mɪst, ○~⁴

16 Wo 1–3 mɪst 4 mɪ·st, stɛm ["usu."] 5–7 mɪst

17 Wa 1 mɪst [ɛ̣ɪzɪ¹ *hazy*] 2 mɪst, ○~¹ 3 fɒg, ○□mɪsts 4–7 mɪst

23 Mon 1–3 mɪst 4 n.a. 5–6 mɪst 7 n.a.

24 Gl 1–2 mɪst 3 mɪst, ○~³ VII.6.4 4–7 mɪst

25 O 1 mɪsk 2–6 mɪst

VII.6.9 FOG

Q. When it is really thick outside, especially in November, you call it . . . .

R. FOG

Note 1—I.m. exs. of FOGGY *adj.* are reproduced below between square brackets untransliterated.

Note 2—FOG meaning *mist* occurs at VII.6.8.

7 Ch 1 fɒg 2 fɔg [fɔgɪ] 3–6 fɒg

8 Db 1 fɒgᵊ 2 fɒg 3 fɒgᵊ 4–7 fɒg

11 Sa 1–7 fɒg 8 fɔ:g 9 fɒg 10–11 fɔ:g

12 St 1–11 fɒg

15 He 1 fɔ:g 2–7 fɒg

16 Wo 1 fɑ·g 2–6 fɑ:g 7 fɔg

17 Wa 1 fɒg 2 fɔg [fɔgɩ; blak fɔg *black f.* (near industrial sites)] 3 fɒg, ○~ [fɒgɩ²] 4–7 fɒg

23 Mon 1–2 fɑ:g 3 fɒg 4 n.a. 5 fɒ̣·g 6 fɑ:g 7 n.a.

24 Gl 1–2 fɑ:g 3 vɑ:g 4 fɑ:g 5–6 fɒg 7 vɒg [fɒgdju¹ *f.-dew* (i.e. mist) VII.6.7]

25 O 1 fɒg 2 fɑg 3 fɒg 4 fɒg [fɒgɩ⁴] 5–6 fɒg

VII.6.10 DULL

Q. When it is dark and gloomy, what sort of day do you say it is?

Rr. DARK, DIRTY, DULL, GLOOMY, HEAVY, MUCKY, MUGGY, OVERCAST

Note—The following, all emotive terms, are u.rr.:—DISMAL, DREARY, MISERABLE.

7 Ch 1 dɷl⁽²ˣ⁾ 2 §mɩ̣zəɹəbl 3 mɷgɩ 4 dɷɫ 5–6 dɷl

8 Db 1 §mɩzɹəbl, s.w. dɷl 2–5 dɷl 6 §mɩzɹəbl, s.w. dɷl 7 §dɹɩəɹɩ

11 Sa 1 dʌl 2 dɷl 3–4 dʌl 5 dɷl 6 n.r., ○dʌl [rec. in «ɒməst mɔ:əʳ ðn̩ dʌl» *almost more than dull*; ɩts ə nəvɛmbəʳ· de: *it's a November day*] 7 dʌl 8 dɷl 9 dʌl, ɛvɩ 10–11 dʌl

12 St 1 §mɩsɹəbl 2–3 dɷl 4 dɔ:tɩ 5 mɷkɩ 6 dɷl 7 §dɹi:əɹɩ 8 dɷl, ○~ 9 dɷl 10–11 §dɹɩəɹɩ

15 He 1–2 dʌɫ 3 dɷɫ, ○~ 4 dʌɫ 5 dɷɫ 6 dɷɫ, ○~ 7 dʌl, §dɹɩəɹɩ, ○dʌl

16 Wo 1 dɷ̣l 2 dɷl 3–6 dɷɫ 7 dɷl, §dɹɩəɹɩ

17 Wa 1 dɷl 2 ɔɷvəkɑ:st, dɷl, ○~ 3 dɒl 4 n.a. 5 dəʳ:ʈɩ, ○~ 6 dɷɫ 7 dɷɫ, ○~

23 Mon 1 dʌɫ, ○~⁴ 2 dɷɫ 3 dʌɫ̣ 4 n.a. 5 dʌ̣̈l 6 dʌɫ 7 n.a.

24 Gl 1 dɷɫ 2 dɷɫ, ○~ 3 dʌɫ 4 dɷɫ 5 dʌɫ 6 dəɫ, §dɩzməɫ 7 məgɩ, ○dəl, ○ɛvɩ

25 O 1 dʌl, dəʳ:k 2 §dɹɩəɹɩ 3 §dɹɩəɽɩ 4 dɷɫ 5 glu:mɩ, dʌɫ 6 dʌɫ, ○~³

VII.6.11 ICICLES

Q. In winter when water freezes, what can you sometimes see hanging down from the spouts?

Rr. DAGGERS, ICICLES, ICKLES

Note—For ICE, see VII.6.12.

7 Ch 1 ɑɪsɪklz 2 aɪsɪ̦klz 3 ɑ:sɪtlz 4–5 ɑɪsɪklz 6 aɪzɪlkz

8 Db 1 aɪsɪtlz 2 ɪklz 3 aɪsɪtlz 4 ɑɪsɪklz 5 ᐞɑɪsɪkl 6–7 ɑ̃·ɪ̃sɪklz

11 Sa 1–7 aɪsɪklz 8 ɒɪsɪklz 9–11 aɪsɪklz

12 St 1–2 ɒɪsɪklz 3 ɒ:ɪsɪklz 4 aɪsɪklz 5–6 ɒ:ɪsɪklz 7 ɒɪsɪklz, ○~ 8–9 ɒɪsɪklz 10 a:ɪsɪklz 11 a̱:ɪsɪklz

15 He 1 æɪsɪkłz 2 ᐞæɪsɪkł 3–6 əɪsɪkłz 7 aɪsɪkəlz

16 Wo 1 ɒɪsɪkłz 2 əɪsɪkłz 3 əi:sɪkłz 4 əɪsɪkłz 5 əɪsɪkɷłz 6 dægəʳz̦, ɒɪsɪkłz 7 əɪsɪkłz

17 Wa 1 ɑɪsɪklz 2 əɪsɪkəlz 3 əɪsɪ̄kłz 4 əɪsəkłz 5–7 əɪsɪklz

23 Mon 1–3 əɪsɪkəłz 4 n.a. 5 əɪ̦sɪkłz 6 əɪsɪkłz 7 n.a.

24 Gl 1–3 əɪsɪkɷłz 4 ɒɪsɪkłz 5 ə̈ɪsɪkłz 6 ʌɪsɪklz 7 ʌɪsɪkłz

25 O 1–2 ə̈ɪsɪklz 3 ʌʏsɪkłz 4 əɪsəkəłz 5 ʌʏssaklz 6 ə̈ɪsakłz

VII.6.12 ICE*

Q. When water freezes, it turns into . . . .

R. ICE

Note—For ICICLES, see VII.6.11.

7 Ch 1 aɪs 2 aɪst 3–4 ɑɪs 5 ɑɪst 6 aɪs

8 Db 1–3 aɪs 4–5 ɑɪs 6 ɑ·ɪs 7 ɑ̃·ɪ̃s

11 Sa 1–7 aɪs 8 ɒɪs 9 haɪs 10–11 aɪs

12 St 1–2 ɒɪs 3 ɒ:ɪs 4 ɒɪs 5 ɒ:ɪs 6 ɛɪs 7 ɒɪs, ○~[1] 8 ɒɪs 9 ɒis 10 aɪs 11 ɑ̊:ɪs

15 He 1–2 æɪs 3–5 əɪs 6 əɪs [əɪsɪ[1] *icy*] 7 aɪs

16 Wo 1 ɒɪs 2 əɪs 3 ɒɪs 4–5 əɪs 6 ɒɪs 7 əɪs, ○~[1]

17 Wa 1 ɑɩs 2 ɔɩs 3 ɔɩs, °~³ 4–7 ɔɩs

23 Mon 1–2 əɩs 3 æɩs 4 əi§ 5 əɩ̨s 6 əɩs 7 n.a.

24 Gl 1–3 əɩs 4 ɒɩs, °~¹ 5 ɔ̈ɩs 6–7 ʌɩs

25 O 1–2 ɔ̈ɩs 3 ʌʏs 4 ɔɩs 5 ʌʏs 6 ɔ̈ɩs

VII.6.13 SNOW*

Q. In winter the ground is often all white and covered with ....

R. SNOW

7 Ch 1 snọ: 2 snọ: 3 snü: 4 snọ: 5 snų: 6 snọ:

8 Db 1–2 sno: 3–4 sno:° 5 sno: 6 sno:° 7 sno·ɷ

11 Sa 1–5 sno: 6 sno:, °~⁴⁽²ˣ⁾ VI.1.3 7 snaɷ 8 snɒɷ 9–11 sno:

12 St 1–2 snoɷ 3 snɷ: 4 snɔɷ 5 snoɷ [¶snɷ:ɩn² *snowing*] 6 snɛɷ, °snoɷ¹
7–8 snoɷ 9 snɷ:, °~² 10 snɛɷ 11 snȍɷ

15 He 1–4 snæɷ 5 sno: 6 snæɷ 7 snoɷ, s.f. snä:⁽²ˣ⁾, °snoɷ¹

16 Wo 1 snɒɷ 2 snoɷ, snaɷ ["older"] 3 snaɷ 4 snaɷ, °~¹ 5 snaɷ
6 snæɷ 7 snɔɷ, °snoɷ¹

17 Wa 1 snọɷ 2 snɔɷ 3 snɒ̈ɷ 4 snọɷ 5–6 snɒɷ 7 snọɷ

23 Mon 1 snæɷ, °~² 2–3 sno: 4 n.a. 5 snou 6 sno: 7 n.a.

24 Gl 1 snæɷ, °snæɷ:¹ 2–3 snæɷ 4 snɒɷ, °snaɷ¹ 5–6 snɑɷ 7 snɒɷ

25 O 1–3 snɔɷ 4 sno:, °~⁴ 5 snọ̈ɷ 6 snoɷ

VII.6.14 SLIPPERY

Q. When the ground is frozen, you must take care, because the roads are very ....

Rr. GREASY, ROUND, SLAKE, SLAPE, SLICK~SLIKE, SLIPLY, SLIPPERY, SLIPPY, TRICKY

7 Ch 1 slɩpɩ̨ 2–3 slɩpɩ 4 slɩ̨pɩ 5 slɩpɩ 6 slɩplɩ

8 Db 1 slɩppɩ 2 sle:p, slɩpɩ 3 slɩppɩ 4–7 slɩpɩ

11 Sa 1 slɩpɩ 2 slɩpɹɩ 3–5 slɩpɩ 6 slɩpəɹɩ 7 slɩpəɹɩ, °ɹaɷnd [rec. in « ðə ˈɹoːd‿z tuː ˈɹaɷnd» *the road's too round* (i.e. slippery)] 8 slɩpɹɩ 9–10 slɩpɩ 11 slɩpɹɩ, °tɹɩkɩ

12 St 1 slɩpɹɩ 2 sl̹ɩpɩ 3 sl̹ɩpɩ, gɹɛɩsɩ 4–5 slɩpɩ 6 gɹiːsɩ, slɩpɩ, °~ 7–8 slɩpɩ 9 slɩpɹɩ, slɩpɩ, °slɩpɹɩ 10 slɩpɩ 11 slɩpəɹɩ

15 He 1 slɩpɩ 2 slɩpəɹɩ, slæɩk ["older"] 3 slɩk, °~ 4 slɩk 5 sləɩk 6 slɩk 7 slaɩk, °~

16 Wo 1 slɩpɩ̹ 2 slɩpɩ 3 slɩpəɹiː 4 slɩpɩ, sleːɩk 5 sleːk 6–7 slɩpɩ

17 Wa 1 slɩpɩ 2 slɩpəɹɩ, s.f. slɩpɩ ["pref."] 3 slɩ̆pɩ 4 slɩpɩ, slɩpəɹɩ 5 slɩpəɹɩ 6 slɩpɩ 7 slɩpəɹɩ

23 Mon 1 slɩk 2 slɩpɹɩ 3 slɩpəɹɩ 4 n.a. 5 slɩpəɹi 6 slɩpɹɩ 7 n.a.

24 Gl 1 slɩpɹɩ 2 slɩpɩ 3 słɩk 4 slɩk 5–6 slɩpɹɩ 7 slɩkʻ

25 O 1 slɩpɩ 2 slɩpəɹɩ 3 slɩpəɽɩ 4 słɩpɩ, °~ 5 slɩpɩ 6 slɩpɹɩ

VII.6.15 THAWING*

Q. When it begins to get warm again and the snow begins to melt, what do you say it is doing?

Rr. GIVING (WAY), THAWING (OUT)

7 Ch 1 θɔ̆ːɩn 2 θɷuɩn 3 θọː-ɩn 4 θɔːɩn, θɔː ["said by old people"] 5 θɔːɩn 6 θɔː-ɩn

8 Db 1 θoːwɩn 2 θɔː 3 θoːᵂwɩn 4–5 θɔːɩn 6 θɒɷɩn 7 θɔːɩn

11 Sa 1 θɔːɩn 2 θɑːɩn 3–10 θɔːɩn 11 θɔːɩn, °gɩvɩn weː

12 St 1–3 θoɷɩn 4 θɔːɩŋg 5 θɔː-ɩn 6 θɛɷɩn, giːɩn wiː 7 θɔː-ɩn 8 θɔːɹɩn 9–10 θɔːwɩn 11 θɔ̣ːɩn

15 He 1–2 θɔːɩn 3 θɑːɩn [θɑː[3] *thaw n.*] 4–6 θɑːɩn 7 θɔ·ɩn, gɩvɩn [pref.], °~[4]

16 Wo 1–3 θɑːɩn 4 fɑːɩn 5–6 θɑːɩn 7 θɔːɩn

17 Wa 1 θɔːɹɩn 2 θɔ·ɩn 3 θɔːɹɩn 4 θɔːɩn 5 əθɔːɩn 6–7 θɔːɹɩn

23 Mon 1 θɑːɩn 2 θɑːɹɩn 3 θɑːɩn 4–5 θɔːɹɩn 6 θɑːɩn [əθɑːd[1] *a-thawed p.p.*] 7 n.a.

24 Gl 1–2 θɑ:ɪn 3 ðɑ:ɪn 4 ðɑ:ɪ̥n əɷt 5 θɔ:ɪn 6–7 ðɔ:ɪn

25 O 1 θɔ:ɪn 2 θa:-ɪn 3 θɔ: 4 θɔ̜ɪn 5–6 θɔ:ɪn

VII.6.16 SLUSH

Q. When the frost breaks and the snow becomes very wet, what might you have to walk through?

Rr. SLOSH, SLOUGH, SLUDGE~SLUTCH, SLURRY, SLUSH, SNOW-BROTH

Note—Some of the above terms also occur at VII.6.17 meaning *mud.*

7 Ch 1 slɷʃ 2 slɷtʃ [slɔpɪ *sloppy* (=*slushy*)] 3 slɷtʃ 4 slɒʃ 5 slɷtʃ 6 slɷʃ

8 Db 1 slɷʃ 2–3 sno:bɹɒθ 4 slɒʃ 5 sno:bɹɒθ 6–7 slɷʃ

11 Sa 1 slʌdʒ 2 slɔ̜dʒ 3 slɷʃ 4 slʌʃ 5 slɷdʒ 6 slʌʃ 7 slʌdʒ, slʌɹɪ 8 slɷdʒ 9 slɒʃ 10 slʌʃ 11 slɒʃ

12 St 1–6 slɷʃ 7 slɒʃ 8 slɷʃ 9 slaɷ 10 slɷʃ 11 slɷʃ ["old"], slɒʃ

15 He 1 slɒʃ 2 slʌʃ 3–4 slɷʃ 5 slɷdʒ 6 sləɷ 7 slʌʃ

16 Wo 1 slɷʃ 2 slɷdʒ, slɷʃ 3 slɷɹi: 4–7 slɷʃ

17 Wa 1–7 slɷʃ

23 Mon 1 slʌʃ 2 slɷʃ 3 slʌʃ 4 n.a. 5 slʌ̤̈ʃ 6 słʌɹɪ 7 n.a.

24 Gl 1 slɷʃ 2 slɷdʒ 3 slɷʃ 4 słɷʃ 5 slɔ̜ʃ 6–7 sləʃ

25 O 1 slʌʃ 2 ʃlʌʃ 3 slɷʃ 4 słɷʃ, ○~[4] 5–6 slʌʃ

VII.6.17 MUD

Q. When you walk along a country road after a heavy rain, your boots may get covered with . . . .

Rr. MUCK, MUD, SLOUGH, SLUDGE~SLUTCH, SLURRY

Note—Some of the above terms also occur at VII.6.16 meaning *slush.*

7 Ch 1 slɷtʃ, ○~[4] 2 mɷd 3 slɷdʒ 4 slɷtʃ 5 mɷd 6 slɷdʒ, ○slɷɹɪ[2]

8 Db 1 slɷtʃ 2–3 slɷdʒ 4–6 mɷd 7 slɷdʒ

11 Sa 1 mʌd 2 mọd 3 mɷd 4 mʌd 5 mɷd 6–7 mʌd 8 mɷd 9 mʌd [mʌd aɷt¹⁽²ˣ⁾ *mud out* IV.2.11] 10 mʌd 11 mɷd

12 St 1–3 slɷdʒ 4 mɷd, slɷdʒ 5 slɷdʒ, mɷd 6 mɷk, slɷdʒ, °~² 7 mɷd 8 mɷd, °slɷdʒ¹ 9–10 mɷd 11 mọd

15 He 1–2 mʌd 3–4 mɷd 5 məd 6 mɷd 7 mʌd, slʌɹɩ

16 Wo 1–3 mɷd 4 mɷ:d 5 mɷd 6 mɷ:d 7 mɷd

17 Wa 1–2 mɷd 3 slɷdʒ 4–5 mɷd 6 mɷd, °~³ 7 mɷd

23 Mon 1 mʌd 2 mɷd 3 mʌd 4 n.a. 5 mʌ̽d 6 mʌd 7 n.a.

24 Gl 1 mɷ:d 2 mɷd 3 sləɷ, °~ 4 mɷd 5 mọd 6 mək 7 mək ["older"], məd

25 O 1–3 mʌd 4 mɷd 5 mʌd 6 mọd

VII.6.18 DUST*

Q. In summer when there has been no rain for a long time, the country roads are covered with . . . .

R. DUST

Note—See also SAW–DUST at I.7.17.

7 Ch 1 dɷst 2 dɷst⁽²ˣ⁾ 3 dɷs 4–6 dɷst

8 Db 1–3 dɷst 4 dɷst [dɷstbɒnɩt³ *d.-bonnet* VI.14.1] 5–7 dɷst

11 Sa 1 dʌst 2 dọst 3–4 dʌst 5 dɷst 6–7 dʌst 8 dɷst 9–11 dʌst

12 St 1–3 dɷst 4 dɷst [dɷstɩ¹ *dusty*] 5–7 dɷst 8 dɷst, °~⁵ 9–11 dɷst

15 He 1 dʌst, °~¹ 2 dʌst 3 dɷst, °~³ [ref. money] 4 dʌst 5 dəst 6 dɷst 7 dʌst

16 Wo 1–5 dɷst 6 dɷ:st 7 dɷst

17 Wa 1 dɷst 2 dɷst, °~ 3 dÿst, dəst 4 dɷst [dɷstlɛɷdz³ *d.-clouds* VII.6.2] 5–7 dɷst

23 Mon 1 dʌst 2 dɷst 3 dʌst, °~² 4 dʌ̽stʰ 5 dʌ̽st 6 dʌst, °~² 7 n.a.

24 Gl 1 dɷ:st 2 n.r. 3 dʌst 4 dɷst 5 dọst 6 dəs 7 dəst

25 O 1–2 dʌst 3 dɷst, °dʌst² 4 dɷst, °~¹ [nɒkəɫdɷstəɽz³ *knuckle-dusters*] 5 dʌst 6 dọst

VII.6.19 DRY

Q. Some years the summer months have almost no rain. So the summer has been very ....

Rr. (A-)DRY, HASK, HASKY

Note—For additional exs. of DRY, see III.1.9, VI.13.10 and VII.6.20.

7 Ch 1 dɹɑɩ, °dɹaɩ[4] 2 dɹaɩ, °~[2] 3 dɹɛɩ 4–5 dɹɑɩ 6 dɹaɩ

8 Db 1 dɹɛɩ 2–3 dɹaɩ 4 dɹɑɩ 5 dɹɑ·ɩ 6–7 dɹɑ̃·ɩ̃

11 Sa 1–7 dɹaɩ 8 dɹɒɩ 9–11 dɹaɩ

12 St 1 dɹɒɩ, ask 2 dɹɒɩ, °~[2] 3 dɹɒ:ɩ, askɩ 4 dɹɒɩ 5 dɹɒ:ɩ, askɩ 6 dɹɛɩ 7 dɹɒɩ 8 dɹɒɩ [askɩ wɩnd *hasky* (=*dry*) *wind*] 9 dɹɒɩ 10 dɹaɩ 11 dɹɑ̈:ɩ

15 He 1–2 dɹæɩ 3–6 dɹəɩ 7 dɹæɩ

16 Wo 1 dɹɒɩ̜ 2 dɹəɩ 3 dɹəi: 4 dɹəɩ, °~[1] 5 dɹəɩ, °~[1], °ədɹəɩ[1] 6 dɹɒɩ 7 dɹɔɩ, °~[4]

17 Wa 1 dɹɑɩ 2 dɹɔ·ɩ, °dɹɔɩ[2] 3–7 dɹɔɩ

23 Mon 1 dɹəɩ, °~[4] 2–3 dɹəɩ 4 n.a. 5 dɹəɩ̜, °~[1,2] 6 dɹəɩ 7 n.a.

24 Gl 1 dɹəɩ 2 dɹəɩ, °dɹɒɩ[1] 3 dɹəɩ 4 dɹɒɩ, °dɹəɩ[3] 5 dɹɔ̈ɩ 6–7 dɹʌɩ

25 O 1 dɹɔ̈ɩ 2 dɹɔ̈ɩ [dɹɔ̈ɩ[1] *dry v.*, dɹɔ̈ɩz[2] *dries 3 pr.pl.* VIII.5.1] 3 dɹʌʏ, °dɹʌɩ[1] 4 dɽəɩ̜, °~[4] 5 dɹʌʏ 6 dɹɔ̈ɩ

VII.6.20 DROUGHT*

Q. And (when the summer has been very dry) *you say there has been a long and serious ....*

Rr. DROUGHT, DRY SPELL/TIME

Note—For exs. of DRY, see VII.6.19 (and refs.).

7 Ch 1 dɹɑɩt 2 dɹɔɷt, dɹaɩ taɩm [usu.] 3 dɹɛɩ spɛl, p. dɹaɷt [rare] 4 dɹɔ:t 5 p. dɹɛɷt [but not used] 6 dɹa̟ɷt

8 Db 1 dɹɛ̝ɷt‘ 2 dɹɔ:t 3 dɹaɩ taɩm, pp. dɹɛ̈ɷt 4 dɹɔ:t‘ 5 dɹɔ:t 6–7 dɹɛ:t

11 Sa 1–2 dɹɔ:t 3 dɹaɷt 4 dɹɛu:t 5 dɹɔ:t 6 dɹaɷt 7 dɹəu:t 8 dɹɛɷt, dɹɔ:t ["older"] 9 dɹɔ:t 10 dɹaɷt 11 dɹau:t

12 St 1 dɹɔ:t 2 dɹaft [*sic*] 3 dɹoɷt 4 dɹæɷt 5 dɹa̜ɷt 6 dɹɛ̜ɷt 7 dɹɔ:t 8 dɹæɷt 9–11 dɹɔ:t

15 He 1 dɹæɷt 2 dɹɔ:t 3–4 dɹəɷt 5 dɹɑ:t 6 dɹəɷθ 7 dɹă̜ɷt [ə vɛɹɩ dɹæ̜̆ɩ ta̜ɩm *a very dry time* (i.e. a long drought)]

16 Wo 1 dɹɑ:t 2 dɹɛɷθ 3 dɹɑ:t 4–5 dɹəɷθ 6 dɹɛu:θ 7 dɹæɷθ

17 Wa 1 dɹæ̜ɷt 2 dɹəɩ spɛl, dɹæɷt 3 dɹəɩ spɛɫ, dɹɛ̜̈ɷt 4–5 dɹɛɷθ 6 dɹɛɷt‘ 7 dɹɛ̈ɷt

23 Mon 1 dɹʌɷt 2 dɹəɩθ 3 dɹɑ:t 4 dɹəut^{h} 5 dɹəut 6 dɹɑ:t 7 n.a.

24 Gl 1 dɹəɷ:θ 2 dɹəɷt 3 dɹɑ:t 4 dɹəɷt 5 dɹʌɷt 6 dɹ^{ɷ}u:t 7 dɹ^{ɷ}u:t‘

25 O 1 dɹɛ̈ɷt 2 dɹæɷt 3 dɹɛɷt 4 dɽəɩ spɛɷ [pref.], s.w. dɽaɷt 5 dɹɛ̈ɷʔ 6 dɹɔ:ʔ

VII.6.21 THUNDER*

Q. What do you call that loud rumbling noise we often hear on very hot summer days?

R. THUNDER

7 Ch 1 θɷndə, θɷnə [but not used loc.] 2 θɷnə 3–4 θɷndə 5 θɷndə. fɷndə 6 θɷndə

8 Db 1 θɷndə$^{ɹ̠}$ 2–3 θɷndə 4 θɷnə 5–7 θɷndə

11 Sa 1 θʌndə^{ɽ} 2 θɷndə 3–4 θʌndə^{ɽ} 5 θɷndə^{ɽ} 6 θʌndə^{ɽ}· 7 θʌndə^{ɽ} [θʌndə^{ɽ}stɔ:m *t.-storm*] 8 θɷnə^{ɽ} 9–11 θʌndə^{ɽ}

12 St 1 θɷndə 2 θɷndə [¶θɷndɹɩn *thundering*] 3–10 θɷndə 11 θɷndə^{ɽ}

15 He 1–2 θʌndə^{ɽ} 3–6 θɷndə^{ɽ} 7 θʌndəɹ

16 Wo 1–6 θɷndə^{ɽ} 7 θɷndə^{ɽ}, °θɷndə^{ɹ}

17 Wa 1 θɷndə 2 θɷndə, θɷnə 3 θʌndə 4 θɷnə^{ɽ}· 5–7 θɷndə^{ɽ}

23 Mon 1–2 θʌndə^{ɽ} 3 θʌndə 4 θʌ̜̆ndʌ̜̆ 5 θʌ̜̆ndə 6 θʌndə^{ɽ} 7 n.a.

24 Gl 1–2 θɷndə^{ɽ} 3 ðʌndə^{ɽ} 4 ðɷndə^{ɽ} 5 θʌndə^{ɽ} 6 θəndə^{ɽ}, s.f. ðəndə^{ɽ} 7 ðəndə^{ɽ}

25 O 1 θʌndə^{ɽ} 2 θʌndə$^{ɹ̠}$ 3 θʌndɽ 4 θɷndəɽ 5 θʌndə^{ɽ} 6 θɷndɽ

VII.6.22 LIGHTNING*

Q. Before we hear the thunder, we see . . . .

R. LIGHTNING

7 Ch 1 lɛɩtnɩn 2–3 li:tnɩn 4 lᵊi̯:tnɩn 5 lɛɩtnɩn 6 lɛ̜ɩtnɩn

8 Db 1–2 li:tnɩn 3–4 lɛɩtnɩn 5 lɑɩtnɩn 6 lɑɩtnɩn, lɛɩtnɩn ["older"] 7 lɑ̃·ĩtnɩn, lɛɩtnɩn ["older"]

11 Sa 1–7 laɩtnɩn 8 lɒɩtnɩn 9–11 laɩtnɩn

12 St 1 lɒɩtnɩn 2 lɒɩtnɩn, lɛɩtnɩn 3 lɛɩtnɩn 4 la̜ɩtnɩŋg 5 lɒ:ɩtnɩn 6 lɛɩtnɩn 7 lɒɩtnɩn 8 lɒɩtnɩŋg 9 lɒɩtnɩn 10 la:ɩtnɩn 11 lɑ̊:ɩtnɩŋg

15 He 1–2 læɩtnɩn 3–6 ləɩtnɩn 7 lǣɩtnɩn

16 Wo 1 lɒɩtnɩn 2 ləɩtnɩn 3 ləi:tnɩn 4–5 ləɩtnɩn 6 ləi:tnɩn 7 ləɩtnɩn

17 Wa 1 lɒɩtnɩn 2–7 ləɩtnɩn

23 Mon 1–3 ləɩtnɩn 4 ləitnɩn 5 ləɩ̜tnɩn 6 ləɩtnɩn 7 n.a.

24 Gl 1–4 ləɩtnɩn 5–7 lʌɩtnɩn

25 O 1–2 lə̈ɩtnɩn 3 lʌʏtnɩn 4 ɫəɩtnɩn 5 lʌʏtnən 6 lə̈ɩtnɩn

VII.6.23 BEGAN† TO RAIN

Q. It was quite fine when we left, but then dark clouds gathered and soon it . . . . to rain.

—August 1953, *to rain* made key-words.

If necessary, suggest *begin* to get *began*.

Rr. BEGAN (/FOR TO RAIN/RAINING/), BEGAN TO /§POUR DOWN/RAIN/, CAME ON TO (RAIN), STARTED /RAINING/TO RAIN/

Note 1—In the above list of rr., BEGAN subsumes BEGIN and BEGUN; and CAME subsumes COME.

Note 2—I.m. exs. of RAIN *v.* and *n.* are reproduced below between square brackets untransliterated. An attached superior ◇ indicates an infin., and superior + a n.

Note 3—For exs. of BEGIN and START, see VIII.6.2.

7 Ch 1 bɩgɷn, bɩgɷn ɹe̜:nɩn 2 bɩgɷn tə ɹe:n, p. bɩgɷn ɹe:n [pref.] 3 bɩgɷn 4 bɩgɷn tə ɹe:ᵊn 5 bɩgɷn tə ɹi:n 6 bɩgɷn tə ɹe:ᵊn

8 Db 1 bɪgɒn fə‿ˀ ɹe:n 2 bɪgɒn tə ɹe:n 3 bɪgɛn‿ˀ ɹe:n 4 bɪgɒn tə ɹi:n 5 bɪgɒn 6 bɪgɒn‿ʔ ɹi:n 7 bɪgɒn tə ɹi:n

11 Sa 1 bɪgʌn tə ɹe:n 2 bɪgɒn tə ɹe̜:n 3–4 bɪgʌn tə ɹe:n 5 bɪgɒn 6–7 bɪgʌn tə ɹe:n 8 bɪgɒn tə ɹe:n 9 bɪgʌn tə ɹe:n 10 bɪgʌn tə ɹe:n [+ɹe:n³] 11 bɪgɒn tə ɹe:n

12 St 1 bɪgan 2 sta:tɪd ɹi:nɪn, bɪgan [¶ɹi:nɪn¹, ɹi:nd² *3 p.t.s.*; +ɹi:n²] 3 bɪgɒn‿t ɹi:n [¶ɹi:nɪn¹, ɹi:nz² *3 pr.s.*] 4 bɪgan 5 bɪgɒn tə ɹe:n [◇ɹi:n²; +ɹe:n²] 6 bɪgan tə ɹi:n [ɹi:nd *p.t.*] 7 bɪgan tə ɹɛɪn [+ɹi:n ("old")] 8 bɪgan, ○kɛɪm ɒn tə ɹɛɪn 9 bɪgan tə ɹi:n 10 bɪgan [pɔ:əd ə ɹɛɪn *poured of* (i.e. with) *rain*] 11 bɪgan, ○stɑ·tɪd tə ɹɛɪn [pɒəɹ (*inf.*) ə ɹɛɪn² *pour of* (i.e. with) *r.*; pɔ̜:d ɒv ɹɛɪn *poured of* (i.e. with) *r.*]

15 He 1 bɪgʌn tə ɹe:ɪn 2 bɪgæn tə ɹæɪn [◇ɹæɪn³⁽²ˣ⁾] 3 bɪgɒn tə ɹæɪn [+ɹæɪn¹; ∼¹ (n.d.g.)] 4 bɪgɒn tə ɹæɪn 5 bɪgɒn tə ɹe:ɪn 6 bɪgɪn tə ɹɒɪn [◇ɹɛn¹] 7 bɪgan tə §pɔ̜əɹ daɒn

16 Wo 1 bɪgɒn tə ɹɛɪn 2 bɪgɒn tə ɹe:ᵊn 3 bɪgæn tə ɹe:ɪᵊn 4–5 bɪgɒn tə ɹaɪn 6 bɪgɒn tə ɹe:ɪn [pæɒəʳɖ ə ɹe:ɪn *poured of* (i.e. with) *rain*] 7 bɪgan tə ɹe̜ɪn [+ɹẽ̜ĩn¹]

17 Wa 1 bɪgɒn tə ɹe̜ɪn 2 sta:tɪd ɹæɪnɪn [pref.], bɪgɒn tə ɹæɪn, pp. bɪgan [+ɹe̜ɪn⁴; ɹɛɪnklæɒd¹ *r.-cloud*] 3 bĭgan tə ɹe̜ɪn 4 bɪgɒn tə ɹe̜·ən 5–6 bɪgɒn 7 bɪgɒn tə ɹe̜ɪn

23 Mon 1 bɪgʌn tə ɹæɪn 2 bɪgɒn tə ɹe:n 3 bɪgʌn tə ɹe:n, ○sta:tɪd ɹe:nɪn 4 kʌ̆m ɒ̥n tʰə, bigan ["rare"] 5 bigʌ̥n 6 bɪgæn tə ɹe:n 7 n.a.

24 Gl 1 bɪgɒn tə ɹæɪᵊn [◇ɹæɪᵊn] 2–3 bɪgɒn tə ɹæɪn 4 bɪgɒn tə ɹaɪn 5 bɪgɒ̜n 6 bɪgɒn 7 bɪgɒn tə ɹe̜ɪn [+ɹæɪn¹]

25 O 1 bɪgʌn 2–3 bɪgɒn 4 bɪgan tə ɽe:n [◇ɽe:n¹; +ɽeɪn¹] 5 bɪgan [ɹe:nz² *3 pr.s.*] 6 bɪgɒn

VII.6.24 WET*

Q. And if something is left out in the rain, it's bound to get . . . .

Rr. (SOPPING) WET

Note—WET *v.* meaning *brew* (ref. tea) occurs at V.8.9.

7 Ch 1–2 wɛt 3 wɛt, wi:t ["older"] 4 wɛt 5 wɛt, wat ["older"], ○∼² 6 wɛt

8 Db 1 wi:t‘, °sɒppɩn wi:t‘, °wi:t[3] 2 wi:t 3–7 wɛt

11 Sa 1 wɛ·t 2–11 wɛt

12 St 1–10 wɛt 11 wɛ̜t

15 He 1–6 wɛt 7 wɛt, °~[1,3,4(2x)] [soɷkt[4] *soaked* (i.e. *very wet*)]

16 Wo 1–2 wɛt 3 wɛt‘ 4–5 wɛt 6 wɛ:t 7 wɛt, °~[1]

17 Wa 1 wɛt 2 wɛt [wɛt[3] *w. 3 p.t.s.*] 3–7 wɛt

23 Mon 1–6 wɛt 7 n.a.

24 Gl 1–7 wɛt

25 O 1–2 wɛt 3 wɛt, °~[1] 4 wɛt 5 wɛʔ 6 wɛʔ, °wɛt[1]

VII.6.25 NORTH*, SOUTH*, EAST*, WEST*

Q. What are the four points of the compass?

Rr. NORTH. SOUTH. EAST. WEST

Note—The rr. to the four parts of the q. are separated below by full stops.

7 Ch 1 nɔ:θ. saɷθ. e̜:st. wɛst 2 nɔ:θ. sæɷθ. i:st[(2x)]. wɛ̜st, °wɛst 3 nɔ:θ. saɩθ. ɛɩst. wɛst 4 nɔ:θ. saɷθ. i:st. wɛst 5 nɔ:θ. sɛɷθ. ɛɩst. wɛst 6 nɔ:θ. sɛ̜ɷθ. i:st. wɛst

8 Db 1 nɔ˞:θ. sɛ̜ɷθ. i:st. wɛst 2 nɔ:θ. sa:θ. i:st, p. ɩəst. wɛst 3 nɔ:θ. sɛɷθ. i:st. wɛst 4 nɔ:θ. sɛ:θ. i:st. wɛst 5 nɔ:θ. sɛ̜:θ. i:st. wɛst 6–7 nɔ:θ. sɛ:θ. i:st. wɛst

11 Sa 1 nɔ:θ. saɷθ. i:st. wɛst 2 nɔ:θ. sæɷθ. ˈi:st. wɛst 3 nɔ˞:θ. saɷθ. i:st. wɛst 4 nɔ˞:θ. sɛu:θ. i:st. wɛst 5 nɔ˞:θ. sɛɷθ. ˈi:st. wɛst 6 nɔ˞:θ. saɷθ. i:st. wɛst 7 nɔ˞:θ. saɷθ. i:st. wɛst 8 nɔ:θ. sɛɷθ. i:st. wɛst 9 nɔ˞:θ. saɷθ. i:st. wɛst 10 nɔ:θ. saɷθ. i:st. wɛst 11 nɔ˞:θ. saɷθ. i:st. wɛst

12 St 1 nɔ:θ. sæɷθ. i:st. wɛst 2 nɔ:θ. saɷθ. i:st. wɛst 3 nɔ:θ. saɷθ. saɩθ. ɛɩst [ask wɩnd[2(2x)] *hask wind* (ref. east wind)]. wɛst 4 nɔ:θ. sæɷθ. i:st. wɛst 5 nɔ:θ. saɷθ. i:st. wɛst 6 noɷθ. sæɷθ. ɛist. wɛst 7 nɔ:θ. sa:θ, °~[4]. i:st. wɛst 8 nɔ:θ. sæɷθ. i:st. wɛst 9–10 nɔ:θ. sa:θ. i:st. wɛst 11 nɔ:θ. sæɷθ. i:st. wɛst

15 He 1–2 nɔ:θ . sæɷθ . i:st . wɛst 3–4 nɑʳ:θ . səɷθ . i:st . wɛst 5 nɑ:θ . səɷθ . i:st . wɛst 6 nɑʳ:θ . səɷθ . i:st . wɛst 7 nɔɹθ, ○~[3] . səʉθ . i:st . wɛst

16 Wo 1 nɑ:θ . saɷθ . i:st . wɛst 2–3 nɑ:θ . sɛɷθ . i:st . wɛst 4 nɑʳ:θ . səɷ:θ . i:st . wɛ:st 5 naʳ:θ . səɷ:θ . i:st . wɛst 6 nɑ:θ . sɛu:θ . i:st . wɛ:st 7 nɔʳθ, ○nɑʳθ[1] . sæɷθ, ○~[3] . i:st, ○~[3] . wɛst

17 Wa 1 nɔ:θ . sæɷθ . ei:st . wɛst 2 nɔ:θ . sæɷθ [sæɷθwɛst[1] *s.-west*] . i:st, s.f. ɛɪst ["older"], ○~ . wɛst 3 nɔ:ᵊθ . sɛ̈ɷθ . i:st . wɛst 4 nɔ:θ . sɛɷθ . i:st . wɛst 5 nɔʳ:θ . sɛɷθ . i:st . wɛst 6 nɔ:θ . sɛɷθ . i:st . wɛst 7 nɔ:θ . sɛ̈ɷθ . i:st . wɛst

23 Mon 1 nɑʳ:θ . sʌɷθ . ˈi:st . wɛst 2 nɑ:θ . sʌɷθ . i:st . wɛst 3 nɑ:θ . səɷθ . i:st . wɛst 4 nɔ:θ . səuθ . i:st . wɛst 5 nɔ:θ . səuθ . ɨ:st . wɛst 6 nɑ:θ . səɷθ . i:st . wɛst 7 n.a.

24 Gl 1 naʳ:θ [naʳ:ðəʳɳ[3] *northern*] . səɷ:ᵊθ . i:s . wɛs 2 nɑʳ:θ . səɷθ . ɩi:st . wɛst 3 nɑʳ:θ . səɷθ . ˈi:st . wɛst 4 naʳ:θ . səɷθ . ˈi:st . wɛst 5 nəʳ:θ . sʌɷθ . e:st, jɷst . wɛst 6 nəʳ:θ . sᵚu:θ . ɛɩs . wɛst 7 nɔʳ:θ . sᵚu:θ . i:st . wɛ·st

25 O 1 nɔʳ:θ, nəʳ:θ ["older"] . sɛ̈ɷθ . i:st . wɛst 2 nɔ˞:θ . sæɷθ . eˈst . wɛst 3 nɔʳ:θ . sɛɷθ . e:st . wɛst 4 nɔ:θ . saɷθ [sæwɛst[4] *s.-west*] . i:st . wɛs, wɛst, ○~[4] 5 nɔəʳθ . sɛ̈ɷθ . i:st . wɛst 6 nɔʳ:θ . sɛ̈ɷθ . i:st . wɛst

VII.6.26 WHAT DIRECTION IS THE WIND?

Q. If you wanted to know where the wind was coming from, you would ask . . . .

Rr. WHAT QUARTER IS THE WIND (IN)?, WHERE /DO THE WIND BLOW/DOST RECKON THE WIND IS/?, WHERE IS IT BLOWING FROM?, WHERE IS THE WIND (/BLOWING/ COMING FROM /LAYING/)?, WHICH ROAD BE THE WIND? WHICH ROAD IS THE WIND (BLOWING)?, WHICH WAY DOES THE WIND BLOW?, WHICH WAY IS THE WIND /BLOWING/COMING (FROM)/

Note 1—I.m. exs. of ROAD meaning *direction* are included below between square brackets untransliterated.

Note 2—For additional exs. of COME, see VIII.3.1 and IX.3.4 (and refs.); of WAY, see IX.10.7; and of WHERE, see IX.9.7.

7 Ch 1 wɩə‿z‿ð wɩnd kɷmɩn fɹɷm 2 wɩə‿z‿t wɩ̣nd 3 wɩə‿z‿ð wɩnd 4 wɩə‿z ðə wɩnd 5 wɩtʃ ɹu:d‿z‿ð wɩnd blo·ɩn 6 wɩtʃ ɹo:d‿z ðə wɩnd

8 Db 1 wɩtʃ ɹo:d‿z‿t wɩnd blo:ɷɩn 2 wɩtʃ we: ɩs‿t wɩnd blɔ:ɩn 3 wɩə‿s‿θ wɩnd 4 wɩə‿s‿t wɩnd blo:ʷ-ɩn 5 wɩə‿z‿t wɩnd kɷmɩn fɹɒm 6 wɩtʃ ɹü:d‿z‿ð wɩnd 7 wɩə‿z‿ð wɩnd

11 Sa 1 wəʳ:‿z̨ ɩt blo:ɩn fɹam 2 wɩtʃ wę:‿z ðə wɩnd 3 wɩtʃ we:‿z ðə wɩnd 4 wɩtʃ we: ɩz ðə wɩnd blo:ɩn 5 wɩtʃ ɹo:d‿z ðə wɩnd 6 wɛəʳ:‿z̨ ðə wɩnd 7 wɩtʃ ɹo:d‿z ðə wɩnd 8 wɩtʃ we:‿z ðə wɩnd kɷmɩn 9 wɩtʃ we:‿z ðə wɩnd 10 wɩtʃ ɹo:d bi: ðə wɩnd 11 wɩtʃ wa:ɩ‿z ðə wɩnd

12 St 1 n.a. 2 wɩə‿z ðə wɩnd kɷmɩn fɹɒm 3 wɩtʃ wi:‿z‿θ wɩnd blɷ:ɩn [wɩndɩ *windy adj.*] 4 wɛ:‿z ðə wɩnd 5 wɩtʃ we:‿z ðə wɩnd əblɷ:ɩn 6 wɩtʃ wi:‿z ðə wɩnd 7 wɛ:‿z ðə wɩnd, wɩtʃ ɹoɷd‿z ðə wɩnd bləɷɩn 8 wə:‿z ðə wɩnd [ɹoɷd[1(2x)]] 9 ir.r. 10 wɩtʃ ɹoɷd‿z ðə wɩnd əbloɷwɩn 11 wɩtʃ wɛɩ‿z ðə wɩnd, °wə:ɹ‿z ðə wɩnd

15 He 1 wəʳ:‿z ðə wɩnd 2 wəʳ du: ðə wɩnd blɒɷ 3–4 wɩtʃ wæɩ‿z ðə wɩnd 5 wəʳ:‿z̨ ðə wɩnd 6 wɒt kwɑʳ:ʈəʳ‿z̨ ðə wɩnd 7 wɩtʃ weɩ ɩz ðə wɩnd, °wəɹ‿z ðə wɩnd əbloɷɩn

16 Wo 1 wɩə‿z ðɩ wɩnd əkɷmɩn fɹɷm 2 wəʳ:‿z̨ ðə wɩnd 3 wɩtʃ we:ɩ‿z ðə wɩnd 4 wɩtʃ waɩ dɷz ðə wɩn blaɷ 5 wɩtʃ waɩ‿z ðə wɩnd əblaɷɩn 6 wɩtʃ ɹoɷd‿z ðə wɩnd əblæɷɩn 7 wɛə‿z ðə wɩnd əkɷmɩn fɹɒm [ɹɷ·d[3], ɹoɷd[4]]

17 Wa 1 wɩtʃ ɹǫɷd‿z ðə wɩnd əblǫɷɩn 2 wɩtʃ weɩ‿z ðə wɩnd [ɹoɷd[1]] 3 wɩtʃ wɛɩ‿z ðə wɩnd 4 wɩə‿z ðə wɩn 5 wɒt kwɔ:təʳ‿z̨ ðə wɩnd ɩn 6 wɩə‿z ðə wɩnd əkɷmɩn fɹɒm 7 wɩtʃ wɛɩ‿z ðə wɩnd

23 Mon 1 wɩtʃ wæɩ‿z ðə wɩnd əkʌmɩn fɹɑ:m 2 wɩtʃ we:‿z ðə wɩnd 3 wɛə‿z ðə wɩnd 4 n.a. 5 wɛ:‿z ðə wɩnd 6 wəʳ:‿z̨ ðə wɩnd le:-ɩn 7 n.a.

24 Gl 1 wɩtʃ wæɩ‿z ðə wɩnd əblæɷɩn 2 wɩtʃ ɹæɷd‿z ðə wɩnd əblæɷɩn 3 wɩtʃ wæɩ‿z ðə wɩnd əblɒɷɩn 4 wɩtʃ waɩ‿z ðə wɩnd əblaɷɩn 5 wɩtʃ wæɩ ɩz ðə wɩnd 6 wəʳ:‿z̨ ðə wɩnd 7 wəʳ:‿ʂʈ ɹɛkn ðə wɩnd ɩz

25 O 1 wɛəʳ‿z̨ ðə wɩnd əkʌmɩn fɹɒ:m 2 wɩtʃ wɛɩ‿z ðə wɩnd 3 wɩtʃ we:‿z ðə wɩnd 4 wəɽ‿z̨ ðə wɩnd 5 wɩtʃ we:ˡ‿z ðə wɩn 6 wɛəʳ‿z̨ ðə wɩnd

VII.7.1 HALFPENNY*. HALFPENNYWORTH*

Q. □ *What do you call this?*
If a child went into a shop to buy some sweets for a halfpenny, what would she ask for?

Rr. HALFPENNY
HALFPENNYWORTH, HALFPENNY'S WORTH

Note—The rr. to the two parts of the q. are separated below by a full stop.

7 Ch 1 ẹ:pnɩ. ẹ:pəθ 2 ɔ:pnɩ. ɔ:pnɩzwəθ 3 e:pnɩ, i:pnɩ ["older"]. i:pəθ 4 ẹ:pnɩ. ẹ:pəθ 5 i:pnɩ. i:pəf 6 e:pnɩ. e:pəθ

8 Db 1 e:pnɩ. e:pəθ 2 a:pnɩ ["old"], e:pnɩ. e:pəθ 3 e:pnɩ. e:ˈpəθ 4–5 e:pnɩ. e:pəθ 6 apnɩ. e:ˈpəθ 7 e·ɩpnɩ. e·ɩpəθ

11 Sa 1 e:pnɩ. e:pəθ 2 japnɩ. ẹ:pəθ 3–4 e:pnɩ. e:pəθ 5 apnɩ. apəʵθ 6 e:pnɩ. e:pəθ 7 e:pnɩ. e:pəʵ:θ 8 jɛpnɩ. e:pəθ 9 e:pnɩ. e:pəθ 10 e:pnɩ. e:pəʵ:θ 11 japnɩ. japəʵθ

12 St 1–2 ɛɩpnɩ. ɛɩpəθ 3 oɷpnɩ. ɛɩpəθ, °oɷpəθ[1] 4 ɛɩpnɩ. ɛɩpəθ 5 e:pnɩ. e:pəθ 6 ɛɩpnɩ. ɛɩpəθ 7 ɛɩpnɩ. ɛɩpəθ, °~[1,4] 8 ɛɩpnɩ. ɛɩpnɩwə:θ 9 ɛ·ɩpnɩ. ɛ·ɩpəθ 10 ɛɩpnɩ. ɛɩpəθ 11 ɛɩpnɩ. ɛɩpnɩwə:ɹθ

15 He 1 jɛpnɩ. jɛpəʵθ 2 jɛpnɩ. e:ɩpəʵθ 3 æpnɩ. e:ɩpəʵθ 4 jæpnɩ. e:pəʵθ 5 e:ɩpnɩ. e:ɩpəʵθ 6 jɷpnɩ. jɷpəʵθ 7 eɩpnɩ [eɩpnɩnap *h.-nap* (ref. card-game)]. eɩpəθ, °æɩpəθ[4], °eɩpəs[4] VIII.9.7 [rec. in «ˈsʌtʃ ən‿eɩpəs» *such an halfpennyworth* (i.e. fool)]

16 Wo 1 ɛɩpnɩ. ɛɩpəθ 2 ɛɩpnɩ. e:ˈpəθ 3 e:ɩpnɩ. e:ɩpəθ 4 jæpnɩ. e:pɷθ 5 jɒpnɩ. e:pɷθ 6 e:ɩpnɩ [θɹi:-e:ɩpɷns[2] *three-halfpence*]. e:ɩpɷθ 7 eɩpnɩ. eɩpnɩwə:θ[(2x)] [pref.], s.w. eɩpəθ

17 Wa 1 ẹɩpn [*sic*]. ẹɩpnɩwə:θ 2 apnɩ. apəθ 3 ɛɩpnɩ. ɛɩpəθ 4 ẹɩpnɩ. ẹɩpəθ 5 apənɩ. apəθ 6 ɛɩpnɩ, e:ᵊpnɩ [old]. e:ᵊpəθ 7 ɛɩpnɩ, apnɩ [older]. apɷθ

23 Mon 1 jʌpnɩ. e:ɩpəθ 2–3 e:pnɩ. e:pəθ 4 ẹˈpni. ẹˈpʰʌ̈θ 5 □ẹ:pni:z. ẹ:pəθ 6 e:pnɩ. e:pəθ 7 n.a., °he:pni[1]. n.a., °eɩpniwœ:θ[1], °e:pəθ[1]

24 Gl 1 e:pənɩ. e:pəʵθ 2 e:pnɩ. e:pɷθ 3 jʌpnɩ. jʌpəʵθ 4 japnɩ. japəʵθ [dɹˈi:-e:pɷns[3] *three-halfpence*] 5 jɷpnɩ. jɷpəθ [e:pəns[2] *halfpence*] 6 jəpnɩ. jəpəθ 7 ɛpnɩ. ɛpəθ

25 O 1 jɷpnɩ. jɷpnɩwəʳ:θ 2 e:pnɩ, °e:pmɩ[1]. ɛˈpəθ 3 e:pnɩ. e:pəθ 4 e:pnɩ [e:pnɩnap[5] *h.-nap*; θɽi:-e:pəns[4] *three-halfpence*]. e:pəθ[(2x)] 5 eˈpnɩ, °e:pnɩ[2]. e:pəθ, °e:pəʳθ[2] 6 eɩpmɩ. eɩpəθ

VII.7.2 FARTHINGS

Q. A halfpenny is worth two . . . .

R. FARTHING(S)

Note—Uninflected FARTHING was freq. rec. in the rr. This is the case, too, in the SOUTH (cf. *Vol. IV, ad loc*) and in the EAST MIDLANDS (cf. *Vol. III, ad loc*). These uninflected forms were also often rec. in the Northern rr. (cf. *Vol. I, 1st Ed., ad loc*). Unfortunately in the last case the forms in question were, perhaps incorrectly, marked with a superior ▵, our conventional sign for singular number in nn., the assumption being that they were genuine sg. forms. The only certain sgs. are the i.m. forms at 5.3, 6.9/17/18 and the s.f. at 6.17.

7 Ch 1 fa:ðɩnz 2 fa:ðɩn 3 fe:dɩnz 4 fa:ðɩnz 5 fa:ɹɩn 6 fa:ðɩn

8 Db 1 faꜝ:ðɩn 2–3 fa:ðɩn 4–7 fa:ðɩnz

11 Sa 1–3 fa:ðɩnz 4 faʳ:ðɩn 5 faʳ:ɖɩnz 6–7 faʳ:ðɩnz 8 fɔ:ðɩnz 9 faʳ:ðɩnz 10 fa:ðɩnz 11 fɔʳ:ɖɩnz

12 St 1–3 fa:ðɩnz 4 fɑ:ðɩnz 5–7 fa:ðɩnz 8 fɑ:ðɩnz 9 fa:ðɩnz 10 fa̱:ðɩnz 11 fɑ̣:ðɩŋgz

15 He 1 fa:ðɩnz 2 fa:ðɩn 3 faʳ:ɖɩnz 4 fɑʳ:ɖɩn 5 faʳ:ðɩn 6 fædɩn 7 fɑɹðɩnz

16 Wo 1 fɑ:dɩnz 2 fa:dɩnz 3 fa:ðɩnz 4 fɑʳ:ðɩnz 5 fa:dɩnz 6 fɑ:ðɩn 7 fɑʳɖɩnz, °▵fɑ:dɩn[3]

17 Wa 1 fa:ðɩn 2 fa:ðɩnz, s.f. fa:dɩnz [pref.], °~ 3–4 fa:ðɩnz 5 faʳ:ðɩnz 6 fa:ðɩn 7 faʳ:ɖɩnz

23 Mon 1 faʳ:ðɩn 2–3 fa:ðɩnz 4 n.a. 5–6 fa:ðɩnz 7 n.a.

24 Gl 1 faʳ:ðɩn 2 fa:dnz 3 vaʳ:ðɩn 4 va:dnz 5 fəʳ:ɖɳ 6 vaʳ:ɖɩnz 7 vaʳ:ðɩnz

25 O 1 faʳ:ɖɳ 2 faꜝ:dn 3 faʳɖɩn 4 faɽðɩnz, °fɑɽɖɳʐ[1] 5–6 faʳ:ɖɳʐ

VII.7.3 THREEPENNY-BIT. THREEPENCE

Q. □ *What do you call this?*

And when a thing costs that amount, you say it costs how much?

Rr. JOEY, THREEPENNY-BIT/JOE(Y)/PIECE THREEPENCE

Note 1—The rr. to the two parts of the q. are separated below by a full stop.
Note 2—For THREE, see VII.1.3 (and refs.). -PENCE occurs at VII.7.1/4.

7 Ch 1 θɹɪpnɪbɪt. θɹɪpns 2 θɹᶖpnɪbɪt. θɹᶖpəns 3 θɹɪpnɪbɪt. θɹɪpns 4 θɹɪpnɪbɪt. θɹɪpəns 5 θɹɪpnɪbɪt, ○fɹɪpnɪbɪt [pref.]. θɹɪpns, ○fɹɪpns [pref.], ○~[2] 6 θɹəpnɪbɪt. θɹəpəns

8 Db 1 θɹɪpnɪbɪt. θɹɪpəns 2 θɹɛpnɪbɪt. θɹɛpns 3 θɹɛpnɪbɪt. θɹɛpəns 4 θɹɛpnɪbɪt. θɹɛpns 5 θɹɪpnɪbɪt. θɹɪpns 6 θɹɛpnɪbɪt. θɹɛpns 7 θɹɪpnɪbɪt, ○~[1]. θɹɛpəns, ○θɹɪpəns[1]

11 Sa 1 θɹʌpnɪbɪt. θɹʌpəns 2 θɹɛpnɪbɪt. θɹɛpəns 3 θɹɪpnɪbɪt. θɹɪpəns 4 θɹɛpnɪbɪt. θɹɪpɪns 5 fɹɪpnɪbɪt. fɹɪpəns 6 θɹɛpnɪbɪt. θɹɛpəns 7 θɹɛpnɪbɪt. θɹɪpəns 8 θɹɛpnɪbɪt. θɹəpəns 9 θɹɛpnɪbɪt. θɹɪpəns 10 θɹɛpnɪbɪt. θɹʌpəns 11 θɹɛpnɪbɪt. θɹɪpɪns

12 St 1 θɹɛpnɪbɪt. θɹɷpəns 2 θɹɪpɪnɪbɪt. θɹɪpəns 3 θɹᶖpnɪbᶖt. θɹɪpəns, fɹɪpəns ["old"] 4 θɹɪpnɪbɪt. θɹɪpəns 5 θɹɛpnɪbɪt. θɹɛpəns 6 θɹɪpnɪbɪt. θɹɪpəns 7 θɹɛpnɪbɪt. θɹɛpəns 8 θɹɛpnɪbɪt, ○θɹɛpnɪjoɷ. θɹɛpns 9–10 θɹɛpnɪbɪt. θɹɪpəns 11 θɹɛpnɪbɪt. θɹɛpəns

15 He 1 θɹɛpnɪbɪt. θɹɛpəns 2 θɹɛpnɪbɪt. dɹɪpəns 3 θɹɛpnɪbɪt. θɹɷpəns 4 dɹɪpnɪbɪt. n.r. 5 θɹɛpnɪbɪt. θɹəpəns 6 dɹɷpnɪbɪt. dɹɷpəns 7 θɹɛpnɪbɪt, ○θɹɛpnɪdʒoɷɪ. θɹɛpəns [θɹi:pɛnəθ *threepennyworth*]

16 Wo 1 θɹɛpnɪbᶖt. θɹɛpəns 2 θɹɛpnɪdʒoɷɪ. θɹɛpəns 3 θɹɛpnɪbɪt. θɹɛpəns 4 fɹɷpnɪbɪt. fɹɷpɷns 5 θɹɛpnɪbɪt. θɹɷpɷns 6 θɹɛpnɪbi:t θɹɛpɷns 7 θɹɛpnɪbɪt. θɹɛpəns

17 Wa 1 θɹɛpnɪbᶖt. θɹɛpəns 2 θɹɪpnɪbɪt. θɹɪpəns 3 θɹəpnɪbɪt. θɹəpəns 4 θɹɛpnɪbɪt. θɹɛpɷns 5 θɹɪpənɪbɪt. θɹɪpɷns, ○~[1] 6 θɹɛpnɪbɪt. θɹɛpəns 7 θɹɛpnɪbɪt. θɹɛpɷns

23 Mon 1 θɹɛpnɪbɪt. θɹʌpəns 2 θɹɛpnɪbət, ○□θɹəpnɪbɪts. θɹəpəns 3 θɹɛpnɪbɪt. n.r. 4 n.a. 5 θɹʌ̣̈pnibɪt. θɹʌ̣̈ppʌ̣ns 6 θɹɛpnɪbɪt. θɹɛpəns 7 n.a. n.a., ○θɹʌ̣pəns[1]

24 Gl 1 θɹɛpnɪbɪt. θɹɛpɷns, ○~[1] 2 θɹɛpnɪbɪt, dʒo:ɪ [usu.]. θɹɛpɷns 3 dɹɪpnɪbɪt. dɹɪpəns 4 dɹɪpnɪbɪt. dɹɪpɷns 5 θɹɛpnɪbɪt. θɹɛpns 6 dɹəpnɪbɪt. dɹɪpəns 7 dɹɪpnɪbɪt. dɹɪpənts

25 O 1 θɹʌpnɪbɪt. θɹəpəns 2 θɹəpnɪbɪt. θɹɛpəns 3 θɹəpnɪ̞piːs. θɹɛpəns 4 θɽɛpnɪbɪt. θɽɪpəns 5 θɹɪpnɪbɪt. θɹəpəns 6 θɹɪpnɪbɪt. θɹɪpns

VII.7.4 SIXPENCE

Q. What do you call this?

Rr. (SIXPENNY-)JOEY, SIXPENCE, TANNER

Note—For SIX, see VII.1.5 (and refs.). -PENCE occurs at VII.7.1/3.

7 Ch 1 tanə, sɪkspəns 2 sɪkspəns 3 tanə [usu.], p. sɪkspəns 4–6 sɪkspəns

8 Db 1 sɪkspəns, tanəʳ ["pref."] 2 sɪkspəns 3 tanə [pref.], sɪkspəns 4 sɪks-pəns 5 tanə, sɪkspəns 6 tanə, sɪkspənts 7 tanə, p. sɪkspəns

11 Sa 1 tanəʳ 2 sɪkspəns 3 tanəʳ· 4 sɪkspɪns 5 sɪkspəns 6 sɪkspəns, tanəʳ 7 sɪkspəns 8 tanəʳ, sɪkspɪns 9 sɪkspəns 10 sɪkspəns, tænəʳ 11 sɪkspəns

12 St 1 sɪkspəns. tanə 2 tanə 3 tanə, sɪkspəns 4 tanə 5 sɪkspəns, tanə 6–8 tanə 9 tanə, sɪkspəns 10 sɪkspəns 11 sɪkspəns, °tanə

15 He 1–2 sɪkspəns, tænəʳ [usu.] 3 sɪkspɒns, tænəʳ ["usu."] 4 sɪkspəns 5 sɪkspɛns 6 zɪkspəns 7 sɪkspəns, tanəɹ

16 Wo 1 sɪ̞kspəns 2 tanəʳ 3–5 sɪkspɒns 6 sɪkspɒns, °~[2] 7 sɪkspə̣ns

17 Wa 1 sɪkspəns 2 sɪkspəns, tanə 3 sɪkspəns 4 sɪkspɒns 5 sɪkspɒns, °~[1] 6 tanəʳ, sɪkspəns 7 tanəʳ, sɪkspɒns

23 Mon 1 sɪkspəns, °sɪkspʌns[1] 2–3 sɪkspəns 4 n.a. 5 sɪkspʌ̣̈ns 6 sɪkspəns 7 n.a.

24 Gl 1–2 sɪkspɒns 3 zɪkspɒns 4 zɪkspɒns, tanəʳ 5 tanə, sɪkspɒns 6–7 zɪkspəns

25 O 1–2 sɪkspəns 3 sɪkpənts 4 sɪkspəns, °tanəɽ[4] 5 tanəʳ, sɪkspəns 6 sɪkpns [*sic*], °sɪkspnɪjoɒɪ[3], °joɒɪ[3] [*sic*]

VII.7.5 SHILLING*

Q. What do you call this?

Rr. BOB, SHILLING

Note—I.m. exs. of BOB and SHILLING, all of which are uninflected plural forms, are reproduced below between square brackets untransliterated.

7 Ch 1 ʃɪlɪn 2 ʃɪ̢lɪn 3–5 ʃɪlɪn 6 ʃɪ̢lɪn

8 Db 1 bɒbᵊ [pref.], ʃɪlɪn 2 ʃɪlɪn 3 bɒb, ʃɪlɪn, ○~ 4 ʃɪlɪn 5 ʃɪlɪŋg, ʃɪlɪn 6 bɒb, p. ʃɪlɪn 7 bɒb [pref.], p. ʃɪlɪn

11 Sa 1 ʃɪlɪn 2 ʃɪlɪn, ○~[3] 3–5 ʃɪlɪn 6 ʃɪlɪn, bɒb 7 ʃɪlɪn 8 ʃɪlɪn, bɒb 9 ʃɪlɪn 10 ʃɪlɪn, bɒb 11 ʃɪlɪn

12 St 1 bɒb, ʃɪ̢lɪn, ○bɒb [ʃɪlɪn[2]] 2 ʃɪlɪn 3 bɒb, ʃɪlɪn [bɒb[1]] 4 ʃɪlɪn 5 ʃɪlɪn, bɒb [ʃɪlɪn[2]] 6 bɒb, ʃɪlɪn 7 ʃɪlɪn, ○~, ○bɒb 8 ʃɪlɪn, ○bɒb [bɒb[2]] 9 bɒb, ʃɪlɪn 10–11 ʃɪlɪn

15 He 1 ʃɪlɪn, bɔ:b 2 ʃɪɫɪn, bɒb 3 ʃɪɫɪn, bɑʳ:b, ○ʃɪɫɪn[2] 4–5 ʃɪɫɪn 6 zɪɫɪn 7 ʃɪlɪn, bɒb

16 Wo 1 ʃɪ̢lɪ̢n 2 ʃɪlɪn 3 ʃɪlɪn [ʃɪlɪn[1,2]] 4 ʃɪ̢lɪn [ʃɪɫɪn[3]] 5 ʃɪɫɪn [ʃɪlɪn[1]] 6 ʃɪlɪn, bɑ:b 7 ʃɪlɪn

17 Wa 1 ʃɪlɪn 2 ʃɪlɪn, ○bəb[1,3] [ʃɪlɪn[2(2x)]] 3–7 ʃɪlɪn

23 Mon 1 ʃɪɫɪn 2 ʃɪɫən 3 ʃɪɫɪn, ○~[2] 4 ʃɪlɪ̢̈n 5 ʃɪlɪn [ʃɪlɪn[2]] 6 ʃɪɫɪn 7 n.a.

24 Gl 1–2 ʃɪɫɪn 3 ʒɪɫɪn 4 ʃɪɫn 5 ʃɪlɪn [bɒb[1]] 6 bɒb, ʃɪlən 7 ʃɪlɪn

25 O 1 ʃɪlɪn, ○~[2] 2–3 ʃɪlɪn 4 ʃɪɫən, ○□ʃɪɫɪnz[5] [ʃɪɫɪn[3]; bɒb[4]] 5 ʃɪlɪn, ○bɒ·b 6 ʃɪlɪn

VII.7.6 HALF-A-CROWN

Q. □ *What do you call this?*

Rr. HALF(-A)-CROWN

Note—For HALF, see VII.5.4 (and refs.).

7 Ch 1 ẹ:fəkɹaɪn 2 a:fəkɹæɒn, s.f. e:fəkɹæɒn [pref.] 3 ẹ:fəkɹaɪn 4 ẹ:fəkɹaɒn 5 e:fəkɹa:n 6 ɔ:fəkɹạɒn

8 Db 1 e:fəkɹɛ̢ɒn 2 ɔ:fəkɹa:n, ○e:fəkɹa:n[2] 3 e:fəkɹɛ̢̈ɒn 4 e:fəkɹɛ:n 5 e:fəkɹɛ̢:n 6 e:ˈfəkɹɛ:n 7 e·ɪfəkɹɛ:n

11 Sa 1 e:fkɹaɒn 2 e:fəkɹæɒn 3–4 a:fəkɹaɒn 5 ẹ:fəkɹɛɒn, ○a:fəkɹɛ̢ɒn[1], ○a:fəkɹɛɒn[3] 6–7 e:fkɹaɒn 8 e:fəkɹɛɒn 9 e:fəkɹaɒn 10 e:fkɹaɒn 11 ɔ:fkɹaɒn

12 St 1 a:fəkɹaɒn 2 ɛɪfəkɹaɪn, ○~[1] 3 ɔ:fəkɹaɪn 4 a:fkɹaɒn 5 ɛɪfəkɹaɒn 6 ɛɪfəkɹæ:n 7 ɑ̊:fəkɹæɒn 8 ɑ:fəkɹæɒn 9 ɛɪfəkɹa:n 10 a:fəkɹæɒn 11 ɑ:fəkɹæɒn

15 He 1 a:fəkɹæɷn 2 i:fəkɹæɷn 3 aʳ:fəkɹəɷn 4 ɛfəkɹəɷn 5 a:fəkɹʌɷn 6 ɑ:fəkɹəɷᵊn 7 a:fəkɹaɷn, eɪfəkɹaɷn [freq.]

16 Wo 1 ɑ:fəkɹɛɷn 2 ɑ:fəkɹɛɷᵊn 3 a:fəkɹɛu:n 4 aʳ:fəkɹəɷ:n 5 a:fəkɹɷn, °a:fəkɹɷn[1] 6 ɑ:fəkɹɛu:n 7 ɑ:fəkɹæɷn

17 Wa 1 a:fəkɹæɷn 2 ä:fkɹæɷn, °a:fəkɹæɷn[3] 3 a:fəkɹɛ̈ɷn 4–7 a:fəkɹɛɷn

23 Mon 1 a:fkɹʌɷn 2 a:fəkɹʌɷn 3 a:fəkɹəɷn 4 n.a. 5 a:fəkɹəun 6 a:fkɹəɷn 7 n.a.

24 Gl 1 æ:fkɹəɷ:n 2 a:fəkɹəɷn 3 æ:fkɹəɷn, °æ:fəkɹəɷn[4] 4 a:fəkɹəɷn 5 a:fəkɹʌɷn 6–7 a:fəkɹ°u:n

25 O 1 a:fəkɹɛɷn 2 a:fkɹæɷn 3 a:fkɹɛɷn 4 a:fəkɽa̢ɷn 5 a:fəkɽɛɷn 6 a:fəkɹɛ̈ɷn

VII.7.7 SILVER*

Q. □ *What's it* (viz. half-a-crown) *made of?*

R. SILVER

7 Ch 1 sɪlvə 2 sɪlvə [sɪlvəbəɪtʃ[2] *s.-birch* IV.10.1] 3–5 sɪlvə 6 sɪɫvə

8 Db 1 sɪlvəɹ̠ 2–7 sɪlvə

11 Sa 1 sɪlvəʳ 2 sɪlvə 3–4 sɪlvəʳ 5 n.r. 6–11 sɪlvəʳ

12 St 1–10 sɪlvə 11 sɪlvəɹ

15 He 1–2 sɪɫvəʳ 3 sɪɫvəʳ, °~[1] 4–6 sɪɫvəʳ 7 sɪlvəɹ

16 Wo 1–2 sɪɫvə 3–6 sɪɫvəʳ 7 sɪlvəʳ, °sɪlvə[3] VI.14.12

17 Wa 1–2 sɪlvə 3 sɪɫvə, °~ 4–5 sɪlvə 6–7 sɪɫvəʳ

23 Mon 1–2 sɪɫvəʳ 3 sɪɫvə 4 s̬ɪlvə, °sɪlvə[1] 5 sɪlvɐ 6 sɪɫvəʳ 7 n.a.

24 Gl 1 sɪɫvə 2–4 sɪɫvəʳ 5 sɪlvəʳ 6 zɪɫvəʳ 7 zɪlvəʳ

25 O 1 sɪɫvəʳ 2 sɪlvə 3 sɪlvəʳ 4 sɪɫvəɽ 5–6 sɪlvəʳ

VII.7.8 POUND* NOTE

Q. □ *What do you call this?*

Rr. BRADBURY, POUND/QUID NOTE

Note 1—I.m. exs. of POUND and QUID meaning *twenty shillings* are reproduced below between square brackets untransliterated. An attached superior × indicates an uninflected plural.

Note 2—For additional exs. of POUND meaning *twenty shillings*, see VII.7.9. For exs. of POUND ref. weight, see VII.8.2–4.

7 Ch 1 paɪnd nǫ:t 2 pæ̧ɪnd ᵔnɔ:ts [×pᵊu:nd¹ *p.* (n.d.)] 3 paɪn nǫ:t [×paɪnd³] 4 paɷn nǫ:t 5 pɛɷn nų:t 6 pɛ̧ɷn no:t

8 Db 1 pɛ̧ɷn ᵔno:ts 2 pa:n no:t [pa:nd⁴] 3 pɛ̧:n noᵒt 4 pɛ:n no:ᵒt 5 pa:n no:t 6 pɛ:n no:ᵒt 7 pɛ:n no·ɷt

11 Sa 1 paɷn no:t 2 pæɷn no:t [×pæɷnd³ *p.* (n.d.)] 3–4 paɷn no:t 5 pɛɷ no:t 6–7 paɷn no:t 8 pɛɷn no:t 9–11 paɷn no:t

12 St 1 pæɷnd noɷt [×pɷn⁴] 2 paɪnd noɷt 3 paɪnd nɷ:t 4 n.a. 5 pa:nd noɷt 6 pa:nd nɛɷt, kwɪd nɛɷt, °bɹadbɹɪ 7 pæ:ɷnd noɷt 8 pæɷnd noɷt 9 pa:ɷnd nɷ:t 10 pa:n noɷt 11 pæɷnd noɷt [×pæɷnd²]

15 He 1 pæɷ no:t 2 pæɷn no:t 3 pɛɷnd no:t 4 pəɷn no:t [pəɷn²] 5 pʌɷn no:t 6 pəɷn no:t 7 p. pə̆ųnd noɷt

16 Wo 1 paɷn noɷt 2 pɛɷn noɷt 3 pɛu:n noɷt 4 pəɷ:n no:t 5 pəɷ:n no:t [kwɪd¹; ×pəɷ:nd *p.* (n.d.)] 6 pɛu:nd noɷt 7 pæɷn noɷt, °bɹadbəɹɪ [×pæɷn³, ×pæɷnd³,⁴⁽²ˣ⁾]

17 Wa 1 pæɷn nǫɷt 2 pæɷn nəɷt 3 pɛ̈ɷn nǫɷt 4 pɛɷn noɷt 5–6 pɛɷn nǫɷt 7 pɛɷn noɷt

23 Mon 1 pʌɷn no:ɷt 2 pʌɷn no:t 3 pəɷn no:t [pəɷn] 4 pəun no:t [kwɪd] 5 pəun no:ᵊt 6 pəɷn no:t [pəɷnd¹; ×pəɷnd] 7 n.a.

24 Gl 1 pəɷᵊnd no:ɷt 2 pɛɷn no:ɷt 3 pəɷ no:ɷt 4 pəɷnd no:ɷt 5 pʌɷn no:t 6–7 pᵒu:n no:t

25 O 1 pɛɷnd no:t 2 pæɷn nɷət 3 pɛɷnd nǫɷt 4 paɷn no:t, °bɹadbəɽɪ⁴⁽²ˣ⁾, °bɽadbɽɪ⁴⁽²ˣ⁾, °ᵔbɽadbəɽɪz⁴, °ᵔbɽadbɽɪz⁴ [×paɷnd⁴] 5 s.f. pɛɷn nɷət 6 pɛ̈ɷn noɷt

VII.7.9 ALMOST

Q. I paid 19/–, that is, not quite a pound, but . . . . a pound.

Rr. ABOUT, ALL BUT, CLOSE (ON), (VERY) CLOSE TO, (AL)MOST, (DAMN/PRETTY/VERY) NEAR, NEAR ENOUGH, NEARISH, NEARLY, NIGH ON, NOT FAR OFF, PUSHING, VERY NIGH, WELLY (NEAR)

Note 1—When rec. in the rr., A POUND is reproduced below.

Note 2—For additional exs. of NEAR, see IX.2.10 (and refs.); of POUND, see VII.7.8 (and refs.); of ENOUGH, see III.8.4a (and refs.); of PRETTY, see VI.5.18; and of VERY, see VIII.3.2 (and refs.).

7 Ch 1 ɔ:mʏ:st ə paɪnd 2 nə [prec. by «ɽ» *is*] fɔ:ɹ əf ə pæɪnd, °vɛɹɪ nɪəɹ[1] [+ V.], °vɛɹɪ nɪə[2] [+ C.], °nɪə[4] 3 ɔ:məst 4 vɛɹɪ nəɪəɹ, °ɒməst[2] 5 vɛɹɪ nɛɪə, °ɒməst[1] 6 ɒməst, °~[1,2,3]

8 Db 1 naʳ:ɽ ɪnɷf 2 əba:t, p. ɒməst 3 nɪəɹ ənɷf 4 vəɹɪ nɛɪ 5 nɪəɹ ənɷf 6 vəɹɪ nɪə 7 vəɹɪ tlᵒü:s tɛɷ

11 Sa 1 ɒməst 2 ɒməst, °~[1,2] 3 ɒməʳ:ʂt 4 ɒməst 5 ɒməst, °ɒməst[1,2] 6 ɒməst, °~[4] 7 ɒməʳʂt 8 ɒməʳʂt, °ɒməst[2] 9 ɒməst, °~[1], °ɒməʳʂt[1(3x)] 10 ɒməʳ:ʂt, °pəʳ:ɖɪ nɪəʳ[3] [+ C.] 11 ɒməʳ:ʂt, °ɒməʳʂt[2], °pɷʃɪn[2(2x)] [rec. in «ˈi:z ˈpɷʃɪn ˈaɪtɪ» *he's pushing* (=*almost*) *eighty* (ref. age)]

12 St 1 nɪəlɪ 2–3 wɛlɪ ə paɪnd 4 nɪəlɪ 5 vɛɹɪ nɪə, wɛlɪ nɪə 6 nɪəlɪ 7 nɪəlɪ ə pæɷnd 8 nɪ̣əlɪ 9 vɛɹɪ nɪə 10 nɪəlɪ ə pa:nd 11 ɔ̣:lmoɷst ə pæɷnd, ɔ:l bɷt ə pæɷnd

15 He 1 ɒməs ə pæɷn, °ɒmɷs[2] 2 ɒməst, °vɛɹɪ næɪ ə pæɷn 3 ɒməʳʂt 4 njəʳɽ ənʌf 5 ɑ:ɬməst 6 ɒmɷst 7 vɛɹɪ nɪəɹ, nɪəɹ ənʌf, °vɛɹ nɪəɹ[1] [+ C.], °moɷst[3]

16 Wo 1 ɒməst 2 ɑ·moɷst, °nɒɪ ɒn[2] 3 ɑ:lmoɷst ə pɛu:n, °vɛɹɪ nɒɪ[2] 4 nɪəʳɽ ɪnɷf 5 ɒmɷst, °ɑ:mɷs[1] 6 ɑ:moɷst, °əmɷs[2] 7 vɛɹɪ nɪəɹ [+ V.], p. vɛɹɪ nɪəʳ [+ pause]

17 Wa 1 vəɹɪ nɪə 2 nɪəlɪ ə pæɷnd, °nɪəlɪ[1(2x)], °vɛɹə nɪə[1] 3 ɔ:lmo̧ɷst 4 vɛɹɪ nɪəʳ 5 vɛɹɪ nɪə 6 klo̧ɷs tü: 7 nɪəlɪ

23 Mon 1 ɑ:məst 2 ɑ:ɬməst 3 vɛɹɪ nɪə 4 n.a. 5 ɔ:lmo:st 6 dæm nɪəʳ, nɪəʳɭɪ 7 n.a.

24 Gl 1 njəʳ:ɭɪ, °ɑ:məst[1] 2 nɪəʳ 3 ɑ:mo:st 4 ɒmɷst 5 vəɹɪ nɪəʳ· 6 nɪəɹ ənəf 7 nəʳ:ɽ ənə·f

25 O 1 klo:s ɒn, vəɹɪ nɪəʳ 2 vəɹɪ nɪə̠ɪ 3 vəɽɪ nʌʏ 4 pəɽɪ nɪəɽ, °nɪəɽɪʃ[3] 5 nɪəʳ ənʌf 6 nɪəʳɭɪ

VII.7.10 GOLD*

Q. What is a sovereign made of?

R. GOLD

7 Ch 1 gɛɷld 2 gɷuld, s.f. gæɷd(2x) [pref.; older], °gu:ld[1] 3 gɛ̈ɷld 4 gu:ld 5 gɛɷɫd 6 go:ld

8 Db 1–2 go:ld 3 gɛ̈ɷd 4 gɛɷd 5 go:ld 6 go:ᵊld 7 go·ɷld

11 Sa 1 go:ld 2 gaɷld 3 go:ld 4 go:l 5–6 go:ld 7 gaɷd 8–9 gaɷld 10 gaɷd 11 go:ld

12 St 1 goɷld 2 gɛɷld 3 gæ̣ɷd 4 goɷld 5 goɷld, °gaɷld[2] 6 gɛɷd 7 gọɷld 8 goɷld 9 goɷ·ld 10–11 goɷld

15 He 1–2 go:ɫd 3 gɒɷɫd 4 gæɷɫd 5 go:ɫd 6 gæɷɫd 7 go:ᵊld

16 Wo 1 goɷld 2–3 goɷɫd 4 go:ɫd 5 gɒɷɫd 6 goɷɫd 7 goɷld

17 Wa 1 gọɷld 2 gɔɷld 3 gɒɷɫd 4 goɷɫd 5 goɷɫd, °~ 6 gɒɷɫd 7 gọɷɫd

23 Mon 1 go:ɷɫd 2–3 go:ɫd 4 go:ᵘld [gọ:ldn *golden*] 5–6 go:ɫd 7 n.a.

24 Gl 1 gæɷᵊɫd 2 gæɷɫd 3 gɒɷᵊd 4 gɒɷɫd 5 gɑɷld 6 gɑɷɫd 7 gɒɷᵊɫd

25 O 1 gọɷɫd 2 gɔɷɫd 3 gɔɷɫd, °gɔ̣ɷɫd[1] 4 go:ld [go:ɫdɪn[4] *golden*] 5 gɔɷɫd 6 goɷd

VII.8.1 QUART*

Q. What's your word for two pints?

R. QUART

7 Ch 1 kwa:t(2x) 2 kwa:t 3 kwe:t 4–5 kwa:t 6 kwɔ:t

8 Db 1 kwaᶦ:t 2–4 kwa:t 5 kwa:tʻ 6 kwɔ̃:t 7 kwɔ:t, p. kwa:t

11 Sa 1 kwaʳ:ʈ 2 kwɔ:t 3 kwɔʳ:ʈ 4 kwɔʳ:əʳʈ 5–10 kwɔʳ:ʈ 11 kwɔʳ:ʈ, °□kwaʳʈʂ[1]

12 St 1 kwɔ:t 2–3 kwa:t 4 kwɔ:t 5 kwɔ:t, kwa:t ["old"] 6 kwoɷt 7–10 kwɔ:t 11 kwɔ:t, °□kwa̱:ts1(2x)

15 He 1–2 kwɔʳ:ʈ 3–5 kwɑʳ:ʈ 6 kwɑ:t 7 kwɔɹt

16 Wo 1 kwɑ:t 2–4 kwɑʳ:ʈ 5–6 kwɔʳ:ʈ 7 kwɑʳʈ

17 Wa 1–2 kwɔ:t 3 kwɔʳ:ʈ 4 kwɔ:t 5 kwɔʳ:ʈ 6 kwaʳ:ʈ 7 kwɔʳ:ʈ, s.f. kwaʳ:ʈ [old]

23 Mon 1 kwaʳ:ṭ 2–3 kwɑ:t 4 kʰwɔ:tʰ 5 kwɔ:t 6 kwɑʳ:ṭ 7 n.a.

24 Gl 1–4 kwɑʳ:ṭ 5 kwəʳ:ṭ 6–7 kwəʳ:ṭ

25 O 1 kwəʳ:ṭ 2 kwæʳ:ṭ 3 kwɔʳ:ṭ 4 kwɔ·ṛṭ 5–6 kwəʳ:ʔ

VII.8.2 POUND*

Q. How do you buy your tea? By the . . . .

R. POUND

Note—For additional exs. of POUND, see VII.8.3/4; and for exs. of POUND meaning *twenty shillings*, see VII.7.8/9.

7 Ch 1 paɪnd 2 pæɷnd⁽²ˣ⁾ ["modern"], pæ̨ɪnd⁽²ˣ⁾ [pref.] 3 paɪnd 4 pæɷnd 5 pɛɷnd⁽²ˣ⁾ 6 pɛ̨ɷn

8 Db 1 pɛ̨ɷnd 2 pɷnd 3 pɛ̨:nd 4 pɛ:nd 5 pa:n 6–7 pɛ:nd

11 Sa 1 paɷnd 2 pæɷn 3–4 paɷnd 5 pɛɷn 6 paɷnd 7 paɷn 8 pɛɷn 9 pɒɷnd 10 paɷn 11 paɷn ,○~

12 St 1 paɷnd 2 paɪnd, ○~¹ 3 paɪnd, ○~¹ 4 pæɷnd 5 paɷnd 6 pa:nd, ○~ 7 pa:nd 8 pæɷnd 9 paɷnd, ○~ 10 pa:nd 11 pæɷnd, ○~²

15 He 1 pænd [*sic*] 2 pæɷn 3 pɛɷnd 4 pəɷnd 5 pʌɷn 6 pəɷn 7 pɑɷnd, ○□pɑ̆ɷnd³, ○pɔ̣̆ɷnd³

16 Wo 1 paɷnd 2 pɛɷnd 3 pɛu:nd 4–5 pəɷ:n 6 pɛu:nd 7 pæɷnd, ○□pæɷnz³

17 Wa 1 pæɷn 2 pæɷnd, ○~ 3 pɛ̈ɷnd 4 pɛɷn 5–6 pɛɷnd 7 pɛ̈ɷnd

23 Mon 1 pʌɷn, ○pʌɷnd¹ 2 pʌɷn 3 pəɷn 4 pʰəund 5 pəun 6 pəɷnd 7 n.a.

24 Gl 1 pəɷ:ᵊn 2 pəɷ:nd 3–4 pəɷnd 5 pʌɷnd 6 pᵒu:n 7 pᵒu:nd

25 O 1 pɛ̈ɷnd 2 pæɷnd 3 pɛɷnd 4 paɷnd, ○□~¹, ○pɑɷnd¹ 5 pɛ̈ɷnd 6 pɛ̈ɷn

VII.8.3 POUND* of TEA*

Q. So, when buying some (tea) *in a grocer's shop, you might ask for a . . . .*

Rr. POUND (OF) TEA

Note 1—Though not a keyword, OF was always rec. in the rr., except at 17.3, where a full stop is used to separate POUND and TEA. At 25.1 TEA alone was rec.

Note 2—I.m. exs. of TEA are reproduced below between square brackets untransliterated.

Note 3—For additional exs. of POUND, see VII.8.2/4; for POUND meaning *twenty shillings*, see VII.7.8/9. For additional exs. of TEA(-), see V.7.20 and V.8.9/15.

7 Ch 1 paɪnd ə ti: 2 pæ̨ɪnd ə te:⁽²ˣ⁾ [te:²⁽²ˣ⁾,³⁽³ˣ⁾,⁴] 3 paɪnd ə te: 4 paɷnd ə tị: 5 pɛɷnd ə ti: 6 pɛɷnd ə tẹ:

8 Db 1 pɛ̨ɷnd ə te: 2 pɷnd ə ti: 3 pɛ̨:nd ə ti: 4 pɛ:nd ə ti: 5 pa:nd ə ti: 6 pɛ:nd ə ti: [ti:¹] 7 pɛ:nd ə ti:

11 Sa 1 paɷn ə te: [te:⁴] 2 pæɷn ə tẹ: [ẹ:tˡi: *hay-t.* (i.e. water in which hay has been boiled)] 3 paɷn ə ti: 4 paɷnd əv ti: 5 pɛɷn ə tẹ: 6 paɷnd ə te: 7 paɷn ə te: [te:] 8 pɛɷn ə te: [te:] 9 pɒɷnd ə te: 10 paɷn ə te: [te:³] 11 paɷn əv te:

12 St 1 pɷn ə tɛɪ [ti:⁴; ti:pɒt² *t.-pot*] 2 paɪnd ə ti: [ti:⁵] 3 paɪnd ə tɛɪ [tɛɪ¹⁽²ˣ⁾; tɛɪpɒt¹ *t.-pot*] 4–5 pæɷnd ə ti: 6 pa:nd ə tɛɪ [□tɛɪz¹] 7 pæɷnd ə ti: [ti:¹,²] 8 pæɷnd ə ti: [ti:³,⁶] 9 paɷnd ə tɛ̨ɪ 10 pa:nd əv ti: 11 pæɷnd əv ti:

15 He 1 pæn ə ti: 2 pæɷn ə ti: [ti:kʌp² *t.-cup*] 3 pɛɷn ə te:ɪ 4 pəɷn ə ti: 5 pʌɷn ə ti: 6 pəɷn ə te: 7 pɑ̆ɷnd ə ti: [ti:³,⁴]

16 Wo 1 paɷnd ə ti: 2 pɛɷnd ə te:ˡ [te:²] 3 pɛu:n ə te:ɪ [te:ɪ²] 4 pəɷ:n ə te: 5 pəɷ:nd ə te: 6 pɛu:nd ə te:ɪ 7 pæɷnd əv ti: [tɛɪkɛtl³ *t.-kettle*]

17 Wa 1 pæɷnd ə tᵉi: 2 pæɷnd ə ti:, p. pæɷnd ə tɛɪ [pref.; tɛɪ³⁽²ˣ⁾; tɛɪkadɪ³ *t.-caddy*] 3 pɛ̈ɷnd . ti: [ti:¹] 4 pɛɷnd ə ti: [tɛɪ¹] 5 pɛɷnd ə tɛɪ [tɛɪ¹] 6 pɛɷnd ə tɛ̨ɪ 7 pɛ̈ɷnd ə tɛɪ

23 Mon 1 pʌɷn ə tˡi: 2 pʌɷn ə ti: 3 pəɷn ə ti: 4 pʰəun ə tʰị: [tʰi:¹] 5 pəund ə ti: 6 pəɷn ə ti: 7 n.a. [ti:j¹; ti:klɔ:θ¹ *t.-cloth* V.9.6]

24 Gl 1 pəɷ:ᵊn ə te: 2 pəɷ:nd ə tɛɪ 3 pəɷn ə tˡi: [te:¹³] 4 pəɷnd ə te: [te:²] 5 pʌɷnd ə te: [te:²] 6 pᵊu:n ə ti: [ti:¹] 7 pᵊu:nd ə ti:

25 O 1 ir.r. tæɪ 2 pæɷnd ə teɪ [teɪ³, ti:¹] 3 pɛɷnd ə te: 4 paɷnd ə ti: [ti:⁴] 5–6 pɛ̈ɷnd ə ti:

VII.8.4 A‡ POUND

Q. If you wanted to know the price (of a pound of tea), *you'd ask: How much . . . .?*

Rr. (A) POUND, A §QUARTER

Note—For additional exs. of POUND, see VII.8.2 (and refs.).

7 Ch 1 ə paɪnd 2 ə pæ̧ɪnd(2x) 3 ə paɪnd 4 ə paɷnd 5 ə pɛɷnd 6 ə pɛ̧ɷnd

8 Db 1 n.a. 2 ə pɒnd 3 ə pɛ̧:nd 4 ə pɛ:nd 5 ə pa:nd 6–7 ə pɛ:nd

11 Sa 1 ə paɷn 2 ə pæɷn 3 ə paɷn 4 ə paɷnd 5 ə pɛɷn 6 n.r. 7 ə paɷn 8 ə pɛɷn 9 ə pɒɷn 10–11 ə paɷn

12 St 1 ə paɷnd 2–3 ə paɪnd 4 ə pæɷnd 5 ə paɷnd 6 ə pa:nd 7–8 ə pæɷnd 9 ə pa:ɷnd 10 ə pa:nd 11 ə pæɷnd

15 He 1–2 ə pæɷn 3 ə pɛɷn 4 ə pəɷn 5 ə pʌɷn 6 ə pəɷnd 7 ə pɑ̆ɷnd

16 Wo 1 ə paɷnd 2 ə pɛɷnd 3 ə pɛu:nd 4 ə pəɷ:n 5 ə pəɷ:nd 6 ə pɛu:nd 7 ə pæɷnd

17 Wa 1–2 ə pæɷnd 3 ə pɛ̈ɷnd 4–6 ə pɛɷnd 7 ə pɛ̈ɷnd

23 Mon 1–2 ə pʌɷn 3 ə pəɷn 4–5 ə pəund 6 ə pəɷn 7 n.a.

24 Gl 1 ə pəɷ:ən 2 ə pəɷ:nd 3 ə pəɷn 4 ə pəɷnd 5 ə pʌɷnd 6 ə pᴼu:n 7 ə pᴼu:nd

25 O 1 ə pɛ̈ɷnd 2 ə pæɷnd 3 ə pɛɷnd 4 ə §kwɔ·ɽtəɽ 5 ə pɛ̈ɷnd 6 ə pɛ̈ɷn

VII.8.5 OUNCE*

Q. *You buy your sweets by the . . . .*—Spring 1955, *tobacco* replaced *sweets*.

R. OUNCE

Note—The r. at 8.3 has a proclitic «n-» from the (unrecorded) indef. art. The same feature also characterises the i.m. form at 8.3 and the 2nd i.m. form at 15.7.

7 Ch 1 aɪns 2 æ̧ɪns 3 aɪns 4 aɷns 5 aɪns 6 ɛ̧ɷns

8 Db 1 ɛ̧ɷns 2 a:ns 3 nɛ̈ɷnts, ○nɛ̈ɷnts [rec. in «ə nɛ̈ɷnts» *an o.*] 4 ɛ:ns 5 ɛ̧:nts 6–7 ɛ:ns

11 Sa 1 aɷns 2 æɷns 3–4 aɷns 5 ɛɷns 6–7 aɷns 8 ɛɷns 9–11 aɷns

12 St 1 aɷns 2 aɪns 3 pp. aɪns 4 æɷns 5 ạɷns 6 a:ns 7 aɷnz [*sic*] 8–10 aɷns 11 æɷns

15 He 1–2 æɷns 3 ɛɷns 4 əɷns 5 ʌɷns 6 əɷns 7 əuns, °əu̯ns[3], °nǎu̯ns[4] [rec. in «ə nǎu̯ns» *an o.*]

16 Wo 1 aɷns 2 ɛɷns 3 ɛu:ns 4–5 əɷ:ns 6 ɛu:ns 7 æɷns

17 Wa 1–2 æɷns 3 ɛ̈ɷns 4 ɛɷnts 5 ɛɷns, °~[1] 6 ɛɷns 7 ɛ̈ɷns

23 Mon 1–2 ʌɷns 3 əɷns 4 əunʂ̬ 5 əɷns 6 əɷns 7 n.a.

24 Gl 1 əɷns 2 əɷ:ns 3–4 əɷns 5 ʌɷns 6 ᵊu:ns 7 ᵊu:nts

25 O 1 ɛ̈ɷns 2 æɷnts 3 ▫ɛɷnsɪz 4 ạɷns, °~[4] 5–6 ɛ̈ɷns

VII.8.6 PINCH

Q. What do you call a very small quantity of sugar or salt [g.]?

Rr. BIT, MITE, NIP, PINCH, SPOONFUL~SPOONTLE

Note 1—Some ii. used different expressions acc. substance. Accordingly, when rec., OF SUGAR and OF SALT are reproduced below untransliterated.

Note 2—The 1st r. at 12.3 represents SPOONFUL.

Note 3—For additional exs. of SALT(–), see III.12.5; and of SUGAR, see V.8.10.

7 Ch 1 pɪnʃ(2x) 2 pɛnʃ(2x) 3 pɛnʃ 4 pɪnʃ(2x) 5–6 pɪnʃ

8 Db 1 pɪntʃ 2–4 pɪnʃ 5–6 pɪntʃ 7 pɪnʃ, °pɪnʃ ə sɔ:t

11 Sa 1–11 pɪnʃ

12 St 1 pɪnʃ 2 pɪnʃ ə sɒlt 3 spɛɷntl, pɪntʃ ə soɷt 4–5 pɪnʃ 6 pɪntʃ ə sɒlt, °mɒ:ɪt ə ʃɷgə 7 bɪt ə ʃɷgə, bɪt ə sɒlt 8 pɪntʃ 9–11 pɪnʃ

15 He 1 bɪt 2–6 pɪnʃ 7 pɪnʃ ["salt"], bɪt ["sugar"]

16 Wo 1–4 pɪnʃ 5 pɪntʃ 6 pɪ:nʃ 7 pɪnʃ ə sɒlt, spu:nfɷl ə ʃɷgəʳ

17 Wa 1 pɪ̣nʃ 2 pɪnʃ əv sɔ:lt, spu:nfɷl əv ʃɷgə 3 nɪp 4 bɪt 5–7 pɪnʃ

23 Mon 1–3 pɪnʃ 4 n.a. 5–6 pɪnʃ 7 n.a.

24 Gl 1–4 pɪnʃ 5 pɪntʃ 6 pɪnʃ 7 pɪntʃ

25 O 1–2 pɪntʃ 3 pɪnʃ 4 pɪnʃ [ref. salt] 5 pɪnʃ 6 pɪntʃ

VII.8.7 A LOT OF MONEY

Q. A man is rich when he has . . . .

Rr. A LOT/POCKETFUL OF MONEY, §GOT MONEY, HANTLE OF MONEY, PLENTY ({OF} MONEY), PLENTY OF BRASS

Note 1—I.m. exs. of A LOT OF and comparable expressions are reproduced below between square brackets together with their context. These are followed by exs. of MONEY, untransliterated. Cross-refs. have been given only when the entire quotation is included in some other article.

Note 2—In the i.m. below, OF is frequently represented by ON.

Note 3—Expressions comparable with some of those listed above also occur at VII.8.8 and VII.8.13. Expressions for MONEY also occur at VII.8.8. For additional exs. of LOT, see VII.2.12.

7 Ch 1 plɛntι mɷnι 2 s.w. plɛntι mɷnι [ιz mɷnι ιn ιz pɒkιt *he's* (= *he has*) *m. in his pocket* (i.e. he is wealthy); ιz sɷm mɷnι^(2x) *he's* (= *he has*) *some m.* (i.e. he is wealthy); mɷnι[2]] 3 plɛntι ə mɷnι [ə lɒt ə land[2] *a lot of land*] 4 plɛntι ə mɷnˡι 5 plɛntι ə mɷnι 6 ə lɒt ə mɷnι

8 Db 1 plɛntι ə bɹas 2 plɛntι ə mɷnι, °~ 3–4 plɛntι ə mɷnι 5 ə lɒt ə mɷnι 6 plɛntι ə mɷnι 7 plɛntι

11 Sa 1 plɛntι ə bɹa:s 2 plɛntι ə mɷnι [ə lɒt n‿əm[2] *a lot of them*; mʌnι[2]] 3 plɛntι ə mʌnι 4 plɛntι ə mʌnι [plɛntι ə ðɛm[2] *p. of them*; mʌnι[2]] 5 plɛntι ə mɷnι 6 plɛntι ə mʌnι [plɛntι ɒn ιt[1] *p. of it*; plɛntι ə nιtιn[3] *p. of knitting*] 7 plɛntι ə mʌnι [plɛntι ə tιts[1] *p. of teats* III.8.4a; ə lɒt əv wɔ:təʳ[1] *a lot of water*] 8 plɛntι ə mɷnι [plɛntι ɒn ιt[1] *p. of it*; plɛntι ɒn əm[2] *p. of them*; sɷm kwɒntιtι ə stɛps[1] *some quantity of steps* (i.e. a lot of ss.); pɹιtι wɛl ə pasəndʒəz[2] *pretty well of passengers* (i.e. a lot of ps.)] 9 plɛntι ə mʌnι [plɛntι ɒn əm[1] *p. of them*; lɒts ə dιfɹənt ne:mz[1] *lots of different names*; mʌnι[1]] 10 plɛntι mʌnι [mʌnι[3]] 11 plɛntι ə mʌnι, plɛntι

12 St 1 plɛntι ə mɷnι [plɛntι ə stɒk *p. of stock*; ə lɒt əv əs stɷf[1] *a lot of us* (i.e. our) *stuff*] 2 plɛntι ə mɷnι [plɛntι ə fɹɛnz[2] *p. of friends*] 3 plɛntι ə mɷnι [ə lɒt ə kɔ:n[2] *a lot of corn*; ə ˈtɹιmɛndəs lɒt ə tʃi:ndʒιz[1] *a tremendous l. of changes*; pɹιtι wɛl ə lɛιbə[2] *pretty well of labour* (i.e. a lot of l.)] 4 §gɒt mɷnι 5 plɛntι ə mɷnι, °~[1] 6 p. ə lɒt ə mɷnι, °antl ə mɷnι[1] [bɹas[1] *brass* (i.e. money)] 7 plɛntι ə mɷnι [mɷnι[3]] 8 ə pɒkιtfɷl ə mɷnι [plɛntι ə fi:lɹu:m *plenty of field-room*; mɷnι[2] *money*; poɷk[2] *? poke* (i.e. money)] 9 ə lɒt ə mɷnι [mɷnι[2]] 10 plɛntι ə mɷnι 11 ir.r. [lɒts ə tɒιmz[2] *lots of times*]

15 He 1–2 plɛntι ə mʌnι 3 plɛntι ə mɷnι [plɛntι ə dɷst *p. of dust* (i.e. money)] 4 plɛntι ə mʌnι [plɛntι ɒn əm[2] *p. of them*; ə lɒt ən əm[1] *a lot of them*] 5 plɛntι ə mɷnι 6 plɛntι ə mɷnι [plɛntι ə ɹɷm[1] *p. of room*; mɷnι[1]] 7 ə lɒt ə mʌnι [ə lɒt ə stoɷn[2] *a l. of stone*; lɒts ə flăʉəɹz[1] *ls. of flowers*; lɒts ə stʌf[3] *ls. of stuff*; lɒts ə faɹməɹz[3] *ls. of farmers*]

16 Wo 1 plɛntι ə mωnι [ə lɒt ɒn ιt[1] *a lot of it*] 2 plɛntι ə mωnι 3 plɛntι ə mωni: 4 plɛntι ə mωnι [lɒts ə waιz[1] *lots of ways*; mɒnι[3]] 5 plɛntι mωnι 6 plɛntι ə mωnι 7 plɛntι ə mωnι, plɛntι ə bɹɑ:s [pref.; ə lət əv ɹẽĩn[1] *a lot of rain*; ə lət ə pi:pl[3] *a l. of people*; ə lət ə bωtə[4] *a l. of butter*]

17 Wa 1 plɛntι ə mωnᵊι 2 plɛntι ə mωnι [ə lət ən ιt[2] *a lot of it*; ə lət ən əm[2(2x)] *a l. of them*; plɛntι ə θιŋz[4] *plenty of things*] 3 plɛntˈĭ, plɛntι əv mʌnι 4 plɛntι ə mωnˈι 5 ə lɒt ə mωnι 6 plɛntι ə mωnᵊι [ə lɒt əv ωntιn[3] *a lot of hunting*] 7 plɛntι ə mωnι

23 Mon 1 plɛntι mʌnι 2 plɛntι ə mωnι 3 plɛntι ə mʌnι [mʌnι[2]] 4 n.a. 5 ə lɒ̤̂·t ə mʌ̤̃nι [ləuzi wι mʌ̤̃ni *lousy with money* (i.e. very rich)] 6 plɛntι ə mʌnι [ωf *? huff* (="*money*")] 7 n.a.

24 Gl 1 plɛntι ə mωnι [məω:nts ɒn əm[3] *amounts of them* (i.e. a lot of them)] 2 plɛntι ə mωnι [ə lɑ:t ə ðɑ:t[2] *a lot of that*; ə lɒt ɒn ιt[3] *a l. of it*; dæω[3] *dough* (i.e. money; "old")] 3 plɛntι ə mωnι [plɛntι ə ðæι[2(2x)] *p. of those*; plɛntι ɒn əm[2] *p. of them*] 4 plɛntι ə mωnι [dɒω *dough* (i.e. money)] 5 plɛntι ə mωnι 6 plɛntι ə mənι 7 plɛnι ə mə·nι

25 O 1 plɛnʔι ə mʌnι, ○~[2] 2 ə lɑt ə mənι 3 plɛntι ə mʌnι 4 ə łɒd̥ əv mωnι, ○ə łɒt əv mə̃nι[5] [ə łɒd̥ əv θιŋz[4] *a l. of things*; ə łɒd̥ əv bəɽɖʐ[4] *a l. of birds*; ə łɒt əv kωzənz[5] *a l. of cousins*; mωnι[4]] 5 plɛnι ə mʌnι [ə lɒʔ ə mιłkιn[2] *a lot of milking*] 6 plɛnʔι ə mω̣nι

VII.8.8 IF

Q. We could and would do lots of things in this world [rattle some coins] . . . . *we had the money.*

R. IF

7 Ch 1 ιf, ○~ [plus «wι‿d mωnι ʔ dʏ: ιt wιð» *we'd money to do it with*], ○~[2(2x)] 2 ι̹f [plus «wι ad mωnι» *we had money*], ○ιf[1(4x),2(6x),3(2x),4(5x)] 3 ιf [plus «wι‿d gɛtn‿ð mωnι» *we'd got the money*], ○~[1(2x),2] 4 ιf, ○~[1,2(2x)] 5 ιf, ○~[1(4x)] 6 ιf, ○~[1,2(2x)]

8 Db 1 ιf 2 ιf, ○~ [plus «ðι‿d plɛntι ə mωnι» *they'd plenty of money*], ○~[4] 3–5 ιf 6 ιf, ○~[1] 7 ιf, ○~[1(2x),2]

11 Sa 1 ιf 2 ιf, ○~[3] 3 ιf, ○~[2(2x)] 4–6 ιf 7 ιf, ○~[1] 8 ιf, ○~[2(4x)] 9 ιf, ○~[1(3x)] 10 ιf, ○~[3(3x)] 11 ιf, ○~[1(2x),2]

12 St 1 ɪf, ○~$^{1(2x),2}$ 2 ɪf [plus «wɪ‿d gɒt ðə mɷnɪ» *we'd got the money*], ○~^{1,2} 3 ɪf [plus «wɪ‿d gɒt plɛntɪ ə mɷnɪ» *we'd got plenty of money*], ○~$^{1(4x),2(5x)}$ 4 ɪf, ○~$^{2(3x)}$ 5 ɪf [plus «jə‿d oɷnlɪ gɒt ðə mɷnɪ» *you'd only got the money*], ○~$^{2(7x),3(3x)}$ 6 ɪf [plus «wɪ‿d gɒt ðə dɛɷ-ɪnz *we'd got the doings*], ○~$^{1(9x),2(4x),3}$ 7 ɪf [plus «wɪ‿d gɒt sɷm ɛl ɛs di:» *we'd got some L.s.d.*], ○~$^{1(2x),2,3}$ 8 ɪf [plus «wi: ad gɒt plɛntɪ ə mɷnɪ» *we had got plenty of money*], ○~$^{1(4x),2(2x)}$ 9 ɪf [plus «wɪ‿d gɒt sɷmət ɪn ə pɒkɪt» *we'd got somewhat in our pocket*], ○~$^{1(2x),2(3x),3(2x)}$ 10 ɪf [plus «wɪ ad gɒt ðə mɷnɪ» *we had got the money*] ,○~^{6} 11 ɪf [plus «jə wəz nɒt ʃɔ:t ə mɷnɪ» *you were not short of money*], ○~$^{1(3x),2(2x)}$

15 He 1 ɪf, ○~^{1,2} 2 ɪf, ○~^{2,3} 3 ɪf, ○~$^{2(3x)}$ 4 ɪf, ○~^{2} 5–6 ɪf 7 ɪf [plus «wɪ ad ðə kaʃ» *we had the cash*], ○~$^{1(6x),2,3(5x),4(6x)}$

16 Wo 1 ɪf, ○~^{1,2} 2 ɪf, ○~^{1} 3 ɪf, ○~$^{1(2x),2}$, ○f^{1} [rec. in «tə ˈsi: ˈf‿i:z . . . .» *to see if he's . . . .*] 4 ɪf, ○~^{2} 5 ɪf, ○~$^{1(2x)}$ 6 ɪf, ○~^{1} 7 ɪf [plus «wi:‿d gɒt ðə doɷ» *we'd got the dough (=money)*], ○~$^{1(2x),3(5x),4(2x)}$

17 Wa 1 ɪf, ○~^{1} 2 ɪf [plus «wɪ‿d gət ðə kaʃ» *we'd got the cash*], ○~$^{1(3x),3(6x),4(7x)}$ 3–4 ɪf 5 ɪf, ○~$^{1(10x)}$ 6 ɪf, ○~$^{4(2x)}$ 7 ɪf, ○~$^{1(2x),2}$

23 Mon 1 ɪf, ○~$^{2(3x)}$ 2 ɪf 3 ɪf, ○~^{1} 4 ɪf, ○~$^{1(5x),2}$ 5 ɪf, ○~$^{1(3x),2(5x)}$ 6 ɪf, ○~^{2} 7 n.a., ○ɪf^{1}

24 Gl 1 ɪf, ○~^{1} 2 ɪf 3–4 ɪf, ○~^{1} 5 ɪf, ○~^{2} 6 ɪf, ○~$^{1,2(2x)}$ 7 ɪf

25 O 1 ɪf, ○~^{1} 2 ɪf, ○~$^{2(2x)}$ 3 ɪf, ○~$^{1(3x)}$ 4 ɪf [plus «wɪ‿d gɒt ðə mɷnɪ» *we'd got the money*], ○~$^{1(6x),3,4(6x),5}$ 5 ɪf, ○~$^{2(8x)}$ 6 ɪf, ○~$^{1(3x)}$

VII.8.9 MISER

Q. What do you call a man who has a lot of money, but still goes on saving every penny?

Rr. MISER(D), ? SCRAWMER, §SCROUNGER, SKINFLINT

7 Ch 1 mɑɪzəᴵ, mɛɪzəᴵ ["older"] 2 maɪzə 3 mɛɪzə 4 mɑɪzə 5 mɛɪzə 6 mɑɪzə

8 Db 1 mɛɪzə, maɪzə 2 mɑɪzə 3 maɪzə 4 mɑɪzəᴵ 5 mɑɪzə 6–7 mɑ̃·ɪ̃zə

11 Sa 1 maɪzəʳ 2 maɪzə 3 mɛɪzəʳ 4–7 maɪzəʳ 8 mɒɪzəʳ 9 maɪzəʳ:ɭ 10 maɪzəʳ 11 mɒɪzəʳ

12 St 1 mɒɪzə 2 mɒɪzə, skɹoɷmə ["older"] 3 mɒ:ɪzə, §skɹɔ:ndʒə 4 mɒɪzə 5–6 mɒ:ɪzə 7–9 mɒɪzə 10 mɑɪzə 11 maɪzəɹ

15 He 1–2 mæɪzəʳ 3 məɪzəʳd̨ 4–6 məɪzəʳ 7 maɪzəɹ

16 Wo 1 mɒɪzə 2 məɪzəʳ 3 mɒɪzəʳ:d̨ 4–5 məɪzəʳ 6 mɒɪzɷd 7 p. skɪnflɪnt, məɪzəʳ [usu.]

17 Wa 1 mɒɪzə 2–3 məɪzə 4–7 məɪzəʳ

23 Mon 1–2 məɪzəʳ 3 məɪzə 4 n.a. 5 məɪzzɐ 6 məɪzəʳ 7 n.a.

24 Gl 1 məɪzəʳ 2–3 məɪzəʳd̨ 4 məɪzəʳ 5 mə̈ɪzəʳ 6–7 mʌɪzəʳ

25 O 1 mə̈ɪzəʳ 2 mə̈ɪzəɹ̣ 3 mə̈ɪzəʳ 4 məɪzəɽ 5 mʌʏzəʳ 6 mə̈ɪzəʳ

VII.8.10 HANDFUL, DOUBLE HANDFUL, ARMFUL

Q. What do you call this much [*i.*]*?*

Rr. FISTFUL, HANDFUL~HANTLE

COUPLE OF HAND(S)FUL, DOUBLE HANDFUL~HANTLE, TWO FISTFULS/HAND(S)FUL/HANDFULS/HANTLE

ARMFUL, ARMTLEFUL, BOLTING

Note 1—The rr. to the three parts of the q. are separated below by full stops.

Note 2—For additional exs. of ARM(–), see VI.6.7/8; of DOUBLE–, see VI.5.7; of FIST, see VI.7.4; of HAND, see VI.7.1 (and refs.); of –FUL, see V.1.16/17 and V.10.5; and of TWO, see VII.1.2 (and refs.).

7 Ch 1 anfɷl . dɷbl anfɷl . a:mfɷl 2 anfɷl . tü: anfɷl . a:mfɷl 3 anfɷl, antl ["older"] . dɷbl antl . a:mfɷl, °a:mtlfɷl 4 anfɷl . dɷbl anfɷl . ɑ:mfɷl 5–6 anfɷl . dɷbl anfɷl . a:mfɷl

8 Db 1 ɒnfɷl . tʏ: ɒnfɷl . aɹ̣:mfɷl 2 anfɷl . dɷbl anfɷl . n.r. 3 anfɷl, ɒnfɷl ["older"] . tü: ɒnfɷl . a:mfɷl 4 anfɷl . dɷbl anfɷl . a:mfɷl 5 anfɷl . tɛɷ anzfɷl . a:mfɷl 6 anfɷl . dɷbl anfɷl . a:mfɷl 7 anfɷl . dɷbl anfɷl . a:mfɷl

11 Sa 1 anfəl . kʌpl ə anfəl . aʳ:mfəl 2 anfəl . tɪu anfəl . a:mfəl 3 fɪsfəl . tu: fɪsfəlz . aʳ:mfəl 4 a:nfəl . dʌbl a:nfəl . aʳ:mfəl 5 anfəl . dɷbl anfəl . aʳ:mfəl 6 fɪsfəl . kʌpl əv a·nfəl . aʳ:mfəl 7 æ:nfəl . dʌbl æ:nfəl . aʳ:mfəl 8 ɒnfl . dɷbl ɒnfl . aʳ:mfl 9 ænfəl . dʌbl æ·nfəl . aʳ:mfəl 10 ænfəl . dʌbl ænfəl . aʳ:mfəl 11 ɒnfl . dɷbl ɒnfl . aʳ:mfl

12 St 1 andfɷl. dɷbl andfɷl. a:mfɷl 2 andfɷl, antl. tɛɷ antl. a:mfɷl 3 ɒntl. dɷbl ɒntl. a:mfəl 4 andfɷl. dɷbl andfɷl. a:mfɷl 5 andfɷl, ɑntl ["old"]. tü: andzfɷl, dɷbl antl. a:mfɷl 6 ɒndfəl, antl. dɷbl ɒndfəl. a:mfəl 7 andfɷl. tü: andfɷlz. a:mfɷl 8 andfɷl. dɷbl andfɷl. ɑ:mfɷl 9 andfɷl, antl. dɷbl andfəl. a:mfɷl 10 andfɷl. kɷpl əv andzfɷl. a:mfɷl 11 anfɷl. dɷbl anfɷl. ȧ:mfɷl

15 He 1 ænfəɫ. dʌbl ænfəɫ. aʳ:mfəɫ 2 ænfəɫ. tu: ænfəɫz. aʳmfəɫ 3 ænfəɫ. dɷbɫ ænfəɫ. aʳ:mfəɫ 4 ɒnfəɫ. dɷbɫ ɒnfɫ. ɑʳ:mfəɫ 5 ænfəl. dɷbɫ ænfəɫ. aʳ:mfəl 6 ænfəɫ. dɷbɫ ænfəɫ. aʳ:mfəɫ 7 anfɷl. kʌpəl ə anfɷl. aɪmfɷl

16 Wo 1 ɒnfəl. dɷbl ɒnfəl. ɑ:mfəl 2 anfəɫ. dɷbɫ anfəɫ. a:mfəɫ 3 ænfəɫ. dɷbɫ ænfəɫ . aʳ:mfəɫ 4 ɒnfɷɫ. dɷbɫ ɒnfɷɫ. ɑʳ:mfɷɫ 5 ɒnfɷl. dɷbɫ ɒnfɷɫ. aʳ:mfɷɫ 6 ænfɷl. dɷbl ænfɷɫ. aʳ:mfɷɫ 7 anfɷl. dɷbɫ anfɷl. ɑ:mfɷl

17 Wa 1 anfɷl. dɷbl anfɷl. a:mfɷl 2 anfɷl. dɷbl anfɷl. ä:mfɷl 3 ænfɷɫ. dʌbɫ ænfɷɫ. a:mfɷɫ 4 anfɷl. tü: anfɷlz. a:mfɷɫ 5–7 anfɷɫ. dʌbɫ anfɷɫ. aʳ:mfɷɫ

23 Mon 1 ænfəɫ. dʌbɫ ænfəɫ. aʳ:mfəɫ 2 ænfəɫ. dɷbɫ ænfəɫ. a:mfəɫ 3 a:nfəɫ, ○∼². dʌbl a:nfəɫ. a:mfəɫ 4 n.a. 5 anfɷɫ. tu: anfɷɫz. a:mfɷɫ 6 ænfəɫ. dʌbɫ ænfəl. bo:ɫtɩn 7 n.a.

24 Gl 1–2 ɒnvəɫ. dɷbɫ ɒnvəɫ. aʳmfəɫ 3 ænvəɫ. dʌbɫ ænvəɫ. aʳ:mvəɫ 4 anvəɫ. dɷbɫ anvəɫ. aʳ:mvəɫ 5 anfɷɫ. dʌbɫ anfɷɫ, dɷbɫ anfɷɫ. əʳ:mfɷɫ 6 anfɷɫ, anvɷɫ ["older"]. dɷbl anvɷɫ. aʳ:mvɷɫ 7 anvɷɫ, ○□anvɷɫz¹, ○□anfɷɫz¹. dɷbɫ anvɷɫ. aʳ:mvɷɫ

25 O 1–2 anfɷɫ. dʌbl anfɷɫ. aʳ:mfɷɫ 3 anfɫ. dʌbl anfɫ. aʳ:mfɫ 4 anfɷɫ. dɷbɫ anfɷɫ. äʳmfɷl 5 anfɫ. dʌbɫ anfɫ. aʳmfɫ 6 anfɷɫ. dʌbɫ anfɷɫ. aʳ:mfɷɫ

VII.8.11 HOW MANY?

Q. You go to the grocer's shop for eggs, and the grocer asks . . . .

R. HOW MANY?

Note 1—I.m. exs. of MANY are reproduced below between square brackets untransliterated.

Note 2—For additional exs. of HOW, see VI.12.4 and VIII.2.8.

7 Ch 1 aɪ mɛnɪ$^{(2x)}$ 2 s.w. æɷ mɛnɪ [mɛnɪ$^{2(3x),3(3x),4(2x)}$] 3 aɪ mɛnɪ 4 aɷ mɛnɪ$^{(2x)}$ 5 aɪ mɛnɪ, a: mɛnɪ 6 aɷ mɛnɪ [mɛnɪ$^{2(2x),3}$]

8 Db 1 ɛ̧ɷ mɛnɪ [mɒnɪ^{1}] 2 a: mɛnɪ 3 ɛ: mənə, °ɛ: mənɪ, °ɛɷ mɛnɪ^{2} 4 ɛ: mɛnɪ, °~ [mɛnɪ^{2}] 5 ɛ̧:^{ə} mɒnɪ 6 ɛ: mɛnɪ [mɛnɪ^{1}] 7 ɛ: mɛnɪ

11 Sa 1 aɷ mɛnɪ 2 æɷ mɛnɪ 3 aɷ mɛnɪ [mɛnɪ^{2}] 4–5 ɛɷ mɛnɪ 6 aɷ mɛnɪ [mɛnɪ$^{1(2x)}$] 7 aɷ mɛnɪ [mɛnɪ^{1}] 8 ɛɷ mɛnɪ$^{(2x)}$ [mɛnɪ^{1,2}] 9 aɷ mɛnɪ 10–11 aɷ mɛnɪ [mɛnɪ^{2}]

12 St 1 a mɛnɪ [mɛnɪ$^{1(2x)}$, mɛnɪ·^{3}, mɛnə^{1}] 2 a: mɛnɪ [mɛnɪ$^{2(2x),3,5}$] 3 a: mɛnɪ, °~^{1} [mɛnɪ$^{1(2x)}$] 4 æɷ mɛnɪ [mɛnɪ^{3}; æɷ mɷtʃ^{1} *how much*] 5 a: mɛnɪ [mɛnɪ$^{1,2(3x),3(2x)}$] 6 æ: mɛnɪ [mɛnɪ$^{1(3x),2(2x)}$] 7–8 a: mɛnɪ 9 aɷ mɛnɪ [mɛnɪ$^{1,2(3x)}$] 10 a: mɛnɪ 11 æɷ mɛnɪ [mɛnɪ$^{1(2x)}$]

15 He 1 æɷ mɛnɪ [mɛnɪ^{1}] 2 æɷ mɛnɪ 3 ɛɷ mɛnɪ, °~^{2} [mɛnɪ^{1}] 4 əɷ mɛnɪ 5 ʌɷ mɛnɪ 6 əɷ mɛnɪ [mɛnɪ^{1}] 7 ăɷ mɛnɪ, °u: mɛnɪ^{2} [mɛnɪ$^{2,3(2x),4}$]

16 Wo 1–2 ɛɷ mɛnɪ 3 ɛu: mɛni: [mɛnɪ^{3}] 4 əɷ: mɛnɪ [mɛnɪ^{1,2}] 5 əɷ: mɛnɪ [mɛnɪ$^{1(2x)}$] 6 ɛu: mɛnɪ [mɛnɪ^{2}] 7 æɷ mɛnɪ [mɛnɪ$^{1(3x),3(2x),4(2x)}$]

17 Wa 1 æɷ mɛn^{e}ɪ 2 æɷ mɛnɪ [mɛnɪ$^{1(2x),2(3x),3(2x)}$] 3 ɛ̈ɷ mɛnɪ̈ 4 ɛɷ mɛnɪ 5 ɛɷ mɛnɪ [mɛnɪ$^{1(2x)}$] 6 ɛɷ mɛnɪ [mɛnɪ^{4}] 7 ɛ̈ɷ mɛnɪ

23 Mon 1–2 ʌɷ mɛnɪ 3 əɷ mɛnɪ [mɛnɪ^{1}] 4 n.a. [mɛni̯^{2}] 5 əu mɛni [mɛni^{2}] 6 əɷ mɛnɪ 7 n.a.

24 Gl 1 əɷ: mɛnɪ [mɛnj^{1} rec. in «mɛnj‿ə təɪ^{ə}m» *many a time*] 2–3 əɷ mɛnɪ 4 əɷ mɛnɪ [mɛnɪ^{2}] 5 ʌɷ mɛnɪ [mɛnɪ] 6–7 ^{ɷ}u: mɛnɪ

25 O 1 ɛ̈ɷ mɛnɪ 2 æɷ mɛnɪ, °æ̧ɷ mɛnɪ^{1} [mɛnɪ^{2}] 3 ɛɷ mɛnɪ [mɛnɪ^{1,2}] 4 aɷ mɛnɪ [mɛnɪ$^{5(3x)}$] 5–6 ɛ̈ɷ mɛnɪ

VII.8.12 ONLY

Q. If your little girl Mary did something wrong, you wouldn't be so hard on her as a grown-up, you'd say: After all, Mary is . . . . a child.

Rr. (NOUGHT) BUT, ONLY

7 Ch 1 o:nɪ, nɛɷt bət 2 s.w. o̧:nlɪ 3–4 o:nɪ 5 o̧:nɪ 6 o:nɪ

8 Db 1 nɒbət, o:nɪ 2 nɒbət, °o:nɪ^{2} 3–4 o:nɪ 5–6 o:^{ɷ}nɪ 7 o:nɪ, °~

11 Sa 1 o:nlɪ 2 o:nɪ 3 o:nlɪ 4–7 o:nɪ 8 o:nɪ, °~$^{1(2x)}$ 9 o:nlɪ, °~^{1} 10 o:nɪ, °~^{3} 11 o:nɪ, °bʌt^{2}

12 St 1 oɷnlɩ, °bɷt^{1} 2 oɷnlɩ 3 oọnlɩ, oɷnlɩ^{1}, oɷnɩ^{2} 4 oɷnlɩ 5–6 oɷnlɩ, °ɷ:nlɩ^{2} 7 oɷnlɩ, °~^{4}, °oɷnɩ^{1} 8 oɷnlɩ, °~^{1,3} 9–11 oɷnlɩ

15 He 1 o:nɩ 2 o:nɫɩ 3–5 o:nɩ 6 o:nɩ, °~^{1} 7 oɷnlɩ, °~^{4}, °o:nlɩ^{4}

16 Wo 1 ɒɷnlɩ, °~^{2} 2 oɷnɩ 3 oɷnɩ$^{(2x)}$, °oɷnlɩ^{2,3} 4 o:nɩ, °ɒɷnɫɩ^{1} 5 ɒɷnɫɩ, °bɷt^{1} 6 oɷnɩ, °~^{2} 7 p. ɔ:nlɩ, s.w. ɔ:nɩ, °~$^{1,3(2x),4(5x)}$, °ɔ:nlɩ^{3}

17 Wa 1 ọɷnlɩ 2 ɔɷnɩ, °ɔ:nɩ^{1,2}, °ɔ:nlɩ^{1}, °ənɩ^{3}, °bət^{2} 3 ọɷnɩ$^{(2x)}$ 4 ọɷnlɩ 5 ɔ:nɩ, °ọɷnɩ^{1} 6 ọɷnlɩ 7 ọɷnɫɩ

23 Mon 1 o:ɷnɫɩ 2–3 o:nɫɩ 4 n.a., °o:nli^{2} 5 ọ:ni 6 o:nɫɩ 7 n.a.

24 Gl 1 o:ɷnɫɩ 2 o:ɷnɩ 3 ɷnɩ, °ɷnɫɩ^{3} 4 ɒɷnɩ 5–6 o:nɩ 7 o:nɩ, °~$^{1(2x)}$

25 O 1 ɷnlɩ 2 ɔɷnɩ, °ənɩ^{1}, °oɷnɩ^{2} 3 ọɷnlɩ 4 o:nɩ, °~$^{2,4(3x),5}$ 5 ɔ·ɷnɩ 6 oɷnɩ

VII.8.13 A GOOD DEAL MORE*

Q. You are doing some work, but you've so far done only very little of it. So you still have how much to do?

Rr. A /DEVIL OF A/GREAT/GOOD/LARGE/TERRIBLE/ LOT MORE, A LOT (MORE), A SMARTISH /BIT MORE/LOT/, EVER SO MUCH, (A /GOOD {BIT}/{GOOD} DEAL/) MORE, QUITE A BIT

Note 1—Some ii. included (FOR) TO DO in their r. When so rec., this has been reproduced below. Occ. the TO was here absorbed in the adjacent sounds.

Note 2—Occ. the f.ws. omitted to rec. the wanted MORE. I.m. exs. of MORE are reproduced below between square brackets untransliterated.

Note 3—Expressions comparable with some of those listed above also occur at VII.8.7. For additional exs. of MORE, see V.1.17 and VI.12.4.

7 Ch 1 ə lɒt mʏ:əɹ 2 ə lət dü:, ə lət fə‿t dü: [mɷə$^{1,2(2x),3,4(2x)}$] 3 ə gɷd lɒt mˈʏ:ə 4 ɛvə sə mɷtʃ ["usu."], p. mọə 5 ə gɷd dɛɩl mʏ:ə [mˈʏə^{1}] 6 ə lɒt mo·ə

8 Db 1 ə gɷd lɒt mʏ·ə̱ [mʏ·ə̱] 2 ə gɷd lɒt mɷə 3 ə de:ˈl mo·ə 4 ə lɒt mo·ə 5 ə gɷd lɒt mo:ᵊ 6 ə lɒt, p. ə lɒt mu·ə 7 ə gɹɛt lɒt mo·ə

11 Sa 1 ə lɒt məɽ: 2 ə lɒt mo:ə 3 ə lɒt məɽ:əɽ 4 ə lɒt mɔ:ᵊ 5 ə lɒt mo:əɽ 6 ə lɒt mɔ:əɽ 7 ə lɒt mo:əɽ [nɒt ə gɹe:t lɒt *not a great lot*] 8 ə lɒt moəɽ 9 ə lɒt moəɽ [moəɽ^{1}] 10 ə lɒt moəɽ [mo:əɽɽ‿^{3} (+ V.)] 11 ə lɒt moɔ:ɽ

12 St 1 ə lɒt mɷə [mɷə[1], mɔ:[2], moɷə[4]] 2 ə lɒt moɷə 3 ə lɒt mɷ:ə· [mɷə[1,2]] 4 ə lɒt mɔ: 5 ə lɒt mɷ·ə [mɔ:ɹ[2] (+ V.)] 6 ə lɒt dɛɷ, ə lɒt mɷ:ə [mɔ:[1], mɷə[1], mɷ:ə[2]] 7 ə la:dʒ lɒt mɔ: 8 ə lɒt mɔ: tə dü: [mɔ:[1]] 9 ə lɒt mɷə [mɷə[1], mɔ:ɹ[2] (+ V.)] 10 ə lɒt mɔ: 11 ə lɔt mọə

15 He 1 ə gɷd bɪt mo:əʳ 2 ə lɒt mo:əʳ [mo:əʳ[2] (+ V.), mo:əʳ[3]] 3–4 ə lɒt mo:əʳ 5 ə lɒt mo:əʳ [mo:əʳ[4]] 6 ə lɒt mo:əʳ 7 ə lɒt mɔəɹ tə du: [mɔəɹ[1] (+ V.), mɔ·ɹ[2], mɔ·əɹ[3]]

16 Wo 1 ə lɒt mɔ:ə 2 ə lɒt mo:əʳ 3 ə lɒt mo:əʳ [mo:əʳ[1], məʳ:[1]] 4 ə lɒt moəʳ [mɑʳ:[2]] 5 ə lɒt mo:əʳ 6 ə lɑ:t moɷəʳ [mɷəʳ[3]] 7 p. ə lɔt tə du:, pp. ə lɔt moəʳ tə du: [moə[3(2x),4], mɷə[3(2x)], mọə[3]]

17 Wa 1 ə gɷd mɔ: 2 ə lɔt mɔə tə du: [mɷə[3]] 3 ə lɒt moə 4 ə gɷd lɒt mọ·ə 5 ə dɛvɬ əv ə lɒt mo·əʳ [mɒɷəʳ[1]] 6 ə tɛɹəbl lɒt mo·əʳ 7 ə lɒt moɷəʳ

23 Mon 1–2 ə lɒt mo:əʳ 3 ə lɒt mo:ə 4 kwəitʰ ə bitʰ [mɔ:[3]] 5 ə lɒ̥·t˳ mọ: [mọu[1]] 6 ə ɬɒt mo:əʳ 7 n.a.

24 Gl 1 ə lɒt mo:əʳ [nə mo:əʳ[1] *no more*] 2 ə lɒt mo:əʳ 3–4 ə lɒt mɒɷəʳ 5 ə lɒt mo·əʳ 6 ə gɷd lɒt mo·əʳ 7 ə lɒt mo:ɽ [+ V.]

25 O 1 ə smaʳ:ʔɪʃ lɒt 2 ə gɷd lɑt mɷəʳ, ○~[1] 3 ə lɒt mɷəʳ 4 ə ɬɒt mɔ·əɽ tə du: [mɔ·ɽ[5]] 5 ə smaʳ:ʔɪʃ bɪʔ moəʳ 6 ə lɒʔ moəʳ tə du:

VII.8.14 NOTHING

Q. What's in my pocket [show an empty pocket]?

Rr. NOTHING, NAUGHT

Note—For additional exs. of NAUGHT, see VII.8.12. For ANYTHING and AUGHT, see V.8.16.

7 Ch 1 nɛɷt 2 næɷt, ○~[1,2,3(2x)], ○~[2] VI.13.15, ○nɔɷt[2], ○nɛɷt[2], ○nɛ̈ɷt[2], ○~[2] VI.7.14, ○naɷt[3] 3 nɛ̈ɷt, ○nɛɷt[3] 4 nɒɷt, ○nɷθɪn[2] IX.1.10 5 nɛɷt, ○~[3], ○naɪt[1] [rec. in «naɪt əbaɪt ɪt» *n. about it*] 6 nɒɷt

8 Db 1 nɒɷt, ○~[3] 2 nɒɷt, ○~[4] 3 nɛ̈ɷtʻ 4 nɛɷt, ○~[3] 5 nɛɷt, ○nɒɷt[1] 6 nɛɷt, ○~[1] 7 nɛɷt

11 Sa 1 naɷt 2 næɷt 3 nʌθɪn, ○nʌðɪn[2] 4 nʌθɪn 5 nɷθɪn, ○nɒθɪn[2] 6 nʌθɪn, ○~[3,4] 7 nʌθɪn, ○~[1] 8 nɛɷt, ○nɷθɪn[1(2x),2] 9 nʌθɪn, ○nʌðɪn[1], ○nɒθɪn[1] 10 nʌθɪn, ○nɒθɪn[3] 11 nɷðɪn, ○nɒθɪn[2], ○no:t[(2x)]

12 St 1 nɷθɩŋ, noɷt ["older"], °~, °nɷθɩŋ[1] 2 nɛɷt 3 næɷt, °~[2], °naɷt[1], °nɷθɩŋk[2] 4 nɷθɩŋk, °~[2] 5 næɷt, °naɷt[3], °nɷθɩŋk[1] 6 nɛɷt, °~[2], °nɛɷt[2], °noɷt[1(2x)], °nɷθɩŋk[2] 7 nɷθɩŋk, °~[1(2x)] 8 noɷt 9 nɛɷt, °noɷt[2], °nɷθɩŋk[1,2], °nɷθɩn[3] 10 nɷθɩŋk, noɷt, °~[5] 11 nɷθɩŋk, °~[1,2], °nɷtn[2], °nɷθɩn[2]

15 He 1 nʌθɩn, °nʌfɩn[1] 2 nʌθɩn 3 nɷfɩŋ, °nɷθɩn[1] 4 nɷθɩn, °nʌθɩnt[2] 5 nɷθɩn, °~[4], °nʌθɩn[1] 6 nɷðən 7 nʌθɩn, °~[3], °nʌθɩŋ[1]

16 Wo 1 nɷθɩŋk 2 nɷθɩŋk, °nɷθɩnk[2] [? error for «-ŋk», Edd.] 3 nɷθɩn, °nɷθɩŋk[1] 4 nəɷ:t 5 nɷθɩŋk, °~[1(2x)] 6 nɷθɩn, °nɷθɩŋ[1], °nɷθɩŋg̊[2] 7 nəθɩŋk, °nɷθɩŋk[3(2x)]

17 Wa 1 nɷθɩŋk 2 nɷθɩŋk, p. nəɷt, °nɷθɩŋ[1,4(2x)], °nɷθɩŋk[4(3x)] 3 nɷθɩŋk 4 noɷt, nɷθɩŋ 5 nɷθɩn 6 nɛɷt 7 nɷθɩn, p. nɛɷt

23 Mon 1 nʌθɩn, °~[2,3] 2 nɷθɩn, °~[3] 3 nʌθɩn, °~[1,2] 4 n.a. 5 nʌ̰̈θɩn, °~[2] 6 nʌθɩn 7 n.a.

24 Gl 1 nɷθɩn, °~[2,3] 2 nɷθən, °nɷθɩn[3] 3 nʌθɩn 4–5 nɷθn 6 nəθɩn 7 nəθɩn, °~

25 O 1 noɷt 2 nəɷt, °nʌθɩn[1], °nɷθn[1] 3 nəθɩn 4 nɷθən, °nɷ̰̈ðən[5] 5 nəɷt 6 nʌθɩŋk

VII.8.15 SOMETHING

Q. But in this one [*show a full pocket*] *there's not* nothing, *there's . . . .*

Rr. SOMETHING, SOMEWHAT

Note—For additional exs. of SOME(-), see V.8.4.

7 Ch 1 sɷməʔ, °sɷmθɩn[4] 2 sɷmət, °~[2(3x),3,4], °sɷmθɩŋ[1] 3 sɷmət 4 sɷmət, °~[2] 5 sɷmət 6 sɷmət, °~[3(2x)]

8 Db 1 sɷmət, °~[1(3x),3] 2 sɷmət 3 sɷmətʻ 4 sɷmət 5 sɷmət, °~[2,4] 6–7 sɷmət

11 Sa 1 səmət 2 sɷmət, °~[2(2x)], °sɷmθɩŋk[3] 3 sʌmθɩn 4 sʌmθɩŋk 5 sɷmət, °~[3], °sɷ̜mət[1] 6 sʌmθɩn, °~[3], °sʌmət[1] 7 sʌmθɩŋk, °~[1(3x)] 8 sɷmət, °~[2(2x)] 9 sʌmət, °~[1(2x)] 10 sʌmθɩnk [? error for «-ŋk», Edd.], °sʌmθɩŋk[2,3] 11 sɷmθɩŋk, °sʌmət[2]

12 St 1 sɷmət, °~[2,5] 2 sɷmət, °~[2] 3 sɷmət, °~[1(2x)], °sɷmθɩŋk[1] 4 sɷmət, sɷmθɩŋk, °sɷmət[2], °sɷmθɩŋk[1,2,3], °sɷnθɩŋk[1] 5 sɷmət, °~[2,3], °sɷmθɩŋk[3] 6 sɷmət, °~[1], °sɷmθɩŋk[1] 7 sɷmθɩŋk, °~[4], °sɷmət[1,3] 8 sɷmθɩŋk, °sɷmət[1] 9 sɷmət, °~[2] 10 sɷmθɩŋk, sɷmət, °sɷmθɩŋk[3(2x)], °sɷmɩŋk[5] 11 sǫmθɩŋk, °sɷmθɩŋk[2(2x)], °sɷmət[1,2]

15 He 1 sʌmət, °~[2(2x)] 2 sʌməʳʈ, °~[2] 3 sɷməʳʈ, °~[3(2x),4(2x)], °sɷmɷ:t[4], °sɷmθɩŋk[3] 4 sɷməʳʈ 5 sɷmθɩn 6 zɷməʳʈ 7 sʌmθɩn, sʌmət, °~[1,2,4(3x)], °sɷmθɩŋ[3]

16 Wo 1 sɷmət 2 sɷməʳʈ 3 sɷməʳʈ, °~[1,4], °sɷmθɩŋg̊[1] 4 sɷmɷt, °~[1(2x),3] 5 sɷmɷt, °~[1], °sɷmɷ:t, °sɷmət[1] 6 sɷmɷ:t, °sɷmɷt[2,3], °sɷməʳʈ[3] 7 sɷmθɩŋk, s.w. sɷmət, °~[2,3], °sɷmθɩŋk[3(2x),4(2x)]

17 Wa 1 sɷmθɩŋk 2 sɷmθɩŋk, s.w. sɷmət [pref.], °~[1(2x),3,4(3x)], °sɷmɷt[4], °sɷmθɩŋk[1(2x),4] 3 sɷmθ̬ɩŋ, °sɷmət[3] 4 sɷmət, °sɷmθɩŋk 5 sɷmət, °~[1] 6 sɷmət 7 sɷmɷt

23 Mon 1 sʌmθɩn 2 sɷmət 3 sʌmət, °~[1(3x),2(2x)], °sʌməʳʈ[3] 4 n.a. 5 sʌ̰̈mʌ̰̈tʰ, °sʌ̰̈mət[1], °sʌ̰mət[2] 6 sʌməʳʈ 7 n.a.

24 Gl 1 sɷmɷt, °sɷmɷ:t[1], °sɷməʳʈ[1] 2 sɷmɷt, °sɷmət[3] 3 sʌmət, °~[3] 4 zɷməʳʈ, °~[1], °zɷmɷt[3(2x)] 5 sɷmət 6 səmət 7 zɷmət, °zəmət

25 O 1 n.a. 2–3 sʌmət 4 sɷmət, sɷmθɩŋ, °~[3], °sɷmθɩŋk[4] 5 sɷməʔ 6 sʌmθɩŋk, °sɷmʔn[3]

VII.8.16 WHAT KIND OF‡

Q. A little girl comes to your door and says: My mother wants to borrow a knife. You'd say to her: . . . . a knife?

Rr. WHAT KIND OF, WHAT SORT (OF~ON)

Note 1—The f.w. occ. omitted to rec. the required OF. Such rr. are, strictly speaking, u.rr. Where rec., A or (A) KNIFE has been reproduced in the r.

Note 2—I.m. exs. of KIND/SORT OF are reproduced below between square brackets untransliterated.

Note 3—For additional exs. of WHAT KIND/SORT (OF), see VII.8.17. KNIFE occurs at I.7.18.

7 Ch 1 wat sǫ:ᵊt 2 p. wət sɷət ə nɑɩɣ [kaɩnd əv[1], kɑɩnd ə[1]] 3 wɒt sɷət əv ə nɛɩf 4 wɒt sɔ:t əv 5 wat sɔ:t əv 6 wɒt kaɩnd əv

8 Db 1 wɒt sʏ·ə̠ᵗt 2 wat soət 3 wɒt so:t ə 4 wɒt so·ət əv 5 wat sɷət 6 wɒt so·ət ə 7 wɒt so·ət

11 Sa 1 wɒt sɔʳ:ʈ əv ə 2 wɒt sɔ:t n‿ə 3 wɒt sɔʳ:ʈ əv 4 wɒt sɔʳ:ʈ əv ə 5 wɒt sɔʳ:ʈ n‿ə 6 wɒt sɔʳ:ʈ əv 7 wɒt sɔʳ:ʈ ɒn 8 wɒt sɔ:t ən ə 9 wɒt sɔ:ʳʈ ɒn ə 10 wɒt sɔʳ:ʈ ɒn 1 wɒt sɔʳ:ʈ əv

12 St 1 wɒt sɔ:t əv ə nɒɪf 2 wɒt soʊt ə nɒɪf [kɒɪnd əv ə[2]] 3 wɒt sɔ:t əv ə nɒ:ɪf 4 wɒt sɔ:t əv ə nɒɪf [sɔ:t əv[1], sɔ:t ə[2(2x)]] 5 wɒt sɔ:t əv ə nɒ:ɪf 6 wɒt sɔ:t 7 wɒt sɔ:t əv ə nɒɪf 8 wɒt kɒɪnd əv nɒɪf [sɔ̣:t ə[1]] 9 wɒt sɔ:t əv ə nɒɪf [sɔ:t ə[2]] 10 wɒt sɔ:t əv ə naɪf [sɔ:t ə[5]] 11 wɒt sɔ:t əv ə nɒɪf [ɔ:l sɔ:ts ə[1] *all sorts of*]

15 He 1 wɒt sɔʳ:ʈ n̩ ə næɪf 2 wɒt sɔʳ:ʈ n‿ə næɪf 3 wɒt sɑ:ʳʈ əv ə nəɪf 4 wɒt sɑʳ:ʈ n‿ə nəɪf 5 wɒt sɑʳ:ʈ n‿ə nəɪf 6 wɒt sɑʳ:ʈ n‿ə nəɪf 7 wɒt sɔɹt ə naɪf [sɔɹts[4] *sorts*]

16 Wo 1 wɒt sɑ:t ən ə 2 wɒt sɑʳ:ʈ ən 3 wɒt sɑʳ:ʈ ə nəi:f 4 wɒt sɑʳ:ʈ ɒn ə nəɪf 5 wɒt sɑʳ:ʈ n‿ə nəɪf 6 wɒt sɑʳ:ʈ n‿ə nɒɪf 7 wət sɔ·ʈʈ əv ə nəɪf

17 Wa 1 wɒt sɔ:t əv 2 wət sɔət əv ə nəɪf, °wət sɔət ə[4] [plus «tɹapʃən» (*con*)*traption*], °wət sɔ:t ə[2] [sɔət əv[1]] 3–4 wɒt sɔ:t əv 5 wɒt sɔʳ:ʈ əv [sɔʳ:ʈ əv[1]] 6 wɒt sɔʳ:ʈ əv 7 wɒt sɔʳ:ʈ

23 Mon 1 wɒt sɑʳ:ʈ 2 wɒt sɑ:t n̩ ə 3 wɒt kəɪnd ə nəɪf 4 wɒ̣·k kʰəind ə nəif 5 wɒ̣·t° sɔ:tʰ əv ə nə̣ɪf 6 wɒt kəɪnd n̩ ə 7 n.a.

24 Gl 1 wɒt sɑ:t n̩ ə 2 wɒt sɑʳ:ʈ n̩ ə nəɪf 3 wɒt zɑʳ:ʈ n̩ 4 wɒt zɑʳ:ʈ n̩ ə 5 wɒt sɔʳ:ʈ əv 6 wɒt sɔʳ:ɖ ə 7 wɒt sɔʳ:ʈ əv ə nʌɪf

25 O 1 wɒt sɔʳ:ʈ əv 2 wɒt kö̈ɪnd əv 3 wət sɔʳ:ʈ 4 wɒt sɒʈʈ 5 wət sɔəʳʔ əv 6 wɒʔ kö̈ɪnd əv

VII.8.17 WHAT KIND‡?

Q. You go into a bootshop and say you want some boots. The shopman would at once ask . . . .

What kind of ones would also be a satisfactory answer.

Rr. WHAT KIND/SORT (OF)

Note 1—I.m. exs. of interrog. WHAT are reproduced below between square brackets untransliterated.

Note 2—For additional exs. of WHAT KIND/SORT (OF), see VII.8.16; and of interrog. WHAT, see VII.5.1, VIII.8.6 and IX.9.4. WHATEVER occurs at VII.8.19.

7 Ch 1 wat sɔ̣:t 2 wət kaɪnd ə [wət[3(2x)]] 3 wɒt soət 4 wɒt sɔ:t[(2x)] [wɒt[3]] 5 wat sɔ:t [wat[2]] 6 wɒt kaɪnd [wɒt[2]]

8 Db 1 wɒt sʏ·ə̠ːt 2 wat soət 3 wɒt soːt ə [wɒt^{2,3}] 4 wɒt so·ət 5 wat sɷət [wɒt^{2,3,4}] 6 wɒt so·ət [wɒt^{1}] 7 wɒt so·ᵓət, ᴼwɒt so·ət^{1}

11 Sa 1 wɒt sɔʳːʈ [wɒt^{4}] 2 wɒt sɔːt 3–4 wɒt sɔʳːʈ 5 wɒt sɔʳːʈ [wɒt^{1}] 6 wɒt sɔʳːʈ [wɒt$^{3(2x)}$] 7 wɒt sɔʳːʈ 8 wɒt sɔːt [wɒ dʒə^{2} . . . . *what d'you* . . . .] 9 wɒt sɔʳːʈ [wɒt^{1}] 10 wɒt sɔʳːʈ 11 wɒt sɔʳːʈ [wɒt^{2}]

12 St 1 wɒt sɔːt 2 wɒt kɒɪnd [wɒt$^{1(2x)}$] 3 wɒt sɔːt [wɒt$^{1(5x)}$] 4 wɒt sɔːt 5 wɒt sɔːt [wɒt^{2}] 6 wɒt sɔːt [wɒt$^{1(2x),2(3x)}$] 7 wɒt sɔːt 8 wɒt kɒɪnd 9 wɒt kɒɪnd [wɒt$^{1(2x),2}$] 10 wɒt sɔːt [wɒt^{2,4}] 11 wɒt kɒɪnd [wɒt^{1,2}]

15 He 1 wɒt sɔʳːʈ [wɒt$^{2(2x)}$] 2 wɒt sɔʳːʈ [wɒt^{2}] 3 wɒt sɑʳːʈ, ᴼ~ 4–5 wɒt sɑʳːʈ 6 wɒt kəɪnd [wɒt^{1}, ~^{1} VI.5.8] 7 wɒt sɔɹt [wɒt$^{1,4(2x)}$]

16 Wo 1 wɒt sɑːt 2 wɒt sɑʳːʈ 3 wɒt sɑʳːʈ [wɒt^{1,2,3}] 4 wɒt sɑʳːʈ 5 wɒt sɑʳːʈ [wɒt^{1}] 6 wɒt sɑʳːʈ 7 wət kəɪnd əv ə [wət$^{1(4x),2(3x),4(3x)}$]

17 Wa 1 wɒt sɔːᵊt 2 p. wət sɔət ə [wət$^{1,2,3,4(2x)}$, wat$^{4(2x)}$, wəd$^{2,4(4x)}$ (+ V.)] 3 p. wɒt sɔːt 4 wɒt sɔːt 5 wɒt sɔʳːʈ 6 wɒt kəɪnd [wɒt^{4}] 7 wɒt sɔʳːʈ [wɒt^{1,2}]

23 Mon 1 wɒt sɑʳːʈ 2 wɒt sɑːt 3 wɒt kəɪnd 4 wɒ̟̣·k kʰəind [wɒ̟̣·t∘^{1}] 5 wɒ̟̣·t∘ sɔːtʰ [wɒ̟·t^{2}] 6 wɒt sɑʳːʈ 7 n.a.

24 Gl 1 wɒt sɑːt [wɒt$^{1(2x)}$] 2 wɒt sɑʳːʈ [wɒt$^{3(3x)}$] 3 wɒt zɑʳːʈ [wɒt^{3}] 4 wɒt zɑʳːʈ [wɒ̣ dʒə wɒn tə naɷ^{1} *what d'you want to know*] 5 wɒt sɔʳːʈ [wɒt^{1,2}] 6 wɒt sɔːd̥ [wɒt$^{2(2x)}$] 7 wɒt sɔːt

25 O 1 wɒt kɔ̈ɪnd [wɒt^{2}] 2 wɒt kɔ̈ɪnd [wɒʔ^{1}] 3 wət sɔʳːʈ 4 wɒt sɒɽʈ [wɒt^{3,5}; wɒ‿s^{1} rec. in «wɒs ɛnɪ nɒɪsəɽ» *what's any nicer*] 5 wət sɔʳət [wət^{3}, wəʔ^{1,3}] 6 wɒt sɔəʳʈ [wɒʔ^{3}]

VII.8.18 WHICH ONE‡

Q. If you offered a boy the choice of six apples, you'd ask him: . . . . will you have?

Rr. WHICH (ONE)

Note—When rec., the remainder of the q. is given below between square brackets.

7 Ch 1 wɪtʃ [+ «ə ðə gʏ·ɪn ʔ‿av» *art thou going to have*] 2 wɪtʃ [+ «dɷst wɒnt» *dost want*] 3 wɪtʃ [+ «jə want» *you want*] 4 wɪtʃ wɒn 5 wɪtʃ [+ «dɷn jə want» *do you want*] 6 wɪtʃ

8 Db 1 wɩtʃ wɒn 2–4 wɩtʃ 5 wɩtʃ wɒn [+ «dɷn jə» *do you*] 6 wɩtʃ 7 wɩtʃ [+ «jə‿l av» *you'll have*]

11 Sa 1–2 wɩtʃ 3 wɩtʃ wʌn 4 wɩtʃ ən 5–7 wɩtʃ 8 wɩtʃ n̩ 9 wɩtʃ [+ «ɭ jə æ·v» *'ll you have*] 10–11 wɩtʃ

12 St 1 wɩtʃ wɷn 2 wɩtʃ [+ «dɷst wɒnt» *dost want*] 3 wɩtʃ [+«wət av» *wilt have*] 4–5 wɩtʃ [+ «wɩl j‿av» *will you have*] 6 wɩtʃ wɒn [+ «ʃat av» *shalt have*] 7 wɩtʃ wɷn [+ «d‿jə wɒnt» *d'you want*] 8 wɩtʃ wɒn 9 wɩtʃ wɒn [+ «ɭ j‿av» *'ll you have*] 10 wɩtʃ wɷ̜n 11 wɩtʃ wɒn

15 He 1–2 wɩtʃ [+ «ɫ jə æv» *'ll you have*] 3 wɩtʃ 4 wɩtʃ ən 5 wɩtʃ [+ «ɫ» *'ll*] 6 wɩtʃ wən [+ «bɩ jə gwɒɩn tə æv» *be you going to have*] 7 wɩtʃ [+ «wəd jə laɩk» *would you like*]

16 Wo 1–2 wɩtʃ 3 wɩtʃ wɷn [+ «wɩɫ jə æv» *will you have*] 4 wɩtʃ ɷn 5–6 wɩtʃ 7 wɩtʃ [+ «wɩl jə æv» *will you have*]

17 Wa 1 wɩtʃ wɒn 2 wɩtʃ [+ «wɩl jə av» *will you have*] 3 wɩ̜tʃ [+ «wɩl j‿av» *will you have*] 4 wɩtʃ wɷn, wɩtʃ 5 wɩtʃ, ~ [+ «ju: ɭ av» *you 'll have*] 6 wɩtʃ [+ «wəd jə» *would you*] 7 wɩtʃ

23 Mon 1–3 wɩtʃ 4 wɩtʃ [+ «wɷd ju· ləik» *would you like*] 5 wɩtʃ [+ «ɭ ju: av» *'ll you have*] 6 wɩtʃ ən [+ «əɫ jə a:v» *will you have*] 7 n.a.

24 Gl 1–2 wɩtʃ ɷn 3 wɩtʃ ən 4 wɩtʃ 5 wɩtʃ ən [plus «ɷ‿t ɛv» *wilt have*] 6 wɩtʃ wən 7 wɩtʃ [+ «dəst wɔ:nt» *dost want*]

25 O 1 wɩtʃ [+ «əl j‿av» *'ll you have*] 2 wɩtʃ wən 3 wɩtʃ wɷn 4 wɩtʃ [+ «də jə wɒnt» *do you want*] 5 wɩtʃ wʌn 6 wɩtʃ, °~ [+ «ə jə goɷɩn av» *are you going* (to) *have*]

VII.8.19 EVERY

Q. You don't milk the cows on Tuesdays and Fridays only, you milk them .... day.

R. EVERY

Note 1—I.m. exs. of EVERYBODY and EVERYTHING, as well as of EVER and NEVER, are reproduced below between square brackets untransliterated.

Note 2—For additional exs. of EVERY–, see VI.14.20; and of NEVER, see IX.5.5 and IX.6.3. –EVER occurs at VII.8.17.

7 Ch 1 εvɹι [εvə^{2}; nεə^{1}, nιvəɹ^{1} (+ V.)] 2 εvəɹι [εvə^{3}; nεvə$^{1(2x),2,3(2x),4(3x)}$, nεvəɹ$^{2(2x),3}$ (+ V.)] 3 εvɹι [nεvə$^{3(2x)}$] 4 εvɹι [εvə^{3} VII.8.13] 5 εvɹι 6 εvɹι [εvə^{2}]

8 Db 1 εvɹι [nεvə^{4}] 2 εvɹι [ιvɹιbɒdι^{4}; nιvə$^{2,3,4(2x)}$] 3 εvɹι 4 ιvɹι 5 ιvɹι, ◦~ [nιvə^{1}] 6–7 ιvɹι

11 Sa 1–3 εvɹι 4 εvɹι [nεvəʳ^{1,2}] 5 εvɹι, ◦~^{3} 6 εvɹι [εvəʳ^{3}; nεvəʳ$^{3(3x)}$, nεvəʳɽ‿^{4} (+ V.), nεvəɹ^{3} (+ V.)] 7 εvɹι [εvəʳ$^{1(2x)}$; nεvəʳ$^{1(4x)}$] 8 εvɹι, ◦~^{2} [nεvəʳɽ‿^{1} (+ V.), nεvəʳ$^{1(3x),2(3x)}$] 9 εvɹι [εvɹιbɒdι$^{1(2x)}$; nεvəʳ$^{1(5x)}$] 10 εvɹι [nεvəʳ$^{2,3(3x)}$, nεvəʳɽ‿^{3} (+ V.)] 11 εvɹι, ◦~^{1} [nεvəʳ$^{1(2x),2(2x)}$]

12 St 1 ιvɹι, ◦~^{2} [εvɹιθιŋg^{2}; ιvə^{1}; nιvə^{1,3}, nεvə^{2}] 2 ιvɹι [ιvəɹ^{1} (+ V.); nιvəɹ^{1} (+ V.), nεvə^{2}] 3 ιvɹι [nεvə^{1}, nεvəɹ^{1,2} (+ V.)] 4 εvɹι [εvɹιθιŋk^{1}; nεvəɹ^{3} (+ V.)] 5 ιvɹι, ◦~$^{1(2x),2}$ [εvə^{2}; nιvə^{1}, nεvə^{1,2}, nεvəɹ^{1} (+ V.)] 6 ιvɹι, ◦~^{2} [nεvə$^{1(3x),2(4x)}$, nεvəɹ$^{1(4x)}$ (+ V.)] 7 εvɹι, ◦~^{1,2} [nεvə$^{1(2x)}$] 8 εvɹι, ◦~^{1} [nεvə$^{1(2x),5}$, nεvəɹ$^{1(3x)}$ (+ V.)] 9 εvɹι, ◦ιvəɹ^{2} [nιvə^{1}, nεvə$^{1,2(3x)}$, nεvəɹ$^{1(2x)}$ (+ V.)] 10 εvɹι [nεvəɹ^{6} (+ V.)] 11 εvɹι [εvə^{2} VIII.3.2; nεvə$^{1(2x),2(3x)}$, nεvəɹ$^{1(2x),2(2x)}$ (+ V.)]

15 He 1 εvɹι 2 εvɹι [εvɹιθιŋk^{1}; nεvəʳ^{1,2}] 3 εvɹι [nεvəʳ$^{1(3x),2,4}$] 4 εvɹι [εvɹιbɒdι:^{1}; nεvəʳ^{1}] 5 εvɹι [nεvəʳ$^{1,2(3x)}$, nεvəʳɽ^{1} (+ V.)] 6 εvɹι [nεvəʳɽ‿$^{1(2x)}$ (+ V.)] 7 εvɹι, ◦~^{1} [εvɹιbɒdι^{1,4}; εvɹιwɒn^{4} *everyone*; nεvəɹ$^{1(3x),2,3(5x),4(2x)}$, nεvə$^{3(3x)}$, nιvəɹ^{3}, nιvə^{3}]

16 Wo 1 εvɹι [nεvəʳɽ^{1} (+ V.); nεvəʳ^{1}] 2 εvɹι [εvəʳ^{2}; εvɹιθιn^{2}; εvɹιwəʳ:^{2} *everywhere*; nεvəʳ$^{1,2(2x)}$] 3 εvɹι [nεvə$^{2,3(2x)}$] 4 εvɹι [εvəʳɽ^{1} (+ V.); nεvəʳ$^{1(2x),2,3}$, nεvəʳɽ‿^{2} (+ V.)] 5 εvɹι [nεvəʳ$^{1(2x)}$] 6 εvɹι [εvɹιθιŋk^{2}; εu:-εvəʳ^{3} *however* (=*whether*); nεvəʳ$^{1,2,3(2x)}$] 7 p. εvəɹι [εvə^{3,4}; əu·εvə^{3} *however*; nεvə$^{1(5x),2,3(2x),4(2x)}$, ~$^{1(2x)}$ (+ V.), nεvəɹ$^{1,3(2x)}$ (+ V.), nεvəʳ$^{1(2x)}$]

17 Wa 1 εvɹι [ιvəɹ^{1} (+ V.); nεvəɹ^{1} (+ V.)] 2 εvɹι, ◦~ [εvəɹ^{1} (+ V.), εvə^{1,4}; nιvəɹ^{2} (+ V.), nεvə$^{1,2(3x),4}$, ~$^{4(2x)}$ (+ V.)] 3 ȩvɹι [nεvə$^{1(2x),2,3(2x)}$, nεvəɹ^{2} (+ V.)] 4 εvɹι [nεvə^{2}; fəɹεvə^{1} *forever*;] 5 εvɹι, ◦~ [εvə^{1}; nεvəɹ^{1} (+ V.), nεvə$^{1(2x)}$ IX.6.3] 6–7 εvɹι

23 Mon 1 εvɹι [nεvəʳ^{2}] 2 εvɹι, ◦~^{2} [nεvə^{3}, nεvəʳ$^{3(4x)}$] 3 εvɹι [nεvə^{1}, ~^{1} (+ V.), nεvəʳɽ^{2} (+ V.)] 4 n.a. [εvə^{2}; nεvə$^{2(2x)}$] 5 εvɹi [nεvə^{1,2}, nεvɐ^{2}, nεvəɹ^{2} (+ V.)] 6 εvɹι [nεvəʳ^{1,2}] 7 n.a.

24 Gl 1 εvɹι [εvɹιθιŋ;^{3} nεvəʳ$^{1(2x),3(2x)}$] 2 εvɹι [εvəʳ^{3}] 3 εvɹι 4 εvɹι [nεvəʳ, ~^{3} (+ V.)] 5 εvɹι [nεvə^{1}, nεvəɽ^{2} (+ V.)] 6 εvɹι [εvə^{1}; nεvə$^{2(2x)}$] 7 εvɹι [nεvəɹ, nεvəɽ]

25 O 1 ɛvɹɪ, °~^{1} [nɛvəɽ^{2}] 2 ɛvɹɪ, s.f. ɪvɹɪ ["old and rare"; nɛvəɹ̣] 3 ɛvɽɪ [ɛvɹɪbɒdɪ^{1}; ɛvɽɪθɪŋk^{2}; nɛvəɽ^{1} (+ V.)] 4 ɛvɽɪ, °~^{1} [ɛvɽɪbɒdɪ^{4}; ɛvɽɪθɪŋk^{4}; nɛvəɽ$^{1,3,4(2x),5(3x)}$, nɛvəɹ^{1}] 5 ɛvɽɪ [nɛvəɽ$^{2(2x)}$, nɛvəɽɽ^{2}] 6 ɛvɹɪ [ɛvɹɪθɪŋk^{1}; ɛvəɽ^{1}; nɛvəɽ^{3}]

VII.8.20 LITTLE

Q. If you are asked whether you take milk in your tea, you might answer: Yes, but only ....

Rr. A /BIT/(SMALL) DROP/LITTLE (DROP~SPOT)/SPOONFUL/ SPOT/SUP/, DROP, LITTLE

Note 1—I.m. exs. of LITTLE in other contexts are reproduced below between square brackets untransliterated.

Note 2—LITTLE *adj.* occurs at III.8.2 and IX.9.4, and DROP *n.* and SUP *n.* at III.13.12.

7 Ch 1 ə dɹɒp 2 ə spuːnfʊl, p. ə lɪtl dɹəp 3 ə dɹɒp 4 ə dɹɒp [lɪtl^{2} IV.7.1] 5 ə spɒt [lɪtl^{1}] 6 lɪtl dɹɒp

8 Db 1 ə dɹɒp [lɪtl^{1}] 2 ə dɹɒp 3 ə sʊpʻ 4–5 ə dɹɒp 6 ə sʊp [lɪtl$^{1(2x)}$] 7 ə dɹɒp

11 Sa 1 ə dɹɒp, ə lɪtl 2 ə lɪtl [lɪtl^{2} IV.9.9] 3 ə lɪtl 4 lɪtl 5 ə dɹɒp 6 lɪtl 7 ə lɪtl [lɪtl^{1}] 8 ə dɹɒp 9–10 ə lɪtl 11 ə bɪt [lɪtl^{2}]

12 St 1–2 ə dɹɒp 3 ə lɪtl spɒt [lɪtl^{2}] 4–5 ə dɹɒp 6 ə dɹɒp [lɪtl^{1,2}] 7 ə lɪtl, ə dɹɒp [usu.] 8 ə lɪtl 9 ə dɹɒp [lɪtl^{1}] 10 ə lɪtl, ə dɹɒp 11 ə lɪtl dɹɒp [lɪtl$^{2(4x)}$]

15 He 1 ə dɹɔːp 2 ə smɔːl dɹɒp 3 lɪtɫ 4 ə dɹɑːp 5–6 ə dɹɒp 7 ə dɹɒp, °~ [lɪtl$^{1,2(2x),4}$, lɪtl̩əɹ^{4} *littler*]

16 Wo 1 ə lɪtl 2 ə dɹɒp [lɪtəɫ^{2} VIII.9.1] 3 ə dɹɒp 4 ə dɹɑɽːp 5 ə lɪtɫ 6 ə dɹɑːp [lɪtɫ^{3}] 7 ə lɪtl dɹɔ·p [lɪtl$^{3(3x),4(2x)}$]

17 Wa 1 ə dɹɐp [lɪtl^{1}] 2 ə dɹəp [lɪtl$^{1,4(2x)}$] 3 ə lɪtɫ dɹɑp 4 ə dɹɒp [lɪtɫ^{1}, ~^{1} III.12.2] 5 ə dɹɒp 6 ə dɹɒp [lɪtɫ^{3}] 7 ə dɹɒp [lɪtl^{1}, lɪtɫ^{2}]

23 Mon 1 ə dɹɒp 2 ə lɪtɫ 3 ə dɹɑːp 4 n.a. 5 ə bɪt 6 ə smaːɫ dɹɑːp [lɪtl^{2}] 7 n.a.

24 Gl 1 ə dɹɑ:p 2 ə spɑ:t 3–4 ə dɹɑ:p 5 ə dɹɑp [lɩʔɫ², lɩtl] 6 dɹɒp 7 ə dɹɒpʻ

25 O 1 ə lɩtɫ 2 ə lɩʔɫ 3 ə lɩtɫ 4 ə ɫɩtɫ dɽɒp [ɫɩtɫ¹⁽²ˣ⁾, ɫɩʔɫ²,⁵] 5 ə sməɫ dɽɔ·p 6 ə lɩʔl

VII.8.21 A FEW

Q. I might ask you if there are any foxes round here, and you might answer: Yes, but only . . . .

Rr. AN ODD ONE, A SCATTERING/SKITTERING, (A) /FEW/TWO-THREE/, ODD ONES, ONE OR TWO

Note 1—I.m. exs. of pronominal FEW are reproduced below between square brackets untransliterated.

Note 2—For expressions comparable with some of those above used adjectivally, see VII.1.19.

7 Ch 1 ə fɩʏ: 2 ə fjü: 3 ə skatɹɩn 4 ə tu:θɹɩ 5 ə fju: 6 fju:

8 Db 1 ə to:θɹɩ, ɒd ənz, ə fjʏ: 2 ə fju:, °fu:, °ə tu:θɹɩ⁴ 3 tɛɷθɹɩ 4 ə f°ü: 5 ɒd n̩z 6 tɛɷθɹɩ 7 ə f°ü:

11 Sa 1 wɒn ə tu: 2 ɒd ənz, ə fʿu: 3–4 ə fɩu: 5 ə fju: 6 ə fɩu: 7 ə fju: 8 ə fju:, °ə tɷθɹɩ 9 fɩu: 10 ə fɩu: 11 ə fjaɷ

12 St 1 ə tü:θɹɛɩ 2–3 ə tɛɷθɹɩ 4 ə fju: 5 ə fjü:, ə skɩtəɹɩn, ə tü:θɹɩ 6 wɒn ə tæɷ, ə tɛ̢ɷθɹɩ 7–8 ə fju: 9 ə ɒd n̩, ə tɩɷθɹɩ 10 ə fjü:, s.w. ə tü:θɹi: 11 ə fjü:, ə tu:θɹi: ["older"]

15 He 1–4 ə fjæɷ 5 ə fjæɷ, °ə fju:² 6 ə vjæɷ 7 ə fju:

16 Wo 1 ə fɩu: 2 wɷn əʳ tu: 3 ə fju: 4 ə fjaɷ, °~¹ [fju:¹, fjaɷ²] 5 ə fjaɷ, °ə fɩaɷ¹ 6 ə fjæɷ 7 ə fju:, p. ə fjaɷ, °ə fju:³,⁴

17 Wa 1–3 ə fju: 4 ə fɩu: 5 ə fjɒɷ 6 ə fjü: 7 ə fjaɷ

23 Mon 1 ə fjæɷ 2–3 ə fju: 4 n.a. 5 ə fjɩu 6 ə fju: 7 n.a.

24 Gl 1 ə fjæɷ, °~² 2 ə fjæɷ, °~³ 3 ə vjɒɷ 4 ə vjaɷ, °~² [vjaɷ²] 5 ə fjɑɷ 6 ə vjaɷ 7 ə vju:

25 O 1 ə fju: 2 fu: ["old and rare"], °ə fju:¹ 3 ə fjʏ: 4–5 ə fju: 6 ə fü:

RESPONSES: BOOK VIII

VIII.1.1 FATHER*, MOTHER*

Q. Who are the two most important members of a family?

Rr. FATHER

MOTHER

Note 1—The rr. to the two parts of the q. are separated below by a full stop.

Note 2—For additional exs. of FATHER, see IX.9.4. FATHER'S occurs at IX.8.6. For GRANDFATHER and GRANDMOTHER, see VIII.1.7.

7 Ch 1 fẹ:ðə, ○∼[2]. mɷðə 2 fa:ðə, s.f. fe:ðə [pref.], ○fa:ðə[4], ○□fe:ðəz[4]. mɷðə, ○mɷðəɹ[4] [+ V.], ○mɷðəz[3] *poss.* 3 fẹ:ðə. mɷðə 4 fẹ:ðə. mɷðə 5 fe:ðə, ○fi:ðə[1]. mɷðə 6 fe:ðə. mɷðə

8 Db 1 fe:ðəɽ. mɒðəɽ, ○mɷðəz[1] *poss.* [stɛpmɷðəz[3] *step-m.'s poss.* VI.7.11] 2 faðə, ○∼[3]. mɷðə 3 fe:ðə. mɒðə 4 fe:ðə, ○∼[1], ○fe:də[1]. mɒðə 5 fe:ðə. mɒðə 6 fe:ˈðə, ○∼[1]. mɒðə, ○∼[1] 7 fe·ɪðə. mɒðə

11 Sa 1 faʵ:ðəʵ. mʌðəʵ 2 fe:ðəʵ. mɷðəʵ, ○∼[1] 3 faðəʵ. mʌðəʵ 4 faʵ:ðəʵ. mʌðəʵ 5 fẹ:ðəʵ. mɒðəʵ, ○mɷdəʵ[3] 6 fe:ðəʵ, ○fa:ðəʵ·[4]. mʌðəʵ 7 fe:ðəʵ. mʌðəʵ 8 fe:ðəʵ. mɒðəʵ 9 fe:ðəʵ, ○∼[1]. mʌðəʵ 10 fe:ðəʵ. mʌdəʵ 11 fe:ðəʵ. mɒdəʵ

12 St 1 fɛɪðə, ○∼[3], ○fa:ðə[2]. mɒðə, ○mɷðə[2,4,5] [mɷðəd[2] *mothered 3 p.t.s.*] 2 fɛɪðə, ○∼[2]. mọðə, ○mɷðə[2] 3 fɛɪðə, ○∼[1(2x)]. mɷðə, ○∼[2] 4 fɛɪðə. mɷðə 5 fɛɪðə, ○∼[1(2x)]. mɷðə, ○∼[2] 6 fɛɪðə. mɷðə, ○∼[1,2], ○mɒðə[1] 7 fa:ðə, ○∼[4]. mɷðə, ○∼[3], ○mɷðəɹ[4] [+ V.] 8 fa̱:ðə. mɷðəʴ 9 fɛɪðə, ○∼[2(2x)], ○fa:ðə[1]. mɷðə, ○mɒðə[1] 10 fa:ðə. mɷðə, ○∼[5] III.7.1 11 fa:ðə. mɵ̣ðə

15 He 1 fe:ðəʵ. mɷðəʵ 2 fi:ðəʵ, ○∼[2(2x)], ○fe:ðəʵ[2]. mʌðəʵ 3 fe:ðəʵ, ○∼[2]. mɷðəʵ 4 fe:ðəʵ. mʌðəʵ 5–6 fe:ðəʵ. mɷðəʵ 7 fæ̣:ðəɹ, ○fæ̣:ðəɹ[3], ○fạ:ðəɹ[3], ○fa:ðəɹ[3,4]. mɷðəɹ, ○mʌðəɹ[3]

16 Wo 1 fe:ðə. mɷðə 2 fe:ᵊðəʵ. mɷðəʵ, ○∼[1] 3 fɛ:əðəʵ. mɷðəʵ, ○∼[1] 4 fɛ:ᵊðəʵ. mɷðəʵ 5 fe:ðəʵ. mɷðəʵ 6 fe:ɪðəʵ. mɷðəʵ 7 fɑ:ðəʵ, fe:ðəʵ ["older"], ○fɑ:ðə[3], ○fɛ:ðə[2]. mɷðəʵ, ○mɷðə[4(2x)]

17 Wa 1 fa:ðə. mɷðə 2 fe:ðə, ○∼[4(2x)], ○fe:ðəʴ[4]. mɷðə, ○∼[3(2x)], ○mɷðəɹ[4] [+ V.] 3 fẹ:ᵊðə, ○fẹ·əðəɹ[3] [+ V.], ○fadə[3]. mɷðə 4 fa:ðə, ○fẹəðə[1]. mɷðəʵ 5 fẹ·əðəʵ. mɷðəʵ 6 fa:ðəʵ, ○fe·əðəʵ[3]. mɷðəʵ 7 fa:ðəʵ. mɷðəʵ

23 Mon 1 fe:ɩðəʳ, ○~[1]. mʌðəʳ 2 fa:ðəʳ. mɷðəʳ 3 fa:ðə. mʌðə 4 fa:ðə. mʌ̤̈ðə 5 fa:ðə. mʌ̤̈ðə [fɒ̤̝˖stəmʌ̤̈ðə[1] *foster-m.*] 6 fa:ðəʳ. mʌðəʳ 7 n.a., ○mʌ̤ðə[1]

24 Gl 1 fe:ðəʳ, ○~[2], ○fæ:ðəʳ[1(2x)]. mɷðəʳ, ○mɷðəʳɽ[1] [+ V.] 2 faʳ:ðəʳ. mɷðəʳ 3 ve:ᶥðəʳ, ○~[3], ○fæ:ðəʳ[3(2x)]. mʌðəʳ 4 fjɛðəʳ, ○~[1]. mɷðəʳ 5 fa:ðəʳ. mɷðəʳ 6 fjaðəʳ, ○fjɛðəʳ[1]. məðəʳ 7 fa:ðə. məðəʳ

25 O 1 fa:ðə. məðəʳ, ○mʌðə[2], ○mʌðəʳʐ[2] *poss.* 2 fa:ðəʴ̠, ○feəðəʴ̠[1]. mʌðəʴ̠ 3 fa:ðəʳ, ○fa:ðə[2]. mʌðəʳ 4 fɑ:ðəɽ, ○~[5]. mɷðəɽ, ○~[1(2x)] 5 faðəʳ, ○faðə[2]. mʌðəʳ 6 faðəʳ. mʌðəʳ

VIII.1.2 CHILDREN. CHILD

Q. In the olden days, families often had up to five or six ....
But nowadays many of them have only one ....

Rr. BAIRNS, CHILDER~CHILDREN, CHILDS, KIDDIES, KIDS, YOUNGSTERS

BAIRN, CHILD, KID

Note—The rr. to the two parts of the q. are separated below by a full stop.

7 Ch 1 tʃɩldə. tʃɑɩld 2 tʃɩldə, ○~[2(3x),3], ○tʃɩldəɹ[2] [+ V.]. tʃaɩld, ○~[2], ○tʃɑɩld[2] 3 tʃɩldə, ○tʃɩldəʴ[2]. tʃɑɩlt 4 tʃɩldɹən, ○tʃɩldən[2]. tʃɑɩld 5 tʃɩldən, ○kɩdz. tʃɑɩld 6 tʃɩldən, ○~[3]. tʃaɩl

8 Db 1 tʃɩldəɽ, kɩdz. tʃaɩld 2 tʃɩldə, ○~[3]. tʃɑɩld 3 tʃɩldə. tʃaɩld, ○tʃaɩld̥[2] 4 tʃɩldə, ○~[1]. tʃɑɩld 5 tʃɩldə. tʃɑɩld, ○tʃɑɩlt[4] 6 tʃɩldɹən, kɩdz [pref.]. tʃɑ̃ɩ̃ld 7 kɩdz, p. tʃɩldə. kɩd, tʃɑ̃·ɩ̃lt

11 Sa 1 tʃɩldəʳ:ɳ. tʃaɩld 2 tʃɩldəʳ:ɳ. tʃa:ᶥld 3 tʃɩldəʳ:ɳ. tʃaɩld 4 tʃɩldɹən. tʃaɩld 5 tʃɩldəʳɳ, ○~[2]. tʃaɩld 6–7 tʃɩldəʳ:ɳ. tʃaɩld 8 tʃɩldɹəʳ:ɳ. tʃɒɩld 9 tʃɩldɹən. tʃaɩld 10–11 tʃɩldəʳ:ɳ. tʃaɩld

12 St 1 tʃɩldɹən. tʃɒɩld 2 tʃɩldə, kɩdz, ○tʃɩldə[5]. kɩd, ○tʃɒɩlt[2] 3 tʃɩldə, ○~[1(2x)], ○kɩdz[1]. tʃɒ:ɩld 4 tʃɩldɹən. tʃɒɩld 5 kɩdz, tʃɩ̱ldɹən. kɩd, tʃɒ:ɩld 6 kɩdz ["old"], tʃɩldɹən. kɩd, tʃɒ:ɩld, ○kɩd[1] 7 tʃɩlən, ○tʃɩlɹən[1], ○kɩdɩz[4]. kɩd[(2x)] 8 tʃɩlɹən, kɩdz ["old"]. kɩd 9 bɛ:nz, ○kɩdz[2]. bɛ:n, ○tʃɒɩld[1(2x)] 10 tʃɩlɹən. tʃa:ɩld, ○tʃaɩld[2] 11 tʃɩlɹən, ○tʃɩlən[2]. tʃaɩld, ○~[2]

15 He 1 kɩdz, tʃɩɫdəʳɳ. kɩd, tʃæɩᵊɫ, ○kɩd[2] 2 kɩdz, ○~[3]. kɩd 3 tʃɩɫdəʳɳ, ○kɩdz[2]. tʃəɩɫd, ○~[3] 4 tʃɩɫdɹən. tʃəɩᵊɫd 5 tʃɩɫdɹən. tʃəɩɫd 6 tʃɩɫdəʳɳ. tʃəɩᵊɫ 7 tʃɩɫdɹən, ○jɷŋstəɹz[4]. n.r.

16 Wo 1 tʃɩldən, ○tʃɩldɹən^{2}. tʃɒɩld 2 tʃɩldɹən. tʃɒɩɫd 3 tʃɩldəʳ:ɳ, ○tʃɩlɷn^{1}. tʃɒɩɫd, ○tʃəi:ɫd^{5} 4 tʃɩɫdɹən, kɩdz. tʃəɩɫd 5 tʃɩɫdɹɷn. tʃəɩɫd 6 tʃɩɫdəʳɳ. tʃɒɩɫ 7 jɷŋstəz, s.w. tʃɩldɹən, ○~^{4}. tʃəɩld, ○~$^{3(2x)}$

17 Wa 1 tʃɩldɹən. tʃɑɩld 2 tʃɩldɹən, ○kɩdɩz ["familiar"], ○kɩdz ["familiar"], ○~^{4}, ○~^{4} *poss.* tʃəɩld, ○~^{1,4} 3 tʃɩldɹɵ̈n. tʃəɩld, ○tʃəɩɫ^{2} 4 tʃɩɫdɹən. tʃəɩɫd 5 tʃɷɫdɹən. tʃəɩɫd 6 tʃɩɫddəʳ·ɳ, ○tʃɩɫdəʳ:ɳ^{4}. tʃəɩɫd 7 tʃɩldɹɩn, ○kɩdz. tʃəɩld

23 Mon 1 kɩdz, tʃɩɫdəʳɳ. kɩd, tʃəɩɫd 2 tʃɩɫdɹən. tʃəɩɫ 3 tʃɩɫdɹən. tʃəɩɫd 4 n.a., ○tʃɩlɹʌ̰̈n^{3}. n.a. 5 tʃɩldɹʌ̰̈n. tʃəiɫd, ○tʃəɩ̹ɫd^{2} 6 tʃɩɫdɹən. tʃəɩᵊɫd 7 n.a.

24 Gl 1 tʃɩɫdɹɷn, tʃəɩɫdz. tʃəɩɫd 2 kɩdz, tʃɩɫdɹɷn. tʃəɩᵊɫ 3 kɩdz, tʃɩɫdən. tʃəɩᵊɫd, kɩd 4 tʃɩɫdɹən. tʃɒɩᵊɫd 5 tʃɩldəʳ:n, ○kɩdz^{1,2}. tʃə̈ɩᵊɫd 6 tʃɩldəʳɳ, kɩdz. tʃʌɩld 7 tʃɩɫdɹɩn, kɩdz. tʃʌɩld

25 O 1 tʃɩldəʳɳ, ○tʃɩldən^{2}, ○tʃɩɫdəʳ:ɳ^{2}. tʃə̈ɩld 2 tʃɩɫdɹən. tʃə̈ɩɫd 3 tʃɩldɽən. tʃʌʏɫd, ○tʃʌʏld^{1} 4 tʃɩ̈ɫdɽən. tʃɑɩɫd, ○~^{4} 5 tʃɩɫdɽən, s.f. tʃɩldəʳ [old]. tʃʌʏld, ○tʃə̈ɩld^{2} 6 tʃɩɫdɹən. tʃə̈ɩɫd

VIII.1.3 BOYS, GIRLS

Q. Children may be of either sex: they're either . . . . , or . . . .

Rr. BOYS, CHAPS, KIDS, LADS

GIRLS, LASSES, △MAID, WENCHES

Note 1—The rr. to the two parts of the q. are separated below by a full stop.

Note 2—For additional exs. of BOY, see IX.9.4; of LAD, see VIII.8.3 and IX.9.4. For expressions comparable with some of those listed above, see VIII.1.4.

7 Ch 1 ladz, ○~^{4}. wɛnʃɩz, ○△wɛnʃ^{4} 2 bɔɩz, ○△bɔɩ^{1}, ○△bɑɩ^{2}. gjəl:z, ○△gjə:l^{4} 3 ladz. wɛntʃɩz, ○△wɛnʃ^{3} 4 ladz, ○△lad^{1}. wɛnʃɩz, ○~^{2} 5 ladz. wɛnʃɩz 6 ladz, bɒɩz, baɩz. wɛnʃɩz, gəɹ̩:lz

8 Db 1 bɒɩz. gəɹ̩:lz, galz 2 bɒɩz, ladz ["older"]. gə:lz, lasəz ["older"], ○△wɛnʃ^{4} 3 ladz. wɛntʃəz 4 ladz. wɛntʃəz, ○△wɛntʃ^{2} VIII.1.4 5 ladz, ○△lad^{4}. lasəz 6 ladz. wɛntʃəz, ○△wɛntʃ^{1} 7 ladz. wɛntʃəz

11 Sa 1 bɒɩz. gəʳ:ɭʐ 2 ladz, ○△lad^{3}, ○baɩ^{3}. wɛnʃɩz, ○gəʳ:ɭʐ^{3}, ○△wɛnʃ^{3}, ○△gˡə:l^{2}, ○△gəʳ:ɭ^{3} 3 ladz. lasɩz 4 bɒɩz. gəʳ:ɭʐ 5 bɒɩz, ladz ["older"]. gəʳ:ɭʐ, wɛnʃɩz ["older"] 6 ladz, bɒɩz. lasɩz, wɛnʃəz, ○△la·s^{4} 7 ladz, ○bɷi:z^{1}, ○△læd. la:sɩz [səʳ:vəndwɛnʃ^{1} *servant-w.*] 8 ladz, bɒɩz ["*modern*"]. lasɩz, gəʳ:ɭʐ ["*modern*"] 9 bɷɩ:z, ○△bɷɩ^{1}. gəʳ:ɭʐ 10 bɷi:z [*usu.*], ladz. gɩəʳ:ɭʐ [*usu.*], lasɩz 11 bɒɩz. gɩəʳ:ɭʐ

12 St 1 baɪz, ○△baɪ[2], ○△lad[1]. gəːlz, ○△gəːl[1] 2 ladz, ○△lad[2]. wɛnʃɪz, ○△gəːl[2] 3 ladz, ○~[1], ○△lad[2]. wɛnʃɪz, ○~[1] 4 kɪdz, ○ladz[1]. wɛntʃɪz, ○△gəːl[2] 5 ladz, ○△bɒ̈ɪ[1]. wɛnʃɪz 6 ladz, ○~[1,2]. wɛnʃɪz, ○△wɛntʃ[1], ○△gɛl[1(3x)] 7–8 kɪdz. wɛnʃɪz 9 bo̜ɪz, ladz ["older"], ○△lad. gɛlz, wɛnʃɪz ["older"], ○gɛlz[2], ○△wɛnʃ[2(2x)], ○△las[1], ○△mɛɪd[2] 10 kɪdz, ladz. wɛntʃɪz 11 bəɪz, ○△bɒ̈ɪ[2]. gəːlz, ○△wɛntʃ

15 He 1 bɒɪz, lædz ["older"], ○△bwɒɪ[3]. gəʳːɭz̧, wɛnʃɪz ["older"] 2 △bwɒɪ. gəʳːɬz̧, wɛnʃɪz ["older"], ○△gəʳːɬ[3] 3 bɒɪz, ○△bʷɒɪ[2]. gˈəʳːɬz̧, wɛnʃɪz ["older"] 4 bwæɪz. gjəʳːɬz̧, ○△wɛnʃ[2] 5 bwɒɪz, ○△bwɒɪ[4]. wɛnʃɪz 6 △bwɒɪ. △wɛnʃ 7 △bəɪ, ○△~[3,4], ○△bω̆ɪ[2]. gəɽɭz̧, ○△gə·ɹl[3]

16 Wo 1 bɒɪz. gəʳːɭz̧ 2 bwɒɪz. gɒɫz, ○△wɛnʃ[2] 3 bɒɪz. wɛnʃɪz 4 bwɒɪz, ○bʷɒɪz[1] [bwɒɪkɪn[1] *boykin* (i.e. little b.)]. gˈəʳːɬz̧ 5 bwɒɪz, ○△bwɒɪ[1(4x)]. gɪəʳːɬz̧, ○△gˈəʳːɬ[1(2x)] 6 bwɒɪz, ○~[2], ○△bwɒɪ[2]. wɛnʃɪz 7 p. bəɪz, ○~[1,4], ○△~[4] *poss.* [plæωbəɪ[2] *plough-b.* I.8.1]. wɛnʃɪz, ○△gəːl[3]

17 Wa 1 △bɒɪ. △gəl 2 bəɪz, p. tʃaps [*pref.*]. gəːlz, p. wɛnʃɪz [*pref.*], ○△wɛnʃ[4] 3 bəɪz. gəːlz, ○△gɛl[3] 4 bɒɪz. gəːlz, ○wɛnʃɪz 5 ladz, ○△lad[1]. wɛnʃɪz 6 bəɪz. wɛnʃɪz, ○△wɛnʃ[3] 7 bwɒɪz. wɛnʃɪz

23 Mon 1 lædz, ○bɒɪz[4]. wɛnʃɪz, ○△gəʳːɬ[4], ○△gjəʳːɬ[4] 2 laːdz. wɛnʃɪz 3 bɒɪz. gœːɫz 4 n.a. 5 bɔiz, ○bəɪz[2]. gœ̣̈ːɫz, ○△gœ̣̈ːl[2] 6 bɒɪz, ○△bɒɪ[1]. gəʳːɬz̧, wɛnʃɪz ["older"] 7 n.a. n.a., ○△gœːᵊl[1]

24 Gl 1 bwɒɪz, ○bwæɪz[1], ○△bwæɪ[1], ○△bwɒɪ[1,2(3x)]. wɛnʃɪz, ○△wɛnʃ[1(2x)] 2 bɒɪz, ○bwɒɪz[3], ○△bæɪ[2]. wɛnʃɪz, ○~[3] 3 bwɒɪz, ○~[1], ○△bwɒɪ[1]. wɛnʃɪz, ○△wɛnʃ[1] 4 bwɒɪz, ○△bwɒɪ[3]. wɛnʃəz, ○△wɛnʃ[3] 5 bwɒɪz, ○△bwɒɪ[2(2x)]. gəʳːɬz̧ 6 △bwɒɪ. △gəʳːɭ 7 bwɒɪz. gəʳːɭz̧, ○△wɛnʃ

25 O 1 bəɪz. wɛnʃɪz 2 boɪz, ○△bʷoɪ[1]. gɛɫz 3 bwo̜ɪz. gɛɫz, ○gəʳɭz̧[1] 4 bəɪz, ○△bəɪ[3]. gəɽɬz̧, wɛnʃɪz, ○△gəɽɬ[3(2x)], ○△gəɽəɫ[5], ○△gaɫ[5(2x)], ○△wɛnʃ[5] 5 bo̜ɪz, ○~[3]. gɛɫz 6 boɪz. gɛlz, ○△gɛɫ[3], ○△wɛntʃ[3(2x)]

VIII.1.4 SON, DAUGHTER

Q. □ *He [p.] is their [p.] . . . . , and she is their . . . .*

Rr. BOY, LAD, SON

DAUGHTER, GIRL, LASS, MAID, WENCH

Note 1—The rr. to the two parts of q. are separated below by a full stop.

Note 2—For expressions comparable with some of those listed above, see VIII.1.3. DAUGHTER– and SON'S occur at VIII.1.18 (and refs.).

7 Ch 1 lad. wɛnʃ, dɔ:tə ["modern"] 2 sɒn, °~¹. dɔɒtə, °~⁴ 3 lad. wɛntʃ 4 lad. wɛnʃ 5 sɒn, lad [*pref.*]. dɛɒtə, wɛnʃ [*pref.*] 6 lad. wɛnʃ

8 Db 1 lad. dɛ̝ɒttə 2 lad, sɒn [less common], °lad³. las, dɔ:tə [less common] 3 □ladz. □wɛntʃəz, p. dɛɒttə 4 lad, sɒn [rare]. las, dɛɒtə [rare], °wɛntʃ² VIII.1.3 5 sɒn. dɛɒtə 6–7 lad. wɛntʃ

11 Sa 1–2 sɒn. dɔ:təʳ 3–4 sʌn. dɔʳ:təʳ 5 sɒ̣n. daʳ:təʳ 6–7 sʌn. dɔʳ:təʳ 8 sɒn. dɔ:təʳ 9 sʌn. dɔʳ:təʳ 10 sʌn. dɔ:təʳ 11 □sʌnz. dɔ:təʳ

12 St 1 sɒn. dɔ:tə 2 □sɒnz. dạɒtə 3 sɒn. dæɒtə, °da:təɹ¹ [+ V.] 4 sɒn. dɔ:tə 5 sɒn. doɒtə 6 sɒn, °~¹. daɒtə 7 sɒn. dɔ:tə 8 sɒn. dọ:təɹ, °dɔ:tə¹ 9 sɒn. dọ:tə 10 sɒn. □dɔ:təz 11 sɒn. dọ:tə

15 He 1 sʌn. dɔʳ:təʳ 2 sʌn. dɔ:təʳ 3 sɒ:n, °~². dɑ:təʳ 4–5 sʌn. dɑ:təʳ 6 zɒn, °sɒn¹. dɒɒtəʳ 7 sɒn. dɔ:təɹ

16 Wo 1–2 sɒn. dɑʳ:ʈəʳ 3 sɒn, °~². dɑ:təʳ 4 sɒn. dɑʳ:ʈəʳ 5 sɒ:n, °sɒn¹. dɑʳ:ʈəʳ, °~¹ 6 sɒ:n. dɑʳ:ʈəʳ 7 sɒn, °~¹. dɔ:təʳ, °dɔɒtəɹ⁴ [+ V.]

17 Wa 1 sɒn. dọ̈:tə 2 sɒn. dɔ:tə 3 lad. gə:l, °gɛɫ³ 4 lad. wɛnʃ 5 sɒn. dɔ:təʳ, °dɔ:tə¹ 6 sɒn. dɔʳ:ʈəʳ 7 bwɔɩ. gɛɫ

23 Mon 1 sʌn. dɑʳ:ʈəʳ, °~⁴ 2 sɒn. dɑ:təʳ 3 sʌn. dɑ:tə 4 n.a. 5 sʌ̥̈n. dɔ:tə, °□dɔ:təz¹ 6 sʌn, °~¹. dɑ:təʳ 7 n.a.

24 Gl 1 sɒn. daʳ:ʈəʳ 2 sɒ:n. dɑʳ:ʈəʳ 3 sʌn. dɑ:təʳ 4 zɒn. dɑ:dəʳ 5 sɒn. dɔ:təʳ 6 sən. dɔ:tə, wɛnʃ ["older"] 7 sə·n. gəʳ:ɭ ["usu"], mæ̝ɩd

25 O 1 sɒn. □daʳ:ʈəʳʐ 2 □sʌnz. □dɔ̝ʳ:ḍəʳʐ 3 sʌn. dɔ·ᵊtɽ 4 sɒn, °~³. n.r. 5 sʌn. dɔ:t͜ʔəʳ 6 sɒ̣n. dɔ:ᵊʔəʳ

VIII.1.5 BROTHER*

Q. □ *He is her . . . .*

R. BROTHER

7 Ch 1–6 bɹɒðə

8 Db 1–4 bɹɒðə 5 bɹɒdə 6–7 bɹɒðə

11 Sa 1–2 bɹɷðəʳ 3–4 bɹʌðəʳ 5 bɹɷðəʳ, °bɹɷdəʳ³ 6–7 bɹʌðəʳ 8 bɹɷðəʳ 9–11 bɹʌðəʳ

12 St 1 bɹɷðə 2 ᵔbɹɷðəz 3–4 bɹɷðə 5 bɹɷðə, °bɹɷðəɹ² [+ V.] 6–7 bɹɷðə 8 bɹɷðəɹ 9 bɹɷðə, °ᵔbɹɷðəz² 10 bɹɷðə 11 bɹə̣ðə

15 He 1–2 bɹʌðəʳ 3 bɹɷðəʳ 4 bɹʌðəʳ, °~² 5 bɹʌðəʳ 6 bɹɷðəʳ 7 bɹɷðəɹ

16 Wo 1 bɹɷðə 2 bɹɷðəʳ 3 bɹɷðəʳ, °bɹɷðəʳɽ² [+ V.] 4–6 bɹɷðəʳ 7 bɹɷðə, °~⁴

17 Wa 1 bɹɷðə 2 bɹɷðə, °~⁴ 3 bɹɷðə, °~³ 4 bɹɷðə 5 bɹɷðəʳ 6 bɹɷðə 7 bɹɷðəʳ

23 Mon 1 bɹʌðəʳ 2 bɹɷðəʳ, °~³, °ᵔbɹɷðəz 3 bɹʌðə 4 bɹʌ̹̆ðə 5 bɹʌ̹̆ðə, °~³ 6 bɹʌðəʳ [ˈbɹʌðəʳˈlɑː¹ *b.-in-law*] 7 n.a.

24 Gl 1–2 bɹɷðəʳ 3 bɹʌðəʳ 4–5 bɹɷðəʳ 6 bɹəðəʳ· 7 bɹɷðəʳ

25 O 1 bɹɷðə 2 bɹʌðəɹ̠ [bɹɷðəɽɪnlaː² *b.-in-law*] 3 bɹʌðəʳ 4 bɽɷðəɽ, °~³ [+ V.], III.3.7 5 bɹʌðəʳ 6 bɹọðə

VIII.1.6 MAN*. WOMAN*

Q. A boy grows up into a youth and then into a . . . .
A girl grows up into a . . . .

Rr. MAN

WOMAN

Note 1—The rr. to the two parts of the q. are separated below by a full stop.

Note 2—For additional exs. of MAN, see III.3.7, VIII.1.25, VIII.8.3 and IX.9.5; of WOMAN, see VIII.1.24 and VIII.5.3a; -MAN occurs at I.2.2–4, II.3.7, II.6.11, III.11.9, VIII.1.19, VIII.5.7a and VIII.8.1. WOMEN occurs at VIII.1.10.

Note 3—I.m. forms of MEN, though irrelevant here, are reproduced below because of their intrinsic interest.

7 Ch 1 mɒn, °~². wɷmən, °~² 2 man, mən [pref.], °man²,⁴, °mən¹,²,⁴⁽⁵ˣ⁾, °ᵔmɛn¹. wɷmən, °~² 3 mɒn. wɷmən 4 mɒn, °~²⁽²ˣ⁾,³. wɷmən 5 mɒn, °~¹⁽²ˣ⁾,³⁽²ˣ⁾ [jɛdmɒn¹ *head-m.* (i.e. headmaster)]. wɷmən 6 mɒn, °man³. wɷmən

8 Db 1 mɒn. wɷmən 2 man, mɒn. wɷmən 3–4 mɒn. wɷmən 5 man. wɷmən 6 mɒn, °~¹⁽²ˣ⁾. wɷmən 7 mɒn. wɷmən

11 Sa 1 man. wɷmən 2 mɒn, ○~², ○man¹ [de:ˈmɑn³ *day-m.*; ˈɹo:dˈmɪn³ *road-men*]. ɷmən, ○~ 3 ma:n. wɷmən 4 ma·n. wɷmən 5 mɒn. ɷmən, ○~³ 6 mɒn⁽²ˣ⁾. wɷmən 7 mɒn, ○manz¹ *poss.* VII.4.11. ɷmən, ○~¹ 8 mɒn. ɷmən, ○~² 9 mɒn, ○~¹. wɷmən 10 mɒn. ɷmən, ○~³ 11 mɒn. ɷmən, ○~²

12 St 1 mɒn, ○~¹,²,³. wɷmən 2 mɒn, ○~¹⁽²ˣ⁾,³,⁵, ○man², ○mɒns⁵ *poss.* [rec. in «mɒns fɛɪs» *m.'s face*], ○□mɛn⁵. wɷmən 3 mɒn, ○~¹⁽³ˣ⁾,². wɷmən, ○~¹⁽²ˣ⁾ 4 mɒn, ○~, ○man¹, ○□mɛn¹. wɷmən 5 mɒn, ○~¹⁽⁴ˣ⁾,²⁽²ˣ⁾, ○man², ○□mɛn¹. wɷmən, ○~¹,², ○wɷməz¹ [*sic*] 6 mɒn, ○~¹⁽²ˣ⁾. wɷmən 7 mɒn, ○~³⁽²ˣ⁾. wɷmən 8 mɒn, ○man⁶. wɷmən 9 mɒn, ○~², ○~² VIII.5.7a, ○□mɛn¹. wɷmən, ○wɷmə² [*sic*] 10 man. wɷmən 11 mæn, ○man², ○mɒn¹, ○□mɛn²⁽²ˣ⁾. wɷmən

15 He 1 mɒn. ɷmən, ○~ 2 mɒn, ○~¹,². ɷmən, ○~²⁽²ˣ⁾, ○~² VIII.1.18 3 mɒn, ○~¹⁽²ˣ⁾. n.r. 4 mɑ:n, ○~³. ɷmən 5 mɒn. ɷmən, ○~³,⁴ 6 mɒn. ɷmən 7 man, ○~¹⁽²ˣ⁾,³⁽²ˣ⁾,⁴⁽²ˣ⁾, ○□mɛn³. wɷmən

16 Wo 1 mɒn, ○man¹. wɷmən 2 mɒn, ○ma·n². ɷmən 3 mɒn. ɷmən 4 mɒn, ○~³, ○□mɛn³. ɷmɷn 5 mɒn, ○~¹⁽³ˣ⁾. ɷmɒn, ○ɷmən¹ 6 mɑ:n, ○mɒn¹,². ɷmɷn, ○ɷmən²,³ 7 man, s.f. mən [pref.], ○man¹,⁴⁽²ˣ⁾, ○mən⁴⁽⁴ˣ⁾, ○mɑ:n¹, ○mə·n¹, ○□mɛn¹ [twɛntɪmɷn¹ *twenty-m.* (i.e. twenty-first child in a family) VII.1.12]. ɷmən, ○~⁴

17 Wa 1 man, ○mɒn¹. wɷmən 2 man, s.f. mən [pref.], ○man¹⁽³ˣ⁾,², ○ma·n¹, ○mən⁴⁽³ˣ⁾, ○□mɛn¹. ɷmən, ○~¹,⁴⁽⁴ˣ⁾ 3 man, ○~³. wɷmən 4 man. wɷmɷn 5 mɒn, ○~¹⁽³ˣ⁾, ○□mɛn¹. ɷmən, ○~¹ 6 man. wɷmɷn 7 man, ○~². ɷmɷn ["very old"]

23 Mon 1 mɑ:n. ɷmən, ○~² 2 mɑ:n, ○mɑ:n³. ɷmən, ○~³ 3 mɑ:n. ɷmən, ○~²⁽³ˣ⁾ 4 ma·n, ○□mɛ·n. wəmʌ̣n 5 mɑ:n. wɷmʌ̣n 6 mɑ:n, ○~¹⁽²ˣ⁾. ɷmən, ○~² 7 n.a., ○mɑ:n¹⁽²ˣ⁾. n.a.

24 Gl 1 mɑ:n, ○mɒn¹⁽²ˣ⁾. ɷmɷn, ○ɷmən¹ 2 mɑ:n [ˈmɪłkˈmɷn³ *milkman*]. ɷmən 3 mɒn, ○mɑ:n¹ [vɒɹəstmɒn¹ *forest-m.*]. ɷmən, ○ɷmən³ VIII.1.20 4 mɑ:n, ○~¹,³. ɷmən 5 man, ○~². ɷmən, ○~², ○wɷmən² 6 mɒn. ɷmən, ○~² 7 man. ɷmən

25 O 1 man. ɷmən, ○~¹ 2 man. ɷmən 3 man, ○~². ɷmən 4 man, ○män³⁽³ˣ⁾, ○□mɛn¹,³, ○□~⁵ VIII.5.7a. ɷman, ○~ 5 man, ○~². ɷmən 6 man, ○~³⁽²ˣ⁾. wɷmən

VIII.1.7 GRANDFATHER. GRANDMOTHER

Q. □ *This boy speaks of him as his . . . .*
And of her as his . . . .

Rr. GRAND–DAD, GRANDFATHER

GRANDMOTHER, GRANNY

Note 1—The rr. to the two parts of the q. are separated below by a full stop.

Note 2—Expressions comparable with some of those listed above also occur at VIII.1.8. For FATHER and MOTHER, see VIII.1.1.

7 Ch 1 gɹanfẹ:ðə. gɹanmɷðə 2 gɹɔnfe:ðə. gɹɔnmɷðə 3 gɹanfe:ðə. gɹanmɷðə 4 gɹanfẹ:ðə. gɹanmɷðə 5 gɹanfi:ðə. gɹanmɷðə 6 gɹanfe:ᵊðə. gɹanmɷðə

8 Db 1 gɹɒnfe:ðəɽ. gɹɒnmɒðəɽ, °gɹanmɷðə[3] 2 gɹanfaðə, gɹɒnfaðə ["older"]. gɹɒnmɷðə 3 gɹɒnfe:ðə. gɹɒnmɒðə 4 gɹɒnfe:də. gɹɒnmɒðə, gɹɒnmɷdə 5 gɹanfe:ðə. gɹanmɒðə 6 gɹanfe:ˡðə, °gɹanfeɩðə[1]. gɹanmɷðə 7 gɹanfẹ·ɩðə. gɹanmɒðə

11 Sa 1 gɹanfa:ðəʴ. gɹanmɷðəʴ 2 gɹandfe:ðəʴ. gɹanmɷðə 3 gɹanfa:ðəʴ. gɹanmʌðəʴ 4 gɹanfaʴ:ðə. gɹanmʌðəʴ 5 gɹanfe:ðəʴ. gɹanmɷðəʴ 6 gɹandfe:ðəʴ. gɹanmʌðəʴ 7 gɹanfe:ðəʴ. gɹanmʌðəʴ 8 gɹanfe:ðəʴ. gɹanmɒðəʴ 9 gɹænfe:ðəʴ. gɹænmʌðəʴ 10 gɹanfe:ðəʴ. gɹanmʌdəʴ 11 gɹanfe:ðəʴ. gɹanmɒdəʴ

12 St 1 gɹanfeɩðə. gɹanmɷðə 2 gɹanfɛɩðə, °gɹanfɛɩðəz[1] *poss.* gɹanmɷðə 3–4 gɹanfɛɩðə. gɹanmɷðə 5 gɹanfɛɩðə. gɹanɩ, gɹanmɷðə 6 gɹanfɛɩðə. gɹanmɒðə 7 gɹanfa:ðə. gɹanɩ 8 gɹanfȧ:ðə. gɹanmɷðə 9 gɹanfɛɩðə. gɹanmɷðə 10 gɹandfa:ðə. gɹanmɷðə 11 gɹanfȧ:ðə. gɹanmʌðə

15 He 1 gɹænfe:ðəʴ. gɹænmɷðəʴ 2 gɹænfi:ðəʴ. gɹænmʌðəʴ 3 gɹænfe:ðəʴ. gɹænmɷðəʴ 4 gɹænfe:ðəʴ. gɹænmʌðəʴ 5–6 gɹænfe:ðəʴ. gɹænmɷðəʴ 7 gɹandad, °~[4]. gɹanɩ

16 Wo 1 gɹanfe:ðə. gɹanmɷðə 2 gɹanfe:ᵊðəʴ. gɹanmɷðəʴ 3 gɹænfɛ:əðəʴ. gɹænmɷðəʴ 4 gɹænfɛ:ᵊðəʴ. gɹænmɷðəʴ 5 gɹænfe:ðəʴ. gɹænmɷðəʴ 6 gɹænfe:ɩðəʴ. gɹænmɷðəʴ 7 gɹandad, s.f. gɹɒndad. gɹanɩ

17 Wa 1 gɹanfa:ðə. gɹanmɷðə 2 gɹanfe:ðə. gɹanmɷðə 3–4 gɹanfa:ðə. gɹanmɷðə 5 gɹanfẹ·əðəʴ. gɹanmɷðəʴ 6 gɹanfa:ðəʴ, °gɹanfe·əðəʴ[3]. gɹanmɷðəʴ 7 gɹanfa:ðəʴ. gɹanmɷðəʴ

23 Mon 1 gɹænfe:ˈðəʳ. gɹænmʌðəʳ 2 gɹænfa:ðəʳ. gɹænmɷðəʳ 3 gɹænfa:ðə. gɹænmʌðə 4 n.a. 5 gɹænfa:ðə. gɹammʌ̣ðə 6 gɹænfa:ðəʳ. gɹænmɷðəʳ 7 n.a., °gɹanfa:ðə[1]. n.a.

24 Gl 1 gɹænfe:ðəʳ, °gɹænfæ:ðəʳ[1]. gɹænmɷðəʳ 2 gɹænfaʳ:ðəʳ. gɹænmɷðəʳ 3 gɹænve:ˈðəʳ. gɹænmʌðəʳ 4 gɹanfjɛðəʳ. gɹanmɷðəʳ 5 gɹanfa:ðə. gɹanmɷðə 6 gɹanfjaðəʳ. gɹanməðəʳ 7 gɹanfa:ðəʳ. gɹanməðəʳ

25 O 1 gɹanfa:ðə. gɹanmɷðəʳ 2 gɹanfa:ðə!. gɹanmʌðə 3 gɹanfa:ðəʳ. gɹanmʌðə 4 gɽandad. gɽanι 5 gɹanfaðəʳ. gɹanmʌðəʳ 6 gɹanfaðə. gɹanmʌðəʳ

VIII.1.8 GRAND-DAD. GRANNY

Q. And, to call them (viz. his grandparents) *into a room, the boy would shout: Come in . . . .*

Rr. GAMP, GONGOG, GRAMP, GRAMPY, GRAND-DAD/FATHER/PA/PAP/SIRE, GRANFER, GRANFEY, TAID

GRAMMER, GRAN, GRANDMA, GRANDMAM, GRANNY, NANNA, NANNY

Note 1—The rr. to the two parts of the q. are separated below by a full stop.

Note 2—The r. TAID at 11.1 represents Welsh *taid* (*=grandfather*).

Note 3—I.m. exs. of GRANNY-REARED (i.e. brought up by a grandmother) are reproduced between square brackets below untransliterated.

Note 4—Expressions comparable with some of those listed above occur at VIII.1.7. NANNY- occurs at IV.8.10.

7 Ch 1 gɹandad. gɹanma: 2 gɹəndad, °gɹandad[4]. gɹanι 3–5 gɹandad. gɹanι 6 gɹandad. gɹanmam, gɹanι

8 Db 1 gɹɒndad. gɹɒnma: 2 gɹɒnfaðə. gɹanι 3 gɹɒnfe:ðə. gɹɒnι 4 gɹɒndad. gɹɒnma: 5–7 gɹandad. gɹanι

11 Sa 1 gɹandad, taιd ["older"]. gɹanι 2 gɹandad. gɹanmam [gɹanιɹιəʳɖ[2]] 3 gɹandad. gɹanmam 4 gɹandad. nanι 5 gɹandad. gɹanma: 6 gɹandad. gɹanι 7 gɹanfəʳ. gɹanι 8 gɹandad. gɹanma: [gɹanιɹιəʳɖ[1]] 9 gɹændæ·d. gɹænι 10 gɹandad. gɹanmam [gɹanιɹəʳ:ɖ[2]] 11 gɹandad. gɹanι [gɹanιɹəʳ:ɖ[2]]

12 St 1–3 gɹandad. gɹanι 4 gɹandad. gɹanι(2x) 5–6 gɹandad. gɹanι 7 gɹandad, °~. gɹanι, °~[3] [gɹanιɹιəd[4]] 8 gɹandad. gɹan 9–10 gɹandad. gɹanι 11 gɹandạd. gɹanι

15 He 1 gɹændæd. gɹæn 2 gɹændæd. gɹæn [gɹænɪɹaʳ:ɖ[2]] 3–4 gɹændæd. gɹæni: 5 gɹænfəʳ. gɹæni: [gɹænɪɹɛəʳɖ[2]] 6 gɹændæd. gɹænma: 7 gɒŋgɒg ["baby word"], ○~[4(2x)]. nanə [gɹanɪɹɛəɹd[4] V.7.11]

16 Wo 1 gɹandad. gɹanɪ 2 gɹandad. gɹanɪ [gɹanɪɹɛ·əʳɖ[2]] 3 gɹændæd. gɹænɪ 4 gɹændæd. gɹænmɑʳ: 5 gɹændæd. gɹænɪ 6 gɹændæ:d. gɹæn [gɹænɪɹɪəʳ:ɖ[3]] 7 gɹandad, s.f. gɹɒndad. gɹan, ○~[1]

17 Wa 1 gɹandad. gɹanᵉɪ 2 gɹandad, ○~. gɹanma:, ○gɹanɪ[4] *poss.* [rec. in «məɪ gɹanɪ bɹɷðə» *my granny*('s) *brother*] 3 gɹandad. gɹanɪ 4 gɹanpap. gɹanᴵɪ· 5 gɹandad. gɹanma: 6 gɹandad. gɹanᵊɪ 7 gɹandad. gɹanɪ

23 Mon 1 gɹænʃəʳ. gɹænɪ 2 gɹænʃ. gɹæn 3 gɹænʃə. gɹænɪ 4 n.a. 5 gɹamp. nanə 6 gɹæmp. gɹænɪ 7 n.a.

24 Gl 1 gɹændæ:d. gɹænɪ 2 gɹæmp. gɹæn 3 gɹænʃəʳ. gɹænɪ 4 gɹamp, ○gɹanpə[1]. gɹan 5 gɹamp. gɹanɪ 6 gɹanʃɪ. gɹanɪ 7 gɹanfɪ. gɹanɪ

25 O 1 gɹampɪ, ○gɹamp[1]. gɹan, ○~[2(2x)], ○gɹanɪ[2] 2 gɹampɪ. gɹanɪ 3 gɹampɪ. gɹamə 4 gɽamp, ○~[5], ○gamp ["baby talk"]. gɽan 5 gɹamp. gɹanɪ 6 gɹampɪ [old]. gɹanɪ

VIII.1.9 RESEMBLES

Q. □ *Look at their faces now. Don't you think this boy . . . . his grandfather?*

Rr. FAVOURS, ir.r. FEATURE ONE ANOTHER, FEATURES, FOLLOWS (HIM IN LOOKS), IS LIKE, IS THE SPIT, IS THE (VERY) SPIT OF, RESEMBLES, TAKES AFTER

Note 1—In the lists above, IS subsumes BE, and uninflected 3 pr.s. forms are not separately listed.

Note 2—The rr. at 11.1, 12.2/4 and 25.1(2nd r.) are regarded here as 3 pr.ss.

Note 3—In the r. at 8.7, the expected prep. was not rec.

7 Ch 1 favəz 2 fe:vəz, ○~[2] 3 favəz 4 fi̞:tʃəz [ɪz ðə dɛd spɪt ɒn jə *he's the dead spit on* (=*of*) *you*] 5 fɛɪtʃəz 6 fe:tʃəᶦz

8 Db 1 favəᶦz 2 favəz 3 fe:vəz 4 tɛks aftə 5 fi:tʃəz 6 fe:ᴵvəz 7 ɪz ðə spɪt

11 Sa 1 te:k aʳ:ftəʳ 2 fi:tʃəz 3 te:ks aftəʳ 4 te:ks aʳ:ftə 5 fę:tʃəʳʐ 6 te:ks aftəʳ 7 te:ks æftəʳ 8 fe:tʃəʳʐ 9 te:ks æ·ftəʳ 10 te:ks a:ftəʳ 11 te:ks a:ftəʳ [dɷnəɹ‿i: fi:tʃəʳɽ‿ɪm *doesn't he feature* (=*resemble*) *him?*]

12 St 1 ɪz lɒɪk 2 fɛɪvə 3 ɛɪz [=*he's*] lɒ:ɪk, fi:tʃɪz 4 fi:tʃə 5 ɪz lɒ:ɪk 6 ir.r. fi:tʃə wɒn ənɷðə 7–11 fi:tʃəz

15 He 1 fi:tʃəz 2 fɒlo:z [jɷnt i: ləɪk ɪz fi:ðəʳ *isn't he like his father?* VIII.1.1] 3–6 fi:tʃəʳʐ 7 feɪvəz, ɪz ðə vɛɹɪ spɪt ɒv

16 Wo 1 fɛɪtʃəz 2–5 fi:tʃəʳʐ 6 fe:ɪtʃəʳʐ 7 bi: ðə spɪt əv

17 Wa 1 fi:tʃəz 2 fələz ɪm [=*him*] ɪn lɷks, fələz 3 ɪz ləɪk 4 fi:tʃəʳʐ 5 fi:tʃəʳ 6 fi:tʃəʳʐ 7 fi:tʃəʳ:ʐ

23 Mon 1 fʻi:tʃəʳʐ 2 fi:tʃəz 3 fe:vəz [do:n‿ɪ fe:vəɹ‿ɪm *doesn't he f. him?*] 4 n.a. 5 z‿lə̞ɪk [ðə lɪvɪn ɪmɪdʒ *the living image*] 6 fi:ɪtʃəʳʐ 7 n.a.

24 Gl 1 fi:tʃəʳʐ 2 fe:tʃəʳʐ 3 vʻi:tʃəʳʐ 4 fʻi:tʃəz 5 ɪz lə̈ɪk 6 vi:tʃəʳʐ 7 ɹɪzɛmblz

25 O 1 ɪz lə̈ɪk, fe:tʃəʳ ["older"] 2 fɛɪvəʳʐ 3 fe:vəʳʐ 4 ɪz łaɪk 5 feɪvəʳʐ 6 feɪvəz, ○feɪvəʳʐ[3] [i:z ðɪ ɪmɪdʒ əv ju: *he's the image of you*]

VIII.1.10 WOMEN*

Q. □ *You wouldn't call these two* [*p.*] men, *would you? They are . . . .*

R. WOMEN

Note—For WOMAN, see VIII.1.6 (and refs.).

7 Ch 1–6 wɪmɪn

8 Db 1 wɷmən 2–6 wɪmɪn 7 wɪmɪn, ○~[2]

11 Sa 1–6 wɪmɪn 7 wɪmən 8–11 wɪmɪn

12 St 1 wɪmɪn, ○~[2] 2 wɪ̞mɪn 3–6 wɪmɪn 7 wɪmɪn, ○~[1] 8–11 wɪmɪn

15 He 1–2 wɪmɪn 3 wɪmən 4–7 wɪmɪn

16 Wo 1–4 wɪmɪn 5 wɪmɪ:n 6 wɪmɪn 7 p. wɪmɪn, ○~[1]

17 Wa 1 wɪmɪn 2 wɪmɪn, ○~[1] 3–7 wɪmɪn

23 Mon 1–3 wɪmɪn 4 wɪm:ɪ̃n 5 wɪ̃mɪn 6 wɪmɪn 7 n.a.

24 Gl 1 wɪmɪn, ○~[1] 2–6 wɪmɪn 7 wɪmɪn, ○~[1]

25 O 1–2 wɪmɪn 3 wɪmɪn, ○~[2] 4–6 wɪmɪn

VIII.1.11 BROUGHT† HER UP

Q. This girl's mother died, so her grandmother took her and . . . .

If necessary, suggest *bring up* to get *brought up*.

Rr. BROUGHT HER UP, KEPT/MOTHERED HER, REARED HER (UP)

Note 1—This q. was intended to elicit the local form of BROUGHT. But REARED frequently and KEPT occ. emerged as the 1st r., obviously indicating the appropriateness of both words in this context. Strictly speaking, these are u.rr.

Note 2—At 7.4 (2nd r.) and 7.6, the f.w. omitted to rec. the pronominal obj. At 7.2, 16.7 and 17.2, P.W. used the 4th version of the Qr., in which the q. read: *This boy's mother died, so his grandmother took him and . . . .* Hence at the locs. concerned the rr. contain HIM not HER.

Note 3—I.m. exs. of BRING and BROUGHT, as well as of HER when used as a pronominal obj., are reproduced below between square brackets untransliterated. An attached superior ◇ denotes a p.p.

Note 4—For additional exs. of HER as pronominal obj., see III.3.6 and IV.6.8. HER as pronominal subj. occurs at III.1.7/10–12, III.4.6, III.8.10, III.13.14, VI.14.14, VIII.9.5, IX.7.2/3/6–10 and IX.9.7; HER *poss.* occurs at III.1.11, III.3.6, III.4.6 and III.7.4; HERS at IX.8.5. GRANNY-REARED *adj.* occurs at VIII.1.8.

7 Ch 1 bɹɛɷt əɹ ɷp 2 bɹɔ:t ɪm ɷp [bɹɪŋ[1,2], bɹɪŋɪn[2] (n.d.g.)] 3 bɹɛ̈ɷt əɹ ɷp 4 ɹɪəd ə, p. bɹɛɷt [bɹɪŋ[2], bɹɪŋɪn[1] (n.d.g.); ə[1,2,3]] 5 ɹɪəd ə [pref.], p. bɹɛɷt əɹ ɷp 6 ɹɪəɹd [ə[2]]

8 Db 1 bɹɒɷt əɹ ɷp [ə[3]] 2 bɹɒɷt əɹ ɷp [¶bɹɪŋɪn[2]] 3 bɹɛɷt əɹ ɷp 4 bɹɒɷtt‿əɹ‿ɷp [bɹɪŋg[3]] 5 bɹɛɷt əɹ ɷp, ɹɪəd ə ["older"; bɹɪŋg[1] (+ V.)] 6 bɹɛɷ̆t əɹ ɷp [ə[1(2x)]] 7 bɹɛɷt əɹ ɷp

11 Sa 1 bɹɔʴ:ʈ əʴ: ʌp 2 ɹɪəd əʴ, bɹɔ:t əʴɽ ɷp 3 bɹɔʴ:ʈ əʴɽ‿ʌp, ɹəʴ:ɖ ə 4 bɹɔʴ:ʈ əʴ· ʌp 5 bɹɔ:t əʴɽ ɷp, kɛp əʴ [əʴ[3(3x)]] 6 bɹɔʴ:ʈ əʴ·ɽ‿ʌp, ɹəʴ:ɖ əʴ 7 bɹɔʴ:ʈ əʴɽ‿ʌp 8 bɹɔ:t əʴɽ ɷp [əʴ:[1]] 9 bɹɔʴ:ʈ əʴɽ‿ʌp, ɹəʴ:ɖ əʴ· 10 bɹɔʴ:ʈ əʴɽ‿ʌp [əʴ:[3]] 11 bɹɔ:t əʴ:ɽ ʌp [əʴ:[2]]

12 St 1 bɹɔ:t əɹ ɷp, mɷðəd ə [ə[2], ə:[5]] 2 ɹɪəd ə [ə[1], ə:[1]] 3 ɹɪəd ə, bɹɛɷt əɹ ɷp [bɹɪŋgɪn[1] (n.d.g.), bɹɪŋgz[1]; ə:[1]] 4 bɹɔ:t əɹ ɷp 5 bɹoɷt əɹ ɷp [bɹɪŋ[1]] 6 kɛpt ə, bɹɔ:t əɹ ɷp [◇bɹɔ:t ɪm ɷp[1] *brought him up*; ə[1,2(2x)], ə:[1], əɹ (+ V.; pres. ref. knife, Edd.), ə:ɹ[2] (+ V.)] 7 bɹɔ:t əɹ ɷp, ɹɪəd ə [ə[3(2x)]] 8 bɹɔ:t əɹ ɷp [bɹɪŋg[1] (+ C.)] 9 ɹɛ:d ə, bɹɔ:t əɹ ɷp [bɹɪŋ[1]] 10 ɹɪəd ə: [usu.; "*bring* rare"] 11 bɹɔ:t əɹ ɷp, ◦◇ɹɪəd əɹ ɷp [bɹɪŋg[2] (+ V.); ə[2]]

15 He 1 ɹɪəʴɖ əʴ, bɹɔ:t əʴɽ ʌp 2 bɹɔ:t əʴɽ ʌp, ɹaʴ:ɖ əʴɽ ʌp [əʴ[2]] 3 bɹɑ:t əʴɽ ɷ:p [bɹɪŋ[3]] 4 bɹɑ:t əʴɽ ʌp [əʴ[2]] 5 bɹɑ:t əʴɽ ʌp, ɹɛəʴɖ əʴ [əʴ[3]] 6 bɹɑʴ:ʈ əʴɽ ɷp 7 ɹɛəɹd əɹ, bɹɔ:t əɹ ɷp [◇bɹʌŋ[4]; əɹ[4(2x)]]

16 Wo 1 bɹɑ:t əʵɻ ɷp, ɹɩəd əʵɻ ɷp [əʵ[1(2x)]] 2 ɹɛ·əʵɖ 3 bɹɑ:t əʵɻ ɷp, ɹəʵ:ɖ əʵ [bɹɩŋg[5] (+ V.)] 4 bɹɑʵ:ʈ əʵ:ɻ ɷp, ɹaʵ:ɖ əʵ 5 bɹɑ:t əʵɻ ɷp [əʵ[1]] 6 bɹɑʵ:ʈ əʵɻ ɷp, ɹɛ:əʵɖ əʵ [ɒɩ wəz bɹɑ:t ɷp[2] *I was b. up*; əʵ[2]] 7 bɹɔ:t ɩm ɷp [bɹɔ:t ɷp[4] *b. up*, bɹɩŋ[3], bɹɩŋz[4]; əɹ[3], əʵ[4(2x)]]

17 Wa 1 kɛp ə, bɹɔ:t əɹ ɷp 2 bɹɔ:t ɩm ɷp, p. ɹɛəd ɩm [bɹɔ:t[4]; ə:[1] (ref. a hedge), əɹ[3] (+ V.), ə:[3]] 3 bɹɔ̣:t əɹ ɷp [bɹɩŋ[2]] 4 bɹɔ:t əɹ ɷp [əʵ·[1], əɹ[1] (+ V.; pres. ref. fire, Edd.)] 5 bɹɔ:t əɹ ɷp [əʵ:ɻ[1] (+ V.), ə[1]] 6–7 bɹɔ:t əɹ ɷp

23 Mon 1 bɹɑʵ:ʈ əʵɻ ʌp 2 bɹɑ:t əʵɻ ɷp, ɹɛəʵɖ əʵ 3 bɹɑ:t əɹ ʌp, ɹɛəd ə 4 bɹɔ:tʰ əɹ ʌ̣̈pʰ [◇bɹɔ:tʰ] 5 ɹɛ:d ə, p. bɹɔ:t əɹ ʌ̣̈pʰ 6 bɹɑʵ:ʈ əʵɻ ʌp [bɹaʵ:ʈ[1]; əʵɻ[1] (+ V.), əʵ[1]] 7 n.a.

24 Gl 1 bɹɑ:t əʵɻ ɷ:p 2 bɹɑ:t əʵɻ ɷ:p 3 bɹɑ:t əʵɻ ʌp 4 bɹɑ:t əʵɻ ɷp [əʵ:[3]] 5 bɹɔ:t əɹ ɷp 6 bɹɔ:t əɹ əp [ə[1]] 7 bɹɔ:d əɹ əp

25 O 1 bɹɔ:t əɻ ʌp 2 bɹɔ:d̥ əɹ ʌp [əʵ̣:[2]] 3 bɹɔ:t əɹ ʌp [bɹɩŋz[2] *3 pr.pl.* VIII.5.1] 4 bɻɔ̣:d̥ əɻ ɷp [bɻɩŋz[1] *1 pr.s.*] 5 bɹɔ:ʔ əɻ ʌpʻ [əɻ[2] (+ V.)] 6 bɹɔ:ʔ əɹ ʌp [əʵ:[3]]

VIII.1.12 UNCLE*. AUNT*

Q. □ *If this man had a brother, he'd be their . . . .*
And if he had a sister, she'd be their . . . .

Rr. (N)UNK, (N)UNCLE

AUNT(IE), NAUNT

Note 1—The rr. to the two parts of the q. are separated below by a full stop.
Note 2—For additional exs. of NUNK and (N)UNCLE, see IX.9.6.

7 Ch 1 ɷŋkl. ant 2 ɷŋkl, ○□ɷŋklz[4(3x)]. ant, ○□ants[4(2x)] 3 ɷŋkl. ant 4 nɷŋkl. ant 5 nɷŋk, nɷŋkl [“rare”]. nant 6 nɷŋk. ant

8 Db 1 nɷŋkl. nant, ○∼ [foll. «mɩ» *my*] 2 nɷŋkl. nənt, ○∼ [*foll.* «mɩ» *my*] 3–4 ɷŋkl. ɒnt 5 ɷŋkl, ɷntl. ant 6 ɷŋkl. ã:ntɩ 7 ɷŋkl. a:nt

11 Sa 1 ʌŋkl. a:nt 2 ɷŋkl. ant 3 ʌŋkl. ant 4 ʌŋkl. a:nt 5 nɷŋkl. nę:nt 6 ʌŋkl. ant 7 ʌŋkl. a:nt 8 ɷŋkl. a:nt 9 ʌŋkl. æ:nt 10–11 ʌŋkl. a:nt

12 St 1–2 ɷŋkl. ant 3–7 ɷŋkl. a:nt 8 ɷŋkl, ○∼[2]. a̱:ntɩ 9–10 ɷŋkl. a:nt 11 ʌŋkl. a̱:nt

15 He 1 ʌŋkł. ænt 2 ʌŋkł. a:nt 3 ɷŋkł. ænti: 4 ʌŋkł. ȧ:nti: 5 ʌŋkł. ɒnt 6 ɷŋkł. ænt 7 ɷŋkl. ant

16 Wo 1 ɷŋkl . a̠:nt 2 ɷŋkɫ . a:nt 3 ɷŋkɫ, °~[2] . ɑ:nt 4 ɷŋkɫ . æ:nt 5 ɷŋkɫ . a:nt 6 ɷŋkɫ . æ:ntι 7 ɷŋkɫ, °ɷŋkl[3] . ɑ:nt

17 Wa 1 ɷŋkl, ṅɷŋk ["older"] . ä:nt, antᵉι ["older"] 2 ɷŋkl, °~[3] . a:nt, °ɑ:nt[3] 3 ɷŋkɫ . a:nt, °a:ntᵊῐ 4–7 ɷŋkɫ . a:nt

23 Mon 1 ʌŋkɫ . ænt 2 ɷŋkɫ . ænt 3 ʌŋkɫ . a:nt 4 ʌ̰̈ŋkɫ . antʰ 5 ʌ̰̈ŋkɫ . a:nt, °ant[1] 6 ʌŋkɫ . a:nt 7 n.a.

24 Gl 1 ɷŋkɫ, °□ɷŋkɫz[3] . æ:nt 2 ɷŋkɫ . a:nt 3 ʌŋkɫ . ə nænt 4 ɷŋkɫ, °~[2] . a:nt 5 ɷŋkɫ . a:nt 6 nəŋkl . a:nt 7 əŋkɫ . a:nt

25 O 1 ɷŋkɫ . a:nt 2 ʌŋkl . a:nt 3 ɷŋkl . a:nt 4 ɷŋk . a:nt 5 ʌŋkɫ . a:nʔ 6 ɷŋkɫ . a:nʔ, °anʔ[3]

VIII.1.13 NEPHEW*

Q. □ *And this boy would be the brother's . . . .*

R. NEPHEW

7 Ch 1 nɛfjʏ: 2 s.f. nɛfι 3 nɛfjʏ: 4 nɛvjɷ, °nɛvjə[1] 5 nɛfjɷ 6 nɛvju:

8 Db 1 nɛfjʏ: 2 nɛfι, °~[4] 3–7 nɛfι

11 Sa 1 nɛfu: 2 nɛvιu: 3 nɛvəʳ 4 nɛfu: 5 nɛvju: 6 nɛfιu: 7 nɛfι 8 nɛvι 9 nɛvu: 10 nɛvιu: 11 nɛfιu

12 St 1 □nɛfju:s 2 nɛfju 3–4 nɛfju: 5 nɛvju: 6–7 nɛfju: 8 nɛvju: 9 nɛfju:, °nɛfju[2] 10 nɛfjü: 11 nɛfju:

15 He 1 nɛvju:, °~[1] 2–6 nɛvju: 7 nɛvju:, °~

16 Wo 1 nefιu: 2 nɛfju: 3 nɛfιu: 4 nɛfju: 5 nɛvju: 6 nɛvιu: 7 nɛvju:, °~[3]

17 Wa 1–6 nɛfju: 7 nɛvju:

23 Mon 1 nɛvjɷu: 2 nɛvju:, °~[1,3] 3 nɛvju: 4 ir.r. 5 nɛvjιu 6 nɛvju: 7 n.a.

24 Gl 1–2 nɛvju: 3 nɛvj°u:, °nɛvju:[1] 4 nɛvjɷu: 5 nɛfju: 6 nɛvι 7 nɛvju:

25 O 1 nɛvju: 2 nɛvju:, s.f. nɛvι 3 nɛvι 4 nɛvιu 5 nɛvju: 6 nɛvι

VIII.1.14 NIECE*

Q. □ *And this girl would be the brother's . . . .*

R. NIECE

7 Ch 1 nẹ:s 2 s.w. ni:s 3 nɛɩs 4 nị:s 5 nɛɩs 6 ni:s

8 Db 1–3 ni:s 4 ir.r. 5 ni:s 6–7 nɛɩs

11 Sa 1–2 ni:s 3 nʻi:s 4 ni:s 5 nɩi:s 6–11 ni:s

12 St 1 □ni:sɩz 2 ni:s 3 nɛɩs 4–11 ni:s

15 He 1–6 ni:s 7 ni:s, ○~

16 Wo 1–5 ni:s 6 ne:ɩs 7 ni:s

17 Wa 1–7 ni:s

23 Mon 1 nʻi:s 2–3 ni:s 4 nị:s̬ 5–6 ni:s 7 n.a.

24 Gl 1 ni:^{ə}s 2 nɩi:s 3 ne:ʻs 4 nʻi:s 5–7 ni:s

25 O 1–6 ni:s

VIII.1.15 COUSINS*

Q. □ *And the children of the brothers are their . . . .*

R. COUSINS

7 Ch 1 kɷznz 2 kɷzɩnz [e:fkɷzənz[4] *half-cs.*] 3–6 kɷznz

8 Db 1–6 kɷznz 7 △kɷzn

11 Sa 1 kʌzənz 2 kɷznz 3 kʌzənz 4 kɒznz 5 kɷznz 6 kʌzənz 7 kʌznz 8 kɷznz 9–11 kʌznz

12 St 1–11 kɷznz

15 He 1 kʌznz 2 kʌznz, ○△kʌzn[1] 3 kɷzənz 4–5 kʌznz 6 kɷzənz 7 kɷzənz, ○△kʌzən[4]

16 Wo 1 kɷzənz 2–3 kɷzɩnz 4 kɷzəns 5–6 kɷzənz 7 kɷznz

17 Wa 1 kɷznz 2 kɷzənz 3–5 kɷznz 6 △kɷzn 7 kɷznz

23 Mon 1 kʌznz 2 kɷznz 3 kʌznz 4 k^{h}ʌ̣̈znz 5 kʌ̣̈znz 6 kʌzənz 7 n.a.

24 Gl 1 kɷzənz 2 kɷzɷnz 3 kʌznz 4 kɷzɩnz 5 kɷznz 6–7 kəznz

25 O 1 kɷznz 2–3 kʌznz 4 kɷzənz, ○~^{5} 5 kʌznz 6 kɷznz

VIII.1.16 READY

Q. Jack, waiting to go out with Mary, shouts: Have you got your things on yet? And she answers: Yes, I'm quite . . . .

Rr. FIT, READY

Note—For additional exs. of READY, see IV.7.2 and V.10.5.

7 Ch 1 ɹɛdɩ [ɔ: bɷt ɹɛdɩ *all but* (i.e. nearly) *r.*] 2 ɹɛdɩ, ○~^{3} 3 ɹɛdɩ 4 ɹɛd^{ɩ}ɩ 5–6 ɹɛdɩ

8 Db 1–5 ɹɛdɩ 6 ɹɛdɩ, ○~ 7 ɹɛdɩ

11 Sa 1–6 ɹɛdɩ 7 ɹɛdɩ, ○~^{1} IV.8.6 8 ɹɛdɩ 9 ɹɛdɩ, ○~^{1} II.3.5 10–11 ɹɛdɩ

12 St 1 ɹɛdɩ 2 ɹɛ·dɩ, ○ɹɛdɩ^{1} 3–10 ɹɛdɩ 11 ɹɛdi

15 He 1–2 ɹɛdɩ 3 ɹɛdɩ, ○~^{1} 4–6 ɹɛdɩ 7 ɹɛdɩ, ○~

16 Wo 1–6 ɹɛdɩ 7 fɩt, ○ɹɛdɩ^{1}

17 Wa 1 ɹɛ̣d^{e}ɩ 2 ɹɛdɩ, ○~ 3 ɹɛd^{ɩ}ɪ̈ 4–5 ɹɛdɩ 6 ɹɛd^{ə}ɩ 7 ɹɛdɩ

23 Mon 1–3 ɹɛdɩ 4–5 ɹɛdi 6 ɹɛdɩ 7 n.a.

24 Gl 1–5 ɹɛdɩ 6 ɹɛdɩ, ○~ 7 ɹɛdɩ

25 O 1 ɹɛdɩ 2 ɹɛdɩ, ○~^{3} 3 ɹɛdɩ [əɽɛdɩ^{2} *already*] 4 ɽɛdɩ, ○~$^{1,2(2x),5}$ 5 ɹɛdɩ, s.w. fɩt 6 ɹɛdɩ

VIII.1.17 MARRIED

Q. If your son Jack is not single, he must be . . . .

Rr. MARRIED, TIED UP, WED

Note 1—In the i.m. below, an attached superior × denotes a p.p.
Note 2—For additional exs. of MARRIED and WED, see VIII.1.19 and IX.7.2/3.

7 Ch 1 maɹɩt 2 maɹɩd, ○maɹɩt^{4} 3 maɹɩt 4–6 maɹɩd

8 Db 1 wɛd 2 maɹɩd, wɛd ["older"] 3–7 maɹɩd

11 Sa 1 maɹɩd 2 wɛd 3–4 maɹɩd 5 mɒɹɩd 6–8 maɹɩd 9–10 mæɹɩd 11 maɹɩd, wɛd ["older"]

12 St 1 maɹɪd, °×~⁴, °~² [n.d.g.] 2 maɹɪd, °~² 3 maɹɪd, tɛɪd ɷp [pres. facetious, Edd.], °maɹɪd¹ *3 p.t.pl.*, °×~¹ 4 maɹɪd 5 maɹɪd, °~³, °~³ *3 p.t.s.* 6–10 maɹɪd 11 maɹɪd, °~²

15 He 1–3 mæɹɪd 4–6 mɒɹɪd 7 mæɹɪd

16 Wo 1 maɹɪd 2 maɹɪd, °wɛd *3 p.t.s.* 3 wɛ:d 4 mɒɹɪd, °mæɹɪd³ 5 mɒɹɪd 6 wɛd 7 maɹɪd, °~⁴

17 Wa 1–7 maɹɪd

23 Mon 1 mæɹɪd, °×~¹ 2 mæɹɪd, °~³ 3 mæɹɪd 4 n.a. 5 maɹid 6 ma:ɹɪd 7 n.a.

24 Gl 1 wɛd, °~ 2 mæɹɪd 3 wɛd, °~ 4 mɒɹɪd 5 maɹɪd, °~² 6 maɹɪd̥ 7 maɹɪd

25 O 1–3 maɹɪd 4–5 maɽɪd 6 maɹɪd

VIII.1.18 MY DAUGHTER-IN-LAW

Q. *If* (your son) *Jack had married someone called Mary, you'd speak of her as . . . .*

Rr. (MY) DAUGHTER-IN-LAW, (OUR) JACK'S WIFE, JACK'S WOMAN, OUR /§BILL'S WIFE/JACK'S MARY~MISSIS/MARY/, (MY) SON'S WIFE

Note 1—The f.w. often omitted to rec. an expression for MY.

Note 2—I.m. exs. of MY are reproduced below between square brackets untransliterated.

Note 3—For additional exs. of MY, see VI.2.2, VI.5.2, VII.5.2 and VIII.1.24/25; MYSELF occurs at IX.11.1/3. For exs. of DAUGHTER, see VIII.1.4; of WOMAN, see VIII.1.6; of expressions for WIFE, see VIII.1.24; and of OUR, see VI.3.3 and VIII.8.8.

7 Ch 1 a: mɛ:ɹɪ 2 dɔ:təɹɪnlɔ:, s.w. æɷə dʒaks wæ̞ɪf [mɪ¹⁽²ˣ⁾,²⁽⁶ˣ⁾,⁴⁽³ˣ⁾, mɑɪ²,³] 3 a: dʒaks wɛɪf [mɪ³] 4 dɔ:təɹɪnlɔ: [mɪ¹] 5 a: dʒaks wɛɪf [mɪ²⁽³ˣ⁾, mɑɪ³] 6 aɷə dʒaks mɛ:ɹɪ

8 Db 1 mɪ dɒɷttəɹɪnlɔ: [mɪ⁵, maɪ³] 2 a: dʒaks wɑɪf [mɪ²,⁴⁽²ˣ⁾, mɑ:⁴] 3 dɛɷttɹɪnlɔ: [mɪ¹, ma:²] 4 a dʒɛks wɑɪf [mɪ³] 5 a: mɛ:ɹɪ 6 mɪ dɛɷtəɹɪlɔ: [mɪ¹⁽²ˣ⁾] 7 dʒaks wɑ̃·ɪ̃f, mɪ dɛɷtəɹɪnlɔ:

11 Sa 1 dʒaks waɪf [mɪ⁴] 2 dʒaks wæɪf [mɪ³, maɪ²⁽²ˣ⁾] 3 dʒaks wɛɪf 4 dʒaks waɪf 5 dʒaks waɪf [mɪ³⁽²ˣ⁾] 6 maɪ dɔʳ:ʈəʳlɔʳ:, dʒaks waɪf [usu.; mɪ³, maɪ³,⁴] 7 dʒæ·ks waɪf 8 dʒaks wɒɪf 9 dʒæ·ks waɪf 10 dʒæks waɪf 11 dʒaks waɪf [mɪ²⁽²ˣ⁾, maɪ²]

12 St 1 mɒɩ dɘ:tɹɪnlɘ: [mɩ$^{2(2x),4}$] 2 mɒɩ daɷtɹɩlaɷ 3 mɒ:ɩ dɛɷtɹɪnlɘ: [mɩ$^{1(2x),2}$, mɒ:ɩ^{2}] 4 dɘ:tɹɪnlɘ: [mɩ^{2,3}, maɩ^{1}] 5 mɒ:ɩ dɘ:tɹɪnlɘ: [mɩ$^{1(2x)}$, mɒ:ɩ^{1}] 6 mɒ:ɩ dɘ:tɹɪnlɘ: [mɩ$^{1(2x),2}$] 7 mɒɩ dɘ̣:tɹɪnlɘ̣: [mɩ^{3,4}, mɒɩ^{1}, ~^{1} VIII.8.12] 8 mɒɩ dɘ̣:tɹɪnlɘ̣: [mɒɩ^{2}] 9 mɒɩ dɘ:tɹɪnlɘ: [mɩ$^{1,2(2x)}$, mɒɩ$^{1(3x)}$] 10 ma: dɘ:tɘɹɪnlɘ: [mɩ^{5}] 11 dɘ:tɹɪnlɘ:

15 He 1 mɩ dɘ:tɘ˞lɘ˞: 2 dʒæks wɘɩf, dʒæks ɷmɘn ["usu."] 3 dʒæks wɘɩf, °mɩ dɑ˞:ʈɘ˞lɑ:^{1} [mɩ^{2}, mɘɩ^{4}] 4 dʒæks wɘɩf [mɩ^{2}, mɘɩ^{1}] 5 dʒæks ɷmɘn [mɩ^{1}] 6 dʒæks wɘɩf [mɩ^{1}, mɘɩ$^{1(2x)}$] 7 dɘ:tɘɹɪnlɘ: ["more polite"], [mɩ^{3,4}, maɩ$^{2,3(5x),4(3x)}$, mɑɩ^{4}]

16 Wo 1 dʒaks wɒɩf [mɩ^{1}] 2 dʒaks wɘɩf [mɩ^{2}, mɒɩ^{2}] 3 dʒæks wɘi:f [mɩ^{1,2}, mɘi:^{1} VIII.9.4] 4 dʒæks wɘɩf [mɒɩ^{1}] 5 dʒæks wɘɩf [mɩ^{1}, mɒɩ$^{1(3x)}$, mɘɩ^{1}] 6 dʒæks wɒɩf [mɒɩ$^{3(2x)}$] 7 dɑ:tɘɹɪnlɘ̣:, s.w. æɷɘ dʒaks wɘɩf [mɩ$^{3,4(2x)}$, ~^{4} IX.8.1, ~^{4} IX.11.3, mɘɩ$^{1(8x),2(2x),4(4x)}$]

17 Wa 1 dɘ:tɹɪnlɘ: [mɑɩ^{1,2}] 2 dɘ:tɘɹɪnlɘ:, p. sɷnz wɘɩf [pref.; mɩ$^{1,3,4(3x)}$, mɘɩ$^{3(4x),4(10x)}$, mɑɩ^{2}] 3 s.w. ɛɷɘ dʒaks wɘɩf [mɘɩ^{1}] 4 mɩ sɷnz wɘɩf 5 mɘɩ sɷnz wɘɩf [mɩ$^{1(2x)}$, mɘɩ^{1}] 6 dɘ:tɘɹɪnlɘ: 7 ɛɷɘ˞ dʒaks wɘɩf [mɘɩ^{2}]

23 Mon 1 dʒæks wɘɩf [mɩ^{1}] 2 dɑ:tɘ˞lɑ: [mɘ^{3}, mɘɩ^{3}] 3 dʒæks wɘɩf [mɘɩ$^{1(2x)}$] 4 n.a. 5 dɘ:tɘɹɪnlɘ̣: [mɘi$^{1(3x)}$] 6 mɩ dɑ˞:ʈɘ˞lɑ: [mɩ^{1}; bɹʌðɘ˞lɑ:^{1} *brother-in-l.* VIII.1.5] 7 n.a.

24 Gl 1 dʒæks wɘɩf 2–3 dʒæks wɘɩf [mɘɩ^{3}] 4 da˞:ʈɘ˞lɑ: [mɘɩ^{2}] 5 ʌɷɘ˞ dʒaks wɘ̈ɩf [mɩ^{2}, mɘ̈ɩ$^{2(2x)}$] 6 °u:ɘ˞: dʒaks mɩsɩs [mɩ^{1}, mʌɩ^{2}] 7 °u:ɘ˞ §bɩlz wʌɩf [mɩ^{1}, ~^{1} IX.11.1, mʌɩ^{1}]

25 O 1 mɘɩ da˞:ʈɘ-ɪnla: [mɘɩ^{2}, mɘ̈ɩ^{2}] 2 da˖:tɘ˞ɽɪnlɘ: [mɩ^{3}, mɘ̈ɩ^{3}; bɹɷðɘɽɪnla:^{2} *brother-in-l.* VIII.1.5] 3 dʒaks wʌɩf 4 aɷɘɽ mɛɘɽɩ$^{(2x)}$, dɘ:tɘɽɪnɫɘ: ["polite"; mɩ$^{3,4(2x)}$, mɘɩ^{1,5}] 5 dɘ:ʔɘɽɪnlɘ: [mɘ̈ɩ^{2}, mʌʏ$^{2(2x)}$] 5 dʒaks wɘ̈ɩf [mɘ̈ɩ$^{3(2x)}$]

VIII.1.19 TO‡

Q. If your daughter's husband is a Frenchman, you could say: She's [using his word] *married . . . . a Frenchman.*

Rr. A (FOREIGNER/FRENCHMAN/FRENCHY), MARRIED A (FOREIGNER/FRENCHMAN/FRENCHY/FROGGY), MARRIED TO A (FROGGY), (MARRIED) OF, ON, TO (A {FOREIGNER/ FRENCHMAN/FROGGY}), WED (TO) A FRENCHMAN, *Zero*

Note 1—This q. was intended to ascertain what prep., if any, was used after married, or its equivalent, in response to VIII.1.17. However, the grammatical functions of MARRIED at VIII.1.17 and here are dissimilar. At VIII.1.17, it is a p.p. adj., whereas here it is either a p.p. or a p.p. adj. The rr. over the whole of the network now show clearly that this particular q. has produced results that are not comparable, since the r. would be affected by whether the i. understood the SHE'S of the q. to mean SHE IS or SHE HAS.

Note 2—When rec. in the r., MARRIED, or its equivalent, is reproduced below.

Note 3—For additional exs. of MARRIED and WED, see VIII.1.17 (and refs.).

7 Ch 1 ə fɒɹənə 2 maɹɪd ə fɹɛnʃmən 3 ə fəɹɪnə 4–5 maɹɪd ə 6 ə fɒɹɪnə

8 Db 1 ə fɒɹɪnə 2 wɛd ə 3 ə 4 maɹɪd ə fɒɹɪnə 5 ə fɹɛnʃɪ 6 maɹɪd ə fɒɹɪnə 7 maɹɪd ə

11 Sa 1 tu: 2 wɛd tu: ə fɹɛnʃmn̩ 3 tə 4 tʊ 5 tu: 6 tʊ 7 maɹɪd tu· ə 8 ɒn 9 tu: ə 10 tu: 11 əv [əʳ maɹɪd əv sʌtʃ ə fɛlə *her* (=*she*) *married of* (pres. = *on*, Edd.) *such a fellow*]

12 St 1 tü: 2 zero 3 ə fɹɛnʃmɒn 4 tü: 5–6 zero 4 tü: 8 tü: ə fɒɹɪnə 9 ə fɹɛnʃɪ 10 tü: 11 s.w. tu:

15 He 1 mæɹɪd ə fɹɛnʃmɒn 2 tu: ə fɹɒgɪ 3 tu: ə 4 ə fɹɛnʃmɒn 5–6 tu: ə 7 maɹɪd ə fɹɒgɪ

16 Wo 1–2 tʊ 3 wɛ·d tu: ə fɹɛnʃmn̩ 4 mɒɹɪd ə fɹɛnʃmən 5 mɒɹɪd ə fɹɛnʃmʊn 6 tʻu: ə fɹɛnʃmɒn 7 ə fəɹənə

17 Wa 1 maɹɪd ə fɹɛnʃɪ 2 maɹɪd ə fəɹənə 3 maɹɪd ə 4 tʊ ə 5 maɹɪd ʊ 6–7 maɹɪd ə

23 Mon 1 tʊu: ə 2–3 tu: ə 4 tu· ə 5 tʊ̜ 6 tu: 7 n.a.

24 Gl 1–2 tu: 3 tʊu: 4 tʊu 5 maɹɪd ə fʊɹənəʳ 6 ə vɒɹɪnəʳ 7 maɹɪd ə

25 O 1 maɽɪd ə fɒɽənəʳ 2 maɹɪd ə 3 ə 4 maɽɪd tʊ ə fɽɒgɪ 5 ə 6 maɽɪd ə

VIII.1.20 OLD*

Q. I am a young man, and you are . . . .

R. OLD

Note 1—I.m. exs. of OLDEST, OLD–FASHIONED and OLDEN DAYS are reproduced below between square brackets untransliterated.

Note 2—For additional exs. of OLD, see III.6.5, V.7.21, VII.3.5 (and ref.), VII.4.10, VIII.1.22/24/25, VIII.3.5, VIII.8.3 and VIII.9.4. For OLDER, see VIII.1.21.

7 Ch 1 εɷd, ○~[4], ○ɒɷld[4] 2 n.a., ○ɔɷd[1], ○ɛ̈ɷd[1,2(2x),3,4], ○~[3] VIII.4.2, ○εɷd[1,2(2x),4(2x)] [ɷ:ldɪst[1]] 3 ɛ̈ɷd, ○~[2] [εɷdn di:z[2]] 4 εɷd, ○ɒɷd[2] 5 εɷd[(2x)], ○~[1(2x),2] 6 εɷd, ○~[3]

8 Db 1 ɒɷd, ○~[1], ○ɛ̧ɷd[2] 2 ɒɷd, ○~[3,4(2x)] 3–6 εɷd 7 ɛ̧ɷd, ○εɷd[2(2x)]

11 Sa 1 aɷd 2 ɛ̧ɷd, ○o:ld[1,3], ○æɷd[2] 3 ɒu·d 4 o:ld 5 εɷd, ○~[2], ○ɛ̧ɷd[1], ○εɷt[3] [+ «plɛ̧:s» *place*; εɷdfaʃən[2]] 6 aɷd, ○~[1], ○o:ld[4] 7 aɷd, ○~[1] 8 aɷd, ○~[2] [aɷdɪst[1]] 9 aɷd, ○~[1], ○ɔ:d[1] 10 aɷd, ○~[3(2x)], ○aɷld[2] [aɷdəst[2]] 11 ɒɷd, ○~, ○ɔ:d[2(2x)] [aɷdɪst[1]]

12 St 1 oɷd, ○~[2(2x)], ○aɷd[1,2] [εldɪst[2]] 2 εɷd, ○~[2(3x),5] 3 æɷd, ○~[1(4x),2(2x)], ○εɷd[1] [æɷdfaʃnd[1]; æɷdən di:z[1]] 4 oɷd, ○aɷd[2], ○oɷld[3] [oɷldən taɪmz[1] *olden times*] 5 ạɷd, ○aɷd[1,2(7x),3(5x)], ○æɷd[2(2x)], ○oɷd[1] [aɷdən di:z[1]] 6 ạɷd, ○oɷd[1,2], ○εɷd[2(4x)], ○æɷd[1(3x),2] [oɷldən dεɪz[1]] 7 oɷld, ○oɷl[3], ○oɷd[3] [oɷdn dεɪz[1]] 8 oɷd, ○~[1(2x)], ○oɷld[1] [oɷdɪst[1]] 9 εɷd, ○~[2], ○æɷd[1,2], ○oɷld[1], ○oɷd[1(2x)], ○aɷd[1,2,3] 10 oɷld 11 oɷld, ○~[2(2x),3], ○oɷl[2(4x)], ○oɷd[2(4x)] [oɷldən dεɪz]

15 He 1 ɒɷd, ○aɷld[1,3], ○a:l[2], ○ɔ:ɫd[2] 2 ɔ:ɫd, ○o:ɫd[2], ○æɷɫ[2], ○æɷl[2] [ɒɷɫfa:ʃn n̩z[1] *o.-fashioned ones* II.4.5] 3 ɒɷd, ○æɷd[1] 4 æɷɫd, ○ɔɷɫ[1], ○æɷɫ[1,2,3] 5 æɷɫd, ○æɷl[3] 6 ɒɷɫd, ○ɒɷd[1], ○ɒɷɫ[1], ○o:ɫ[1] 7 o:ɫ, o:ɫd, ○o:l[2], ○ǫ:ld[2], ○o:ld[1,3,4], oɷl[3,4]

16 Wo 1 ɒɷld, ○~[3] 2 æɷd, ○oɷld[1] 3 εu:ɫd, ○oɷl[5], ○oɷɫ[5], ○oɷld[5] 4 ɒɷɫ, ○ɒɷɫd[2], ○ɒɷd[3], ○aɷd[1,2(2x)] 5 aɷɫd, ○~[1(3x)], ○aɷd[1] 6 ɒɷɫd, ○εu:ɫd[3] 7 n.a., ○ɑɷl[4], ○ɔɷld[1,3,4(6x)], ○ɔɷl[1(4x),3(2x),4(7x)], ○oɷl[4]

17 Wa 1 ǫɷld 2 n.a., ○ɔɷld[1(2x),3(4x)], ○ɔɷl[1(2x),3(4x),4(3x)] [ɔɷldfaʃənd[3]] 3 ɒɷɫ, ○ɒɷl[3] 4 oɷɫd, ○oɷɫ[1] 5 ɒɷɫ, ○ɒɷɫd[1] 6 ɒɷɫd, ○ǫɷɫd[4] 7 ɒɷɫd, ○ɒɷɫ[1]

23 Mon 1 ɒɷɫ, ○~[4], ○æɷɫ[2], ○ɒɷɫd[1] 2 o:ɫ 3 o:ɫ, ○o:ɫd[2(2x)] [o:ɫfaʃn[2]] 4 ọ:ld [ọ:ldn dˈẹ:ˈz] 5 o:ɫd, ○ouɫ[2], ○oul[2], ○ǫ:ᵊɫd[2], ○o:ɫ[3] 6 o:ɫ, ○ɑ:ɫ[1] 7 n.a.

24 Gl 1 æɷᵊɫd, ○ɑ:ɫ[1], ○æɷɫ[1(3x),3] [æɷɫfæʃɒn[1]] 2 æɷɫd, ○~, ○ɒɷɫ[1,2] [ɒɷdɪst[2]] 3 ɒɷᵊɫ, ○ɒɷd[1], ○ɒɷɫ[3], ○ɒɷɫd [rec. in «ɒɷɫd ɷmən» *o. woman* VIII.1.6] 4 aɷɫd, ○ɒɷd[1] 5 ɒɫd 6 ɒɫ 7 ɒɷɫ, ○~[1] VIII.8.1

25 O 1 ɒɷɫd 2 oɷɫd 3 ɔ̣ɷld 4 o:ɫd, ○~[1(2x),4,5], ○o:ɫ[1,3,4(3x),5(2x)] 5 ɔɷɫd, ○~[3], ○ɔ̣ɷɫd[1], ○ɔɷld[2] 6 oɷɫd, ○~[3(2x)], ○oɷld[1]

VIII.1.21 OLDER† THAN

Q. Talking of people's ages: most husbands are not younger but . . . . their wives.

Rr. OLDER ({TH}AN/NOR/TILL~TIN)

Note 1—Unfortunately, the f.w. occ. omitted to record THAN or an equivalent expression.

Note 2—I.m. exs. of OLDER are reproduced below between square brackets untransliterated.

Note 3—For exs. of OLD, see VIII.1.20 (and refs.); and for additional exs. of THAN foll. comparative adjs., see VI.12.4.

7 Ch 1 εɷdə ðn̩ 2 εɷdə tɪn 3 ëɷdə ðən 4 εɷdə ðən, °εɷdə tl̩[1(2x)] [ɒɷdə wə:d tl̩ ðat[1] *o. word till that*] 5 εɷdə tl̩ 6 εɷdə tl̩, °εɷdə tɪl[3]

8 Db 1–2 ɒɷdə nə 3 εɷdə ðən 4 εɷdəɹ ən 5 εɷdə ðən 6 εɷdə 7 εɷdə ðən

11 Sa 1 aɷdəʳ ðn̩ 2 ε̧ɷdəʳɽ‿ən 3 ɒu·dəᶦ ðən 4 aɷdəʳɽ‿ən 5 εɷdəʳɽ‿ən 6 aɷdəɹ‿ən 7–8 aɷdəʳɽ‿ən 9 aɷdəʳ ðn̩ 10 aɷdəʳɽ‿ən 11 ɒɷdəɹ‿ən

12 St 1 oɷldə ðən 2 εɷdə ðən, °aɷdə‿n[2] 3 æ̧ɷdə ðən 4 oɷldə ðən 5 aɷdə ðən 6 ạɷdə ðən 7–8 oɷldə ðən 9 εɷdə ðən 10 oɷldə ðən 11 o̧ɷldə ðən

15 He 1 ɒɷdəʳɽ‿ən 2 ɒɷɫdəʳɽ‿ən 3 ɒɷdəʳɽ‿ən 4–5 æɷɫdəʳɽ‿ən 6 ɒɷɫdəʳɽ‿ən 7 o:ldəɹ ðən[(2x)], °ä:ldəɹ ðən[4]

16 Wo 1 ɒɷldəʳɽ‿ən 2 æɷdəʳɽ‿ən 3 εu:dəʳɽ‿ən 4 ɒɷɫdəʳɽ‿ən 5 aɷdəʳɽ‿ən [aɷdəʳ[1]] 6 ɒɷɫdəʳɽ‿ən 7 ɔɷldə ðən [ɔɷldə[1,3(2x)]]

17 Wa 1 o̧ɷldə ðən [ɒɷldə[2]] 2 ɔɷldə, p. ɔɷldə nə 3 ɒɷɫdəɹ ɷn 4 oɷɫdəɹ ɷn 5 ɒɷɫdəɹ ɷn 6 ɒɷɫdəɹ ə 7 ɒɷɫdəʳ ðən

23 Mon 1 ɒɷɫdəʳɽ‿ən 2 o:ɫdəʳɽ‿ən 3 o:ɫdəɹ‿ən 4 o̧:ldə 5 o:ɫdə 6 o:ɫdəʳɽ‿ən 7 n.a.

24 Gl 1 æɷᵊɫdəʳɽ‿ən 2 æɷɫdəʳɽ‿ən [æɷdəʳ[3]] 3 ɒɷᵊdəʳɽ‿ən 4 aɷɫdəʳɽ‿ən 5 ɒɫdə nə 6 ɒɫdə ðən 7 ɒɷɫdəɽ‿ən

25 O 1 ɒɷɫdəʳ 2 oɷɫdə ðən 3 ɔɷldəʳ ðən 4 o:ɫdəɽ ðən 5 ɔɷɫdɽ nə 6 oɷɫdəɽ‿ən

VIII.1.22 SO‡ OLD AS

Q. Maybe you've known cases where the husband was not quite . . . . his wife.

Rr. AS/SO OLD (AS)

Note 1—The f.w. freq. omitted to rec. AS or its equivalent.

Note 2—I.m. exs. of AS/SO . . . . AS foll. a neg. are reproduced below between square brackets.

Note 3—For exs. of (AS/SO) . . . . AS not foll. a neg., see VIII.9.4; and for OLD, see VIII.1.20 (and refs.).

7 Ch 1 əz ɛɷd 2 əz ɛɷd əz 3 əz ɛ̈ɷd 4–5 əz ɛɷd 6 sə ɛɷd

8 Db 1–2 əz ɒɷd 3–5 əz ɛɷd 6 əz ɛɷd əz 7 əz ɛɷd

11 Sa 1 əz aɷd əz 2 əz ɛ̨ɷd əz 3 əz ɒu·d əz 4 sə o:ld 5 sə ɛɷd 6–10 əz aɷd əz 11 əz ɒɷd əz

12 St 1 əz oɷld əz 2 əz ɛɷd əz 3 sə æ̣ɷd əz [əz fə:ɹ əz² *as far as*; sə bad əz² *so bad as*] 4 soɷ oɷld əz 5 so oɷld əz 6 əz ạɷd əz 7 əz oɷld əz 8 soɷ oɷld əz 9 soɷ ɛɷd əz 10 sɛɷ oɷld əz 11 sɛɷ oɷld əz

15 He 1 əz ɒɷd əz 2 əz ɒɷɫd 3 əz ɒɷd əz 4 sə æɷɫd əz [sə vɷɫgəʳɽ əz¹ *so vulgar as*] 5 əz æɷɫd 6 sə ɒɷɫd əz 7 soɷ o:ld əz

16 Wo 1 əz ɒɷld 2 əz æɷd əz 3 sə oɷɫd əz 4 sə ɒɷɫd 5 əz aɷɫd əz 6 sə ɒɷɫd 7 əz ɔɷld əz

17 Wa 1 sᵊ ọɷld 2 s.w. əz ɔɷld əz 3 s‿ɒɷɫd 4 əz oɷɫd 5 əz ɒɷɫd [sə θɩk əz¹ *so thick as*] 6 sə ɒɷɫd 7 soɷ ɒɷɫd

23 Mon 1 əz ɒɷɫd əz 2 əz o:ɫd 3 sə o:ɫd 4 əz o:|d əz 5 soɷ o:ɫd əz 6 sə o:ɫd 7 n.a.

24 Gl 1 s‿æɷᵊɫd 2 əz æɷɫd 3 əz ɒɷɫd əz 4 sə aɷɫd əz 5 sə ɒɫd [sə bɩg əz² *so big as*] 6 sə ɒɫd əz 7 sə ɒɷɫd

25 O 1 so: ɒɷld 2 s‿oɷɫd 3 sə həɷld, əz ọɷld ["pref."] 4 so: o:ɫd əz 5 sə ɔɷɫd 6 soɷ oɷɫd

VIII.1.23 LOOK AFTER

Q. Mary had to leave the baby at home while she went out shopping, so she said to her husband: Jack, will you . . . . the baby?

Rr. KEEP YOUR EYE ON, LOOK AFTER, MIND, WATCH OVER

Note—A few exs. of LOOK AFTER not ref. a human are reproduced below between square brackets untransliterated. Additional exs. of LOOKS (*3 pr.s.*) AFTER occur at III.3.7. For exs. of LOOK, see III.13.18 (and refs.); and of AFTER(–), see VII.3.11 (and refs.).

7 Ch 1 lʏ:k aftə 2 lu:k aftə 3 lʏ:k aftə 4 lu:k aftə 5 lʏ:k aftə 6 maɩnd

8 Db 1 lʏ:k aftə 2 lu:k aftə 3 maɪnd(2x) 4 lᵒu:k aftə 5 watʃ o·ə 6–7 lɛɷk aftə

11 Sa 1 maɪnd 2 lʏʉ:k aftə 3 lɷk a·ftəʳ 4 maɪnd 5 maɪnd, maɪn 6–7 maɪnd 8 mɒɪn 9 maɪnd 10–11 maɪn

12 St 1 lü:k aftəɹ [+ V.] 2 lü:k aftə 3 lɛɷk aftə 4 mɒɪnd 5–6 mɒ:ɪnd 7 mɒ̣ɪnd 8–9 mɒɪnd 10 mǫɪnd 11 lɷk aftə

15 He 1 lɷk ætəʳ 2 mæɪnd 3 məɪnd [lɷk ætəʳ jəsɛɫvz³ *look after yourselves* V.8.13] 4 lɷk ætəʳ [lɷks (*1 pr.s.*) ætəʳ²] 5 lɷk ɒftəʳɽ [+ V.] 6 lɷk ætəʳ 7 maɪnd, °lɷk aftəɹ, °lɷkt [*p.p.*] ạ:ftəɹ⁴

16 Wo 1 lɷk a̱:tə 2 məɪnd 3 mɒɪn 4–5 məɪnd 6 mɒɪnd, lɷk æ:təʳ 7 məɪnd [lɷk ɑ:təɹ⁴ (+ V.), lɷks ɑ:təʳ⁴ *looks after* (i.e. for)]

17 Wa 1 lɷk aftə 2 lɷk a:ftə, °lɷk ɑ:təɹ⁴ [+ V.], °lɷkt [*p.p.*] ɑ:ftəɹ⁴ [+ V.] 3 lɷk a:f, °lɷkt [*p.p.*] a:ftəɹ² [+ V.; lɷkt (n.d.g.) a:ftə³] 4 lɷk aʳ:ʈə 5 məɪnd, lɷk aʳ:ʈəʳ 6 məɪnd 7 məɪnd, lɷk aʳ:ʈə ["older"]

23 Mon 1 lʌk æftəʳ 2 lɷk æftəʳ 3 lɷk a:ftə 4 n.a. 5 ki:p jəɹ əij ɒ̣·n 6 lɷk a:ftəʳɽ [+ V.] 7 n.a.

24 Gl 1 məɪnd 2 lɷk a:təʳ 3 məɪn 4 lɷk atəʳ, °lɷk atəʳɽ³ [+ V.] 5 lɷk aʳ:ʈəʳ [lɷkt (*1 p.t.s.*) aʳ:ʈə²] 6 lu:k aʳ:ɽʔə 7 lɷk aʳ:ʔə(2x)

25 O 1 lɷk aʳ:ʈəʳ 2 lɷk aʳ:ʈə, °lɷk aʳ:ʔəɽ² [+ V.] 3 lɷk a:ftəʳ 4 ɫɷk ɑ·ɽʈəɽ 5 lɷk a:ftəʳ, lɷk aʳ:ʈəʳ [pref.] 6 lɷk a:ftə, p. lɷk aʳ:ʔəʳ ["older"]

VIII.1.24 MY WIFE

Q. If you asked Mr. Smith, the farmer, at the door if he could let you have a dozen eggs, he'd probably say: It's nothing to do with me, you'll have to ask . . . .

Rr. MY~THE /MISSIS/OLD WOMAN/WIFE/, THE /OLD LADY/ WOMAN/

Note 1—Exs. of WIFE, as well as of MISSIS and OLD WOMAN both meaning *wife*, are reproduced below between square brackets untransliterated.

Note 2—For additional exs. of OLD, see VIII.1.20 (and refs.); and of WOMAN, see VIII.1.6 (and ref.). MRS. occurs at VIII.2.3 and WIFE at VIII.1.18.

7 Ch 1 ð̩ mɪsɪs [wɛɪf¹] 2 t‿mɪsɪz [wæ̣ɪf⁴] 3 mɑɪ mɪsɪs 4–5 ðə mɪsɪz 6 ðə mɪsɪs

8 Db 1 t‿mɪsɪs, °maɪ mɪsɪsɪz[3] *poss.* 2–3 t‿mɪsɪs 4 t‿ɛɷd wɷmən, t‿mɪsɪz 5 t‿mɪsɪs [t‿wɑɪf[4] *the wife*] 6 t‿mɪsɪs 7 ð̩ mɪsɪs

11 Sa 1 ðə mɪsɪs 2 ðə waɪf 3 ðə wɛɪf 4–9 ðə mɪsɪs 10 ðə mɪsɪs [wɑɪf[3] V.7.21] 11 ðə ɷmən

12 St 1 ðə mɪsɪs 2 ð̩ mɪsɪs [wɛɪf[1]] 3 mɪsɪz(2x), ð‿æɷd wɷmən, °mɒːɪ mɪsɪz[1] 4 ðə mɪsɪs 5 ðə mɪsɪs [mɪsɪs[2(3x)]] 6–7 ðə mɪsɪs 8 ð‿oɷl lɛɪdɪ 9 ðə mɪsɪz [wɒɪf[2], ▫wɒɪvz[2]] 10 ðə waːɪf, maːɪ mɪsɪs, ðə mɪsɪs 11 ðə wɒɪf

15 He 1–2 ðə mɪsɪs 3 ðə wəɪf 4 ðə mɪsɪs [æɷɫ ɷmən] 5–6 ðə mɪsɪs 7 ðə mɪsɪz, °maɪ mɪsɪz[3] VI.14.14 [▫waɪvz[4]]

16 Wo 1 mɪ wɒɪf 2–6 ðə mɪsɪs 7 məɪ ɔɷld ɷmən, °ðə mɪsɪz[1(2x),4], °məɪ mɪsɪz[3], °ðə mɪsɪzɪz[3] *poss.*, °məɪ mɪsɪzɪz[1] *poss.* [mɪsɪz[4]]

17 Wa 1 ðə mɪsɪs [wɑɪf[2]] 2 ðə wəɪf, °~, °ðə wəɪfs[1] *poss.*, °mɪ mɪsɪz[1] III.3.7 3 ðə mɪsɪs 4 ðə wəɪf 5 ðə mɪsɪs 6 ðə wəɪf [wəɪf[4]] 7 ðə mɪsɪs

23 Mon 1–2 ðə mɪsɪs 3 ðə wəɪf [wəɪf[3]] 4 n.a. 5 məi wəif, ðə mɪssɪs [wə̹ɪf[2]] 6 ðə mɪsɪs 7 n.a.

24 Gl 1–2 ðə mɪsɪs 3 ðə mɪsɪs(2x) 4 ðə mɪsɪs [wəɪf[3]] 5 ðə mɪsɪs [wə̈ɪf[1,2]] 6 ðə mɪsɪs 7 ðə mɪsɪz

25 O 1 ðə mɪsɪs(2x) 2 mə̈ɪ mɪsɪs 3 ðə mɪsɪs 4 ðə mɪsəz, °~[4], °ðə mɪsɪz[4] [wəɪf[5]] 5 ðə mɪsɪs 6 ðə wə̈ɪf

VIII.1.25 MY HUSBAND

Q. And if you asked Mrs. Smith (the farmer's wife) *if you could have a sack of potatoes or a load of dung, she'd probably say: It's nothing to do with me, you'll have to ask . . . .*

Rr. GAFFER, (MY/THE) /HUSBAND/OLD MAN/, (OUR/THE) MASTER, MY/THE BOSS, /MY/THE OLD/ CHAP, THE GAFFER (-MAN)/GOVERNOR

Note 1—I.m. exs. of BOSS, GAFFER, HUSBAND and MASTER, all meaning *husband*, are reproduced below between square brackets untransliterated.
Note 2—For additional exs. of OLD, see VIII.1.20 (and refs.); and of MAN, see VIII.1.6 (and refs.). Expressions comparable with some of those listed above occur at VI.14.14.

7 Ch 1 ð̩ bɒs 2 s.w. t‿mastə 3 mɪ ɷzbən 4 ðə bɒs, ðə mɛstə 5 ð̩ bɒs, mɛstə ["rare"] 6 ðə gafə, ðə bɒs

8 Db 1 t‿bɒs 2 a: mɛstə 3 a: mɛstə(2x) 4 t‿ɛɷd tʃap 5 t‿mɛstə 6 t‿bɒs 7 ð̩ mɛstə

11 Sa 1 ðə ma:stəʳ, ðə gafəʳ· 2–3 ðə bɒs 4 ðə bɒs, ðə ga·fəʳ 5 ðə gafəʳ 6 ðə bəʳ:ʂ 7 ðə gæfəʳ 8 ðə gafəʳ 9–10 ðə bɔ:s 11 ðə bɔ:s, ðə gafəʳ ["older"]

12 St 1 ðə mastə, θ‿ɷzbənd 2 ð‿ɛɷd mɒn 3 gafə, æɷd mɒn 4 ðə mastə [bɒs³; mastə³] 5 ðə gafə, ðə bɒs 6 ðə mastə, ðə bɒs, ðə gafə ["old"] 7 ðə bɒs 8 mɒɩ tʃap 9 ðə gafə 10 ðə bɒs [ɷzbən⁶] 11 mɒɩ ɷzbənd

15 He 1–2 ðə gæfəʳ 3 ðə gˡæfəʳ [gˡæfəʳ³] 4 ðə æɷɫ mɒn 5 ðə bɒs 6 ðə gjæfəʳ 7 ðə bɒs, ðə gafəɹ ["old; rare"]

16 Wo 1 ðə gafəʳ 2 ðə gafəʳmɒn 3 ðə bɑ:s 4 ðə gˡæfəʳ, ɷzbɷn 5 ðə bɒs 6 ðə gæfəʳ 7 məɩ əɷld mɒn(2x)

17 Wa 1 ðə mastə, ðə bɒs, °mɑɩ bɒs² 2 ðə bɔs, məɩ ɷzbənd ["polite"] 3 ðə bɒs, ðə ma:stə 4 ð‿oɷɫ man 5 ðə mastəʳ 6–7 ðə bɒs

23 Mon 1 ðə gæfəʳ 2 ðə ma:stəʳ 3 ðə bɑ:s 4 n.a. [ʌ̥̈zbʌ̥̈nd¹] 5 məi ʌ̥̈zbʌ̥̈nd, ðə gaffə 6 ðə bɑ:s 7 n.a.

24 Gl 1 ðə bɑ:s 2 ðə gjæfəʳ 3 ðə bɑ:s 4 ðə aɷɫ mɒn 5 ðə bɔ:s 6 ðə bɒs, ðə gjafəʳ 7 ðə bɒs

25 O 1 ðə bɒs 2 ðə ma:stəʳ 3 ðə ma:stɽ 4 ðə gɷvnəɽ 5 mʌʏ ʌzbən 6 mö̈ɩ ʌzbən

VIII.1.26 EARNED

Q. Talking of a man's living, you can say: That man is a regular wastrel, he has never . . . . his living.

Rr. ADDLED, $DONE /ANY GOOD/NO WORK/, EARNED, GET *3 pr.s.*, WORKS *3 pr.s.* (HARD) FOR

Note 1—When rec. in the r., the pron. obj. IT has been included below.

Note 2—At 7.2, 15.7, 16.7, 17.2 and 25.4, the f.w. used the fourth version of the Qr., in which the q. read: *A mother looks after the house, but the money she spends comes from the father; and he doesn't steal it, of course, but he . . . . it.* Hence at the locs. concerned the rr. contain a *3 pr.s.* These are marked with a superior ×.

7 Ch 1 əɹ:nd 2 ˣwə:ks fɔɹ ɩt, s.w. ə:nz ɩt 3 s.w. əɹ:nd 4 ə:nd 5–6 a:nd

8 Db 1 əɹnd 2 ə:nd, ɛdld 3 ə:nt ɩt 4 ə:n [n.d.g.] 5 a:nd 6–7 ə:nd

11 Sa 1 əʳ:ɳɖ 2 əʳ:ɳʈ 3–4 əʳ:ɳɖ 5 əʳ:ɳʈ 6 əʳ:ɳɖ 7–8 əʳ:ɳʈ 9–10 əʳ:ɳɖ 11 əʳ:ɳʈ

12 St 1 əʴ:nd 2 ɔ:nd 3 §dɷn noɷ wɔ:k, adlt, ɔ:nd ɩt 4–5 ɔ:nd 6 §dɷn ɒnɩ gɷd, adld, ɔ:nd 7 ɔ:nt 8 əʴ:nd 9–10 ɔ:nd 11 ɔɹ:nd

15 He 1–6 əʳ:ɳʈ 7 ×gɛt, ×ɔ·ɹn, ○ɔ·ɹnz[3] *1 pr.s.*

16 Wo 1–2 əʳ:ɳɖ 3 əʳ:ɳʈ 4–6 əʳ:ɳɖ 7 ×wɔ:ks ɑ:d fɔɹ ɩt, s.w. ×ɔ:nz ɩt, ○əʳɳɖ[4] *3 p.t.s.*

17 Wa 1 ɔ̣̂:nd 2 ×ɔ:nz 3 s.w. ɔ:nd 4–5 əʳ:ɳʈ 6–7 əʳ:ɳɖ

23 Mon 1–2 əʳ:ɳʈ 3 œ:nt 4 n.a. 5 œ:nd 6 əʳ:ɳɖ 7 n.a.

24 Gl 1–4 əʳ:ɳʈ 5 əʳ:ɳɖ 6 jaʳ:ɳɖ 7 jəʳ:ɳɖ

25 O 1 əʳ:ɳɖ 2 əʳ:ɳʈ ["older"], əʳ:ɳɖ 3 jaʳ:ɳʈ 4 ×gɛt, ○əɽɳɖ *3 p.t. pl.* 5 əʳ:ɳɖ 6 əʳ:ɳʔ, ○~[3]

VIII.2.1 NEIGHBOURS*

Q. The people who live next to you, you call your . . . .

R. NEIGHBOURS

7 Ch 1 nẹ:bəz 2 ne:bəz 3 △ni:bə, ○ni:bəz[3] 4 nẹ:bəz 5 ni:bəz, ○△nị:bə[3] 6 ne:bəz

8 Db 1–3 ne:bəz 4 ni:bəz 5 nẹ:ˈbəz 6–7 ni:bəz

11 Sa 1 ne:bəʳ:ʐ 2 nẹ:bəʳʐ 3–4 ne:bəʳ:ʐ 5 nẹ:bəʳʐ 6–11 ne:bəʳʐ

12 St 1 neɩbəz 2 nɛɩbəz 3 ni:bəz, ○~[1] 4 nɛɩbəz 5 ni:bəz 6 nɛɩbəz, ni:bəz 7–10 nɛɩbəz 11 nɛɩbəz, ○□nɛɩbə[2]

15 He 1 ne:bəʳʐ 2 næɩbəʳʐ 3 nɛɩbəʳ:ʐ, ○△næɩbəʳ[1] 4 næɩbəʳʐ 5 ne:ɩbəʳʐ 6 næɩbəʳʐ 7 △nẹɩbəɹ [nɛɩbɹɷd[4] *neighbourhood*]

16 Wo 1 nɛɩbəz 2 nɛ:ᵊbəʳʐ 3 ne:ɩbəʳ:ʐ 4 naˈbəʳʐ 5 naɩbəʳ:ʐ, ○~[1], ○naɩbəʳʐ[1] 6 ne:ɩbəʳʐ 7 nɛɩbəʳʐ, ○△nẹɩbə[3]

17 Wa 1 nẹɩbəz 2 nẹɩbəz(2x) 3 næɩbəz, ○~ 4 nẹəbəʳʐ 5 nɛɩbəʳ·ʐ 6 nɛɩbəʳʐ 7 ne:ᵊbəʳ·ʐ

23 Mon 1 næɩbəʳʐ 2 ne:bəʳʐ 3 ne:bəz 4–5 nẹ:bəz 6 ne:bəʳʐ 7 n.a.

24 Gl 1 næɩbəʳ:ʐ, ○△næɩbɷ[1] 2–3 næɩbəʳʐ 4 naɩbəʳʐ 5 næ̣ɩbəʳ·ʐ 6 næɩbəʳ·ʐ 7 nẹɩbəʳʐ

25 O 1 næɪbəʳʐ 2 nɛɪbəᶦz 3 nȩˡbɽʐ 4 △ne:bəɽ, ○~[5], ○△neɪbəɽ[1] *adj.* [△ne·ˡbəɽ[5(2x)] (= *friend*)] 5 nɛɪbəʳʐ 6 neɪbəʳʐ

VIII.2.2 LEND*

Q. You want a spade for a short time, and yours is broken, so you ask your neighbour: Will you . . . . me yours?

R. LEND

Note—When rec., the indirect objs. I, ME, and US, all = *me*, are reproduced below untransliterated. For additional exs. of I, see VII.5.8 and IX.8.3–4; and of ME and US, see VII.5.8 and IX.8.2–4.

7 Ch 1 lɛn 2–3 lɛn mɪ 4 lɛnd 5–6 lɛn mɪ

8 Db 1 lɛn 2 lɛn mɪ 3 lɛn, ○~ 4 lɛn mɪ 5 lɛn 6 lɛn əz 7 lɛn mɪ

11 Sa 1 lɛnd [rec. in «kan aɪ lɛnd jɷəʳ spe:d» *can I lend your spade*] 2 lɛnd mɪ 3–4 lɛn 5 lɛnd 6–9 lɛn 10 lɛnd 11 lɛn

12 St 1 lɛn mɪ 2 lɛn ɷz 3–6 lɛn mɪ 7–8 lɛn 9 lɛnd 10 lɛn 11 lɛnd

15 He 1 lɛnd ʌz 2 lɛnd əz 3–5 lɛn mɪ 6 lɛnd əz 7 lɛnd əz̥, ○lɛnd[4] [lɛnd[4] *l. n.*]

16 Wo 1–2 lɛnd 3–4 lɛn mɪ 5 lɛn ɷz 6 lɛn mɪ 7 lɛn mi:, ○lɛnd[4(2x)]

17 Wa 1 lɛnd 2 lɛn mi: 3 lɛnd əs 4 lɛn mɪ 5 lɛn 6 lɛnd mɪ 7 lɛn mɪ

23 Mon 1 lɛnd 2 lɛn 3 lɛn mɪ 4 lɛn mi· 5 lɛnd 6 lɛn 7 n.a.

24 Gl 1 lɛn mɪ 2 lɛn ɷz 3 lɛn 4 lɛnd əs 5 lɛn mɪ 6 lɛnd ʌɪ 7 lɛnd

25 O 1 lɛn mɪ 2 lɛn, ○lɛn mɪ[2] 3 lɛn mɪ, lɛnd əz 4 ɫɛnd əs, ɫɛn əs 5 lɛn 6 lɛn, ○lɛn mɪ[3]

VIII.2.3 MRS.* MR.*

Q. Among friends, you speak of your neighbour as Mary White, but among strangers you speak of her as . . . . White.
And of her husband as . . . . White.

Rr. MRS.
MASTER, MR.

Note 1—The rr. to the two parts of the q. are separated below by a full stop.
Note 2—Additional exs. of MRS. occur at VIII.1.24; and of MASTER, at VIII.1.25.

7 Ch 1 mɪsɪs . mɛstə 2 mɪ̞sɪz, °mɪsɪz[3(3x),4] . mɪ̞stə, °mɛstə 3 mɪsɪz . mɛstəɹ 4–6 mɪsɪz . mɛstə

8 Db 1 mɪsɪs . mɪstəɹ 2 mɪsɪs . mɪstə 3 n.r. mɪstə, mɛstə 4 mɪsɪs . mɛstə 5 mɪsɪs . mɛstə 6 mɪsɪz . mɛstə 7 mɪsɪs . mɛstə

11 Sa 1–11 mɪsɪs . mɪstəʵ

12 St 1 mɪsɪs . mæstə 2 mɪ̞sɪs . mɛstə 3 mɪsɪs . mastə 4 mɪsɪz . mɪstə 5 mɪsɪs, °~[2] . mɪstə 6 mɪsɪz . mɪstə, °mastə[1] VIII.6.5 7 mɪsɪs . mɪstə 8 mɪsɪs . mɪstə 9 mɪsɪz . mɪstə, °mɛstə[1] 10–11 mɪsɪs . mɪstə

15 He 1–6 mɪsɪs . mɪstəʵ 7 mɪsɪs, °~[1,4], °mɪsɪz[2,4], °mɪsɪzɪz[4] *poss.* mɪstəɹ, °mɪstəɹ[3] (+ V.)

16 Wo 1 mɪsɪs . mɪstə 2–6 mɪsɪs . mɪstəʵ 7 mɪsɪz . mɪstə

17 Wa 1 mɪsɪs . mɪstə 2 mɪsɪz, °~[1] . mɪstə 3 mɪsɪs . mɪstə 4 mɪsɪz . mɒstə 5 mɪsɪs . mɪstəʵ [mastəʵ *m.* (ref. a bachelor)] 6 mɪsɪs . mɪstəʵ 7 mɪsɪs, °mɪsɪz[2] . mɪstəʵ

23 Mon 1–2 mɪsɪs . mɪstəʵ 3 mɪsɪs . mɪstə 4 mɪs̬ɪz . mɪs̬tʰə 5 mɪsɪz . mɪstə 6 mɪsɪs . mɪstəʵ 7 n.a.

24 Gl 1–4 mɪsɪs . mɪstəʵ 5 mɪsɪs . mɪstə 6–7 mɪsɪz . mɪstəʵ

25 O 1 mɪsɪs . ma:stəʵ 2 mɪsɪz . mɪstə 3 mɪsɪz . mɪstɽ 4 mɪsɪz, °mɪsəs[4] . mɪstəɽ 5 mɪsɪz . mɪstɽ 6 mɪsəs . mɪstəʵ

VIII.2.4 RELATIVES

Q. If people are connected with you by birth, they are your . . . .

Rr. RELATIONS, RELATIVES

7 Ch 1 ɹɛlətɪvz 2 ɹɪle:ʃənz 3 ɹɪle̞:ʃnz 4 ɹɪle̞:ʃnz, ɹɛlətɪvz ["older"] 5–6 ɹɪle:ʃənz

8 Db 1 ɹɛlətɪvz, ɹɪle:ʃnz 2 ɹɪle:ʃənz 3 ɹɪle:ʃnz 4 ɹɪli:ʃnz 5 ɹɛlətɪvz 6 ɹɪli:ʃnz 7 ɹɪle̞·ɪʃnz

11 Sa 1–4 ɹɪle:ʃnz 5 ɹɪle̞:ʃnz 6–10 ɹɪle:ʃnz 11 ɹɪlɛ:əʃnz, °~

12 St 1 ɹɛlətɪvz 2 ɹɪlɛɪʃənz 3 ɹɪli:ʃənz 4 ɹɪlɛɪʃənz 5 ɹɪle:ʃənz 6 ɹɪlɛɪʃənz 7 ^ɹɪlɛɪʃən 8–10 ɹɪlɛɪʃənz 11 ɹɛlətɪvz

15 He 1 ɹɪle:ʃnz 2 ɹɪle:ɩʃnz 3 ɹɪłe:ʃənz 4 ɹɪle:ʃənz 5 ɹɪle:ɩʃnz 6 ɹɪle:ʃənz 7 ɹɪleɪʃənz

16 Wo 1 ɹɪlɛɪʃnz 2 ɹɪle:^{ə}ʃənz 3 ɹɪle:ʃnz 4–6 ɹɪ·le:ʃɷnz 7 ɹɪlɛɪʃənz

17 Wa 1 ɹɛlətɪv̥z̥ 2 ɹɪlẹɪʃənz 3 ɹɪlɛɪʃnz 4 ɹɪlẹɪʃənz 5 ɹɪlɛɪʃənz 6 ɹɛlətɪvz 7 ɹɪlẹɪʃnz [ɹɪlɛɪtɪd *related p.p. adj.*]

23 Mon 1 ɹɪłe:ˈʃən [*sic*] 2 ɹɪłe:ʃnz 3 ɹɪłe:ʃənz 4 n.a. 5 ɹɛlətɪvz̥, ○ɹɛlətɪvz^{2} 6 ɹɪłe:ʃənz 7 n.a.

24 Gl 1 ɹɪłe:ʃɷnz 2 ɹɪłɛɪʃɷnz 3 ɹɪłe:ˈʒnz 4 ɹɪłaɪʃɷnz 5 ɹɪle:^{ə}ʃɷnz 6 ɹɪle:ʃənz̥ 7 ɹɪle:ʃənz

25 O 1 ɹɪleəʃnz 2 ɹɪlẹɪʃənz 3 ɹɪle:ʃənz 4 ɽɪłeɪʃənz, ○∼^{5}, ○ɽɪleɪʃənz^{5} 5 ɹɛlətɪvz 6 ɹɪleɪʃənz

VIII.2.5 SAW†

Q. Our cousin Jim from Canada actually came to see us three times, but unfortunately I never once . . . . him.

Rr. SAW, SEE, SEED, SEEN

Note 1—In the i.m. below, an attached superior + denotes a 3 p.t.s., superior ɑ denotes a 3 p.t.pl., and superior ◇ denotes a p.p.

Note 2—For SEE *pr.t.*, see VI.3.2 (and refs.).

7 Ch 1 sẹ:d 2 sɔ:, s.f. si:d [pref.], ○∼$^{1,2(2x),3}$, ○sɔ:^{2}, ○si:d^{2} *1 p.t.pl.*, ○ɑ∼^{4}, ○◇si:n^{1} 3 sɛɪd, ○◇sɛɪn^{3} 4 sɩ:d, ○◇sɪn^{2} 5 sɛɪd, ○◇sɪn^{1}, ○◇sɛɪn^{1} 6 si:d, ○◇si:n^{2,3}

8 Db 1 sɔ:, si:d ["older"] 2 sɔ:, ○◇si:n^{4}, ○◇sˈi:n^{4} 3 si:d 4 sɛɪn, ○◇∼^{1,2,3} 5 sɔ:, ○◇si:n^{4} 6 sɛɪd 7 sɛɪd, ○◇sɛɪn^{1}

11 Sa 1 si:d 2 si:d, ○+∼^{3}, ○◇si:n^{3} 3 si:d 4 sɔʳ:ɖ 5 sɪd, ○◇∼^{2} 6 si:d, ○◇sɪn^{3}, ○◇si:n^{4} 7 si:d, ○◇sɪn^{1} 8 sɪ̇d, ○∼^{2}, ○◇∼$^{2(2x)}$, ○◇sɪ^{1} 9 si:d, ○◇∼^{1}, ○◇sɪd$^{1(2x)}$, ○◇sɪn$^{1(2x)}$ 10–11 sɪd

12 St 1 soɷ, ○∼^{1}, ○sɒɷ^{2}, ○+soɷ^{2}, ○ɑsɛn^{3}, ○◇si:n^{1}, ○◇sɛɪn$^{2,3(2x)}$ 2 sɛɪd, ○∼^{5} *p.t.*, ○◇sɛɪn$^{1(2x)}$, ○◇si:n^{2} 3 sɛɪd, ○∼^{1}, ○si:d^{1}, ○◇sɛɪn$^{1,2(2x)}$ 4 sɔ:ɹ, ○◇si:n^{1,2}, ○∼^{2} [n.d.g.], ○◇sɛɪn^{4} 5 sɔ:, ○+sɛɪd^{1}, ○◇si:d^{1}, ○◇sɛɪn$^{1(3x),3}$ 6 sɔ:ɹ, sɛɪd, ○∼^{1}, ○◇∼^{2}, ○◇sɛɪn$^{1(4x)}$ 7 si:n, ○◇si:d^{1,2} 8 sọ:, ○sɪd^{1} *2 p.t.pl.*, ○◇si:n^{2} 9 si:d, ○◇si:n^{1}, ○◇sɛɪn^{2} 10 sɔ:, ○si:d^{1} *p.t.*, ○◇si:n$^{4(2x)}$ 11 sɔ:, si:n, ○si:^{2}, ○◇sɪd$^{1(2x)}$

15 He 1 sɪn, ○◇~[1] 2 sɪn, ○~[2] *1 p.t.pl.* 3 si:n, ○◇sɪn[1(3x),3] 4 sɪn, ○~[1], ○~[1] *1 p.t.pl.*, ○◇~[1,2] 5 sɪd, ○sɪn[2], ○◇~[1(3x)] 6 sɪn, ○◇~[1] 7 sɔ:, ○si:[1], ○◇əsɪn[1,3], ○◇sɪn[4(5x)], ○◇əsi:n[1], ○◇si:n[1,2,3(2x)], ○◇si:d[1]

16 Wo 1 sɪd, ○◇sɪn[1] 2 sɪd 3 si:d, ○sɪn[2,3], ○◇~[2,3] 4 sɪn, ○~[1], ○◇~[3] 5 sɪn, ○si:[1], ○◇sɪn[1(2x)] 6 sɪn, ○+~[2], ○◇~[2,3(2x)] 7 sɔ:, si:n, ○si:[1(2x)], ○sɪn[4], ○◇~[4], ○◇si:n[3]

17 Wa 1 si:d 2 sɔ:, p. si:n [pref.], ○~[2], ○sɪn[4], ○si:[3], ○si:n[3] *2 p.t.pl.*, ○◇sɪn[2,4], ○~[4(2x)] [n.d.g.] 3 si:n 4 sɪn, ○□~[2], ○si:n[2] *2 p.t.pl.* 5 sɔ:, ○◇sɪn[1(3x)] 6 si:n, ○◇sɪn[3(2x)] 7 sɪn, ○si:[2], ○◇sɪn[2]

23 Mon 1 sɪn, ○◇~[2(3x)] 2 sɪn, ○~[3(3x)], ○si:n[2], ○◇~[1,3(2x)] 3 si:n, ○◇sɪn[3] 4 sị:n 5 sɔ:, ○◇si:n[1,2], ○◇si:n[2], ○◇sị:n[2] 6 sɪn, ○+si:n, ○◇~[1(2x)] 7 n.a.

24 Gl 1–2 sɪn, ○~[3] 3 sɪd, ○+sˈi:n[1], ○◇sɪn[1,2] 4 sɪd, ○zɪm[2] [rec. in «zɪm ɷm» *seen* (=*saw*) *them*], ○◇sɪd[2], ○◇sɪn[2,3(2x)], ○◇zɪn[3] 5 sɪn, ○~[2], ○◇~[2] 6 zɪd, ○~[1], ○◇~[2] 7 zɪd, ○◇~[2]

25 O 1 sɪn, ○~[1,2], ○si:[2], ○sɪn[2] *2 p.t.pl.*, ○◇~[2,3], ○~[2] [n.d.g.] 2 si:, ○sɪn[2], ~[1(2x),2], ○◇si:[1] 3 sɔ:, si: ["older"], ○◇~[1(3x)] 4 sɪn, ○si:n[3], ○si:[4], ○◇si:n[1,4(4x)] 5 sɔ:, ○si:[2], ○◇sɪn[2(3x)] 6 si[(2x)], ○[1(2x),2], ○sɔ:[3], ○◇si:n[3], ○◇sɪn[3(2x)]

VIII.2.6 HEARD*†

Q. I've been told you knocked at my door three or four times, but I'm deaf and can honestly say I never . . . . you.

R. HEARD

Note 1—In the i.m. below, an attached superior ◇ denotes a p.p., and superior × denotes a form that may be either a p.t. or a p.p.

Note 2—For HEAR, see VI.4.2.

7 Ch 1 ẹəd, ○ɛəd 2 ə:d, s.f. ɪəd 3 əɹ:d 4 ɪəd, ○◇~[2] 5 ɪəd, ○◇~[3] 6 ɪəd

8 Db 1 jəɹ:d 2 ɪəd 3 ɪəd, ○◇~[1] 4 ɪəd, ○◇ə:d[1] 5–7 ɪəd

11 Sa 1 əɽ:ɖ 2 ɪəɽɖ 3 əɽ:ɖ 4 əɽ:ɖ, ɪəɽ:ɖ ["older"] 5 ɪəɽɖ, ○~[3], ○◇~[1,3] 6 əɽ:ɖ, ɪəɽ:ɖ ["older"], ○əɽ:ɖ[3,4(2x)] 7 ɪəɽ:ɖ 8 ɪəɽ:ɖ, ○ɪəɽɖ[1] 9 ɪəɽ:ɖ, ○ɪəɽɖ[1(2x)], ○◇~[1], ○◇ɪəɽ:ɖ[1] 10 ɪəɽ:ɖ, ○əɽ:ɖ[3] 11 ɪəɽ:ɖ, ○◇~[2(2x)], ○◇əɽ:ɖ[2]

12 St 1 ə:d, ○i·əd[4] 2 ɪəd, ○◇~[5] 3 iəd, ○◇ə:d[2] 4 ə:d, ○×~[3] 5 ə:d 6 ɪəd, ○◇~[1(2x)] 7 ɪ̣əd, ○◇ɪəd[4] 8 ə:d, ○×ɪəd[1], ○×~ 9 i·əd, ○◇iəd[1], ○×~[2] 10 ə̣:d, ○◇ɛ:d[2,3], ○×iəd[6] 11 ə:ɹd, ○◇ɛ̣:d[2], ○×iəd[1]

15 He 1 ιəʵɖ, ○~[2], ○◇~[2] 2 əʵ:ɖ 3 ιəʵɖ, ○◇~[4], ○◇jəʵ:ɖ[1(3x),4] 4 ιəʵɖ 5 əʵ:ɖ 6 əʵ:ɖ, ○◇ιəʵɖ[1(3x)] 7 əɹd, ○~[3], ○◇əɹd[3]

16 Wo 1 i:d, ○ιəd[1], ○◇~[2] 2 ιəʵɖ, ○jəd[2] 3 jəʵ:ɖ, ○jəd[3] 4 ιəʵɖ, ○jəʵ:ɖ[3], ○◇~[1], ○◇ιəʵ:ɖ[1(2x),2(2x),3] 5 ιəʵɖ, ○◇jəʵ:ɖ[1], ○◇ιəʵɖ 6 ιəʵ:ɖ[(2x)], ○jəʵ:ɖ[1,2], ○◇jιəʵɖ[1], ○◇ιəʵɖ[1] 7 ιəd, ○ɜ:d[3,4], ○×ιəd[1,4], ○◇~[3(2x)]

17 Wa 1 ɜ̣̈:d, ○ιəd[1] 2 ɜ:d, s.f. ιəd, ○~[4], ○ɜ:d[1], ○×~[4], ○◇ιəd[4(4x)] 3 ɜ:d, ○×ιəd[2] 4 ιəd 5 əʵ:ɖ, ○ιəd[1] 6–7 əʵ:ɖ

23 Mon 1 jəʵɖ, ○◇~[4], ○◇jəʵ:ɖ[2,3] 2 ιəʵɖ, ○ιəʵɖ[3], ○jɛd[3(2x)], ○◇ιəʵɖ[3], ○◇jəʵɖ[3] 3 œ:d, ○◇jœ:d[3] 4 œ:d 5 hœ̣̈:d, jœ̣̈:d, ○◇~[2], ○◇œ̣̈:d[1] 6 jəʵ:ɖ 7 n.a., ○hœ:d[1], ○×~[1]

24 Gl 1 jəʵ:ɖ, ○ιəʵɖ[1], ○◇~[1(3x)] 2 jəʵ:ɖ, ○~[3], ○◇~[2] 3 əʵ:ɖ 4 ιəʵɖ, ○~[3] 5 əʵ:ɖ 6 jəʵ:ɖ 7 jəʵ:ɖ, ○əʵ:ɖ[1]

25 O 1 jəʵ:ɖ, ○◇~[2] 2 ə̶:d 3 əʵ:ɖ, ○×ιəʵɖ 4 jəɽɖ, ○◇əɽɖ[3,4] 5–6 əʵ:ɖ

VIII.2.7 FRIENDS

Q. If you know some people very well, and like them, you speak of them as your . . . .

Rr. △BUTTY, FRIENDS, △MATE, PALS

Note—For exs. of BUTTIES, (-) MATES and PALS, see VIII.4.1/2; FRIENDS occurs at VIII.4.2.

7 Ch 1–6 fɹɛnz

8 Db 1 fɹɛnz 2–3 fɹɛndz 4 fɹɛnz, ○palz 5–7 fɹɛnz

11 Sa 1–11 fɹɛnz

12 St 1 fɹɛnz 2 palz 3 fɹɛnz, ○~[1] 4 fɹɛnz 5 fɹɛnz, ○△fɹɛnd[1,2], ○△me:t[2] 6–10 fɹɛnz 11 fɹɛnz, ○~[1]

15 He 1–5 fɹɛnz 6 vɹɛnz 7 fɹɛnz

16 Wo 1–6 fɹɛnz 7 fɹɛnz, △fɹɛnd

17 Wa 1–4 fɹɛnz 5 fɹɛnz, ○△fɹɛnd[1] 6 fɹɛnz, ○~[4] 7 fɹɛnz

23 Mon 1–2 fɹɛnz 3 fɹɛnz, ○△bʌtι[1] 4 n.a. 5 fɹɛndz, ○fɹɛnz[2] 6 fɹɛnz 7 n.a.

24 Gl 1–3 fɹɛnz 4 vɹɛnz 5 fɹɛnz 6 fɹɛnz, ○△me:t, ○△pal 7 fɹɛnz

25 O 1 fɽɛnz 2–3 fɹɛnz 4–5 fɽɛnz 6 fɹɛnz

VIII.2.8 HOW ARE YOU?

Q. On meeting a friend in the street and inquiring about his health, you would say to him . . . .

Rr. HOW AM YOU (GETTING ON)?, HOW ARE YOU (/GETTING ALONG~ON/GOING ON/)?, HOW BE/DO?, HOW'S THINGS?, HOW YOU GETTING/GOING ON?

Note 1—In the list of rr. above, ARE subsumes ART, BE, BEEN and BEES(T), and YOU subsumes THOU, THEE and YE.

Note 2—For additional exs. of HOW, see VII.5.1 and VII.8.11.

7 Ch 1 aɷ a: ðə 2 æɷ ə jə gɛtɩn ən 3 ɛ̈ɷ a jə 4 aɷ jə gɷɩn ɒn 5 aɩ jə gɷɩn ɒn 6 aɷ bɩn jə

8 Db 1 ɛ̨ɷ‿t go:ɩn ɒn, °ɛɷ‿t gʏ:ɩn ɒn[1] 2 aɷ a: tə 3 ɛɷ a:‿t 4 ɛ:‿t g^{ɷ}u:ɩn ɒn 5 ɛ̨: jə go:ən ɒn 6 ɛ:‿t gü:ɩn ɒn 7 ɛ: jə g^{ɷ}u:ɩn ɒn

11 Sa 1 aɷ bɩst ðɩ 2 æɷ am jə 3 aɷ bɩn i: gɛtn ɒn 4 aɷ a^{ɽ}:ɽ jə 5 ɛɷ bɩst ðɩ, °ɛɷ bɩst[2] 6 aɷ bɩn i:, °aɷ bɩst ðɩ 7 aɷ bɩst ðɩ 8 aɷ bɩst 9 aɷ bi: gɛtɩn ɔ:n 10 aɷ bɩst, °aɷ bɩst gɛtɩn ɔ:n 11 aɷ bɩst, °aɷ bɩst ɩ[2]

12 St 1 aɷ a: jə 2 a:‿t gɷɩn ɒn 3 a:‿t gɷ:ɩn ɒn 4 aɷ‿t gɛtɩn ɒn 5 aɷ a: jə 6 a: ju: gɷ:ɩn ɒn 7 ạ: jə gɛtɩn ɒn 8 aɷ jə gɛtɩn ɒn 9 aɷ a: jə 10 a:ɷ ə jọ: əgɛtɩn ɒn 11 aɷw ɑ: ju:

15 He 1 æɷ bi: jə 2 æɷ bɩst gɛtɩn ɔ:n 3 əɷ bi: jə^{ɽ} 4 əɷ bi: jə 5 ʌɷ bi: jə 6 əɷ bɩs ðɩ 7 aɷ ɑ: jə, °aɷ ə jə gɛtɩn ɒn[4]

16 Wo 1 ɛɷ am jə gɩtɩn ɒn 2 ɛɷ bɩn ðɩ 3 ɛu: bɩ jə goɷɩn ɑ:n 4 əɷ: bɩs ðə gwaɩn ɑ:n 5 əɷ: bɩst ə gu:ɩn ɑ:n 6 ɛu: bɩ jə 7 æɷz θɩŋz[(2x)]

17 Wa 1 æɷ ə jə gọɷɩn ɒn 2 æɷ ɑ: jə, æɷ du: 3–4 ɛɷ a: jə 5 ɛɷ jə gɛḍɩn ɒn 6 ɛɷ ə^{ɽ} ju: 7 ɛɷ ə jü:

23 Mon 1 ʌɷ bɩs ðɩi:, °ʌɷ ə j^{ɷ}u:[4] 2 ʌɷ bɩ ju: gɛtɩn ɒn 3 əɷ a: jə 4 əu bɩst^{h}, əu bi:, °əu bɩst^{h}[1], °əu bi:j[1], °əu bɩs ði[1] 5 əu bij u: 6 əɷ a^{ɽ}: jə 7 n.a.

24 Gl 1 əɷ: bɩst ði: 2 əɷ bɩst ði: 3 əɷ bɩst 4 əɷ b^{ɩ}i: 5 ʌɷ bɩst 6 ^{ɷ}u: bɩst 7 ^{ɷ}u: bɩst gɛtɩn ɒ·n

25 O 1 ɛ̈ɷ bɩ gɛʔɩn lɒŋ 2 æ̨ɷ bi:, æɷ ɔɹ jü:, °æɷ bi: gɷɩn ɔ:n[1] 3 ɛɷ ə ju: 4 aɷ bi: 5 ɛ̈ɷ bɩ gɛʔn ɑn 6 ɛ̈ɷ ju: gɩʔn ɒn

VIII.2.9 SIGHT*

Q. Some people you know to talk to, but others you just know by . . . .

R. SIGHT

7 Ch 1 sɛɪt 2 saɪt 3 sɛɪt 4 sɑɪt‘, p. si:t‘ [“older”] 5 sɛɪt 6 saɪt

8 Db 1 si:t‘ 2 si:t 3–4 sɛɪt 5 sɑɪt 6–7 sɛɪt

11 Sa 1–3 saɪt 4–5 sɛɪt 6–7 saɪt 8 sɒɪt 9–11 saɪt

12 St 1 sɒɪt 2 sɛɪt 3 sɒ:ɪt, sɛɪt [“older”] 4 sɒɪt 5–6 sɒ:ɪt 7–9 sɒɪt 10 sa:ɪt 11 sa:ɪt [ɷnsa:ɪtlɪ² *unsightly*] .

15 He 1–2 sæɪt 3–5 səɪt 6 zəɪt 7 saɪt⁽²ˣ⁾

16 Wo 1 sɒɪt 2 səɪt 3 səi:t 4–5 səɪt 6 sɒɪt 7 səɪt, ○∼¹

17 Wa 1 sɑɪt‘, ○sɒɪt² 2 səɪt, ○∼¹ 3 səït 4–7 səɪt

23 Mon 1–3 səɪt 4 səɪtʰ 5 sə̨itʰ 6 səɪt, ○∼¹ 7 n.a.

24 Gl 1 səɪt, ○∼² 2 səɪt 3 zəɪt 4 zɒɪt 5 sö̆ɪt 6 sʌɪt 7 zʌɪt

25 O 1 sö̆ɪt, ○∼² 2 sö̆ɪʔ 3 sʌʏt, ○∼², ○□sʌʏts² 4 səɪt [əɪsəɪt³ *eye-s.*] 5–6 sö̆ɪʔ

VIII.2.10 STRANGERS

Q. And if you don’t know certain people at all, you say they are . . . .

Rr. FOREIGNERS, STRANGERS

7 Ch 1 stɹẹ:ndʒəz 2 stɹe:ndʒəz 3–4 stɹẹ:ndʒəz 5 stɹi:ndʒəz 6 stɹe:ndʒəz

8 Db 1 ᐞstɹe:ndʒə̠ 2 stɹe:ndʒəz, ○ᐞstɹe:nʒə⁴ 3 stɹe:nʒəz 4 ᐞstɹi:ndʒə 5 ᐞstɹe:ˈnʒə 6 stɹi:ndʒəz 7 stɹe·ɪndʒəz

11 Sa 1 ᐞstɹe:ndʒəʳ 2 stɹe:ndʒəz 3 ᐞstɹe:ndʒəʳ 4 stɹe:ndʒəʳ:z̜ 5 stɹẹ:ndʒəʳz̜ 6–11 stɹe:ndʒəʳ:z̜

12 St 1 stɹeɪndʒəz 2 stɹɛɪndʒəz 3 stɹɒndʒəz 4 stɹɛɪndʒəz 5 stɹe:ndʒəz 6 stɹɛɪndʒəz, ○∼ 7–8 stɹɛɪndʒəz 9 stɹɛɪndʒəz, ○fɒɹɪnəz 10–11 stɹɛɪndʒəz

15 He 1 stɹe:ndʒəʳz̜ 2 stɹæɪndʒəʳz̜ 3 stɹɛɪnʒəʳz̜ 4 ᐞstɹæɪnʒəʳ 5 stɹe:ɪnʒəʳz̜ 6 ᐞstɹɒɪnʒəʳ 7 ᐞstɹeɪndʒəɹ, ○ᐞ∼⁴

16 Wo 1 stɹɛɪndʒəz 2 stɹe:ndʒəʳz̜ 3 stɹe:ɪndʒəʳz̜ 4 stɹaɪndʒəʳz̜ 5 stɹa̱:ndʒəʳz̜ 6 stɹe:ɪndʒəʳz̜ 7 stɹeɪndʒəʳz̜, ○stɹeɪndʒəʴz[1]

17 Wa 1 stɹȩɪndʒəz 2 stɹȩɪndʒəz 3 stɹɛɪndʒɷz 4 stɹȩəndʒəʳz̜ 5 stɹɛɪndʒə·ʳz̜ 6 stɹɛɪndʒəʳz̜ 7 stɹɛɪndʒəz

23 Mon 1 △stɹe:ˈnʒəʳ 2 stɹe:nʒəʳz̜ 3 stɹe:ndʒəz 4 n.a. 5 stɹȩ:ndʒəz 6 stɹe:nʒəʳz̜ 7 n.a.

24 Gl 1–2 stɹæɪnʒəʳz̜ 3 △stɹæɪnʒəʳ 4 stɹaɪnʒəʳz̜ 5 △stɹæɪndʒəʳ, ○△stɹæɪnʒə[2] 6 △stɹæɪnʒə, ○△~ 7 stɹȩɪndʒəʳz̜, ○~

25 O 1 △stɹæɪdʒəʳ [*sic*] 2 stɹɛɪnʒəʴz 3 stɹȩ:ndʒəʳz̜ 4 △fɒɽənəɽ, s.w. △stɽeɪndʒəɽ, ○△fɒɽənəɽ[5] 5 stɽeˈndʒəʳz̜ 6 stɹeɪndəʳz̜

VIII.2.11 FROM

Q. You might say: Who's that queer-looking stranger over there? I wonder where he comes ....

Rr. FRO, FROM

Note—FROM also occurs at VII.6.26.

7 Ch 1 fɹɒm 2 fɹəm(2x), ○fɹe:[1], ○fɹəm[2] 3 fɹɒm 4 fɹɒm, ○~[2], ○fɹəm[1] 5 fɹɒm 6 fɹɒm [dɪfɹənt tɬ naɷ[2] *different till* (i.e. from) *now*]

8 Db 1 fɹəm 2 fɹu:, ○fɹəm[3] 3 fɹɷm, ○~ 4 fɹɷm 5 θɹˈu: 6–7 fɹɷm

11 Sa 1 fɹɒm 2 fɹəm, ○~[1,2] 3 fɹɒm, ○~[2] VII.2.6 4 fɹɒm 5 fɹam 6 fɹɒm 7 fɹɔ:m, ○fɹəm, ○fɹɒm 8 fɹɒm, ○fɹəm[2] 9–11 fɹɒm

12 St 1 fɹɒm, ○~[4], ○fɹəm[1] 2 fɹǫm, ○fɹɒm 3 fɹɒm, ○~[1(2x),2], ○fɹəm[1(3x),2] 4 fɹɒm, ○~[4] IX.9.4 5 fɹɒm, ○~[1,3], ○fɹəm[2(2x),3] 6 fɹɒm, ○~[1] 7 fɹɒm, ○~[1], ○fɹəm[1,4], ○~[1] IX.9.4 9–10 fɹɒm 11 fɹɒm, ○fɹəm[1]

15 He 1–2 fɹɒm 3 fɹɑ:m 4–5 fɹɒm 6 vɹæm, ○fɹəm[1] 7 fɹɒm, ○fɹəm[3(2x)]

16 Wo 1 fɹɷm, ○fɹəm[1] 2–4 fɹɒm 5 fɹɑ:m 6 fɹɒm 7 fɹəm, ○~[3], ○fɹəm[1(3x),3(2x),4], ○fɹɷm[4]

17 Wa 1 fɹɒm 2 fɹəm 3–7 fɹɒm

23 Mon 1–2 fɹɒm 3 fɹɑ:m, ○~[2] 4 fɹɒ̟·m, ○~[2] 5 fɹɒ̟·m 6 fɹɑ:m 7 n.a.

24 Gl 1 fɹɑ:m, ○fɹəm[1] 2–3 fɹɑ:m 4 vɹɑ:m 5 fɹɒm 6 vɹɑm 7 vɹɒm

25 O 1–3 fɹɒm 4 fɽɒm, ○~[1,5], ○fɹɒm[4], ○fɽəm[1,4] ○fɹəm[4] 5 fɽɒm, ○fɹəm[2] 6 fɹɒm

VIII.2.12 PEOPLE

Q. If your wife comes home from a meeting and you want to know if it was well attended, you'd ask her: . . . . **Were there many people** *there?*—March 1953, **were there many** *not rated as key-words.*

Rr. FOLK(S), PEOPLE

The following, since they omit an expression for PEOPLE, are u.rr. and have been so designated below:—HOW MANY WAS THERE THERE?, WAS IT CROWDED?, WAS THERE MANY AT IT?, WAS/WERE THERE MANY THERE?

7 Ch 1 fo̜:ks 2 pi:pl, s.w. fɷək, °fɷ:k[1], °fɷəks[1], °pi:pl[2] 3 fo̜:k 4 fo:ks 5 fu̜:ks, °fεɷks[2] 6 fo:k[(2x)]

8 Db 1 fɒɷks 2 fɷəks, °~[4], °foəks[3] 3 fo:k 4 fo:kʻ 5–6 fo:[ɷ]ks 7 fo·ɷks

11 Sa 1 fo:k 2–5 fo:ks 6 fo:k, °pi:pl[3] 7–11 fo:ks

12 St 1 §wɒz ɩt kɹaɷdɩd 2 §wɒz ðə mεnɩ ðiə 3 §wə: ðə mεnɩ ðiə 4 §wɒz ðə mεnɩ ðε:, °foɷks[2,3] 5 §wɒz ðə mεnɩ at ɩt, °pi:pl[2] 6 foɷks 7 §a: mεnɩ wɒz ðə ðεə, °fɔɷks[2] 8 §wɒz ðə mεnɩ ðε: 9 §wɒz ðə mεnɩ ðε:, °pi:pl[1], °foɷks[3], °foɷk[3] 10 §wɒz ðə mεnɩ ðɩə, °pi:pl[3] 11 §wε: ðə mεnɩ ðε:, °foɷk[2]

15 He 1 fo:ɷks 2 pi:pł 3 fo:ks 4 pi:pl, °fo:ks[1] 5 pi:pl 6 fɒɷks 7 foɷk, °pi:pl[3], °foɷks[4]

16 Wo 1 fɒɷks 2 foɷks, °~[2] 3 foɷks 4–5 fo:ks 6 foɷks, °~[3] 7 pi:pl, s.w. fɔ̜ɷk, °fɔɷks[1,4], °pi:pl[1,3(2x)]

17 Wa 1 pi:pl, s.w. fo̜ɷks ["older"] 2 pi:pl, fɔɷks, °~[1,4(2x)], °pi:pl[1] 3 foɷks 4 foɷks, °pi:pł[1] 5 fɒɷks 6 fo̜ɷks 7 pi:pł, p. foɷks

23 Mon 1 fo:[ɷ]ks 2–3 pi:pł 4 n.a., °pʰi:pł[3] 5 pʰi:pł, °~[1], °pi:pł[2] 6 pi:pł 7 n.a.

24 Gl 1 pi:pɷł, °~[1] 2 fo:ɷks 3–4 pʻi:pł 5 fo:ks 6 vo:k 7 vo:[ɷ]k

25 O 1 fɔɷks 2 pi:pl 3 pi:pł 4 pi:pɷł, °pi:pł[4(3x)] 5 pi:pł 6 pi:ˀpł

VIII.3.1 COME IN

Q. What do you say to a caller at the door if you want him to enter?

Rr. BE COMING IN, COME (THOU) IN, COME INSIDE (WITH THEE), COME ON (IN {WITH THEE}), SHALL YOU COME IN?, STEP INSIDE

Note—Exs. of COME, *imp.* also occur at II.3.5 and VII.5.8. For exs. of COME and its parts, see IX.3.4.

7 Ch 1–6 kɷm ɩn

8 Db 1–5 kɷm ɩn 6 kɷm ɩnsɑ̃ɩ̃d wɩ ðɩ 7 kəm ɩn

11 Sa 1 kʌm ɩn 2 kɷm ɩn 3 kɷm ɒn ɩn 4 kʌm ɩn 5 kɷm ɩn 6–7 kʌm ɩn 8 kɷm ɩn 9–10 kʌm ɩn 11 kɷm ɩn

12 St 1 kɷm ɩn 2 kɷm ɩ̥n 3–4 kɷm ɩn 5 kɷm ɩn, ○~[2] 6–8 kɷm ɩn 9 ʃal jə kɷm ɩn 10 kɷm ɩnsaɩd 11 kɷm ɩn, kɷm ɩnsaɩd

15 He 1–2 kʌm ɩn 3 kɷm ɩn 4–5 kʌm ɩn 6–7 kɷm ɩn

16 Wo 1 kɷm ɒn ɩn 2 kɷm ɑ·n 3–5 kɷm ɩn 6 kɷm ɩ:n 7 kɷm ɩn

17 Wa 1 kɷm ɩn 2 stɛp ɩnsɔɩd, ○kɷm ɩn[1] 3–4 kɷm ɩn 5 kɷ̢m ɩn 6–7 kɷm ɩn

23 Mon 1 kʌm ɩn 2 kɷm ɩn 3 kʌm ɩn 4 kʌ̢̆m ɒ̢̆·n 5 kʌ̢̆m ɩnsəɩ̢d 6 kʌm ɩn 7 n.a.

24 Gl 1 kɷm ɩ:n 2 kɷm ɩn 3 kʌm ðə ɩn 4 kɷm ɩn 5 kʌm ɩn 6 kəm ɒn ɩn 7 kəm ɩn

25 O 1 kʌm ɒn ɩn wɩ θə 2 kʌm ɩn, bɩ kʌmən ɩn ["older"] 3 kʌm ɩn 4 kɷm ɩn 5–6 bɩ kʌmɩn ɩn

VIII.3.2 GLAD TO SEE YOU. VERY

Q. And if the caller was a rare visitor, though a good old friend of yours, you'd say: I'm . . . .

If he answers without an intensifier, then ask him—

And if you felt it more strongly, you'd say: I'm . . . . glad to see you.

Rr. FAIN TO SEE YOU, (RIGHT/TERRIBLE/VERY) GLAD TO SEE YOU, (/EVER SO/MIGHTY/RIGHT/VERY/) PLEASED TO SEE YOU, (MIGHTY/VERY) PROUD TO SEE YOU, §THAT'S NICE TO SEE YOU

Intensifiers rec. as rr. to the supplementary q.:—DAMNED, EVER SO, PROPER, REALLY, RIGHT, UNCOMMON, VERY

Intensifiers rec. in the i.m.:—AWFUL, DAMN, GRADELY, JOLLY, PRETTY, PROPER, RIGHT, VERY

Note 1—In the list of rr. above, YOU subsumes THEE and YE.

Note 2—Rr. to the supplementary q. are separated from the rr. to the main q. by a full stop. Intensifiers from the i.m., since they do not occur in the present context, are reproduced below between square brackets untransliterated.

Note 3—For additional exs. of intensifiers, see IV.11.5, VI.13.1, VI.13.19, VII.7.9 and VIII.8.5.

7 Ch 1 vəɹɪ glad‿ˀ sẹ: ðɪ 2 glad si: ðɪ . ɹi:t [vɛɹɪ$^{1(6x),2(10x),3(2x)}$, vɛ̧ɹɪ^{2}, vɛɹ^{2} (+ C.); gɹe:dlɪ^{4}] 3 vəɹɪ pɹaɪd sɛɪ ðɪ [vɛɹɪ^{3}; ɹi:t^{1}] 4 dlad tə sɪ̧: jə . vɛɹɪ [vɛɹɪ$^{2(2x)}$, vəɹɪ^{2}] 5 plɛɪzd tə sɛɪ ðɪ . vɛɹɪ [vɛɹɪ^{3}] 6 ple:zd tə sɪ jə . vɛɹɪ

8 Db 1 fe:n‿ˀ si: jə . ɹi:t 2 vɛɹɪ glad tə si: jə . ɹɛɪt 3 pli:zd‿ˀ sɛɪ ðɪ . ɹɛɪt [dam^{1}] 4 vəɹɪ plɛɪzd‿ˀ sɛɪ ðɪ 5 vaɹɪ pli:zd tə si: ðɪ 6 ɹɛɪt pli:zd‿ʔ sɛɪ ðɪ [vɛɹɪ^{1}] 7 ɹɛɪt dlad sɛɪ ðɪ [vəɹɪ^{1}]

11 Sa 1 glad tə si: jə . ʌnkɒmən 2 pli:zd tə si: jə . ɹaɪt 3 pɹaᴼd tə si: jə . ɹaɪt [vɛɹɪ^{2}] 4 pli:zd tə si: jə . ɹɛɪt 5 plˡi:z tə sˡi: ðɪ . vɛɹɪ [vɛɹɪ^{1}] 6 §ðat‿s naɪs tə si: jə, glad tə si: jə [vɛɹɪ$^{2,4(3x)}$] 7 glæd tə si: ðɪ . ɹaɪt 8 glad tə si: ðɪ . ɹɒɪt [vɛɹɪ^{1}] 9 pli:zd tə si: jə . ɹaɪt [vɛɹɪ$^{1(2x)}$] 10 glad tə si: jə . ɹaɪt [pəʳ:ɖɪ^{3}, pɹɪdɪ^{3}] 11 glad tə si: jə . ɹaɪt [vɛɹɪ$^{1(2x)}$; dʒɒlɪ^{1}]

12 St 1 vɛɹɪ pli:zd tə si: jə [vɛɹɪ^{1}; ɔ:fɷl^{1}] 2 glad sɛɪ ðɪ . pɹɒɪd 3 pli:zd sɛɪ ðɪ . vɛɹɪ [vɛɹɪ$^{1(4x),2}$] 4 pli:zd tə si: jə . vɛɹɪ [vɛɹɪ$^{1(2x),2}$] 5 pli:zd tə si: jə . vɛɹɪ [vɛɹɪ$^{1(2x),2(7x),3(3x)}$] 6 pli:zd tə sɛɪ jə . vɛɹɪ [vɛɹɪ$^{2(4x)}$] 7 pli:zd tə si: jə . vɛɹɪ [vɛɹɪ^{1,4}] 8 pli:zd tə si: jə . vɛɹɪ [vɛɹɪ$^{1(2x)}$] 9 pli:zd tə sɛɪ jə . vɛɹɪ [vɛɹɪ$^{1(4x),3}$; dam^{2}] 10 vɛɹɪ pli:zd tə si: jə [vɛɹɪ^{3,6}] 11 pli:zd tə si: jə . ɛvə soɷ [vɛɹɪ$^{1,2(4x)}$; ɪts naɪs tə si: jə^{2} *it's nice to see you*]

15 He 1 pli:zd tə si: jə . vɛɹɪ 2 glæd tə si: θə$^{(2x)}$ 3 pli:zd tə si: jɷ . vɛɹɪ [vɛɹɪ^{4}] 4 pli:zd tə si: θə . dæmd 5 glæd tə si: jə . dæmnd [with non-syllabic «n»] 6 pli:zd tə si: ðɪ . vəɹɪ 7 pli:zd tə si: jə . vɛɹɪ [vɛɹɪ$^{1(2x),2(2x),3(3x),4(6x)}$, vɛɹ^{1}; pɹɪtɪ$^{4(2x)}$, pɹətɪ^{3}; ɔ:fəl^{2}]

16 Wo 1 glad tə si: jə . ɹɒɪt 2 glad tə si: ðɪ . ɹəɪt [vɛɹɪ^{2}] 3 ple:ɪzd tə si: jə . vɛɹɪ [vɛɹɪ^{2}, vɛɹi:^{1}] 4 glæ·d tə si: ðɷ . vɛɹɪ [vɛɹɪ$^{1(2x)}$] 5 glæd tə sɪ jɷ . ɹəɪt [vəɹɪ^{1}, vɛɹɪ$^{1(2x)}$] 6 glæd tə si: jə . vɛɹɪ [rec. in «vɛɹɪ glæd jɷ bɪ kɷ:m» *very glad you be come*] 7 vɛɹɪ pli:zd . vɛɹɪ [vɛɹɪ$^{1(2x),3(7x),4(2x)}$, vɛʳ^{1}, vɛɽɪ^{2}]

17 Wa 1 pli:zd tə si: jə. ɹɪəlɪ 2 pli:zd tə si: jə. vɛɹɪ [rec. in «vɛɹɪ glad tə si: jə» *very glad to see you*; vɛɹɪ[1(6x),3,4(3x)], vɛɹə[1]; pɹɪtɪ[2]] 3 pl̥ɪ:zd tə sɪ jə. vɛɹɪ [vɛɹɪ[2(2x)]] 4 ɛvə sə plɛɪzd tə si: jə 5 vɛɹɪ pli:zd tə si: jə [vɛɹɪ[1(3x)]] 6 pli:zd tə si: jə. vɛɹɪ 7 pli:zd tə sɪ jə. vɛɹɪ [vɛɹɪ[1]]

23 Mon 1 pli:zd tə s'i: jəʳ. vɛɹɪ 2 gla:d tə si: jə. vɛɹɪ 3 glæd tə si: jə. vɛɹɪ [vɛɹɪ[2]] 4 n.a. [vɛɹi[1]] 5 glad tə si: ju:. vɛɹi [rec. in «vɛɹi pli:st tə si: ju:» *very pleased to see you*; vɛɹi[2]; pɹɪtɪ[2]] 6 pli:zd tə si: jə. vɛɹɪ [pɷtɪ[2]] 7 n.a.

24 Gl 1 glæd tə si: jə. vɛɹɪ 2 pli:z tə si: θə. vɛɹɪ 3 ple:'z tə z'i: ðə. vɛɹɪ 4 vɛɹɪ pɫi:zd tə s'i: 'i: 5 pli:zd tə sɪ jə, ple:zd tə sɪ ðə [pref.; "older"]. vɛɹɪ [vɛɹɪ[2]] 6 vɛɹɪ ple:zd tə zɪ ðə 7 vəɹɪ pli:zd tə zɪ ðə

25 O 1 ple:zd tə sɪ θə. vɛɽɪ [vəɽɪ[2]] 2 pli:zd tə si: jə. vəɹɪ [vɛɽɪ[2]; ɹəɪt[1]; pɹɒpə̠] 3 tɛɹəbl glad tə si: jɷ [vəɽ[1]] 4 pɫi:zd tə si: jə. vɛɽɪ [vɛɽɪ[1(2x),3,4], vəɽɪ[3(2x),4], vɛ̈ɹɪ[4]; pəɽtɪ[4]] 5 mʌʏtɪ pli:zd tə si: ɪ [vɛɹɪ[3]] 6 pli:zd tə si: jə. vəɽɪ

VIII.3.3 SIT DOWN

Q. And what do you say when you offer him (viz. a caller) *a chair?*

Rr. HAVE (A) SIT–DOWN, SET DOWN, SIT (YOU/YOURSELF) DOWN, SQUAT DOWN, TAKE A SEAT

Note 1—In the above list YOU and YOURSELF subsume THEE and THYSELF resp.
Note 2—For additional exs. of DOWN, see VIII.3.6 (and refs.).

7 Ch 1 sɪt ðɪ da:n 2 sɪ̞t dæɷn 3 sɪt jə daɪn 4 sɪt daɷn 5 sɪt daɪn 6 sɪt da̙ɷn

8 Db 1 sɪt ðɪ dɛ̝ɷn 2–3 sɪt ðɪ daɷn 4 sɪt ðɪ dɛ:n 5 sɪt ðɪ dɛ̝:ᵊn 6–7 sɪt ðɪ dɛ:n

11 Sa 1 sɪt daɷn 2 sɪt dæɷn 3 sɪt daɷn 4 sɪt jə dɛɷn 5 sɪt ðɪ dɛɷn 6 sɪt daɷn 7 sɪ daɷn 8 sɪt dɛɷn 9 sɪt daɷn 10 sɪt jəsɛlf daɷn 11 sɪt ðə daɷn

12 St 1 sɪt ðɪ da:n 2–3 sɪt ðɪ daɪn 4 sɪt jə dæɷn 5 sɪt jə da:n 6 sɪt ʃə dæ:n 7 sɪt da:n 8 sɪt jə dæɷn 9 sɪt da:n 10 sɪt jə da:n 11 sɪt dæɷn

15 He 1 sɪt dæɷn 2 skwæt dæɷn 3–4 sɪt dəɷn 5 sɪt dʌɷn 6 zɪt dəɷn 7 sɪt jə dəɷn

16 Wo 1 sɩt dɛɷn 2 sɩt dɛɷᵊn 3 sɩt dɛu:n 4 sɩt dəɷ:n 5 sɩ dəɷ:ᵊn 6 sɩ dɛu:n 7 sɩt ðɩsɛlf dæɷn

17 Wa 1 sɩt dæ̧ɷn 2 tɛ̧ɩk ə si:t, p. sɩt dæɷn(2x), s.f. sɩt jə dæɷn [only said to a child] 3 sɩt dɛ̈ɷn 4 sɩt dɛɷn 5 sɩd̥ dɛɷn 6 sɩt dɛɷn 7 sɩt dɛ̈ɷn

23 Mon 1 sɩt dʌɷn 2 æv sɩtdʌɷn 3 sɩt dəɷn 4 n.a. 5 sɩt̥ dəun 6 sɩ dəɷn 7 n.a.

24 Gl 1 sɩt dəɷ:ᵊn 2 æv ə sɩtdəɷ:n 3 sɩt ðə dəɷn 4 sɩt dəɷᵊn 5 sɛt dʌɷn 6–7 zɩt dᵒu:n

25 O 1 sɛʔ dɛ̈ɷn 2 sɩʔ dæɷn 3 sɩt dɛɷn 4 sɛt dạɷn 5 sɩd dɛ̈ɷn 6 sɩʔ doɷn

VIII.3.4 CHAT

Q. And when you had both sat down comfortably you'd start to have a....

Rr. CANK, CANT, CHAT, CHATTER, CHINWAG, CHOPS, CONFLABERATION, GOSSIP, LARRAP, TALK

Note—Verbs corresponding to some of the nn. listed above occur at VIII.3.5.

7 Ch 1–2 tʃat 3 tʃat, tʃɒps ["older"] 4–6 tʃat

8 Db 1 tʃatʻ 2–7 tʃat

11 Sa 1–2 tʃat 3 tʃa·t 4–6 tʃat 7 tʃæt 8 tʃat, laɹəp 9–10 tʃæt 11 tʃat, laɹəp ["older"; ant əʳ gɒt ə laɹəp *hasn't she got a l.?* (i.e. doesn't she talk a lot?)]

12 St 1–2 tʃat 3 tʃɒps, toɷk 4–11 tʃat

15 He 1–3 tʃæt 4 kjæŋk 5 tʃɒt 6 tʃæt 7 tʃat, °tʃɩnwag[4]

16 Wo 1–2 tʃat 3–5 tʃæt 6 tʃæ:t 7 p. ta:k, kɒnflabəɹeɩʃən, °tʃɩnwag[1]

17 Wa 1–3 tʃat 4 tʃatəʳɽ 5 tɔ:k, s.w. tʃat 6–7 tʃat

23 Mon 1 kjænt 2 tʃa:t 3 ka:nt 4 n.a. 5 tʃat 6 tʃa:t 7 n.a.

24 Gl 1 tʃæ:t 2–3 tʃæt 4 tʃɛt 5 tʃɩnwag, tʃat 6 tʃɩnwag 7 tʃat

25 O 1 gɒʃəp ["older"], tʃat 2 tʃatəʳ 3 gɒsəp, tɔ:k 4 tʃat 5–6 tʃaʔəɽ

VIII.3.5 GOSSIPING. GOSSIP

Q. What's your word for spending a lot of time doing this (viz. chatting) *and spreading tales?*
And have you a special word for a woman who does this?

Rr. CAG–MAG(GING), CANKING, (A–)CANTING, CHOPSING, GALLIVANTING, (A–)GOSSIPING, HAVING A NATTER, HAWCHING, NATTERING, TONGUE–WAGGING

BUSYBODY, CAG–MAG, CANK, CANT, CANTER, CHATTERBOX, GALLIVANTER, GAS/NEWS/WIND–BAG, ({PROPER/RARE}OLD) GOSSIP, GOSSIPER, MAGGER, NEWS–CANTER, (REGULAR) OLD CANT, RATTLE(–BOX), RATTLER, SCANDAL–MONGER, TONGUE–WAG

Note 1—The rr. to the two parts of the q. are separated below by a full stop.
Note 2—See also VIII.3.4.

7 Ch 1 gɒsəpɪn. bɪzɪbɒdɪ, gɒsɪp 2 gəsɪpɪn, °~. pɹɔpəɹ ɛɷd gəsɪp 3 gɒsəpɪn. gɒsəp 4 gɒsɪpɪn, kantɪn ["old"]. gɒsɪp, kant 5 gɒsəpɪn. gɒsəp 6 kaləvantɪn. kalɪvantə

8 Db 1 gɒsəppɪn. gɒsəppə 2 gɒsəpɪn. gɒsəp 3–4 gɒsəpɪn. gɒsəpə 5 kantɪn. kantə 6–7 gɒsəpɪn. gɒsəpə

11 Sa 1 gɒsəpɪn. gasbag 2 gə:zəpɪn. gə:zəpəʳ 3 gɒsəpɪn. tʃatəʳbɒks 4 gɒsəpɪn. gɒ·sɪp, ga·sba·g 5 gɒsɪpɪn. kant, °~ 6 gɒsəpɪn. gɒsəpəʳ 7 gə:səpɪn. gə:sɪp 8 gɒsəpɪn. gɒsəpəʳ 9 gə:səpɪn. gə:səp 10 gə:səpɪn. gə:səp, °ɹe:əʳɽ‿aɷd gə:səp 11 gə:səpɪn. gə:səp, ɹatl

12 St 1 gɒsəpɪn, °atʃɪn[2]. gɒsəpə 2 kantɪn. gɒsəpə, °~ 3 tʃɒpsɪn ["old"], gɒsəpɪn. gɒsəp, °ɹatlə[1] 4 gɒsəpɪn. gɒsəpə 5 gɒsəpɪn. gɒsəpə 6 gɒsəpɪn. gɒsəp 7 gɒsəpɪn [ɹatlɪn *rattling* (= *talking*)]. gɒsəpə 8 gɒsəp. gɒsəpə 9 gɒsɪpɪn. gɒsəpə 10 n.r. gɒsəp, skandlmɷŋgə 11 kantɪn, əkantɪn. nju:zbag

15 He 1 gə:səpɪn. ɹætłbɒks 2 kæntɪn. gə:səpəʳ 3 kʽæntɪn. kʽænt 4 kjæŋkɪn. gɒsɪp 5 kjæntɪn. gɒsəpəʳ 6 kjæntɪn. kjæntəʳ 7 gɒsəpɪn, natəɹɪn. wɪnbag

16 Wo 1 gɒsəpɪn. gɒsəp 2 gɑ·səpɪn. gɑ·səp 3 kæŋkɪn. gɑ·səpəʳ 4 əkʽæntɪn, °~. kʽæntəʳ 5 əgɒsəpɪn. gɒsəpəʳ 6 gɑ:səpɪn. gɒsəpəʳ 7 p. gəsɪpɪn, °~. tɷŋwag

17 Wa 1 gɒsəpɪn. gɒsəp 2 kaŋkɪn, °tɷŋwagɪn[4]. gəsɪp, əɷl gəsɪp, kaŋk 3–4 gɒsɷpɪn. gɒsɷp 5 gɒsəpɪn. gɒsəpə 6–7 gɒsɷpɪn. gɒsɷp

23 Mon 1 kjæntɪn. kjænt, °ɹɛgłəʴ ɒɷłd kjænt 2 kæntɪn. kænt, °o:łd kænt 3 gɑ:səpɪn. ka:nt 4 n.a. 5 gɒ̟̈‹sʌ̟̈pɪn. gɒ̟̈‹sʌ̟̈pə 6 gɑ:səpɪn. kænt 7 n.a.

24 Gl 1 kæntɪn, əkæntɪn. kæntəʴ 2 kjæntɪn. kjæntəʴ 3 kæntɪn. kæntəʴ 4 gɑ:səpən. gɑ:səp 5 kagmag, °kjantɪn[2], °kægmægɪn[2]. kjant, °gɒsəp[2] 6 kjagmagɪn. nju:zkantəʴ 7 gɒsəpɪn. magəʴ, kagmag, gɒsəpəʴ ["oldest"]

25 O 1 gɒʃəpɪn. gɒʃəpəʴ 2 gɒsəpɪn. gɒsəp 3 gɒsəpɪn. gɒsəpəʴ 4 avən ə natəɽ, s.w. gɒsəpən, °natəɽɪn. gɒsəpəɽ, °gɒsɪp[5(2x)], °natəʴ[5] ["malicious"] 5 gɒsəpɪn. gɒsəp, °bɪzɪbɒdɪ 6 gɒsəpɪn. gɒsəp

VIII.3.6 LIE* DOWN*. LAY†

Q. *You might say to your visitor: If you are not feeling well, here's the sofa, why not come and . . . .*
The visitor thought it a good idea, came in and . . . . down.

Rr. HAVE /A DOSS/A LAY–DOWN/(YOU) A LIE–DOWN/, LAY (YOURSELF) DOWN, LIE (YOU) DOWN, LIG YOU DOWN, REST YOURSELF FOR A BIT

LAY ({HER/HIM} DOWN), LAID (HIMSELF) DOWN, LIGGED HIM DOWN, SWACKED HIMSELF DOWN

Note 1—The rr. to the two parts of the q. are separated below by a full stop.

Note 2—Acc. the view taken here, LAY *v*. occurs in the r. to the 1st part of the q. at 7.5, 11.8, 12.10, 23.4 and 25.2-5.

Note 3—I.m. forms of LIE *v*. and its parts, as well as of DOWN, are reproduced below between square brackets untransliterated. In the case of LAY *v*. and its parts, however, transliterations are given.

Note 4—In the lists above, YOU and YOURSELF subsume resp. THEE and THYSELF.

Note 5—When rec. in the r. to the second part of the q., DOWN is included below.

Note 6—For additional exs. of LAY (eggs), see IV.6.4 (and refs.). Additional exs. of DOWN occur at III.1.12, III.8.10, III.12.9, III.13.10, IV.2.3/4, VI.5.13, VII.6.5, VIII.3.3 and VIII.7.8.

7 Ch 1 lɑɪ daɪn [daɪn[4(2x)]]. le: daɪn 2 av ə lɑɪdæɷn, le: ðɪsɛn dæɷn [¶lɑɪ-ɪn[1] dæɷn[1(2x),2(5x),3], dæn[3,4], dæ:n[4], dæ̜:n[3(2x),4], da:n[1], daɷn[2], d[ə]un[2]; dæɷnspæɷt[3] *d.-spout*]. le:d ɪzsɛn dæ̜ɷn 3 lɑɪ ðɪ daɪn [daɪn[3(4x)], ~[2] IV.4.1]. lɛɪ ɪm daɪn 4 lɑɪ daɷn. lẹ: 5 lɛɪ daɪn. li: daɪn 6 laɪ dɛ̜ɷn [dɛɷn[2,3], daɷn[2(2x),3]]. lẹ: dɛɷn [le:[ə]d[2] *laid* (=*plashed*) IV.2.4]

8 Db 1 laɩ dɛ̞ɷn, lɩg ðɩ dɛ̞ɷn [old; dɛɷn¹]. lɩgd ɩm dɛ̞ɷn 2 laɩ ðɩ da:n [da:n¹,²]. le:d da:n 3 laɩ ðɩ dɛɷn [dɛ:n³]. le:d dɛɷn 4 lɑɩ dɛ:n [dɛ:n³⁽²ˣ⁾]. li: dɛ:n 5 lɑɩ dɛ̞:n. le:ˡ 6 lɑɩ ðɩ dɛ̞n [dɛ:n¹]. le:ˡ ɩm dɛ̞:n 7 lɑ̃·ĩ ðɩ dɛ:n [dɛ:n¹]. le·ɩ dɛ:n

11 Sa 1 lɛɩ daɷn. lɛɩd daɷn 2 laɩ dæɷn [dæɷn¹,²⁽²ˣ⁾]. le: dæɷn 3 lɛɩ daɷn. lɛɩ daɷn 4 laɩ dɛɷn. laɩd dɛɷn 5 laɩ dɛɷn [dɛɷn²]. lȩ:d dɛɷn 6 laɩ daɷn [daɷn¹⁽²ˣ⁾,³]. laɩd daɷn 7 laɩ daɷn [daɷn¹⁽⁴ˣ⁾]. laɩd daɷn 8 lɛɩ dɛɷn [dɛɷn¹,², ~² V.3.8]. lɛɩd dɛɷn 9 laɩ daɷn [daɷn¹]. le: 10 laɩ daɷn [daɷn¹⁽²ˣ⁾,²⁽³ˣ⁾,³⁽³ˣ⁾]. laɩd daɷn 11 laɩ daɷn. laɩd daɷn

12 St 1 laɩ daɷn [daɷn¹]. lɛɩ daɷn 2 lɒɩ ðɩ daɩn [lɒɩ², ¶lɒɩ-ɩn¹; daɩn¹⁽²ˣ⁾,⁵, da:n², daɷn²,³]. lɛɩ daɩn 3 lɒ:ɩ ðɩ daɩn [lɒ:ɩ² *inf.*; daɩn¹⁽⁹ˣ⁾,²⁽⁴ˣ⁾, dan²; li: *lay inf.*]. swakt ɩmsɛlf daɩn, li:d daɩn 4 lɒɩ dæɷn [dæɷn²]. lɛɩ dæɷn 5 lɒ:ɩ jə daɷn [daɷn³]. le: ə [=*her*] daɷn 6 lɒ:ɩ dæ:n [dæ:n¹,²]. lɛɩ dæ:n 7 lɒɩ da:n. lɛɩ dạ:n 8 lɒɩ dæɷn [daɷn¹, dæɷn¹]. lɛɩ dæɷn 9 lɒɩ da:n [lɒɩ¹,²; da:n²⁽⁴ˣ⁾,³⁽²ˣ⁾]. lɛɩ da:n 10 lɛɩ da:n [da:n⁴⁽²ˣ⁾]. lɛɩ da:n 11 la:ɩ daɷn [daɷn¹, da:n², dæɷn²⁽²ˣ⁾]. lɛɩ dæɷn

15 He 1 læɩ dæɷn [dæɷn¹]. le: dæɷn 2 læɩ dæɷn [dæɷn²]. le:ɩ dæɷn 3 ləɩ dəɷn [dəɷn¹]. læɩ dəɷn 4 ləɩ dəɷn [dəɷn¹]. læɩd dəɷn 5 ləɩ dʌɷn [dʌɷn¹,³,⁴]. le:ɩ dʌɷn 6 ləɩ dəɷn. læɩ dəɷn 7 laɩ dɑɷn [laɩ⁴ *3 pr.pl.*; dɑɷn¹, dɑ̆ɷn⁴, daɷn¹,⁴, ~⁴ VII.6.23, dɑ̆ɷn¹, dɑ̈ɷn³, də̆ɷn¹,², dəɷn², dᵊu:n², dᵊʉ̞:n²; dɑ̆ɷnəɹ *downer* (i.e. a lie-down) *n.*]

16 Wo 1 laɩ dɛɷn [dɛɷn³⁽²ˣ⁾, daɷn¹]. lɛɩ dɛɷn 2 ləɩ dɛɷn [dɛɷn²]. le: dɛɷn 3 ləi: dɛu:n [leɩ¹ *p.p.* (*sic*); dɛu:n¹⁽²ˣ⁾, dɛu:ᵊn²]. le:ɩ dɛu:n 4 ləɩ dəɷ:n [dəɷ:n¹,²⁽²ˣ⁾³]. ləɩ dəɷ:n 5 ləɩ dəɷ:n, °æv jə ə ləɩdəɷ:n. laɩ dəɷ:n [ləɩ¹ *lay 3 p.t. p.l.*; dəɷ:n¹⁽³ˣ⁾, dɒn¹; laɩd *laid p.p.*;]. laɩ dəɷ:n 6 lɛɩ dɛu:n [dɛu:n¹,³⁽²ˣ⁾]. læɩ dɛu:n, °le:ɩ dɛu:n² 7 ɹɛst ðɩsɛlf fəɹ ə bɩt, ləɩ dæɷn, °lɛɩ dæɷn¹ [¶ləɩ-ɩn⁴; dæɷn¹⁽²ˣ⁾,²,³⁽⁷ˣ⁾,⁴⁽⁴ˣ⁾]. lɛɩ dæɷn

17 Wa 1 lɑɩ dæɷn [dæɷn¹⁽³ˣ⁾]. lȩɩ dæɷn 2 av ə dɔs, p. ləɩ dæɷn [dæɷn¹⁽³ˣ⁾,³,⁴⁽³ˣ⁾]. lɛɩ dæɷn 3 lɛɩ dɛ̈ɷn. lɛɩd dɛ̈ɷn 4 ləɩ dɛɷn. ləɩd dɛɷn 5 lɛɩ dɛɷn [dɛɷn¹⁽³ˣ⁾, daɷn¹]. lɛɩ 6 ləɩ dɛɷn [dɛɷn³,⁴]. lɛɩ dɛɷn 7 ləɩ dɛ̈ɷn. lɛɩ dɛ̈ɷn

23 Mon 1 ləɩ dʌɷn [dʌɷn¹⁽²ˣ⁾]. le:ɩ dʌɷn 2 ləɩ dʌɷn. lɛd dʌɷn 3 ləɩ dəɷn, °~¹ [dəɷn¹⁽²ˣ⁾,²,³; ʌpsɩddəɷn² *upside-d.*]. le: 4 lei dəun [dəun¹]. lɛd dəun 5 ləi dəun [dəun²,³]. lɛd˚ dəun, °lɛd dəun¹ 6 ləɩ dəɷn [¶le:-ɩn dəɷn¹⁽³ˣ⁾ *laying d.*]. le: dəɷn 7 n.a.

24 Gl 1 ləɩ dəɷ:ᵊn [dəɷ:ᵊn[1(2x),2], dəɷᵊn[1], dəɷ:n[2], du:ᵊn[1]]. lɛɩ 2 ləɩ dəɷ:n [dəɷ:n[3]]. le: dəɷ:n 3 ləɩ dəɷn [dəɷᵊn[4]]. le:ˈ dəɷn 4 ləɩ dəɷᵊn dəɷn[1(2x),2(2x),3]. laɩ 5 lə̈ɩ dʌɷn. lɛd dʌɷn 6 lʌɩ dᴼu:n. le: dᴼu:n 7 lʌɩ dᴼu:n [le:ˈdᴼu:n *lay-down n.* III.13.14]. ləd dᴼu:n

25 O 1 lə̈ɩ dɛ̈ɷn [dɛ̈ɷn[1]]. læɩ dɛ̈ɷn 2 lɛ̣ɩ dæɷn. lɛ̣ɩ dæɷn 3 le: dɛɷn [le:d[2] *laid p.p.*; lɩgd[1] *ligged* (*sic*; =*lodged*) *1 p.t.pl.*; dɛɷn[1(2x),2(3x)], dæɷn[1]]. le: dɛɷn 4 lɛ̣ɩ dæ̜ɷn, ᴼɬe: dɑɷn[1] [ɬɛd[3] *laid 1 p.t.s.*; dɑɷn[1(2x),3(2x),4], dɑ̣ɷn[2,3], dæ̜ɷn[4], dɑɷn[1]]. lɛ̣ɩd dæ̜ɷn 5 le: dɛɷn [dɛɷn[1,2(3x)], dɛ̈ɷn[2] V.6.12, dɛ̈ɷn[3]]. le:d dɛɷn 6 av ə leɩdɛ̈ɷn, leɩ dɛ̈ɷn [dɛ̈ɷn[1,3]]. leɩ dɛ̈ɷn

VIII.3.7 DO YOU REMEMBER‡

Q. In talking over with an old friend the happy times you had together long ago, you'd ask him from time to time: . . . . how we . . . . ?

Rr. CAN YOU MIND, CAN (YOU) REMEMBER, §CAN'T YOU REMEMBER, DO YOU RECOLLECT, §DON'T YOU REMEMBER, (/DO YOU {EVER}/YOU/) REMEMBER

Note 1—In the list of rr. above, CAN subsumes CANST; DO YOU subsumes DOES THEE, DON YOU, DOST and D'YOU; DON'T YOU subsumes DOSTN'T THEE; and YOU subsumes THEE.

Note 2—I.m. exs. of REMEMBER *inf.* and of MIND *inf.* meaning *remember* are reproduced below between square brackets untransliterated. MIND meaning *look after* (ref. a baby) occurs at VIII.1.23.

7 Ch 1 dɷz ðə ɹɩmɛmbə 2–3 dɷst ɹɩmɛmbə 4 djə ɹɩmɛmbə 5 dɷs ðɛɩ ɹɩmɛmbə 6 kan jə ɹɩmɛmbə

8 Db 1 kan tə ɹɩmɛmbə 2 dɷst ɹɩmɛmbə [ɹɩmɛmbə[3]] 3 dɷz tə ɹɛkəlɛkt 4 dɷst ɹɩmɛmbə 5 dɷz ðə ɹɩmɛmbə 6 kɒst ðɛɩ ɹɩmɛmbə 7 kɒnst ɹɩmɛmbə

11 Sa 1 dɷst ɹɩmɛmbəᵗ 2 kan jə ɹɩmɛmbəᵗ 3 də jə ɹɩmɛmbəᵗ 4 dɷ jə ɹɩmɛmbəᵗ 5 dɷst ɹɩmɛmbəᵗ [ɹɩmɛmbəᵗ[3]] 6 dʌst ðə ɹɩmɛmbəᵗ 7 dʌs ðɩ ɹɩmɛmbəᵗ 8 dɷs ðɩ ɹɩmɛmbəᵗ 9 dʌst ðɩ ɹɩmɛmbəᵗ 10 dʌs θi: ɹɩmɛmbəᵗ [ɹɩmɛməᵗ[2]] 11 §dɷsnə ði: ɹɩmɛmbəᵗ

12 St 1 n.k. [a kɒnə dʒɷst kɷm tü: ɩt *I cannot just come to* (i.e. remember) *it*] 2 kɒst ɹɩmɛmbə 3 dɷst ɹɩmɛmbə 4 dʒu: ɹɩmɛmbə 5 dɷn jə ɹɩmɛmbə 6 də joɷ ɹɩmɛmbə 7 də jə ɹɩmɛmbə [ɹɩmɛmbə[5]] 8 də joɷ ɹɩmɛmbə 9 dɷn joɷ ɹɩmɛmbə [ɹɩmɛmbə[1]] 10 djə ɹɩmɛmbə 11 dju: ɹɩmɛmbə

15 He 1 dʒə ɹɪmɛmbəʳ 2 dɷsnt θi: ɹɪmɛmbəʳ 3 dɷ jɷ ɹɪmɛmbəʳ 4 kɒn jə ɹɪmɛmbəʳ 5 də jə ɹɪmɛmbəʳ 6 dɷs ði: ɹɪmɛmbəʳ 7 də ju: ɹɪmɛmbəɹ [ɹɪmɛmbə¹]

16 Wo 1 də jə ɹɪmɛmbə 2 kən ði: ɹɪmɛmbəʳ 3 dɷs ði: ɹɪmɛmbəʳ 4 dɷst ɹɪmɛmbəʳ 5 dɷs ði: ɹɪmɛmbəʳ 6 dɷz ði: ɹɪmɛmbəʳ 7 p. dɪ jə ɹɪmɛmbə

17 Wa 1 dɪ jə ɹɪmɛmbə 2 də jə ɹɪmɛmbə 3 dɪ jə ɹɪmɛmbə 4 §dọ·ən tʃə ɹɪmɛmbə, §do:ən jə ɹɪmɛmbə 5 ju: ɹɛmɪmbəʳ 6 kan jə ɹɪmɛmbəʳ 7 §ka:nt jə ɹɪmɛmbəʳ

23 Mon 1 dʌs ðɪ ɹɪmɛmbəʳ 2 du: jə ɹɪmɛmbəʳ 3 də jə ɹɪmɛmbə 4 ɹi:mɛm:bə 5 ɹimɛmbɐ 6 kæn jə ɹɪmɛmbəʳ [ɹɪmɛmbəʳ *1 pr.s.*)] 7 n.a.

24 Gl 1 kənst ði: ɹɪməmbəʳ 2 dɷst ɛvəʳ ɹɪmɛmbəʳ 3 kɒst ɹɪmɛmbəʳ 4 dᵒu: ɪ ɹɪmɛmbəʳ 5 kan jə ɹɪmɛmbəʳ 6 dəst ðɪ: ɹɪmɛmbəʳ 7 kəst ði: mʌɪnd [mʌɪn²]

25 O 1 dəs ði: ɹɪmɛmbəʳ 2 kan jə ɹɪmɛmbəʳ 3 dɪ jɷ ɹɪmɛmbəʳ [ɹɪmɛmbə¹] 4 dʌst ɽɪmɛmbəɽ 5 dɪ jə ɽɪmɛmbəʳ 6 kan jə ɹɪmɛmbəʳ

VIII.4.1 WORK-MATES

Q. What's your word for the men that you work with?

Rr. BUTTIES, CHUMS, (WORK-)MATES, PALS

Note—For additional exs. of BUTTIES, (-)MATES and PALS, see VIII.2.7 and VIII.4.1. MATE also occurs at VIII.2.7, and CHUMS at VIII.4.2.

7 Ch 1 wə:kmẹ:ts 2 me:ts 3 mẹ:ts 4 △mẹ·t 5 me:ts 6 me:ᵊts

8 Db 1 me:ts, ○△me:t¹ 2–3 me:ts 4 mi:ts 5 △me:ˈt 6 me:ˈts 7 me·ɪts

11 Sa 1 me:ts 2 mẹ:ts 3 me:ts 4 me:əts, ○~² 5 bɷtɪz, mẹ:ts ["modern"] 6–11 me:ts

12 St 1 palz 2–4 mɛɪts 5 me:ts 6–7 mɛɪts 8 △wəɹ:kmɛɪt 9 palz 10 mɛɪts, palz 11 mɛɪts

15 He 1 me:ts 2–3 me:ɪts 4 me:ts 5 me:ɪts 6 me:ts 7 meɪts, △meɪt, wəɹkmeɪts

16 Wo 1 mɛɪts 2 me:ᵊts 3 bɷtɪz 4–5 me:ts 6 me:ɪts 7 tʃɷmz

17 Wa 1 mɛɪts, ○△mẹɪt¹ 2 bɷtɪz 3 mẹɪts, ○△mɛɪt² 4 mɛ·əts 5 mɛɪts 6 △mɛɪt 7 wəʳ:kmɛɪts

23 Mon 1 ᐃme:ˈt 2 bɷtɩz 3 me:ts 4 wœ:kmẹ:ts, bʌ̹̈tʰɩ̹z [colliers' word] 5 bʌ̹̈tʰi:z 6 bʌtɩz 7 n.a.

24 Gl 1 me:ᵊts 2 me:ɩts 3 bʌtɩz 4 bɷtɩz 5 wəʳ:kme:ts 6–7 me:ts

25 O 1 mẹ:ᵊts 2 mɛɩts 3 me:ts 4 mẹɩts 5 mɛᵊts 6 meɩts

VIII.4.2 COMPANIONS

Q. And, when you were a young man, what did you call those you went about with when you weren't at work?

Rr. BUTTIES, CHUMS, FRIENDS, (PLAY-)MATES, (OLD) PALS

Note—Some of the above expressions also occur at VIII.2.7 and VIII.4.1.

7 Ch 1 palz 2 ɛ̈ɷd päłz 3–6 palz

8 Db 1 palz, ○ᐃpal[1] 2–7 palz

11 Sa 1–6 palz 7 pælz 8 palz 9 pælz 10 palz 11 palz, bɷtɩz

12 St 1 palz 2 pli:mɛɩts 3–6 palz 7 fɹɛnz 8 mɛɩts 9 mɛɩts, ○ᐃmɛɩt[3] 10 palz 11 plɛɩmɛɩts

15 He 1–2 pæłz 3 pɒłz 4 pæ̣łz 5–6 bɷtɩz 7 palz

16 Wo 1 palz 2 pałz 3 pæłz, ○~[4] 4 pˈælz 5–6 pæłz 7 meɩts

17 Wa 1 pałz 2 palz 3 pałz, ○~[3] 4–7 pałz

23 Mon 1 bʌtɩz 2 pæłz, ○ᐃpæł[3] 3 bɷtɩz, ○ᐃbʌtɩ[1] 4 pʰalz 5 palz 6 pæłz 7 n.a.

24 Gl 1 bɷtɩz, ○ᐃbɷtɩ 2 pæłz 3 me:ˈts 4 pałz 5–6 palz 7 me:ts, tʃəmz

25 O 1 palz 2 pałz 3 pæᵊłz 4 bɷtɩz 5 ᐃpæł 6 tʃɷmz ["older"], ᐃpæᵊł

VIII.4.3 CARPENTER, JOINER

Q. What do you call the man who makes things out of wood?

Does he distinguish between the two?

Rr. (ROUGH) CARPENTER, CHIPPY, JOINER

Note—In the rr. below, an attached superior + denotes 'does more highly skilled work', and superior ɑ 'does heavier, less skilled work'. Superior ★ attached to the first r. denotes 'no difference in meaning between the two rr.' The f.w., however, often omitted to ascertain the distinction, if any. The rr. are, as usual, reproduced in the same order as given by the f.w.

7 Ch 1 dʒɒɪnə, ka:pɪntə [rare] 2 dʒɑɪnə, +kja:pɪntə ["makes furniture"], °dʒæɪnə2(x) 3 ★dʒɛɪnə, s.w. ka:pɪntə [but not used] 4 ᵒdʒɑɪnə, +ka:pɪntə 5 ᵒdʒɛɪnə [a "carpenter makes furniture"] 6 +dʒaɪnə, ᵒka:pɪntə

8 Db 1 ★dʒɛɪnə: 2 dʒɒɪnə, +ka:pɪntə 3 dʒaɪnə 4 dʒɑɪnə 5 dʒɔɪnə 6–7 dʒɑ̃·ĩnə

11 Sa 1 ᵒka:pəntəʳ, +dʒɒɪnəʳ 2 ★dʒaɪnəʳ, ka:pɪntəʳ 3 ★kaʳ:pəntəʳ, dʒɒɪnəʳ 4 ★kaʳ:pəntə, dʒɒɪnəʳ 5 kaʳ:pɪntəʳ, ᵒdʒaɪnəʳ 6 +dʒɒɪnəʳ, ᵒkaʳ:pəntəʳ 7 kaʳ:pəntəʳ, ᵒdʒɒɪnəʳ 8 ★kaʳ:pəntəʳ, dʒɒɪnəʳ 9 ᵒkaʳ:pəntəʳ, +dʒɒɪnəʳ 10 ★kəʳ:pəntəʳ, dʒɒɪnəʳ 11 ᵒka:pəntəʳ, +dʒɒɪnəʳ

12 St 1 dʒa:ɪnə, ka:pɪntə, °□dʒa:ɪnəz 2 ★dʒɛɪnə ["carpenter" polite term] 3 ★ka:pɪntə, dʒɒɪnə 4 ᵒdʒɔ:ɪnə, +ka:pɪntə 5 dʒɒ̂ɪnə, ka:pɪntə 6 +ka:pɪntə, ᵒdʒɒɪnə, °dʒaɪnə, °tʃɪpɪ [i.e. carpenter, joiner or wheel-wright] 7 ka:pɪntə(2x) 8 +kɑ:pɪntə, ᵒdʒɒɪnə [an assistant] 9 ★ka:pɪntə, dʒa̠ɪnə 10 ka:pɪntə, dʒɔɪnə [also "makes wheels"] 11 ★kɑ̂:pɪntə, dʒɔ̂ɪnə

15 He 1 ★kʲa:pɪntəʳ, dʒɒɪnəʳ 2 ★ka:pɪntəʳ, dʒæɪnəʳ 3 ★kʲɑʳ:pəntəʳ, dʒɔɪnəʳ 4 ★kjɑ̣ʳ:pɪntəʳ, dʒæɪnəʳ 5 ᵒkjaʳ:pɪntəʳ, +dʒɒɪnəʳ 6 ★kjaʳ:pəntəʳ, dʒæɪnəʳ 7 kaɹpntəɹ, s.w. dʒɔɪnəɹ

16 Wo 1 kɑ:pəntə, +dʒɒɪnə 2 ★kɑʳ:pəntəʳ, dʒɔɪnəʳ 3 ★kəʳ:pəntəʳ, dʒɒɪnəʳ 4 ★kʲəʳ:pɪntəʳ, dʒɒɪnəʳ ["makes coffins" also] 5 ★kʲaʳ:pɪntəʳ, dʒaɪnəʳ 6 ★dʒɒɪnəʳ, kʲɑʳ:pəntəʳ 7 kɑʳpəntəʳ, s.w. dʒɔɪnəʳ

17 Wa 1–2 ka:pɪntə 3 ★ka:pɪntə 4 ᵒka:pɪntə, ɹʊf ka:pntəʳ·, +dʒɒɪnə 5 +käʳ:pɪntəʳ ["joiner would work in a factory"] 6 ka:pɪntəʳ ["joiner was undertaker"] 7 ᵒkaʳ:pɪntəʳ, +dʒɒɪnəʳ

23 Mon 1 +kjaʳ:pəntəʳ, ᵒdʒæɪnəʳ 2 +ka:pəntəʳ, ᵒdʒɒɪnəʳ [assisted in building houses] 3 ★ka:pəntə, dʒɒɪnə 4 n.a. 5 ka:pɪntə [he cuts it (ref. wood) out] dʒəinə [he puts it together] 6 kaʳ:pəntəʳ, +dʒɒɪnəʳ 7 n.a.

24 Gl 1 +kjaʳ:pəntəʳ, ᵒdʒæɪnəʳ 2 ★kjaʳ:pəntəʳ, dʒæɪnəʳ 3 ★kaʳ:pəntəʳ, dʒɒɪnəʳ 4 ★kaʳ:pntəʳ, dʒaɪnəʳ 5 kjəʳ:pntəʳ ["joiner would make furniture"] 6 kjaʳ:pntəʳ, ᵒdʒɒɪnəʳ 7 ★kjaʳ:pɪntəʳ

25 O 1 kjaʳ:pntəʳ [joiner is a wheel-wright] 2 kaʳpɪntə ["makes wagons"], ᵒdʒoɪnə ["makes doors, window-frames, tables"] 3 kaʳ:pntəʳ 4 ᵒkɑɽpntəɽ, dʒɔɪnəɽ 5 kaʳ:ɽpntəʳ 6 kaʳ:pntəʳ, +dʒoɪnəʳ

VIII.4.4 WRIGHT

Q. What do you mean by **wright?**

Rr. CART/MILL/WAIN/WHEEL-WRIGHT

Note 1—When the f.w. recs. the i.'s pron. of WRIGHT, this is reproduced after the full stop.

Note 2—In the rr. below, a superior ◇ attached to the r., or to the first r. when more than one, denotes that WRIGHT was not used independently.

Note 3—For WHEEL, see I.9.5 (and refs.).

7 Ch 1 ◇wẹ:lɹɑɩt 2 ◇wi:lɹạɩt, s.w. kja:tɹạɩt 3 wɛɩlɹɛɩt, wɩlɹɛɩt 4 ◇wi:lɹɑɩt 5 ◇wi:lɹi:t, wi:lɹɛɩt 6 ◇wi:lɹaɩt

8 Db 1 ◇wɩlɹi:t 2 wïlɹɑɩt 3 ◇we:nɹɛɩt 4 ◇wɛɩlɹɛɩt 5 wi:lɹɑɩt. ɹɑɩt 6 ◇wɛɩlɹɛɩt 7 wɛɩlɹɛɩt, mɩlɹɛɩt, ○wɛɩlɹɛɩt[2]

11 Sa 1 wi:lɹɪt 2–3 wɩlɹɪt 4 wɩlɹaɩt 5 wɩlɹɪt 6 ◇wɩlɹət 7–11 wɩlɹɪt

12 St 1 n.a. 2 wɛɩlɹɛɩt. ɹɛɩt 3 n.r. ɹɒ:ɩt 4 wi:lɹɒɩt 5 wi:lɹɒ:ɩt 6 wɛɩlɹɒ:ɩt 7 wɩlɹɒɩt 8 n.r. [but he is the «man əz mɛɩks kɑ:twɩ:lz» *man as* (=*who*) *makes cart-wheels*] 9 wi:lɹɒɩt 10 n.r. [but he is «ə man əz mɛɩks wi:lz» *a man as* (=*who*) *makes* (cart-)*wheels*] 11 wi:lɹaɩt, mɩlɹaɩt

15 He 1 wi:ɫɹæɩt 2–3 wɩɫɹəɩt 4 n.a. 5–6 wi:ɫɹəɩt 7 wi:lɹaɩt, ○wi:lɹaɩts[4] *poss.*

16 Wo 1 wi:lɹɒɩt 2 wˡi:ɫɹɪt 3 wi:ɫɹɒɩt 4 wi:ɫɹəɩt 5 wi:ᵊɫɹəɩt 6 wɩɫɹɒɩt 7 □wi:lɹəɩts, ○□∼[1]

17 Wa 1 s.w. ◇wi:ᵊɫɹɑɩt 2 ◇wi:lɹəɩt 3–6 ◇wi:lɹəɩt 7 wɩᵊɫɹəɩt, mɩɫɹəɩt

23 Mon 1 wˡi:ɫɹəɩt 2–3 wi:ɫɹəɩt 4 ◇wị:ḷɹəitʰ 5 ◇wi:ɫ̥ɹəit 6 wi:ɫɹəɩt 7 n.a.

24 Gl 1 wi:ɫɹəɩt 2 wɩi:ɫɹəɩt 3 wɩɫɹəɩt 4 wˡi:ɫɹəɩt 5 ◇wi:ᵊɫɹə̈ɩt 6 ◇wi:ɫɹʌɩt 7 ◇wi:ᵊɫɹʌɩt

25 O 1 ◇wɩlɹə̈ɩt 2 ◇wɩɫɽə̈ɩt 3 ◇wɩɫɹʌʏt'. ɹʌʏt [but not used] 4 ◇wɩəɫɽə̣ɩt 5 ◇wɩᵊɫɽʌʏt 6 ◇wɩᵊɫɹə̈ɩʔ. ɹə̈ɩʔ

VIII.4.5 COBBLER

Q. What do you call the man who mends boots and shoes?

Rr. COB, COBBLER, NOBBY, SHOE-MAKER, (SHOE-)SNOB, SNOBBER, SNOBBLER

7 Ch 1 kɒbləˑɹ 2 kəbɫə, °kəbləz² *poss.* 3–5 kɒblə 6 kɒbləˑɹ̱

8 Db 1 kɒbləˑɹ̱ 2–7 kɒblə

11 Sa 1–4 kɒbləʴ 5 nɒbɩ 6 kɒbləʴ, °ʃu:mɩkəʴ:z̨⁴ *poss.* 7–11 kɒbləʴ

12 St 1–2 kɒblə 3 kɒblə, snɒb, °kɒblə¹ 4 kɒblə 5 kɒblə, snɒb, °□kɒbləz² 6 kɒblə, snɒb ["older"], °~ 7–8 kɒblə 9 kɒblə, °~², °snɒb² 10 kɒblə 11 kɒblə, °□snɒbz ["old"]

15 He 1 snɒbəʴ 2 snɔ:b ["usu."], °kɒbləʴ 3–4 snɑ:b 5 kɒbləʴ 6 snɒb 7 kɒbləɹ, snɒb

16 Wo 1 kɒbləʴ, snɒb [occ.] 2 snɑ·b, °snɑ:b² 3 kɒbləʴ, snɒb ["usu."] 4 snɑ:b 5–6 kɒbləʴ, snɑ:b [usu.] 7 snɒb ["older"], kɒblə [snɒb¹ *s.* (=*cobble*) *inf.*]

17 Wa 1 snɒb, kɒblə 2 kəbɫə 3 kɒblə, snɒb, kɒb 4 snɒb [¶snɒbɩn¹ *snobbing*] 5 kɒbləʴ, s.w. snɒb ["rare"] 6 kɒbləʴ, snɒb ["old"] 7 snɒb

23 Mon 1–2 snɒb 3 snɑ:b 4 n.a. 5 ʃu:me:kə ["makes shoes"], kɒ̝·bɫə [mends shoes] 6 snɑ:b 7 n.a.

24 Gl 1–2 snɑ:b 3 snɒbɫəʴ 4 snɑ:b 5 kɒbləʴ 6 kɒbləʴ, ʃu:snɒb 7 ʃu:snɒb, snɒb

25 O 1–3 kɒbləʴ 4 snɒb 5 snɒb, °ʃu:snɒb³ 6 kɒbləʴ

VIII.4.6 BUTCHER

Q. What do you call the man who sells meat?

R. BUTCHER

7 Ch 1 bʊtʃəˑɹ 2–5 bʊtʃə 6 bʊtʃəˑɹ̱

8 Db 1 bʊtʃəˑɹ̱ 2–7 bʊtʃə

11 Sa 1 bʌtʃəʴ 2 bʊtʃəʴ 3–4 bʌtʃəʴ 5 bʊtʃəʴ 6–7 bʌtʃəʴ 8–11 bʊtʃəʴ

12 St 1–2 bʊtʃə 3 □bʊtʃəz 4–7 bʊtʃə 8 bʊtʃəˑɹ 9–11 bʊtʃə

15 He 1 bʌtʃəʴ 2–6 bʊtʃəʴ 7 bʊtʃəɹ

16 Wo 1–7 bʊtʃəʴ

17 Wa 1–3 bʊtʃə 4–7 bʊtʃəʴ

23 Mon 1–2 bʊtʃəʴ 3–5 bʊtʃə 6 bʊtʃəʴ 7 n.a.

24 Gl 1 bʊtʃəʴ 2 bʊʃəʴ [*sic*] 3–7 bʊtʃəʴ

25 O 1–3 bʊtʃəʴ 4 bʊtʃəɽ 5 bʊtʃɽ 6 bʊtʃəʴ

VIII.4.7 FARMER*

Q. What do you call the man who works the land?

R. FARMER

Note—FARM(-) occurs at I.1.2 (and refs.).

7 Ch 1 fa:mə[ɹ] 2 fa:mə 3 fa:mə, ○□fa:məz[2] 4–5 fa:mə 6 fa[ɹ]:mə[ɹ]

8 Db 1 fa[ɹ]:mə[ɹ] 2–7 fa:mə

11 Sa 1 fa[ɽ]:mə[ɽ] 2 fa:mə[ɽ] 3–5 fa[ɽ]:mə[ɽ] 6 fa[ɽ]:mə[ɽ·] 7 fa[ɽ]:mə[ɽ] 8 fa[ɽ]:mə[ɽ], ○~[2] 9 fa[ɽ]:mə[ɽ], ○□fa[ɽ]:mə[ɽ]ʐ[1] 10–11 fa[ɽ]:mə[ɽ]

12 St 1–7 fa:mə 8 fɑ:mə[ɹ] 9–10 fa:mə 11 få̂məɹ

15 He 1–2 fa[ɽ]:mə[ɽ] 3 fɑ[ɽ]:mə[ɽ] 4–5 fa[ɽ]:mə[ɽ] 6 va[ɽ]:mə[ɽ] 7 faɹməɹ, ○□faɹməɹz[3], ○□fɑɹməɹz[1] [faɹməɹz glo:ɹɪ[1] *f.'s glory* I.7.3]

16 Wo 1 fɑ:mə 2–3 fa[ɽ]:mə[ɽ] 4 fɑ[ɽ]:mə[ɽ] 5 fa[ɽ]:mə[ɽ] 6 fə[ɽ]:mə[ɽ] 7 fɑ[ɽ]mə[ɽ], ○~[4] [¶fɑ[ɽ]mɪn *farming*]

17 Wa 1 fä:mə 2 □fa:məz, ○□~[1], ○~[1] *poss.*, ○fa:mə[1] 3 fa:mə 4 fa:mə[ɽ] 5–7 fa[ɽ]:mə[ɽ]

23 Mon 1 fa[ɽ]:mə[ɽ] 2 fa:mə[ɽ] 3–5 fa:mə 6 fa[ɽ]:mə[ɽ] 7 n.a.

24 Gl 1 va[ɽ]:mə[ɽ] 2 fa[ɽ]:mə[ɽ] 3–4 va[ɽ]:mə[ɽ] 5 fa[ɽ]:mə[ɽ] 6 va[ɽ]:mə[ɽ] 7 va[ɽ]:mə[ɽ], ○~[1]

25 O 1–2 fa[ɽ]:mə[ɽ] 3 fa[ɽ]ɽmə, ○□fa[ɽ]məz[1] 4 fa·ɽməɽ, ○faɽməɽ[1(2x)], ○faɽməɽʐ[2] *poss.* 5 fa:ɽmə[ɽ] 6 fa[ɽ]:mə[ɽ]

VIII.4.8 WORK*. WORKING*

Q. All those people (viz. tradesmen) *are busy on weekdays, but on Sunday they usually rest and don't do any . . . .*

Nowadays, some men retire at 65, but other men, who have been busy all their lives, still go on . . . .

Rr. WORK

WORKING

Note 1—The rr. to the two parts of the q. are separated below by a full stop.

Note 2—A superior ◇ attached to an i.m. form below marks an inf.,; superior ×, a 3 pr.s.; superior ᴅ, a p.t. sg. or pl.; superior ɑ, a p.p.; and superior ‼, a form which is n.d.g.

Note 3—Since the q. was asked for phonological purposes, i.m. exs. of the v. used transitively have not been specially distinguished below.

Note 4—WORK *v.* occurs at IV.8.6 and VIII.1.26; and WORK(ING)- at I.2.4, VI.14. 20, VII.4.6 and VIII.4.1.

7 Ch 1 wəˑ:k. wəˑ:kɪn 2 wə:k, s.f. wa:k ["rare"]. wə:kɪn, °wəˑkɪn¹, °◇wə:k², °~² *v.*, °×wə:ks¹ 3 wəˑ:k. wəˑ:kɪn, °~³ 4 wə:k. wə:kɪn 5 wəˑ:k⁽²ˣ⁾, °‖wa:k¹ [wə:kaɪs¹ *w.-house*]. wa:kɪn⁽²ˣ⁾, °¶wakən 6 wəˑ:k. wəˑ:kɪn

8 Db 1 wəˑk, °waˑ:k². wəˑkkɪn, °~² 2 wə:k. wə:kɪn, °ᴰwə:kt⁴ 3 wə:k. wə:kɪn 4 wə:k. wə:kkɪn 5 wɛ:k, °wək². wɛ:ᵊkɪn 6 wək. wəkɪn 7 wə:k. wə:kɪn

11 Sa 1–6 wəʳ:k. wəʳ:kɪn 7 wəʳ:k. wəʳ:kɪn, °ᴰwəʳ:kt¹ 8–9 wəʳk. wəʳ:kɪn 10 wəʳ:k [pætʃwəʳ:k kwɪlts³ *patch-w. quilts*]. wəʳ:kɪn 11 wəʳ:k. wəʳ:kɪn, °¶~², °ᴰwəʳ:kt²

12 St 1 wə:k. wə:kɪn, °◇wə:k²⁽²ˣ⁾ 2 wə:k. wə:kɪn, °¶~⁵ 3 wə:k, °~¹⁽²ˣ⁾. wə:kɪn, °◇~¹⁽²ˣ⁾·² 4 wə:k. wə:kɪn, °◇wə:k³ 5 wə:k. wə:kɪn, °¶~² 6 wə:k, °~¹. wə:kɪn, °×wə:ks 7 wə:k, °~³. wə:kɪn 8 wəˑ:k. wəˑ:kɪn, °◇wə:k² 9 wə:k. wə:kɪn, °×wə:ks¹ 10 wə:k. wə:kɪn 11 wə:ɹk. wə:ɹkɪn, °ᵈwə:kd̥²

15 He 1 wəʳ:k. wəʳ:kɪn, °¶~¹ 2 wəʳ:k. wəʳ:kɪn, °wəʳ:k² *1 pr.s.* 3 wəʳ:k. wəʳ:kɪn, °~¹ *pr.p. adj.* 4 wəʳ:k. wəʳ:kɪn, °¶əwəʳ:kɪn²⁽²ˣ⁾ 5 wəʳ:k. wəʳ:kɪn 6 wəʳ:k. wəʳ:kɪn, °¶~¹, °◇wəʳ:k¹⁽²ˣ⁾ 7 wəɹk, °~¹·³⁽²ˣ⁾·⁴ [wəkmən³ *w.-man*]. wəɹkɪn, °~², °◇wəɹk¹, °ᴰwəɹkt³, °ᵈ~¹

16 Wo 1 wəʳ:k. wəʳ:kɪn 2 wəʳ:k. wəʳ:kɪn, °ᴰwəʳkt¹ 3 wəʳ:k. wəʳ:kɪn, °wəʳ:ks¹ *3 pr.pl.* 4 wəʳ:k. wəʳ:kɪn, °¶əwəʳ:kɪn³, °‖wəʳ:k¹ 5 wəʳ:k. əwəʳ:kɪn, °ᵈwəʳ:kt¹ 6 wəʳ:k, °~²·³. wəʳ:kɪn 7 wəʳk, °~¹⁽²ˣ⁾·³. wəʳkɪn, °¶əwə:kɪn⁴, °◇wə:k⁴, °◇wəʳk¹

17 Wa 1 wə:kʻ. wə:kɪn 2 wə:k, °~²·³. wə:kɪn⁽²ˣ⁾, °ᴰwə:kt¹ 3 wə:k. wə:kɪn 4 wəʳ:k. wəʳ:kɪn 5 wə:k. wəʳ:kɪn, °◇wə:k¹ [=*knead*] 6–7 wəʳ:k. wəʳ:kɪn

23 Mon 1 wəʳ:k [pætʃwəʳ:ks³ *patch-ws.*] 2 wə:k. wə:kɪn 3 wœ:k. wœ:kɪn 4 wœ:kʰ [sti:lwœ:ks¹ *steel-ws.*]. wœ:kʰɪn, °×wœ:ks 5 wœ̞̈:k, °wœ:k². wœ̞̈:kɪn, °~¹ 6 wəʳ:k. wəʳ:kɪn, °¶~¹ 7 n.a., °‖wœ:k¹

24 Gl 1 wəʳ:k, °~². əwəʳ:kɪn 2 wəʳ:k. əwəʳ:kɪn 3 wəʳ:k. əwəʳ:kɪn, °wəʳ:k¹ *v.* 4 wəʳ:k. əwəʳ:kɪn, °‖wœ:k³ 5–7 wəʳ:k. wəʳ:kɪn

25 O 1 wəʳ:kʻ. wəʳ:kɩn, ○‖wəʳ:k² 2 wəʳ:k. wəʳ:kɩn 3 wəʳ:k. wəʳ:kɩn, ○ᵈwəʳ·kt² 4 wəɽk, ○~1(2x),4 [wəɽkmən⁵ *w.-man*; aɷswəɽk³ *house-w.* V.1.1 b; o:vəɽwəɽk⁴ *over-w.*]. wəɽkɩn, ○‖~4 5 wəʳ:k, ○~1,2(2x). wəʳ:kɩn 6 wəʳ:k, ○~3. wəʳ:kɩn, ○¶~1, ○wəʳ:k³ *pr.t.*, ○‖~2, ○ᴰwəʳ:kt³

VIII.4.9 TINKER

Q. What do you call the man who mends, or used to mend, pots and pans?

Rr. TINKER, TINKLER, TINSMITH

7 Ch 1 tɩŋkəɹ 2 tɩ̞ŋkə 3–5 tɩŋkə 6 tɩnsmɩ̞θ, tɩŋkəɹ̱ ["older"]

8 Db 1 tɩŋkləɹ̱ 2 tɩŋkə 3 tɩnklə 4–7 tɩŋkə

11 Sa 1–11 tɩŋkəʳ

12 St 1 tɩŋkə 2 tɩnsmɩθ 3–7 tɩŋkə 8 tɩŋkəɹ 9–10 tɩŋkə 11 tɩŋkəɹ

15 He 1–6 tɩŋkəʳ 7 tɩŋkəɹ

16 Wo 1 tɩŋkə 2–3 tɩŋkəʳ 4 □tɩŋkəʳ:z̧ 5–6 tɩŋkəʳ 7 tɩŋkəʳ

17 Wa 1 tɩŋkə 2 tɩŋkə [tɩŋkəz lɛ̧ɩn *T.'s Lane* (pl.n.)] 3 tɩŋkə 4 tɩŋkəʳ 5 tɩŋkləʳ 6 tɩŋkə 7 tɩ́ŋkəʳ

23 Mon 1–2 tɩŋkəʳ 3 tɩŋkə 4 n.a. 5 tɩŋk·kʰə, ○~2 6 tɩŋkəʳ 7 n.a.

24 Gl 1–7 tɩŋkəʳ

25 O 1–3 tɩŋkəʳ 4 tɩŋkəɽ 5 tɩŋkɽ 6 tɩŋkəʳ

VIII.4.10 ANVIL

Q. By the way, we haven't mentioned the blacksmith, but what does he hammer things on?

R. ANVIL

7 Ch 1 anvəl 2 änvɩl 3 anvɩl 4 anvəɫ 5 anvɩl 6 anvəɫ

8 Db 1–7 anvɩl

11 Sa 1 anvəl 2–3 anvɩl 4 a·nvɩl 5 ɒnvɩl 6 anvə̣l 7 ænvɩl 8 ɒnvɩl 9 ɒnvəl 10–11 ɒnvɩl

12 St 1–8 anvɩl 9 anvəl 10–11 anvɩl

15 He 1 ænvɩɫ, ɒnvɩɫ ["older"] 2–5 ænvɩɫ 6 ænbɩɫ [*sic*] 7 ạnvɩl

16 Wo 1 anvɩɫ 2 ɒnvəɫ 3–4 ænvɩɫ 5 ɒnvɩɫ 6 ænvɩɫ 7 anvɩl

17 Wa 1–2 anvɩl 3 anvɩɫ 4 anvɫ 5 anvɩɫ 6 anvəɫ 7 anvɩɫ

23 Mon 1 ænvɩɫ 2 ænvəɫ 3 ænvɩɫ 4 anvɩl 5 ʔanvɩl 6 ænvɩɫ 7 n.a.

24 Gl 1 ænvɩɫ 2–3 ɒnvɩɫ 4 anvɩɫ 5 anvəɫ 6–7 anvɩɫ

25 O 1 anvəɫ 2 anvɩᵊɫ 3 anvɩᵊɫ, °anvɩɫ[1] 4 anvɩɫ 5 anvəɫ 6 anvɫ

VIII.4.11 BUSY

Q. The blacksmith might tell a man who dropped in to see him: I can't stop my work to talk to you now: I'm far too . . . .

Rr. BUSY, THRONG

7 Ch 1–6 bɩzɩ 7 bɩ̣zɩ

8 Db 1 bɩzɩ 2 bɩzɩ, °~[4(2x)] 3–4 bɩzɩ 5 θɹɒŋg 6 bɩzɩ 7 bɩzɩ

11 Sa 1–6 bɩzɩ 7 bɩzɩ, °~[1] 8–11 bɩzɩ

12 St 1 bɩzɩ 2–3 bɩ̣zɩ 4–6 bɩzɩ 7 bɩ̣zɩ 8–10 bɩzɩ 11 bɩzɩ, °~[2]

15 He 1–2 bɩzɩ 3 bɩzi:, °~[2] 4 bɩzi: 5–7 bɩzɩ

16 Wo 1–2 bɩzɩ 3 bɩzi: 4 bɩzɩ, °~[1] 5–6 bɩzɩ 7 bɩzɩ, °~[1(2x),4]

17 Wa 1 bɩzᵉɩ 2 bɩzɩ 3 bɩzᵊɩ 4–5 bɩzɩ 6 bɩzᵊɩ 7 bɩzɩ

23 Mon 1–3 bɩzɩ 4–5 bɩzi 6 bɩzɩ 7 n.a.

24 Gl 1–7 bɩzɩ

25 O 1 bɩzɩ, °~[2] 2–4 bɩzɩ 5 bɩzɩ [bɩzɩbɒdɩ[3] *b.-body*] 6 bɩzɩ

VIII.4.12 GIPSIES

Q. What do you call those dark-skinned people who move about the country in caravans?

Rr. DICKIES, DIDDIES, DIDDIKIES, GIPPOES, GIPPOTS, GIPS, GIPSIES, LONG COMPANIES, ROMANIES, TURNPIKE(-ROAD)-SAILORS

7 Ch 1 dʒɩpsɩz [dʒɩpsɩ fɩnɩ *G. Finny* (nickname)] 2 dʒɩ̣psɩz 3 dʒɩpü:z 4–6 dʒɩpsɩz

8 Db 1 n.a. 2–7 dʒɪpsɪz

11 Sa 1 dʒɪpsɪz 2 dʒɪpo:z 3–4 dʒɪpsɪz 5 dʒɪpo:z 6 dʒɪpsɪz, lɷŋ kəmpənɪz 7 dʒɪpsɪz, dʒɪpo:z ["older"] 8 dʒɪpo:z 9 dʒɪpsɪz, ˈdɪkɒɪz 10 dʒɪpsɪz, dʒɪpo:z 11 dʒɪpo:z

12 St 1–5 dʒɪpsɪz 6 dʒɪpsɪz, dʒɪpoɷz ["older"], ○∼[1] 7 dʒɪpoɷz 8 dʒɪpsɪz 9 dʒɪpoɷz 10 dʒɪpsɪz 11 dʒɪpsɪz [usu.], dɛdɪkəɪəz

15 He 1–3 dʒɪpo:z 4 dʒɪpo:z, dɪdɪkəɪz 5 dʒɪpo:z 6 dʒɪpɷts 7 dʒɪpo:ᶸz, dɪdɪkəɪz [fr. i.'s daughter], ○∼[4]

16 Wo 1 dʒɪpɒɷz 2–3 dʒɪpoɷz 4 dʒɪpo:z, tˈəʳ:ɳpəɪksaɪɬəʳʐ 5 dʒɪpo:z, tˈəʳ:ɳpɪkɹo:dsaɪɬəʳʐ 6 tʃɪps 7 p. dʒɪpsɪz, ɹoɷmənɪz

17 Wa 1–3 dʒɪpsɪz 4 dʒɪpoɷz 5 dʒɪpǫɷz 6 dʒɪpǫɷz, dɪdɪkəɪz ["older"], ○dʒɪpsɪz 7 dɪdɪkəɪz, dʒɪpoɷz

23 Mon 1 dɪdɪkjæɪz 2 dʒɪps, dɪdɪkæɪz 3 dɪdɪkəɪz, dʒɪpo:z 4 n.a. 5 dɪdikeiz 6 dɪdɪkəɪz, ○△dɪdɪkəɪ[1] 7 n.a.

24 Gl 1 dɪdɪkəɪᵊz 2 dɪdɪkæɪz 3 dɪdɪkəɪz 4 dɪdɪkɒɪz 5 dʒɪpsɪz, ○∼[2] 6 dʒɪpo:z, dʒɪpsɪz, ○∼[1] 7 dɪdɪkʌɪz

25 O 1 dʒɪpoᶸz 2 dʒɪpəɷz, ○dʒɪpsɪz[1] 3 dʒɪpǫɷz, ○dʒɪpsɪz[1] 4 dɪdɪkəɪz, dɪdɪz [pref.] 5 △dɪdɪkʌʏ ["old"] 6 dɪdɪkö̈ɪz

VIII.5.1 THEY GO† TO CHURCH*‡

Q. What do good people do on Sunday?

Insist on a complete sentence.

Rr. §SOME GO TO §CHAPEL/CHURCH, THEY CHURCH, THEY GO (TO) CHURCH

Note 1—In the list of rr. above, GO subsumes DO GO, GOES and GON.

Note 2—I.m. exs. of THEY GO and CHURCH are reproduced below between square brackets untransliterated. I.m. exs. of THEY foll. by any other full v. in the pr. t. with –N/–S endings are also included below between square brackets transliterated in their normal spelling. I.m. exs. of THEY foll. by uninflected 3 pr.pl. have not been included here. The cross refs. usu. ref. only to the v.

Note 3—For other parts of GO *v.*, see VIII.6.1 (and refs.). For THEY foll. by vv. in the pr.t., see VI.2.2, VII.5.2, VIII.5.2, VIII.9.5, IX.3.3/4/6/7, IX.5.1/4 and IX.6.1/4. For vv. foll. a n.pl. subj., see III.10.7 and V.7.21. CHURCH– occurs at VIII.5.5.

7 Ch 1 ðι gɷ tʃəɹ:tʃ [ðə gιvn² *t. give* IX.8.2; ðι nọ:n² *t. know*] 2 p. ðε gɷ tʔ tʃə:tʃ [ðε pιkn⁴ *t. pick*; ðε dʒεnəlι sεn⁴ *t. generally say*; ðə stιkn⁴ *t. stick*] 3 ðι gɷn tʃəɹ:tʃ [ðι gɷn³ *t. go*; ðι sεn² *t. say*; ðι ɹɷbn³ *t. rub*] 4 ðι gɷ tə tʃə:tʃ [ðι ɒpnz² *t. open*] 5 ðι gɷn tə tʃə:tʃ [ðι sεn¹, ðə sεn² *t. say*] 6 ðι gɷ tə tʃə:ɹtʃ [ðι kɷtn² *t. cut*; ðι an² *t. have*]

8 Db 1 ðι gʏ: tə tʃəɹtʃ [ðι ki:pn¹ *t. keeps* IV.6.2; ðι tεkn¹ *t. take* VI.12.4; tɷtʃn⁴ (t.) *touch*] 2 ðι gɷ tə tʃə:tʃ 3 ðə gɷ tə tʃə:tʃ [tʃə:tʃ] 4 ðι gᵊu:‿ʔ tʃə:tʃ [ð‿i:tn¹ *t. eat* VI.5.11] 5 ðι gɷ tə tʃətʃ [ðι ka:ts¹ *t. cart*] 6 ðι gɷ‿ʔ tʃə:tʃ [ðι dɹɒpn *t. drop*; ðι ɔ:ləs sεn¹ *t. always say*; ðι sta:tn¹ *t. start*; ðι tεɷz¹ *t. touse* (=*tousle*) VI.2.8] 7 ðι gᵊu:‿ʔ tʃə:tʃ

11 Sa 1 ðι go: tə tʃəʳ:tʃ 2 ðə gɷ tə tʃəʳ:tʃ [ðι kɔ:n¹ *t. call*] 3–4 ðι gɷ tə tʃəʳ:tʃ 5 ðι gɷ tə tʃəʳ:tʃ [tʃəʳ:tʃ³] 6 ðι gɷ tə tʃəʳ:tʃ 7 ðe: go: tə tʃəʳ:tʃ 8 ðι gu: tə tʃəʳ:tʃ 9 ðι go: tə tʃəʳ:tʃ [tʃəʳ:tʃ; ðe: dɹɔʳ:z¹ *t. draw*] 10 ðι go: tə tʃəʳ:tʃ [ðe: skɹεtʃəz³ *t. scratch*] 11 ðι go: tə tʃəʳ:tʃ [ðe: θιŋks² *t. think*]

12 St 1 ðι gɔ: tə tʃə:tʃ 2 ðι gu:n tʃə:tʃ [ðə wɒnts *t. want*] 3 ðι gɷ:n tʃə:tʃ, °ðι gɷn tʃə:tʃ¹ [ðι an¹ *t. have*; ðι sεn¹ *t. say*] 4 ðι goɷ tə tʃə:tʃ 5 ðι goɷ tə tʃə:tʃ 6 ðι gɷ tə tʃə:tʃ [tʃə:tʃ¹; ðι gεn¹ *t. get*] 7 ðει gɷ tə tʃə:tʃ 8 ðει gɷ tə tʃəɹ:tʃ [tʃəɹ:tʃ] 9 ðι gɷ tə tʃə:tʃ 10 ðε tʃə:tʃ [tʃə:tʃ] 11 ðει goɷ tə tʃə:tʃ [tʃə:tʃ]

15 He 1 ðι gɷ tə tʃəʳ:tʃ 2 ðι gɷz tə tʃəʳ:tʃ [ðι du:z² *t. do*] 3 ðæι gɷz təʳ tʃəʳ:tʃ 4 ðι gɷ tə tʃəʳ:tʃ [ðι ævz¹ *t. have*] 5 ðι gɷ tə tʃəʳ:tʃ 6 ðι gɷ dəʳ tʃəʳtʃ 7 ðει goɷ tə tʃəɹtʃ [ðει nɒkəleιts¹ *t. inoculate*; ðει ɹιks¹ *t. rick*; ðει noɷz³ *t. know*; ðe pɷlz ιt ən sεlz ιt³ *t. pull it and sell it*; ðει si:mz³ *t. seem*]

16 Wo 1 ðι gɷ tə tʃəʳ:tʃ 2 ðι gɷ tə tʃəʳ:tʃ [ðι pu:lz *t. pull* VI.2.8] 3 ðι goɷ tə tʃəʳ:tʃ [ðι wəʳ:ks¹ *t. work* VIII.4.8; ðι gεts² *t. get*] 4 ðι gɷ tə tʃəʳ:tʃ [ðι sεz¹ *t. say*; ðaι bəʳ:ŋʐ² *t. burn*; ðaι k'æɹιz ɑʳ:ŋ² *t. carry on*; ðaι dəιz² *t. die* III.7.2; ðaι bιgιnz³ *t. begin* VIII.6.2] 5 ðι gɷ tə tʃ'əʳ:tʃ [ðaι dɹægz¹ *t. drag*; ðι naɷz¹ *t. know*] 6 ðι gɷz tə tʃəʳ:tʃ [ðει fɒιts² *t. fight* III.13.6; ðι sεlz² *t. sell*; ðι ʃιdz *t. shed*; ðe: kɑ:łz³ *t. call*] 7 ðει gɷz tə tʃə:tʃ [ðει bιlz¹ *t. build*; ðει lεts¹ *t. let*; ðει ɹεvəlz¹ *t. revel*; ðει kɔ:lz² *t. call*; ðει u:sιz² *t. use*; ðει wɷndəʳʐ² *t. wonder*; ðει bᵊuθ ku:z⁴ *t. both coo*; ðει ɹεkənz⁴ *t. reckon*; ðει sιts əbæɷt⁴ *t. sit about*]

17 Wa 1 ðι gọɷ tə tʃə̣:tʃ [tʃə:tʃ¹] 2 ðε gɷ: tə tʃə:tʃ [ðe: gεts² *t. get*; ðει az² *t. has*; ðει li:vz² *t. leave*] 3 ðẹι gɷ tə tʃə:tʃ 4 ðẹι gɷ tə tʃəʳ:tʃ 5 ðει gu: tə tʃəʳ:tʃ 6 ðει gɷ tə tʃəʳ:tʃ [tʃə:tʃ⁴] 7 ðει gɷ tə tʃəʳ:tʃ [ðει mjaɷz¹ *t. mew* III.10.6]

23 Mon 1 ðι gɷ tə tʃəʴ:tʃ 2 ðι gɷ tə tʃə:tʃ 3 ðι gɷ tə tʃœ:tʃ [ðe: fιts[1] *t. fit*] 4 ðei də go: tö̞ tʃœ:tʃ [ðei gεts[3] *t. get*] 5 §sʌ̈m də gọ: tə §tʃapɫ, §sʌ̈m də gọ: tə tʃœ̞̈:tʃ [tʃœ̞̈:tʃ[2(2x)], tʃʌ̈tʃ[2]; tʃœ̞̈:tʃwɔ:dn[2] *c.-warden* VIII.5.4; ðe· gọ:z ɒ̞·n[2] *t. go on*] 6 ðι gɷ tə tʃəʴ:tʃ 7 n.a.

24 Gl 1 ðæι gɷz tə tʃəʴ:tʃ [tʃəʴ:tʃ[1]; ðæ du:z[1(2x)] *t. do*] 2–3 ðæι gɷ tə tʃəʴ:tʃ 4 ðaι gɷ tə tʃəʴ:tʃ 5 ðι go:z tə tʃəʴ:tʃ 6–7 ðι go: tə tʃəʴ:tʃ

25 O 1 ðə goɷz tə tʃəʴ:tʃ [ðeι bö̈ιts *t. bite*; ðə kɔ:lz[2] *t. call*] 2 ðει gɷ tə tʃəʴ:tʃ [ðει dιps[2] *t. dip*; ðει dɹö̈ιz[2] *t. dry*] 3 ðe: gọɷ tə tʃəʴtʃ [ðe: bɹιŋz[2] *t. bring* VIII.1.11; ðe kɔ:lz[1] *t. call*; ðe: dɹɒps[1] *t. drop*; ðe: ʃu:ts[1] *t. shoot*] 4 ðeι goɷ tə tʃəɽtʃ [tʃəɽtʃ[5]; go:ᵒ (*inf.*) tə tʃə·ɽtʃ; ðe: wɒnts[1] *t. want*] 5 ðə gəɷ tə tʃəʴ:tʃ 6 ðə goɷ tə tʃəʴ:tʃ [ðeι ɹu:stιs[1] *t. roost*; ðeι dιkeιz[3] *t. decay*]

VIII.5.2 STAY AT HOME*

Q. But some lazy people like to read the Sunday papers, and so they ....

Rr. BIDE/STOP AT HOME, STAY (AT) HOME

Note 1—Periphrastic DO and verbal forms in –S/N are excluded from the list of rr. above.

Note 2—I.m. exs. of (AT) HOME are reproduced below between square brackets untransliterated.

Note 3—For exs. of HOME–, see I.1.2.

7 Ch 1 stɒp ə wɒm [wɒm[2,4]] 2 stɒp ə wäm 3 stɒpn ə wɒm [wɒm[2,3]] 4 stɒp ə wɒm [wɒm[1,2]] 5 stɒp ə wɒm [wɷm[1]] 6 stɒp ə wɒm, stɒp ə wɷm [wɒm[3], wɷm[3]]

8 Db 1 stɒps ə wɒm, ᵒ~ [wɒm[1]] 2 stɒp ə wɒm [ɷəm ("usu."), ɒm[3]] 3 stɒp ə wɒm [ə wɒm[2]] 4 stɒp ə wɷm [wɷm[1]] 5 stɒp ət ɒm, ᵒstɒp ə wɒm[1] [wɒm[1], ɒm[4]] 6 stɒp ə wɒm [wɒm[1]] 7 stɒpn ə wɒm

11 Sa 1 ste: ət o:m 2 stɒp ə wɷm [wɷm[3]] 3–4 ste: ət o:m 5 stɒp ə wɷm [wɷm[2]] 6–7 ste: ət o:m 8 ste: ət wɒm 9 stɒp ət o:m [wɒm[1]] 10 ste: ət wɒm [wɒm[2]] 11 ste: ət wɒm

12 St 1 stει ət oɷm, ᵒstειd [*p.t.*] ə wɔ:m[3] 2 stɒp ə wɒm [wɒm[1(2x)]] 3 stɒp ə wɒm [wɒm[1(4x)]] 4 stɒp ə wɒm, ᵒstɒpt [*1 p.t.s.*] ə wɷm 5 stɒp ət ɷ:m, stɒp ə wɒm 6 stɒp ə wɒm [wɒm[1(2x),2]] 7 stει ə wɒm 8 stɒp ə wɒm, ᵒ~[1] 9 stɒp ət ɒm [wɒm[2]] 10 stει ət ɷm 11 stει ət oɷm, ᵒstɒpt [*p.p.*] ət oɷm[2] [oɷm[2]]

15 He 1 stɒp ət wɒm 2 stɒp ət wɒm [wɷm^{3}] 3 stɒps ət wɷ:m [ət‿o:m^{4}] 4 ste: ət wʌm [wɷm^{2}] 5 stɒp ət o:m [o:m^{3}] 6 stæɩ ə wɷm 7 stɒp ət oɷm [o:m]

16 Wo 1–3 stɒp ə wɷm 4 stɒps ə wɷm [wɷ:m^{1}] 5 stɒp ə wɷ:m [wɷm$^{1(4x)}$] 6 stɒps ə wɷm [oɷm^{1}] 7 stɔps ət oɷm, s.f. stɔps ət wɷm [oɷm$^{1(2x),4}$, wɷm^{1}]

17 Wa 1 stɒp ət ǫɷm 2 steɩ ət ɔɷm [wɷm^{4}, wəm^{4}] 3 steɩ ət ǫɷm 4 stẹɩ ət ǫɷm [ɷm^{1}] 5 stɒp ət wɷm 6 stɒp ət ɷm 7 stɒp ət wɷm

23 Mon 1 stɒp ət o:^{ɷ}m [o:ɷm^{4}] 2 stɒp ət o:m [o:m^{3}] 3 stɒp ət o:m [o:m^{2,3}] 4 də steij ət ǫ:m [ǫ:m$^{2(2x)}$] 5 stẹ:z ǫ:m [oum^{3}] 6 stɒp ət‿o:m [o:m$^{1(2x)}$] 7 n.a. [ho:m^{1}]

24 Gl 1 stɒps ət o:ɷm 2 stɒps ət wɷm 3 stɒp ət‿wɒm [wœ:m$^{1(2x)}$] 4 stɒp ət wɷm 5 stɒps ət o:m 6 stɒp ət wɷəm 7 baɩd ət wəm

25 O 1 stɒps ət o:^{ɷ}m 2 stɒp ət əm [əm^{2}, ɔɷm^{3}] 3 stɒp ət ɔ̣ɷm [ɔ̣ɷm^{1}] 4 p. steɩ ət o:m [o:m^{5}; o:mbɽɛd^{1} *h.-bred* III.7.3] 5 stɒp ət əm [əm^{3}, ɷəm^{3}] 6 steɩ ət oɷm [ət oɷm^{2}; hoɷmkloɷs^{1} *h.-close* I.1.10]

VIII.5.3 WENT†

Q. Last night the parson came to see us, but stayed only a few minutes and then off he . . . .

Rr. GOED, §GOES, GONE, WENT

Note—In the i.m. below, an attached superior × denotes a p.t. form other than the 3 p.t.s.

7 Ch 1 wɛnt 2 wɛnt, ○∼^{3}, ○×∼$^{2(2x),3}$ 3–6 wɛnt

8 Db 1 wɛnt 2 wɛnt, ○×∼^{3} 3–7 wɛnt

11 Sa 1 wɛnt 2 wɛnt, ○×gɒn^{2} 3 wɛn 4 wɛnt 5 wɛnt, ○∼^{3} 6–7 wɛnt 8 wɛnt, ○×∼^{2} 9 wɛnt, ○∼^{1} 10 wɛnt, ○∼^{3}, ○×∼^{3} 11 wɛnt

12 St 1 wɛnt, ○∼^{1}, ○×wænt^{2} 2–3 wɛnt 4 wɛnt, ○×∼^{1} 5–7 wɛnt 8 wɛnt, ○∼^{3} 9 §goɷz 10–11 wɛnt

15 He 1 wɛnt, ○∼^{2} 2–3 wɛnt 4 wɛnt, ○×∼^{1} 5 wɛnt, ○go:d^{3} 6 wɛnt, ○×∼^{1}, ○×wɛn^{1} 7 wɛnt

16 Wo 1 wɛnt 2–3 wɛnt, ○×∼^{2} 4 wɛnt 5 wɛnt, ○∼^{1} 6 wɛnt 7 wɛnt, ○∼^{3}, ○×∼$^{1(2x),3,4}$

17 Wa 1 wɛnt', ○×~[2] 2 wɛnt, ○×~[1,3,4(2x)] 3–5 wɛnt 6 wɛnt, ○×~[4] 7 wɛnt

23 Mon 1–4 wɛnt 5 wɛntʰ, ○~[1], ○×~[2] 6 wɛnt, ○~[1] *inf.* [*sic*] 7 n.a.

24 Gl 1 wɛnt, ○×~[2] 2–7 wɛnt

25 O 1 wɛnt 2 wɛnʔ 3 wɛnt 4 wɛnt, ○~[5], ○×~[3,4(3x)] 5–6 wɛnʔ

VIII.5.3a PERSON

Q. He (viz. the parson) *came* (to see us) *along with his wife*; *she is a very nice . . . .*

Rr. BODY, §LADY, PERSON, §TART, §WOMAN

Note 1—Since the q. did not require a r. ref. sex, LADY, TART and WOMAN are u.rr.

Note 2—For additional exs. of WOMAN, see VII.1.6.

7 Ch 1 §wɷmən, s.w. bɒdɩ 2 §wɷmən 3 pəˠsn 4 p. bɒdɩ 5 bɒdɩ, ○~ 6 s.w. bɒdɩ

8 Db 1 pə:ˠsn 2 pə:sn, bɒdɩ [usu.] 3 §wɷmən 4 pə:sn 5 pɛ:sn 6 §wɷmən 7 pə:sn

11 Sa 1 pəʳ:ʂən 2 bɒdɩ, ○~ 3–4 pəʳ:ʂɳ 5–10 pəʳ:ʂən 11 pəʳ:ʂən, bɒdɩ

12 St 1 pə:sən 2 §wɷmən, §ta:t[(2x)] 3 §li:dɩ, pə:sn 4 pə:sən 5–6 pə:sn 7 §wɷmən 8 §lɛɩdɩ 9 pə:sn, ○□pə:snz[1] 10 pə:sn 11 pə:ɹsn

15 He 1–5 pəʳ:ʂən 6 pəʳʂən 7 §leɩdɩ, pəɹsən

16 Wo 1 bɒdɩ 2 pəʳ:ʂən, bɑ·dɩ ["older"] 3 bɒdɩ 4 p'əʳ:ʂən 5 pəʳ:ʂɒn 6 bɒdɩ 7 pəʳʂən, s.w. bədɩ

17 Wa 1 pə̣̂:sn 2 pə:sən, s.w. bədɩ 3–4 pə:sn 5 §wɷmɒn 6–7 pəʳ:ʂɳ

23 Mon 1 §ɷmən 2 pəsən 3 pœ:sən 4 n.a. 5 pœ̣̈:sn, ○~[2(2x)] 6 pəʳ:ʂən 7 n.a.

24 Gl 1–2 pəʳ:ʂɒn 3 §ɷmən 4 §ɷmɒn 5–6 pəʳʂɳ 7 §ɷmən, pəʳ:ʂɳ ["modern"]

25 O 1 pəʳ:ʂən 2 pəˠ:sn 3 pəʳ:ʂɳ 4 §ɷmən 5 s.w. bɒdɩ, ○pəʳ:ʂɳ[2] 6 bɒdɩ

VIII.5.4 SEXTON*

Q. What do you call the man who looks after the church building, and keeps it warm and clean?

Rr. ir.r. CHURCH–WARDEN, (PARISH–)CLERK, SEXTON, VERGER

7 Ch 1 sɛkstɷn 2–4 sɛkstən 5 sakstən 6 saksən

8 Db 1 sɛksn 2–3 sɛkstən 4 sakstn 5–6 saksn 7 sɛkstən

11 Sa 1–2 sɛkstn 3 sɛksn 4 sɛkstn 5 sɛkstən, klaʵ:k [usu.] 6 saksən 7 sɛkstən 8 sɛkstn 9 sæksn 10 saksən, klaʵ:k [pref.] 11 sɛkstn, klaʵ:k [pref.]

12 St 1 sɛ̧kstən 2–5 sɛkstən 6 və:dʒə, sɛkstən 7–8 sɛkstən 9 sɛkstn 10 və:dʒə, sɛkstən 11 sɛkstən

15 He 1 sɛkstn 2 sɛkstən 3 sɛktəʵ [*sic*], sɛkʃtən 4 sɛkstəʵɳ 5–6 sɛkstən 7 paɹɩʃklaɹk, sɛkstən ["modern"]

16 Wo 1–2 sɛkstən 3–4 sɛkstɷn 5–6 kləʵ:k 7 sɛkstən

17 Wa 1 sɛkstən 2 kla:k, və:dʒə, p. sɛkstən 3 sɛkstən 4 sɛkstɷn 5 vəʵ:ɖʒəʵ, p. saksn 6 vəʵ:ɖʒə, s.w. sɛkstən 7 vəʵ:ɖʒəʵ, p. sɛkstən [but not used]

23 Mon 1–3 sɛkstən 4 sɛk§tʌ̣n [rare] 5 ir.r. tʃœ̣:tʃwɔ:dn, s.w. sɛkstən 6 sɛkstən 7 n.a.

24 Gl 1 sɛkstɷn 2 kləʵ:k ["usu."], sɛkstɷn 3–4 sɛkstɷn 5 p. sɛkstɷn [but "clerk" pref.] 6 vəʵ:dʒəʵ, pp. sɛkstən 7 saksn

25 O 1 sɛkstən 2 sɛkstən, kləʴ̠:k 3–5 sɛkstən 6 vəʵ:dʒəʵ, sɛkstən

VIII.5.5 CHURCHYARD

Q. What do you call the place where all the tombstones are?

Confirm that he means the place round the church.

Rr. CHURCH/GRAVE–YARD

Note—For CHURCH, see VIII.5.1; for GRAVE, see VIII.5.6; and for additional exs. of (–)YARD, see I.1.3 (and refs.).

7 Ch 1 tʃəʴ:tʃja:d 2 tʃətʃja:d 3 tʃəʴ:tʃjaʴ:d 4–5 tʃə:tʃja:d 6 tʃəʴ̠:tʃja:d

8 Db 1 tʃəʴ̠tʃjaʴ̠:d 2–4 tʃə:tʃja:d 5 tʃətʃja:ɑ, °tʃətʃja:d[4] 6 tʃətʃja:d 7 tʃə:tʃja:d

11 Sa 1 tʃəʳ:tʃjaʳ:ɖ 2 tʃəʳ:tʃja:d 3–4 tʃəʳ:tʃjaʳ:ɖ 5 tʃəʳtʃjaʳ:ɖ 6 tʃəʳ·tʃja:d 7–8 tʃəʳ:tʃjəʳ:ɖ 9 tʃəʳ:tʃjaʳ:ɖ 10–11 tʃəʳ:tʃjəʳ:ɖ

12 St 1 tʃə:tʃja:d 2 tʃə:tʃja:d, gɹɛɪvja:d 3 tʃə:tʃjɔ:d 4 gɹɛɪvja:d 5 gɹe:vja:d 6–7 tʃə:tʃja:d 8 tʃəʴ:tʃjɑ:d 9 gɹɛɪvja:d 10 tʃətʃja:d 11 tʃə:ɹtʃja:ɹd

15 He 1–2 tʃəʳ:tʃjaʳ:ɖ 3 tʃəʳtʃjaʳ:ɖ 4 tʃəʳ:tʃjəʳ:ɖ 5 tʃəʳtʃjəʳ:ɖ 6 tʃəʳtʃjəʳ:ɖ, °tʃəʳtʃjəʳɖ 7 gɹeɪvjɑ:ɹd, tʃəɹtʃjɑɹd [fr. i.'s wife, nat.]

16 Wo 1 tʃəʳ:tʃjɑ:d 2 tʃəʳ:tʃja:d, °tʃəʳ:tʃa:d[2] 3–4 tʃəʳ:tʃjəʳ:ɖ 5 tʃəʳ:tʃəʳ:ɖ 6 tʃəʳ:tʃjəʳ:ɖ 7 tʃə:tʃjɑʳɖ

17 Wa 1 tʃə̥:tʃja:d 2–3 tʃə:tʃja:d 4 tʃəʳ:tʃja:d 5 tʃəʳ:tʃa:d 6–7 tʃəʳ:tʃjaʳ:ɖ

23 Mon 1 tʃəʳtʃjəʳ:ɖ 2 tʃə:tʃja:d 3 tʃœ:tʃja:d 4 n.a. 5 gɹe:vja:d 6 tʃəʳ:tʃja:d 7 n.a.

24 Gl 1–2 tʃəʳ:tʃjaʳ:ɖ 3 tʃəʳ:tʃjaʳ:ɖ [bʷənəs *bone-house* (i.e. the churchyard)] 4 gɹe:vjaʳ:ɖ, tʃəʳ:tʃjaʳɖ 5 tʃəʳ:tʃjəʳ:ɖ 6 tʃəʳ:tjaʳ:ɖ [*sic*] 7 tʃəʳ:tʃjaʳ:ɖ

25 O 1 tʃəʳ:tʃjəʳ:ɖ 2–3 tʃəʳ:tʃjaʳ:ɖ 4 tʃəɽtʃjɑɽɖ, tʃəɽtʃjɑd 5 tʃəʳ:tʃjaʳ:ɖ 6 tʃəʳtʃjaʳ:ɖ

VIII.5.6 GRAVE*

Q. What does the tombstone cover?

R. GRAVE

Note—GRAVE- occurs at VIII.5.5.

7 Ch 1 gɹe:v 2 □gɹe:vz 3–4 gɹẹ:v 5 gɹi:v 6 gɹe:v

8 Db 1–3 gɹe:v 4 gɹi:v 5–6 gɹe:ᶦv 7 gɹe·ɪv

11 Sa 1 gɹe:v 2 gɹe:ᵊv 3–4 gɹe:v 5 gɹę:v 6–11 gɹe:v

12 St 1–2 gɹɛɪv 3 gɹi:v 4 gɹɛɪv 5 gɹe:v 6 gɹɛɪv, gɹi:v 7 gɹɛɪv 8 gɹɛɪv [gɹɛɪvstoʊnz *g.-stones*] 9–11 gɹɛɪv

15 He 1–2 gɹe:ɪv 3–4 gɹe:v 5 gɹe:ɪv 6 gɹɛv 7 gɹeɪv

16 Wo 1 gɹɛɪv 2 gɹe:ᶦv 3 gɹe:ɪv 4 gɹaɪv, °~[3] 5 gɹe:v, °gɹi:v[1] 6 gɹe:ɪv 7 s.w. gɹeɪv

17 Wa 1 gɹẹɪv 2–3 gɹɛɪv 4–5 gɹẹɪv 6–7 gɹɛɪv

23 Mon 1 gɹe:ɪv 2 gɹe:ᵊv 3 gɹe:v 4 gɹẹ:v 5 gɹe:v, °~[2] [gɹe:vdɪgʱə[2] *g.-digger*] 6 gɹe:v 7 n.a.

24 Gl 1 gɹe:ᵊv 2 gɹɛɪv 3 gɹe:ˈv 4–7 gɹe:v

25 O 1 gɹeəv 2 gɹɛɪv 3 gɹeˈv 4 gɾẹɪv 5 gɹeˈv 6 gɹeɪv

VIII.5.7 COFFIN

Q. And what is put in the grave?

Rr. BOX, COFFIN

7 Ch 1 kɒfɪn 2 kɔfɪn 3–6 kɒfɪn

8 Db 1–7 kɒfɪn

11 Sa 1–2 kɒfɪn 3 kɔ:fɪn 4 kɒ·fɪn 5 kɒfɪ̣n 6 kɒfɪn 7 kɔ:fɪn 8–9 kɒfɪn 10–11 kɔ:fɪn

12 St 1 kɒfɪn, ○~² 2–5 kɒfɪn 6 kɒfɪn, bɒks 7–8 kɒfɪn 9 kọfɪn 10–11 kɒfɪn

15 He 1–2 kɔ:fɪn 3–6 kɒfɪn 7 kɒfɪn, ○□kɒfɪnz[1,2]

16 Wo 1 kɒfɪn 2 kɑ·fɪn 3–4 kɒfɪn 5 kɒfɪn, ○~[1] 6 kɒfɪn 7 kɔfɪn

17 Wa 1 kɒfɪn 2 kɔfɪn 3–7 kɒfɪn

23 Mon 1–2 kɒfɪn 3 kɑ:fɪn 4 n.a. 5 kɒ̣̀·fɪn 6 kɒfɪn 7 n.a.

24 Gl 1 kɑ:fɪn 2 kɒfɪn 3 kɑ:fɪn 4 kɒfɪn 5 kɑfɪn 6–7 kɒfɪn

25 O 1 kɒfɪn 2 kɒfɪn, ○□kɒfɪnz[2] 3 kɒ·fɪn 4–5 kɒfɪn 6 kɔ:fɪn

VIII.5.7a BODY

Q. What's inside the coffin?

If he doesn't use *dead,* ask what kind of a body.

Rr. (DEAD) BODY/CORPSE

Note 1—When rec. separately in the rr., DEAD is reproduced after a full stop.

Note 2—I.m. exs. of DEAD *adj.* and DEATH are reproduced untransliterated below between square brackets foll. a full stop.

Note 3—BODY– occurs at VIII.5.3a and –BODY at V.8.4 and VII.3.16; DEAD at III.7.2; DEADLY at IV.11.5; DEATH at VI.13.9/18/19; and DIED at III.7.2.

7 Ch 1 n.r. dʒɛd. [dʒɛd (rec. in «ɩ‿z gɒn dʒɛd» *he's gone d.*)] 2 kɔ:ps, s.w. dɛd bədɩ [but not used; bədɩbɹʊʃ[1] *b.-brush* III.5.5] 3 dʒɛd bɒdɩ. [dʒɛd[3(3x)]] 4 p. dʒɛd bɒdɩ. [dɛd[2] VIII.1.9] 5 dʒɛd bɒdɩ. [dʒɛd[1] (rec. in «sʊmbɒdɩ‿z gɒn dʒɛd[1]» *somebody's gone d.*)] 6 dʒɛd bɒdɩ. [dʒɛd[2,3]]

8 Db 1 n.r. dɩəd 2 dɩəd bɒdɩ 3 dʒɛd bɒdɩ. [dʒɛd[1], ~[1] VI.13.8] 4 di:d bɒdɩ 5 dɛd bɒdɩ 6 dʒɛd bɒdɩ, kɔ:ps. [dɛθ[1]] 7 dʒɛd bɒdɩ

11 Sa 1 dɛd bɒdɩ 2 dɛd bɒdɩ. [dʒɛθ[2]] 3 dɛd bɒdɩ 4 dɛd bɒ·dɩ 5 dʒɛd bɒdɩ [dʒɛθ[2]] 6 dɛd bɒdɩ. [dɛθ[3]] 7 dɛd bɒdɩ. [dɛdmanz fe:əʳ[1] *D-man's Fair* VII.4.11; dɛθ[1]] 8–9 dɛd bɒdɩ 10 dɛd bɒdɩ [bɒdɩ[1] *body* (of cart)]. [dʒɛθ[2,3(2x)]] 11 dɛd bɒdɩ, °ka:ps. [dʒɛθ[2]]

12 St 1 bɒdɩ 2 bɒdɩ, kɔ:ps, dʒɛd bɒdɩ. [dɛd[1,2], dʒɛd[5]] 3 bɒdɩ, dʒɛd bɒdɩ. [dʒɛd[2]; dʒɛdmɒn[2] *d.-man* III.11.9; dɛθ[2(2x)]] 4 kɔ:ps. [dɛd[1]] 5 dɛd bɒdɩ. [dʒɛd[2]; dɛθ[1]] 6 bɒdɩ, kɔ:ps. [dʒɛd[2]] 7 kɔ:ps, dɛd kɔ:ps 8 kɔ:ps, bɒdɩ, dɛd bɒdɩ. [dɛd[1]] 9 kɔ:ps. dɛd 10–11 kɔ:ps

15 He 1 kɔʳ:ps, dʒɛd bɒdɩ. [dʒʌθ[1]] 2 kɔʳ:ps. [dʒʌd[1]] 3 dʒʊd bɒdɩ 4 djʌd bɒdɩ. [dʒʌd[1(2x)]] 5 kaʳ:ps 6 dʒʊd bɒdɩ. [dʒʊd[1]] 7 kɒɹps[(2x)], bɒdɩ, °~[4]. [dɛd]

16 Wo 1 dɛd bɒdɩ 2 dɛd ba·dɩ 3 kaʳ:ps, dʒʊd bɒdɩ. [dʒʊd[1]] 4 dʒʊd bɒdɩ 5 djʊd bɒdɩ 6 dʒɛd bɒdɩ, kaʳ:ps 7 bɒdɩ, s.w. dɛd bədɩ [bɒdɩ-ɑʳs[2(2x)] *b.-horse* (i.e. third horse in a team of four)]

17 Wa 1 kɔ:ps, dɛd bɒdɩ. [dʒʊd[1]] 2 bədɩ, s.w. dɛd bədɩ. [djɛd[3,4]] 3 dɛd bɒdˈĭ 4 dʒɛd bɒdɩ. [dʒɛd[1(2x)]] 5 dʒɛd bɒdɩ 6 dɛd bɒdɩ. [dʒɛd[3]] 7 dʒʊd bɒdɩ. [dʒʊd[1]; dʒʊθ[2]]

23 Mon 1 dɛd bɒdɩ 2–3 dɛd bɒdɩ, kɑ:ps 4 n.a. 5 dɛd bɒ̞·di 6 dɛd bɒdɩ 7 n.a.

24 Gl 1 dʒʊ:d bɒdɩ 2 dʒʊd bɒdɩ, kɑ:ps [usu.; bɒdɩ-ɒs[1] *b.-horse* (i.e. middle one of team of three horses) I.6.5]. [dʒʊd[3]; dʒʊθ[3]] 3 dʒʊd bɒdɩ. [dʒʊθ[1]] 4 dʒɛd bɒdɩ 5 dʒɛd bɒdɩ. [dʒɛd[2]; djɛθ[2]] 6 dʒəd bɒdɩ. [djəd] 7 djəd bɒdɩ

25 O 1 dɛdbɒdɩ 2 kɔʳ·ᵊps 3 dɛd bɒdɩ [bɒdɩ[1], bədɩ[1] *b.* (ref. middle horse in a team of three)] 4 bɒdɩ, dɛd ən. [□stɛdɩmɛn *steady-men* (i.e. dead men; "jocular")] 5 kɔʳəps 6 kɔʳ:ps

VIII.5.8 EARTH

Q. What's a grave filled with?

Rr. DIRT, EARTH, MOULD, MUCK, SOIL

Note—MUCK = *dung* occurs at I.3.12 (and refs.). For exs. of DIRTY *v.* and MUCK(Y) *v.*, see V.2.8. EARTH– occurs at V.1.13.

7 Ch 1 sɑɩl 2 sɔɩl, s.f. sæɩl ["older"], s.w. ə:θ [pref.], °sаɩl[2(2x)], °ə·ɹθ[1], °ə:θ[2] [ə:θən[2] *earthen*; ə:θt *earthed p.p.*] 3 dəɹt 4 sɑɩl 5 saɩl, °~[3], °sɑ:l[3] 6 saɩl, °~[2]

8 Db 1 dəɹt 2 ə:θ, sɒɩl 3 saɩl 4 mɷk, °sɑɩl[1] 5 sɔɩl 6 də:t 7 də:t, °sɑ̃·ɩ̃l ["older"]

11 Sa 1 əɽ:θ 2 saɩl 3–4 sɒɩl 5 sɒɩəl 6 sɒɩl 7–8 əɽ:θ 9 sɒɩl 10 əɽ:θ 11 sɒɩl

12 St 1 sɒ·ɩl, °ə:θ[2] 2 ə:θ 3 mɷk, də:t 4 sɒɩl, °saɩl[1] *v.* 5 də:t 6 sɒɩl, °sɒ́ɩl[1] 7 sɒɩl, °sɒ̣ɩl[3] 8 dəɹ:t 9 mɷk, sɒɩl 10 ə:θ 11 sɔ:ɩl

15 He 1 sɒɩɫ 2 əɽ:θ 3–4 dəɽ:ʈ 5 mæɷɫ 6 əɽθ 7 əɹθ [əɹθt[3] *earthed p.p.*]

16 Wo 1–2 sɒɩəl 3 sɒɩəɫ 4 dəɽ:ʈ, sɒɩəɫ [usu.] 5–6 sɒɩəɫ 7 də·ɽʈ

17 Wa 1 ə̣̂:θ 2 sɔɩl, s.w. ə:θ 3 sɒɩəɫ, də:t ["probably older"] 4 də:t 5 əɽ:θ 6 dəɽ:ʈ 7 sɒɩəɫ

23 Mon 1 dəɽ:ʈ 2 mo:ɫd 3 mo:ɫ, mæɷɫ ["older"] 4 œ:θ 5 œ̣̂:θ, °ʌ̣̈f[1] 6 mo:ɫd 7 n.a. [œ:θn̩wɛ:[1] *earthen-ware*]

24 Gl 1 mæɷəɫ 2 dəɽ:ʈ 3–4 mo:ɷɫd 5–6 dəɽ:ʈ 7 mək

25 O 1 sɒɩɫ 2 soɩɫ 3 sɔɩl 4 əɽθ 5 sɔɩɫ, dəɽ:ʔ 6 soɩɫ

VIII.5.9 HEARSE*, BIER

Q. How is the coffin taken from the house to the churchyard?

Rr. (HORSE–)HEARSE
BEARER, (SHALLOW) BIER

Note—The two rr. to the q. are separated below by a full stop.

7 Ch 1 ə:s. n.r. 2 ə:st. bɩə 3 əɹ:st. bɩə 4 ə:st. bɩə, °bɩət 5 ə:st. bɩəd 6 əɹ:s. bɩəɹd

8 Db 1 ɩəꜝst, °ɩəst. bɹɩəꜝ [*sic*] 2 ə:st ["on two wheels in old days"]. n.r. 3 ə:s. bɩə 4 ɩəs. bɛ: 5 ɛ:s. bɩə 6–7 ə:s. bɩə

11 Sa 1–3 əʳ:ʂ. bɩəʳ 4 həʳ:ʂ. bɩəʳ· 5–10 əʳ:ʂ. bɩəʳ 11 əʳ:ʂ. bi:əʳ

12 St 1 ə:st. bɩəʴ 2 ə:s. biə 3 ə:s. biəd 4–5 ə:s. biə 6 ə:st. bi:ə 7 ə:s. □biəz 8 ə:st. bɛ:ɹə 9 ə:s. ʃalə bɛ: 10 ɛ:s. biə 11 ə:s. bɩə

15 He 1–3 əʳ:ʂ. bɩəʳ 4 əʳ:ʂ. bjə:ʳ 5 əʳʂ. bɩəʳɖ 6 əʳ:ʂ. bɩəʳ 7 əɹs, ɒɹs, əɹs ["older"]. bɩəɹ ["old"], °bɩəɹ[4(3x)]

16 Wo 1 əʳ:ʂ. bɩə 2–3 əʳ:ʂ. bɩəʳ 4 əʳ:ʂ. bɛəʳ 5–6 əʳ:ʂ. bɩəʳ 7 ə·ʳʂ. n.r.

17 Wa 1 ə̣̂:s. bɩə 2 ə:s. n.r. 3 ə:s, °ə:st[3] [ə:sə:s[3] *horse-h.*]. bɩə 4 əʳ:ʂ. bɩəʳɖ 5 əʳ:ʂʈ. bɩəʳɖ 6 əʳ:ʂ, °~. bɩəʳ 7 əʳ:ʂ. bɩəʳ

23 Mon 1 əʳ:ʂ. bɩəʳɖ 2 ə:s. bæɩəʳ 3 œ:s. bæɩə 4 œ:§ 5 œ̣̈:s 6 əʳ:ʂ. bɩəʳ 7 n.a.

24 Gl 1 əʳ:ʂ. bɩəʳ: 2 əʳ:ʂ. bjəʳ 3 œ:s. bɩəʳ 4 əʳ:ʂ. bɩəʳ 5 əʳ:ʂ. bɩə ["modern"] 6 əʳ:ʂ. bɩəʳ ["modern"] 7 həʳ:ʂ. bɩəʳ

25 O 1 əʳ:ʂ. bɛəɽə 2 əꜝ:s. bɩəꜝ 3 əʳ:ʂ. bɩəʳɖ 4 əɽʂ ["modern"], °□ə·ɽʂɩz[5]. bɩəɽ ["modern"] 5 əʳ:ʂ. beəʳ 6 əʳ:ʂ. bɩəʳɖ

VIII.5.10 BEARERS

Q. What do you call the men that carry the coffin (from the house to the churchyard)*?*

Rr. BEARERS, CARRIERS

7 Ch 1 bɛ:ɹəz 2 bɛəɹəz 3–4 bɛ:ɹəz 5 bɩəɹəz 6 bɛ:ɹəz

8 Db 1 bɛ:ɹəz 2 bɛəɹəz 3–5 bɛ:ɹəz 6 ᐞbɛ:ɹə 7 bɛəɹəz

11 Sa 1 bɛəʳ:ɽəz 2 bɛ:ᵊɹəz 3 bɛəɹəz 4 bɛ·ᵊɹəz 5 bɛɹə:ʳʐ 6 bɛᵊɹəʳ:ʐ 7 be:əʳɽəz 8 be:ɹəʳ:ʐ 9 be:ɹəʳ·ʐ 10 be:ɹəʳ:ʐ 11 bɛ:əʳɽəz

12 St 1–2 bɛ:ɹəz 3 bɛ̣:ɹəz 4 bɛ·ɹəz 5–9 bɛ:ɹəz 10 bɛ̈:ɹəz 11 bɛ:ɹəz

15 He 1–5 bɛəʳɽəʳʐ 6 bɛɹəʳʐ 7 bɛəɹəz

16 Wo 1 bɛ:əɹəz 2 bɛ:ᵊɹəz 3 bɛ:ɹəʳ:ʐ 4 bɛəɹəʳʐ 5 be:ɹəʳʐ 6 be:əʳɽəʳ:ʐ 7 s.w. bɛəɹəz, °~

17 Wa 1 bɛ̈:ɹəz 2 bɛəɹəz 3 bɛ:ɹəz 4 bɛ:ɹəz, kaɹɪəz ["older"] 5 kaɹɪəʳʐ, ○~¹ 6 bɛ:ɹəʳʐ 7 kaɹɪəʳʐ

23 Mon 1 bɛɹəʳʐ 2–3 bɛɹəz 4 n.a. 5 bɛ̣:ɹəz 6 bɛəʳɽəz 7 n.a.

24 Gl 1 be:ɹəʳ:ʐ 2 bəʳ:ɽəʳʐ 3–4 be:ɹəʳʐ 5 bɛəɹəʳ·ʐ 6 be:ɽəʳʐ, ○~ 7 bɛəɽəʳʐ

25 O 1 kæɹɪəʳʐ 2 bɛəɽəᶦz 3 kaɽɪəʳʐ 4–5 bɛəɽəz 6 bɛəɽəʳʐ

VIII.5.11 BURIED*

Q. A grave is a place in which someone has been . . . .

R. BURIED

7 Ch 1 bɛɹɪd, ○~⁴ 2 bɛɹɪd 3 bəɹɪt 4–6 bɛɹɪd

8 Db 1 bɛɹɪd 2 bəɹɪd 3 bɛɹɪd 4 bəɹɪd 5–7 bɛɹɪd

11 Sa 1–4 bɛɹɪd 5 bɛɹ̩ɪd 6–11 bɛɹɪd

12 St 1 bəɹɪd 2 bɛɹɪd 3 bɛɹɪd, ○~¹, ○~¹ *1 p.t.s.* 4–7 bɛɹɪd 8 bəɹɪd, ○bɛɹɪz⁵ *3 pr.s.* 9–10 bɛɹɪd 11 bɛɹɪd, ○~², ○bɛɹɪ² *pr.t.*

15 He 1–6 bɛɹɪd 7 bɛɹɪd, ○~⁴

16 Wo 1–6 bɛɹɪd 7 bɛɹɪd, ○~⁴

17 Wa 1–7 bɛɹɪd

23 Mon 1–3 bɛɹɪd 4–5 bɛɹ̩ɪd 6 bɛɹɪd 7 n.a.

24 Gl 1–4 bɛɹɪd 5 bɛɹɪd, ○bɛɹɪ² *v.* 6 bɛɹɪd, ○bɛɹɪ² *inf.* 7 bɛɽɪd

25 O 1 bɛɽɪd, ○bɛɹɪ³ *inf.* 2 bəɽɪd 3 bɛɹɪd 4 bɛɽɪd, ○bɛɽɪ⁵ 5 bæɽɪd 6 bɛɽɪd

VIII.5.12 MOURNERS*

Q. What do you call the relatives and friends who attend a funeral?

R. MOURNERS

7 Ch 1 mo:nəz 2 mọənəz 3 mọ:nəz 4 mo:nəz 5 mɔ:nəz 6 mo:nəᶦz

8 Db 1 mɔᶦ:nəᶦz 2 mo·ənəz 3 mo:ᵊnəz 4 mɷənəz 5 mɔ:nəz 6 △mɔ:nə 7 mɔ:nəz

11 Sa 1 mo:nəʳ:ʐ 2 mo:nəz 3 mo:ənəʳ:ʐ 4 məʳ:ɳəʳ:ʐ 5 mɔ:nəʳʐ 6 mo:nəʳ:ʐ 7 mo:əʳɳəʳ:ʐ 8 mo:ənəʳʐ 9–10 mɔ:ənəʳ:ʐ 11 mɔ:əʳɳəʳʐ

12 St 1 mɔ:nəz 2 mɔ̣:nəz 3–6 mɔ:nəz 7 mɔ̣:nəz 8–9 mɔ:nəz 10–11 mɔ̣:nəz

15 He 1 məʳ:ɳəʳʐ 2–4 mo:əʳɳəʳʐ 5 mo:nəʳʐ 6 mɑʳ:ɳəʳʐ 7 məəɹnəɹz

16 Wo 1 mɑ:nəz 2 mo:ᵊnəʳʐ 3 moɷ·ənəʳʐ 4 mɑʳ:ɳəʳʐ 5 mo:nəʳʐ 6 moɷənəʳʐ 7 s.w. mɔ·ənəʳʐ

17 Wa 1 mɔ:nəz 2 mɔənəz 3 mɔ:nə̣z 4 mọ·ənəz 5 mɒɷəʳɳəʳʐ 6 məʳ:ɳəʳʐ 7 mo·əʳɳəʳʐ

23 Mon 1 mo:əʳɳəʳʐ 2–4 mo:nəz 5 mouənəz 6 mɑʳ:ɳəʳʐ 7 n.a.

24 Gl 1 mɑʳ:ɳəʳʐ 2 mo:əʳɳəʳʐ 3–4 mo:ɷnəʳʐ 5–6 mo·əʳɳəʳʐ 7 məʳ:ɳəʳʐ

25 O 1 məʳ:ɳəʳʐ 2 moᵊnəɪz 3 moəʳɳəʳʐ 4 məəɽɳəɽʐ 5–6 məʳ:ɳəz

VIII.5.13 FLOWERS*

Q. On graves, people like to put wreaths of . . . .

R. FLOWERS

7 Ch 1 flaɷəz 2 flæɷəz 3 flaɷəɪz 4–5 flaɷəz 6 flaɷəz, °△flaɷə[2]

8 Db 1 flaɷəɪz 2 flaɷəz 3 flëɷəz 4 flɛɷəz 5–6 flaɷəz 7 flɛɷəz

11 Sa 1 flaɷəʳ:ʐ 2 flaɷəz 3–4 flaɷəʳ:ʐ 5 flɛɷəʳʐ 6–7 flaɷəʳ:ʐ 8 flaɷəʳʐ 9–11 flaɷəʳ:ʐ

12 St 1–3 flaɷəz 4 flæɷəz 5 flaɷəz, °~[1] 6 flaɷəz ,°△flæɷə[1] 7 flæɷəz [flæɷəɹɪ[1] *flowery*] 8 flæɷəz 9 flaɷəz, °fla·ɷəz[1] 10 flɛɷwəz 11 flaɷəz, °△flaɷə[1]

15 He 1–2 flæɷəʳʐ 3 fɫəɷəʳʐ 4 fləɷəʳʐ, °fləɷəʳʐ[3], °△fləɷəʳ[1] 5 flʌɷəʳʐ 6 fləɷəʳʐ 7 flə̆uəɹz, °~, °flăʉəɹz[1] °flăɷəɹz[3]

16 Wo 1 flɛɷəz 2 flɛɷəʳʐ 3 flɛu:əʳʐ 4 fləɷəʳʐ 5 fləɷ:əʳʐ 6 flɛu:əʳʐ 7 flæɷəʳʐ, °~, °flɛɷəʳʐ[2], °flɛɷəz[1]

17 Wa 1 flæɷəz 2 flæɷəz, °~ 3–4 flɛɷəz 5–7 flɛɷəʳʐ

23 Mon 1 flʌɷəʳʐ 2 flʌɷəz 3 fləɷəz 4–5 fləu-əz 6 fləɷəʳʐ 7 n.a.

24 Gl 1 fləɷ:əʳʐ 2 flɛɷəʳʐ 3–4 vɫəɷəʳʐ 5 flʌɷəʳʐ 6 flᵚu:əʳʐ [flʌɷə ʃɑɷ[1] *f. show* VII.4.11] 7 flᵚu:əʳʐ

25 O 1 flε̈ωəʳʐ, ○△flε̈ωəʳ[1] 2 flæωəʳʐ 3 flεωəʳʐ 4 fłaωəɽʐ, fłaωəz 5 flε̈ωəɽʐ 6 flε̈ωəʳʐ, ○△flε̈ωəʳ[1]

VIII.5.14 CROSS*

Q. On some graves, there's not a tombstone, but a [i.] . . . .

R. CROSS

Note 1—I.m. exs. of ACROSS and CROSS–WAYS are reproduced below between square brackets untransliterated.

Note 2—(–)CROSS(–) occurs at I.10.4, IV.3.7, VI.3.6 and IX.1.8.

7 Ch 1 kɹɒs [əkɹɔ:s[2]] 2 kɹɔs, ○□kɹɔsɪz [əkɹɔs[1,2,3(3x),4]; kɹɔs *c. inf.*; kɹɔswe:[1] *c.-way adv.*; kɹɔsɹωədz[3] *c.-roads*] 3–5 kɹɒs 6 kɹɔ:s [kɹɔ:spi:sɪz[2] *c.-pieces* IV.3.6]

8 Db 1 kɹɔs [əkɹɔ:s[1,3]] 2 kɹɒs 3 kɹɒs [kɹɒspi:s[1] *c.-piece* V.1.12] 4–7 kɹɒs

11 Sa 1 kɹɒs 2–3 kɹɔ:s 4 kɹɔʳ:ʂ 5–6 kɹɒs 7–11 kɹɔ:s

12 St 1–3 kɹɒs 4 kɹɒs [əkɹɒs[2]; kɹɒs[2] (rec. in «ə kɹɒs bɪtwi:n ə at ən ə ʃɔ:l» *a cross between a hat and a shawl*)] 5 kɹɒs [əkɹɒs[2(2x)]] 6 kɹɒs [ɔ: kɹɒs[1] *Hoar C.* (pl.n.)] 7 kɹɒs 8 kɹɒs [kɹɒslεgz[3] *c.-legs* I.7.16] 9 kɹɒs [əkɹɒs[1,2]] 10-11 kɹɒs

15 He 1–2 kɹɔ:s 3 kɹɑ:s [əkɹɑ:s[1]] 4–5 kɹɑ:s 6 kɹɑ:s [kɹɑ:sbaʳ:[1] *c.-bar* V.3.5] 7 □kɹɒsɪz [əkɹɒs[3,4(2x)]; kɹɒsweɪz[4]]

16 Wo 1 kɹɒs 2 kɹɑ:s 3 kɹɑ:s [kɹɑ:sstɪk[1] *c.-stick* I.11.1] 4–5 kɹɑ:s 6 kɹɑ:s, ○~[2] [n.d.; əkɹa:s[2]] 7 kɹɔ:s [kɹɔ:s[4] (a)*cross*; kɹɔ:sweɪz[3] VI.3.5]

17 Wa 1 kɹɒs 2 kɹɔ:s [kɹɔ:s[4] (a)*cross*; əkɹɔ:s[4]; kɹɔ:st[4] *crossed p.p.*] 3 kɹɒs [əkɹɔ:s[1]] 4 kɹɔ:s 5 kɹɔ:s [əkɹɔ:s[1(2x)], əkɹɒs[1]; kɹɔ:spi:s[1] *c.-piece*] 6 kɹɔ:s, ○~[4] 7 kɹɔ:s

23 Mon 1–3 kɹɑ:s 4 kʰɹɔ·s 5 kɹɒ̞̈‹s 6 kɹɑ:s [əkɹɑ:s[1]] 7 n.a.

24 Gl 1 kɹɑ:s 2 kɹa:s 3–4 kɹɑ:s 5–7 kɹɔ:s

25 O 1 kɹɔ:s [əkɹɔ:s[1]] 2 kɹɔ:s [əkɹɔ:s[2]; kɹɔ:swę̈ɪz[1]] 3 kɹɔ:s [kɹɔ:st[1] *crossed p.t.*] 4 kɽɒ:s [əkɹɔ:s[1]] 5 kɽɔ:s [əkɹɔ:s[2]] 6 kɹɔ:z

VIII.6.1 GO TO SCHOOL*‡

Q. Children are not taught to read and write at home, they must . . . .

Rr. GO (TO) SCHOOL

Note 1—I.m. exs. of GO *v.* and most of its parts are reproduced below between square brackets untransliterated. An attached superior ◇ denotes an inf. and superior × a 3 pr.s. I.m. exs. of SCHOOL are also included here untransliterated.

Note 2—All the exs. of the 3 pr.pl. form of GO in the i.m. below were rec. with pl. nn. as subjects.

Note 3—Additional exs. of GO *inf.* occur at V.5.9, V.7.10, and VI.11.8; of the pr.p. at III.1.12, III.13.3/10/14, VII.6.5, VII.8.18, VIII.2.8, VIII.8.5 and IX.4.1; of the 3 pr.s. at VIII.6.2; of the 3 pr.pl. at VIII.5.1 and of the 2 pr.pl. at VIII.7.9. For GO *imp.*, see VIII.7.9 (and refs.); for GO AND, see IX.5.8 (and refs.); for WENT, see VIII.5.3; and for the p.p., see IX.5.7 (and refs.). GO *n.* occurs at VII.5.8 and VIII.9.1.

7 Ch 1 gɷ skʏ: [◇gɷ^{4}, ¶gɷɪn^{2}] 2 gɷ‿t skᵊu: [◇gɷ·^{2}, ◇∼^{3} IX.4.1, ◇gɷ:$^{3(2x)}$, ¶gɷɪn$^{2(3x),3}$, ¶gɷɪn^{2} VII.5.8, gɷ^{2} (n.d.g.); sku:^{1,2}] 3 gɷ‿t skᶦʏ: [gü:ɪn^{2,3}] 4 gɷ tə sku:l [¶gɷɪn^{2}, ¶əgɷɪn^{2}] 5 gɷ tə skɪʏ̈: [×gɷz^{1}, ¶gɷɪn^{1,2}] 6 gɷ tə skᵚų̈:ɫ [¶gɷɪn^{2}]

8 Db 1 gɷ tə skʏ: [¶gʏ:ɪn,$^{1(2x)}$, ¶gʏ·ɪn^{2}, gʏ:^{2} (n.d.g.)] 2 gɷ tə skᵚu:l [tə‿t skᵚu:l^{3} *to the s.*] 3 gɷ‿t skɛɷ [◇gɷ^{1}, ×gɷz^{1} VI.14.2] 4 gɷ‿ʔt skɛɷl [◇gᵚu:^{2}, ¶gᵚu:ɪn^{1}, ¶gɷɪn^{1}; gᵚu:^{1} *n.*] 5 gɷ tə skᶦu:l [◇gɷ^{2,3}, ×gɷz^{1} III.3.7, ¶gɷɪn$^{2,3(2x)}$] 6 gü:‿tʔ skɛɷl [×gɷz^{1}] 7 gᵚü:‿t skɛɷl [¶gᵚü:ɪn^{1}]

11 Sa 1 go: tə skᵚu:l 2 gɷ tə skʏʉ:l [¶go:ɪn^{1,2}] 3 gɷ tə sku:l 4 go: tə sku:l 5 go: tə skɪu:l, ᴼgɷ tə skɪu:^{3} [◇go:^{3}, ×gəz^{2}; skɪu:l^{1,2}, skɪu:əl^{1,3}; skɪu:lbɒs *s.-boss* VIII.6.5] 6 gə tə sku:l [¶goɪn$^{1(2x),3}$] 7 go: tə sku:l [◇go:$^{1(3x)}$, ¶go:ɪn^{1}; j‿əd g‿i:n^{1} *you would go in*] 8 gɷ tə sku:l [◇gu:^{2}, ¶gu:ɪn^{2}; gu:^{1} *n.*; sku:lgafəʵ^{2} *s.-gaffer*] 9 go: tə sku:l [sku:l^{1}] 10 go: tə sku:l [◇go:^{3}, ×go:z^{2}, ¶go:ɪn^{2}] 11 go: tə sku:ᵊl [×go:z^{1}, ¶go:ɪn^{2}, ¶gwan$^{2(2x)}$]

12 St 1 goɷ tə sku:l, ᴼgɷɪn tə sku:l^{1}, ᴼgɷɪn‿t sku:l^{3}, ᴼəgɷɪn sku:l^{2} [◇gu:$^{3(3x)}$, ◇gų:^{3}, ¶gɷɪn$^{1(2x),3(2x)}$, ¶əgoɷɪn$^{2(2x)}$, goɷ$^{2(2x)}$ (n.d.g.), gɷɪ^{2} *vbl. n.* (rec. in «fə gɷɪ‿t tʃapəl» *for going to chapel*)] 2 gu: skɛɷl [◇goɷ^{2}, ◇gɷ^{1}, ¶gɷɪn^{1}] 3 gɷ‿t skɛɷl [◇gɷ:^{1,2}, ×gɷ:z^{1,2}, ¶gɷ:ɪn$^{1(4x),2(5x)}$, ¶gɷ:n$^{1(2x)}$] 4 gɷ tə skü:l [◇gɷ:^{2}, ◇goɷ^{2}, ×goɷz^{2}, ¶gɷɪn^{2}, goɷ^{2} (n.d.g.)] 5 gɷ:‿t sku:l [◇gɷ:^{1,2,3}, ¶gɷɪn^{2}] 6 gɷ: tə sku:l [◇gɷ:$^{1(2x),2(2x)}$, gɷ:^{1} *3 pr.pl.*, ¶gɷ:ɪn^{2} III.8.10, ¶gɷ:ɪn$^{1(5x),2(2x)}$, gɷ:^{1} (n.d.g.); gɷ‿n^{1} *go (2 pr.pl.) in*; skü:l^{1}, skɛɷl^{2}; sku:lgafə^{1} *s.-gaffer*] 7 gɷ tə sku:l [¶əgɷɪn^{3}, goɷ^{1} (n.d.g.)] 8 goɷ tə sku:l [◇goɷ$^{1,2(2x)}$, ×goɷz^{1}, ×gɷz^{1}, ¶goɷɪn^{1}, goɷ^{1,2} (n.d.g.)] 9 gɷ‿t skɪɷl [◇gɷ^{2}, ◇gɷ:$^{1,2(2x)}$, ◇gə^{2}, ×gɷ:^{1}, ×gɷz^{3}, gɷ^{3} *3 pr.pl.*, ¶gɷ:ɪn^{1,2}, ¶əgɷ:ɪn^{1}, gɷ:$^{1(3x)}$ (n.d.g.), gɷ:ɪn^{1} (n.d.g.), gɷ·ɪn^{1} *vbl. n.*; skɪɷl] 10 gɛɷ tə skü:l [◇gɷ·^{5}, ◇gə^{5}, ◇goɷ^{4}, gə (n.d.g.)] 11 goɷ tə sku:l [◇gə^{2}, ¶gɷɪn$^{2(2x)}$, ¶gǫɷɪn^{2}]

15 He 1 go: tə sku:ɫ [◇go:ɷ$^{2(2x)}$, ¶gwɛɪn^{1}] 2 gɷ tə sku:ɫ [◇go:$^{3(2x)}$, ¶gwæɪn^{2}, ¶əgwɛɪn^{2}] 3 gɷ tə sku:l [◇gu:$^{1(2x),3}$, go:^{2} *3 pr.pl.*, ¶əgwæɪn^{1}, ¶gu:ɪn^{3}, ¶gwɪn^{1}, ¶gwɒn^{2}, ¶gwæɪn$^{2,3(2x)}$; sku:l^{3} (n.d.g.); sku:lgˈæfəʳ^{1} *s.-gaffer*] 4 gɷ təʳ sku:ɫ [¶gwæɪn^{1} III.8.9, ¶~^{3}, ¶əgu:ɪn^{3}] 5 gɷ tə sku:ᵊɫ [◇go:^{3}, ˣgəz^{3} IX.2.3, ¶gwæɪn^{1}; sku:ɫ^{1} (n.d.g.)] 6 go: tə sku:əɫ [¶gwɒɪn^{1}; sku:əɫ] 7 goɷ tə skuɷl [◇goɷ$^{3(2x)}$, ˣgɷz^{1}, ˣ~^{4} IX.2.3, ˣgoɷz$^{1(2x),3,4}$, ˣgo:z$^{3(2x)}$, ~^{3} *2 pr.pl.*, ~^{1} *3 pr.pl.*, ¶goɷɪn$^{2(2x)}$, ¶gəɪn$^{1(5x),2,4}$, ¶gɷn^{3}, go:z^{3} (n.d.g.); sku:l$^{4(2x)}$; sku:lbɒs^{3} *s.-boss*]

16 Wo 1 gɷ tə skᶷu:l [¶əgu:ɪn$^{2,3(2x)}$] 2 gɷ tə sku:l [◇gu:^{2}, ¶goɷɪn$^{1(2x),2}$, ¶əgwɛɪn^{2}] 3 gɷ tə skɪu:ᵊɫ [◇gu:$^{2(2x)}$, ◇goɷ^{3}, ¶əgwɪn^{1}; sku:ɫma:stəʳ^{2} *s.-master*] 4 gɷ tə sku:ᵊɫ [◇gu:$^{1,2(3x),3(2x)}$, ¶əgu:ɪn^{2}, ¶gwɛn^{3}, ¶əgwɛn^{1}] 5 gɷ tə sku:ɫ [◇gu:^{1}, ¶əgwaɪn$^{1(2x)}$; skɷɫ^{1}] 6 gɷ tə sku:ɫ [◇gu:$^{2(2x),3}$, ¶gu:ɪn^{3}, ¶əgwɪn^{2}] 7 gɷ: tə sku:l [◇gɷ:^{3}, ◇gɷ·^{3}, ˣgɷz$^{3(2x),4}$, goɷz^{1} *2 pr.s.*, gɷz^{3} *1 pr.pl.*, ¶gɷɪn^{1}, ¶gɷn^{3}, ¶əgɷɪn$^{1(2x)}$, ¶əgɷ·ɪn^{3}; sku:l^{3}; skɷltʃɪldɹən^{4} *s.-children*]

17 Wa 1 gǫɷ tə sku:l [◇goɷ^{1}, ˣgǫɷz^{1}; sku:ᵊɫ^{2}] 2 gə tə sku:l [◇goɷ^{1}, ◇gɷ^{2,4}, ◇gɷ:^{4}, ˣgɷz^{1,2}, gɷ$^{1(2x)2,4}$ *3 pr.pl.*, ¶gɷɪn$^{1(2x),3(3x),4(2x)}$, ¶gɷ·ɪn^{1,4}, ¶əgɷɪn$^{4(4x)}$, ¶əgɷ·ɪn^{4}, gɷ:^{2} (n.d.g.); sku:l^{1}] 3 gɷ tə sku:ᵊɫ [¶gǫɷɪn^{1}, ¶əgǫɷɪn^{1}, ¶goɪn^{2}] 4 gɷ tə skü:ᵊɫ [◇goɷ^{1,2}, ¶goɷɪn^{1}] 5 gɷ tə sku:ɫ [◇gu:^{1}, ˣgɷz$^{1(2x)}$, ¶əgɷn$^{1(2x)}$] 6 gɷ tə skü:ɫ [ˣgɷz^{2}] 7 gü: tə skü·əɫ [¶gü:ɪn^{1}, ¶gu:ɪn$^{2(2x)}$]

23 Mon 1 gɷ tə skᶷu:ɫ [◇go:ɷ^{1}, ◇go:ᶷ^{4}; skᶷu:ᵊl^{2}] 2 gɷ tə sku:ɫ [ˣgəz^{3}, ¶gwɷn^{3}] 3 go: tə sku:ɫ [◇go:^{1}, ◇gə^{2}] 4 go· tʰῷ skʰu:ḷ [◇gǫ:^{1}, ◇go:^{3}, ¶go:-ɪn^{1,2}, ¶go·-ɪn^{1,2}, go·^{1} (n.d.g.)] 5 go: tə sku:ɫ [◇go:^{2}, ◇go^{2}, ◇gou^{2} (n.d.g.) II.9.16] 6 go: tə sku:ᵊɫ [◇go:^{1}, go:z^{1} *1 pr.pl.*] 7 n.a.

24 Gl 1 gɷ tə sku:ᵊɫ [◇go:ɷ$^{3(2x)}$, ◇gæɷ^{2}, ¶əgwæɪn^{1}; sku:ᵊɫ$^{1(3x)}$] 2 ga: tə sku:ᵊɫ [gɷz^{3} *1 pr.s.*, ¶gæɷɪn^{3}] 3 gɷ tə skᶷu:ᵊɫ [◇gɒɷ^{4}, ˣgo:ɷz^{3}, ¶gɒɷɪn^{1}, ¶əgɒɷɪn^{3}, ¶gwæɪn^{4}] 4 go:ɷ tə skᶷu:ɫ [◇go:ɷ^{2}] 5 go: tə sku:ᵊl 6 gɷ tə sku:ᵊɫ 7 gɷ tə sku:ᵊɫ [◇go:^{1}, ◇gᶷu:^{1}, ¶gwæ̨ɪn^{1}]

25 O 1 go: tə sku·ᵊɫ [◇gɷ^{1}, ¶gɷn^{2}, ¶əgo:ɪn^{2}, ¶əgo·ɪn^{1}] 2 gɷ tə sku:ɫ [◇gəɷ^{1}, ◇gɷ·^{1}, gɷ^{1} *1 pr.s.*, ¶gɷn$^{1(2x)}$, ¶gɷɪn^{3}, ¶əgɷɪn^{2}, ¶gwe:n^{2}] 3 gǫɷ tə skᶷu:ɫ [◇gɷ^{2}, ¶gwe:n$^{1(3x)}$] 4 go: tə sku: [◇go:$^{1(2x)}$, ◇goɷ^{2}, go:z^{1} *2 pr.pl.*, go:^{1} *2 pr.pl.*, go:$^{1(2x),4}$ *3 pr.pl.*, ¶gəɪn^{1}, ¶go·ɪn^{1,3}, ¶gɷn^{3}, ¶gən^{2}; sku·ɷ^{5}] 5 go: tə skɷᵊɫ [◇gə̨ɷ^{2}, ◇gɷ^{2}, ¶go:ɪn^{2}, ¶goɪn^{2}] 6 goɷ tə sku:ɫ [¶goɷɪn^{1}]

VIII.6.2 BEGINS. FINISHES

Q. There are two times in the day that every schoolboy knows. One is about 9 in the morning, when school . . . . , and the other is about 4 o'clock when school . . . .

Rr. BEGINS, GINS, GOES IN, OPENS, STARTS
CLOSES, COMES OUT, ENDS, FINISHES, GIVES OVER, KNOCKS OFF, LEAVES, SHUTS (UP)

Note 1—The rr. to the two parts of the q. are separated below by a full stop.

Note 2—The inflected 3 pr.s. forms in the above lists subsume the corresponding uninflected 3 pr.s. forms and periphrastic DO.

Note 3—I.m. exs. of BEGIN and FINISH and their parts are reproduced below between square brackets untransliterated. Expressions comparable with some of those listed above also occur at VII.5.9.

Note 4—For BEGAN, see VII.6.23; for GO, see VIII.6.1 (and refs.); OPEN *adj.* occurs at IX.2.7, and START at V.8.13. For COME, see IX.3.4 (and refs.); for FINISHED, see V.7.21; and for SHUT, see IX.2.8.

7 Ch 1 bɪgɪnz. fɪnɪʃɪz 2 sta:ts [bɪgɪn^{1} *3 pr.pl.*]. gɪvz ọɷə [fɪnɪʃ^{1} *2 pr.pl.*] 3 ɒpnz. tlọ:zɪz 4 ọ:pnz. ʃɷts 5 ụ:pnz. ʃɷts, lɛɪvz 6 o:pənz. tlo:zɪz

8 Db 1 staʴ̠:ts. ʃɷts ɷp 2 gɷz ɪn. fɪnɪʃəz 3 o:pns. kɷmz ẹ:t 4 ɒpnz. kɷmz ɛ:t 5 sta:ts. fɪnɪʃɪz 6 ɒpnz. tlü:zəz 7 o·ɷpnz. ʃɷts

11 Sa 1 bɪgɪnz. fɪnɪʃəz 2 sta:ts. fɪnɪʃəz 3 o:pnz. klo:zɪz 4 staʳ:ʈʂ. fɪnɪʃɪz 5 o:pnz. klo:zɪz [fɪnɪʃt^{3} *p.p.*] 6 staʳ:ʈʂ. fɪnɪʃəz 7–8 bɪgɪnz. fɪnɪʃɪz 9 bɪgɪnz. fɪnɪʃəz 10 go:z ɪn, staɽ:ʈʂ. ɛnz 11 bɪgɪnz. fɪnɪʃəz

12 St 1 sta:ts. kloɷzɪz 2 sta:ts. fɪnɪʃɪz 3 sta:ts. kloɷzɪz 4 bɪgɪnz. fɪnɪʃɪz 5 oɷpnz, sta:ts. kloɷzɪz 6 oɷpnz [bɪgɷn^{2} *2 p.t. pl.*]. kloɷzɪz [fɪnɪʃt^{1} *p.p.*] 7 oɷpənz. kloɷzɪz, fɪnɪʃɪz 8 bɪgɪnz. li:vz [fɪnɪʃ^{1} *1 pr.pl.*] 9 sta:ts. kloɷzɪz 10–11 bɪgɪnz. fɪnɪʃɪz

15 He 1 o:pnz. klo:zəz 2 o:pnz. klo:zɪz 3 bɪgɪnz. nɒks ɑ:f 4 bɪgɪnz. klo:zɪz 5 staʳ:ʈʂ. fɪnɪʃɪz 6 bɪgɪnz. fɪnɪʃ, ○~ *3 pr.s.* 7 bɪgɪnz, staɹts. fɪnɪʃɪz

16 Wo 1 bɪgɪnz. klɒɷzɪz 2 sta:ts. fɪnɪʃɪz 3 bɪgɪnz. fɪnɪʃɪz 4 o:pnz [bɪgɪnz^{3} *3 pr.pl.*]. klo:zɪz 5 stəʳ:ʈʂ. fɪnɪʃɪz 6 stəʳ:ʈʂ. fɪnɪʃəz 7 bɪgɪnz [bɪgɪnz^{3} *3 pr.s.* VII.6.5, ~^{4} *3 pr.pl.*, gɪn (be)*gin inf.*]. kɷmz æɷt [fɪnɪʃ (n.d.g.)]

17 Wa 1 bɪgɪnz. fɪnɪʃɪz [fɪnɪʃ^{1} *f. n.*] 2 bɪgɪnz. ɛnz 3 sta:ts. fɪnɪʃɪz 4 oɷpnz. tloɷzɪz 5 bɪgɪnz. ɛnz 6 stæ:ts. fɪnɪʃɪz 7 bɪgɪns [¶bɪgɪnɪn^{2}]. li:vz

23 Mon 1 staʳ:ʈʂ. fɪnɪʃ [fɪnɪʃ *3 pr.s.*, fɪnɪʃt^{3} *p.p.*] 2 bɪgɪnz. klo:zəz 3 sta:ts. də fɪnɪʃ 4 n.a. 5 bigɪnz. fɪnɪʃɪz 6 bɪgɪnz. fɪnɪʃəz 7 n.a.

24 Gl 1 o:pnz. klo:ɷzɩz 2 sta:ts. kɷmz əɷ:t 3 sta^{r}:ʈʂ. vɩnɩʃɩz 4 bɩgɩnz. fɩnɩʃɩz 5 o:pnz. kɷmz ʌɷt 6 dɷ o:pn. dɷ ʃət 7 go:z ɩn. kəmz ^{ɷ}u:t‘

25 O 1 bɩgɩnz. fɩnɩʃɩz 2 sta^{ɹ}:ts. fɩnɩʃɩz 3 sta^{r}ʈʂ. li:vz 4 stɑɽʈʂ, $^{\circ}$gɩnz^{1} [bɩgɩn^{1} *inf.*]. p. kɷmz aɷt 5 bɩgɩnz. fɩnɩʃɩz 6 bɩgɩnz. li:vz

VIII.6.3 A‡ HOLIDAY*

Q. On election day the school is often used for polling, and the children get . . . .

Rr. A §DAY'S HOLIDAY (A/AN) HOLIDAY,

Note 1—I.m. exs. of the indef. art. prec. orthographic *h*- are reproduced below in their full context between square brackets for their morphological interest; cross-references are given only when the whole phrase is included in some other article and is not covered by the list of cross-references in Note 3 (below).

Note 2—An attached superior × indicates that the r. was immediately prec. by a V., and an attached superior + that the f.w. stated that no article was used.

Note 3—For additional exs. of the indef. art. prec. orthographic *h*-, see VI.1.6 and VI.2.2.

7 Ch 1 ɒlədẹ: 2 ə ɔləde: [ə ɔltəɾ^{1} *a halter*; ə ɔg$^{1(2x)}$ *a hog*; ə ɔ:s^{1} *a horse*; ə ɜ:^{ɹ}n^{2} *a heron*; ə ɔlɩ tɹi:^{2} *a holly tree*] 3 ə ɒlɩdɩ 4 $^{+}$ɒləd^{ɫ}ɩ· [ə ɒz^{1} *a horse*] 5 ən ɒlədi: 6 ɒlɩde:, $^{\circ\times}$~

8 Db 1 ə ɒlədɩ 2 $^{\times}$ɒlədɩ [ə ɒst^{4} *a hoast* (=*cough*)] 3 ə ɒlədɩ 4 $^{\times}$ɒlədɩ [ə atʃ^{1} *a hatch* (of chickens)] 5 ə ɒlədɩ, $^{\circ}$~ [ə ɛə^{1} *a hare*] 6–7 $^{\times}$ə ɒlədɩ

11 Sa 1 $^{+}$ɒlɩdɩ 2 $^{\times}$ɒlɩdɩ 3 ə ɒlɩde: 4 ə ɒlɩdɩ 5 ɒlɩdɩ 6 ɒlɩdɩ [ə ɔ^{r}:ʂ^{1} *a horse*; ə ʌk^{3} *a hook*] 7 ɒlɩde: 8 ɒlɩdɩ [ə ɷndə^{r}:ʈ^{2} *a hundred*] 9 ɒlɩde· 10 ə ɒlɩdɩ 11 ɒlɩdɩ

12 St 1 ɒlɩdɩ 2 ɒlɩdi· [ə at^{2} *a hat*] 3 ɒlɩdɩ [ɒlɩdɩ^{1}] 4 ɒlɩdɩ, $^{\circ}$~ [ə at^{2} *a hat*; ə ɔ:s^{2} *a horse*] 5 ɒlɩdɩ [ə ü:k^{2} *a hook*] 6 $^{+}$ɒlɩdɩ, $^{\circ}$~^{1} 7 $^{+}$ɒlɩdɩ 8 $^{+}$ɒlɩdɩ, $^{\circ}$~^{1} [lɛɩ ən ɛdʒ^{1} *lay a*(*n*) *hedge*; əv ən ɛdʒɹoɷ^{1} *of a*(*n*) *hedgerow*; ə atʃ əv tʃɩkɩnz^{4} *a hatch of chickens*] 9 ɒlɩdɩ 10 ə ɒlɩdɩ 11 ɒlɩdɛɩ

15 He 1 ɒlɩdɩ [ə o:^{1} *a hoe*; ə ɒgpɩg^{1} *a hog-pig*] 2 ɒlɩdɩ [ə ɛdʒ$^{1(2x)}$ *a hedge*; o:n ə ɛdʒ^{2} *horn* (i.e. trim) *a hedge*; ə a:^{1} *a hoe*] 3 ɒlɩdɩ 4 ɒlɩdi: [ə ɷsək^{2} *a hussock* (=*cough*)] 5 ɒɫɩde:ɩ [ə ɛp^{1} *a heap*] 6 ɒɫɩde: [$^{\square}$ɒɫɩde:z^{1}] 7 ə ɒlɩdɩ [ə əɹd^{1} *a herd*; ə ɔ̣ɹs^{1} *a horse*; ə ɛdeɩk^{3} *a headache*; dạft əz ə eɩpəθ ə so:p^{4} *daft as a halfpennyworth of soap* VIII.9.4; ə eɩpəθ ə swi:ts^{4} *a halfpennyworth of sweets*; ə anfɷɫ^{4} *a handful*; ə aɷəɹ^{4} *a*(n) *hour*]

16 Wo 1–2 ɒlɪdɪ 3 ə §deːɪz ɒlɪdɪ 4 ɒlɪdɪ [ə ætʃ[2] *a hatch* (of chickens); ə ɑ˞ːɳ[2] *a horn*] 5–6 ɒlɪdɪ 7 ×ɒlɪdɪ [ə ɷndəd jəːz[3] *a hundred years*; ə atʃ[4] a *hatch* (of chickens); ɛðəɹɪn ə ɛdʒ[4] *eddering a hedge*; mɛnɪ ə ɷndəd[4] *many a hundred*; ɪn ə ɷtʃ[4] *in a hutch*; əstɪd əv ə ɛdʒ[4] *instead of a hedge*]

17 Wa 1 ×ɒlədeɪ 2 ə ɔlədɪ [ən ɔːn[1(2x)] *a*(*n*) *heron*; ə ɔːdl[1] *a hurdle*] 3 ×ɒləd'ï 4 +ɒlədɪ 5 ×ɒlədɪ [ɪt‿s ə a˞ːɖ wɪntə˞[1] *it's a hard winter*] 6–7 ×ɒlədɪ

23 Mon 1 ɒɫɪdæɪ [ə ætʃ[1] *a hatch* (of chickens)] 2 ɒɫɪdeː [ə ʌɷə˞[3] *a*(n) *hour*] 3 ɒɫɪdɪ [ə əɷə[1] *a*(n) *hour*] 4 ə ɒ̤·lɪdei 5 ʔɒ̤·lɪdei [ən hɪl[2] *a*(*n*) *hill*; ən əu-ə[2], ən əu-əɹ[1] *an hour*] 6 ɒɫɪdeː [ə əɷə˞[1] *a*(n) *hour*] 7 n.a. [ən əu-ə[1] *an hour*]

24 Gl 1 ɒɫɪdeː 2 ɒɫɪdɪ [ə ɛɫ əv ə ɹætɷɫ[2] *a hell of a rattle*] 3–4 ɒɫɪdɪ 5 +ɑlɪdeː 6 ə ɒlədeː [ə jə˞[1] *a hare*] 7 ə ɒlədeː

25 O 1 ɒlɪdæɪ 2 ɒlədɪ, ×ɒlədɪ 3 ə ɒlɪdeː 4 ə ɒɫədeɪ, °ən ɒɫədeɪ[4] [gɪv ɪm ə ɔɪdɪn[1] *give him a hiding*; ɪn ə əɽɖ[1] *in a herd*; ə ɒg[1] *a hog*; wɪð ə oɷ[1] *with a hoe*; ə eːpəθ ə ɫɒɫɪz[4] *a halfpennyworth of lollies*; ən æ̨ɷəɽ[4] *an hour*; gɪ ðɪ ə ӓnd[4] *give thee a hand* IX.9.5] 5 ə ɒlɪdeː 6 ɒlədeɪ, ×~ [oɷvə˞ ən ɛ̈ɷə˞[3] *over an hour*]

VIII.6.4 PLAY

Q. In their holidays some children like to work, but most like to . . . .

Rr. PLAY (ABOUT), PLAY THEM

Note 1—The refl. use of THEM at 8.6/7 is striking.
Note 2—PLAY also occurs at III.2.10.

7 Ch 1 pleː 2 s.w. pleː 3 pliː, °~[2,3] 4 plẹː 5 pliː 6 pleː

8 Db 1 pleː 2 pleː [pleː[4] *p. n.*] 3 pleː' 4 pliː, °~[2] [n.d.g.], °¶pliː-ɪn[2] 5 pleː' 6 pleː' əm 7 pliːn ɷm, °¶pliːɪn əm

11 Sa 1–4 pleː 5 plẹː 6–7 pleː 8 pleː, °~[2] 9–11 pleː

12 St 1 plɛɪ 2–3 pliː 4 plɛɪ 5 pleː 6–8 plɛɪ 9 pliː 10 plɛɪ 11 plɛi

15 He 1 pleːɪ 2 plæɪ 3 plɛɪ 4 plæɪ 5 pleːɪ 6 pɫɒɪ, °plɒɪ[1] 7 pleː əbaɷt, °¶pleɪ-ɪn[4]

16 Wo 1 plɛɪ 2 pleː' 3 pleːɪ 4–5 plaɪ 6 plæɪ 7 s.w. pleɪ-ɪn

17 Wa 1 plẹɪ 2 s.w. plẹɪ-ɪn 3 plæɪ 4 plẹɪ 5–7 plɛɪ

23 Mon 1 pleː' 2–3 pleː 4 n.a. 5 plei 6 pɫeː 7 n.a.

24 Gl 1 plæɪ əbəɷ:ᵊt 2–3 plæɪ 4 pɫɛɪ 5–6 plæɪ 7 plæ̣ɪ

25 O 1 plæɪ 2 plɛɪ, °plɛɪd² *3 p.t.s.* 3 ple: 4 pɫe: 5 ple:ˑ 6 pleɪ

VIII.6.5 TEACHER

Q. At school, the class is taken by the ....

Rr. SCHOOL–BOSS, TEACHER

Note—For SCHOOL, see VIII.6.1.

7 Ch tḭ:tʃə 2 te:tʃə 3 tɛɪtʃə 4 tẹ:tʃə 5 tɛɪtʃə⁽²ˣ⁾ 6 te:tʃəᶦ

8 Db 1 ti:tʃə 2–4 tɛɪtʃə 5 ti:tʃə 6 tɛɪtʃə 7 ti:tʃə

11 Sa 1–3 ti:tʃəʳ 4 tɪ:tʃəʳ 5 tẹ:tʃəʳ, °skɪu:lbɒs ["boys' name for a teacher"] 6 ti:tʃə·ʳ 7–9 ti:tʃəʳ 10 te:tʃəʳ 11 ti:tʃəʳ

12 St 1 ti:tʃə 2 tɛɪtʃə 3–10 ti:tʃə 11 ti:tʃəɹ

15 He 1–6 ti:tʃəʳ 7 ti:tʃəɹ

16 Wo 1 ti:tʃə 2–5 ti:tʃəʳ 6 □ti:tʃəʳz̨ 7 ti:tʃəʳ, s.f. tɛɪtʃəʳ

17 Wa 1 ti:tʃə 2 ti:tʃə, s.f. tɛɪtʃə ["older"] 3–4 ti:tʃə 5 ti:tʃəʳ 6 ti:tʃəʳ, °∼⁴ 7 ti:tʃəʳ

23 Mon 1 tɪi:tʃəʳ 2 ti:tʃəʳ 3 ti:tʃə 4 n.a. 5 ti:tʃɐ 6 ti:tʃəʳ 7 n.a.

24 Gl 1 ti:tʃəʳ 2 tɪi:tʃəʳ 3 te:ˑtʃəʳ 4–6 te:tʃəʳ 7 ti:tʃəʳ

25 O 1 te:tʃəʳ 2 te·ˑtʃəᶦ 3 te:tʃəʳ 4 ti:tʃəɽ 5–6 ti:tʃəʳ

VIII.6.6 WRITING*‡

Q. If, as a boy, you wrote badly, you could say: I used to be bad at ....

R. WRITING

Note—I.m. exs. of WRITE *v.* and its parts other than the vbl.n. are reproduced below between square brackets untransliterated.

7 Ch 1 ɹɑɪtɪn 2 ɹæɪtɪn 3–5 ɹɑɪtɪn 6 ɹaɪtɪn

8 Db 1 ɹaɪtɪn 2 ɹɑɪtɪn 3 ɹaɪtɪn 4–6 ɹɑɪtɪn 7 ɹɑ̃·ĩtɪn

11 Sa 1 ɹɛɪtɪn 2–4 ɹaɪtɪn 5–6 ɹɛɪtɪn 7 ɹaɪtɪn 8 ɹɒɪtɪn 9–11 ɹaɪtɪn

12 St 1 ɹɒɪtɪŋ 2 ɹɒɪtɪn 3 ɹɒ:ɪtɪn 4 ɹɒɪtɪŋ [ɹoɷt[2] *p.p.*] 5 ɹɒ:ɪtɪŋg [ɹɒ:ɪt[1] *inf.*] 6 ɹɒ:ɪtɪn 7 ɹɒɪtɪn 8 ɹɒɪtɪŋg 9 ɹɒɪtɪn 10 ɹa:ɪtɪn 11 ɹɒɪtɪŋg

15 He 1 ɹæɪtɪn 2 ɹəɪtɪn, °ɹæɪtɪn[3] 3–6 ɹəɪtɪn 7 ɹæ̆ɪtɪn [ɹaɪt[3] *inf.*]

16 Wo 1 ɹɒɪtɪŋg 2 ɹəɪtɪn 3 ɹəi:tɪn 4–5 ɹəɪtɪn 6 ɹɒɪtɪn 7 s.w. ɹəɪtɪn [¶ɹəɪtɪn[3]; ɹəɪt[1,3] *inf.*]

17 Wa 1 ɹɑ̣ɪtɪn 2 ɹəɪtɪn [ɹəɪt[4] *inf.*] 3 ɹəɪtɪn 4 ɹəɪtɪ̣n 5 ɹʌɪtɪn 6–7 ɹəɪtɪn

23 Mon 1–2 ɹəɪtɪn 3 ɹəɪtɪn, °~[1] [n.d.g.] 4 ɹəittʰɪn 5 ɹəitɪn 6 ɹəɪtɪn 7 n.a.

24 Gl 1 ɹəɪᵊtɪn 2 ɹəɪtɪn 3 ɹəɪtɪn [ɹəɪt *inf.*] 4 ɹəɪtən 5 ɹə̈ɪtɪn 6–7 ɹʌɪtɪn

25 O 1–2 ɹə̈ɪtɪn 3 ɹʌʏtɪn 4 ɽəɪtɪn [ɽɑɪt[4] *v.*; ɽɔ:t[3] *p.p.*] 5–6 ɹə̈ɪʔɪn

VIII.7.1 SLIDE

Q. When children find the footpaths or the playground covered with ice, they will at once begin to . . . .

Rr. GLIRRY, SLARE, SLIDE ABOUT, SLITHER, SLUR (ABOUT)

Note—For exs. of (–)SLIDE, meaning *plough-sole*, see I.8.9, and meaning *drag*, see I.11.3.

7 Ch 1 sləˢ:, °slə:[2] 2 slə·ɹ əbæɷt, °slə:[2] *3 pr.pl.* 3 slɑɪd 4–5 sla: 6 slɛ:

8 Db 1 slaɪd 2 slə: 3 slaɪd 4 sləˢ: 5–6 slɑɪd 7 slə: [slə: *slur n.*]

11 Sa 1–2 slɪðəʵ 4 slɛɪd 5–7 slɪðəʵ 8 slɪðəʵ, °slɒɪd[1] 9 slɪðəʵ 10 slɪðəʵ, °slaɪdəd[1] *p.t.* 11 slɪðəʵ

12 St 1 slɒɪd 2 slə:, °~ 3 slɒɪd, slɪðə 4 slɒɪd 5–6 slɒ:ɪd 7 slɪðə 8–9 slɒɪd 10 slɑ̣ɪd 11 sla̱:ɪd

15 He 1 slæɪᵊd 2 sləɪd 3 sɫɛðəʵ 4 slɪðəʵ 5 sləɪd 6 sɫɪðəʵ 7 slaɪd, °slɪðəɹ [slaɪd *slide n.*]

16 Wo 1 slɛðə 2 slɪðəʵ 3 slɛðəʵ, °əslɛðəʵɽɪn[1] [sləi:d[1] *slide* I.9.1] 4–6 slɛðəʵ 7 sləɪdɪn [+ «ən slɪðəɹɪn əbæɷt» *and slithering about*]

17 Wa 1 slɒɪd 2 sləɪd, °¶sləɪdɪn[1] 3–7 sləɪd

23 Mon 1 slɪðəʵ 2–3 sləɪd 4 n.a. 5 sləɪ̣d 6 sɫəɪd 7 n.a.

24 Gl 1 sləɪᵊd 2–3 sləɪd 4 sɫəɪᵊd 5 slə̈ɪd 6–7 slʌɪd

25 O 1 slöɪd, gləʈɪ ["older"] 2 slöɪd 3 slʌʏd 4 słɔɪd 5 slʌʏd 6 slöɪd

VIII.7.2 SEESAW

Q. Children also like to play on a [i.] . . . .

Rr. ? HAYLY-GAYLY, HAYTY-BAYTY, QUEAGLE, SEESAW (-PLANK), SHIGGLY, TWEEDLE, TWEEZLE

7 Ch 1 sẹ:sɔ: 2–5 si:sɔ: 6 sẹ:sɔ:

8 Db 1 si:ssɔ: 2 sˡi:sɔ: 3 kwi:gl [¶əkwi:glɪn *queagling*] 4 sɛɪsɔ: 5 twi:dl 6 si:sɔ 7 twi:dl

11 Sa 1 e:dɪbe:dɪ 2–3 si:sɔ: 4 si:sɔʵ: [sˡi:sɔʵ:[1] *s.* (=*sawing-horse*) I.7.16] 5 sˡi:sɔ: 6 e:lɪge:lɪ 7–11 si:sɔ:

12 St 1 twi:zl 2 si:soɷ, °~ 3 twi:dl 4–5 kwi:gl 6–9 si:sɔ: 10 sisɔ: 11 si:sɔ:

15 He 1–2 si:sɔ: 3–5 si:sɑ: 6 si:sɒ 7 si:sɔ:

16 Wo 1 si:sɑ:plaŋk 2 si:sɔ: 3–6 si:sɑ: 7 si:sɔ:

17 Wa 1–7 si:sɔ:

23 Mon 1 sˡi:sɑ: 2–3 si:sɑ: 4 n.a. 5 ʃɪgłɪ 6 si:sɑ: 7 n.a.

24 Gl 1 si:zɑ: 2 si:sɑ: 3–4 zˡi:zɑ: 5 si:sɔ: 6 zi:zɔ: 7 si:sɔ:

25 O 1 si:sɔ: 2 si:sa: 3–4 si:sɔ: 5 sɪu:sɔ: 6 si:sɔ:

VIII.7.3 BOUNCE

Q. A rubber ball that's punctured won't [i.] . . . .

Rr. BOUNCE, DAP, PLAY, TAMP

7 Ch 1 baɷns 2 bæˡns 3 baɪns 4 baɷns 5 baɪns(2x) 6 bɛ̨ɷns

8 Db 1 bɛ̨ɷnts 2 baɷns 3 bɛɷnts 4 bɛ:nts 5–6 bɛ̨:ns 7 bɛ:ns

11 Sa 1 bɷu·ns 2 bæɷns 3 baɷns 4 bɛɷns 5 bɛɷnts, °~ 6–7 baɷns 8 bɛɷns 9 bəu:ns 10–11 baɷns

12 St 1 baɷns 2 baɪns 3 baɪns, °~ 4 plɛɪ [i. insists] 5 baɷns [baɷnsɪn[2] *bouncing adj.*] 6 bæɷns 7 baɷns 8 bæɷns 9 ba:ns 10 bæɷns 11 baɷns

15 He 1–2 bæɷns 3 bəɷnts 4 bə̀ɷns 5 bəɷnts 6 dæp 7 bə̆ʊ̨ns

16 Wo 1–2 bɛɷns 3 bɛu:ns 4 bəɷns 5 bəɷ:ns 6 bɛu:nts 7 bæɷns

17 Wa 1 bæ̩ɷns 2 bæɷns 3 bɛɷns 4 bɛɷnts 5–6 bɛɷns 7 bɛɷnts

23 Mon 1 bʌɷnts, dæp ["older"] 2 tæmp 3 dæp, °dæpt² *3 p.t.s.* 4 tʰamphʰ
5 dap, tamp 6 da:p 7 n.a.

24 Gl 1–2 bəɷns 3 dæp 4 dap 5 bʌɷns 6 dap 7 dap'

25 O 1 bɛɷns 2 bæ̨ɷnts 3 bɛɷnts 4 bæɷns 5 bɛɷns 6 bɛɷnts

VIII.7.4 CLIMB

Q. If a boy wanted to get to the top of a tree, he'd have to . . . . it.

Rr. CLAMBER, CLIMB/SWARM (UP), CLIMB TO, SCRAWL UP

7 Ch 1 klaɩm 2 swa:m ɷp, p. klaɩm 3–5 tlaɩm 6 tlaɩm

8 Db 1 tlaɩm 2 tlaɩm 3 tlaɩm 4 tlaɩm, swa:m [klaɩmɩnstɛɩl¹ *climbing-stile* IV.2.9] 5 tlaɩm 6 klãĩm 7 tlã:m [tlaɩmstãĩl¹ *c.-stile* IV.2.8]

11 Sa 1–2 klaɩm 3 klɛɩm 4 klaɩm 5–6 klɛɩm 7 klɩm, °swɔʳ:m 8 klɒɩm
9–10 klaɩm 11 klɛɩm

12 St 1 klaɩm 2 klɒɩm ɷp 3 klɒ:ɩm 4 klɒɩm 5–6 klɒ:ɩm 7–9 klɒɩm
10 klɔ̣ɩm 11 klaɩm

15 He 1 klæɩm 2 kləɩm ʌp 3 kləɩᵊm 4 kləɩm tu: 5 kləɩm 6 kɫəɩm
7 klæ̆ɩm, °swɔɹm [when the tree has no branches]

16 Wo 1 klɒɩm 2 kləɩᵊm 3 kləi:m ɷp 4–5 kləɩm 6 klɒɩm 7 ¶kləɩmɩn

17 Wa 1 klɒɩm 2–3 kləɩm 4 tlɒmbə, °~¹, °tlɒmbəɹ¹ [+ V.] 5–7 kləɩm

23 Mon 1–2 kləɩm 3 kɫəɩm ʌp, skɹa:ɫ ʌp 4 n.a. 5 kləim ʌ̤̆p [kləimɩn² *climbing vbl. n.*] 6 kɫəɩm 7 n.a.

24 Gl 1 kləɩᵊm 2–3 kləɩm 4 kɫəɩm 5 tlə̈ɩm 6 klʌɩm ʌp 7 klʌɩm

25 O 1–3 klə̈ɩm 4 kɫə̨ɩm 5 klʌʏm 6 klə̈ɩm

VIII.7.5 STEAL*. BURGLARS STEAL† THEM STOLE†. STOLEN†

Q. What do burglars do? They break into houses and . . . .

So you can say: We ordinary people buy the things we need, but . . . .

Convert for p.t. and p.p.

At 7.2, 15.7, 16.7, 17.2 and 25.4, the f.w. (viz. P. W.) used Version 4 of the Qr., in which the q. read: *What do naughty boys often do when they pass an orchard of ripe apples?* To this the required r. was simply STEAL (not BURGLARS STEAL THEM as above). If the obj. THEM happened to be rec. it has been reproduced below. Note further that at the locs. under consideration, only three, not four, rr. were rec.

Rr. 3 pr.pl.: PINCH, STEAL~STEALEN~STEALS

BURGLARS STEAL(S) THEM, BURGLARS PINCH/STEAL §IT, BURGLARS PINCH/STEAL §IT, BURGLARS PINCH/THIEVEN THEM, §OTHERS/THEY STEAL THEM,

3 p.t.pl.: STEALED, STOLE

p.p.: STEALED, STOLE(N)

Note 1—The rr. to the four parts of the q. are separated below by full stops.

Note 2—In the r. to the 2nd part of the q., the f.w. omitted the subj. BURGLARS at 7.5, 23.5, 24.6 and 25.3; rec. the obj. IT, not THEM, at 17.4; and omitted the obj. at 23.1/5, 23.5, 24.6 and 25.3.

Note 3—Periphrastic DO STEAL at 23.3 is subsumed under STEAL in the list of rr. above.

Note 4—For additional exs. of vv. ending in –N/S with a pl. noun as subj., see III.10.7 and V.7.21.

7 Ch 1 stḭ:ɫ . bə:gləz stḭ:l ɷm . stọ:l . stọ:lən 2 pɩnʃ əm, sti:lɩn, s.f. ste:lɩn [pref.], ○¶~⁴ . stɛ̈ɷl . stɛ̈ɷl 3 sti:l . bəɹ:gɫəz sti:l əm . stɛ̈ɷl . stọ:lən 4 stᵊɩəɫ . n.r. stọ:l . stọ:lən 5 stɛɩl . stɛɩl əm . sto:l, stɛɷl . stɛɷlən 6 ste:ᵊl . n.r. sto:l . sto:lən

8 Db 1 sti:l . bəɹ̠:gləz sti:l ɷm . sto:l . sto:lən 2 stɛɩlz . bə:gləz stɛɩlz əm . sto:l . stɒɷn 3 sti:l . bə:gləz sti:l əm . stɛɷl . stɛɷl 4 stɛɩl . bə:gləz stɛɩlz əm . stɒɷl . stɒɷlən 5 sti:l . bɛ:gləz sti:lz əm . sto:ɷl . sto:ɷlən 6 stɛɩl . bə:gləz stɛɩl əm . sto:ᵚl . sto:ᵚl 7 sti:l . bə:gləz sti:l əm . sto·ɷl . sto·ɷl

11 Sa 1 stᶥi:l . bəʵ:gləz sti:l əm . sto:l . sto:l 2 stę:l . bəʵ:gləz stę:lz əm . sto:l . sto:l 3 sti:l . bəʵ:gləz sti:lz əm . n.r. 4 sti:l . bəʵ:gləz sti:l əm . sto:l . sto:ln 5 stę:l . bəʵ:gləʵʐ stę:lz əm . sto:l . sto:l, ○~ 6 sti:l . bəʵ:gləʵ:ʐ sti:lz əm . sto:l . sto:l 7 sti:l . bəʵ:gləz sti:lz əm . sto:l . sto:l, ○~ 8 sti:l . bəʵ:gləz sti:lz əm . sto:l . sto:l 9 sti:l . bəʵ:gləz sti:lz ðəm . sto:l . sto:l 10–11 sti:l . bəʵ:gləʵ:ʐ sti:lz ðəm . sto:l . sto:l

12 St 1 stiːl. §ðει stiːl ɷm. stoɷl. stoɷl 2 stiːl. bəːgləz ðειvn əm. stoɷl. stoɷl 3 stiːl. bəgləz stiːl əm. stεɷl. stεɷlən 4 stiːl. §dει stιːl ɷm. stoɷl. stoɷlən 5 stiːl. bəːgləz stiːl əm. stoɷl. stoɷl 6 stiːl. bəːgləz stiːl əm. stǫɷl. stoɷl 7 stiːl. bəːgləz stiːl ɷm. stoɷl. stoɷl 8 stiːl. bəːgləz stiːl ɷm. stoɷl. stoɷln 9 stiːl. §ɷðəz stiːl əm. stoɷl, stiːld. stoɷl, stiːld 10 stiːl. bəːgləz pιntʃ əm. n.r. 11 stiːl. bə̈ːgləz stiːl ðəm. stoɷl[(2x)]. n.r.

15 He 1 stiːɫ. bəʳːgləʳʐ stiːɫz əm. stoːɫ. stoːɫən 2 stiːɫz. bəʳːgləʳʐ stiːɫz əm. stoːɫ. stoːɫ 3 stiːɫz, ○¶stiːɫιn[1]. △bəʳːgləʳ stiːɫz əm. stoːɫ. stoːɫ 4 stiːɫ. bəʳgləʳʐ stιɫz əm. stoːɫ. stoɫn. 5 stiːɫ. bəːʳgləʳʐ stiːɫz əm. stoːɫ. stoːɫ 6 stiːᵊɫ. bəʳːgɫəʳʐ stιɫz əm. stoːɫ. stoːɫ 7 stιəl, stiːl əm. stoːl. stoːlən

16 Wo 1 stiːɫ. bəʳːgləz stiːɫz əm. stɒɷl. stɒɷl 2 stιᵊɫ. bəʳːgləz stιᵊɫz əm. stoɷᵊl. stoɷᵊl 3 stiːəɫ. bəʳːgləʳʐ stiːəɫz ɷm. stoɷl. stoɷln 4 stiːɫz. bəʳːgləʳːʐ stiːɫz ɷm. stoːl. stoːɫn 5 stiːɫz. bəʳːgləʳʐ stiːɫz ɷm. stoːl. stoːɫɷn 6 stiːɫ. bəʳːgləʳʐ stiːɫz ɷm. stoɷɫ. stoɷɫn 7 n.r. stειlz [rec. in «ðει gɷ ən stειlz əm» *they go and steal them*]. stoɷl. stoɷlɷn

17 Wa 1 stiːᵊɫ. bəːgləz stịːᵊɫ ðɷm. stǫɷl. stǫɷlən 2 pιnʃ, stιəl əm, s.f. stειl əm ["older"], ○¶stειlιn. stɔɷl. stɔɷln̩ 3 stiːᵊɫ. bəːgləz stiːɫ ɷm. stɒɷɫ. p. stɒɷɫɷn 4 stiːᵊɫ. bəʳːgləz pιnʃ §ιt. stoɷɫ. stoɷɫən 5 stειᵊɫ. bəʳːgləz stειɫ ɷm. stǫɷɫ. stǫɷɫ 6 stiːᵊɫ. bəːgləʳʐ stιəɫ ɷm. stǫɷɫ. stoɷɫ 7 stiːl. bəːgləz stiːl ɷm. stoɷɫ. stoɷɫ

23 Mon 1 stιiːɫ. bəʳːgɫəʳʐ stιlz əm. stoːᵊɫ. stoːᵊɫ 2 stiːɫ. bəʳːgləz stiːɫz əm. stoːɫ. stoːɫ 3 stiːɫ. bœːgləz də stiːɫ əm. stoːɫ. stoːɫ 4 stịːl. n.r. stoːl. stoːl 5 stiːɫ̩. stiːɫ̩. stǫːᵊɫ. stǫːᵊɫ 6 stiːᵊɫz. bəʳːgɫəʳʐ stiːᵊɫz əm. stoːɫ. stoːɫ 7 n.a.

24 Gl 1 steːᵊɫ. bəʳːgɫəʳʐ steːᵊɫz ɷm. stoːɷɫ. stoːɷɫ 2 stιiːᵊɫ. bəʳːgləʳʐ stˡiːᵊɫz ɷm. stɒɷəɫ. stɒɷᵊɫ 3 steːˡɫ. bəʳgləʳʐ steːˡɫz ɷm. stoːɷɫ. stoːɷɫ 4 stˡiːᵊɫ. bəʳːgɫəʳʐ də stˡiːᵊɫ ɷm. n.r. 5 steːl. stjεlz §ιt. stoːl. stoːl 6 steːᵊɫ. steːᵊɫ. stoːɫ. stoːlən 17 steːᵊɫ. bəʳːgləʳʐ steːl əm. stoːᵊɫ. stoːᵊɫ

25 O 1 steᵊɫ. bəʳːgləʳʐ ste·ᵊɫz əm. stɔɷɫ. stɔɷɫ 2 stι̞·ᵊɫ. bəːgləz stιᵊɫ §ιt. stɔɷɫ. stɔɷɫ 3 stιəɫ. stιəɫz. stɔɷl. stǫɷlən 4 stιɷ, ○stιəɫ[5] *inf.* bəɽgɫəɽʐ stιɷ. stoːɫ. stoːɫən 5 stιᵊɫ. bəʳgləz stιᵊɫz əm. stǫɷɫ. stǫɷlən 6 stiːᵊɫ. bəʳːgləʳʐ stiːᵊɫ əm. stoɷɫ. stoɷlən

VIII.7.6 HIDE IT

Q. A dog buries a bone because he wants to . . . .

At 7.2, 15.7, 16.7, 17.2 and 25.4, the f.w. used Version 4 of the Qr., in which the q. read: *If naughty boys* (who were robbing an orchard) *happened to catch sight of the owner as they left the orchard, they'd no doubt slip the apples into their pockets in order to . . . .* Accordingly, the wanted obj. was THEM (as reproduced below), not IT.

Rr. ? COUCH, HIDE EN/HER/HIM/IT/THEM, KEEP THEM OUT OF SIGHT

Note—The f.w. unfortunately often omitted to rec. the wanted obj. IT.

7 Ch 1 ɑɪd 2 aɪd əm 3–4 ɑɪd ɪt 5 aɪd 6 aɪd ɪt

8 Db 1 aɪd ɪt 2 ɑɪd ɪt 3 aɪd ɪt 4 aɪd 5 ɑɪd ɪt 6 ɑ̃·ɪ̃d ə 7 ɑ·ɪd ɪt

11 Sa 1 aɪd ɪt 2 aɪd [aɪdɪnsiːk³ *h.-and-seek*] 3–4 aɪd 5–6 aɪd ɪt 7 aɪd 8 ɒɪd ɪt 9 aɪd 10–11 aɪd ɪt

12 St 1 aɪd ɪt 2 ɒɪd 3 ɒːɪd ɪt 4 ir.r. 5–6 ɒːɪd ɪt 7 ɒɪd ɪt 8 aɪdz *3 pr.s.* 9 ɒɪd ɪt 10 n.a. 11 a̤ɪd ɪt

15 He 1 æɪd ɪm 2 æɪd ɪt 3–4 əɪd ɪm 5 əɪd ɪt 6 əɪd ən 7 aɪd ðəm

16 Wo 1 ɒɪd ɪt 2 əɪd ɪt 3 əiːd ɪt [ə-əiːdɪn ɪt¹ *a-hiding it*] 4 əɪd ɪt [ɪ ˈjəɪdz ɪt³ *he hides it*] 5 əɪd ɪm 6 ɒɪd ɪt 7 p. kiːp əm æɷt əv səɪt

17 Wa 1 ɒɪd ɪt 2 s.w. əɪd əm 3–4 əɪd ɪt 5–6 əɪd 7 əɪd ɪt

23 Mon 1 əɪd ɪt 2–3 əɪd 4 n.a. 5 kɷtʃ [*sic*] 6 əɪd 7 n.a.

24 Gl 1 əɪd ɪt 2 əɪd ɪm 3 əɪd 4 ɒɪd n̩ 5 ə̈ɪd ɪt 6 ʌɪd ɪt, °~ 7 ʌɪd n̩

25 O 1 ə̈ɪd 2 ə̣̈ɪd ɪʔ 3 ʌʏd 4 əɪd ðəm 5 ʌʏd ɪʔ 6 ə̈ɪd ɪʔ

VIII.7.7 THROWING a stone

Q. What would you say a boy was doing, if you saw him doing this [i.]?

Rr. CHECKING, CHUCKING, FLINGING, HOLLING, PEGGING, PELTING, PITCH, THROWING

Note—For exs. of THROW *v.* and its parts, see I.11.5, III.4.6, III.7.4 and VI.13.14.

7 Ch 1 θɹoːɪn 2 pɛgɪn, °θɹuːz² *3 pr.s.* 3 θɹọːɪn, °θɹoː³ 4 tʃɷkɪn⁽²ˣ⁾, °tʃɷk² *pr.t.* 5 θɹɔːɪn 6 θɹoːɪn

8 Db 1 tʃɷkkɪn 2 θɹɔːɪn 3 θɹoːwɪn 4 θɹoːɪn 5 θɹoːɷɪn 6 ɒlɪn, ○~ 7 θɹo·ɷɪn

11 Sa 1 θɹoɪn 2 tʃɷkɪn 3 θɹoːɪn 4 θɹoː, ○θɹoːd[2] *p.t.* VI.13.14 5 tʃɷ̣kɪn 6 θɹoːɪn, ○θɹoː[3] *inf.* 7 θɹoːɪn, ○θɹoːd *p.t.* 8 θɹaɷɪn 9 θɹoːɪn 10 θɹoːɪn, tʃʌkɪn, ○θɹoːd[3(2x)] *p.t.* 11 θɹaɷɪn, ○θɹaɷd *p.t.*, ○θɹoːd[1] *p.t.*

12 St 1 θɹoɷɪŋ, ○θɹoɷd[1] *p.t.*, ○tʃɷks[1] *3 pr.s.* 2 θɹoɷɪn 3 θɹɷːɪn, ○θɹɷː[2] *inf.*, ○θɹuː[1] *p.t.*, ○θɹɷːd[2] *p.t.*, ○tʃɷk[2] *v.* 4 θɹoɷɪn, tʃɷkɪn [older], ○θɹoɷd[2] *p.t.* 5 θɹoɷɪn 6 θɹoɷwɪn 7 θɹoɷɪn, ○tʃɷkɪn [older] 8 θɹoɷɪn, ○θɹoɷ[1] II.6.10, ○θɹoɷz[1] *3 pr.s.*, ○θɹoɷd[2] *p.p.* 9 θɹɷːɪn 10 θɹoɷɪn, pɛltɪn 11 θɹoɷwɪn, ○θɹoɷ[3] *v.*

15 He 1 θɹɒɷɪn 2 θɹæɷɪn 3 θɹɒɷɪn, ○θɹɒɷd[4] *p.p.* 4 əθɹæɷɪn, ○θɹəɷz[1] *3 pr.s.* 5 tʃɛkɪn, ○θɹæɷ[1] *2 pr.pl.* 6 θɹæɷɪn 7 θɾoɷɪn, θɾoɷɪn, ○tʃʌk *imp.*

16 Wo 1 θɹaɷɪn 2 ətʃɷkɪn 3 flɪŋɪn 4 əθɹaɷɪn, ○θɹaːɪn[2] 5 əθɹaɷɪn, ○θɹaɷd[1] *3 p.t.s.* 6 θɹɒɷɪn 7 θɹəɷ, ○~[2] *inf.*, ○θɹəɷd[4] *p.p.*, ○~[3] [n.d.g.], ○θɹɑɷd[4] [n.d.g.]

17 Wa 1 θɹọɷɪn 2 θɹəɷɪn, ○θɹəɷ[3] [n.d.g.], ○θɹɑɷ[2] [n.d.g.], ○θɹəɷd[4] *p.p.* 3 θɹoɷɪn 4 θɹoɷɪn, ○θɹọɷd[1] [n.d.g.] 5 θɹɒɷɪn, ○~ 6 θɹọɷɪn 7 θɹɒɷɪn

23 Mon 1 θæɷɪn [*sic*] 2 fɹoːɪn 3 θɹoːɪn 4 θɹọː, ○pɪtʃ[1] *inf.* 5 θɹou, ○~[2] *inf.* 6 θɹoːɪn 7 n.a.

24 Gl 1 θɹæɷɪn, ○θɹæɷ[3] IV.2.11 2 θɹæɷɪn, ○~[3], ○θɹɒɷd[2(2x)] *p.t.* 3 dɹɒɷɪn, ○dɹɒɷz[1] *3 pr.s.* III.1.11 4 dɹɒɷɪn [dɷŋdɹɒɷɪn[1] *dung-t.*] 5 θɹɑɷɪn 6 tʃəkɪn, flɪŋɪn 7 flɪŋɪn

25 O 1 dʌbɪn, ○tʃɷk[1] [n.d.g.] 2 tʃɷkɪn, ○θɹoɷd[1] *p.p.* 3 θɹọɷən 4 θɹo·ɪn, ○tʃɷkɪn[5] 5 flɪŋɪn 6 θɹoɷɪn

VIII.7.8 DUCK

Q. If you saw a stone coming straight for your head, you'd at once [i.] . . . .

Rr. BOB, DOB, DUCK, DUCK (§HIS HEAD) DOWN, DUCK (§YOUR HEAD)

7 Ch 1 dɷk‘ 2–4 dɷk 5 dɛɷk 6 dɛ̣ɷk‘

8 Db 1 dɷk‘ 2 dɷk 3 dɷk‘ 4–5 dɷk 6 dɷk‘ 7 dɷk

11 Sa 1 daɷk 2 dɛ̧ɷk 3–4 daɷk 5 dɛɷk 6–7 daɷk 8 dɛɷk 9–10 daɷk 11 daɷk §jəʳ jɛd

12 St 1–2 dɷk 3 dɷk jə jɛd 4 dɷk 5 daɷk §ɩz ɛd daɷn 6–7 dɷk 8 daɷk 9–10 dɷk 11 daɷk

15 He 1–2 dæɷk 3 dəɷk 4–5 dʌk 6 dɷk 7 dʌk

16 Wo 1–2 dɛɷk 3 dɛu:k 4 dəɷk 5 dəɷ:k 6 dɛu:k 7 dɷk dæɷn

17 Wa 1 dɷk‘ 2–3 dɷk 4 dü:k 5 dɷk 6 dɛɷk 7 dɷk

23 Mon 1 dʌk 2 dɷk dʌɷn 3 dʌk 4 n.a. 5 dʌ̤̈k jəɹ ɛd 6 dʌk 7 n.a.

24 Gl 1 dɷ:k 2 dɷk 3 dœ:k 4–5 dɷk 6 dək 7 dək‘

25 O 1–2 dʌk 3 dɒb 4–5 dɷk 6 bɒb

VIII.7.9 GO AWAY! Off YOU GO!

Q. To get rid of someone quickly who was being a bit of a nuisance, you'd say ....

Do you know that one beginning: Off ....

Rr. BE/BEGGAR/BOLT/BUGGER/BUZZ/CLEAR/GET/HOP/MESS/MUCK/POTTER/PUSH/SHOVE OFF, CLEAR/GET OFF WITH YOU, CLEAR OUT, GET AWAY/ON, GET OUT (OF~ON IT), GET YOU FROM HERE, GO (AWAY/ON), HOP IT (YOU), PUSH IT, SCOOT, (YOU) SCRAM, TAKE YOUR HOOK,

OFF YOU GO/POP, WITH YOU, YOU GO

Note 1—The rr. to the two parts of the q. are separated below by a full stop.

Note 2—When rec. in the r. to the 2nd part of the q., OFF is reproduced below.

Note 3—In the list of rr. above, GO subsumes GOEN and GOES(T), YOU subsumes THEE and THOU, and YOUR subsumes THY.

Note 4—I.m. exs. of GO *imp.* and of AWAY are reproduced below between square brackets untransliterated. For additional exs. of GO *imp.*, see II.3.5 and IX.5.8; and for other parts of the v., see VIII.6.1 (and refs.). For additional exs. of (–)AWAY, see V.8.14, VII.6.5 and VIII.8.15; and of OFF, see IX.2.13 (and refs.).

7 Ch 1 gɛɹ ɒf [əwe̜:[2]]. ɒf ða go̜:z 2 klɩəɹ æ:t, əp ɩt [əwe:[2(2x),3,4]]. n.r. 3 bɛgəɹ ɒf. ðaɩ gɷz 4 tɛk jəɹ u:k. ɒf jə go: 5 tlɛɩəɹ ɒf, mɷk ɒf. ɒf ðɩ gu̜:st 6 mɛs ɒf. ɒf jə go:

8 Db 1 ɒp ɩt. jə go: 2 gɛt aɷt. ɒf ða go:z 3 go: əwe:. ða go:z 4 tɛk ðɩ ɛɷk [əwi:^{3}]. ðɩ g^{ɷ}ü:z 5 ɒp ɩt. ɒf ða gɷz 6 ɒp ɩt. ɒf ðɩ gü:st 7 tlɩəɹ ɒf [əwi:^{2}]. ɒf jə g^{ɷ}u:n

11 Sa 1 bʌgə^{r}·ɽ ɒf. jə go: 2 bɷgə^{r}ɽ ɒf. jə go: 3 bʌgə^{r}·ɽ ɒf. jə go: 4 bʌgə^{r} ɔ:f. ju: go: 5 gɛt ɛɷt ɒn ɩt. ɒf ðɩ go:st 6 gɛɹ‿ɔ^{r}:f. jə go: 7 bʌgə^{r}ɽɔ:f. jə go: 8 bɷgə^{r}ɽ ɔ:f. ɔ:f jə gu: 9–10 klɩə^{r}ɽ‿ɔ:f. jə go: 11 bʌgə^{r}ɽ‿ɔ:f. jə go:

12 St 1 klɩəɹ ɒf [gɷ^{3}]. wɩð jə 2 gɛɹ ɒf [gɷ^{2}]. ɒf jə gu:n 3 bɷgəɹ ɒf, klɩəɹ ɒf. ɒf ðɩ gɷ:st 4 gɛt ɒf wɩð jə. ɒf jə pɒp 5 gɷ:, klɩəɹ ɒf. n.r. 6 gɛɹ ɒf, joɷ skɹam [gɷ^{1}]. ɒf jə gɷ: 7 gɛt əwɛɩ. jə goɷ 8 gɛt ɒf [əwɛɩ$^{1,2(2x)}$]. jə goɷ 9 ɒp ɩt, kliə ɒf wɩ jə [gɷ:^{1}; əwi$^{1(2x)}$]. n.r. 10 klɩəɹ ɒf. n.r. 11 kliəɹ ɒf, bi: ɒf, gɛt ɒf, pɒtəɹ ɒf [əwɛɩ^{2}]. ɒf jə goɷ

15 He 1 bʌz ɔ:f [əwe:^{1}]. jə go:ɷ 2 bʌgə^{r}ɽ ɔ:f. ju: go: 3 gɛt ɑ:f. jə go:z 4 bʌgə^{r}ɽ ɑ:f [ðɩ ka:n du: ɷˈðæɩ əð ɩt *they can't do away with it*^{3}]. jə gu:z 5 bʌgə^{r}ɽ ɑ:f. jə go:z 6 bɷgə^{r}ɽ ɒf. jə go: 7 klɩəɹ ǝ̆ut, bʌz ɒf, °skɹam [əweɩ^{4}]. ɒf jə go:

16 Wo 1 gɩt ɒf. jə gɒɷz 2 klɩə^{r}ɽ‿ɔ:f [gu:^{1}]. ɒf jə goɷ 3 gɛɹ‿ɑ:f. ɒf jə goɷ 4 ɒp ɑ:f. jə go:z 5 gɛɹ ɑ:f. jɷ gɷz 6 pɷʃ ɩt. ɑ:f jə gɷz 7 teɩk jə^{r} ɷk. n.r.

17 Wa 1 klɩəɹ ɒf [əwẹɩ^{1}]. jə gọɷ 2 klɩəɹ ɔ:f, əp ɩt, °tɛk jəɹ ɷk [əwe:$^{2,3(2x),4}$, əweɩ^{2}]. ɔ:f jə gɔɷ 3 ʃɷv ɔ:f, pɷʃ ɔ:f. p. ɔ:f jə gɷ· [but not used] 4 gɛɹ ɛɷt. jə gọɷ 5 klɩə^{r}ɽ ɔ:f [əwɛɩ^{1}]. ju: gɷ: 6 klɩəɹ ɔ:f [əwɛɩ^{4}]. jə gọɷ 7 bɷz ɔ:f, klɩəɹ ɔ:f [pref.; əwɛɩ^{2}]. ɔ:f jə goɷ

23 Mon 1 te:ɩk jə^{r}ɽ ʌk. jə gæɷ 2 gɛt ʌɷt əv ɩt. jə go: 3 gɛt ɑ:n. jə go: 4 n.a. 5 kliəɹ ɔ:f. ɔ:f ju· go: 6 bʌz ɑ:f. jə go:z 7 n.a.

24 Gl 1 gɛɹ ɑ:f wɩ jə [əwɛɩ^{1}, əwæɩ$^{2,3(2x)}$; fɛnt əwæɩ^{1} *faint away* VI.13.7]. jə go:ɷ 2 ʃɷv ɑ:f [əwɛɩ^{3}, əwæɩ^{3}]. jə go:ɷ 3 gɛt ðə fɹa:m jə^{r}:. jə go:ɷz 4 gɛd ɑ:f. jə gɒɷ 5 bʌgəɹ ɔ:f [əwaɩ$^{2(2x)}$]. jə go: 6 klɩəɹ ɔ:f, skɷt. ɔ:f ðə go:z 7 pɷʃ ɒf, ɒf wɩ ðə

25 O 1 bəɷłt ɔ:f [əwæɩ^{1}]. jə gəɷ 2 gɛḍ ɔ:f. ɒf ju: gəɷ 3 gọɷ ɔ:n [əwe:^{1}, əwe:^{1} II.6.10]. ɔ:f jɷ gọɷ 4 ɒp ɩt jü:, °kłɩəɽ ɔ:f^{5}. ɔ:f ju: go: 5 klɩə^{r} ɔ:f [gɷ^{2}]. ɔ:f jə gọɷ 6 goɷ əweɩ. ju: goɷ

VIII.7.10 WALK

Q. Suppose you missed the last bus or train back to here, then you'd have to set off and . . . .

Rr. FOOT/HOOF IT, /GO/WALK (IT)/ ON SHANKS' PONY, TRAMP, WALK (HER/IT)

Note 1—When rec. in the r. the grammatical obj. IT, referend vague, but perhaps = *distance* or the like, has been reproduced below.

Note 2—For exs. of WALKING *pr.p.*, see IV.8.6; and of -WALK *n.*, see IV.3.11; of -WALKER *n.*, see II.3.4; and of -WALK, -WALKING *n.*, see VII.4.11.

7 Ch 1 wɔ:k, ○~¹ 2 wɔ:k ɩt, ○wɔ:k² 3 wɔ:k ɩt 4 wɔ:k 5 wɔ:k [wɔ:ks *3 pr.pl.*; wɔ:k² *w. n.*] 6 wɔ:k

8 Db 1 wɔ:k ɩt 2 wo:kʻ 3 wɔ:kʻ 4 wɔ:k ɩt 5 tɹamp, wɔ:k 6 wɔ:k ə [=*her*] 7 wɔ:k ɩt

11 Sa 1 fʌt ɩt [pref.], wɔ:k 2 wɔ:k, ○~¹ 3–4 wɔʳ:k 5 wɔ:k, ○~² 6 wɔʳ:k 7–10 wɔ:k 11 wɔ:k, ○~²

12 St 1 wɔ:k 2 woɷk, ○~⁵ 3 wɒɷk ɒn ʃaŋksɩz poɷnɩ, ○woɷk² 4 fɷt ɩt, wɔ:k 5 wɔ:k, ○wɔ:kɩn² 6 wɔ̣:k ɩt 7 wɔ:k 8 wɔ:k, ○~¹ 9 wɔ:k ɩt ɒn ʃanksɩz poɷnɩ 10 wɔ:k 11 wɔ:k, ○~² *2 pr.pl.*

15 He 1–2 wɔ:k 3 wa:k, ○~¹ 4–5 wa:k 6 wa:k, ○~¹ 7 wɔ:k ɩt, ○wɔ:k, ○~⁴, ○ɷf ɩt, ○fɷt ɩt

16 Wo 1–2 wa:k 3 waʳ:k, ○wa:k² 4 waʳ:k, ○wa:kt¹ *2 p.t.pl.* 5 wa:k, ○~¹, ○wa:kst¹ *2 p.t.s.* 6 wa:k, ○~³ 7 wɔ̣:k. ○wɔ:k⁴

17 Wa 1 wɔ:k 2 wɔ:k ɩt, ○¶wɔ:kɩn¹ 3 wɔ̃:k, ○wɔ:k² 4 wɔ:k ɩt, ü:f ɩt ["older"] 5 wɔ:k ɩt 6 wɔ:k 7 wɔ:k ɩt

23 Mon 1–3 wa:k 4 wɔ:k 5 wɔ:k, ○¶wɔ:kɩn¹ 6–7 n.a.

24 Gl 1 wa:k 2 wa:k [wa:k³ *w. n.*] 3 wa:k, ○~⁴ *3 pr.pl.* 4 wa:k 5 wɔ:k 6 wɔ:k ɩt 7 wɔ:kʻ, ○go: ɒn ʃaŋksɩz po:nɩ

25 O 1 wɔ:k 2 wɔ:k ɩt 3 wɔ:k [wɔ:k¹⁽²ˣ⁾ *w. n.* I.3.7/18] 4 wɔ:k ɩt, ○wɔ:k⁴, ○¶wɔ:kɩn³ [wɔ:k⁴ *w. n.*] 5 wɔ:k 6 wɔ:k, ○~³

VIII.8.1 BOGEY

Q. Sometimes, when children are behaving very badly, their mother will tell them that someone will come and take them away. What do you call this mysterious person?

Rr. BLACK-MAN, BOBBY, BOGEY(-MAN/SAM), BOGGART, BUGA-BO/BOWL, COPPER, (THICK) OLD MAN, POLICEMAN, SCUG

Note 1—Expressions comparable with some of those listed above also occur at VIII.8.3.

Note 2—POLICEMAN and the synonymous BOBBY and COPPER, all ref. a local functionary, can hardly be regarded as satisfactory rr.

7 Ch 1 bǫ:gɩmɒn 2 bəbbɩ, p. bɷ:gɩ, p. bɷ:gɩsam 3 bɷgət, skɷg [pref.] 4 bǫ:gɩmɒn 5 bų:gɩmɒn 6 bo:gɩmɒn

8 Db 1 bo:gɩmɒn 2 bo:gɩman 3 bɒgət 4 bɒgəd 5 bo:ᵒgɩ 6 bo:ᵒgɩmɒn 7 boɷgɩmɒn

11 Sa 1 bɷgɩbo: 2 bo:gɩmɒn 3 bɷgɩbo:, ○~ 4 bɷgɩbo: 5 bo:gɩmɒn 6 bɷgɩman 7 bo:gɩmɒn 8 bo:gɩmɒn, ○~ 9 bɷgɩbo: 10 bo:gɩman 11 bo:gɩmɒn, bɷgɩbo:

12 St 1 blakman, boɷgɩ 2 plɛɩsmən(2x) 3 bɒbɩ, bɷ:gɩmɒn 4 boɷgɩman 5 pli:smən, bɷ:gɩmɒn 6 bɒbɩ 7 boɷgɩman 8 boɷgɩ 9 boɷgɩman, ○boɷgɩ 10 boɷgɩman 11 boɷgɩman, ○pli:smən(2x)

15 He 1 bɒbɩ 2 bʌgɩbo: 3 bo:gɩmɒn 4 bɷgɩmɒn 5 bɷgɩbo: 6 bo:gɩmɒn 7 bo:gɩmɒn, pli:smən, blakman, ○pli:sman

16 Wo 1 bɒɷgɩmɒn 2 boɷgɩmɒn 3 bɷgɩboɷ, ○bɷgɩboɷl[1] 4 bɷgɩbo: 5 bo:gɩmɒn 6 boɷgɩmɑ:n 7 s.w. boɷgɩman, kɒpəʴ [usu.]

17 Wa 1 bǫɷgɩman 2 bəɷgɩman 3 bǫɷgɩ 4 bǫɷgɩman 5 bǫɷgɩmɒn, ○bɒɷgɩmɒn 6 bǫɷgɩman 7 boɷgɩman

23 Mon 1 bo:ᵒgɩ 2 bo:gɩ [also called *policeman*] 3 bo:gɩma:n, ○~[1] 4 n.a. 5 bo:gɩ, ○plį:smən 6 bʌgɩbo: 7 n.a.

24 Gl 1 bɷgɩmɒn 2–3 bo:ɷgɩmɒn 4 bo:ɷgɩ 5 bo:gɩman 6 bo:gɩmɒn 7 bo:gɩman, ðɩk ɒɷɫ man ["usu."]

25 O 1 bəɷgɩman 2 bəɷgɩman, ○~ 3 bǫɷgɩ 4 pɫi:smən, s.w. bo:gɩman 5 bǫɷgɩman 6 boɷgɩmæn

VIII.8.2 AFRAID

Q. Nowadays, of course, that trick (of frightening misbelieving children) *does'nt work, for some children are not . . . .*

Rr. FEARED, (A)FRAID, FREET~FRIGHT(ED)~FRIT, FREETENED~FRIGHTENED~FRITENED, SCARED

7 Ch 1 fɹɛɩtnd 2 p. fɩəd, p. fɩət [pref.], °~⁴ 3 fɩət 4 fɹɩtnd, °~² 5 fɹɩtnd [fɹɩtn *frighten v.*] 6 fɹɩtnd

8 Db 1 fɹaɩtnt, fɹi:tnt ["older"], °fɹi:t³ 2 fɹi:tnd, °~² [n.d.g.] 3 fɹɛɩtnt [fɹɛɩtn¹ *frighten inf.*] 4–6 fɹɛɩtnd 7 fɹɩt, °~

11 Sa 1 skɛəʳ:ɖ 2 fɹɩtn 3 fɹɛɩtnd 4 əfɹe:d 5 fɹɩtnd, °~² 6 fɹɩtnd 7–8 fɹɩt 9 fɹɩt, °~ 10 fɹɩt 11 fɹɩt, °~

12 St 1 fɹɒɩtnd 2 fɹɛɩtnt, °~ 3 fɹɛɩtnd, °~ 4 fɹɒɩtnd 5–6 fɹɒ:ɩtnd 7 fɹɒɩtnd 8 əfɹɛɩd 9 əfɹɛɩd, fɹɩt ["older"], °~⁽²ˣ⁾ 10 fɹa:ɩtnd 11 fɹɛɩd

15 He 1 fɹæɩtnd 2–6 fɹəɩtnd 7 fɹæ̆ɩtnd

16 Wo 1 fɹɒɩtnd 2 fɹəɩtnd 3 ske:əʳɖ, °~¹ 4 fɹəɩtnd, °fɹɩt³ 5 fɹəɩtnd 6 fɹɒɩt 7 fɹəɩtənd

17 Wa 1 fɹɒɩtnd 2 skɛəd, °fɹeɩd¹ 3 fɹəɩtnd 4 fɹɩt, °~ 5 fɹʌɩtnd, °fɹɩt¹ 6 fɹəɩtnd 7 fɹɩt, °~

23 Mon 1 fɹəɩtnd 2 əfɹe:d 3 fɹəɩtnd, °~¹ 4 n.a. 5 fɹəɩ̣tnd 6 fɹəɩtnd 7 n.a.

24 Gl 1 fɹəɩtnd 2 fɹəɩtnd, °~, °əfɹɛɩd³ 3–4 vɹəɩtnd 5 fɹə̈ɩtnd 6 fɹʌɩtnḍ 7 fɹʌɩʔnd

25 O 1 fɹə̈ɩʔnd 2 fɹə̈ɩʔnd 3 fɹʌʏtnd, °~ 4 əfɽe:d, °fɽɩt, °fɹɩtnd 5–6 fɹə̈ɩʔnd

VIII.8.3 DEVIL

Q. What do you call that other mysterious person we think of as having horns and a tail?

Rr. DEMON, (THE) DEVIL, OLD HARRY/LAD/MICK/NICK, SATAN, THE BLACK-MAN WITH NO WHITE IN HIS EYES, THE OLD CHAP/DEVIL/FELLOW/LAD/MAN

Note 1—When rec. in the r., the def. art. is reproduced below. Its absence cannot imply that the ii. did not include it in their rr., since the q. unfortunately omitted to instruct the f.w. to note its occurrence.

Note 2—Expressions comparable with some of those listed above also occur at VIII.8.1 and VIII.9.4.

Note 3—OLD occurs at VIII.1.20 (and refs.). For THE plus initial C., see IX.2.3 (and refs.).

7 Ch 1 dɛvl 2 θ‿ɛɷd läd 3–5 dɪvl 6 ð‿ɛɷd lad

8 Db 1 dɛvl 2 ɒɷd nɪk' 3 dɛvl 4 dɪvl 5 t‿ɛɷd lad 6 ð‿ɛɷd lad 7 dɛvl

11 Sa 1 aɷd lad 2 dɛvl 3 dɛvəl 4 dɛvl 5 ɛɷd nɪk 6 ðə aɷd fɛlə, ðə ˈblakˈman wɪð no: waɪt ɪn ɪz aɪz 7 dɛvɪl, ○□dɪvlz¹ 8 ðə aɷd la·d 9 dɛvəl 10 aɷd nɪk 11 ɒɷd nɪk, ○dɛvl², ○~² VIII.9.4

12 St 1 oɷd nɪk, ðə dɛvl 2 si:tn, dɪ̢vl, ○dɛvl² 3 dɛvl, ○~¹ 4 dɛvl 5 ðə dɛvl 6 ðə dɛvl, æɷd nɪk 7 dɛvl 8 dɛvəl 9 ɛɷd nɪk, ðə dɛvl 10–11 dɛvl

15 He 1 ɒɷd nɪk 2 dɛvəɫ, ○ɒɷɫd nɪk 3 ɒɷd nɪk 4 æɷd nɪk 5 æɷɫd nɪk 6 ɒɷd æɹɪ 7 ð‿o:l dɛvl, o:l nɪk

16 Wo 1 dɛvl 2 dɛvəɫ 3 dɛvəɫ, ○□dɛvɪɫz¹ 4 dɛvəɫ 5 ðə aɷl mɒn 6 ɒɷd nɪk 7 s.w. dɛvɫ, ○~¹, ○dɛvl¹

17 Wa 1 ðə dɛvɫ, ○dɛvl² 2 di:mən, s.w. dɛvl, ○~⁽²ˣ⁾ 3 dɛvɫ [ɒɷɫ nɪk *Old Nick* (ref. a person who might catch someone in a dark lane; not the devil; pres. a bogey, Edd.)] 4 dɛvɫ 5 dɛvɫ, ○~¹⁽³ˣ⁾, ○~¹ VII.8.13 6–7 dɛvɫ

23 Mon 1 ɒɷɫd nɪk 2 ðə o:ɫ ma:n 3 o:ɫ nɪk 4 n.a. 5 dɛvɫ 6 o:ɫd æɹɪ 7 n.a.

24 Gl 1 dɛvɷɫ, ðɪ æɷᵊɫ mɒn ["usu."] 2 æɷɫ nɪk 3 ɒɷɫ nɪk, ○ðə ɒɷᵊɫ tʃæp³ 4 dɛvɫ 5 dɛvl, ○~¹,² 6 dɛvɫ, ○~ 7 dɛvɫ [dɷmɫdɛvɫ¹ *dummel-d.* (a term of abuse)]

25 O 1 dɛvɫ, ○□dɛvɫz² 2 dɛvl, ○sɛɪtən 3 davl 4 dɛvɷ 5 dɛvɫ, ○□davɫz² 6 dɛvɫ

VIII.8.4 TRIED

Q. That boy didn't manage to win a prize at the sports, but I will say, to his credit, he at least . . . .

Rr. DID /AS WELL AS HE COULD/HIS BEST/, DONE /HIS BEST/ WELL/, HAD A GOOD TRY, TRIED (/HIS BEST/{VERY} HARD/), §WAS VERY NEAR IT

7 Ch 1 tɹɑɪd 2 p. tɹaɪd ɪz bɛst, dɪd əz wi:l əz ɪ kɒd, °tɹɑɪd¹ *p.p.*, °tɹɑɪ¹ *inf.* 3–4 tɹɑɪd 5 dɪd ɪz bɛst 6 tɹaɪd

8 Db 1 tɹaɪd 2 tɹɑɪd 3 tɹaɪd 4 tɹɑɪd [tɹɑɪ *t. n.*] 5 tɹɑɪd 6–7 tɹɑ̃·ɪ̃d

11 Sa 1 tɹɛɪd 2 ad ə gɒd tɹaɪ 3–4 tɹɛɪd 5–7 tɹaɪd 8 tɹɒɪd 9–11 tɹaɪd

12 St 1–2 tɹɒɪd 3 tɹɒ:ɪd vɛɹɪ a:d 4 tɹɒɪd a:d 5–6 tɹɒ:ɪd 7–9 tɹɒɪd 10 tɹa:ɪd 11 dɒn wɛl, tɹa̤:ɪd ɑ̊:d, °tɹɒɪz¹ *3 pr.s.*

15 He 1 tɹæɪd 2 tɹəɪd, °~¹ *p.p.* 3–6 tɹəɪd 7 tɹaɪd, °tɹaɪ⁴ *inf.*

16 Wo 1 tɹɒɪd 2 tɹəɪᵊd, °tɹəɪ² *inf.* III.13.18 3 tɹəi:d, °tɹɒɪ² *inf.*, °¶tɹɒɪn¹ 4–5 tɹəɪd 6 tɹɒɪd, °¶ətɹɒɪ-ɪn¹ 7 §wəz vɛɹɪ nɪəʳ ɪt, s.w. tɹəɪd ɪz bɛst

17 Wa 1 tɹɑɪd, °tɹɑɪ¹ [n.d.g.] 2 tɹəɪd, dɒn ɪz bɛst 3 tɹə·ɩd 4 ad ə gɒd tɹəɪ, °¶tɹəɪ-ɪn, °tɹəɪ¹ *v.* 5–7 tɹəɪd

23 Mon 1–3 tɹəɪd 4 n.a. 5 tɹə̜id 6 tɹəɪd 7 n.a.

24 Gl 1–4 tɹəɪd 5 tɹə̈ɪd 6–7 tɹʌɪd

25 O 1–2 tɹə̈ɪd 3 tɹʌʏd 4 s.w. tɽəɪd, °tɽəɪ¹˒³ *v.*, °¶tɽɑɪ-ɪn¹, °¶tɹæ̜ɪn¹ [tɽəɪ⁵ *t. n.*] 5–6 tɹə̈ɪd

VIII.8.5 SHAPING WELL

Q. Of a boy who is getting on nicely at his work, you would say: He is . . . .

Rr. DOING /ALL RIGHT/FINE/TIDY/(MIDDLING~RIGHT~VERY) WELL/, GETTING ON (/ALL RIGHT/FINE/GRAND/WELL/), GOING /ON FINE~WELL/STRONG/, §IMPROVING, §MAKING A GOOD LAD, §PROGRESSING, SHAPING /ALL RIGHT/PRETTY FAIR/, SHAPING /OFF VERY/PRETTY/RIGHT/UP/) WELL, §TAKING AN INTEREST, §TRYING, §VERY SMART

Note—I.m. forms of WELL *adv.* are included below between square brackets untransliterated. WELL *adv.* also occurs at VI.14.2. For WELL *adj.*, see VI.13.1. For DOING, see IX.5.3 (and refs.); and for GOING, see VIII.6.1 (and refs.). VERY occurs at VIII.3.2 (and refs.).

7 Ch 1 dɪʏ:ɪn ɔ: ɹɛɪt 2 ʃe:pɪn wɛl [wɛl³, wi:l³⁽²ˣ⁾] 3 dᶦʏ:ɪn ɔ: ɹɛt 4 gɛtɪn ɒn gɹand, du:ɪn wɛl 5 dɪʏ:ɪn wɛɫ [wɛɫ³] 6 d°ʉ̜:ɪn ɔ:l ɹaɪt

8 Db 1 dʏ:ɪn mɪdlɪn wi:l [wi:l[1]] 2 du: ɪn ɹɛɪt wi:l 3 dɪüɪn wɛl 4 go·ɪn ɒn faɪn 5 gɛtɪn ɒn ɔ: ɹɛɪt 6 ʃe̜:ˈpɪn wɛl 7 dɛɷɪn wɛl

11 Sa 1 ʃe:pɪn wɛl 2 ʃe:pɪn wɛl [wɛl[2] IV.1.4] 3 ʃe:pɪn ɹɛɪt wɛl, °dɷɪn ɹaɪt wɛl[2] 4 ʃe:pɪn wɛl [wɛl[2]] 5 ʃe̜:pɪn pɹɪtɪ wɛl 6 ʃe:pɪn wɛl, dɷɪn wɛl 7-8 ʃe:pɪn wɛl 9 gɛtn ɔ:n wɛl 10 ʃe:pɪn wɛl 11 ʃe:pɪn wɛl, du:ɪn taɪdɪ [wɛl[1]]

12 St 1 du:ɪn vɛɹɪ wɛl 2 §tɹɒɪ-ɪn 3 §takɪn ən ɪntɹɛst, gɛtɪn ɒn wɛl 4 gɛtɪn ɒn wɛl, gɷɪn stɹɒŋg 5 gɛtɪn ɒn wɛl 6 gɷ:ɪn ɒn wɛl 7 gɛtɪn ɒn wɛl 8 gɛtɪn ɒn 9 gɛɹɪn ɒn 10 dü:ɪn wɛl 11 ir.r.

15 He 1 gɛtɪn ɔ:n ɔ:ɫ ɹæɪt 2 gɛtɪn ɔ:n fəɪn 3 du:ɪn wɛɫ 4 ədu:ɪn wɛɫ 5 du:ɪn wɛɫ 6 ədu:ɪn wɛɫ 7 dɷɪn wɛl

16 Wo 1 ʃɛɪpɪn wɛl 2 ʃe:ᵊpɪn wɛɫ [wɪl[1]] 3 əʃe:ɪpɪn wɛɫ 4 ʃe:ɪpɪn wɛɫ 5 əʃe:pɪn pɹɪtɪ fe:əʳ 6 du:ɪn ɑ:ɫ ɹɒɪt, ədu:ɪn wɛɫ [wɛl[1], wɛɫ[2]] 7 ədɷɪn fəɪn [wɛl[1,2,3(2x),4]]

17 Wa 1 du:ɪn wɛl 2 §pɹəgɹɛsɪn, gɛtn ən wɛl 3 §mɛkɪn ə gɷd lad, §ɪmpɹu:vɪn, °duɪn wɛl[1] 4 du:ɪn wɛɫ 5 ədu:ɪn vɛɹɪ wɛɫ 6–7 du:ɪn wɛɫ

23 Mon 1 ʃe:ˈpɪn wɛɫ 2 ʃe:pɪn wɛɫ 3 ʃe:pɪn ɑ:ɫ ɹəɪt [wɛɫ[1]] 4 n.a. 5 §vɛɹi sma:t, du-ɪn wɛl 6 ʃe:pɪn wɛɫ 7 n.a.

24 Gl 1 ədu:ɪn ɑ:ɫ ɹəɪt 2 ʃe:pɪn wɛɫ 3 ʃe:ˈpɪn ɑ:f vɛɹɪ wɛɫ 4 əd°u:ən wɛɫ 5 gɛtn ɑn ɔ: ɹöɪt 6 du:ɪn vɛɹɪ wɛɫ 7 du:ɪn fʌɪn

25 O 1 duɪn ɔ:l ɹöɪt 2 du:-ɪn wɛᵊɫ [wɛᵊɫ] 3 duɪn wɛl 4 dɷɪn ɔ:ɫ ɽəɪt 5 ədu:ɪn wɛl 6 ʃɛɪpɪn ʌp wɛᵊɫ

VIII.8.6 WHY‡

Q. If you found your wife had done something extraordinary, you'd certainly ask her: . . . . did you do that?

Rr. WHAT DID YOU /(WANT TO) DO THAT/DO THIS/ FOR?, WHATEVER DID YOU DO THAT FOR?, WHAT (DID . . . . THAT) FOR?, WHAT HAVE YOU DONE THAT/THIS FOR?, WHAT'S YOUR IDEA OF DOING THAT?, WHY (/DID YOU DO IT/HAVE YOU DONE THIS/)?

Note 1—Any r. comprising a complete sentence is reproduced below in full.

Note 2—In the list of rr. above, DID YOU subsumes DIDST THOU, and HAVE YOU subsumes HAST THOU and HAN YOU. The aux. DID has been absorbed at 15.7; and HAVE at 8.4, 12.1/5/6/9. Further, DIDST THOU appears in a reduced form at 24.7 and likewise DID YOU at 17.6, 24.2 and 25.4(2x).

Note 3—For additional exs. of DO *inf.*, see IX.5.5; of DID, see IX.5.4; and of DONE, see IX.5.6. Additional exs. of HAVE YOU occur at VI.5.8. For additional exs. of WHAT, see VII.5.1 and VII.8.16/17; of THAT, see IX.10.1 (and refs.); and of THIS, see IX.10.2.

7 Ch 1 wɒt‿s ðə dɷn ðat fəᶦ: 2 wət ə jə dɷn ðɪs fɔ: 3 wɒt . . . . fɔ: 4 wɒt . . . . fɒ 5 wɒt dɪd . . . . ðat fə [wɒt dɷn jo: want ɪt fɔ:[2] *what do you want it for?*] 6 wɒt dɪd jə want tə dᵒu: ðat fɒ

8 Db 1 wɒt‿s tə dɷn ðat fəᶦ 2 wɒt‿s tə dɷn ðat fɔ: 3 wɒt an jə dɷn ðat fə 4 wɒt jə dɷn ðat fɒ 5 wɒt‿s tə dɷn ðat fɔ: 6 wɒt əs‿t dɷn ðat fɔ: 7 wɒt an jə dɷn ðat fɔ:, ○wɑɪ[1]

11 Sa 1–7 waɪ 8–9 wɒɪ 10 waɪ, ○~[3] 11 waɪ

12 St 1 wɒt jə dɷn ðat fɔ: 2 wat‿s dɷn ðat fɔ:, ○wɛɪ[1] 3 wɒt‿s dɷn ðat fɔ: 4 wɒt dɪd jə dü: ðat fɔ: 5 wɒt jə dɷn ðat fɔ: 6 wɒ:ɪ, wɒt jə dɷn ðat fɔ: 7 wɒt jə dü: ðat fɔ: [wɒt ʃə wɒnt ɪt fɔ:[4] *what you want it for?*] 8 wɒt dɪd jə du: ðat fɔ̣:, wɒɪ dɪd jə du: ɪt 9 wɒt jə dɷn ðat fɔ: 10 wa:ɪ 11 waɪ, ○wɒt dɪd jə du: ɪt fɔ:

15 He 1–2 wæɪ 3–6 wəɪ 7 wɒt jə du: ðat fɔɹ

16 Wo 1–2 wɒɪ 3 wəi: 4 wɒɪ 5 wəɪ 6 wɒɪ 7 wɒts jəɹ ɔɪdɪə ə dɷ-ɪn ðat, s.w. wəɪ

17 Wa 1 wɒt ə jə dɷn ðat fɔ: [wɒd̥ ə jə bla:tɪn (VIII.8.11) fɔ: *what are you blarting* (i.e. screaming) *for?*] 2 wəɪ ɛv jə dɷn ðɪs 3 wɒt . . . . fɔ̣: 4 wɒd̥ dɪd jə dü: ðat fɔ: 5 wɒd̥ ə jə dɷn ðat fɔ: 6 wɒt d‿ʒə du: ðat fɔʳ: 7 wɒt . . . . fɔʳ:

23 Mon 1–3 wəɪ 4 wəi 5 wəɪ̣, ○wɒ̣̈˂t . . . . fɔ: 6 wəɪ 7 n.a.

24 Gl 1 wəɪ 2 wəɪ d‿ʒə du: ɪt 3–4 wəɪ 5 wɒt . . . . fɔʳ: 6 wɒt dɪdst ðɪ: du: ðat vɔʳ: 7 wɒt‿s du: ðɪs fɔ:ʳ

25 O 1 wɒʔ ju: dʌn ðaʔ fɔʳ: 2 wə̈ɪ 3 wʌʏ 4 wɒdɛvəɽ d‿jə du: ðat fɔ·ɽ, s.w. wɒt d‿jə du: ðat fɔ·ɽ 5 wə̈ɪ, ○wʌʏ[2] 6 wəɪ

VIII.8.7 LAUGHING*

Q. What am I doing now [i.]?

Rr. CHUCKLING, GAUSTERING, GIGGLING, LAUGHING, NICKERING

Note 1—An attached superior ◇ below marks an inf.
Note 2—For additional exs. of LAUGHING, see IX.2.14.

7 Ch 1 lafɪn 2 lä:fɪn 3–5 lafɪn 6 la:fɪn

8 Db 1 la:fɪn, gɪdlɪn 2 lafɪn 3 la:ffɪn 4 lafɪn 5 gɒstɹɪn ["older"], lafɪn 6 lafɪn 7 lɒfɪn

11 Sa 1 la:fɪn 2 lafɪn 3–4 la:fɪn 5 lɒfn̩ 6 laˠ:fɪn 7 lɔ:fɪn 8 lɒfɪn 9 lɔ:fɪn 10–11 lɒfɪn

12 St 1 lafɪn 2 lafɪn, °nɪgɹɪn[1] 3–7 lɒfɪn 8 lafɪn 9 lɒfɪn 10 lafɪn 11 lafɪn, °◇laf[2], °nɪgəɹɪn

15 He 1 lɔ:fɪn 2 lɒfɪn 3 łɒfɪn 4–6 lɒfɪn 7 la:fɪn

16 Wo 1 lɒfɪn 2 əlɒfɪn 3 lɒfɪn, °◇łæf[1] 4 əlɒfɪn 5 lɒfɪn, °lɒft[1] *1 p.t.s.* 6 lɑ:fɪn, °lɑ:f[2] [n.d.g.] 7 tʃɷklɪn, s.w. la:fɪn

17 Wa 1 lafɪn [la:f *l. n.*] 2 la:fɪn, lɔ:fɪn ["older"], °¶lɔ:fɪn, °◇lɑ:f[4] 3–4 la:fɪn 5 əla:fɪn 6–7 la:fɪn

23 Mon 1 əlæfɪn 2–4 la:fɪn 5 la:fɪn, °◇la:f[2] 6 łɑ:fɪn 7 n.a.

24 Gl 1 əlɒfɪn, °læ:fs[2] *3 pr.pl.* III.10.3 2 əlɒfɪn, °~ 3 əlæ:fɪn 4–7 la:fɪn

25 O 1 la:fɪn 2 la:fn̩ [la:f[2] *l. n.*] 3 la:fɪn, °la:f[3] *v.* 4 łɑ:fɪn, °◇łɑ:f[3] 5–6 la:fɪn

VIII.8.8 OUR† OWN

Q. We have stopped borrowing the neighbour's tractor because we now have . . . .

At 7.2, 16.7 and 17.2, the f.w. used Version 4 of the Qr. in which the q. read: *The football match got rough and we couldn't play the game properly because we all got upset and lost . . . .* OUR† tempers. In which case the wanted r. was OUR (as reproduced below), not OUR OWN.

Rr. OUR, (ONE OF) OUR/US OWN, US

Note 1—When rec., the r. ONE OF OUR OWN is reproduced below in full.

Note 2—D.R.S. alone of the five f.ws. here concerned thought it necessary to indicate that the –R of OUR was closely connected phonetically with the foll. OWN. Though a "linking *r*" is a normal feature in English pronunciation, the Edd. have, in accordance with their usual editorial practice, used the transcription [ɹ‿] or [ɽ‿] whenever D.R.S. has noted this feature in his recordings below.

Note 3—I.m. exs. of OUR, US (= *our*) and OWN (used anaphorically) are reproduced below between square brackets untransliterated.

Note 4—For additional exs. of OUR see VI.3.3 and VIII.1.18; and of OWN, see VIII.9.6. For ONE, see VII.1.1 (and refs.).

7 Ch 1 əɹ o:n(2x) 2 a, əz [pref.; ɔ:n³] 3 əz o̤:n 4 aɷəɹ o:n [aɷə²; o:n] 5 əɹ o:n [a:ɹ¹ (+ V.)] 6 aɷəɹ o:n

8 Db 1 əz o:n [əz⁴] 2 əz o:n [a:²,⁴(2x)] 3 əɹ o:n 4 əɹ o:ᵚn 5 əz o:ᵚn [a:¹(2x)] 6 əɹ o:n 7 əɹ o·ɷn

11 Sa 1 aɷəʳ o:n 2 aɷəʳɽ‿o:n 3 aɷəɹ‿o:n 4 aɷə o:n 5 əɹ‿o:n 6 aɷɹ‿o:n 7 aɷəʳɽ‿o:n 8 ˈaɷəʳɽ‿o:n 9–11 aɷəʳɽ‿o:n

12 St 1 a:ɹ oɷn [əz¹; oɷn²] 2 ɷz oɷn [ɷz⁵; əz¹,²] 3 wɒn əv əɹ oɷn 4 wɒn əv a:ɹ oɷn 5 wɒ̣n əv əɹ oɷn [əz²; oɷn¹(2x)] 6 wɒn əv əz oɷn, ᵚəɹ oɷn² [əz¹] 7 wɒn əv a:ɹ oɷn 8 aɹ oɷn 9 wɒn əv əz oɷn 10 wɷn əv əz oɷn 11 aɷ˞ oɷn

15 He 1 əɹ æɷn 2 əʳɽ‿o:n, ᵒ∼³ 3 əʳɽ‿ɒɷn 4 əʳɽ‿æɷn 5–6 əʳɽ‿æɷn 7 wɒn əv əɹ o:n [o:ᵚn²,⁴(2x); oɷn³; o:n³]

16 Wo 1 əɹ‿ɒɷn 2 əɹ oɷᵊn 3 əɹ‿oɷn [əʳ:¹] 4 əɹ‿aɷn 5 əɹ‿aɷn [aɷəʳ¹; o̤:n¹] 6 əɹ‿oɷn 7 ə [ɔɷn¹,³; ɑɷn⁴]

17 Wa 1 wɒn əv əɹ o̤ɷn 2 n.a. 3 æɷəɹ o̤ɷn [ɛɷə³] 4 əɹ o̤ɷn 5 əɹ ɒɷn [ɛɷəʳ¹] 6 əɹ o̤ɷn 7 əɹ oɷn

23 Mon 1 əɹ‿ɒɷn 2 əɹ o:n 3 əɹ‿o:n 4 əuɹ o̤:n 5 əuɹ o̤:n 6 əɹ‿o:n [o:n¹] 7 n.a.

24 Gl 1 əʳɽ æɷn 2 əɹ æɷn [əɷ:əʳɽ² (+ V.)] 3–4 əɹ‿ɒɷn 5–6 əɹ ɑɷn 7 ᵚu:əɽ ɒɷn

25 O 1 əʳɽ ɔɷn [ɛ̈ɷəʳ²] 2 əɹ oɷn 3 əɽ ɔ̣ɷn 4 wɷn əv əɽ o:n, əɽ ɔ:n¹ [ɒn əɽ oɷn⁵ *on our own*; əɽ¹,⁵, aɷəɽ⁴; o:n⁴, o̤:n¹,⁴] 5 wʌn əv əɽ ɔ̣ɷn [əɽ²] 6 wən əv əɽ oɷn

VIII.8.9 CURSING* and SWEARING*

Q. Of a person who uses a lot of bad language, you'd say: He is always . . . .

Rr. BLACKGUARDING, CURSING
BLINDING, SWEARING

Note—The two rr. to the q. are separated below by a full stop.

7 Ch 1 kɒsɪn. swɛəɹɪn 2 kə:sɪn, s.f. kəsɪn [pref.]. swɛəɹɪn(2x) 3–4 kɒsɪn. swɛ:ɹɪn 5–6 kɒsɪn. swɛəɹɪn

8 Db 1 kɷssɪn. swɪəɹɪn 2 kə:sɪn. swɛ·əɹɪn 3 kəssɪn. swɛəɹɪn 4 kə:sɪn. swɛ:ɹɪn 5 kɒsɪn. swɛ:əɹɪn 6 kəsɪn. swɛ:ɹɪn 7 kəsɪn. swɛəɹɪn

11 Sa 1 kʌsɪn. swɛəʳ·ʈɪn 2 kəʳ:ʂɪn, °kɷs² *inf.* swɛ:əɹɪn 3 kəʳ:ʂɪn. swəʳ:ʈɪn 4 kʌsɪn. swɛ·ᵊɹɪn 5 kɷsɪn. swaʳ:ʈɪn 6 kəʳ:ʂɪn. swɛəʳʈɪn 7 kəʳ:ʂɪn. swe:əʳʈɪn 8 kəʳ:ʂɪn. swe:ɹɪn 9 kəʳ:ʂɪn. swɛəʳʈɪn 10 kəʳ:ʂɪn. swe:əʳʈɪn 11 kəsɪn. swe:ɹɪn

12 St 1 kɷsɪn. swɛ:ɹɪn 2 kɒsɪn, °~(2x). swɛ·ɹɪn, °swɛ:ɹɪn 3 kɒsɪn, °~. swɛ:ɹɪn 4 kɷsɪn. swɛ:ɹɪn 5 kɒsɪn. swɛ:ɹɪn 6 kɒsɪn, °~. swɛ:ɹɪn, °~ 7 kɷsɪn. swɛ:ɹɪŋg 8 kəᶦ:sɪn. sɛ:ɹɪn [*sic*] 9 kɒsɪn, °~. swə:ɹɪn, °~ 10 kɛ:sɪn, kɷsɪn. swɛ:ɹɪn 11 kə:sɪŋ. swɛ:ɹɪn, °~

15 He 1 kəsɪn. swe:ɹɪn 2 kʌsɪn. swɛəʳʈɪn 3 kəʳʂɪn. swɛəʳʈɪn 4 kɷsɪn. swɛəʳʈɪn 5 kəʳ:ʂɪn. swɛəʳʈɪn 6 kəsɪn. swɛəʳʈɪn 7 kʌsɪn. swɛ̣əɹɪn

16 Wo 1 kəʳ:ʂɪn. swɛ:ᵊɹɪn 2 kɷsɪn. swɛ:ᵊɹɪn 3 kɷsɪn. swe:əɹɪn 4 kɷsɪn. swaʳ:ʈɪn 5 kɒsɪn. swəʳ:ʈɪn 6 kəʳ:ʂɪn. swe:əɹɪn 7 kɷsɪn swɪəɹɪn

17 Wa 1 kɷsɪn, °~. swɛ̈:ɹɪn, °blɑɪndɪn 2 kɷsɪn. swɛəɹɪn 3 kɷsɪn. swɛ:ɹɪn, °~² [n.d.g.], °¶əswɛ:ɹɪn¹ [swɛ:wə:d³ *swear-word n.*] 4 kɷsɪn. swɛəɹɪn 5–6 kɷsɪn. swɛ:ɹɪn 7 kɷsɪn. swɛ·əɹɪn

23 Mon 1 kəʳʂɪn. swɛəʳʈɪn 2 kɷsɪn. swɛɹɪn 3 kœ:sɪn. swe:ɹɪn 4 kʰœ:ʂʂɪn. swɛ̣ɪɹɪn 5 kœ̣̈:sɪŋ. swɛ̣ᵊ:ɹɪn 6 kʌsɪn. swɛəʳʈɪn 7 n.a.

24 Gl 1 əkɷsɪn. əswəʳ:ʈɪn 2 kɷsɪn. swəʳ:ʈɪn 3 kɷsɪn. swe:ɹɪn 4 kɒsɪn. swe:ɹɪn 5 əkəʳ:ʂɪn. əswəɹɪn 6 kəsɪn. zweəʈɪn 7 kəsɪn. swɛəʈɪn

25 O 1 kɷsɪn, °əblakgaʳ:ɖɪn. swəʈɪn, °swɛ̈:ɹɪn¹ 2 kəʳ:ʂɪn. swɛəɹɪn 3 kəʳ:ʂɪn. swɛəʈɪn 4 kɷsɪn. swɛəʈɪn 5 kəʳ:ʂɪn. swɛəʈɪn 6 kʌsɪn. swɛəʈɪn

VIII.8.10 BEAT

Q. When a boy had been very naughty indeed, his father might put him across his knee and . . . . him on the buttocks.

Rr. BASTE, BEAT, BELT, CLOUT, FETTLE, GIVE HIM A /GOOD HIDING~SMACKING~THRAPING~THRASHING~WINDING/ THRASHING/, MARK, RATTLE/TAN HIS ARSE, SLAP (HIS ARSE/BEHIND/BOTTOM), SMACK (HIS ARSE), SPANK, STRIPE, TAN, TANK, THRAPE, THRASH, WALED *1 p.t.s.*

Note 1—Any r. comprising a phrase is reproduced below in full.

Note 2—Comparable expressions ref. beating but not clearly to beating on the buttocks are reproduced below between square brackets.

Note 3—BEAT (= *tired*) occurs at VI.13.8. For additional exs. of GIVE, see IX.8.2; and of ARSE, see VI.9.2 (and refs.). I'LL and I SHALL occur at IX.4.3 and i.m. exs. occurring below have not been provided with cross-refs. Their inclusion here does not therefore preclude their citation at IX.4.3.

7 Ch 1 smak [al spaŋk ðɩ[2] *I'll spank* (i.e. beat) *thee*] 2 smak, p. klæɷt [al gɩv ɩt ðɩ[3] *I'll give it thee* (i.e. I'll beat you); næɷtʃt[2] *nowched* (i.e. beaten) *p.p.*; kla:t[3] *clout* (=blow) *n.*] 3 bɛlt 4 smak [al ɹatl jəɹ a:s *I'll rattle* (i.e. beat) *your arse*] 5 ɹatl ɩz a:z, smak 6 spaŋk

8 Db 1 smɛk 2 smak, spaŋk 3 smak, °we:lt [rec. in «a we:lt ɩz a:s fɒɹ ɩm» *I waled* (=beat) *his arse for him*] 4 smak ɩz a:s [al gɩ ðɩ wɒn[2] *I'll give thee one* (i.e. a blow)] 5 slap, °slap ɩz a:s 6 smak [al be:ˈs[1] *I'll baste* (i.e. beat)] 7 bɛlt

11 Sa 1 spaŋk 2 slap ɩz a:s [aɩl smak jə[3] *I'll smack you*] 3 smak [al bɛlt jə[2] *I'll belt* (i.e. beat) *you*] 4 θɹa:ʃ, bi:t ["older"] 5 ɹatl ɩz aʵ:ʂ 6–7 slap 8 smak 9 smæ:k 10 smæk, spæŋk 11 smak ɩz aʵ:ʂ

12 St 1 bɛɩst [¶bɛɩstɩŋ[2] *basting*; ʃəl skɷft ðɩ[3] (I) *shall scuft* (i.e. beat) *thee*] 2 taŋk, °smak ɩz a:s[1] [ɒɩl skɷft ðɩ iəz[5] *I'll scuft* (i.e. beat) *thy ears*] 3 slap ɩz a:s, gɩv ɩm ə gɷd wɛɩndɩn [ɒɩl tansl[2] *I'll tancel* (i.e. beat)] 4 θɹaʃ ["usu."], θɹɛɩp ["older"; aɩl θɹɛ·p[4] *I'll thrape* (i.e. beat); aɩl klaɷt jəɹ iəɹoɷl[4] *I'll clout* (i.e. strike) *your ear-hole*] 5 slap ɩz bɩ-ɒ:ɩnd [ɒ:ɩl flɒg jə[3] *I'll flog you*] 6 spaŋk, klæɷt, θɹɛɩp ["older"], gɩv ɩm ə gɷd ɒ:ɩdɩn [ɒ:ɩl taŋk jə[1] *I'll tank* (i.e. beat) *you*; ɒ:ɩl gɩv ɩt jə[1] *I'll give it you* (i.e. I'll beat you)] 7 smak [ɒɩl skɷf jə[1] *I'll scuff* (i.e. strike) *you*] 8 θɹaʃ [aɩl klaɷt joɷ[2] *I'll clout* (i.e. strike) *you*] 9 slap ɩz bɒtəm, spaŋk, °fɛtl[2] [rec. in «ɒɩl fɛtl ðɒɩ a:s[2]» *I'll fettle* (i.e. beat) *thy arse*; ɒɩl skɷf jəɹ iə[2] *I'll scuff your ear*] 10 θɹɛɩp [a:ɩl gɩv jəɹ ə θɹaʃɩn[4] *I'll give you a thrashing*] 11 gɩv ɩm ə gɷd smakɩn, tan [ʃəl smak jə[2] (I) *shall smack you*]

15 He 1 θɹeːˈp [ɒɪɫ ʃɪft jə[2] *I'll shift* (i.e. beat) *you*] 2 tæn ɪz aʳːʂ [æɪɫ dɹɛs jɷəʳɽ‿æɪd[3] *I'll dress* (i.e. beat) *your hide*] 3 smæk ɪz aːs [əɪɫ kləɷt jəʳ[1] *I'll clout* (i.e. beat) *you*] 4 smæk ɪz aːs [əɪɫ kɪk jəʳɽ aːs[1] *I'll kick your a.*] 5 slæp [əɪɫ smæk jə[3] *I'll smack you*] 6 slæp ɪz aːs [əɪl kɪk jɷəʳɽ æs[1] *I'll kick your a.*] 7 spaŋk, p. tan, °gɪv ɪm ə gɷd ʔɪdɪn [aɪl dɹɒp sʌmət əkɹɒs jə *I'll drop somewhat across you* (i.e. I'll beat you with something)]

16 Wo 1 klɛɷt [al tan jə[1] *I'll tan* (i.e. beat) *you*] 2 spaŋk [aɪɫ wɒləp ðɪ[2] *I'll wallop* (i.e. beat) *thee*] 3 smæk ɪz aʳːʂ [ɒɪɫ æv jə[2] *I'll have* (i.e. beat) *you*] 4 smæk ɪz aʳːʂ [ɒɪɫ θɹeːp jɷ[3] *I'll thrape* (i.e. beat) *you*] 5 smæk ɪz aʳːʂ [əʳːɖ θɹeːp jə[1] *she'd thrape you*; ɒɪ ʃɫ fɷt jəɹ aʳːʂ[1] *I shall foot* (i.e. kick) *your arse*] 6 smæks [? *3 pr.s.*] ɪz æːs [ɒɪɫ θɹeːɪp jɷ[3] *I'll thrape you*; ə gɷd ɒɪdɪn[2] *a good hiding*] 7 gɪv ɪm ə gɷd θɹaʃɪn, s.w. gɪv ɪm ə gɷd θɹeɪpɪn [ə gɷd ɔɪdɪn[3] *a good hiding*]

17 Wa 1 slap [al gɪv ɪt jə[2] *I'll give it you*] 2 spaŋk, smak, °gɪ ɪm ə gɷd θɹeːpɪn [jəl gɛt jəɹ aːs smakt[4] *you'll get your arse smacked*] 3 slap [pref.], spaŋk 4 biːt, θɹaʃ 5 slap 6–7 smak

23 Mon 1 smæk ɪz æs [əɪɫ kɪk jəʳɽ aʳːʂ[1] *I'll kick your a.*] 2 smæk ɪz aːs 3 smæk ɪz a·s [əɪɫ flɒg jə[2] *I'll flog you*] 4 n.a. [əil wɸ̞·l̞ʌ̞p[1] *I'll wallop*] 5 smak, gɪv ɪm ə θɹaʃɪn [əiɫ gɪv ju· ə θɹaʃɪn[2] *I'll give you a thrashing*] 6 stɹəɪp 7 n.a.

24 Gl 1 slæp [əɪ ʃəɫ θɹeːᵊp jə[2] *I shall thrape you*] 2 smæk ɪz aːs [əɪ ʃɫ flɪp jə[3] *I shall flip you*] 3 tæn ɪz æːs 4 smak 5 spaŋk 6 slap 7 smak, smak ɪz aʳːʂ

25 O 1 bæɫt [al kɷf jəɹ ɪəʳɽɢɷɫ[3] *I'll cuff your ear-hole*] 2 smak 3 maʳːk [biːtɽ[1] *beater* (a wooden tool for beating) *n.*] 4 θɽaʃ [ɑɫ gɪv juː ə gɷd ɔɪdɪn[4] *I'll give you a good hiding*; biːt[1] *beat n.*, ¶biːtɪn[1] *beating*; ɔɪdɪn[1] *hiding n.*] 5 smak [al tan jɷəʳ aʳːʂ[2] *I'll tan your arse*] 6 smak [ɔ̈ɪɫ smak[3] *I'll smack*]

VIII.8.11 SCREAM

Q. If a child nipped her fingers in a door very badly, she'd most likely begin at once to . . . .

Rr. BAWL, BELL, BELLOCK, BLART, CRY, HOWL, SCREAM, SKRIKE/SQUAWK (OUT), SQUALL, SQUEAL, YELL, YELP OUT

Note 1—The r. at 24.1 may perhaps represent SQUEAL.

Note 2—The r. at 11.1 and the 2nd r. at 15.7 do not fit the context and are doubtless vbl. nn. Strictly speaking, they are u.rr.

Note 3—For comparable material see VI.5.15.

7 Ch 1 skɹɑɩk, ○~[2] 2 skɹaɩk 3 bla:t, skɹɑɩk, ○skɹɑɩkɩn[1] [n.d.g.] 4 skɹaɩk 5 skɹɑɩk 6 skwe:ᵊl, skɹaɩk

8 Db 1 jɛl· 2 kɹɑɩ 3 jɛl, ○¶jɛllɩn 4 jɛlɩn 5 skwɔ:k, jɛl 6 aɷl 7 kɹɑ̃·ɩ̃

11 Sa 1 skɹaɩkɩn, ○bɛləkɩn[3] *vbl. n.* 2 skɹaɩk 3 skɹi:m 4 skɹaɩk 5 ɛɷl 6 bɔʳ:ɭ 7 skɹi:m 8 skɹaɩk 9 skwɔ:l 10 skɹi:m 11 skɹaɩk aɷt

12 St 1 kɹaɩ 2 blɑ:t, skɹɒɩk 3 skɹɒɩk aɩt 4 kɹɒɩ 5–6 kɹɒ:ɩ 7 kɹɒɩ 8 skɹi:m 9 kɹɒɩ, bɛlək ["old"] 10 skwɩəl 11 kɹa:ɩ

15 He 1 skɹi:m 2 skwɔ:k 3–4 skwɑ:k 5–6 skwi:ᵊɫ 7 skɹi:m, ɘ̨ǫlɩn [jɛl *yell* (if being naughty)]

16 Wo 1 skwi:ɫ 2 skɹi:m 3 skɹi:ᵊm 4 swɑʳ:ʈ 5 skwɑ:k əɷ:t 6 bɛɫ 7 bɛlɷk, p. skɹi:m

17 Wa 1 skɹi:m, blä:t', ¶bla:tɩn 2 skwɩəl, skwɛɩl ["older"], ○¶skwɛɩlɩn 3 kɹəɩ 4 jɛɫ, kɹəɩ 5 ɛɷᵊɫ 6 kɹəɩ 7 ɛɷɫ, kɹəɩ

23 Mon 1 skwɩi:ᵊɫ 2–3 skɹi:m 4 n.a. 5 skɹi:m 6 əɷɫ 7 n.a.

24 Gl 1 ske:ᵊɫ 2 skwʲi:ᵊɫ 3–4 skwɑ:ɫ 5 bɔ:ɫ 6 skwɔ:ɫ 7 ○u:ᵊɫ

25 O 1 skwɩᵊɫ, skwɔ:k ["older"] 2 kɹə̈ɩ, skwɩᵊɫ 3 jəɫp ɛɷt 4 skwɩɷ 5 ɛ̈ɷᵊɫ 6 kɹə̈ɩ, skwɩəl [pref.]

VIII.8.12 AGREE

Q. When your friend is of the same opinion as yourself and will support what you say, you can say: I can always count on him to . . . . with me.

Rr. AGREE (WITH ME), BACK/BEAR ME UP, BE ON MY SIDE, HELP ME (OUT), HOLD IN WITH ME, SIDE (WITH {ME}), STAND BY ME, SUPPORT ME, UPHOLD

Note 1—A r. comprising a phrase is reproduced below in full. UPHOLD pres. presupposes a direct obj.

Note 2—In the 2nd r. at 7.1 and 17.3, US is used for the direct obj. ME.

Note 3—For additional exs. of WITH ME, see IX.8.4.

7 Ch 1 əgɹẹ:, bak əz ɷp [pref.] 2 stan baɩ mɩ, s.f. stən baɩ mɩ [pref.] 3 əgɹɛɩ, ○əgɹɛɩn *1 pr.pl.* 4 bak mɩ ɷp 5 bak mɩ ɷp' 6 bak mɩ ɷp' [əgɹi:d[2] *agreed p.p.* (ref. food suiting the stomach)]

8 Db 1 əgɹi: 2 bak mɩ ɷp' 3 ɷpɛ̧ɷd 4–6 bak mɩ ɷp 7 stand bɑɩ mɩ, bak mɩ ɷp

11 Sa 1 sɛɩd, bak mɩ ʌp ["older"] 2 bak mɩ ɷp 3–4 əgɹi: 5 bak mɩ ɷp 6 əgɹi: 7 bæk mɩ ʌp 8 bak mɩ ɷp 9 bæk mɩ ʌp 10 bak mi: ʌp 11 saɩd wɩð mɩ, bak mɩ ʌp

12 St 1 ɛlp mɩ aɷt 2 əgɹɛɩ 3 əgɹi: wɛɩ mɩ 4 ɛlp mɩ, stand bɒɩ mɩ 5 əgɹi: wɩð mɩ 6 bak mɩ ɷp 7 bi: ɒn mɒɩ sɒɩd 8 sɒɩd wɩ mi: 9 bak mɩ ɷp 10 saɩd wɩð mɩ 11 stand ba̱ɩ mɩ, əgɹi:

15 He 1 bæk mɩ ɷp 2 bæk mɩ ʌp 3 bæk mɩ ɷp 4 bæk mɩ ʌp 5–6 bæk mɩ ɷp 7 bɛəɹ mɩ ʌp, bak mɩ ʌp

16 Wo 1–2 bak mɩ ɷp 3 bæk mi: ɷp 4 bæk mɩ ɷp 5 bæk mɷ ɷp 6 bæk mə ɷp 7 s.w. əgɹi: wɩð mɩ

17 Wa 1 s.w. bak mɩ ɷp [old] 2 əgɹi: wɩð mɩ 3 bak mɩ ɷp, bak əs ɷp ["older"] 4 bak mɩ ɷp 5 səpɒɷəʳʈ mɩ, bak mɩ ɷp [pref.] 6–7 bak mɩ ɷp

23 Mon 1 bæk mɩ ʌp 2–3 bæk mɩ ɷp 4 n.a. 5 əgɹi: 6 bæk mɩ ʌp 7 n.a.

24 Gl 1 bæ:k m‿ɷ:p 2 stɒnd bəɩ mɷ 3 əgɹˈi: 4 bak m‿ɷp 5 ɒld ɩn wɩ mə 6 bak mɩ əp 7 əgɹi: wɩ mɩ

25 O 1 gɹi: wɩ mə 2 bak mɩ ʌp 3 əgɽi: 4 bak mɩ ɷp [ə ˈfɽɛnd ɩz ə ˈman ðət ju: ˈbak ɷp ɩn ˈɛnɩθɩŋk ɩ ˈsɛz[5] *a friend is a man that you back up in anything he says*] 5 əgɽi: 6 bak mɩ ʌp

VIII.8.13 YES, NO. YES

Q. If I asked you: Have you met that man, you could say: . . . .

If I said to you: You haven't met that man, have you?, and you had, you'd answer: . . . . I have.

Rr. Yes:—AH~AW~AYE, OH AYE, YES
No:—NAY, NO
Yes (contradictory):—AH (I HAVE), (OH/WELL) AYE, OH AH, (OH) YES

Note 1—The alternative rr. to the 1st part of the q. are separated below by a semi-colon, while the rr. to both parts are separated by a full stop.

Note 2—I.m. expressions for YES which are not identical in sense with those required here are reproduced below between square brackets, untransliterated, after the r. to the 2nd part of the q.

7 Ch 1 aɩ; nɛɷ, °~[2]. jɑɩ 2 a:, °jɩs[2], °aɩ[3], °ɑ:[3]; ne:, °næɷ . a: 3 a:; nɛ̈ɷ . a: 4 aɩ, °~[3]; no: . aɩ 5 a:; nʉ: . a: 6 a:; no: . aɩ

8 Db 1 a:; nɒω. jɛs 2 aι; nɒω. jɛs 3 a:; nɛ̞ω. a: 4 ɑ:; nɒω. jɛs 5 ɑ·ι; no:ᶷ. ɑ: 6 a:; no:ᶷ. a: 7 a:; no:ω. a:

11 Sa 1 aι; no:. jɛs 2 a:ᶥ, ○a·ι[3(2x)]; no:. jιs 3 aι; no:. jɛs 4 jɛs; no:. jɛs 5 ɔ:; nɛω. ɔ: aι av 6 aʵ:, ○~[4]; no:. jιs 7 aʵ:; no:. jɛs 8 aʵ:, ○~[2]; no:. jɛs 9 aι; no:. jɛs 10 ɒι; no:. jɛs 11 ɒι, ○~[2], ○ɔʵ:[2]; no:. jɛs

12 St 1 ɑ:[(2x)]; noω. jɛs 2 ɑ:; nɛω, ○~[1,5]. ɑ: 3 ɑ:; nω:. ‖ɑ: 4 a:; noω. jɛs 5 jɛs, a:; noω. jɛs 6 a̠:; noω. jɛs 7 ɑ:; noω. jɛs 8 ɑ:, ○~[2]; noω. ɑ: 9 ɑ:; nɛ:. ɑ:, ○~ 10 a:; nɛω. a̠: 11 jɛs; nɛω. jɛs

15 He 1 a:, ○~[3]; no:. jɛs 2 a:ι, ○ɔʵ:[3]; næω. jɛs 3 ɑ:ι, ○æι[1], ○ɑι[4], ○aʵ:[4]; no:. jɛs 4 æι, ○ɑʵ:[2]; no, ○nɒω[2]. jɛs 5 æι, ○~[2]; no:. jɛs 6 æι, ○~[1(2x)]; nɒω, ○næω[1]. jɛs 7 æ:, ○o: æ:, ○a:[1]; nọ:, ○no:[4]. oω æ:, wɛl æ:

16 Wo 1 ɑ:, ○~[1]; nɒω, ○noω[1]. jɛs 2 ɑ:, noω. jɛs 3 ɒι, ○ai:[2]; noω. jɛs 4 ɑʵ:, ○ɑʵ:ᶥ[1] [*sic*], ○ɑʵ:[3]; no:. jɛs 5 ɑ:, ○~[1(3x)]; no:. jɛs 6 ɑ:ι, ○ɑ:[1], ○ɑʵ:[3]; noω, ○~[3]. jɛs 7 ɑ:, ○~[1]; noω. oω i:s

17 Wa 1 jɛs; nǫω. ǫω jɛs 2 jιs, p. ɑ:, ○~[4(2x)], ○ǫ:[4]; nɔω. ɔω jιs 3 a:; nɐ. s.w. ǫω a:ɹ 4 a:; nǫω. jɛs 5 aʵ:; nǫω. jɛs, ○jas 6 a:; noω. jɛs 7 aʵ:; noω. jɛs

23 Mon 1 æι, ○~[4]; nɒω. æι 2 æι, ○~[1(2x),2]; no:. æι 3 æι, ○~[1]; no:. æι 4 jɛ̞:; nọ:. jɛ:s 5 ir.r. 6 æι, ○~[1]; no:, ○nɒω[1]. æι 7 n.a. [nou[1]]

24 Gl 1 ɑ:, ○~[1], ○ɑʵ:[1]; no:ω. ɑ: 2 ɑ:; no:ω. jɛs 3 ɒι; no:ω. ɒι 4 ɑ:ι, ○~[1(2x)]; nɒω. ɑ:ι 5 a:; no:. jɛs 6 a:; nuə. a:, o: a: 7 a:; no:. a:

25 O 1 aʵ:, ○~[2]; nɔω. jəs 2 aʴ:, ○~[1,3]; nɔω. aʴ: 3 aʵ:, ○~[2]; nọω. aʵ: 4 jɛs, s.f. ɑ: [usu.]; no:. jɛs 5 aʵ:, ○~[3], ○o: aʵ:[2]; nɔω. aʵ: 6 aʵ:, jɛs; noω. jɛs

VIII.8.14 STICKY

Q. When eating bread and treacle, a little girl's hands would soon get....

Rr. BALMED/STICKIED/STUCKED UP, MUCKY, STICKY, TACKY

7 Ch 1 stιkι 2 stιkkι 3–6 stιkι

8 Db 1 stιkkι 2–3 stιkι 4 stιkkι 5–7 stιkι

11 Sa 1–4 stɩkɩ 5 stɩ̞kɩ̞ 6 stɩkɩ 7 tækɩ 8 stɩkɩ, takɩ ["older"] 9–10 stɩkɩ 11 takɩ

12 St 1 stɩkɩ 2 boɷmd ɷp$^{(2x)}$, stɩkɩ 3 stɩkɩd ɷp, bɔ:md ɷp 4 stɩkɩ 5 stɩkɩ, bɔ:md ɷp ["old"] 6 stɩkɩ, bɔ:md ɷp$^{(2x)}$ 7 stɩkɩ 8 stɩkɩ̞ 9 stɩkɩ, bɔ:md ɷp$^{(2x)}$ 10 stɩkɩ 11 stɩkəɩ̞

15 He 1–6 stɩkɩ 7 stɩkɩ [ɔ:l mʌkt ʌp *all mucked up*, fr. i.'s wife, nat.]

16 Wo 1–6 stɩkɩ 7 mɷkɩ, s.w. stɩkɩ

17 Wa 1 stɩkᵉɩ 2 stɩkɩ 3 stɩkᵊɩ 4 stɩkᶦɩ· 5 stɩkɩ 6 stɩkᵊɩ 7 stɩkɩ

13 Mon 1–3 stɩkɩ 4 n.a. 5–6 stɩkɩ 7 n.a.

24 Gl 1–2 stɩkɩ 3 stʌkt ʌp 4–5 stɩkɩ 6 məkɩ, stɩkɩ 7 stɩkɩ

25 O 1–4 stɩkɩ 5 stɩkɩ̞ 6 stɩkɩ

VIII.8.15 COLLECT

Q. A tidy little girl, before going to bed, will not leave her toys lying about, but will [*i.*] . . . . *them.*

Rr. §BRUSH THEM ASIDE, CHUCK THEM UP TOGETHER, CLEAR THEM (ALL) UP, COLLECT (/§IT TOGETHER/THEM UP~TOGETHER), §FOLD/SCOOP/SCRAPE/STRAIGHTEN THEM UP, GATHER (/THEM TOGETHER/THEM {ALL} UP/UP/), LAP, PACK THEM /AWAY/UP (TOGETHER)/, PICK THEM /(ALL) UP/UP AGAIN/, PULL THEM TOGETHER, PUSH THEM UP TOGETHER, PUT THEM /AWAY/TOGETHER/UP (TIDY)/, SIDE (THEM AWAY), TIDY (/THEM UP/OFF/UP/)

Note 1—When rec. in the r., the pronominal obj. THEM is reproduced below only when it separates the two els. of a phrasal v.

Note 2—The 2nd r. at 7.2 may contain TIDY with loss of its final V. before the initial V. of the following word.

Note 3—For additional exs. of PACK *v.*, see VII.2.9, and of PUT, see IX.3.3 (and refs.). GATHER (=*fester*) occurs at VI.11.8.

7 Ch 1 saɩd, saɩd ɷm əwẹ: 2 stɹɛɩtən əm ɷp, taɩd ɒf 3 gɛðəɹ əm ɷp 4 lap 5 skɹi:p əm ɷp, pak əm ɷp 6 pak əm ɷp‘

8 Db 1 gɛðə 2 taɩdɩ əm ɷp 3 pɷt əm təgɛðə 4 stɹɛɩtn əm ɷp‘ 5 taɩdɩ əm, gɛðəɹ əm ɷp 6 pak əm əwi: 7 tã·ĩdɩ əm ɷp

11 Sa 1 pʌt ðəm əwe: 2 pɷt əm ɷp 3 klɪəʳɽ əm ɔ:l ʌp 4 kəlɛkt 5 pak əm ɷ̜p 6 klɪəʳɽ əm ɔʳ:ɭ ʌp 7 kəlɛkt 8 pak əm ɷp təgɪðəʳ, tʃɷk əm ɷp təgɪðəʳ 9 pʌt əm ʌp 10–11 gɛðəʳɽ əm ʌp

12 St 1 taɪdɪ ɷp 2 gɛðəɹ ɷm ɷp 3 gaðəɹ əm ɷp 4 kəlɛkt 5 pɷt ðəm ɷp 6 kəlɛkt 7 kəlɛkt ɷm ɷp 8 gaðə ðəm ɔ:l ɷp 9 kəlɛkt əm ɷp 10 klɛkt əm təgɛðə 11 gaðə ðəm təgɛðə

15 He 1 gʲæðəʳɽ əm ʌp 2 gæðəʳɽ əm ʌp 3 kɫɛkt 4 gæðəʳɽ əm ʌp 5 pɷl əm təgjɛðəɽ 6 gjɛðəʳɽ ɷp 7 klɪəɹ əm ʌp [pakɪn ʌp ðəɹ tɔɪz *packing up their toys*]

16 Wo 1 pɷt əm ɷp təgɪðə 2 klɪəʳɽ əm ɷp 3 kəlɛkt 4 klɛkt ɷm ɷp 5 pɪk ɷm ɷp 6 bɹɷʃ ɷm əsɒɪd 7 sku:p ðəm ɷp

17 Wa 1 pɷt ðəm əwɛɪ, klɪə ðəm ɷp 2 sku:p əm ɷp 3 gaðɹ əm ɷp 4 pɷt əm ɷp 5 kəlɛkt əm ɷp 6 klɪəɹ əm ɷp 7 kəlɛkt ðəm ɷp

23 Mon 1 gjæðəʳɽ əm ʌp 2 kəɫɛkt əm ɷp 3 pʌt əm ʌp 4 n.a. 5 ga:ðə 6 pɷʃ əm ʌp təgɛðəʳ 7 n.a.

24 Gl 1 gjæðəʳɽ ɷm ɷp 2 pɷt ɷm ɷp 3 pɪk əm ʌp 4 pɪk ɷm ɷp 5 pɷt əm ʌp 6 kəlɛkt əm əpʻ 7 pɷt əm əwɛ̝ɪ

25 O 1 §fəɷɫd əm ʌp 2 pak əm əwɛɪ 3 pɪk əm ɔ:l ʌp, gaðəɽ əm ʌp 4 pɷt əm ɷp tɔɪdɪ, p. klɛkt §ɪt təgɛðəɽ 5 pɷʔ əm əweʲ 6 pak əm ʌp

VIII.9.1 ACTIVE

Q. A strong healthy child who is never content to be still, but must always be doing something, you say is very . . . .

Rr. ACTIVE, BUSY, ENERGETIC, FIDGETY, FULL OF /BEANS/ LIFE/, §INDUSTRIOUS, LISSOM, LIVELY, NEVER AT REST, NIMBLE, (ALWAYS) ON THE GO, QUICK, RESTLESS, SHARP, UNEASY, §WIRY

7 Ch 1 aktɪf 2 ɛnədʒɛtɪk, p. ɔ:ləs ɒn ðə gɷ: 3 lɑɪvlɪ 4 ɹɛsləs, ɷnᵊɪəzɪ [pref.] 5 ɒn ðə gʉ̜: 6 fɪdʒɪtɪ, aktɪv [pref.]

8 Db 1 s.w. ɛktɪv 2 n.r., ᴼbɪzɪ⁽²ˣ⁾ [ɒn ðə ɹɒn *on the run*] 3 ɒn‿t go:ᴼ 4 lɑɪvlɪ 5 fɪdʒɪtɪ 6 ɒn‿t gü: 7 s.w. aktɪv, ɒn ðə gᴼü:

11 Sa 1 ɹɛstləs 2 ɛnədʒɛtɪk 3 a·ktɪf 4 ɹɛsləs 5 ɛnəʳdʒɛtɪk 6 aktɪv 7 æktɪv, ɔ·n ðə go: 8 ɹɛslɪs 9 æktɪv, 10 aktɪv, ɛnəʳdʒɛtɪk [əʳ: wəz ə lɪm *her* (=*she*) *was a limb* (i.e. very energetic)] 11 ɹɛslɪs

12 St 1 ɔ:lwɩz ɒn ðə goɷ 2–4 aktɩv 5 §ɩndɷstɹəs, aktɩv 6 nɩmbl 7 aktɩv 8 kwɩk 9 lɒɩvlɩ, §wɒɩɹɩ, aktɩv, °wɛ:ɹɩ [*sic*; ?=*wiry*] 10 aktɩv 11 fɩdʒɩtɩ, °lɩzəm[2]

15 He 1–2 fɩdʒɩtɩ 3 ɹɛsłəs 4 fɩdʒɩtɩ 5 fɩdʒɩti: 6 æktɩv 7 æktɩv, ɑ:lwɩz ɒn ðə go:ᵒ, fɩdʒətɩ

16 Wo 1 aktɩf 2 n.r. [əʳ· ɩz ə ɹɛgləʳ lɩtəł i:l *her* (=*she*) *is a regular little eel*; ju: am ə fɩdʒɩt *you am* (=*are*) *a fidget*] 3 fɩdʒɩti: 4 ɹɛstlɩs 5 ɹɛslɛs 6 fɩdʒɩtɩ 7 s.w. aktɩv ["modern"], ɔ:ləs ɒn ðə fɩdʒət, nɛvəʳ ət ɹɛst

17 Wa 1 lɑɩvlᵉɩ 2 ən ðə gəɷ, p. ɛnədʒɛtɩk 3 fɩdʒɩtᵊɩ 4 ʃa:p 5 haktɩv, aktɩv 6 aktɩv 7 ɹɛslɩs

23 Mon 1 ɹɛsłɛs 2 æktɩv 3 ɛnədʒɛtɩk 4 n.a. 5 a:ktɩv 6 ɹɛsłɛs 7 n.a.

24 Gl 1 ɛnəʳdʒɛtɩk 2 ləɩvłɩ 3 æktɩv, vʌł ə łəɩf 4 aktɩf 5 ɛnədʒɛtɩk 6–7 lʌɩvlɩ

25 O 1–2 aktɩv 3 p. aktɩv, bɩzɩ 4 s.w. aktɩv, fɷł ə bi:nz 5 aktɩv 6 lӧɩvlɩ

VIII.9.2 SHY

Q. Some children are very quiet and easily blush in company, because they are far too . . . .

Rr. BASHFUL, ? DOMICILED, SENSITIVE, SHY, TIMID

7 Ch 1–2 ʃɑɩ 3 ʃɑɩ [pref.], sɛnsɩtɩf 4 ʃɑɩ 5–6 ʃɑɩ

8 Db 1 ʃaɩ 2 ʃɑɩ 3 ʃaɩ 4 ʃɑɩ 5 ʃɑ·ɩ 6–7 ʃɑ̃·ɩ̃

11 Sa 1 ʃɛɩ 2 ʃaɩ, °tʃɩmɩd 3–4 ʃaɩ 5 ʃɒɩ 6–7 ʃaɩ 8 ʃɒɩ 9 ʃaɩ 10 ʃai: 11 ʃaɩ

12 St 1 ʃaɩ 2 ʃɒɩ 3 ʃɒ:ɩ 4 ʃɒɩ 5 ʃɒ:ɩ 6 ʃɒ:ɩ, °~[1] 7 ʃɒɩ 8 baʃfɷl ["old"] 9 ʃɒɩ 10 ʃɑ:ɩ 11 ʃɔ:i

15 He 1 ʃæɩ 2–6 ʃəɩ 7 ʃɑɩ

16 Wo 1 ʃɒɩ 2 ʃəɩ 3 ʃəi: 4–5 ʃəɩ 6 ʃɒɩ 7 dɒməsəɩl [*sic*], s.w. ʃəɩ

17 Wa 1 ʃɑɩ 2 ʃɔ·ɩ 3–7 ʃəɩ

23 Mon 1–3 ʃəɩ 4 n.a. 5 ʃəi, °~[2] 6 ʃəɩ 7 n.a.

24 Gl 1 ʃəɩᵊ 2–4 ʃəɩ 5 ʃӧɩ 6–7 ʃʌɩ

25 O 1–2 ʃӧɩ 3 ʃʌʏ 4 ʃə̜ɩ(2x) 5–6 ʃӧɩ

VIII.9.3 SILLY

Q. A man who is always doing ridiculous things and behaving stupidly, you say is quite . . . .

Rr. BARMY, BATTY, CAKEY, CRANKY, CRAZY, DAFT, DOPEY, DOTTY, DOZY, GAUMY, KIMIT, NOGGEN, OFF HIS HEAD, POTTY, SILLY, SIMPLE

Note—Expressions comparable with some of those listed above occur at VIII.9.4.

7 Ch 1 daft 2 ba:mɩ 3–5 daft 6 do:pɩ, nɒgən

8 Db 1 daft, dɒtɩ 2–3 daft 4 do:zɩ 5 daft 6 sɩlɩ 7 kɹe·ɩzɩ

11 Sa 1–2 daft 3–4 da:ft 5 baʳ:mɩ 6 daʳ:ft 7 dæ·ft 8 daft 9 dæ:ft 10 daft 11 da:ft

12 St 1 sɩlɩ 2 daft, s.w. kɛɩkɩ [kɛɩkɩə[1] *cakier*] 3 gɔ:mɩ, ke:kɩ 4 daft 5 s.w. kɛɩkɩ 6 sɩmpl, daft, kɛɩkɩ ["old"] 7 kɹaŋkɩ 8 daft 9 ba:mɩ 10–11 daft

15 He 1–2 dæft 3–4 da:ft 5–6 dæft 7 da:ft, °kjaɩmət[4]

16 Wo 1–2 daft 3 da:ft 4–5 dæft 6 dæ:ft 7 da·ft

17 Wa 1 pɒtɩ 2 s.w. da:ft, sɩlɩ, ɔ:f ɩz ɛd [klɛɩn gən *clean gone* (i.e. completely stupid)] 3 dǫɷpɩ(2x) 4 da:ft 5 daft 6–7 da:ft

23 Mon 1–2 dæft 3 da:ft 4 n.a. 5–6 da:ft 7 n.a.

24 Gl 1 dæ:ft 2 da:ft 3 dæ:ft 4 da:ft 5–6 sɩlɩ 7 da:ft

25 O 1 baʳ:mɩ 2 daft 3 pɒtɩ, sɩlɩ 4 bɑ:mɩ, batɩ 5 ba:mɩ 6 sɩlɩ

VIII.9.4 AS

Q. (A man who is always doing ridiculous things and behaving stupidly, you say is quite . . . . SILLY.) *And you can add: He's as [using his word] . . . .*

Rr. AS /A BATTLE–TWIG/A BROOM/A BRUSH/A DOORNAIL/A MADMAN/AN IDIOT/CAN BE/LATHERON'S DOG/THEY MAKE THEM/, BARMY AS A /BOAT–HORSE/DUCK/, CAKEY AS ANY FOOL, DAFT AS A /BAT/BRUSH/COOT/CUCKOO/DONKEY/ (GATE–)POST/GOOSE/HALFPENNYWORTH OF SOAP/MONKEY/ MOP/, DAFT AS /AN ASS/BLAZES/DISHWATER/HELL/HE LOOKS ~LOOKED/MUCK/MY ARSE/OLD HARRY/THE DEVIL/THE

HILLS/THEY BE MADE/(THEY) CAN BE/THEY~YOU MAKE THEM/, DOPEY AS SOAP, /DOTTY/DOZY/SOFT/ AS THEY MAKE THEM, §OLD NICK, POTTY AS /CAN BE/HELL/, SILLY AS A CUCKOO/GOOSE/SHEEP, SOFT AS BARM

Note 1—The *as* of the q., when repeated by the i., has been reproduced in the rr. but not in the list above.

Note 2—In the above list, THEY MAKE subsumes THEY MAEN~MAKEN~MAKES.

Note 3—The following complements in the similies rec. in the rr. also occur at the foll. refs.:—ARSE VI.9.2, BAT IV.7.7, BROOM V.9.10, BRUSH III.5.5, V.2.11, V.9.11, DEVIL and OLD HARRY VIII.8.3, DONKEY III.13.16, DUCKS IV.6.14, FOOL VII.4.10, (GATE–)POST IV.3.2, GOOSE IV.6.15, HALFPENNYWORTH VII.7.1, SHEEP III.6.1.

Note 4—For comparable material, see VIII.1.22. Expressions for SILLY occur at VIII.9.3.

Note 5—The f.w. omitted to rec. a complement at 7.5.

7 Ch 1 daft əz ble:zız [əz tɒf əz lıŋg[4] *as tough as ling*] 2 əz pɒttı əz kən bi: [ız əz læızı əz æɷt[2] *he's as lousy as aught*; əz ɹæɷnd əz ðat ðɛə[3] *as round as that there*; əz wi:l əz ı kɷd[3] *as well as he could*] 3 daft əz ðı mẹ:k əm [ɷŋgɹı əz ə ɹɒt[3] *hungry as a rat*] 4 sılı əz ə kɷku: [əz dʒɛf əz ə pü̯əst[2] *as deaf as a post*] 5 daft əz 6 do:pı əz so:pʻ

8 Db 1 daft əz ə də̟:ne:l, dɒtı əz ðı mɛkn əm 2 daft əz ðı kan bı, °sɒft əz ba:m[2] 3 daft əz ðə dɛvl 4 do:zı əz ðı mɛk əm 5 daft əz ə kɷku:, daft əz ðı mɛk əm 6 əz sɒft əz ðı mɛkn əm 7 əz ə batltwıg

11 Sa 1 daft əz ə ku:t 2 daft əz ə do:əne:l [əz fat əz ə snɛg[1] *as fat as a sneg* (="*eel*"); plẹ:n əz ə paksadl[3] *plain as a pack-saddle*] 3 əz ə bɹu:m 4 əz ə bɹʌʃ 5 baʳ:mı əz ə bo:təʳ:ʂ 6 daʳ:ft əz ə dɒŋkı [ız əz aɷd əz mi:[1] *he's* (ref. a straw-twister) *as old as me*; ə bʌtı əz lɒŋ əz mı aʳ:m[3] *a butty as long as my arm*; jə si: əz mʌtʃ əz jəʳ· kan[4] *you see as much as you can*] 7 əz dæ·ft əz ə ku:t 8 daft əz ə po:st 9 dæ:ft əz ə pɒst 10 daft əz ə ge:tpo:st [ðə staʳ:ʐ əz aɷt əz ki:n əz ɹazəʳ·ʐ[3] *the stars is (=are) out as keen as razors*] 11 əz da:ft əz ðə dɛvl

12 St 1 əz ə madmən 2 əz ðı mak ɷm, əz ðı mɛın ɷm 3 əz ke:kı əz ɒnı fɛɷl [flat əz ə flu:k[2], əz flat əz ə flu:k[2] (*as*) *flat as a fluke* (i.e. a flat-fish); əz faɷ əz ə tɷ:d[2] *as foul as a toad*; am ə soɷbəɹ əz ðɛı a:[2] *I'm as sober as they are*; əz fə:ɹ əz[2] *as far as*] 4 əz daft əz ı lü:kt 5 əz ən ıdıət [əz su:n əz jə kɒn[1] *as soon as you can*; vɛɹı nıə əz bıg əz ə dɷk[2] *very near as big as a duck*; əz lɷŋg əz fɹəm iə tə ðat wɔ:l[3] *as long as from here to that wall*] 6 əz kən bi: 7 §oɷd nık 8 əz daft əz ı lɷks, əz daft əz ə bɹɷʃ[6] [əz dɛd əz ə nıt[1] *as dead as a nit*] 9 əz lıðəɹəmz dɒg [apı əz ðə di:z lɒŋg[1] *happy as the day's long*] 10 əz daft əz mɷk 11 daft əz dıʃwɔ:tə

15 He 1 dæft əz ðe:ɹ me:k əm 2 dæft əz ə dɒŋkɩ 3 da:ft əz ðaɩ bɩ me:d 4 da:ft əz ɛɫ 5 dæft əz ðə dɛvɩɫ 6 dæft əz ɛɫ 7 əz da:ft əz ðeɩ meɩks əm, əz da:ft əz ə eɩpəθ ə so:p [ə apəl əz bɩg əz θɩk tɩn[2(2x)] *a apple as big as thick* (=*that*) *tin*; əz ʃaɹp əz ə pi:[3] *as sharp as a pea*]

16 Wo 1–2 daft əz ə mɷŋkɩ 3 da:ft əz məi: aᶦ:ʂ, da:ft əz ə mɒp ["more polite"] 4 dæft əz ðə dɛvəɫ 5 dæft əz ə mɷŋkɩ 6 dæ:ft əz ə mɑ:p 7 əz da:ft əz ðeɩ meɩks ɷm [əz ɔɩ əz ə man kəd tʃək ɩt ɷp[1] *as high as a man could chuck* (i.e. throw) *it up*; əz kwɩk əz jə kən[1] *as quick as you can*; ɔɩ nɛvə nəɷd ɩt sɛt sə bɑ:d əz ɩt av ðɩs tɔɩm[1] *I never knowed it set so bad as it have this time*; dɷɩn əz mɷtʃ dɑmɩdʒ əz əm kɑn[1] *doing as much damage as them can*; ɛld ðə stɹɔ:ɹ ɩn pleɩs əz fa:st əz ðeɩ gəd ɩt ɒn[2] *held the straw in place as fast as they got it on*; əz bɩg əz ə fɑ:dɩn[3] *as big as a farthing*; ə: bi: əz ɹɔɩt əz nɔɩnpəns[3] *her be as right as ninepence*; əz lɔŋ əz ə wɩk[4] *as long as a week*]

17 Wa 1 pɒtɩ əz ɛl [əz gɷd əz nu:[2] *as good as new*] 2 əz sɩlɩ əz ə ʃi:p [əz djɛd əz ə nɩt[3] *as dead as a nit*; ɩts əz ɹæɷnd əz ə kɷku:bɔ:l[4] *it's as round as a cuckoo-ball* (i.e. a small ball); ðat bləɷks əz stɹɛ̝ɩt əz ə da:t[4] *that bloke's as straight as a dart*] 3 n.r. 4 əz da:ft əz o̜ɷld aɹɩ [əz ɔɩ əz ɔɩ bi:[2] *as high as I be*] 5 daft əz ə po̜ɷst 6 da:ft əz ðɩ ɩlz [əz fɷl ə fli:z əz ðe̜ɩ kən ɒɷɫd[3] *as full of fleas as they can hold*; əz tɷf əz wɔɩəᶦ[3] *as tough as wire*] 7 da:ft əz ðɛɩ mɛɩk ɷm

23 Mon 1 dæft əz ðə dɛvəɫ 2 əz dæft əz ðe: də me:k əm 3 da:ft əz ɛɫ 4 n.a. 5 əz ju· me:k əm 6 da:ft əz ə bæt 7 n.a.

24 Gl 1 dæ:ft əz ə dɒŋkɩ [əz blæk əz jɷəᶦɳ[1] *as black as yourn* (=*yours*)] 2 da:ft əz ə kɷku: 3 dæ:ft əz ə mɒp 4 da:ft əz ɛɫ 5 sɩlɩ əz ə kɷku: 6 sɩlɩ əz ən as [əz va:st əz ju: kəd dɩg[1] *as fast as you could dig*] 7 da:ft əz kən bi:

25 O 1 əz ə ku:t [əz kli:n əz[2] *as clean as*] 2 daft əz ə gu:s 3 sɩlɩ əz ə ʃi:p [əz mʌtʃ əz jə lʌʏk[1] *as much as you like*] 4 əz sɩɫɩ əz ə kɷku: 5 ba:mɩ əz ə dʌkʻ 6 sɩlɩ əz ə gu:s, sɩlɩ əz ə dɒŋˀkɩ

VIII.9.5 (a) WE ARE†. I AM†. SHE IS†. THEY ARE†

Q. We drink water when . . . . thirsty.

Convert for I am, she is, they are.

Rr. WE ARE~'N~'RE, WE BE/BIN, WE'M

I AM~'M, I BE/BIN, I'SE

HER BE/IS~'S, HOO'S, SHE BE/IS~'S

THEY AM~'M/ARE~'N~'RE/'S, THEY BE/BIN, THEY'M BE

Note 1—The rr. to the four parts of the q. are separated below by full stops.

Note 2—Because of their special morphological interest, unstressed i.m. exs. of YOU ARE and THOU ART used as full vv. are included below between square brackets untransliterated. The exs. of YOU ARE follow the rr. to the 1st part of the q., and those of THOU ART are placed (for the sake of convenience) after the rr. to the 2nd part. No cross-refs. are given, and the inclusion of a form here does not preclude its citation elsewhere.

Note 3—Stressed exs. of some of the pr. t. forms of BE used as a full v. occur at IX.7.7.

7 Ch 1 wɩ. am, ○~^{4}. ʏz, ○ʏ:z$^{2(2x)}$. ðɩ 2 wɩə [jə^{2,3}]. əm, ○am$^{2(3x)}$, ○əm$^{3(3x)}$. əz, ○ʃɩz$^{1(4x)}$, ○u:z$^{2(3x),4}$. ðɩ, ○~^{1}, ○ðɩɹ^{2} [+ V.], ○ðə^{3}, ○ðəɹ^{3} [+ V.] 3 wɩ [jəɹ^{3} (+ V.)]. am. əz. ðɩ 4 wɩ [jə^{2}]. am. u:z. ðə 5 wɩn. am. əz, ○ə:z$^{1(3x)}$. ðɩ, ○ðəɹ^{1} [+ V.] 6 wɩn. am. əɻ:z, ○ə:z$^{3(2x)}$. ðə

8 Db 1 wə. am. ʃɩz, ○ʏ:z^{1}. ðə 2 wɩ. am. ʃɩz, ○~^{2}. ðɩ 3 wɩə. am [ða a:t^{1}]. ɷz, ○əz^{1}. ðɩə 4 wɩ. am [ðat^{3}]. ɛɷz, ○~$^{1(2x),3(2x)}$, ○ə:z^{1}. ðɩ 5 wɩ. am, ○~^{1,4}. ɛɷz. ðɩ 6 wə. am, ○~^{1}. əz. ðə, ○ðɩ^{1} [+ V.] 7 wɩ. am. əz, ○ə:z^{1}. ðə

11 Sa 1 wɩ. əm. əʳ·ʐ. ðɩ 2 wɩn [jɷəɹ^{1} (+ V.)]. əm. əz, ○ə:z^{2}, ○əʳ:z$^{1(3x),2}$. ðɩn, ○ðe:m^{2}, ○~^{2} [+ ð] 3 wɩ. am. əʳ:ʐ, ○ə:ʳ ɩz^{2}. ðɩ 4 wɩ. am. ʃɩz. ðɩ 5 wɩm. əm. əʳʐ, ○~^{2}. ðɩm 6 wɩ. əm. əʳ·ʐ, ○ʃɩz$^{2(2x),4}$. ðɩ 7 wɩ. am. əʳʐ, ○əʳ:ʐ^{1}, ○ʃɩz^{1}. ðɩ, ○ðe: bi:$^{1(2x)}$, ○ðe:m bi:^{1} 8 wɩ. am. əʳʐ, ○əʳ:ʐ^{1}. ðɩ, ○~^{1}, ○ðe:m$^{2(2x)}$ 9 wɩ, ○wi: bɩ^{1} [jo: bɩ$^{1(3x)}$]. əm, ○aɩm^{1}. əʳʐ, ○əʳ:ʐ$^{1(2x)}$. ðɩ, ○ðe: bɩ$^{1(2x)}$, ○ðe: bɩn^{1}, ○ðe:m^{1} 10 wɩ, ○wi:m^{3} [jo:əʳ^{3}]. əm. əʳʐ, ○əʳ:ʐ$^{2(2x)}$. ðɩ, ○ðe:m^{3} [ðe:m bɩ kɩlɩn^{3} *they'm be* (=*they're*) *killing*] 11 wɩm [jəʳɽ^{2} (+ V.); wɛn ju:m ʃɛl əm *when you'm shell* (i.e. you shell) *them*]. əm, ○aɩm$^{1,2(2x)}$. əʳʐ, ○əʳ:ʐ$^{2(2x)}$. ðɩm, ○ðe:m$^{2(2x)}$, ○ðe: am^{2}, ○ðe: bɩ^{2}

12 St 1 wi: ə. am, ○~^{2}. əz. ðɛɩ ə, ○ðɛ:ɹ^{2} [+ V.] 2 wɛɩ ə. ɒɩm [ðɛɩ at^{1}]. əz, ○ə:z^{1}, ○ʃi:z^{1}. ðɩə 3 wɩə. ɒ:ɩm, ○a:m^{1}, ○am^{1,2}. ə:z, ○~$^{1(2x)}$. ðiə 4 wi: ə. aɩm. ə:z. ðɛɩ ə 5 we: ə, ○wɩn^{3} [jə^{2}]. ɒ:ɩm, ○~^{3}, ○am,^{1,2,3}. ə:z, ○~$^{2(4x),3}$. ðɛɩ ə, ○ðəɹ^{2} [+ V.] 6 wɛɩ ə [ju:m]. ɒ:ɩm. ə:z, ○~$^{1,2(2x)}$. ðɛ:, ○ðɛ:ɹ^{2} [+ V.], ○ðəɹ^{2} [+ V.], ○ðɩ a:^{1} 7 wi: ɑ:. ɒɩ am, ○am$^{2,3(2x)}$. ə:ɹ ɩz, ○ə:z^{3}. ðɛ: 8 wi: bɩn. ɒɩ bɩn. ə:ɹ ɩz. ðɛɩ ɑ:, ○ðə^{4} 9 wɛɩ ə. ɒɩm [ða:t^{2}]. ə:z, ○~$^{1(5x),2}$. ðɛɩm 10 wi: ə [jɷm^{4}]. a:ɩm. ə:z. ðɛ:ə 11 wɩ əɹ [ju:m^{1}]. a:ɩ əm, ○a·ɩm^{2}, ○a:m^{2}, ○am^{2}. ʃi: ɩz, ○ʃɩz^{2}, ○ə:ɹz^{1,2}. ðɛɩ ə, ○ðɛɩn^{1,2}, ○ðɛɩm^{2}

15 He 1 wɪ, ○wi: bɪ[2]. əm. əz, ○əʳ:ʐ[3]. ðɪ, ○ðɛɪ bɪ[1(2x)], ○ðe:ɪ bɪ[2] 2 wɪ. əm, ○æɪm[2(2x)]. əʳʐ, ○~[1(2x)]. ðɪ, ○ðæɪ bɪ[2] 3 wɪ. əm, ○əɪm[3], ○æɪz[4], ○əz[4]. əʳʐ, ○~[1]. ðɪ, ○ðæɪ bɪ[1,4] 4 wɪ [ju: bɪ[2]]. əm. əʳʐ, ○~[1]. ðæɪ bɪ, ○~[1] 5 wɪ. əm, ○~[4]. əʳʐ, ○~[2]. ðɪ 6 wɪə. əɪm, ○~[1]. əʳʐ, ○~[1]. ðɛəʳ, ○ðæɪ bɪ[1(2x)] 7 wɪɹ, ○wɪəɹ[4] [ju: bi:[1], jɷəɹ[3]]. aɪm, ○ɑɪm[4(2x)]. əɪz, ○~[2(2x)], ○əɹ bɪ[4], ○ʃɪz[1(3x),2,3,4], ○ʃi:z[4]. ðɛəɹ, ○ðeɪm[1(3x)], ○ðeɪz[1], ○ðeɪ bɪ[1,3], ○ðeɪ bi:[2]

16 Wo 1 wɪ. əm. əz, ○əʳʐ[2(3x)]. ðɪ 2 wɪ [ju: am[2]]. əm [ði: bɪst[2]]. əz, ○əʳ· ɪz[2]. ðɪ, ○ðe: bɪ[1(3x)], ○ðe:m[2] 3 wɪm. əm. əʳʐ, ○~[2(4x),4], ○əʳ:ʐ[5(2x)]. ðɪm, ○ðe:m[1] 4 wɪ. əm, ○ɒɪm[3]. əʳʐ, ○~[1,2(2x)], ○əʳ:ʐ[2]. ðaɪ bɪ, ○~[1,2(5x)] 5 wɪ bɪ. ɒɪ bɪ, ○~[1]. əʳ:ʐ, ○~[1(2x)], ○əʳʐ[1(2x)]. ðaɪ bɪ, ○~[1] 6 wɪ [ju: bɪ[2]]. əm, ○ɒɪm[3(2x)]. əʳʐ, ○~[2(5x),3], ○əʳ:ʐ[1,3], ○əʳ: bɪ[2]. ðɪ, ○ðe: bɪ[1,3(2x)], ○ðe:ɪ bɪ[2(3x),3], ○ðe: bi:[2], ○ðe:ɪ bi:[3] 7 wi: bi:, ○wi:m[4]. əɪ bi:, ○əɪ bɪ[1], ○əɪm[1,4] [ði: bɪst[1,4(2x)], ði:z[3]]. ə:z, ○ə: bi:[3], ○ʃɪ bɪ[3], ○ʃi:z[4], ○ʃɪz[1,3(4x)]. ðeɪ bi:, ○ðeɪm[1(2x),4(7x)], ○ðeɪ bɪ[3,4(3x)], ○ðeɪ bi:[1,3], ○ðɛ bɪ[3]

17 Wa 1 wɪə. am. ə̣:z. ðɛ:ə 2 wɪə, ○wi:m[4] [ɷs ə gɷ·ɪn[4] *us (=we) are going*; jəɹ, ju:m[4(3x)]]. p. əɪm, ○~[1(2x),4(3x)], ○əm[1], ○am[4(2x)]. ə:z, ○~[4], ○əɹ ɪz[4], ○ʃɪz[1,2,3(8x)], ○ʃi:z[2]. ðə, ○~[3], ○ðɛə[1], ○ðe̞ɪm[1], ○ðe̞ɪm[1], ○ðeɪm[4], ○ðɛm[4] 3 wɪ [jə]. am. ʃɪz. ðɛ, ○ðɛə[1] 4 wɪə [jəɹ[1] (+ V.)]. əɪ bɪ. ʃi: bɪ, ○ʃɪz[1]. ðɛɪ bɪ 5 wɪ ə. əɪ əm, ○əɪm[1]. əʳ:ʐ, ○~[1], ○ə:z[1(3x)]. ðɛɪ ə 6 wɪ. am. əʳ:ʐ, ○~[4]. ðɛɪ əʳ, ○ðɛə[3] 7 wɪ [ʌs ə gü:ɪn[1] *us (=we) are going*]. əɪm. əʳ:ʐ. ðɛɪ bɪ, ○~[2]

23 Mon 1 ir.r., ○wɪ bɪ[2]. əɪm, ○~[2], ○əɪ bɪ[4]. əʳʐ, ○~[2]. ðæɪ bɪ, ○~[2(2x)] 2 wɪ. əɪm, ○~[3], ○əɪ bɪ[3]. əz, ○əʳʐ[3], ○ʃɪz[1]. ðɪ, ○ðe: bɪ[1] 3 wɪ, ○wi: bɪ[2] [ju: bɪ[1]]. əm. ʃɪz. ðɪ, ○ðe: bɪ[3(2x)] 4 wi̜·m [ju·m]. ə̜im. ʃiz, ○ʃi̜·z[1], ○ʃi̜:z[1]. ðeiɹ 5 wi:m, ○~[2] [jü̜:m[2]]. əɪ̜ bi, əɪ̜m. ʃi: bi, ○ʃi:z[2(2x)], ○ʃi·z[2], ○ʃ‿[2] [rec. in «ʃ‿o:ni lɪt·ɫ» *she* (is) *only little*]. ðei bi, ○ðei bi·[2], ○ðei bi:[2], ○ðeiɹ[1] [+ V.] 6 wɪ. əm. ʃɪz. ðɪ, ○ðe: əʳ[1] 7 n.a.

24 Gl 1 wɪə. əɪm, ○əɪ bɪ[1] [ði: bɪs[1]]. əʳʐ, ○~[1]. ðɪ, ○ðæɪ bɪ[1] 2 wi: bɪ. əɪ bɪ, ○~[3] [əɪz dʒɷst əθɪŋkɪn[1] *I's (=I'm) just a-thinking*]. əʳ bɪ, ○əʳ:ʐ[3]. ðæɪ bɪ 3 wɪ bɪ [j○u: bɪ[1]]. əɪ bɪ. əʳʐ. ðæɪ bɪ 4 wɪ bɪ. əɪ bɪ, ○~[3]. əʳʐ. ðaɪ bɪ, ○~[2,3] 5 wɪ bɪ. ə̈ɪ bɪ. əʳ: bɪ, ○əʳ:ʐ[2]. ðæɪ bɪ, ○~[2] 6 wɪ bɪ. ʌɪ bɪ, ○~[2(2x)]. əʳ: bɪ. ðæɪ bɪ 7 wi: bɪ. ʌɪm. əʳ:ʐ. ðe̞ɪ bɪ, ○~[1]

25 O 1 wi: bɪ. ə̈ɪ bɪ. ʃi: bɪ, ○ʃi:z[1]. ðɛɪ bɪ, ○ðeɪ bɪ[2] 2 wi: bi:. ə̈ɪ bɪ. ʃi: bɪ. ðɛɪ bɪ, ○~[1,2], ○ðeɪ bɪ[2], ○ðə[2] 3 wi: bi: [ɷs bɪ gwe:n[1] *us be (=we are) going*]. ʌʏ bɪ, ○ʌʏ bi:[1]. ʃi: bɪ, ○ʃɪz[2(2x)]. ðe: bɪ 4 wɪɽ, ○wɪəɽ[5]

[jəɽ[3], juə[3], ju: bi:[5]]. əɪm, ○~[1,2,4], ○ɑɪm[4], ○aɪm[5]. ʃi:z, ○ʃɪz[1(2x),4]. ðεəɽ, ○ðεɽ[1] [+ V.], ○ðəɹ[3] [+ V.] 5 wɪ bi: [ju: bi:[2]]. ʌʏ bɪ, ○~[3(2x)]. ʃɪz, ○ʃi:z[2]. ðe: bɪ, ○~[2] 6 wɪ ə˞. ʊ̈ɪ bɪ. ʃi: bi:, ○ʃɪz[1]. ðeᶥ ə˞.

VIII.9.5 (b) WE WERE†. I WAS†. SHE WAS†. THEY WERE†

Q. We drank water because . . . . thirsty.

Convert for **I was, she was, they were.**

Rr. US WAS, WE WAS/WERE(N)

I WAS/WERE(N)

HER WAS/WERE, HOO WAS/WERE, SHE WAS/WERE

THEM WAS, THEY WAS/WERE(N)

Note 1—The rr. to the four parts of the q. are separated below by full stops.

Note 2—All i.m. exs. are of the p.t. of the full v. BE, except for some of those transliterated between square brackets.

Note 3—At 7.5/6 and 8.6, it is not clear whether the third r. represents HER or HOO WAS/WERE. At 25.5, the f.w. omitted to rec. the prons. But the forms of SHE at IX.7.9 should be compared.

7 Ch 1 wɪ wə. a wəz. ʃɪ wəz, ʏ: wəz. ðɪ wə 2 n.a. a wə. n.a., ○u: wəɹ[3] [+ V.]. ðɪ wə 3 wɪ wən, ○~[3]. a wə. ε̈ω wə. ðẹ: wən, ○ðɪ wən[3] 4 wɪ wəz. a wəz. u: wəz. ðɪ wəz 5 wɪ wən. a wəz. ə wə. ðə wən, ○ðị: wən[3] 6 wɪ wən. a wəz. ə wəz. ðɪ wən, ○~[2]

8 Db 1 wɪ wə. a wə. ʃɪ wə. ðɪ wə 2 wɪ wə. a wə, ○~[2], ○aɪ wəɹ[3] [+ V.]. ʃɪ wə. ðɪ wə 3 wɪ wə. a wə. εω wə. ðɪ wə 4 wɪ wə. a wə, ○~[1]. εω wə. ðɪ wə 5 wɪ wə. a wə. ε‿wə. ðɪ wə 6 wεɪ wə. a wə. ə wə. ðɪ wə 7 wεɪ wə. a wə. ə: wə. ðeɪ wə

11 Sa 1 wɪ wə. ə‿wə. ə˞ wə. ðɪ wə 2 wɪ wən, ○wi: wəz[2]. ə wə. ə˞ wə. ðe: wən, ○~[2] 3 wɪ wəz. a wəz. ə˞: wəz. n.r. 4 wɪ wə. a wəz. ʃɪ wəz. ðɪ wə 5 wɪ wən. ə wən. ə˞ wəz. ðɪ wən 6 wɪ wə. a wə, ○aɪ wəz[3,4]. ə˞ wə. ðɪ wə 7 wɪ wə. a wə. ə˞ wə. ðɪ wə, ○ðe: wən[1(2x)] 8 wɪ wə. a wə. ə˞ wə. ðɪ wə 9 wɪ wə. aɪ wə. ə˞ wə. ðe: wə 10 wɪ wə, ○wi: wən[1]. ə wə. ə˞ wə, ○ə˞: wəz[2(2x)]. ðɪ wə 11 wɪ wə, ○wi: wən[1]. a wə. ə˞ wə, ○a˞: wəz[1], ○ə˞ wəz[2]. ðɪ wə, ○ðe: wə˞:[2]

12 St 1 wɛι wə, wi: wə. aι wəz, ○a wəz[1]. ɔ: wəz, ○ɔ wəz[1]. ðɛι wə[(2x)] 2 wɛι wən, ○wɛι wə[2]. ɒι wəz. ɔ: wəz. ði: wən 3 wɛι wə[(2x)]. ɒ:ι wəz ○a wə[2]. ɔ: wə. ðι wə, ði: wə 4 wi: wə, wi: wəz. ɒι wəz. ɔ: wəz. ðɛι wəz[(2x)] 5 we: wə[(2x)]. ɒ:ι wəz. ɔ: wəz. ðɛι wə[(2x)] 6 wɛι wə, wɛι wəz. ɒ:ι wə, ○a wəz[1]. ɔ: wə. ðɛι wə, ðɛι wə· 7 wi: wɒz, wι wəz, ○wi: wəz[2]. ɒι wəz, ○a wəz[4]. ɔ: wəz. ðɛι wə, ðɛι wəz, ○ðɛι wɒz[4] 8 wi: wɒz, wi: wəz, wi: wə, ○wi: wəz[1]. ɒι wɒz, ɒι wəz. ɔ: wəz, ○ɔ: wɒz[1]. ðɛ̣ι wə:, ðɛι wə: 9 wɛι wəz, wɛι wə, ○wɛι wəz[2]. ɒι wəz. ɔ: wəz. ðɛι wə[(2x)] 10 wi wə, wi: wəz. a:ι wəz. ɔ: wəz, ○~[4]. ðɛι wɒz[(2x)] 11 wi: wə. a:ι wəz, ○a: wəz[1]. ʃi: wəz. ðɛι wəɹ

15 He 1 wι wə. ə wə. əʳ wə. ðι wə 2 wι wəz, ○wi: wəz[3]. ə wəz. əʳ wəz. ðι wəz 3 wι wəz, ○wi: wəz[2]. ə wəz. əʳ wəz. ðι wəz, ○ðι wɷz[1] 4 wι wə. ə wə. əʳ wə. ðæι wəz 5 wι wə. ə wə, ○əι wəz[1]. əʳ wə. ðæι wə 6 wι wəʳ. ə wəʳ. əʳ wəʳ. ðæι wəʳ, ○əm wəz[1] 7 wι wəɹ. aι wəz, ○~[3(2x)], aι wəɹ[3]. əɹ wəz, ○~[4]. ðeι wəɹ, ○~[4]

16 Wo 1 wι wə. ə wə. əʳ wə. ðι wə 2 wι wə [wi: wən ɑ:lwιz ədu:ιn ιt[2] *we weren (=were) always a-doing it*]. ə wə. ə wə. ðι wə, ○ðe: wəz[1], ○ðe: wəʳɽ[2] [+ V.] 3 wι wə. ə wə. əʳ wəz. ðι wə 4 wι wə. ə wə, ○ɒι wəz[1]. əʳ wə. ðəι wə 5 wι wɷz, ○~[1]. ɒι wɷz, ○~[1(2x)]. əʳ wɷz. ðaι wɷz 6 wι wə. ɒι wə. əʳ wə, ○əʳ wəz[3]. ðι wə 7 n.a., ○wi: wəz[1], ○wi: wəɹ[1] [+ V.]. n.a., ○əι wəz[4]. n.a. n.a., ○ðeι wɷz[4]

17 Wa 1 wι wəz. ɑι wə. ɔ: wəz. ðɛ̣ι wə 2 n.a., ○wi: wə[4], ○wi: wəɹ[4] [+ V.]. n.a., ○əι wəz[3,4]. n.a., ○ʃι wəz[3]. n.a. 3 wi: wəz. əι wəz. ʃi: wəz. ðɛι wəz 4 wι wə. əι wə. əʳ: wə. ðɛι wə 5 wι wəz, ○wi: wəz[1]. əι wəz, ○~[1]. əʳ: wəz. ðɛι wəz 6 wι wəz. əι wəz. əʳ: wəz. ðɛι wəz 7 wι wəz. əι wəz, ○~[2]. əʳ: wəz, ○~[1], ○ə wəz[2]. ðɛι wəz

23 Mon 1 wι wə, ○~. ə wə. əʳ wə. ðæι wə 2 wι wə. əι wə. əʳ wə. ðe: wə 3 wι wə. ə wə. ʃι wə. ðι wə 4 wi̞· wə, wi̞· wəz. əi wəz. ʃi wəz. ðei wəz, ðei wə 5 wi: wə, wi· wəz, ○wi: wəz[2]. əi̞ wəz, ○~[1,2], ○əi wəz[1(2x)]. ʃi: wəz, ○ʃi: wəz[1]. ðe: wəz[(2x)] 6 wι wə. ə wə. ʃι wə. ðι wə 7 n.a.

24 Gl 1 wι wə, ○wi: wəz[1]. ə wə, ○əι wəz[2]. əʳ wə. ðæι wə, ○ðæι wəz[1] 2 wι wə. əι wə. əʳ wə. ðæι wə 3 wι wəz. ə wəz. əʳ wəz. ðæι wəz 4 wι wə. əι wə. əʳ wə. ðaι wə 5 wι wəz. öι wəz, ○~[2], ○öι əwəz[1,2] [*sic*]. ɔ: wəz. ðæι wəz 6 wι wəz. ʌι wəz. əʳ: wəz. ðæι wəz 7 wi: wəz. ʌι wəz. ɔ: wəz. ðɛ̣ι wəz

25 O 1 wɩ wəz. ðɩ wəz. ʃɩ wəz, ᵒəʳ: wəz². ðɛɩ wəz 2 wi: wəz. ðɩ wəz. ʃi: wəz. ðɛɩ wəz 3 wi: wəz, ᵒʌs wəz². ʌʏ wəz. ʃi: wəz. ðe: wəz 4 wi: wəʈ, wɩ wəʈ. ʒɩ wəz, ᵒəɩ wəz³. ʃi: wəz. ðeɩ wəʈ 5 wɩ wəz. ðɩ wəz. ʃɩ wəz. ðeɩ wəz 6 wɩ wəz. ðɩ wəz. ʃɩ wəz. ðeɩ wəz

VIII.9.6 OWN FAULT

Q. If a foolish man, in spite of your advice, does something and comes to grief and nobody else is to blame, you could say: Well it serves him right, it's his . . . .

Rr. FAULT, OWN DOINGS/FAULT

Note 1—The f.w. unfortunately omitted to rec. OWN at 17.1.

Note 2—I.m. exs. of OWN *adj.* are reproduced below between square brackets untransliterated. For additional exs. of OWN, see VIII.8.8.

7 Ch 1 o:n fɔ:t 2 o:n fɔ:t [ɔ:n⁴ VI.8.8] 3 o̧:n fo̧:t 4–6 o:n fɔ:t

8 Db 1–2 o:n fɒlt 4 ɒɷn fɛɷt 5 ɔ:n fɔ:t 6 ɔ̃:n fɔ̃:t 7 o·ɷn fɔ:t

11 Sa 1 o:n fɔʳ:lt 2–3 o:n fɔ:lt 4 o:n fɔʳ:lt 5 o:n fɔ:t 6–11 o:n fɔ:lt

12 St 1 oɷn fɒlt 2 oɷn foɷt 3 oɷn fɒlt, oɷn foɷt 4–5 oɷn fɔ:lt 6 oɷn fɒlt [oɷn¹ VIII.1.26] 7 oɷn fɔ:lt 8 oɷn fɔ̧:lt 9 oɷn fɔ:lt 10 oɷn fɔ:lt [oɷn³] 11 oɷn fɔ:lt

15 He 1–2 o:n fɔ:ɫt 3 ɒɷn fɒlt 4 æɷn fa:ɫt 5 o:n fa:ɫt 6 æɷn fɒɫt 7 o̧:n fɒlt

16 Wo 1 ɒɷn fa:lt 2 oɷn fɒɫt 3 oɷm fɒɫt 4 o:n faʳ:lt 5 o:n fa:ɫt 6 æɷn fa:ɫt 7 ɔɷn fɔ:lt [ɔɷn³]

17 Wa 1 fɔ:lt 2 ɔɷn dɷ·ɩnz 3–4 o̧ɷn fɒɫt 5 ɒɷn fɒɫt [ɒɷn¹] 6 o̧ɷn fɒɫt 7 ɒɷn fɒɫt

23 Mon 1 ɒɷn fɒɫt 2–3 o:n fa:ɫt 4 n.a. 5 oun fɒ̧·ɫt 6 o:n fa:lt 7 n.a.

24 Gl 1 æɷᵊn fa:ɫt 2 æɷn fa:ɫt 3–4 ɒɷn va:ɫt 5 ɑɷn fɔ:t 6 o:n fɒɫt 7 ɒɷn fɔ:t

25 O 1 ɔɷn fɒɫt 2 ɔɷn fɒɫt [ɔɷn¹] 3 ɔ̧ᵒn fɒɫt 4 o:n fɔ:ɫt [o:n⁴, o̧:n⁴] 5 ɔ̧ᵒn fɒlʔ 6 oɷn fɔ:ɫʔ

VIII.9.7 SUCH A‡

Q. You might go on to say: What a fool! You can't get any sense out of him at all. I've never come across . . . . fool.

Rr. SUCH (A)

Note 1—When rec. in the r., the word FOOL is reproduced below. Isolated i.m. forms of SUCH are reproduced between square brackets untransliterated.

Note 2—For exs. of FOOL, see VII.4.10.

7 Ch 1 sɩtʃ ə fʏ: [sɩtʃ ə plẹ:s[2] *s. a place*] 2 sɷtʃ ə [sɩtʃ[2]] 3 sɷtʃ 4–6 sɷtʃ ə

8 Db 1–3 sɷtʃ ə 4 sɩtʃ ə 5 sɷtʃ ə [sɩtʃ[4]] 6 sɷtʃ ə fɛɷl 7 sɩtʃ ə

11 Sa 1 sʌtʃ ə 2 sɷtʃ ə 3 sʌtʃ ə 4–5 sɷtʃ ə 6 sɩtʃ ə 7 sʌtʃ ə 8 sɷtʃ ə 9–10 sʌtʃ ə 11 sʌtʃ ə [sʌtʃ ə fɛlə[2] *s. a fellow*]

12 St 1 sɷtʃ ə 2 sɷtʃ ə [sɷtʃ[3]] 3 sɷtʃ ə fɛɷl 4 ʃɷtʃ ə fü:l 5 sɷtʃ ə 6 sɷtʃ ə fɛɷl 7 sɷtʃ ə fü:l 8–9 sɷtʃ ə 10 sətʃ ə dam [=*damned*] fü:l 11 sɷtʃ ə [sɷtʃ ə wa:ɩl[2] *s. a while*; sɷtʃ[2]]

15 He 1 sɷtʃ ə 2 sʌtʃ ə 3 sətʃ ə 4 sʌtʃ ə 5–6 sɷtʃ ə 7 sʌtʃ ə fu:l [sʌtʃ ən‿eɩpəs *s. a ? halfpennyworth*]

16 Wo 1–3 sɷtʃ ə 4 sɩtʃ ə 5 sɷtʃ ə, ○~ 6 sɷtʃ ə fu:əɫ 7 sɷtʃ ə fu:l [sɷtʃ ə ɩdɩɷt[1] *s. a*(n) *idiot*; sɷtʃ ə skələd[3] *s. a scholar*]

17 Wa 1 sɷtʃ ə 2 sɷtʃ ə [sɩtʃ[2(2x)]] 3–4 sɷtʃ ə 5 sɷtʃ ə [sɷtʃ[1]] 6–7 sɷtʃ ə

23 Mon 1 sʌtʃ ə 2–3 sɷtʃ ə 4–5 sʌ̩̈tʃ ə 6 sətʃ ə 7 n.a.

24 Gl 1–2 sɷtʃ ə 3 sʌtʃ ə 4 sɛtʃ ə 5 sɷtʃ ə 6 sətʃ ə 7 sətʃ

25 O 1 sɩtʃ ə [sɷtʃ[2]] 2 sɷtʃ ə 3 sɩtʃ ə fu:ɫ 4 sɷtʃ ə fuɷɫ 5 sətʃ ə 6 sɷtʃ ə

RESPONSES: BOOK IX

IX.1.1 ROUND*

Q. A ball isn't square, it is . . . .

R. ROUND

Note 1—In the i.m. below, an attached superior $\diamond$ denotes an adv., superior $\times$ a prep. and superior $\triangleleft$ n.d.g. Exs. of AROUND *adv.* or *prep.* are reproduced below between square brackets untransliterated.

Note 2—ROUND also occurs at II.7.1; -ROUND at I.2.4; ROUND *adv.* and *prep.* at II.9.5, and ROUNDS *n.pl.* meaning (ladder-)*rungs* at I.7.15. ROUNDABOUT(S) is included at VII.2.8.

7 Ch 1 ɹaɪnd, $^{\circ\times}$~^{2}, $^{\circ}$ɹaɒnd^{3} *n.* V.6.10 2 ɹæɒnd, $^{\circ}$~^{3}, $^{\circ\diamond}$~^{3} VIII.6.4, $^{\circ\times}$~^{2} VII.6.4, $^{\circ\times}$~$^{2(5x),4}$, $^{\circ\diamond}$ɹaɒnd^{2} IV.6.20 3 ɹaɪnd, $^{\circ\times}$~^{1} VII.6.4, $^{\circ\diamond}$ɹaɪn^{1} 4 ɹaɒnd 5 ɹaɪnd, $^{\circ\diamond}$~^{1}, $^{\circ\times}$ɹaɪn^{1} 6 ɹɛ̞ɒnd, $^{\circ\triangleleft}$ɹɛɒnd^{1}

8 Db 1 ɹɛ̞ɒnd, $^{\circ\times}$~^{3} [ɹɛ̞ɒndəts *roundets* (=*rounders*; ref. a children's game)] 2 ɹa:nd 3 ɹɛ̈ɒnd 4 ɹɛ:n, $^{\circ\times}$ɹɛ:nd^{1} 5 ɹa:nd, ɹɛ̞:nd 6 ɹɛ:nd, $^{\circ\times}$~^{1} 7 ɹɛ:nd

11 Sa 1 ɹɛɒn 2 ɹaɒnd, $^{\circ\triangleleft}$ɹæɒn^{2} 3 ɹaɒn 4 ɹɛɒnd 5 ɹɛɒn, $^{\circ\times}$ɹɛɒnd$^{2(2x)}$ 6 ɹaɒnd [ə ɹaɒnd wi:k^{3} *a round* (i.e. full) *week*] 7 ɹaɒn, $^{\circ}$ɹaɒnd^{1} [="*slippery*"] VII.6.14 8 ɹɛɒnd 9 ɹaɒn, $^{\circ\times}$~ 10 ɹaɒn 11 ɹau:n

12 St 1 ɹæɒnd 2 ɹaɪnd, $^{\circ}$~^{1} 3 ɹaɪnd, $^{\circ\diamond}$~^{1,2}, $^{\circ\times}$~^{1} 4 ɹæɒnd, $^{\circ\diamond}$~^{1}, $^{\circ\times}$~^{1}, $^{\circ\times}$ɹaɒnd^{1} 5 ɹaɒnd, $^{\circ\diamond}$~^{1,2}, $^{\circ\diamond}$ɹæɒnd^{2} 6 ɹæɒnd, $^{\circ\times}$~^{1}, $^{\circ\diamond}$ɹæ:nd$^{1(2x)}$ [əɹæɒnd^{1}] 7 ɹæɒnd 8 ɹæɒnd, $^{\circ\times}$~^{1,5,6}, $^{\circ}$ɹaɒnd 9 ɹa:nd, $^{\circ}$ɹaɒnd^{3} 10 ɹaɒnd, $^{\circ\times}$~^{3}, $^{\circ\diamond}$ɹa:nd^{5} 11 ɹæɒnd, $^{\circ}$~^{1,2}, $^{\circ\triangleleft}$~^{1}, $^{\circ\times}$ɹæ:nd^{1}

15 He 1 ɹæɒn, $^{\circ\times}$~^{1}, $^{\circ\triangleleft}$~^{1}, $^{\circ\diamond}$ɹæɒnd^{1} 2 ɹæɒn, $^{\circ}$~, $^{\circ\times}$~^{3} 3 ɹəɒnd, $^{\circ\times}$~^{3} [əɹəɒnd^{2}] 4 ɹəɒnd, $^{\circ}$~^{1} *n.* V.6.10, $^{\circ\triangleleft}$ɹəɒn^{2} 5 ɹʌɒn 6 ɹəɒnd, $^{\circ\times}$~ 7 ɹə̆ʉ̞nd, $^{\circ\diamond}$ɹaɒnd^{1}, $^{\circ\times}$~^{1}, $^{\circ}$ɹəɒnd^{2}

16 Wo 1 ɹæɒnd 2 ɹɛɒ^{ə}nd, $^{\circ}$ɹɛɒnd^{1} 3 ɹɛu:n, $^{\circ\times}$ɹɛu:nd^{1}, $^{\circ\triangleleft}$~^{1} 4 ɹəɒ:nd 5 ɹəɒ:^{ə}n, $^{\circ}$ɹəɒ:nd$^{1(3x)}$, $^{\circ\diamond}$~^{1} 6 ɹɛu:nd, $^{\circ\times}$ɹɛu:n^{1} 7 ɹæɒnd, $^{\circ\diamond}$~$^{1(3x),3}$, $^{\circ\times}$~$^{3,4(2x)}$, $^{\circ\times}$ɹæɒn^{1}

17 Wa 1 ɹæɒnd 2 ɹæɒnd, $^{\circ}$~, $^{\circ\diamond}$~^{1,3}, $^{\circ\times}$~^{1,4} 3 ɹɛ̈ɒnd 4 ɹɛɒn, $^{\circ\diamond}$~^{1} 5 ɹɛɒn, $^{\circ}$ɹɛɒnd^{1}, $^{\circ\diamond}$ɹæɒnd^{1} 6 ɹɛ̈ɒnd, $^{\circ\times}$ɹɛɒnd^{4} 7 ɹɛ̈ɒnd

23 Mon 1 ɹʌɒnd 2 ɹʌɒn, $^{\circ\triangleleft}$~^{1} [əɹʌɒn^{1}] 3 ɹəɒnd 4 ɹəund 5 ɹəund, $^{\circ\times}$~^{1} [əɹəund$^{2(3x)}$] 6 ɹəɒnd 7 n.a.

24 Gl 1 ɹəɷ:ənd, °◇ɹəɷnd³ 2 ɹəɷ:nd, °×~³, °ɹəɷ:n³ 3 ɹəɷnd 4 ɹəɷənd 5 ɹʌɷnd 6 ɹᵒu:n 7 ɹᵒu:nd

25 O 1 ɹɛ̈ɷnd, °ɑ~² 2 ɹæ̣ɷnd, °◇~² 3 ɹɛɷnd 4 ɽɑɷnd, °◇ɹaɷnd¹, °◇ɽaɷnd²·⁴, °×ɹaɷnd¹, °×ɽaɷnd⁴, °×ɽạɷnd³ 5 ɹɛ̈ɷnd, °◇ɹɛɷnd¹ 6 ɹɛɷnd

IX.1.2 STRAIGHT*

Q. This line is curved [*i.*], *but this one* [*i.*] *is* . . . .

R. STRAIGHT

Note—An attached superior ◇ below marks an adv. and superior × a form that is n.d.g.

7 Ch 1 stɹɛɪt 2 stɹɛɪt, p. stɹe:t ["older, rare"] 3–5 stɹɛɪt 6 stɹæɪt

8 Db 1 stɹɛɪtʻ 2–3 stɹɛɪt 4 stɹɛɪtʻ 5 stɹaɪt 6 stɹẹɪt 7 stɹɛɪt

11 Sa 1 stɹe:t 2 stɹɛɪt 3 stɹɛɪt, °◇stɹe:t² 4 stɹe:t 5 stɹɛɪt 6 stɹe:t, °◇stɹɛɪt³ 7 stɹe:t 8 stɹe:ˈt 9 stɹe:t 10 stɹɛɪt 11 stɹe:t

12 St 1 stɹɛ·ɪt 2 stɹɛɪt 3 stɹɛɪt, stɹaɪt, °~, °stɹi:t², °◇~¹ 4 stɹɛɪt 5 stɹe:t, °~, °stɹɛɪt³, °stɹi:t⁵ 6 stɹi:t, °~, °◇~¹ 7 stɹɛɪt 8 stɹɛɪt, °~¹ 9 stɹi:t 10–11 stɹɛɪt

15 He 1 stɹe:ˈt, °×stɹæɪt¹ 2–3 stɹɛɪt 4 stɹæɪt, °×~² 5 stɹæɪt 6 stɹɒɪt 7 stɹe:ˈt

16 Wo 1–2 stɹɛɪt 3 stɹe:ɪt 4 stɹaɪt, °×~¹ 5 stɹaɪt 6 stɹæɪt 7 stɹɛɪt, °◇~⁴ [stɹɛɪtn³ *straighten inf.*]

17 Wa 1 stɹẹɪt 2 stɹẹɪt, °~ 3 stɹɛɪt 4 stɹẹɪt 5 stɹɛɪt 6 stɹɛɪtʻ 7 stɹe:ət

23 Mon 1 stɹæɪt 2–3 stɹe:t 4 stɹẹ:ˈt 5 stɹeit, °~², °◇~² 6 stɹe:ɪt 7 n.a.

24 Gl 1 stɹæɪt, °◇~¹ 2–3 stɹæɪt 4 stɹɛɪt 5 stɹæɪt 6–7 stɹẹɪt

25 O 1 stɹæɪt, °×~¹⁽²ˣ⁾ 2 stɹɛɪʔ 3 stɹe:t 4 stɽe:t, °◇~¹, °×~³, °◇stɽɛɪt⁵ 5 stɹe:t 6 stɹeɪt

IX.1.3 ASKEW

Q. A picture not hanging straight, is hanging [*i.*] . . . .

Rr. ALL OF A ONER, (ALL) ASKEW, COBWOBBLY, COCK(S)EYED, CROOKED, LOP-ENDED/SIDED, ON THE /SKEW(-WIFFED)/ SQUINT/TILT, (ALL ON) ONE SIDE, SKEW(-WAY{S}/ WIFF{ED}/WIFTED), SKEWDY-WHIFFED, SKUMJOT, SKWIFT, SLANTING, TWISTED, UNLEVEL

Note—Expressions comparable with some of those listed above occur at IX.1.8.

7 Ch 1 ɒn‿ð skwɪnt 2 skɪɷwɪ̞ft 3 skɪʏ:wɪft 4 kɹɷʉ̞:kɪd 5 kɹ'ʏ:kɪd 6 kɹu:kəd

8 Db 1 kɹʏ:kɪdᵊ, kɒkaɪd·ᵊ 2 slantɪn 3 kɹɛ̈ɷkt 4 twɪstɪd 5–7 kɹɛɷkɪd

11 Sa 1 skɪu:wɪf 2 lɒpsaɪdɪd 3 kɹʌkɪd 4 kɹu:kɪt 5 əskju: 6 kɹʌkɪt 7 əskɪaɷ 8 skɪu:wɪftɪd 9 ʌnˈlɛvəl 10 skɪu:wɪf 11 skɪu:wɪft, °ɒn ðə skɪu:wɪft

12 St 1 skju:wɪftɪd, ɒn ðə skju: 2 skjü:wɪft 3 kɹɛɷkɪd, lɒpsɒ:ɪdɪd, skju:wɪft 4 ɒn ðə tɪlt 5 ɒn ðə skju:, skju:wɪft, °~⁵ 6 skju:wɪft, °~ 7 lɒbsɒɪdɪd 8 kɹɷkɪd 9 kɒbwɒblɪ ["pref."], s.f. skju:wɪf, °kɒbwɒblɪ² 10 kɹɷkɪd, skjü:wɪf 11 ɔ:l ə wɒ̣n sɒ:ɪd

15 He 1 ɒn ðə skju:-ɪft 2 ɒn ðə skjæɷ 3 skju:-ɪftɪd 4 skju:wɪftɪd 5 kɹʌkɪt 6 kɹɷkəd 7 əskju:, skju:wɪf, °~

16 Wo 1 skɪu:-ɪftɪd 2 skɪu:-ɪft 3 ɑ:ɫ əskɪu: 4 lɒpɛndɪd 5 skju:-ɪftɪd 6 skᶦu:wæɪz 7 skju:

17 Wa 1–2 kɹɷkɪd 3 skju: 4 skɪu:wɪft 5 əskju: 6 əskᶦü: 7 kɹɷkɪd

23 Mon 1 skjᵒu: 2 skju:wɪf 3 skju:dɪwɪf 4 n.a. 5 skjɪuwɪf⁽²ˣ⁾ 6 skwɪft 7 n.a.

24 Gl 1 ɒn ðə skju: 2 əskju: 3 ɑ:ɫ əskjɷu:, °skjɒmdʒɒɷt 4 kɹɷkəd 5 əskju: 6 kɹəkɪd 7 əskju:

25 O 1 ɔ:l əv ə wʌnə 2 skju:wɛɪ 3 əskju: 4 kɽɷkɪd, °~⁴ 5 wʌnsɔ̈ɪd 6 kɒksɔ̈ɪd

IX.1.4 BRITTLE

Q. Thin cups and saucers that come to pieces very easily in your hands, you say are very . . . .

Rr. BRICKLE, BRITCHELLY, BRITCHER, BRITTLE, BRITTLY, ir.r. CHEAPJACK, EASY BROKE(N), FRAGILE, FRAIL, JOTTY, NESH, ROTTEN, SOFT, ? TINGEY

7 Ch 1 bɹɪtl 2 i:zɪ bɹɔkn 3 p. bɹɪtl 4–5 bɹɪtl 6 dʒɒtɪ

8 Db 1–7 bɹɪtl

11 Sa 1 fɹe:l 2 bɹɪkl 3 bɹɪtəl 4 bɹɪtl 5 nɛʃ 6–8 bɹɪtl 9 bɹɪtəl 10 bɹɪtl 11 fɹe:ᵊl, bɹɪtəl

12 St 1 nɛʃ, bɹɪtɪl 2 bɹɪtl 3 bɹɪtl, bɹɪtʃəlɪ, ○bɹɪtʃlɪ[2] 4 bɹɪtl 5 i:zɪ bɹoɷk, s.w. nɛʃ 6 bɹɪtl, s.w. nɛʃ 7 bɹɪtl 8 ir.r. tʃi:pdʒak 9 bɹɪtl, bɹɪtʃə 10 bɹɪtl, fɹadʒaɪl 11 bɹɪtl

15 He 1 fɹægɫ 2 nɛʃ 3 bɹɪtəɫ 4 nɛʃ 5 bɹɪkəɫ 6 nɛʃ 7 bɹɪtl

16 Wo 1 bɹɪtl 2–4 bɹɪtɫ 5 bɹɪtɫɪ 6 bɹɪtɫ 7 s.w. bɹɪtl

17 Wa 1 fɹagɒɪl, bɹɪtl ["older"] 2 sɔ:ft[(2x)] 3 bɹɪtɫ 4 fɹɛɪɫ, s.w. bɹɪtɫ 5–7 bɹɪtɫ

23 Mon 1 bɹɪkɫ 2 bɹɪtɫ 3 bɹɪkəɫ 4 n.a. 5 fɹe:l, fɹadʒəiɫ 6 bɹɪtəɫ 7 n.a.

24 Gl 1 tɪŋʒɪ 2 bɹɪtɫ 3 bɹɪtəɫ 4 zɑ:ft 5–7 bɹɪtɫ

25 O 1 ɹaʔn 2 ɹɒʔn, bɹɪtl ["older"] 3 bɹɪtɫ 4 bɽɪ̈tɫ 5–6 bɹɪʔl

IX.1.5 ON PURPOSE

Q. If in drying the cups and saucers, someone breaks four or five cups, you might begin to think he was doing it . . . .

Rr. §CARELESSLY, (/FOR~TO THE/ON/) PURPOSE, PURPOSELY, WILFUL, WILFULLY

7 Ch 1 ə pəʴ:pəs 2 ɒn pə:pəs, p. ə pəʴpəs [pref.] 3 ə pəʴ:pəs 4 pə:pəslɪ, ɒn pə:pəs 5 ə pə:pəs, ○~[1(2x)] 6 ə pəʴ̣:pəs

8 Db 1 ə pəʴ̣:pəs 2–4 ə pə:pəs 5 ɒn pɒpəs 6 ə pə:pəs 7 pə:pəslɪ

11 Sa 1 ə pəʵ:pəs 2 fə ðə pəʵ:pəs 3 ə pəʵ:pəs 4 ə pəʵ·pəs 5 ə pəʵ:pɷs 6–7 ə pəʵ:pəs 8 fə ðə pəʵ:pəs 9 ə pəʵ:pəs 10–11 fə ðə pəʵ:pəs

12 St 1 ə pə:pə [? error for «ə pə:pəs», Edd.], ○ə pə:ps[2] 2–3 ə pə:pəs 4 ɒn pə:pəs 5 ə pə:pəs, ○~[5], ○pə:pəslɪ[5] 6–7 ə pə:pəs 8 wɪlfɷlɪ 9 ɒn pə:pəs, ə pə̣:pəs ["older"], ○~[2] 10 ə pə:pəs 11 ə pə:ɹpəs

15 He 1 fə ðə pəʵ:pəs 2 fəʵ: ðə pəʵpəs 3 fəʵ ðə pəʵ:pɷs 4 fəʵ ðə pəʵpəs 5 fə ðə pəʵpəs, ○ə pə̣ʵpəs[4] 6 fə ðə pəʵpəs 7 ɒn pəɹpəs, fə ðə pəɹpəs, ○ɒn pəɹpəs, ○ə pəɹpəs[4]

16 Wo 1–2 fə ðə pəʳ:pəs 3–4 ə pəʳ:pɷs 5 tə ðə pəʳ:pɷs, ○ə pəʳ:pɷs[1] 6 fəʳ ðə pəʳ:pɷs 7 ə pəʳpəs, ○~[4], ○ə pə:pəs[4]

17 Wa 1 ɒn pə̞:pəs 2 ən pə:pəs, ○ə pəʴpəs[1], ○ə pə:pəs[1] 3 ə pə:pəs 4 ə pəʳ:pəs 5 ə pəʳ:pɷs, ○~[1] 6 §kɛ·ələslɩ, p. ɒn pəʳ:pəs 7 ɒn pəʳ:pəs

23 Mon 1 fə ðə pəʳpəs 2 ɒn pəʳpəs 3 ɑ:n pəʳpəs 4 n.a. 5 wɩlfɷɫ 6 pəʳ:pəslɩ 7 n.a.

24 Gl 1 fəʳ ðə pəʳ:pɷs 2 ɒn pəʳ:pɷs 3–4 ə pəʳ:pəs 5 ə pəʳ:pɷs 6 ɒn pəʳ:pəs, ə̩ pəʳ:pəs ["older"] 7 ə pəʳ:pəs

25 O 1–2 ə pəʴ:pəs 3 pəʳ:pəslɩ 4 pəɽpəsɫɩ, ○pəɽpəs[1] 5–6 pəʳ:pəslɩ

IX.1.6 GREAT*

Q. To marry the wrong woman isn't a little mistake, but a . . . . mistake.

Rr. BIG, GREAT

7 Ch 1 gɹe̩:t 2 s.w. gɹe:t, ○gɹɛt[1] 3 gɹi:t, ○~[2] 4 gɹe̩:t, ○~[2] 5 gɹi:t, ○~[2] 6 gɹe:ᵊt

8 Db 1 gɹe:t 2 gɹɛt 3 gɹi:t 4 gɹi:t, ○~[1] 5 gɹɛt 6 p. gɹɛt 7 gɹɛt, ○~[1] VII.8.13

11 Sa 1–3 gɹe:t 4 bɩg 5 gɹe̩:t 6 gɹe:t 7 gɹe:t, ○~[1] 8–11 gɹe:t

12 St 1 gɹɛɩt, ○gɹi:t[2] 2 gɹi:t 3 gɹi:t, gɹɛt, ○gɹi:t[1] [gɹi:tlɩ[1] *greatly*] 4 gɹɛɩt 5 gɹe:t, ○gə:t[1], ○gɹɛɩt[5] 6 p. gɹi:t 7–8 gɹɛɩt 9 p. gɹi:t, ○~[2] 10–11 gɹɛɩt

15 He 1–2 gɹe:ɩt 3 gɹe:t 4 gɹe:ɩt 5 gɹæɩt 6–7 gɹe:t

16 Wo 1 gɹɛɩt 2 gɹe:t 3 gɹe:ɩt 4–5 gɹe:t 6 gɹɩt 7 gɹeɩt, gɹɛt [pref.], ○~[4]

17 Wa 1 gɹɛ̞ɩt 2 pp. gɹɛ̞ɩt, ○gɹɛt[1] [gɹɛɩt bɩg *g. big*] 3 gɹɛɩt 4 gɹɛ̞ɩt 5 gɹɛt, ○~ 6 gɹɛt 7 gɹɛɩt, gɹe:ᵊt ["older"]

23 Mon 1 gɹe:ɩt 2–6 gɹe:t 7 n.a.

24 Gl 1–2 gɹe:ᵊt 3 gɹe:ᶦt 4–5 gɹe:t 6 gəʳ:ʈ, ○~[2,3] 7 gɹe:t, gəʳ:ʈ ["older"]

25 O 1 gɹɛt, ○~[2] 2 gɹɛɩt 3 gɹɛt 4 gɽɛ:t, ○~[1(2x)] 5 gɹɛt 6 gɹɩʔ

IX.1.7 BACKWARDS. FORWARDS

*Q. Here are two ways of walking. This way I'm walking . . . .
And this way . . . .*

Rr. BACKWARD(S)

FORWARD(S), FRONTWARDS

Note—The rr. to the two parts of the q. are separated below by a full stop.

7 Ch 1–2 bakəts . fɒɹət 3 bakət . fəɹəd 4 bakədz . fɒɹədz 5 bakəts . fɒɹəts 6 bakədz . fɒɹəts

8 Db 1 bakwəd, bakə·ts ["older"] . fɒɹəd 2 bakədz . fɒɹədz 3 bakət . fɒɹəd 4 bakəts, °bakət[2] . fɒɹəts 5 bakədz . fɹɒntədz 6–7 bakədz . fɒɹədz

11 Sa 1 bakəʳ:ɖʂ [? error for «bakəʳ:ɖʐ», Edd.] . fɒɹət 2 bakəʳʈʂ, °bakəts[3] . fɒɹədz 3 bakwəʳ:ɖʐ . fɔ:wədz 4 bakəʳ:ʈʂ . fɒɹəd 5 bakəʳʈʂ . fɒɹəts 6 bakəʳ:ʈʂ . fɔʳ:wəʳ:ɖ 7 bakəʳʈʂ . fɒɹəts 8 bakəts . fɒɹəts 9 bakəʳ:ʈʂ . fɒɹəd 10 bækəʳ:ʈʂ . fɒɹəʳ:ʈʂ 11 bakəʳʈʂ . fɒɹəts

12 St 1 ba:kədz . fɒɹədz 2 bakədz . fɹɒntədz 3 bakədz, °~[2] . fɒɹədz 4 bakədz, °~[2] . fɒɹədz, °fɔ:wəd[3] 5 bakədz, °~[2], °bakwədz[5] . fɔ:wəd, °fɔ:wədz[5] 6 bakədz, °~ . fɒɹəd, °~[2] 7 bakədz . fɒɹədz 8 bakədz, °~[3] . fɒɹədz 9 bakədz, °~[1] . fɒɹəd, °fɒɹədz[1] 10 bakədz . fɔ:wəd, fɒɹəd 11 bakwɒdz . fɔ:wɒd

15 He 1 bækədz . fɒɹədz 2 bækəʳʈʂ . fɒɹəʳʈʂ 3 bækəʳɖʐ . fɒɹəʳɖʐ 4 bækəts . fɒɹəts 5 bækəʳʈʂ . fɒɹədz 6 bækəʳɖʐ . vɒɹəd 7 bakədz . fɒɹədz

16 Wo 1 bakədz . fɒɹədz 2 bakədz . fɹɒntədz 3 bækɒdz . fɒɹɒdz 4 bækɒts . fɒɹɒts 5–6 bækɒdz . fɒɹɒdz 7 bakədz, °bakədz[1,3,4] . fɒɹədz, °~[3]

17 Wa 1 bakədz . fɹɒntədz 2 bakədz . fəɹədz 3 bakwəd . fɒɹəd 4 bakəʳɖʐ . fɒɹədz 5 bakəʳɖʐ, °bakədz[1] . fɒɹəd 6 bakəʳɖ . fɒɹəd 7 fɒɹədz . bakəʳ·ɖʐ

23 Mon 1 bækəts . fɒɹədz 2 bækwədz . fɒɹədz 3 bækwəʳɖ . fɒɹəd 4 n.a. 5 bakwɒdz . fɹʌ̜ntwɒdz, fo:wɒdz 6 bækwəʳɖʐ . fɒɹədz 7 n.a.

24 Gl 1 bækwəʳ:ɖʐ . fɒɹɒdz 2 bækɒdz . fɒɹɒdz 3 bækəʳɖʐ . vɒɹədz 4 bakədz . vɹɒntədz 5 bakəʳ:ɖ . fɒɹɒd 6 bakəʳɖʐ . vɒɹəʳɖʐ, 7 bakəʳɖʐ . vɒɹəd

25 O 1 bakəʳ:ɖʐ. fɒɽəʳ:ɖʐ 2 bakəɹdz. fɒɹəɹdz 3 bakəʳɖʐ. fɹʌntəʳɖʐ 4 băkəɽɖʐ, °bakədz[1]. fɒɽəd, °fəɽwədz[1] 5 bakəʳɖʐ. fɒɹədz 6 bakəʳɖʐ. fɒɽəʳɖʐ

IX.1.8 DIAGONALLY

Q. To harrow a field, you can go this way [g. along the side], but sometimes you go [i.] . . . .

Rr. ACROSS (THE CORNER), ASKEW, ATHWART, CATER-AMBLE/CORNER(ED)/CORNERWAYS/SWISH/, CORNERWAYS, CROSS-/CORNERED/HARROW/HARROWING/ROADS/WARDS/WAY(S)/, FROM CORNER TO CORNER, ON /A SLANT/THE SKEW/, SKEW(-ACROSS/CORNERED/WAYS), /SKEWTING/THWART AND/ ACROSS, SLANTING, SLANTWAY(S), SQUINT-ROADS/WAYS

Note—Expressions comparable with some of those listed above occur at IX.1.3. For CROSS, see VIII.5.14 (and refs.), where exs. of ACROSS are also included.

7 Ch 1 skwɩntɹɷədz 2 kɹɔsəts °kɹɔswe:[1] 3 ki:təkɔ:nəd 4 skwɩntwe:z 5 skwɩntɹọ:dz 6 slantwe:ᵊz

8 Db 1 slantwe: 2–3 slantɩn 4 ki:tɩkɔ:nə 5 əkɹɒs‿t kɔ:nə 6 ke:təswɩʃ 7 ke:tə-ɒmɩl, °kɛɩtə-ɒmɩl[2]

11 Sa 1 əkɹɔʳ:ʂ 2 kɹɒswe:z 3 əkɹɔ:s 4 əkɹɔʳ:ʂ 5 skju:wẹ:z 6–7 əkɹɔ:s 8 kɹɔ:swe:z 9 skɩu:tɩn əkɹɔ:s 10 əkɹɔ:s 11 ɒn ðə skɩu:

12 St 1 kɛɩtɩkɔ:nəd 2 kɹɒsɹoɷdz 3 kɛɩtɩkọ:nə 4 kɹɒswɛɩz 5 skju:we:z, °kɹɒswɛɩz[5] 6 kɔ:nəwɛɩz, kɹɒswɛɩz, kɛɩtəswɩʃ, p. kɛɩtɩkɔ:nəwi:z [oldest] 7 kɔ:nəwɛɩz 8 kɹɒsaɹəɹɩn, kɹɒswɛɩz 9 kɛɩtɩkọ:nəd 10 kɛɩtɩkɔ:nəd 11 kɹɒswɛɩz

15 He 1 əkɹɔ:s 2 skjæɷ-aʳ:w [+ V.] 3 kɹɑ:swɛɩz 4–5 kɹɑ:swæɩz 6 kɹɑ:swəɩz 7 əskju:, p. kɹɒskɒɹnəɹd, °ə̣skju:

16 Wo 1 kɹɒswɛɩz 2 əkɹɑ:s 3 kɹɑ:swe:ɩz 4 kɹɑʳ:ʂwaɩz 5 skju:kəʳ:ɳɷd 6 kɹɑ:swæɩz 7 skju:weɩz

17 Wa 1 skju:wẹɩz 2 ən ə slɑ:nt 3 skju:-əkɹɔ:s 4 kɹɔ:swẹɩz 5 əskju:, °~[1] [skju: *skew v.* (i.e. harrow or plough diagonally)] 6 əskᵗü: 7 skju:wẹɩz

23 Mon 1 əskjᵒu: 2–3 kɹɑ:swe:z 4 n.a. 5 kɹɒ̝·sweiz 6 kɹɑ:swe:z 7 n.a.

24 Gl 1 skju:wæɪz 2 kɹɑ:swæɪᵊz 3 skjᵒu:wæɪz 4 kɹɑ:swaɪz 5 əθəʵ:ʈ 6 əskju: [əsku: ə ðə gɹᵒu:nd *askew of the ground* (i.e. 'across the field")] 7 skju:

25 O 1 kɹɔ:swæɪz, əskju: 2 kɹɔ:swɛɪ, °kɹɔ:swȩɪz[1] 3 əskju: 4 fɽəm kəɽɳəɽ tə kəɽɳəɽ, θəɽʈ n̩ əkɽɒs 5 kɹɔ:swe:z 6 kɹɔ:sweɪz

IX.1.9 CREEP*, CREPT† *p.t.* and *p.p.*

Q. To please the children, I often go down on hands and knees and . . . .

If he says *crawl*, ask for the meaning of *creep*, and then convert for p.t. and p.p. **crept**.

Rr. 1 pr.s.:—(S)CRAWL, CREEP, (S)CROBBLE
p.t.:—CREEPED, CREPT
p.p.:—CREPT

Note 1—A full stop separates the rr. to the two parts of the q. below. Since the forms of the p.t. and p.p. of CREEP are identical throughout, it is convenient to reproduce the one form concerned.

Note 2—At 7.2/5, 12.5 (2nd r.), 16.7, 17.2, and 25.4 (1st r.), pr.pp. were wrongly rec. instead of 1 pr.ss.

Note 3—In the rr. below, an attached superior ᴅ means that CREEP is identical in meaning with the alternative r. and superior × that CREEP implies furtiveness.

Note 4—In *Vols. I* and *IV*, the rr. to the 1st part of the q. were by an oversight designated inf., not 1 pr.s.

7 Ch 1 kɹȩ:p, skɹɔ:l ["pref."]. kɹɛpt 2 kɹɔ:lɪn [usu.], s.w. ᴰkɹi:pɪn, °kɹɔ:lɪn [ref. a snail]. kɹɛpt 3 kɹɔ:l, p. ᴰkɹɛɪp. kɹɛpt 4 kɹi:pʻ. kɹɛpt 5 skɹɔ:lɪn, p. kɹɛɪp. kɹɛp 6 kɹɔ:l, s.w. ᴰkɹi:p. kɹɛpt

8 Db 1–2 kɹi:p. kɹɛpt 3 kɹɔ:l. p. kɹɛpt 4 kɹɔ:l, p. kɹɛɪp. kɹɛpt 5 kɹi:p. kɹɛpt 6 kɹɛɪp. kɹɛpt 7 kɹɔ:l, kɹɛɪp. kɹɛpt

11 Sa 1–2 kɹi:p. kɹɛpt 3 kɹi:p. kɹɪpt 4 ᴰkɹi:p, kɹɔʵ:ɭ. kɹɛpt 5 kɹȩ:p. kɹɛp 6 kɹi:p. kɹɛpt 7–8 kɹi:p. kɹɛp 9 kɹi:p. kɹɛpt 10–11 kɹi:p. kɹɛp

12 St 1 skɹǫ:l, ᴰkɹi:p. kɹɛpt 2 skɹoɷl, ᴰkɹɛɪp. kɹɛɪpt 3 kɹɔ:l, kɹɛɪp [kɹɛɪpɪndʒɪnɪ *creeping-jenny* (ref. one who curries favour)]. kɹɛpt 4 kɹɔ:l, ˣkɹi:p. kɹɛpt 5 skɹɔ:l, ᴰkɹi:pɪn, °skɹɔ:l[5(2x)]. kɹɛpt 6 skɹɔ:l, ᴰkɹɛɪp, °skɹɔ:l[1], °skɹɔ:lɪn *vbl.n.*. kɹi:pt 7 kɹɔ:l, kɹɛɪp ["old"]. kɹɛpt 8 kɹɔ:l, ˣkɹi:p. kɹɛpt 9 kɹɔ:l, ᴰkɹi:p. kɹɛpt 10 kɹi:p. kɹɛpt 11 skɹɔ:l, ᴰkɹi:p. kɹɛpt

15 He 1–3 kɹi:p. kɹɛp 4 kɹi:p, °skɹɒbɫ ["usu."]. kɹɛp 5 ᴰkɹi:p, °skɹɑ:ɫ ["usu."]. kɹɛp 6 kɹi:p, skɹɑ:ɫ ["usu."]. kɹɛp 7 skɹɔ:lz, ˣkɹi:p [skɹɔ:ləɹ *scrawler* (ref. baby) *n.*]. kɹɛpt

16 Wo 1 kɹi:p. kɹɛp 2 kɹi:p, °kɹɑ:ɫ. kɹɛp 3 kɹe:ɩps. kɹe:ɩpt 4 ᴰkɹi:p, kɹɒbɫ ["usu."]. kɹɛp 5 kɹi:ps. kɹɛp 6 ᴰkɹi:p, skɹɒblɩn. kɹɛ:p 7 ᴰəskɹɒblɩn, s.w. kɹi:pɩn, °¶əskɹəblɩn[4] [kɹi:pəz *creepers* (= *lice*) *n.pl.* IV.8.1]. kɹɛp, °~[4] *p.p.*

17 Wa 1 kɹi:p. kɹɛp 2 skɹɒbl̩ɩn, kɹi:pɩn. kɹɛpt 3 kɹi:p. kɹɛpt 4 kɹɔ:ɫ, kɹi:p ["proper name"]. kɹɛp 5 kɹi:p. kɹɛpt 6–7 kɹɔ:ɫ, p. ᴰkɹi:p. kɹɛpt

23 Mon 1 kɹɑ:ɫ, ˣkɹˈi:p. n.r. 2 kɹi:p. kɹɛp 3 kɹi:p, skɹɑ:ɫɩn ["usu."]. kɹɛp 4 kɹi̞:p. kɹɛp 5 kɹi:p. kɹi:pʰ 6 kɹi:p. kɹɛp 7 n.a.

24 Gl 1 skɹɑ:ᵊɫ ["usu."], kɹi:ᵊp. n.r. 2 kɹˈi:p, skɹɒbɫ ["usu."]. kɹɛp 3 kɹe:ˈp. kɹɛp 4 kɹˈi:p. kɹɛp 5 kɹi:p. kɹɛpt 6 kɹɔ:l, p. ˣkɹi:p. kɹɛpt 7 kɹɔ:l. s.w. ˣkɹɛpt

25 O 1 kɹɩp. kɹɛp 2 kɹi:p, kɹɔ:l. kɹɛpt 3 kɹɔ:l, s.w. kɹi:p ["older", but not used]. kɹɛpt 4 kɽɔ:ɫɩn, ˣkɽi:p, °~ [kɽi:pɩn θɩsɷ[1] *creeping thistle n.*; kɽi:pǫɷɫ[2] *creep-hole n.*]. kɽɛp 5 kɹɔ:l, s.w. kɹi:p ["not used"]. s.w. kɹɛpt 6 kɹi:p. kɹɛp

IX.1.10 HEAD OVER HEELS

Q. In going backwards downhill, you might stumble and go over like this [i. a somersault with your arms]. How?

Rr. ARSE OVER /(YOUR) HEAD/TIP/, ARSEWARDS, BOX-NECK(ED), FLOP OVER, HEAD AND/OVER HEELS, HEAD-LONG, HEAD OVER THE HEEL, HEELS OVER HEAD, NECK OVER NOTHING, PITCH-POLL (OVER), ROLY-POLY, SOMERSAULT, TOPSY-TURVY, (TIPPLE OVER) TOP-TAIL

Note 1—The 1st r. at 7.5 and the r. at 12.11 look like vv. The rr. at 24.1/2 are here regarded as advs.

Note 2—For additional exs. of ARSE, see VI.9.2 (and refs.); of HEAD, see VI.1.1 (and refs.); and of OVER, see V.6.8 (and refs.).

7 Ch 1 jɛd ǫəɹ ẹ:lz 2 jɛd ən ɩilz 3 jɛd oəɹ ɛɩlz 4 nɛk oə nɷθɩn, jɛd oəɹ ˈi̞:lz, °jɛd oəɹ i:lz[1] 5 flɒp ǫə, p. jɛd ǫəɹ ɛɩlz 6 jɛd oəɹ i:lz

8 Db 1 jɛd o·əʳ ˀθ‿i:l 2 i:lz o·ə jɛd 3 jɛd o·ə t‿i:l 4 jɛd o·əɹ ɛɩlz, °jɛdlɷŋk 5 jɛd o·əɹ i:lz 6 jɛd o·əɹ ɛɩlz 7 jɛd o·əɹ ɛ̧ɩlz

11 Sa 1 ɛd o:əʴɹ i:lz 2 a:s o:vəʳ tɩp 3 ɛd o:vəʴɹ i:lz 4 ɛd o:vəʳ i:lz 5 aʳ:ʂ o:vəʳ jɛd 6 ɛd ovəʴ:ɹ i:lz, °ɹo:lɩpo:lɩ 7–8 ɛd o:vəʴɹ i:lz 9 ɛd o:vəʴɹ i:lz, °bɒksnɛkt 10 ɛd o:vəʴɹ i:lz 11 aʳ:ʂ o:vəʳ jə jɛd

12 St 1 tɒpti:l 2 tɩpl ɷə tɒpti:l 3 jɛd owəɹ ɛɩlz 4 ɛd oɷvəɹ i:lz 5 tɒpsɩtə:vɩ, ɛd oɷvəɹ i:lz, °∼[5] 6–8 ɛd oɷvəɹ i:lz 9 jɛd ɷvəɹ i:lz 10 tɒpsɩtə:vɩ 11 sɷməsɔ:lt

15 He 1 bɒksnɛk [ɩ bɒksnɛkt o:vəʳ *he box-necked over*] 2 pɩtʃpæɷɫ o:vəʳ 3 a:s o:vəʳ jɷd 4 a:s o:vəʳ jʌd 5 bɒksnɛkt 6 æs o:vəʳ jɷd 7 ɛd o:vəɹ ɩəlz [ɩ pɩtʃpo:ld o:vəɹ *he pitch-polled over*]

16 Wo 1 jɛd oɷvəɹ i:lz 2 ɛd oɷvəʴɹ i:ɫz 3 aʳ:ʂ oɷvəʳ jɷd 4 jɷd o:vəʴɹ i:ɫz 5 aʳ:ʂ o:vəʳ jɷd 6 jɷd oɷvəʴɹ i:ɫz 7 jɛd oɷvəʳ i:ɫz

17 Wa 1 ɛd o̧ɷvəɹ i:lz, s.w. as o̧ɷvə tɩp ["older", pref.] 2 jɛd ən ɩəlz 3 a:s o̧ɷvə tɩp, °jɛd o̧ɷvəɹ i:ɫz 4 jɛd o̧ɷvəɹ i:əɫz 5 aʳ:ʂ o̧ɷvəʳ jɛd 6 jɛd o̧ɷvəɹ i:ɫz 7 jɷd o̧ɷvəɹ i:ɫz

23 Mon 1 æsədz 2 a:s o:vəʴɹ ɛd 3 a:s o:vəɹ ɛd 4 n.a. 5 ɛd o:vəɹ i:ɫz 6 aʳ:ʂ o:vəʴɹ ɛd 7 n.a.

24 Gl 1 pɩtʃpæɷəɫ 2 pɩtʃpɒɷɫ 3 æ:s o:ɷvəʳ tɩp 4 a:s o:ɷvəʳ tɩp 5 aʳ:ʂ ɒvəɹ jɷd, °a:s ɒvə jɛd[2] 6–7 aʳ:ʂ o:və jəd

25 O 1 ɛd ɔɷvəɹ ɩəɫz 2 s.w. ɛd ɔɷvəɽ iəɫz 3 a:s o·vəɹ ɛd 4 ɛd o:vəɽ ɩəɫz 5 ɛd ɔɷvəɽ i:əɫz 6 aʳ:ʂ oɷvəʳɽ ɛd

IX.1.11 GIDDY

Q. When you turn round and round, you soon begin to feel . . . .

Rr. DIZZY, GIDDY, MAZY, SWIMY, WANKY

7 Ch 1 dɩzɩ̧ 2–3 dɩzɩ 4 dɩ̧zɩ 5 gɩdɩ 6 gɩdɩ, dɩzɩ ["older"]

8 Db 1 dɩzɩ, wɒŋkɩ 2–3 dɩzɩ 4 dɛzɩ 5–6 dɩzɩ 7 gɩdɩ, dɷzɩ ["older"]

11 Sa 1 dɩzɩ 2–6 gɩdɩ 7 gɩdɩ, dɩzɩ 8–11 gɩdɩ

12 St 1 mɛɩzɩ, dɩzɩ 2 mɛɩzɩ 3 gɩ̧dɩ, gjɩdɩ 4 gɩdɩ 5 gɩdɩ, °∼[5] 6 dɩzɩ, gɩdɩ ["old"], °∼ 7–11 gɩdɩ

15 He 1–7 gɩdɩ

16 Wo 1 gɪdɪ 2 gɪ̣dɪ̣ 3–5 gɪdɪ 6 gɪdɪ, swɒɪmɪ ["older"] 7 gɪdɪ

17 Wa 1 gɪdᵉɪ 2 gɪdɪ(2x) 3 gɪdᶤɪ 4 dɪzᶤɪ, gɪdᶤɪ ["older"], °gɪdɪ[1] 5 gɪdɪ
6 gɪdɪ· 7 gɪdɪ, °~[2]

23 Mon 1–3 gɪdɪ 4 n.a. 5 gɪdi 6 gɪdɪ 7 n.a.

24 Gl 1–4 gɪdɪ 5 gɪdɪ, swɔ̈ɪmɪ 6–7 gɪdɪ

25 O 1 gɪdɪ 2 gɪdɪ, dɪzɪ ["older"] 3 gɪdɪ 4 gɪdɪ, s.w. dɪzɪ 5–6 gɪdɪ

IX.2.1 FURTHER*†

Q. Paris is rather a long way from here, but Australia is much . . . .

Rr. FARTHER, FURTHER

7 Ch 1 fə:ðə, fa:ðə, °fəᶥ:ðəɹ 2 fə:ðə 3 fəᶥ:ðə 4 fə:ðə, °fa:ðə 5 fə:ðə
6 fəᶥ̣:ðə

8 Db 1 fəᶥ̣:ðə 2 fa:ðə, fə:ðə 3 fa:ðə 4 fə:ðə 5 fa:ðə 6–7 fə:ðə

11 Sa 1 fəʵ:ðəʵ 2 fa:ðəʵ 3–4 fəʵ:ðəʵ 5 fa:ðəʵ 6 fəʵ:ðəʵ 7 fəʵ:ðəʵ [ðə fa:ðəmo:st[1] *the farthermost*] 8–10 fəʵ:ðəʵ 11 faʵ:ðəʵ

12 St 1 fə:ðə 2 fə:ðə [fə:ðɪst[5] *farthest* IX.10.6] 3 fə:ðə 4–5 fa:ðə 6 fə:ðə
7 fa:ðə 8 fɑ:ðə 9 fa:ðə 10 fa:ðə, fə:ðə 11 fȧ:ðə

15 He 1 fa:ðəʵ 2 fəʵ:ðəʵ 3 fəʵ:ðəɽ, °~[1] 4 fəʵ:ðəɽ, °vəʵ:ðəʵ[2] 5 faʵ:ðəʵ
6 vəʵðəʵ 7 fɑɹðəɹ, fəɹðəɹ

16 Wo 1 fəʵ:ðə 2 fa:ðəʵ 3 fəʵðəʵ 4 fɑʵ:ðəʵ 5 fəʵ:ðəʵ 6 fa:ðəʵ 7 fəʵðəʵ

17 Wa 1 fa:ðə 2 fə:ðə, °~[1] 3–4 faʵ:ðə 5 fəʵ:ðəʵ 6 faʵ:ðə 7 fəʵ:ðəʵ
[faʵ:ðəməst[2] *farthermost*]

23 Mon 1 fəʵðəʵ 2 fə:də 3 fa:ðə 4 fœ:ðʌ̤̈ 5 fa:ðə 6 fa:ðəʵ 7 n.a.

24 Gl 1 faʵ:ðəʵ 2 fəʵ:ðəʵ 3 vəʵ:ðəʵ 4 vəʵ:ɖəʵ 5 fəʵ:ɖəʵ 6 vəʵ:ɖəʵ·
7 vəʵ:ɖəʵ

25 O 1 fəʵðəʵ, °fa:ðəʵ[1] 2 fəᶥ̣:ðə 3 fəʵ:ɽðə 4 fäɽðəɽ, °fəɽðəɽ[1], °fɑ·ɽðəɽ[4]
[fɑ̈ɽðəst[4] *farthest*] 5 fəʵðəʵ 6 faʵ:ðəʵ

IX.2.2 TILL

Q. You usually can't see a first-class football match on a Tuesday; you have to wait . . . . Saturday.

Rr. THAN, TILL~TIN, TO, UNTIL, WHILE

Note 1—The rr. at 15.1 and 17.6 look like reduced forms of TILL; and the r. at 12.7 and the 2nd r. at 12.10 may well be so, rather than a reduction of TO.

Note 2—For TILL *conj.*, see IX.2.3.

7 Ch 1 tl 2 tɩl, p. ðən, s.w. tɩn(2x), s.w. waɩl(3x), ○~1(2x),3, ○tɩn1(2x),4(2x), ○tɩl1,3, ○ðən 3 tɩl 4 tl 5 tɩl 6 tl

8 Db 1–2 tɩl 4 tl, ○~2 5 waɩl 6 tl 7 tɩl

11 Sa 1–4 tɩl 5 tl 6–8 tɩl 9 tɩl, ○~1 10–11 tɩl

12 St 1 tɩl 2 tən 3–4 tɩl, ○~2 5 tɩl 6 tɩl, ○~1 7 ə 8–9 tɩl 10 tɩl, ɒ, ○tɩl4,5 11 tɩl

15 He 1 tə 2 tɫ 3–4 tɩɫ 5 tɩl 6 tl 7 tɩl

16 Wo 1 tɩl 2 tɩɫ 3 tl 4–5 tɫ 6 tɩɫ 7 tɩl

17 Wa 1 tɩl 2 tɩl(2x) 3–4 tɫ 5 tl 6 əɫ 7 tɫ

23 Mon 1 tɫ 2 tɩɫ 3 tl 4 n.a. 5 tɩl 6 tɩɫ 7 n.a., ○ʌntɩl1

24 Gl 1–4 tɫ 5 tɫ 6 təɫ 7 tl

25 O 1 tl 2 tl, ○tɩɫ2 3 tɩl, ○~1,2 4 tɫ 5 tl 6 tə

IX.2.3 TILL THE‡ SUN*

Q. In summer you don't water your garden in the middle of the day; you wait [g. the sun going down] . . . . goes down.

Rr. ir.r. OF THE SUN, THAN/TILL~TIN/WHILE THE SUN, TILL /§AFTER SUNSET/§SUNDOWN/, TILL SUN

Note 1—The r. at 25.6 is regarded here as a reduced form of TILL.

Note 2—I.m. exs. of the advs. TILL and WHILE (=*till*), of THE + C., and of SUN are reproduced below in this order between square brackets. The exs. of TILL, WHILE and SUN are not transliterated. The various groups are separated by full stops and the individual items in the groups by semi-colons. Only a proportional number of the types of THE + C. rec. for each loc. are given below. Omission of the def. art. is shown by its insertion unitalicized, in round brackets at the appropriate point in the transliteration concerned.

Note 3—For TILL *prep.*, see IX.2.2. For additional exs. of THE + C., see I.5.1, II.9.5, III.1.7/11/12, III.2.11, III.3.6–8, III.5.2, III.7.8, III.10.7, III.12.9, IV.2.11, IV.4.1, IV.6.2/20, V.2.5/12, V.3.8, V.6.6, V.7.21/24, V.8.9/12/14, VI.1.4/6/7, VI.5.2/8, VI.6.2, VI.7.9, VI.9.7, VI.14.14, VII.2.6/11/12/14, VII.3.6/7/13, VII.5.1, VII.6.5/26, VII.8.8, VIII.1.9/24/25, VIII.8.3, VIII.9.1/4, IX.1.3/5/8, IX.2.5/7, IX.5.9, IX.8.8 and IX.10.3/5/6.

Note 4—The i.m. citations are not given cross-refs. unless the whole of the item concerned is reproduced elsewhere.

7 Ch 1 tl‿ð sɷn [ðə bɔ:ks^{1} *the box*; pɷl ðə kɒtəz^{1} *pull the cotters*; ɒn‿ð kɒp^{1} *on the cop* (i.e. turf at bottom of hedge); ɪn‿ð ʃɪpən^{1} *in the shippon*; dɹɛsɪn‿ð ɹɒps^{2} *dressing* (=*cleaning*) *the ropes* (=*entrails*); ð kɛɪz^{2} *the cows*; jʏ:st av‿ð ʃɒp^{2} *used* (to) *have the shop*; ɒf ð flɪʏ:ə^{2} *off the floor*; tə‿θ faɪə^{3} *to the fire*; ɒn‿ð ʃɪlf^{4} *on the shelf*; ð̩ last^{4} *the last*; ɪn‿ð bɒtəm^{4} *in the bottom*] 2 ðən‿tʔ sɷn$^{(2x)}$, tɪn‿tʔ sɷn [tɪn$^{1(4x),4}$; tɪl^{1}; ðən$^{2(2x)}$; waɪl$^{1(2x),3}$. əv ðə kja:t^{1} *of the cart*; tə:nɪn ðə gja:dɪn ɔ:və^{1} *turning the garden over* I.7.8; ðə wo:l ladə^{1} *the whole ladder*; ðə wo:l wi:l^{1} *the whole wheel*; ðə ɹi:l ɷ:ldɪst^{1} *the real oldest*; ən ðə mɷðə^{1} *on the mother*; θ‿taɪə^{1} *the tyre*; θ‿ɹɪdʒ^{1} *the ridge*; θ‿fle:l^{1} *the flail*; θ‿ɹɪtlɪn$^{1(2x)}$ *the ritling* (=*weakling*); θ‿ɹɑɪn^{1} *the rind*; θ‿li:f^{1} *the leaf*; θɹu:‿t mɪdl^{1} *through the middle*; ɪ‿t mɪlk^{1} *in the milk*; ən‿t fɹɷntbɷəd^{1} *and the front-board* (of cart); wɪ‿t wɪnd^{1} *with the wind*; wə‿t kwaɹɪ^{1} *was the quarry*; ɪntə‿tθ bɑ:k^{1} *into the bark*; ɪntə‿tθ fəɹə^{1} *into the furrow*; wɪə‿tθ wa:tə ɹɷnz^{1} *where the water runs*; fɪl‿tʔ kja:t^{1} *fill the cart*; lɷ:d‿tʔ kja:t^{1} *load the cart*; ðə bagɪnz$^{2(2x)}$ *the baggings* (=*snack*); ən‿t gɹɪndlstən^{2} *on the grindle-stone*; kli:nɪn‿t dɪtʃ^{2} *cleaning the ditch*; ɷp‿t slu:p^{2} *up the slope*; gɛt‿t ge:t^{2} *get the gate*; t‿kɔk^{2} *the cock*; ɪ‿t gɹaɷnd^{2} *in the ground*; əmɷŋ‿t bi:z^{2} *among the bees*; ɪ‿t ɹɷəd^{2} *in the road*; gɛt‿tʔ gɷə^{2} *get the gore*; ə‿tʔ tɒp^{2,3} *at the top*; ɪn ðə fɹɷnt^{3} *in the front*; pɷt ðə bagskɪnz ɪn t‿kɷm ðə kɹɷd^{3} *put the bagskins* (=*rennet*) *in to come the crud* V.5.7; kɪnlɪn ðə fæɪə^{3} *kindling the fire*; ən‿t flɷə^{3} *on the floor*; aɷt ə‿t ɹɷəd^{3} *out of the road*; pətəɹɪn‿t faɪə^{3} *pottering* (= *stirring*) *the fire*; wɪə‿t blu:bæ̞:lɪz^{3} *where* (are) *the blow-bellows*; fə‿t tʃɪldə^{3} *for the children*; ɪ‿t mɔ̝:nɪn^{3} *in the morning*; ən‿t dɹɛsə$^{3(2x)}$ *on the dresser*; pɷə‿tʔ te:^{3} *pour the tea*; te:n‿tʔ tʃans^{3} *taken the chance*; bɹu:‿tʔ te:^{3} *brew*(ed) *the tea*; ət wi:kɛnd^{3} *at* (the) *weekend*; θɹu:‿t kɪi-ɔ̝:l^{4} *through the key-hole*; ən‿t nɷəz^{4} *on the nose*; ɪ‿t gəb^{4} *in the gob* (=*mouth*); t‿bɔ:l ə jəɹ and^{4} *the ball of your hand*; bɪ‿t ɹü:ts^{4} *by the roots*; dæɷn‿t ʃɛlf^{4} *down* (from) *the shelf*; lu:k aftə‿t be:bɪ^{4} *look after the baby*; ðɛm ə‿tʔ nɷəzɷəlz^{4} *them are the noseholes*; fɹəm‿tʔ təp^{4} *from the top*; mɛnɪ əʔ^{t} tʃapɪl^{4} *many at the chapel*] 3 tɪl‿ð sɷn [ð‿wɛðə ɹaɪnd‿ð mʏ:n^{1} *the weather* (=*ring*) *round the moon*; ɷdə ðə wi:t^{2} *hooder the wheat* (i.e. put two sheaves across the top of the stook to keep it dry); ɪ‿ð spɹɪŋ^{2} *in the spring*; ð̩ ɹɪdʒ^{2} *the ridge*; ɪ‿ð wɪntə$^{2(2x)}$ *in the*

winter; wɛn‿ð faːməz[2] *when the farmers*; bɩ‿ð ɹọːd[2] *by the road*; ɩ ðə dɹeːn[3] *in the drain*; sɷm ə‿ð skɔːdɩd pɩg ɛː[3] *some of the scalded pig hair*; ɩ‿ð bɒtəm[3] *in the bottom*; ə‿ð lɒt[3] *of the lot*; ɷp ð fɛɩlt[3] *up the field*; θ‿kɔːf[3] *the calf*; θ‿kɔːk[3] *the cork* (ref. pith of a boil); ɩn‿θ ʃəɹːt[3] *in the shirt*; ɩ‿t mɩdl[3] *in the middle*] 4 tɩl‿ð sɷn [ðə wɒn[1] *the one*; fə ðə ɹɩvə[1] *for the river*; ɒn ðə mɛdəz[2] *on the meadows*; paɩzn ðə katl[2] *poison the cattle*; ðə ɹeːzn[2] *the reason*; ɩntə ðə pọːst[2] *into the post*; ɒn‿ð fẹːld[2] *on the field*; an ðə bakɛnd[3] *have* (*inf.*) *the backend*] 5 tɩl ðə sɷn [ðə mɩdɩn[1] *the midden*; ɒn ðə lɒftʻ[1] *on the loft*; ɩn ðə bɩŋg[1] *in the* (food-)*bing*; ðə wəːkaɩs[1] *the workhouse*; kɷt ðe bakswaθ[1] *cut the backswath*; ɩf ðə mɒn[1] *if the man*; ðə naɩz[2] *the noise*; ðə jɛdmɒn[1] *the headman*; fə‿ð dʒɒb[1] *for the job*; ət ðə wɷl[2] *at the wool* (=*hair*); ðə balɩ-iːk[2] *the bellyache*; ɒn‿ð gɹɛs[2] *on the grass*; fə‿ð kɔːvz[2] *for* the *calves*; ðə bɒtɷm[3] *the bottom*] 6 tl‿ð sɷn [tl[3]. ɩn ðə fɩʃ[2] *in the fish*; θɹuː ðə bɹɷkʻ[2] *through the brook* IV.1.3; ɩn ðə kɔːf kɩt[3] *in the calf kit* (=*pen*); ðə lam[3] *the lamb*; ðə kaɷəs[3] *the cowhouse*]

8 Db 1 tɩl‿t sɷn [t‿bɛk loːn[1] *the back loan* (=*lane*); kiːpn‿t dɒg[1] *keep* (*3 pr.pl.*) *the dog*; nɒk‿t woːz dɛɷn[1] *knock the walls down*; bɩ‿ˀ tɒpɩn[1] *by the topping*; θɹʏː‿t kɛɩ-oːl[3] *through the keyhole*; ɒn‿ˀ fiːlz[4] *on the fields*] 2 ir.r. ə‿t sɷn [+ "going down". wɑɩl[3,4]. tə‿t skᵒuːl[3] *to the school*; ɒn‿t ɹoːd[3] *on the road*; sam‿t ʃiːp ɷp[4] *sam* (=*collect*) *the sheep up*; ʃɩlɩn‿t pɛɩz[4] *shelling the peas*] 3 tl‿t sɷn [ðə θɔ̈ːtɹiː[1] *the thwart-tree* (=*curb*); ɩn ðə fɒdə[1] *in the fodder*; θ‿wɔːl[1] *the wall*; θ‿tlɛnzɩn[1] *the cleansing*; fə‿t pɩgz[1] *for the pigs*; t‿biːs[1] *the beast*; maɩnd‿ˀ tʃaɩl̥d[2] *mind the child*] 4 tl‿t sɷn [ə‿t pagᵊ[1] *of the peg*; av sɛɩn‿t nɛst[1] *I've seen the nest*; kiːp‿ˀ bəːdz ɒf[1] *keep the birds off*; təːnz‿ˀ ʃɛɩf[1] *turns the sheaf*; ˀ‿tɒp[1] *the top*; ət‿ˀ doəɹ[1] *at the door*] 5 waɩl‿t sɷn [lɛft‿t kaːt[1] *left the cart*; fɩl‿t kaːt[1] *fill the cart*; ɩz‿t pɹɒpə neɩm[1] *is the proper name*; wɩ‿t sɩkl[1] *with the sickle*; ə‿t jɛd[1] *of the head*; wɩə‿t biəs[1] *where the beast* (=*cattle*); ɩ‿t jaːd[1] *in the yard*; ət‿ˀ jɩəz ɛnd[1] *at the year's end*; ə‿t bak[1] *at the back*; ɩn‿t paːlə[2,3] *in the parlour*; fə‿t wɩntə[2,3] *for the winter*] 6 tl‿ð sɷn [ɩ‿ð nɛɩt[1] *in the night*; ɩ‿ð ɹɩkjaːd[1] *in the rickyard*; tə‿ð bɹɔːn[1] *to the brawn*; ɩ‿ð jaːd *in the yard*; θ‿kɹɷpə[1] *the cropper*; ɔː‿θ faːm[1] *all the farm*; θ‿pantɹɩ[1] *the pantry*; t‿bɩgɩst[1] *the biggest*; ɩ‿t lɒt[1] *in the lot*] 7 tɩl‿ð sɷn [ə‿ð ɹʻuːf[2] *of the roof*; ɩ‿θ pɩn[2] *in the pin* (ref. the middle place of a team of three horses in tandem)]

11 Sa 1 tɩl ðə sʌn [wɒts ðə matəʳ[4] *what's the matter*; ðə miːzlz[4] *the measles*] 2 tɩl ðə sɷn [ðə tɹɛd[2] *the tread*; noːd ðə ɹoːd[2] *knowed the road*; θɹuː ðə kiː-oːl[2] *through the keyhole*; ðat wəz ðə neːm[2] *that was the name*; ðə waɩt ə tɹæɷzəz[2]

the weight of (the) *trousers*; tə ðə kæʊz[3] *to the cows*; ðə ka:z[3] *the cows*] 3 tɪl ðə sʌn 4 tɪl ðə sʌn [spɛnt ðə mʌnɪ[2] *spent the money*] 5 tl ðə sʊn [ðə klɛnzɪn[1] *the cleansing* (=*placenta*); ðə kɹaft *the croft* (=*paddock*); ʊp ðə tɒp ə ðə ɹe̜:kɪn[2] *up* (to) *the top of the Wrekin* (pl.n.); ðə tʃɪəʳ[2] *the chair*; ðə swe̜:p[3] *the sweep*; ðə wɪnd[3] *the wind*; ɪn ðə lɛtəʳɖ[3] *in the letter*] 6 tɪl ðə sʌn [tɪl[3]. ɪn ðə gʌlɪt[1] *in the gullet*; te:k ðə tɒpməst[1] *take the topmost*; kɔ:l ɪt ðə tʃanəl[1] *call it the channel* (=*drain*); ɪn ðə wʊl ə ðə ʃɪp[2] *in the wool of the sheep*; ɒn ðə kaʊ[2] *on the cow*; ə ðə wɔ:ʳɖʐ[3] *of the words*; ðats ðə wəʳ:ɖ[3] *that's the word*; at ðə ki:-o:l[4] *at the keyhole*; ɪts ðə se:m[4] *it's the same*; bɹɪŋ ðə mɪlk ba:k[4] *bring the milk back* VI.13.14] 7 tɪl ðə sʌn [ðə læd[1] *the lad*; ðə fa:ðəmo:st[1] *the farthermost* IX.2.1; dɹɔ:z ðə bɛst[1] *draws* (out) *the best*] 8 tɪl ðə sʊn [ðə slɪps[1] *the slips* (ref. a halter); pʊt ðə stanz dɛʊn[1] *put the stands down*; fə ðə wʊst[1] *for the worst*; ɒn ðə se:m lɛbl[2] *on the same level*] 9 tɪl ðə sʌn [ðə kɛtl[1] *the cattle*; ðə bɪŋɹe:ndʒ[1] *the bing-range*; o:vəʳ ðə kɹəpəʳ[1] *over the crupper*] 10 tɪl ðə sʌn [mʌtʃ ðə se:m[1] *much the same*; ɪn ðə ple:s[1] *in the place*; ɔ:l ðə me:n ə ðə mʌk[1] *all the main* (part) *of the muck*; æd ðə bi:st[2] *had the beast* (=*bull*); ðə ʃe:p[2] *the shape*; ðə nækəʳmɒn[2] *the knacker-man*; bæk ʌp ðə faɪəʳ[3] *back up* (i.e. put ashes on top of) *the fire*; ðæt ɪz ðə bɛst[3] *that is the best*; ɔ:l ðə bɪts[3] *all the bits*] 11 tɪl ðə sʌn [wɒnt ðə vɛɹɪ aʊdɪst[1] *want the very oldest*; ə ðə plaʊ[1] *of the plough*; aɪ no: ðə ne:m[1] *I know the name*; ðə tɹʊθ[2] *the truth*; ðə blaʊbɛlɪs[2] *the blow-bellows*; ɪn ðə gaʳ:ɖɳ[2] *in the garden*]

12 St 1 tɪl sʊn [tɪl[1,3]. oʊldz ðə ʃavz[1] *holds the shafts*; stɛdɪz ðə wi:ɫ[1] *steadies the wheel*; ðə pʊəɹ ənz[1] *the poor ones*; ð ɹɪm[1] *the rim*; ət‿θ bak[1] *at the back*; ʊp‿θ ɹɪvə[1] *up the river*; ɪn‿θ mɪdl[1,4] *in the middle*; tʃʊks ʊm ɒf lʊɹɪ[1] *chucks them off* (the) *lorry*; ə‿θ bɪldɪn[2] *of the building*; stɒp‿θ wɔ:tə[2] *stop the water*; meɪk‿θ kɒfɪn[2] *make the coffin*] 2 tɪl sʊn [pʊt ðə pe̜g ɒn ðə wʊʊ tə sɛɪ ðə mɒn[1] *put the pig on the wall to see the man*; əz ðə wɛɪf[1] *as the wife*; aftə‿ð babɪ[1] *after the baby*; ɪn‿ð moʊnɪn[1], ɪ‿θ moʊnɪn[1] *in the morning*; kɪnt‿θ fɒɪə[1] *kint* (=*kindle*) *the fire*; θ‿si:sɒɪd[1] *the seaside*; ʊndə‿θ tʃɪn[2] *under the chin*; ðə loʊ-aŋgɪn wɒnz[2] *the low-hanging ones*; ð̩ ɹɪdʒ[2] *the ridge*; ɪn‿ð mɪdl[2] *in the middle*; stɒkɪn‿θ bag[2] *stocking the bag* (=*udder*); tə‿θ pɪt[2] *to the pit* (=*pond*); ə‿θ pɪt[2] *of the pit* (=*pond*); θ‿pʊlɪboʊn[2(2x)] *the pulling-bone* (=*wishbone*); θ‿tɹɛd[2] *the tread*; mɛks‿θ bɛst[2] *makes the best*; da:n‿θ fɛɪld[2] *down the field*; pʊl ðə tʃi:n[3] *pull the chain*; stʊə‿ð kɔ:n[3] *store the corn*; θ‿pɛtɪfɛlt[3] *the petty field* (=*pasture*)] 3 tɪl‿θ sʊn [tɪl[1(3x),2]. ðə kɹʊdz[1] *the curds*; wɒt ðɛ dɛvl[1] *what the devil*; ð‿ɹaɪt ni:m[1] *the right name*; θ‿ɹɛʊf[1] *the roof*; θ‿ɹɪdʒ[1] *the ridge*; ɪn‿θ pantɹɪ[1] *in the pantry*; ɒn‿θ tʃiə[1] *on the chair*; θ‿swɛɪ[1] *the sway* (=*crane*); bloʊ‿θ fɒɪəɹ[1] *blow the fire*; nɛɪdɪn‿θ dɒf[1]

kneading the dough; tə‿θ fə:ɹ ɛnd[1] *to the far end*; ðə ɹoɷsɩəst[2] *the rosiest*; ðə pɹɒpə[2] *the proper*; ðə mɩlk[2] *the milk*; ðɛnz ðə tɒ:ɩm[2] *then's the time*; ən ðə fatɩst[2] *and the fattest*; θ‿kaɷəs[2] *the cowhouse*; fɛtʃ‿θ tɩts[2] *fetch the tits* (=*horses*); ə‿θ kaɷz[2] *of the cows*; θ fɷt[2] *the foot*; ə‿θ dɷə[2] *of the door*; ɒn‿θ bɒtəm nɩb ə‿θ sɒ:ɩð[2] *on the bottom nib* (=*handle*) *of the scythe*] 4 tɩl ðə sɷn [ʃɛɩk ðə swaθs aɷt[1] *shake the swaths out*; stə: ðə kə:n[1] *store the corn*; kə:ld ðə mɩlkaɷs[1] *called the milkhouse*; ðə bɷlk[1] *the bulk*; ɩn‿θ fɛɩs[1] *in the face*; wɷn sɒɩd ðə fɛns[2] *one side* (of) *the fence*; mɛɩks ðə gɛɩt[2] *makes the gate*; ɩn ðə bɹɔ:d[2] *in the broad*; noɷz ðə ɹoɷd[2] *knows the road*; kə:l ðə mastə ðə bɒs[3] *call the master the boss*; ɹɛɩd ðə pɛɩpəz[3] *read the papers*; tə‿ð də:ə[3] *to the door*; wɒts ðə matə[4] *what's the matter*] 5 tɩl ðə sɷn [θɹaʃ ðə kə:n[1] *thresh the corn*; tə ðə bɩldɩnz[1] *to the buildings*; oɷvə ðə kaɷʃɛd[1] *over the cowshed*; ə ðə wə:d[1] *of the word*; ðə di: ə ðə wɩk[2] *the day of the week*; ðə tɒp ə ðə ɹu:f[2] *the top of the roof*; fɹɒm ðə ɹɷf[3] *from the rough*; ɒn ðə te:bl[3] *on the table*; gɒt ðə gaɷt[3] *got the gout*; ðə ɹɩvəz ɷp[4] *the river's up*; ɷp ðə baŋk[4] *up the bank*; ət ðə tʃɒkoɷlz[4] *at the chuck-holes* (=*puddles*); ðə sɷfs stɒpt ɷp[4] *the sough's stopped up*; kɷtɩn‿θ bɒŋk[4] *cutting the bank*] 6 tɩl ðə sɷn [ðə mi:t[1] *the meat*; ɷndə ðə sɒ̈ɩl[1] *under the soil*; ɷp ðə tɹɷnk ət ðə tɒp[1] *up the trunk at the top*; ðə gɛl[1] *the girl*; bɒ:ɩ ðə gɹæ:ɷndflɔ:[1] *by the groundfloor*; ðə mastə wɩ ðə bɷk[1] *the master with the book*; ‿ðmi:poɷl[1] *the May-pole*; ju:z ðə swɩplz[2] *use the swipples*; dɹɔ: ðə kə:n[2] *draw the corn*; si: ðə bladə[2] *see the bladder*; ɩn ðə ɹak[2] *in the rack*; ðə tɹɒfs[2] *the troughs*; ɩn ðə sɷmə[2] *in the summer*; ɩn ðə kɒfə[2] *in the coffer*; ‿ðʃɩp[2] *the sheep*; ɩn‿θ fɛɩld[2] *in the field*; kɷt‿θ gɹɛs[2] *cut the grass*; bɩ‿t pa:nd[2] *by the pound*] 7 tɩl §sɷndæɷn [ɩn ðə spɹɩŋ[1] *in the spring*; ɒn ðə ka:ts[1] *on the carts*; wɛ: ðə mənjɷ:əɹ ɩz[1] *where the manure is*; ðə ja:d[1] *the yard*; dɹɔ:d ðə mɷnɩ[2] *drawed* (=*drew*) *the money*; ɔ:l ðə wɒɩl[4] *all the while*; mɷtʃ ðə sɛɩm[4] *much the same*; ðə wɒn bɩfɔ: ðə las[4] *the one before the last*] 8 tɩl §aftə sɷnsɛt [bɹɩŋg ðə land[1] *bring the land*; tə ðə mənju:ə[1] *to the manure*; kə:l ðat ðə bɒtɷm[1] *call that the bottom*; əmɷŋgst ðə tɛɩtəz[2] *amongst the potatoes*; stə·ɹɩn ðə gɹɛɩn[3] *storing the grain*; ðə pɹɒpə nɛɩm[3] *the proper name*; ə ðə stakja:d[3] *of the stockyard*; ðə ɹu:k[4] *the rook*; ðə ploɷvəɹ[4] *the plover*; ɹæɷnd ðə tʃə:tʃ[5] *round the church*; ɹæɷnd ðə mu:n[6] *round the moon*; ə ðə dɷl dɛɩz[6] *of the dull days*; ɩn ðə ti:[6] *in the tea*. sɷn[1]] 9 tɩl ðə sɷn [tɩl[3(2x)]. ɩn ðə ba:n[1] *in the barn*; ðə gɒs[1] *the gorse*; ɩn ðə mɩdl[1] *in the middle*; bɹɷʃɩn ðə twɩgz[1] *brushing* (=*trimming*) *the twigs*; ɒn ðə ʃu:z[2] *on the shoes*; pɷt ðə kɛtʃ ɒn[2] *put the catch on*; ɩn ðə wɔ:l[2] *in the wall*; gɒt ðə gɩft ə ðə gab[2] *got the gift of the gab*; gɒt‿θ mɷnɩ[2] *got the money*; tə ðə pɩt[3] *to the pit* (=*pond*); ɒf ðə də:t[3] *off the dirt*] 10 tɩl ðə sɷn [ðə pi:s[1] *the piece*; ðə ɹoɷd[1] *the road*; ðə tü:[1] *the two*; gɒt ðə mɷnɩ[2] *got the money*; ɩn ðə panʃən[3] *in the panchion*; ɩn ðə bak[4] *in the back*; ɒn ðə tɛɩbl[4] *on the table*; tü:k ðə tʃans[4] *took the chance*; wɒz ə maɹə[5] *what's the matter*; lɒk ðə wi:l[5] *lock the wheel*; loɷd ðə ka:t[5] *load the cart*] 11 tɩl ðə sɷn [tɩl[1(2x)] . ɒn ðə fɷɹəz[1] *on the furrows*; stɩk ðə ʃɒfs[1] *stick the sheaves*; ðə wɔ:l əv ðə θatʃ[1] *the wall of the thatch*; ɒn ðə spɛ:ɹ əv ðə moɷmənt[2] *on the spur of the moment*; tə ðə wɒʃ[2] *to the wash*; fə ðə ʃi:p[2] *for the sheep*]

15 He 1 tɬ ðə sʌn [ðə dɹɩp[1] *the drip* (=*drain*); ɩn ðə tælɩt[1] *in the tallet*; si: ðə ɹɩdʒɩz[1] *see the ridges*; ðə fɹe:m ə ðə dɔ:əʵ[2] *the frame of the door*] 2 tɩl ðə sʌn [ðə ʃæf[1] *the shaft*; ðə gɹa:s[1] *the grass*; gɩvz ðə stʌf[3] *gives the stuff*; æks ɩm ðə wæɩ[3] *ask him the way*] 3 tɩl ðə sɷ:n [ðə fɹɷnt ɷ:n[1] *the front one*; ðə bəʵ:ɖʐ[1] *the birds*; ə ðə ɹɩk[1] *of the rick*; tɩklɩn ðə fɩʃ[2] *tickling the fish* IV.9.10; bɹɩŋ ðə bɹɷm[3] *bring the broom*; ðə bɛlɩs[3] *the bellows*; ə ðə jɔ:ʵ[4] *of the year*. sɷn[1]] 4 tɩɬ ðə sʌn [ðə stɹɩpɩn[1] *the stripping*] 5 tl ðə sɷn [ðə nɛm[1] *the name*; ðə bo:əʵɖ[1] *the board*; fɩl ðə kjəʵ:ʈ[1] *fill the cart*; ðə klɛn[2] *the clean* (=*placenta*); ðə se:ɩm[2] *the same*; gɒt ðə twæŋ[2] *got the twang*; ðə tɷŋz[3] *the tongs*; ðə kʌɷ[3] *the cow*] 6 tl ðə zɷn [əv ðə jɷd[1] *of the head*. ¶əzɷnɩn[1] *a-sunning* (=*sun-bathing*)] 7 tɩl ðə sʌn [ɩn ðə sɛntəɹ əv ðə stɒk[1] *in the centre of the stack*; fɷl ðə ɹoɷd[1] *full* (=*fill*) *the road*; ə ðə man[1] *of the man*; ɒn ðə fɩəlz[1] *on the fields*; əltəɹ ðə lɷk[1] *alter the look*; bɹoɷk ðə baɹn[1] *broke the barn*; pɷt ðə ʃa:f[1] *put the shaft*; ɩn ðə ʃa:vz[1] *in the shafts*; ðə tu: tɹeɩsɩz[1] *the two traces*; ɒn ðɩ gɹɑɷnd[1] *on the ground*; sɷks ðɩ ju:[1] *sucks the ewe*; ðɩ ju:z[1] *the ewes*; wɛə ðə dɷks gɷz[2] *where the ducks go*; ðə lɑ:dʒɜɩst[2] *the largest*; o:vəɹaŋɩn ðə gjɑ·ɹdɩn[3] *overhanging the garden*; kʌvəɹ ðə ɹɩdʒ[3] *cover the ridge*; ɩts ðə kəɹdz[3] *it's the curds*; tə ðə bəɩl[3] *to the boil*; baɩ ðɩ lɒb[3] *by the lob* (ref. part of the ear); gɒt ðə ki: ə ðə dɔəɹ[4] *got the key of the door*; ɩn ðə bɩnz[4] *in the bins*. sʌnʃæ̜ɩn[4] *s.-shine*]

16 Wo 1 tɩl ðə sɷn [tɩl[1] . fə ðə bɷtʃəʵ[1] *for the butcher*; ə ðə plɛɷ[1] *of the plough*; fɹəm ðə tanəs[1] *from the tan-house* (=*knacker's*); ti:tʃɩn ðə tʃɩldɹən[2] *teaching the children*; ðə se:ˈm[2] *the same*; ðə pɹɒpəʵ[2] *the proper*; ə ðə mɛɷθ[3] *of the mouth*; gɒt ðə bɛlɩ-ɛɩk[3] *got the belly-ache*; ðə gɹaɷsəʵʐ[3] *the grocers*] 2 tɩɬ ðə sɷn [ðə se:m[1] *the same*; ə ðə kɩaʵ:ʈ[1] *of the cart*; ðə ʃɛlɩn[1] *the shelling*; ðə skɹu:z[2] *the screws*; θɹu: ðə ki:-oɷl[2] *through the key-hole*; ðə kwɩk[2] *the quick*] 3 tɩɬ ðə sɷn [spɹɛd ðə tɹe:ˈsɩz[1] *spread the traces*; fəʵ: ðə kɛ:uz[1] *for the cows*; ðə mɛdɩlænd[1] *the meadowland*; pɛu:əʵ ðə te:ɩ[2] *pour the tea*; ðə nɒɩ-ɩst[2] *the nighest*; əfo:əʵ ðə təi:m[2] *afore the time*; ðə nɷt[3] *the nut*; ðə bæbɩ[3] *the baby*; ðə bæbɩz[4] *the babies*; ɩn ðə spɹɩŋg ə ðə jəʵ:[5] *in the spring of the year*] 4 tɬ ðə sɷn [ðə faʵ:mjəʵ:ɖ *the farmyard*; ə ðə pləɷ[1] *of the plough*; ðə pɒɩnt[1] *the point*; wɛn ðə mɩɬk[2] *when the milk*; ðə wɷn səɩd[2] *the one side*; ðə fi:d[2]

the feed; ðə bɛlɪs[3] *the bellows*; ðə gɹəɷnz[3] *the grounds*; ðə bɷsəʳks[3] *the bussocks* (=*coughs*)] 5 tɬ ðə sɷn [ðə tɹɷθ[1] *the truth*; ðə bæbɪ[1] *the baby*; ðə se:ᵊm[1] *the same*] 6 tɪɬ ðə sɷn [tə ðə fɛəʳ *to the Fair*; ðə wɛðəʳ[1] *the weather*; ðə se:ɪm[1] *the same*; ðə tɷŋz[1] *the tongs*; ðə bɛlɪs[2] *the bellows*; ðɪ ʃɪp[2] *the sheep*; θɹu: ðə ki:-oɷl[3] *through the keyhole*; ðə flɛu:əʳ[3] *the flour*; ðə bæbɪ[3] *the baby*] 7 tɪl ðə sɷn [tɪl[1]. ðə θɹɛʃəz[1] *the threshers*; ðə ɹɷŋ[1] *the wrong*; ðə bɛɪlɪf[1] *the bailiff*; ɪntə ðə fɪəl[2] *into the field*; ðə ʃe:p[2] *the shape*; tə ðə ɹɪkjɑʳɖ[2] *to the rickyard*; ðə səɪd ðə ʃä:f[3] *ıhe side* (of) *the shaft*; ðə skwə·ʳ[4] *the squire*; ðə wɪdθ[4] *the width*; ðə bɑ:[4] *the bar*]

17 Wa 1 tɪl ðᵊ sɷn [ðə mɷk'[1] *the muck*; kɷt ðə swi:dz[1] *cut the swedes*; ðə wɔ:tə[1] *the water*; ɔ:f ðə lǫɷf[2] *off the loaf*; ɪn ðə gɹæɷnd[2] *in the ground*; ðə kɔ:ɹ[2] (+ V.) *the core*] 2 tɪl ðə sɷn [tɪl[4]. ə ðə dɹɪp[1] *of the drip* (=*drain*); ɷndəni:θ ðə ʃa:ft[1] *underneath the shaft*; skətʃ ðə wɪəl ɷp[1] *scotch* (=*chock*) *the wheel up*; ɪz ðɪ mɛɪn θɪŋ[1] *is the main thing*; ət ðə pɹəɪs[2] *at the price*; ən ðə ɹɪk[2] *on the rick*; ə ðə ɹu:f[2] *of the roof*; ðə ɹəɷd[3] *the road*; ðə kæɷz[3] *the cow's*; ɪn ðə tʃɒps[4] *in the chops*; əfɷə ðə fɷst[4] *before the first*; ðə matəɹ[4] *the matter*] 3 tɬ ðə sɷn [tl[1]. ɒvə ðə jəʳ:ɖ[1] *over the yard*; ðə ka:ts[1] *the carts*; ðə ɹǫɷd[1] *the road*; wɪð ðə wɪnd[2] *with the wind*; gɛt ðə kǫ:ɹ[2] *get the core*] 4 tɬ ðə sɷn [fə ðə wɪntə[1] *for the winter*; ðə blak a:nt[1] *the black ant*; kɛp ðə mɪlk[1] *kept the milk*; ɪn ðə ɹɪkja:d[2] *in ıhe rickyard*; fɪl mɷkka:t[2] *fill* (the) *muck-cart*; sɪ ðə sta:z[3] *see the stars*; ðə koɷɬdɪst[3] *the coldest*; ðə blak fɹɔ:st[3] *the black frost*] 5 tl ðə sɷn [ɪn ðə sɛntəʳ[1] *in the centre*; tə ðə baɹə[1] *to the barrow*; ɪn ðə wɪntəʳ[1] *in the winter*; ki:p ðə fɹɔ:st ɔ:f[1] *keep the frost off*; fɪlɪn mɷkkaʳ:ʈ[1] *filling* (the) *muck-cart*. sɷn[1]] 6 tɬ ðə sɷn [kɛp ðə wɛɪt əf[1] *kept the weight off*; ɷp ðə səɪd[3] *up the side*; ɪntə ðə mɷd[2] *into the mud*; ɒn ðə tɛɪbɬ[4] *on the table*; ðə ɹɪəl dʒɪpsɪz[4] *the real gipsies*] 7 tɬ ðə sɷn [tə ðə ɹɪkbɪldəʳ[1] *to the rick-builder*; ɒn ðə lɛvɬ flɒɷəʳ[1] *on the level floor*; pɷlɪn ðə θatʃ[2] *pulling the thatch*; əpɷlɪn ðə wɷd[2] *a-pulling the wood*; ðə ɹoɷst[2] *the Roast* (ref. a local festival)]

23 Mon 1 tɬ ðə sʌn [ðə fɹʌnt ən[1] *the front one*; ɔ:l ðə sʌməʳ[1] *all the summer*; ðə klɛn[2] *the clean* (=*placenta*); ðə tɹɷθ[2] *the truth*; ðə gɹʌɷnz[3] *the grounds*; stæŋk ðə wɑ:təʳ[4] *stank* (=*dam*) *the water*] 2 tɪɬ ðə sɷn [ðə klɛn[1] *the clean* (=*placenta*); ɒn ðə mɷtʃ[3] *on the mooch* (ref. begging for money); ɹɪŋ ðə bɛɬ[3] *ring the bell*] 3 tɪɬ ðə sʌn [ðə ja:d[1] *the yard*; ðə bo:θ[1] *the both* (i.e. both of them)] 4 tʰɪl ðə sʌ̣̈n [ʌ̣̈p ðə dou[1] *up* (to) *the door*; ðə tʰɹa:m[1] *the tram*; ðə jɛlo[2] *the yellow*; ðə kʰənal[2] *the canal*; ðə mi:zlz[2] *the measles*; ðə katɬ[3] *the cattle*] 5 tɪl ðə sʌ̣̈n [ɪn ðə sʌ̣̈mmə[1] *in the summer*; ðə wʌ̣̈ns o:və[1]

the once over; ɒ̣ˑn² ðə tœ:f¹ *on the turf*; ðə katˑl² *the cattle*; ðə kɔ:n² *the corn*] 6 tł ðə sʌn [ðə ne:m¹ *the name*] 7 n.a.

24 Gl 1 tł ðə sɷn [kɩp ðə fəɷəɫ¹ *keep the fowl*; fəʳ ðə bʌtʃəʳ¹ *for the butcher*; swe:ps (*2 pr.pl.*) ðə le:vz¹ *sweeps the leaves*; ðə bɒtɷm² *the bottom*; ðə sɛkənt³ *the second*] 2 tl ðə sɷn [ðə gɷts ə ðə pləɷ:¹ *the guts* (=*middle*) *of the plough*; ðə ɹæftəʳʐ² *the rafters*] 3 tł ðə zɷn [ðə ɹe:ˈzn¹ *the reason*; kɑ:t ðə jœdz¹ *called the heads* (ref. corn); sˈi: ðə kɩdz² *see the kids* (=*children*); ɩn ðə sləɷ³ *in the slough*; æt ðə do:əʳ³ *at the door*] 4 tł ðə zɷn [ɩn əv ðə gɹəɷn¹ *in off the ground*; ðə kɒɹɩdz¹ *the carriage*; ðə łɒɷłanz² *the lowlands*; ə ðə bɹɩm³ *of the brim*] 5 tl ðə sʌn [te:k ðə bɹɩtʃɩn ɔ:f¹ *take the breeching off*; ki:p ðə wi:l¹ *keep the wheel*; ɒn ðə ɹɩk² *on the rick*; ðə gɷdnəs² *the goodness*; ɩn ðə stɹɩt² *in the street*] 6 təl ðə zən [le:d ðə bɷɫ¹ *lead the bull*; bɩ ðə məʳ:ɳɩn¹ *by the morning*; mɛɫt ðə flɩk¹ *melt the flick* (=*suet*)] 7 tl ðə zən [dɹu: ðə wɔ:təʳ¹ *through the water* IV.1.3; ðə dʌɩk¹ *the dike*]

25 O 1 tɩl ðə sʌn [ðə vɛnt¹ *the vent*; ɽaʔɭz ðə bɷkɩt¹ *rattles the bucket*; kɛtʃ ðə fat² *catch the fat*] 2 tl ðə sʌn [ɩn ðə fɩəlz¹ *in the fields*; bɩfoəʳ ðə li:f¹ *before the leaf*; fə ðə katl² *for the cattle*; ðə kɛˑ ə ðə duəʳ³ *the key of the door*; pɷt ðə ʃɷk ɒn³ *put the shook* (=*kettle*) *on*] 3 tɩl, °tɩl ðə sʌn [tɩl². ðə we:t¹ *the weight*; kʌts ðə tɒps ɒf¹ *cuts the tops off*; ɩf ðə land¹ *if the land*; ðə kat² *the cat*; θɹʏ: ðə ki:-oɷɫ² *through the keyhole*; wʌʏp ðə swɛt ɔ:f² *wipe the sweat off*] 4 tł ðə sɷn [ɩn ðə baɽɳ¹ *in the barn*; ɩn ðə fɩɷɫz¹ *in the fields*; wɛn ðə länd¹ *when the land*; ʃɷt ðə gɩət² *shut the gate*; tə ðə dəɩk² *to the dike* (=*earthen w.c.*); ðə skɩn³ *the skin*; ðə wəɽʂʈ³ *the worst*; wɩð ðɩ jəɽʐ³ *with the ears*; ðə ki: ə ðə dɔ:ɽ⁴ *the key of the door*; ɩts ðə łast⁴ *it's the last*; əɫɒŋ ðə ɽo:d⁵ *along the road*] 5 tl ðə sʌn [ðə kɛɷz¹ *the cows*; ðə wəʳ:k¹ *the work*; əʔ ðə bak¹ *at the back*; ɩn ðə fö̈ɩəʳ² *in the fire*; əf ə ðə flɩəʳ² *off of the floor*; ðə baŋk² *the bank*; ʔə ðə ʃu:snɒb³ *to the shoe-snob* (=*cobbler*); ðə gɷd³ *the good*] 6 tə ðə sɒ̣n [tɩɫ². fi:dz ðə bɩldəʳ¹ *feeds the* (stack-)*builder*; stɒp ðə gɹa:s¹ *stop the grass*; ðə wɔ:ʔəʳ¹ *the water*; ɹʌn ðə mɩəl³ *run the mill*]

IX.2.4 ASK HIM

Q. If you've lost your way and someone comes along, you'd go up to him and . . . .

Rr. ASK EN/HIM

Note 1—Unfortunately the f.w. occ. omitted to rec. the required obj. pronoun. Such rr. are, strictly speaking, u.rr.

Note 2—I.m. exs. of ASK and its parts not followed by an obj. pronoun are reproduced below between square brackets untransliterated. In the i.m., infs. are unmarked, an attached superior ◇ denotes a p.t., and superior ‖ n.d.g.

7 Ch 1 ask 2 ask, p. ɛks [pref.; ɛks, aks, ~[2], as[4]; ◇a·kst[2]] 3 aks ɪm 4 aks 5 ask 6 asks [¶askɪn[3]]

8 Db 1 ɛks [‖ɛks[1(2x)]] 2 aks, ɛks [‖ɛks[2,4], ‖aks[3]] 3 ɛks [ɛks[2]] 4 aks [‖aks[1,3]] 5 ɛks [‖ɛks[3]] 6 ɛks ɪm 7 ɛks

11 Sa 1 aʳ:ʂk ɪm 2 ask ɪm 3–4 a:sk ɪm 5 aks ɪm 6 a:sk 7 a:sk ɪm 8 a:sk ɪm [ast[2]] 9 æ·sk ɪm 10 a:sk ɪm 11 a·sk ɪm

12 St 1 aks ɪm 2 ask ɪm 3 ɛks ɪm [ɛks[1] *imp.*] 4 ask ɪm 5 ɛks ɪm [‖ɛks[3]] 6 ɛks ɪm [ɛks[1(2x)]; ɛkst[1] *p.p.*; ast ʃə[2] *asked you*] 7 ask ɪm [aks[3] *imp.*] 8 ask 9 ɛks ɪm [aks[1] *imp.*; ¶askɪn[1]] 10 aks ɪm 11 ask ɪm

15 He 1 a:sk ɪm, æks ɪm ["older"] 2 æks ɪm [a:sk[3]] 3 æks ɪm 4 ɛks ɪm [‖ɛks[3]] 5–6 æks ɪm 7 a:sk ɪm [a:sk[4]; ◇æ:st[4]]

16 Wo 1 ask ɪm 2 a:sk ɪm 3–4 æks ɪm 5 ɛks ɪm [æks[1]; æsɪz[1] 3 *pr.s.*; ◇ækst[1], ◇ɛkst[1]] 6 æks ɪm 7 s.w. ɑ:sk ɪm [◇ɑ:st[4]; ɛks[1] *p.p.*]

17 Wa 1 ask [‖ask[1]] 2 ɑ:sk əm [a·sk[1]] 3 a:sk [‖aks[2]] 4 a:sk ɪm [aks] 5 ɛks [‖ɛks[1(2x)]] 6 a:sk, aks [‖aks[3]] 7 ɛks ɪm [ɛks[1]]

23 Mon 1 æks ɪm 2 æsk ɪm 3 a:ks ɪm 4 n.a. 5 ask [◇ast] 6 a:sk ɪm 7 n.a.

24 Gl 1 æks ɪm 2 ɛks ɪm [a:sk[1]] 3 ɛks ən [ɛks[3] *imp.*] 4 ask ɪm [əʳɽ askt əɪ[3] *her* (=*she*) *asked I* (=*me*)] 5 ɛks [ɛks[1] VIII.1.25] 6 a:sk n̩, p. ɛks [◇ɛkst] 7 a:sk, haks [‖haks]

25 O 1 ɛks [a:s[1]; aks[2] *imp.*; ‖ɛkst[2(2x)]] 2 a:sk [‖a:sk[1]] 3 a:sk, ɛks [old, not used now; ‖a:sk[1]] 4 ä:sk ɪm 5 a:sk 6 a:st

IX.2.5 BESIDE

Q. Here's the door, and I'm standing [*stand to one side of it*] . . . . *it.*

Rr. §ABACK ON, AGAIN, AGAINST, ALONGSIDE, ANUN(S)T, ASIDE (OF/ON), AT THE SIDE (ON), §BACKSIDE, BESIDE, BY (THE SIDE ON), §CLOSE (UP) TO, SIDE ON, TO THE SIDE OF

Note—When rec. in the rr., the objs. HIM/IT and THE DOOR are reproduced below.

7 Ch 1 əsaɪd ɒn ɪt 2 əgɛn ɪt, ○əsaɪd ə‿tʔ‿ də:, ○əge:n[1] 3 ə‿t saɪd ɒn‿t 4–5 əsaɪd ɒn ɪt 6 bɪsɛɪd ɪt

8 Db 1 ə‿t saɪd ɒn ɪt 2 ɔ‿t saɪd ɒn ɪt 3 ə‿t saɪd ɒn‿t 4 ə‿t sa:d ɒn ɪt 5 ə‿t saɪd ɒn ɪt 6 sã·ĩd ɒn‿t 7 əsã:d ɒn‿t

11 Sa 1 əsaɪd 2 bɪsaɪd 3–5 ənɒnst 6 ənʌnst 7–10 ənɒnst 11 ənʌnst

12 St 1 ə‿t sɒɪd ɒn ɪt 2 ə‿θ sɒɪd 3 əgɛn ɪt, §klɒ:s tə‿θ dɒə 4 bɒɪ 5 §əbak ɒn ɪt, əsɒ:ɪd ɒn ɪt 6 §baksɒ:ɪd, əgɛn ðə dɒ:ə, ○ɛgɛn[1] 7 bɒɪ 8 baɪ ðə dǫ:ə 9 bɪsɒɪd 10 əlɒŋsaɪd, əgɛnst 11 ba:ɪ ɪt ["older"], əgɛnst ɪt

15 He 1 ənʌnst ɪt 2 ənʌnt ɪm 3 ənɒnt ɪt 4 ənʌnt ɪt 5–6 ənɒnt 7 əsaɪd əv ɪt, ○əsaɪd[1]

16 Wo 1 bɪ ðə sɒɪd ən ɪt 2 baɪ ðə səɪd ən ɪt 3 əgjɒnst ɪt 4 bɪ ðə səɪd ɒn ɪm 5 bə ðə səɪd n̩ ɪt 6 bəɪ ðə sɒɪd ɒn ɪt 7 əgɛnst, s.f. əgɛn, ○~

17 Wa 1 əsaɪd ɒv 2 §kləɒs ɒp tɒ ɪt, ○əgɛn ɪt, ○əsəɪd[1] 3 bɪsəɪd ɪt 4 ət ðə səɪd ɒn ɪt 5 bəɪ ðə səɪd ən ɪt 6 tə ðə səɪd əv ɪt 7 bɪsəɪd ɪt

23 Mon 1 ənʌnt 2 bɪsəɪd 3 bɪ ðə səɪd n̩ t 4 n.a. 5 bəi, bisǫɪd 6 bəɪ ɪt 7 n.a.

24 Gl 1 bɪsəɪᵊd ɪt 2 bɪsəɪd ɪm 3 ənɒnt 4 bɪ ðə zəɪd ɒn‿t 5 ə ðə sɔ̈ɪd ɒn‿t 6 ət ðə zʌɪd ə 7 ət ðə zʌɪd ɑn ɪm

25 O 1–2 bɔ̈ɪ ɪt 3 bɪsʌʏd ɪt 4 əsǫɪd əv ðə dəəɽ 5 ə‿t sʌʏd ɒn ɪʔ 6 bɪsɔ̈ɪd

IX.2.6 IN FRONT OF

Q. And now (I am standing) [stand sideways in front of it] . . . . *it.*

Rr. AFRONT ON, §AGAIN, AT/IN THE FRONT ON, §BACK ON DOOR, §FACING, FRONT OF/ON, IN FRONT (OF/ON)

Note 1—When rec. in the rr., the objs. HIM/IT and THE DOOR are reproduced below.

Note 2—At 16.7 and 17.2, the f.w., P.W., used the 3rd version of the Qr.; it did not include this q.

Note 3—I.m. exs. of FRONT *adj.* and *n.* are reproduced below between square brackets untransliterated. For exs. of FRONT– *adj.*, see V.2.2 and of –FRONTED *adj.*, see VI.14.16; for –FRONTS *n.*, see VI.14.16; and for FRONTWARDS, see IX.1.7.

7 Ch 1 əfɹɒnt ɒn ɪt 2 n.a. [fɹɒnt[1] *adj.*] 3 ə‿t fɹɒnt ɒn‿t 4 ɪn fɹɒnt ɒn ɪt 5 əfɹɒnt ɒn ɪt 6 ɪn fɹɒnt ən ɪt

8 Db 1–2 ɪ‿t fɹɒnt ɒn ɪt 3 ɪ fɹɒnt ɒn‿t 4–5 ə‿t fɹɒnt ɒn ɪt 6 fɹɒnt ɒn‿t 7 ɪn fɹɒnt ɒn‿t

11 Sa 1 ɪn fɹʌnt əv ɪt 2 ɪn fɹɷnt ɒn ɪt 3 ɪn fɹʌnt əv ɪt 4 ɪn fɹʌnt ɒn 5 ɪn fɹɷnt ɒn ɪt 6 ɪn fɹʌnt ɒv 7–8 ɪn fɹɷnt ɒn 9 ɪn fɹʌnt ɒn, °ɪn fɹɷnt ɒn[1] 10 ɪn fɹʌnt ɒn ɪt 11 ɪn fɹʌnt ɒn

12 St 1 §bak ɒn du:ə, °ɪ fɹɷnt[2] 2 ɪn‿θ fɹɷnt ɒn ɪt [fɹɷntslo͡ɷt[3] *front-slote* I.10.1] 3 §fɛɪsɪn ɪt, ɪn fɹɷnt ɒn ɪt, °ə‿θ fɹɷnt ɒn[1] 4 ɪn fɹɷnt əv ɪt 5 ɪn fɹɷnt ɒn ɪt 6 ɪn fɹɷnt əv ɪt 7 ɪn fɹɷnt əv 8 ɪn fɹɷnt ɒf ðə dǫ:ə 9 §əgɛn ɪt, ɪn fɹɷnt əv ɪt 10 ɪn fɹɷnt ɒn ɪt 11 ɪn fɹɷnt əv ɪt

15 He 1 ɪn fɹʌnt n̩ ɪt 2 ɪn fɹʌnt ɒn ɪm °ɪn fɹʌnt ɒn əm[1] 3 ɪn fɹɷnt ɒn ɪt 4 ɪn fɹʌnt n̩ ɪt 5 ɪn fɹʌnt n̩ ɪt [fɹʌnt[1] *f.* (n.d.g.)] 6 ɪn vɹɷnt n̩ ɪt 7 ɪn fɹʌnt əv ɪt, °ɪn fɹʌnt[1], °fɹʌnt ə[3]

16 Wo 1 ɪn fɹɷnt ɒn ɪt 2 ɪn fɹɷnt ən 3 ɪn fɹɷnt ɒn ɪt 4 ɪn fɹɷnt ɒn ɪm, °ɪn fɹɷnt ɒn[1] 5–6 ɪn fɹɷnt ɒn ɪt 7 n.a.

17 Wa 1 ə fɹɷnt ɒv 2 n.a. 3 ɪn fɹɷnt əv ɪt 4–5 ɪn fɹɷnt ɒn ɪt 6 ɪn fɹɷnt əv ɪt 7 ɪn fɹɷnt ən ɪt

23 Mon 1 ɪn fɹʌnt ɒn [fɹʌnt[1] *adj.* I.6.3] 2 ɪn fɹɷnt ɒn ɪt 3 ɪn fɹʌnt n̩ ɪt 4 n.a. 5 ɪn fɹʌ̹̈nt əv, °ɪn fɹʌ̹̈nt[1] [fɹʌ̹̈nt[2] *n.*] 6 ɪn fɹʌnt əv ɪt 7 n.a.

24 Gl 1 ɪn fɹɷnt ɒn ɪt 2 ɪn fɹɷnt ɒn ɪm 3 ɪn vɹɷnt n̩ ən 4 ɪn vɹɷnt n̩ ɪt, °ɪn vɹɷnt əv 5 ɪn fɹɷnt ɒn‿t 6 ɪn ðə fɹənt ə 7 ət ðə fɹənt ɑn ɪm

25 O 1 ɪn fɹʌnt ən ɪt 2 ɪn fɹʌnt əv ɪt 3 ɪn fɹʌnt əv ɪt, ɪn fɹʌnt ʌn ɪt ["older"; fɹʌntladəʳ[1] *f.-ladder* (of cart) I.10.5] 4 ɪn fɾɷnt ɒv ɪt 5 ɪn fɹʌnt ɒn ɪʔ, °ɪn fɹʌnʔ[2] 6 ɪn fɹɷnʔ ɔ:v ɪʔ

IX.2.7 AJAR

Q. A door left like this, you say is . . . .

Rr. /A BIT/HALF/PART/ OPEN, (HALF) AJAR, AJAR A BIT, (ON A/THE) JAR, ON THE JAG, UNDONE, UNLATCHED

Note 1—The r. at 16.4 doubtless represents AJAR.

Note 2—For exs. of OPEN *v.*, see VIII.6.2.

7 Ch 1 ə bɪt ɒpn, ədʒa: 2 ədʒaɹ ə bɪt 3 ɷndɷn, e:f ɒpn [wɪ nɛvə sɛn ədʒa: *we never say ajar*] 4 pa:t ọ:pn 5 ədʒa: 6 ɒn ðə dʒa:

8 Db 1 dʒaˑ̣ɹ: 2 pa:t ɒpn 3–5 ədʒa: 6 ədʒã: 7 ədʒa:

11 Sa 1 ədʒa: 2 ɒn ðə dʒa: 3 ɒn ə dʒa: 4 ɒn ə dʒaʳ: 5 ɒn ðə dʒaʳ: 6 ədʒa: 7 ɒn ə dʒaʳ: 8 ɒn ə dʒəʳ: 9 ɒn ə dʒaʳ: 10 ɒn ə dʒəʳ: 11 ɒn ðə dʒaʳ:

12 St 1–7 ədʒa: 8 ɒn ðə dʒag 9 ədʒa: 10 ədʒəʴ: 11 ədʒɑ̊:

15 He 1 ɒn ðə dʒa: 2 ədʒaʵ: 3 ɒn ðə dʒɑʵ: 4 ədʒaʵ: 5 ɒn ðə dʒa: 6 ɒn ðə dʒɑʵ: 7 ədʒɑ·ɹ

16 Wo 1 ɒn ðə dʒɑ: 2 ədʒa: 3 ədʒəʵ: 4 əʃo:əʵ 5 əʃɑʵ:əʵ 6 ədʒaʵ: 7 ədʒɑ·ʵ

17 Wa 1 ɒn ðə dʒa: 2 ədʒa:, ○∼ 3 ɷnlatʃt ["older", i. insists], ədʒa: 4–7 ədʒaʵ:

23 Mon 1 ədʒəʵ: 2–3 ədʒa: 4 n.a. 5 ədʒaʵ: 6 ədʒaʵ 7 n.a.

24 Gl 1 æ:f ədʒæ: 2–3 ədʒaʵ: 4 ədʒɑʵ: 5 ədʒəʵ: 6 a:f o:pn 7 ədʒaʵ:

25 O 1 ədʒaʵ: 2 ədʒaʴ̠ 3 ədʒäʵɽ 4 ədʒa·ɽ 5–6 ədʒaʵ:

IX.2.8 SHUT

Q. If the door blew open on a cold day, you'd get up at once and . . . . it.

Rr. §LATCH, SHUT (UP)

Note 1—When rec. in the rr., the pronominal obj. IT/EN/HIM/HER is included below.

Note 2—For exs. of SHUT *v.*, see VIII.6.2; of SHUTTING– *n.*, see IV.3.4; and of SHUT– *n.*, see I.7.18.

7 Ch 1 ʃɷt 2 ʃɷt, ○∼[3] *imp.* 3–5 ʃɷt ɪt 6 ʃɷd̥ ɪt

8 Db 1–3 ʃɷt ɪt 4 ʃɷt 5 ʃɷt ɪt 6 ʃɷt ə [=*her*] 7 ʃɷt ɪt

11 Sa 1 ʃʌt 2 ʃɷt ɪt 3 ʃət 4 ʃʌt 5 ʃɷt 6–7 ʃʌt 8 ʃɷt [gɛt ʃɷt ɒn ɪm[2] *get shut on* (=*rid of*) *him*] 9 ʃɛt, ○ʃʌt[1(2x)] 10–11 ʃʌt

12 St 1 ʃɷt 2 n.a., ○ʃɷt[5] 3–6 ʃɷt 7 ʃɷt 8 n.a., ○ʃɷt[1] *p.p.* 9 ʃɷt, ○∼[2] *imp.*, ○∼[1] *p.p.* 10–11 ʃɷt ɪt

15 He 1 ʃʌt ɪt 2 ʃʌt ɪm 3 ʃɷt ɪm 4 ʃʌt ɪm 5 ʃʌt ɪt 6 ʒɷt n̩ 7 ʃʌt ɪt

16 Wo 1–2 ʃɷt 3 ʃɷt ɪm 4 ʃɷt ɪt 5 ʃɷt ɪm 6 ʃɷt ɪt 7 §latʃ ɪt, p. ʃɷt ɪt

17 Wa 1 ʃɷt ɪt 2 ʃɷt ɪt, ○ʃɷt[4] *imp.* 3–5 ʃɷt 6–7 ʃɷt ɪt

23 Mon 1 ʃʌt ɪm 2 ʃɷt ɪt 3 ʃʌt ɪt 4 n.a. 5 ʃʌ̈tʰ 6 ʃʌt ɪt 7 n.a.

24 Gl 1 ʃɷt ɪt 2 ʃɷt ɪm 3–4 ʒɷt n̩ 5 ʃʌt n̩ 6–7 ʃət n̩

25 O 1 ʃʌt ɪt 2 ʃʌd̥ ɪt 3 n.a. 4 ʃɷd̥ ɪt ɷp, ○ʃɷt[2] *imp.*, ○∼[2] *p.p.* 5 ʃɛʔ ["older"], ʃʌʔ 6 ʃɷʔ ɪʔ

IX.2.9 WARP

Q. If a door has been made of unseasoned wood, before long it will be sure to ....

Rr. GO SKELL(ER)ED, §LEAVE CHAUNS IN IT, (§RIFT AND) RUN UP, SAP AND CRACK, SHRINK~SINK, SKELLER, TWIST, WARP

7 Ch 1 wa:p 2 ʃɹɪŋk, wɔ:p, °wa:pt *p.p.* 3–6 wa:p

8 Db 1 waꜝ:p 2 skɛlə 3 ɹɷn ɷp, twɪst 4–5 wa:p 6 wɒp 7 wɔ:p

11 Sa 1 wəʳ:p 2 sɹɪŋk 3–4 wəʳ:p 5 waʳ:p 6 wəʳ:p 7 wəʳ:p 8–9 wəʳ:p 10 wəʳ:p 11 wəʳ:p

12 St 1 go skɛlɪd 2 wa:p 3 §ɹɪft ən ɹɷn ɷp, wɔ:p 4 wɔ:p 5 wɔ:p, wɔ:f [*sic*; sap ən kɹak *sap and crack* (ref. a branch)] 6 wɔ:p 7 wọ:p 8–10 wɔ:p 11 wọ:p [ʃɹɪŋk *shrink*]

15 He 1 wɔ:p 2 sɹɪŋk 3 wɑʳ:p 4 sɪŋk 5 ʃɹɛŋk 6 wɑʳ:p 7 twɪst, wɒ̣·ɹp

16 Wo 1 wɑ:p 2 wɑ:ɽp 3 wɑʳ:p 4 sɪŋk, wəʳ:p 5 sɪŋk 6 sɹɪŋk 7 sɹɪŋks *pr.t.*, §li:v tʃɑʳŋẓ ɪn ɪt, °sɹɪŋks⁴ 3 *pr.pl.*

17 Wa 1 ʃɹɪŋk, wɔ:p 2 wɔ:p, sɪŋk, °wɔ:pt⁴ *p.p.* 3 sɹɪŋks *pr.t.*, wɔ:p 4 wɔ:p 5 wəʳ:pʻ 6 wɔ:p 7 wəʳ:p

23 Mon 1 wɑʳ:p 2 sɹɪŋk 3 ʃɹɪŋk 4 n.a. 5 wɔ:p 6 sɹɪŋk 7 n.a.

24 Gl 1 sɹɪŋk 2 sɹɪŋk, °twɪsɪs 3 *pr.s.* 3 ʃɹɪŋk 4 sɹɪŋk 5 wɑʳ:p 6 waʳ:p 7 wəʳ:p

25 O 1 wæʳ:p 2 sɹɪŋk 3 wəʳ:pʻ 4 wɔ·ɽp, °¶wəɽpɪn⁴, °wəɽpt⁴ *p.p.* 5 wɔ:ɽp 6 sʃɹɪŋk

IX.2.10 NEAR

Q. Our house is not far away; so it must be ....

Rr. CLOSE (AT/HANDY/HERE/TO), HANDY, NEAR (TO), NEAR-HAND

Note 1—In the i.m. below, an attached superior × denotes a prep., superior ᴅ an adj. and superior ★ n.d.g. Exs. of the advs. NEARLY and NEAR = *nearly* and of AGAIN/AGAINST *prep.* = *near* are reproduced below between square brackets untransliterated.

Note 2—For exs. of NEAR(LY), see VII.7.9; and of NEAR(–), see I.6.4 and II.3.4.

7 Ch 1 klǫ:s tʏ: 2 nɪə, °nɪəɹ² [+ V.], °*nɪə², °×~² [nɪə²] 3 tlǫ:s tʲʏ: 4 tlǫ:s tᶱü:, °*nɪə 5 tlǫ:s tɪʏ: 6 tlo:s tɪü̧:

8 Db 1 nɪə꞉ 2 nɪə 3 tlo:s tɛ̈ɷ, °×nɪəɹ¹ [+ V.] 4 nɛ: 5 nɪə 6 tlü:s tɛɷ 7 tlᶱü:s tɛɷ

11 Sa 1–3 nɪəʳ 4 nɪəʳ [ᴰi:məʳ *aimer* (=*nearer*)] 5 klɒs tᶱu: 6 klo:s tu:, °nɪəʳ: 7 nɪəʳ: 8 klo:s at [ᴰnaɪst² *nighest* (=*nearest*); nɪəʳ[ɪ¹] 9 klo:s æt, nɪəʳ, °*~¹ 10 nɪəʳ [nɪəʳ³] 11 klo:s at, nɪəʳ

12 St 1 kloɷs tü: [əgɛn²,⁴] 2 kloɷs tɪɷ [nɪəlɪ³; əgɛnst⁵] 3 nɪə tɛɷ 4 nɪə, °~³ 5 kloɷs tü:, °nɪə tü:³ 6 kloɷs tü: 7 nɪ̧ə 8 kloɷs tü: 9 nɪə 10 kloɷs, niə 11 kloɷs tu:

15 He 1 klo:s æt, °~¹ 2–3 klo:s æt 4 klo:s 5 klo:s ət 6 klo:s æt 7 nɪəɹ, s.w. andɪ, °~ [ᴰnɪəɹəst⁴ *nearest*; nɪəɹ¹,⁴; əgɪn¹]

16 Wo 1 nɪə 2 nɪəʳ 3 nɪəʳ [ᴰnɒɪ-ɪst² *nighest* (=*nearest*)] 4 klo:s æt 5 nɪəʳ 6 kloɷs tu: 7 nɪə, °nɪəʳ VIII.8.4

17 Wa 1 tlǫɷs tu [əgɛn¹] 2 nɪə, °~³, °kləɷs tɷ¹ [nɪə¹; nɪəlɪ¹] 3 klǫɷs tu: [əgɪn¹] 4 nɪəʳ tü: 5 nɪəʳ [nɪə¹] 6 klǫɷs 7 kloɷs tü:

23 Mon 1 klo:ᶱs æt 2 nɪə, °*nɪəʳ³ 3 klo:s æt 4 n.a. 5 nɨ-ə 6 klo:s ændɪ 7 n.a.

24 Gl 1 klo:ɷs æt [klo:ɷsəʳ² *closer*; næɪəʳ² *nigher* (=*nearer*)] 2 klo:ɷs 3 nɪəʳ 4 nɪəʳ [əgɛn¹] 5 klo:s 6 nɪəʳ 7 klo:ᶱs

25 O 1 nɪəʳ 2 nɪəɹand 3 kləɷs ɪəʳ, °×nɪəɽ¹ [+ V.] 4 kło:s, nɪəɽ, °×~², °~⁴ [(+ V.; n.d.g.); nɪəɽłɪ⁴] 5 klǫ̈ɷs 6 nɪəʳ

IX.2.11 BETWEEN

Q. Do you see my teeth? Now I place this pencil . . . . them.

Rr. (IN) BETWEEN, §IN, (A)TWEEN, (BE)TWIXT

7 Ch 1 bɪtwi:n 2 ɪn bɪtwi:n, °bɪtwi:n¹⁽²ˣ⁾, °bɪtwɪin⁴ 3 bɪtwɛɪn 4 bɪtwi̧:n 5 ətwɛɪn, °bɪtwɛɪn¹ 6 bɪtwi:n

8 Db 1 bɪtwi:n 2 bɪʔwi:n, °~⁴ 3–4 bɪtwɛɪn 5 bɪtwi:n 6 bəʔwɛɪn 7 bɪtwɛɪn

11 Sa 1 bɪtwi:n 2 bɪtwi:n, °~³ 3–4 bɪtwi:n 5 §ɪn 6 bɪtwi:n 7 ətwi:n 8–9 bɪtwi:n 10 ətwi:n 11 bɪtwɪkst

12 St 1–3 bɩtwɛɩn 4 bɩtwɩkst 5 bɩtwi:n, °bɩtwɩkst[2] 6 bɩtwɛɩn, °~[1] 7 bɩtwɩkst, °bɩtwi:n[1] 8–9 bɩtwɩkst 10 bɩtwi:n, twɩkst 11 bɩtwi:n, bɩtwɩkst [older]

15 He 1 §ɩn 2 bɩtwi:n 3 bɩtwi:n, °ətwi:n[3] 4 bɩtwi:n, °~[1] 5 bɩtwɩn 6 ɩn bɩtwi:n 7 bɩtwi:n, °~[4], °twi:n[3]

16 Wo 1–2 bɩtwi:n 3 ɩn bɩtwɩn, °bɩtwi:n[1] 4 ətwi:n ["older"] 5–6 bɩtwi:n 7 ɩn bɩtwi:n

17 Wa 1 bɩtwi:n 2 ɩn bɩtwi:n, °twi:n[1] 3–4 bɩtwi:n 5–6 bɩtwi:n, °~[1] 7 bɩtwi:n

23 Mon 1 bɩtw^{ɩ}i:n 2 bɩtwi:n 3 bɩtwɩks 4 n.a., °bi:t^{h}wi:n[3] 5 bit^{h}wi:n 6 bɩtwi:n 7 n.a.

24 Gl 1 twɩ:^{ə}n 2 bɩtwɩn 3 bɩtw^{ɩ}i:n 4 §ɩn 5 bɩtwi:n, twɩkst ["older"] 6–7 bɩtwi̜:n

25 O 1 bɩtwi:n 2 ɩn bɩtwi:n 3 bɩtwi:n 4 bɩtwi:n, °~[1], °twi:n[4] 5–6 bɩtwi:n

IX.2.12 AMONG

Q. Where did you say that rabbit was in the garden? Well, do you see those potatoes? I think it's somewhere . . . . them.

Rr. (IN) AMONG(ST), (IN) BETWEEN, IN, MONG(ST)

7 Ch 1 əmɷŋg 2 əmɷŋ, °~[2,4], °əmɷŋg[2,4] 3 əmɷŋg 4 əmɒŋ 5–6 əmɷŋg

8 Db 1 əmɷŋg 2 əmɒŋ 3–7 əmɷŋg

11 Sa 1 əmʌŋst 2 əmɒŋst 3 əmɷŋ 4 əmɒŋ 5 əmɷŋst 6–7 əmɒŋst 8 əmɷŋst 9–11 əmɒŋst

12 St 1 s.f. əmɷŋst 2 bɩtwɛɩn, °əmɷŋst[1] 3 ɩn əmɷŋg 4 ɩn əmɷŋgst 5 ɩn bɩtwi:n, ɩn, ɩn əmɷŋgst 6 əmɷŋgst 7 ɩn əmɷŋgst 8 əmɷŋgst 9 ɩn əmɷŋgst [old] 10 ɩn, əmɷŋg 11 ɩn əmɷŋgst

15 He 1 əmɒŋ, °əmɒŋst[1] 2 əmʌŋ 3 əmɷŋs, °əmɒŋ[2] 4–5 əmɷŋ 6 əmɒŋ 7 əmʌŋst, °əmɷŋst[2]

16 Wo 1–3 əmɷŋst 4 əmɒŋ 5 ɷmɷŋst 6 ɩn ɷmɷŋst 7 əmɷŋ

17 Wa 1 əmɷŋ 2 əmɷŋst, °~[4] 3–6 əmɷŋ 7 mɷŋ

23 Mon 1 əmʌŋ 2 ɪn əmɷŋst 3 əmʌŋ 4 n.a. 5 əmɒ̤·ŋ 6 ɪn əmʌŋst 7 n.a.

24 Gl 1 mɷŋst 2–4 əmɷŋst 5 mɷŋ, °əmɷŋst^{2} 6 əməŋ 7 əmɷ̣ŋst

25 O 1 əmɒŋ 2 əmɑŋ, mɑŋ 3 əməŋ 4 əmɷŋst 5 ɪn, əməŋ 6 ɪn əmɒŋ

IX.2.13 OFF‡

Q. Smith was so bad at riding that he fell . . . . his horse.

Rr. OFF (OF/ON)

Note 1—I.m. exs. of OFF *adv.* are reproduced below between square brackets untransliterated.

Note 2—For exs. of OFF *prep.*, see V.8.2; and of OFF *adv.*, see II.3.5(b), II.4.3, II.6.8/9, II.9.5, III.1.9/12(b), III.7.10, IV.12.5, V.7.10/24, V.8.14, VI.5.3, VI.13.1/16, VII.5.8 and VIII.7.9. For (-)OFF-, see I.6.4, II.3.4 (a) and VII.5.9.

7 Ch 1 ɔ:f, °~^{2} 2 pp. əf, ~^{2,3} [əf$^{1,3(2x),4(2x)}$, ~^{3} VIII.8.15] 3 ɒf [ɒf^{2,3}] 4 ɒ·f [ɒf^{1,2}] 5 ɒf, °~^{1} [ɒf^{1}] 6 ɔ:f, °~^{2} [ɔ:f^{3}]

8 Db 1 ɔ:f, °~^{1,4} [ɔ:f$^{1(3x)}$] 2 ɒf 3 ɒf [ɒf^{1} IV.7.2] 4 ɒf [ɒf^{1}] 5 ɒf [ɒf^{4}] 6–7 ɒf

11 Sa 1 ɔ^{ɽ}:f 2–3 ɒf 4 ɔ:f 5 ɒf [ɒf^{3}, a:f^{2}] 6 ɔ:f [ɔ:f^{1}] 7 ɔ:f 8 ɔ:f [ɒf$^{2(2x)}$; a:f^{2} (n.d.g.)] 9 ɔ:f 10 ɔ:f [ɔ:f^{1,2}] 11 ɔ:f [ɒf^{2}]

12 St 1 ɒf$^{(2x)}$, °~$^{1(2x)}$, °ɒf ṇ^{2} [ɒf$^{1(3x)}$] 2 ɒf [ɒf$^{2(2x)}$] 3 ɒf, °~^{1} [ɒf$^{1,2(4x)}$] 4 ɒf 5 ɒf, °~^{2} 6 ɒf [ɒf$^{1(2x),2(2x)}$, ~$^{2(2x)}$ I.7.19] 7 ɒf [ɒf^{1}] 8 ɒf, °~^{3} [ɒf^{1}] 9 ɒf [ɒf$^{1(3x),2}$] 10 ɒf [ɒf$^{4(2x),5}$] 11 ɒf, °~^{2} [ɒf$^{1(2x),2}$]

15 He 1 ɔ:f [ɔ:f$^{1(2x)}$] 2 ɔ:f, °~^{2} 3 ɑ:f [ɑ:f^{4}] 4 ɑ:f [ɑ:f^{2}] 5 ɑ:f 6 ɑ:f [ɒf$^{1(2x)}$, ɒf^{1} V.5.9] 7 ɒf, °~$^{3(5x)}$, °ɒf ɒn^{2} [ɒf$^{1(2x),2,3(5x),4(5x)}$, ɒ:f^{4}, ɒ̣:f^{4}]

16 Wo 1 ɒf [ɒf^{2,3}] 2 ɑ:f 3 ɑ:f [ɑ:f^{2,3}] 4 ɑ:f [ɑ:f$^{2(2x)}$] 5 ɑ:f 6 ɑ:f [ɑ:f^{1,2}, ɒf^{2}] 7 ɔ:f, °~$^{4(4x)}$, °~^{3} V.7.23 [ɔ:f$^{1(5x),2,3(2x),4(2x)}$, ~^{4} IV.1.9, ɒf^{4}]

17 Wa 1 ɒf, °ɔ:f^{2} 2 ɔ:f, °~^{2,3}, °əf əɹ^{3} [ɔ:f$^{1(8x),3(3x),4(3x)}$, ɔ:f^{4} VIII.9.3, əf^{2}; ɔ:fspɹɪŋ^{1} *offspring*] 3 ɔ:f [ɔ:f^{1}] 4 ɔ:f [ɔ:f$^{1(2x)}$] 5 ɔ:f [ɔ:f$^{1(4x)}$, ~^{1} II.6.10] 6 ɔ:f [ɔ:f^{1,4}] 7 ɔ:f [ɔ:f^{2}, ɑ:f^{2}]

23 Mon 1–2 ɑ:f 3 ɑ:f, °~^{2} 4 ɔ:f, °~^{1} [n.d.g.] 5 ɔ:f, °~^{1} 6 ɑ:f [ɑ:f^{1} III.1.4] 7 n.a.

24 Gl 1 ɑ:f, °əf^{1} 2 ɑ:f 3 ɑ:f [ɑ:f, ~^{3}, ~^{4} VIII.8.5] 4 ɑ:f [ɑ:f^{1}] 5 ɔ:f [ɔ:f^{1}, ~^{2} VI.14.2] 6 ɔ:f [ɔ:f$^{2(2x)}$] 7 ɔ:f [ɔ:f]

25 O 1 ɔ:f 2 ɔ:f, ○~[2] [ɔ:f[1,3]] 3 ɔ:f, ○~[1] [ɔ:f[1,2(2x)], ɒf[1]] 4 ɒf, ○~[1], ○ɒf əv[1,4], ○ɒf ə[1(2x)], ○ɔ:f[1,5], ○ɔ:f əv[2] [ɒf[1,4(3x)], ɒ:f[5] VIII.5.3, ɔ:f[1,3,5]] 5 ɔ:f ○~[2] ○~[2] [n.d.g.; ɔ:f[2]] 6 ɔ:f [~[3] (n.d.g.)]

IX.2.14 LAUGHING‡

Q. Some of those who saw it thought it rather funny and just couldn't help [*i. laughing*] . . . .

Rr. (A–)LAUGHING, BUT LAUGH

Note—For additional exs. of LAUGHING, see VIII.8.7.

7 Ch 1–5 lafɪn 6 la:fɪn

8 Db 1–5 lafɪn 6 bə lɒf, ○lɒfɪn 7 lɒfɪn

11 Sa 1 la:fɪn 2 lɒfɪn 3 la:fɪn 4 laʳ:fɪn 5 lɒfɪn 6 la:fɪn 7 lɔ:fɪn 8 lɒ:fɪn 9–11 lɒfɪn

12 St 1 lɒfɪn 2 lafɪn 3 lɒfɪn 4–5 lafɪn 6 bət lɒf, lɒfɪn 7 lɒfɪn 8 lafɪn 9 lɒfɪn 10 lafɪn, lɒfɪn 11 lafɪn

15 He 1 la:fɪn, lɔ:fɪn ["older"] 2 əlɒfɪn 3–6 lɒfɪn 7 la:fɪn

16 Wo 1–3 lɒfɪn 4 əlɒfɪn 5 lɒfɪn 6 əlɒfɪn 7 p. lɑ:fɪn

17 Wa 1 la:fɪn 2 lɑ:fɪn 3–7 la:fɪn

23 Mon 1 əla:fɪn 2 læfɪn 3–5 la:fɪn 6 ła:fɪn 7 n.a.

24 Gl 1 læ:fɪn 2 lɒfɪn 3 læ:fɪn 4–5 la:fɪn 6 bət la:f 7 la:fɪn

25 O 1–3 la:fɪn 4 łafɪn, s.f. łɑ:fɪn 5–6 la:fɪn

IX.2.15 OUT OF† IT†

Q. A man who has been in the Army a long time is usually very thankful, not to stay in it, but to get . . . .

Rr. OUT OF/ON IT

Note 1—At 12.7 the f.w. omitted to rec. the wanted OF IT.

Note 2—I.m. exs. of OUT *adv.* and *prep.* are reproduced below between square brackets untransliterated.

Note 3—OUT OF/ON IT also occurs at VIII.7.9. For additional exs. of OUT, see II.4.2, II.9.5/11 (a), III.3.4/8, III.11.2, IV.1.4, IV.2.11, IV.6.20, V.3.8, V.8.8, VI.5.4, VI.13.1/8, VII.5.8, VIII.6.2, and VIII.7.9. OF + the 3rd s. pronominal obj. *also* occurs at VII.2.12, VII.8.7, IX.2.5/6 and IX.11.5.

7 Ch 1 aɪt n̩ ɪt 2 æ:t ən ɪt 3 aɪt ɒn‿t 4 aɷt n̩ ɪt [aɷt²⁽⁴ˣ⁾] 5 aɪt ɒn ɪt [aɪt¹·²⁽³ˣ⁾, ɛɷt¹] 6 a̜ɷt əv ɪt [aɷt³; aɷt n̩² *out on* (=*of*)]

8 Db 1 ɛ̜ɷt ɒn ɪt [aɷt¹] 2 a:t ɒn ɪt [a:t²·³·⁴] 3 ɛ:t ɒn ɪt [ɛ̈ɷt¹⁽³ˣ⁾, ɛɷt²] 4 ɛ:t ɒn ɪt [ɛ:t¹⁽²ˣ⁾·³] 5 ɛ̜:t ɒn‿t [ɛ̜:t²·⁴, ɛ̜·ət¹] 6 ɛ:t ɒn‿t [ɛ:t¹⁽⁸ˣ⁾] 7 ɛ:t ɒn‿t [ɛ:t¹, ɛɷt¹]

11 Sa 1 ɛɷt ɒn ɪt 2 æɷt n̩ ɪt 3 aɷt əv ɪt 4 ɛɷt ən ɪt 5 ɛɷt n̩ ɪt 6–7 aɷt ɒn ɪt 8 ɛɷt ɒn ɪt 9 aɷt n̩ ɪt 10–11 aɷt ɒn ɪt

12 St 1 aɷt ɒn ɪt 2 aɪt ɒn ɪt 3 aɪt ɒn‿t 4 n.a. 5 aɷt ɒv ɪt 6 æɷt ɒn ɪt, °æ:t ɒn ɪt 7 æɷt 8 æɷt ɒn ɪt 9–10 a:t ɒn ɪt 11 aɷt əv ɪt

15 He 1–2 æɷt n̩ ɪt 3 əɷt ɒn ɪt 4 əɷt n̩ ɪt 5 ʌɷt n̩ ɪt 6 əɷt n̩ ɪt 7 ə̆ɷ̜t əv ɪt, s.f. əʉ̜t ən ɪt, s.f. əʉ̜t n̩ ɪt

16 Wo 1 ɛɷt ən ɪt [ɛɷt¹⁽²ˣ⁾·²·³⁽²ˣ⁾, ~³ VI.8.1] 2 ɛɷt ən ɪt [ɛɷt¹⁽²ˣ⁾·²] 3 ɛu:t ɒn ɪt 4 əɷ:t ɒn ɪt 5 ir.r. 6 ɛu:t ɒn ɪt 7 æɷt əv ɪt

17 Wa 1 æɷt ɒv ɪt [æɷt²⁽²ˣ⁾, ɛ̜ɷt²] 2 æɷt ən ɪt [æɷt¹ IV.4.4] 3 ɛ̈ɷt əv ɪt [ɛ̈ɷt², ɛ̜ɷt¹ II.9.11, æɷt³; ɛ̈ɷtsəɪd², ɛ̈ɷtsɑɪd² *outside*] 4 ɛɷt ɒn ɪt 5 ɛɷt əv ɪt 6 ɛɷt ɷv ɪt 7 ɛ̈ɷt ɒn ɪt

23 Mon 1–2 ʌɷt n̩ ɪt 3 əɷt n̩ ɪt 4 əutʰ əv ɪtʰ 5 əutʰ əv ɪt 6 əɷt n̩ ɪt 7 n.a.

24 Gl 1 əɷ:ᵊt n̩ ɪt 2 əɷ:t ɑ:n ɪt 3 əɷt ɒn‿t 4 əɷt ɒn‿t [əɷt³ VII.6.15] 5 ʌɷt ɑn‿t 6 °u:t ɒn‿t 7 °u:t ɑn ɪt, °u:t ɑn‿t ["older"]

25 O 1 ɛ̈ɷt ɒn ɪt 2 æɷt əv ɪt 3 ɛɷt ən ɪt 4 æɷt əv ɪt 5 ɛ̈ɷʔ ɒn ɪʔ 6 ɛ̈ɷʔ ɒv ɪʔ

IX.3.1 LOSE

Q. If there's a hole in the pocket where you keep your knife, you're almost certain to . . . . it.

Rr. LOSE, LOSS

Note 1—When rec. in the rr., the pronominal obj. EN/HER/HIM/IT is reproduced below.

Note 2—In the i.m. below, an attached superior + denotes a p.p., and superior × n.d.g.

Note 3—LOST occurs at III.2.7.

7 Ch 1 lʏ:z ɪt 2 lɔ:s, °¶lu:zɪn⁴, °lɔst³ *3 p.t.s.*, °~³ *1 p.t.pl.* 3 lᶦʏ:z 4 l°ü:z 5 lɛɷz 6 l°u:z ɪt

8 Db 1 lo:z 2 lɒɪz, °×~⁴, °×lo:z⁴ 3 lü:z ɪt, lo:z ɪt ["older", pref.] 4 l°ü:z, lɛɷz ["older"] 5 lɒs. 6 lo:°z ə [=*her*] 7 lo·°z

11 Sa 1 lu:z 2 lu:z, °¶lu:zɪn² 3 lu:z 4 lu:z, °×lɔ:st² 5 lɪu:z 6 lu:z 7 lu:z, °lu:st *p.t.*, °+lɔʳ:ʂʈ 8 lu:z 9 lo:z 10–11 lu:z

12 St 1 lü:z ɪt, loɷz ɪt 2 lɛ̩ɷz ɪt 3 lɛɷz ɪt 4 lü:z ɪt 5 lü:z 6 lu:z ɪt 7 lü:z ɪt, °lɒst¹ *3 p.t.s.* IX.9.6 8 lü:z ɪt, °¶lu:zɪn¹ 9 lɛɷz ɪt 10–11 lü:z ɪt

15 He 1 lu:z ɪm 2 ɫu:z ɪt 3 lu:z 4 lu:z ɪm 5 lu:z 6 lu:z ən 7 lu:z ɪt

16 Wo 1–2 lu:z 3 lu:z ɪm 4 lu:z 5 lu:z ɪm, °¶əlu:zɪn¹ VII.6.5 6 lu:z ɪ:t 7 lu:z ɪt, °+lɔ:st⁴, °×~¹

17 Wa 1 lu:z ɪt 2 lu:z ɪt, °lu:z, °lɔ:st² *1 p.t.s.*, °+~¹, °×~⁴ 3 lü:s 4 lü:z 5 lü:s 6 lu:s ɪt 7 lu:z

23 Mon 1 l°u:z ɪm 2 lu:z ət 3 lu:z 4 lu̜:z 5 lü:z, °+lɒ̩·st¹ 6 lu:z ɪt 7 n.a.

24 Gl 1 lu:ᵊz 2 l°u:z 3 l°u:z n̩ 4 l°u:z 5 lu:z n̩, °+lɔ:st² 6–7 lu:z n̩

25 O 1 lu:s 2 lu:z 3 l°uz 4 ɫu:z ɪt, °+ɫɒst¹ 5 lü:z ɪʔ 6 lu:z, °×~³ VII.6.5

IX.3.2 FIND*. FOUND† (*3 p.t.s.*). FOUND† (*p.p.*)

Q. He was looking for his knife but couldn't . . . . it.
Next day he looked for it again and this time he . . . . it.
He came back looking pleased and told us that he had . . . . it.

Rr. inf.:—FIND

3 p.t.s.:—FOUND

p.p.:—FOUND

Note 1—The rr. to the three parts of the q. are separated below by full stops, except when the 3 p.t.s. and the p.p. are identical. In this case the form concerned is, when practicable, marked with superior ◇, and only one full stop is used.

Note 2—V.4 of the *Qr.* was used by P.W. at 7.2, 16.7 and 17.2. The q. then read as follows,—*I was looking for my knife but couldn't . . . . it. Next day, however, I looked for it again and . . . . it. Then I came back looking pleased and said that I had . . . . it.*

Note 3—FIND *inf.* also occurs at III.13.8.

7 Ch 1 faɪnd. ◇fɷnd 2 fæɪnd, °faɪnd¹˒². fɷn *1 p.t.s.*, °fɷnd² *3 p.t.s.* fɷn 3 faɪnd. fɷnt. fɷnd, °fɷnt² 4 faɪnd. ◇fɷnd 5 faɪnd. fɷnt, °fɛɷnd¹ [n.d.g.]. fɷnt 6 faɪnd. ◇fɷnd

8 Db 1 faɪnd. ◇fɷn 2 fɑɪnd. fɷn. fɷn, ○~[2] 3 faɪnd. ◇fɷnd 4 fɑɪnd, ○~[3]. fɷnd. fɷnd, ○fɷn[1] 5 fɑɪnd. ◇fɷn 6 fɑ̃·ɪ̃nd. fɷnd, ○~[1] *1 p.t.s.* fɷnd 7 fɑ̃·ɪ̃nd. ◇fɷnd

11 Sa 1 faɪnd. ◇fʌn 2 faɪnd, ○fɷnd[2] *1 p.t.s.*, ○fɷn[2] *1 p.t.s.* ◇fɷnd 3 fɛɪnd. ◇faɷnd 4 faɪn. ◇fɛɷnd 5 faɪnd. ◇fɷn 6 faɪn. ◇faɷnd 7 faɪn. fʌn. fʌnd 8 fɒɪnd, ○faɪ[2] [rec. in «aɪ kə: (IX.4.16) faɪ nɷθɪn (VII.8.14)» *I can't find nothing*]. ◇fɷn 9 faɪnd. fʌnd, ○~[1] [n.d.g.]. faɷnd, ○fʌn[1] 10 faɪnd. ◇fʌn 11 faɪn. ◇fʌn

12 St 1 fɒɪnd, ○~[2] *3 pr.pl.*. ◇fɷnd 2 fɒɪnd. ◇fɷnt 3 fɒ:ɪnd, ○~[1]. fɷnd, ○~[1] *1 p.t.s.* fɷnd, ○fɷnt[2], ○faɪnd[1] [rec. in «ə:z faɪnd ɪt aɪt[1] *her's (=she's) f. it out*] 4 fɒɪnd. fæɷnd, ○fɷn[2] *1 p.t.s.* fæɷnd 5 fɒ:ɪnd, ○~[2]. faɷnd, fɷnd, ○fɷn[2] *3 p.t.pl.* fɷnd, ○~[3] 6 fɒ:ɪnd. fɷnd. fɷnd, ○fɷn 7 fɒɪnd. fɷn, ○faɷnd[1]. fɷn 8 fɒɪnd. fa̦ɷnd, ○fɷn[1(2x)]. fa̦ɷnd 9 fɒɪnd, ○fa:nd[2] [n.d.g.]. ◇fɷn 10 faɪnd. fæɷnd 11 fɒ·ɪnd. ◇fæɷnd

15 He 1 fæɪnd. ◇fʌnd 2 fæɪnd. fʌn. fʌnd 3 fəɪnd. fɷn, ○~[2]. fɷnd 4 vəɪnd. ◇vʌnd 5 fəɪnd. fʌɷnd. fɷnd 6 vəɪnd. vəɷnd. vɷnd 7 fa̦ɪnd, ○~. ◇fə̆ɷ̜nd

16 Wo 1 fɒɪnd. fɷn, ○~[1(2x)]. fɷn 2 fəɪnd. ◇fɛɷnd, ◇fɷn [older]. 3 fəi:n. ◇fɷnd 4 fəɪnd. ◇fɷn 5 fəɪnd. ◇fɷnd 6 fɒɪnd. ◇fɷnd 7 fəɪnd, ○~[1], ○fəɪndz[1] *3 pr.s.* fæɷnd. fæɷnd, ○~[1]

17 Wa 1 fɑɪnd, ○~[1]. fɛɷnd. fɛ̧ɷnd 2 fəɪnd, ○~[1,4], ○~[1] *2 pr.s.* fæɷnd *1 p.t.s.*, ○fæɷnd[1,4] *1 p.t.s.* fæɷnd 3 fəɪnd. ◇fɛ̆ɷnd 4 fəɪnd. ◇fɛɷnd 5 fəɪnd. fɛɷnd, ○fɛɷn[1]. fɛɷnd 6 fəɪnd. ◇fɛɷnd 7 fəɪnd. ◇fɛɷnd

23 Mon 1 fəɪnd, ○¶əfəɪndɪn[4]. ◇fʌɷnd 2 fəɪnd. ◇fʌɷnd 3 fəɪnd. ◇fəɷnd 4 fə̧ind. ◇fəund 5 fəɪ̧nd. ◇fəund, ○~[2] 6 fəɪnd. ◇fəɷnd 7 n.a., ○fəund[1] *p.p.*

24 Gl 1 vəɪ^{ə}n. ◇vəɷ:n 2 fəɪnd. ◇fɷnd 3 vəɪnd, ○~[4]. ◇vəɷnd 4 vəɪnd, ○~[3]. ◇vəɷnd 5 fə̈ɪnd. ◇fʌn 6 vʌɪnd. ◇v^{ɷ}u:nd 7 vʌɪnd. ◇v^{ɷ}u:nd

25 O 1 fə̈ɪnd. ◇fɛ̈ɷnd 2 fə̈ɪnd. ◇fɷ̜n 3 fə̈ɪnd. fæɷnd, s.f. fɷnd. s.f. fɷnd 4 fəɪnd. ◇fæɷnd 5 fʌʏnd. ◇fɛ̈ɷnd 6 fə̈ɪnd. ◇fɛ̈ɷnd

IX.3.3 PUT† (*p.p.*). PUT† (*1 p.t.s.*). PUT* (*inf.*)

Q. Father says: Jane, I've lost my collar studs. Where have you . . . . them?
She answers: Well, last night I . . . . them away.
He doesn't hear what she says, so he asks again: Where did you . . . . them?

Rr. p.p.:—(A-)PUT
1 p.t.s.:—PUT
inf.:—PUT(TEN)

Note 1—The rr. to the three parts of the q. are separated below by full stops except in those cases covered by Note 2.

Note 2—Where practicable, an attached superior + denotes that the form concerned was rec. as the r. to all three parts of the q.

Note 3—In the rr. and i.m. below, an attached superior ◇ denotes that the form concerned was foll. by THEM without the initial cons., and superior × that it was foll. by IT or HIM (without initial cons.). Superior ‖ denotes a form foll. by a word beginning with a V. of any other word, and superior ɑ denotes a form n.d.g.

Note 4—PUT also occurs at I.5.1, III.3.8, III.5.2, V.2.12, VI.5.9 and VIII.8.15.

7 Ch 1 ◇pɷt. ◇pɷʔ. pɷt [‖pɷtn *3 pr.pl.*] 2 ×pɷt. ×pɷt. pp. pɷt, ○×~, ○~^{2}, ○pü:t^{2} [pɷt^{2} *2 pr.s.*; ~^{1} *3 pr.s.*; ~^{3} *2 pr.pl.*, ~$^{1(2x)}$ *3 pr.pl.*; ɑ×~^{1}, ɑ‖~$^{2(2x)}$; pɷtn^{4} *2 pr.s.*; ○pɷtɪn^{2,3}; ɑ×pɷɹ^{2}, ɑ‖~^{3}] 3 +pɷt 4 ◇pɷt. pɷt. pɷt, ○‖~^{2} [ɑ×pɷt^{1}] 5 +pɷt [ɑ‖pɷt^{1}] 6 +pɷd̥ [ɑ×pɷd̥^{3}]

8 Db 1 ◇pɷt, ○◇~. pɷt. pɷt [pɷtn^{1} *3 pr.pl.*] 2–3 +pɷt 4 +pɷt [pɷtn^{1} *1 pr.pl.*] 5 ×pɷɹ, ◇~. ◇pɷɹ. ◇pɷɹ, ○‖pɷt 6 +pɷt 7 ◇pɷt. pɷt. pɷt

11 Sa 1 +pʌt 2–4 +pɷt 5 +pɷt [◇¶pɷtɪn^{1}] 6 pʌt. pʌt. pʌt, ○pɷt^{4} [pɷt^{3} *imp.*] 7 +pʌt [pʌt^{1} *2 pr.pl.*] 8 +pɷt [ɑpɷt^{1}] 9 +pɷt [ɑpʌt^{1}] 10 +pɷt 11 +pʌt

12 St 1 pɷt. pɷt. pɷt, ○◇~^{1}, ○‖~^{1} 2 pɷt, ○◇~. ◇pɷt. pɷt, ○~^{2} [pɷt^{2} *1 pr.pl.*; ~^{5} *3 pr.pl.*] 3 +◇pɷt [¶pɷtɪn^{2}; ɑ×pɷt$^{1(2x)}$, ɑ~^{1}, ɑ‖~^{2}, ɑ~^{2}] 4 +pɷt 5 +pɷt [ɑpɷt^{1}, ɑ‖~$^{2(2x)}$, ɑ×~^{3}, ɑ◇pɷtɪn^{1}] 6 +◇pɷt [ɑ×pɷt^{1}, ~ɑ‖, ~^{1}, ɑ◇~^{2}, ɑ‖~$^{2(2x)}$] 7 +◇pɷt 8 ◇pɷt, ○~^{4}. ◇pɷt. ◇pɷt, ○‖~$^{1(2x)}$ [ɑ‖pɷt^{1}, ɑ~^{2}] 9 pɷt. pɷt. pɷt, ○×~^{1}, ○‖~^{1}, ○~^{3} [pɷt^{1} *3 pr.pl.*; ɑ~^{2}, ɑ‖~^{3}] 10 ◇pɷt. pɷt. pɷt [ɑpɷt^{4}, ɑ‖~^{5}] 11 ◇pɷt. ◇pɷt. pɷt [ɑ‖pɷt^{2}]

15 He 1 pɷt. ◇pɷd. ◇pɷd 2 ◇pʌt. ◇pʌt. ◇pʌt, ○‖~^{2} 3 pɷt, ○‖~^{1}. pɷt. pɷtn [*sic*], ○×~^{2} 4 ◇pɷt. pɷt. pɷt 5 +pɷt 6 +◇pɷt [ɑ×pɷt^{1}] 7 ×pɷd̥, ○pɷt^{3}, ○×~^{4}, ○əpɷt^{4}. ×pɷt. ×pɷt [¶pɷtn^{2}; ‖pɷts^{4} *3 pr.s.*; ~^{1} *2 pr.pl.*; ‖~^{3} *3 pr.pl.*; ɑpɷt$^{1(2x),3}$]

16 Wo 1 +pɷt [pɷt^{1} *1 pr.pl.*] 2 pɷt, ○~^{2}. pɷt. pɷt [ɑpɷt^{1}, ɑ×~^{2}] 3 +pɷt 4 +pɷt [¶əpɷtɩn^{1}] 5 +pɷt [pɷtn^{1} *vbl.n.*] 6 +pɷt [×pɷts^{2} *1 pr.pl.*] 7 ◇pɷt, ○~^{3}, ○‖~$^{4(2x)}$. ◇pɷt. ◇pɷt, ○~^{4} [pɷt^{1} *imp.*; ¶pɷtɩn^{4}, ¶‖əpɷtɩn^{2}, ¶~^{4}; ɑ×~^{2}, ɑ×~^{3}, ɑ‖~^{3}, ɑ~$^{3(2x)}$]

17 Wa 1 +◇pɷt [ɑpɷt^{1}] 2 +×pɷɹ [×pɷt^{1,2} *3 pr.pl.*; ɑ×~^{1,3}, ɑ~$^{1(2x),3(2x)}$, ɑ‖~^{3}] 3 pɷt. ◇pɷt. ◇pɷt [ɑ◇pɷt^{1}] 4 +◇pɷt 5 pɷt, ○~^{1}. pɷt. pɷt, ○~^{1} [ɑ×pɷt^{1}, ɑ~$^{1(2x)}$] 6 +pɷt 7 ◇pɷt. pɷt. pɷt [ɑ×pɷt^{1} II.6.10]

23 Mon 1 +pʌt 2 ◇pɷt. pɷt. pɷt 3 pʌt. pʌt. pʌt, ○×~^{2} [pɷts^{1} *3 pr.pl.*] 4 +pʰɷt [ɑpʰɷtʰ^{2}] 5 pɷt, ○~$^{2(2x)}$. pɷt. pɷt, ○×pɷtʰ^{2}, ○pÿ̆t$^{2(2x)}$ [ɑ‖pɷt^{2}, ɑ~^{2} V.7.7] 6 +pɷt [ɑ×pʌt^{1}] 7 n.a. [ɑpɷt^{1}]

24 Gl 1 ◇pɷt. pɷt. pɷt, ○×~^{2} 2–4 +pɷt 5 ×pɷt, ◇pɷt. ◇pɷt. pɷt, ○‖~^{2} 6 ◇pət. pət. pət 7 +pət [ɑpɷt^{1}]

25 O 1 +pɷt [ɑpʌt^{2}] 2 pɷʔ. pʌʔ. pʌʔ [pɷʔ^{3} *imp.*] 3 pɷt. pɷt. pɷt, ○×~^{1} 4 ×pɷd̥, ○‖pɷt$^{1(2x)}$. ×pɷd̥, ○×~. ×pɷd̥ [◇pɷts^{1} *3 pr.s.*; ‖pɷt^{3} *2 pr,pl.*; ~^{3,5} *imp.*; ɑ×~^{1}, ɑ~^{1}] 5 ◇pɷd. pɷʔ. pɷd̥ [pɷts^{2} *1 pr.s.*; ɑpʌt^{2}] 6 +pɷʔ [ɑ×pɷʔ^{2}, ɑ‖pɷt^{2}]

IX.3.4 CAME†

Q. Afterwards Father went out, but then he remembered that he had forgotten something else, so back he . . . .

Rr. CAME, COME

Note 1—I.m. exs. of COME and its parts are reproduced below between square brackets untransliterated. An attached superior ◇ denotes an inf., superior × a 3 pr.s., superior ‖ a 1–3 pr.pl., superior + a 1–3 p.t.pl., superior ᴅ a p.p., and superior ★ n.d.g. For historical reasons, the 1 p.t.s. CAME immediately follows the r. and is marked with a superior ɑ.

Note 2—COME also occurs at II.3.5, III.1.6/12, III.10.1, V.8.13, VII.4.7, VII.5.8, VII.6.5/26, VIII.3.1 and IX.9.4/5.

7 Ch 1 kɷm, ○ɑ~$^{2(2x)}$ [◇kɷm^{4}; ¶kɷmn^{2}] 2 kɷm, ○~^{1}, ○kü:m^{4} [◇kɷm$^{1(3x),2,4(2x)}$; ~^{4} *imp.*; ¶kɷmɩn^{1,3}, ¶~^{2} IV.1.4, ¶kɷmɩŋg^{3} (+ V.); kɷm^{2} *1 pr.s.*; ×kɷmz$^{1,2(6x),3(2x)}$; +kɷm^{3}; ᴅ~^{2}; keɩm^{3} *p.t.*; ★kɷm$^{2,3(3x)}$] 3 kɷm$^{(2x)}$, ○ɑki:m^{3} [◇kɷm^{3}] 4 kɷm [◇kɷm; ¶kɷmɩn$^{2(2x)}$; ×kɷmz^{2}] 5 kɷm, ○ɑkɒm^{1} 6 kɷm, ○kɷmən^{2} [rec. in «ðə kɷmən ɛvə sə mɛnɩ» *there came ever so many*; ×kɷmz^{3}]

8 Db 1 kɷm [◇kɒm^{1}; ~^{1} *1 pr.s.*; ×~^{1}] 2 kɷm [◇kɷm^{3}] 3 kɷm 4 kɷm, ○ɑke:m^{2} [¶kɷmən^{1}] 5 kɷm [ᴅkɷm^{1} III.1.7; ★~^{4}] 6 kɷm 7 kɒm, ○ɑke·ɩm^{1} [◇kɒm^{2}]

11 Sa 1 kʌm 2 kɷm 3 ke:m [◇kʌm²; ¶kʌmɩn²] 4 ke:m [◇kʌm¹] 5 kọm, ○ɑkę:m² [ᴰkɷm²] 6 kʌm [¶kʌmɩn³] 7 ke:m, ○ɑkʌm¹ [◇kʌm¹; ‖~¹; +~¹; kɷm¹ *p.t.*] 8 kɷm [◇kɷm²; ~² *pr.t.*; ~¹,² *p.t.*] 9 kʌm, ○~¹ 10 ke:m [¶kʌmɩn¹; ×kʌmz¹; kʌm³ *p.t.*] 11 kʌm [◇kɷm²; kʌm² *imp.*; kɷm² *p.t.*; ᴰ~²⁽²ˣ⁾]

12 St 1 kɷm [◇kɷm²,³⁽²ˣ⁾; ×kɷmz¹] 2 kɷm, ○~²,⁵⁽²ˣ⁾ [◇kɷm²,⁵; ×kɷmz¹; ¶kɷmɩn¹; ᴰkɷm¹; ★~¹,²] 3 kɷm, ○~¹⁽³ˣ⁾ [◇kɷm¹,²; ~¹ *imp.*; ¶kɷmɩn²; ×kɷmz¹; +kɷm¹; ᴰ~¹; ★~¹] 4 kɷm, ○kɛɩm, ○ɑkɷm¹,² [◇kɷm²] 5 kɷm, ○~² [◇kɷm²; ~² *imp.*; ¶kɷmɩn²; ~² *1 pr.s.*; ×kɷmz²,³; ᴰ~²; ★~²] 6 kɷm, ○~¹⁽²ˣ⁾ [×kɷm²; ‖~²; ~¹ *imp.*; ×kɷmz¹; ¶kɷmɩn¹; ★kɷm¹] 7 kɷm, ○~¹,³,⁵ [◇kɷm¹; ×kɷmz⁵; +~³] 8 kɷm, ○~¹ [kɷm¹ *1 pr.s.*; ᴰ~⁶; ★kɛɩm⁶] 9 kɷm, ○~¹,²⁽²ˣ⁾ [◇kɒm¹; ◇kɷm²; ~¹ *imp.*] 10 kɛɩm, kɷm [kɷm⁵ *imp.*] 11 kɷm [◇kɷm²; ¶kɷmɩn¹,², ¶əkɷmɩn²⁽²ˣ⁾; ×kɷmz¹,²]

15 He 1 kʌm [¶əkʌmɩn¹] 2 kʌm [◇kʌm²; ~ *imp.*; ×kʌmz¹] 3 kɷm [◇kɷm⁴; ‖kɷmz⁴⁽²ˣ⁾; ¶əkɷmɩn¹; ᴰkɷm¹] 4 kʌm, ○kɷm² [ᴰkʌm²] 5 kɷm [◇kʌm¹] 6 kɷm [¶əkɷmɩn¹] 7 kʌm, ○~¹,²,³,⁴ [◇kʌm⁴; ×kʌmz¹,³⁽⁴ˣ⁾,⁴; ‖kʌm²,³,⁴⁽²ˣ⁾; ¶kʌmɩn²; ᴰkʌm²,⁴]

16 Wo 1 kɷm, ○ɑ~² 2 kɷm, ○ɑ~² [◇kɷm²; ¶əkɷmɩn²; ‖kɷmz¹; +kɷmd¹] 3 kɷm, ○~²⁽³ˣ⁾ [◇kɷm¹; ᴰ~²] 4 kɷm, ○ɑ~² [◇kɷm²; ¶əkɷmɩn²,³; ‖kɷmz³] 5 kɷm, ○ɑ~¹⁽²ˣ⁾ [kɷm¹ *imp.*; ¶əkɷmɩn¹⁽²ˣ⁾; kɷmz *1 pr.s.*; ×əkɷmz¹; ‖kɷmz¹; ᴰkɷm¹] 6 kɷm [ᴰkɷm³ VIII.3.2] 7 kɷm, ○~¹⁽²ˣ⁾,²,⁴⁽²ˣ⁾, ○ɑ~¹ [◇kɷm¹⁽²ˣ⁾,³,⁴; ~¹⁽³ˣ⁾ *imp.*; ¶kɷmɩn¹; ×kɷmz¹,³⁽²ˣ⁾,⁴; ‖~¹,³⁽³ˣ⁾; +kɷm⁴; ᴰ~¹⁽²ˣ⁾,⁴; ᴰkɷmd¹]

17 Wa 1 kẹɩm, s.w. kɷm 2 kɷm, ○~⁴⁽²ˣ⁾ [◇kɷm⁴; ~³,⁴ *imp.*; ¶əkɷmɩn⁴; ×kɷmz⁴; ᴰkɷm¹,²] 3 kɷm, ○~¹ [¶əkɷmɩn¹,²⁽²ˣ⁾; ‖kɷmz²] 4 kɷm [¶kɷmɩn¹] 5 kɷm [+kɷm¹; ᴰkɷmd¹] 6 kɷm [◇kɷm⁴; ¶əkɷmɩn⁴] 7 kɷm

23 Mon 1 kʌm, ○kɛm¹ [◇kʌm⁴; ¶əkʌmɩn¹⁽²ˣ⁾; ×kʌm¹; ★əkʌmɩn¹] 2 kɷm, ○~³ [¶əkɷmɩn³] 3 kɷm, ○ɑke:m² [◇kʌm²,³] 4 kʰʌ̣̈m, ○kʌ̣̈m³ VII.6.23 5 ke:m, ○ɑkeim¹ [¶kʌ̣̈mɩn²,³] 6 kʌm, ○~¹ [★kʌm¹] 7 n.a.

24 Gl 1 kɷ:m [◇kɷ:m²; ~¹ *p.t.*] 2 kɷm, ○ɑ~³ 3 kœ:m [¶kʌmɩn¹, ¶əkʌmɩn¹] 4 kœ:m 5 kọm [◇kọm; ¶əkɷmɩn] 6 kəm [◇kəm²⁽²ˣ⁾] 7 kɷm

25 O 1 kọm [ᴰkʌm²; ★kɷm²] 2 kɷm, ○~¹, ○kʌm¹ [◇kʌm¹; ¶kʌmɩn¹,², ¶əkʌmɩn²; ‖kʌmz²; ★~¹; ★kʌm²] 3 kɷm, ○ɑkʌm¹ [×kʌmz²; ‖ke:m¹; +kɷm¹] 4 kɷm, ○~¹ [◇kɷm¹,³; ~²,³,⁵; ¶kɷmɩn¹; ¶əkɷmɩn¹; ×kɷm⁴; ×kɷmz¹⁽²ˣ⁾,⁴; ‖kɷm¹ ᴰəkɷm¹; ★kɷm⁵] 5 kọm [◇kʌm²; ¶kʌmɩn²; ‖kʌmz¹; +kʌm²] 6 kọm

IX.3.5 BREAK*. BROKE†. BROKEN†

Q. *Never drop a tumbler on the floor, because it's bound to . . . .*
I dropped one yesterday, and, of course, it . . . .
So I had to tell my wife that I had . . . . it.

Rr. inf.:—BREAK

3 p.t.s.:—BROKE

p.p.:—BROKE(N)

Note 1—The rr. to the three parts of the q. are separated below by full stops, except in those cases covered by Note 2.

Note 2—Where practicable an attached superior ◇ denotes that the form concerned was rec. as the r. to the 2nd and 3rd parts of the q.

Note 3—I.m. derivatives of BREAK foll. the r. to the 1st part of the q.

Note 4—BREAK also occurs at III.13.17 and IV.6.20; and BROKE(N) at III.1.7.

7 Ch 1 bɹẹ:k . bɹɒk . bɹɒkn 2 bɹe:k, ○bɹeɪk[2], ○~[2] *1 p.r.s.*, ○bɹɛk[1] *v.*, ○bɹe:k[1], ○~[1], bɹək . bɹəkən, ○~[2], ○bɹəkn[3] IX.1.4, ○~[3] *p.p.*, ○bɹɔ:k[1], ○bɹo:kən[1], ○bɹɷ:k[2] 3 bɹi:k . bɹɒk . bɹɒkn 4 bɹẹ:k . ◇bɹɒk 5 bɹi:kʿ . bɹɒk . bɹɒkn, ○bɹɒk[1], ○bɹɒkən[1] 6 bɹe:ᵊk . bɹak . bɹɒkən

8 Db 1 bɹe:k . bɹɒk . bɹɒkn 2 bɹɛɪk . bɹo:k . bɹɒkn 3 bɹe:k . bɹɒk . bɹɒkn, ○~[3] 4 bɹị:k . bɹo:ᵚk . bɹɒkn 5 bɹe:ᶦk, s.f. bɹɛk . bɹɒk . bɹɒk ., ○bɹɒkn[4] 6 bɹẹɪk . bɹɒk . bɹɒkn 7 bɹe·ɪk . ◇bɹo·ɷk

11 Sa 1 bɹe:k . ◇bɹo:k 2 bɹi:k . ◇bɹo:k 3 bɹe:k . ◇bɹo:k 4 bɹeɪk . bɹo:k . bɹo:kn 5 bɹę:k . bɹo:k . bɹo:k, ○~[3], ○bɹǫk[1] 6 bɹe:k . ◇bɹo:k 7 bɹe:k . bɹo:k . bɹo:k, ○~ 8 bɹɛɪk . ◇bɹo:k 9 bɹe:k . ◇bɹo:k 10 bɹe:k . bɹo:k . bɹo:k, ○~[2] 11 bɹe:k . ◇bɹo:k

12 St 1 bɹi:k . bɹɒk . bɹɒkn, ○~[3] 2 bɹi:k, ○~[1] . bɹɒk . bɹɒkn, ○~[1] 3 bɹɛk, ○~, ○bɹi:k[1] . bɹɒk . bɹɒkn 4 bɹɛɪk . ◇bɹoɷk 5 bɹe:k . bɹoɷk, ○bɹɒk[3] *1 p.t.s.* bɹoɷk 6 bɹɛk . bɹɒk . bɹɒkn, ○~[1] IX.5.5, ○bɹoɷkn[2] 7 bɹɛk . ◇bɹɒk 8 bɹɛɪk . ◇bɹoɷk 9 bɹiək . bɹoɷk . bɹoɷk, ○bɹɒk[2] 10 bɹɛɪk . bɹoɷk . bɹoɷkn 11 bɹɛɪk . bɹȯɷk . bɹoɷkn, ○bɹoɷk[1,2]

15 He 1–2 bɹe:ɪk . ◇bɹo:k 3 bɹe:k . ◇bɹo:k 4–5 bɹe:ɪk . ◇bɹo:k 6 bɹɛ:k . ◇bɹo:k 7 bɹe:ᶦk, ○~ . bɹo:k, ○bɹoɷk[1(2x)], ○~[1] *1 p.t. pl.* . bɹo:kn, s.f. bɹo:k, ○bɹoɷk[2]

16 Wo 1 bɹɛɪk . ◇bɹɒɷk 2 bɹe:k . ◇bɹoɷk 3 bɹe:ɪk, ○~[2] IX.5.5 . bɹoɷk . bɹoɷk, ○~[1] 4 bɹe:ᶦk . ◇bɹoɷk 5 bɹe:k . bɹo:k . bɹo:kn 6 bɹe:ᶦk . ◇bɹoɷk 7 bɹeɪk, ○~[4] IX.5.5 . bɹəɷk . bɹəɷkn, s.f. bɹəɷk [pref.], ○~[4]

17 Wa 1 bɹɛɪk. ◇bɹǫɷk 2 bɹɛɪk, ○~. bɹɔɷk, ○~[4], ○~[3] III.13.17, ○bɹoɷk[1]. bɹɔɷk, ○bɹɔɷk[3,4] 3 bɹɛɪk, ○~[3] *v.* [□bɹɛɪks[1] *breaks* (i.e. pen or field)]. ◇bɹǫɷk 4 bɹɛ̧ɪk, ○bɹɛ̧ək[1] *v.*. ◇bɹoɷk 5 bɹɛɪk. bɹǫɷk. bɹǫɷk [bɹɒkn̩mɛɷðd[1] *b.-mouthed* (of sheep) VI.5.1] 6 bɹɛ̧ɪk. ◇bɹǫɷk 7 bɹɛɪk. bɹoɷk. bɹoɷk, ○~[2]

23 Mon 1 bɹe:ˈk. ◇bɹo:ᵚk 2 bɹe:k. bɹo:k. bɹo:kn 3 bɹe:k. ◇bɹo:k 4 bɹe:kʰ. ◇bɹo:k 5 bɹẹ:k. bɹo:k. bɹo:kn, ○bɹǫ:k 6 bɹe:k. ◇bɹo:k 7 n.a.

24 Gl 1 bɹe:ᵊk. ◇bɹo:ɷk 2 bɹe:ˈk. ◇bɹo:ɷk 3 bɹe:ˈk. ◇bɹo:ɷk 4 bɹe:k. ◇bɹo:ɷk 5 bɹe:k. bɹo:k. bɹo:kn 6 bɹe:k. bɹo:k. bɹo:kn 7 bɹe·ɪk. ◇bɹo:k

25 O 1 bɹeɪk. bɹǫɷk. bɹɔɷkn 2 bɹɪək. bɹɔɷk. bɹɒkn 3 bɹe:k, ○~[1]. ◇bɹɔ̣ɷk 4 bɽe:k, ○~[1], ○~[1] *v.* bɽo:k. bɽo:kn 5 bɹeˈk. bɹɔ̣ɷk. bɹɔɷk 6 bɹeɪk. ◇bɹoɷk

IX.3.6 MAKES†. MAKE* (*inf.*). (HAS) MADE†‡

Q. *A tailor is a man who . . . . suits.*
You go to a tailor and ask him to . . . . a suit.
I might say: That's a nice suit you're wearing. Tell me, who . . . . it?

Rr. 3 pr.s:—MAKE(S)
inf.:—MAKE
p.t.:—MADE
p.p.:—MADE

Note 1—The rr. to the three parts of the q. are separated below by full stops.

Note 2—The f.w. unfortunately did not usu. rec. any distinction between the p.t. MADE and the p.p. in HAS MADE, but when this was noted, a superior attached ★ is prefixed below to the p.p. form.

Note 3—Except for 3 pr.s. forms, i.m. derivatives of MAKE are reproduced after the r. to the second part of the q. An attached superior ᴅ denotes a 1 pr.pl., superior ◇ a 2 pr.pl., superior + a 3 pr.pl., and superior ‖ n.d.g.

Note 4—MAKE also occurs at V.2.8, V.8.9/13 and VIII.9.4, and (-)MAKER *n.* at II.6.11, II.7.8 and VIII.4.5.

7 Ch 1 mẹ:k. me:k, ○~[4], ○‖~[3]. mẹ:d 2 me:ks, s.f. mɛ̧ks. mɛ̧k, ○me:k[1,2(2x)], ○mɛk[1], ○mak[4(2x)], ○‖~[4], ○+me:ks[2], ○+maks[2], ○¶mɛkɪn[2], ○¶me:kɪn[3] [ᴰmɛkn[1]]. me:d, ○~[1], ○★~[2(5x)] 3 mak. mak, ○+mẹ:k. mi:d 4 mị:ks. mị:k. mẹ:d, ○★me:d[2] 5 mi:ks [*pref.*], maks, ○mi:ks. mak. mi:d 6 maks. mak, ○‖me:k[2]. me:ᵊd

8 Db 1 mɛks. mɛk [^{D}mɛkn^{1}]. mɛd 2 mak. mɛk. me:d 3 mak. mak. me:d 4 me:z. mɛk. mi:d 5 me:ιz, mɛks. mɛk, me:ᶥ, ○me:ᶥ, ○me:^{2,3}. me:ᶥd, ○‖me:d^{4} 6 maks. mak, ○‖mɛk^{1}, ○¶makιn^{1}. me:ᶥd 7 mɛks, maks ["older"], ○mɛks^{2}. mak, ○~$^{2(2x)}$ [^{D}makn^{1}]. mę:ιd

11 Sa 1 me:ks. me:k. me:d 2 mɛks. mɛk, ○ᴰ~^{2}, ○‖~^{2}. me:d, ○~^{3}, ○★~^{1} 3–4 me:ks. me:k. me:d 5 maks. mak. mę:d, ○mɛd^{3} 6 me:ks. me:k, ○~^{3}. me:d 7 me:ks, ○~^{1}. me:k. me:d, ○~^{1} 8 maks, ○mɛks^{2}. mak, ○~^{1}, ○¶mɛkιn^{2}. me:d 9 me:ks. me:k, ○~^{1} [^{D}me:k^{1}]. me:d, ○★~^{1} 10 me:ks. me:k, ○~^{3}. me:d, ○~^{1,3} 11 me:ks. me:k. me:d, ○~^{2}

12 St 1 maks. mak, ○mɛk^{2}, ○mɛιk^{1}, ○◇~^{2}, ○‖~^{2}, ○¶makιn^{1}, ○‖mak^{2}. mɛιd, ○★~$^{1(2x),3}$ 2 mɛιz, ○mɛιks^{1}. mɛιk, ○‖~^{1,3}, ○mak^{1}, ○¶mɛkιn^{2}, ○+mɛιn^{1}. mɛιd, ○★mɛd^{3} 3 maks. mak, ○~^{1}, ○‖~^{2}, ○mɛk^{1} *imp.* mɛιd, mɛd, ○~, ○★mɛιd^{1} 4 mɛks, ○~^{1}, ○mɛιks^{3}. mɛk, ○~^{2}, ○¶mɛιkιn^{3}, ○‖mɛιks^{2}. mɛιd, ○★~$^{1(2x)}$ 5 me:ks, ○mɛks^{2}. me:k, ○~^{1}, ○+mɛk^{2}. mɛιd, ○‖~$^{2,3(2x)}$ 6 mɛks. mɛk, ○~^{1}, ○+~$^{1(2x),2}$, ○‖~$^{2(2x)}$, ○‖mak^{2}. mɛιd, ~^{2}, ○~^{1,2} 7 mɛks, ○~^{3}, ○mɛιks^{4}. mɛk, ○¶mɛιkιn$^{1(2x)}$. mɛd, ○◇mɛιd *p.t.*, ○★~^{1}, ○◇~^{1} 8 mɛks, ○mɛιks^{5} VIII.4.4, ○‖mɛιk^{1}, ○◇mɛιks^{5}. mɛk, ○mɛιk^{1}, ○¶mɛιkιn^{3}. mɛιd, ○★~$^{1(2x),2,3}$, ○★mɛd^{2} 9 mɛks, ○~^{2}. mɛk, ○~^{1}, ○mɛιk^{1}, ○¶mɛkιn^{1}. mɛd, ○mɛιd^{2}, ○★~$^{1(2x)}$ 10 mɛιks, ○~^{4}. mɛιk. mɛιd 11 mɛks, ○~^{2}. mɛιk, ○~^{2}. mɛιd

15 He 1 me:ιks. me:ιk. me:ιd, ○★me:d$^{1(3x)}$ 2 me:ιks. me:ιk. me:ιd 3 me:ks. me:k. me:d, ○me:ιd^{1} 4 me:ks. me:k. me:d, ○★~^{2} 5 me:ιks. me:ιk. mæιd, ○mɛd^{1} 6 me:ks. me:k, ○~$^{1(2x)}$. mɛd 7 meιks, ○~^{3}, ○‖~^{3}. meιk, ○~$^{3(3x),4}$, ○¶me:kιn^{2}. meιd, ○★~^{4}

16 Wo 1 mɛιks. mɛιk, ○mɛιk^{3}, ○me:k^{1}. mɛιd 2 me:ks. me:k [^{D}me:ks^{1}]. me:d 3 me:ιks, ○~^{4}. mɛk, ○¶me:ιkιn^{3}. me:ιd 4 me:ᶥks, ○‖maιks^{2}, ○‖me:ιks^{2}. me:ᶥk. me:d 5 me:ks. me:k. maιd 6 me:ᶥks. me:ᶥk, ○¶əme:ιkιn^{3} VII.6.5. me:ᶥd 7 meιks, ○~^{4}, ○~^{3} *2 pr.pl.* s.w. meιk, ○~^{1,4}, ○◇~^{4}, ○¶meιkιn^{1}, ○¶əmeιkιn^{4}. meιd$^{(2x)}$, ○~^{4}, ○★~^{1}, ○‖~^{3}

17 Wa 1 mɛks. mɛk, ○◇~^{1}. mẹιd 2 mɛks. mɛk, ○~^{2,3,4}, ○meιk^{1}, ○¶mɛkιn$^{3,4(2x)}$, ○¶meιkιn^{1}, ○◇mɛk^{2}. mɛd, ★mɛd, ○★~^{4} 3 mɛιks. mɛιk, ○mɛk^{1}, ○¶mɛkιn^{3} VIII.8.5, mẹιd, ○★mɛιd^{2} 4 mẹιks. mẹιk. mẹιd, ○★mɛd^{1} 5 me:ᵊks, ○me:k^{1} *1 pr.pl.* me:ᵊk. me:ᵊd, ○★me:d^{1} 6 mẹιks. mɛιk. mɛιd, mɛd 7 mɛιk. mɛιk. mɛιd, me:ᵊd ["older"]

23 Mon 1 me:ɪks. me:ɪk, ○¶me:ˈkɪn². me:ˈd 2 də me:k. me:k. me:d 3 me:ks. me:k. me:d, ○~² 4 də mˈẹ:k. mˈe:k [ᴰmˈeˈkʰ²]. mˈẹ:d, ○★mẹ:d², ○‖~² 5 me:k⁽²ˣ⁾, ○meiks². mjẹ:k, ○me:k¹,², ○meɪ̞k³ V.5.7. mjẹ:d, ○★me:d², ○★mei:d² 6 me:ks. me:k. me:d 7 n.a.

24 Gl 1 me:ᵊks. me:k. me:k 2 me:ˈks, ○‖me:ks². me:ˈk. me:ˈd 3 me:ˈks. me:ˈk. me:ˈd 4 me:ks. me:k. me:d, ○★~¹ 5 me:ks. me:k. me:d 6 me:k, ○~². me:k. me:d, ○~, ○★~¹ 7 me:ks. me:k. me:d, ○~

25 O 1 meɪ̞ks. meək, ○◇me:k¹. meəd 2 mɛɪks. mɛɪk. mɪəd 3 me:ks. me:k. me:d 4 me:ks. me:k, ○~¹⁽²ˣ⁾, ○meɪk² *v.* me:d, ○★~¹, ○‖~¹ 5 me:ˈks. meɪk, ○me:k³ *imp.*, ○◇~². meɪd 6 meɪks. meɪk, ○~³. meɪd

IX.3.7 TAKE* (*inf.*). TOOK† (*3 p.t.sg.*). TAKEN†. TAKES†

Q. John Smith had the chance to go to college, but didn't . . . . . it.
But his brother was given the chance too, and he gladly . . . . it.
If their sister had had the same chance, she certainly would have . . . . it.
In fact, she never misses any chance; every chance she gets, she . . . .

Rr. inf.:—TAKE
3 p.t.s.:—TOOK
p.p.:—TAKEN, TOOK(EN)
3 pr.s.:—TAKES

Note 1—The rr. to the four parts of the q. are separated below by full stops.

Note 2—Except for 3 pr.s. forms, i.m. derivatives of TAKE are reproduced after the r. to the first part of the q., and i.m. exs. of TOOK *p.t.* after the r. to the second part. An attached superior × denotes an imp., superior + a 3 pr.pl., superior ɑ a 1 p.t.s., and superior ‖ n.d.g.

Note 3—TAKE and its parts also occur at II.6.10, III.1.7, III.3.8, VII.5.8, VIII.1.9 and VIII.7.9.

7 Ch 1 tak. tɷk. tɷk. taks 2 te:k, p. tẹk, ○te:k², ○~² *2 pr.pl.*, ○‖~², ○‖tɛk¹,²⁽²ˣ⁾, ○¶tɛkɪn², ○tak²⁽³ˣ⁾. tü:k, ○tu:k⁴, ○+~²⁽²ˣ⁾, ○ɑ~². te:n. tẹks 3 tak. tʏ:k. takn. taks 4 tak ["probably older"], tɛk, ○‖tak¹⁽²ˣ⁾. tᵒü:k. tᵒü:k. taks 5 tak. tˈʏ:k. te:n. taks 6 tak. tü̹:k. tü̹:k, ○tɷk³. taks, ○te:ks¹

8 Db 1 tɛk, °+tɛkn[1]. tʏ:k. tɛkn. tɛks 2 tɛk, °×tak[2], °¶takɪn[2]. tᵒu:k. tɛkn. tɛks 3 tɛk. tɷk. tɷk, °te:n[2]. tɛks 4 tɛk, °‖te:z[2]. tᵒük, tɛɷk ["older"], °‖tɛɷk[1]. te:n, °~[3]. tɛks, °taks[1] 5 tɛk, te:ˑ, °~, °tɛk[1(2x)]. tɷk, °tɪu:k[4] *3 p.t.pl.* takn, °tɛkn[4]. tɛks 6 tɛk, °‖~[1]. tɛɷk, °ᵈteɪd[1]. tɛɷk. tɛks 7 tak ["older"], tɛk, °tak[1]. tɷk. tɷk. tɛks, taks ["older"]

11 Sa 1 te:k. tʌk. te:kn. te:ks 2 tak, °‖te:k[3]. tɷk, °ᵈtʃɪu:k[2]. tɷk. tɛks 3 te:k. tɷk. tɷk. te:ks 4 te:k. tɷk. te:kn. te:ks 5 tak, °×~[2]. tɷk. tɷk. taks 6 te:k, °~[1] *2 pr.s.* tʌk. tʌk, °te:kn[3]. te:ks 7 te:k, °+~[1]. tɷk. te:kn. te:ks 8 tɛk, °~[2], °¶tɛkɪn[2]. tɷk. tɷk, °~[2]. taks 9 te:k, °+te:ks[1]. tʌk. tʌk, °~[1]. te:ks 10 te:k. tɷk. te:kn, °tɷk[1,3], °tʌk[1]. te:ks 11 te:k, °tak[2] [+ V.]. tʌk. tʌk. te:ks

12 St 1 tak. tɛɪd. tɛɪn, °tɷkən[1]. taks 2 tak, °~[1], °‖~[1,5], °tɛk[1], °¶takɪn[1]. tɪɷk, °tu:k[1]. tɛɪn, °~[1,2]. taks 3 tak, °×~[2], °‖~[2], °¶takɪn[1] VIII.8.5, °¶tɛkɪn[1]. tɛɷk, °tɷk[2]. tɛɷk. taks 4 tɛk. tɷk. tɷk. tɛks 5 tɛk, °‖~[2]. tu:k, tɷ:k, °‖tu:k[1]. tɷk. tɛks 6 tɛk, °‖~[2]. tɷk. tɷkn. tɛks 7 tɛk, °~[2], °tɛɪk[4]. tɒk. tɷk, °~[2]. tɛks 8 tɛɪk. tɷk. tɷk. tɛɪks 9 tɛk, °~[1(3x),2], °~[1] *1 pr.pl.* tɷk. tɷk, °~[2]. tɛks 10 tɛk. tɷ̣k. tü:k, °~[4(2x)]. tɛks 11 tɛɪk, °‖~[2] VI.11.8. tɷk. tɛɪkn, °tɷk[2]. tɛks

15 He 1 te:ɪk. tɷk. tɷk. te:ɪks 2 te:ɪk. tɷk, °tʌk[1]. tɷk, °tʌk[2]. te:ɪks 3 te:k, °te:ɪk[2]. tɷk. tɷk, °~[4]. te:ks 4 te:k. tɷk. tɷk. te:ks, °~[1] 5 te:ɪk. tɷk. tɷk. te:ɪks 6 te:k, °¶te:kɪn[1]. tɷk. tɷkn. te:ks 7 teɪk, °~[4], °+teɪk̦s[3] [teɪkɪnz[3] *takings*]. tɷk, °ᵈ~[1,4]. teɪkn, °~, °tɷk[3]. teɪks

16 Wo 1 tɛɪk. tɷk. tɷk, °~[2]. tɛɪks 2 te:k. tɷk. tɷk. te:ks 3 te:ɪk, °~[1]. tɷk. tɷk. te:ɪks 4 te:ˈk. tɷk. tɷk. te:ks 5 tˈe:k, °~[1]. tɷk. tɷk, °~[1]. tˈe:ks 6 te:ˈk. tɷk. tɷk, °~[1]. te:ˈks 7 teɪk, °~[1], °‖~[3] V.7.23, °+teɪks[1,3,4], °~[1] *1 pr.pl.*, °¶əteɪkɪn[4] [ɷndəteɪkəʳ *undertaker n.*]. tɷk, °~[4] *3 p.t. pl.* tɷk, °~[3(3x),4(2x)]. teɪks, °~[1]

17 Wa 1 tɛk. tök, °tɷk[2]. tɷk. tɛks 2 tɛk[(2x)], °~[2], °×~[4], °‖~[1], °×tɛɪk[1] VIII.3.3, °¶tɛɪkɪn[1], °¶əte:kɪn[3]. s.w. tɷk. tɷk. tɛks 3 tɛɪk. tɷk. tɛ̣ɪkn, °tɷk[3]. tɛɪks 4 tɛ̣ɪk, °tɛ̣ək. tɷk. tɷk. tɛ̣əks 5 te:ᵊk, °‖te:k[1]. tɷk. tɷk, °~[1]. te:ᵊks 6 tɛ̣ɪk. tɷk, °ᵈ~[4]. tɷk. tɛ̣ɪks, tɛks 7 tɛɪk. tɷk. tɷk. tɛɪks

23 Mon 1 te:ᶦk . tʌk . tʌk . te:ᶦks 2 te:k . tɷk . te:kn . te:ks 3 te:k, ○∼[2] [te:kɩnpo:st[3] *taking-post n.* IV.3.4] . tɷk . tɷk, ○∼[2] . te:ks 4 te:k . tʰɷk . tʰɷk, ○∼[3] . te:k 5 teik, ○∼[2], ○te:k[2], ○+teiks[2] . tɷk, ○∼[1] *2 p.t.pl.* tɷk . teiks 6 te:k . tɷk . tɷk . te:ks 7 n.a., ○¶te:kɩn V.7.24

24 Gl 1 te:ᵊk . tɷk . tɷk . te:ᵊks 2 te:ᶦk . tɷk . tɷk . te:ᶦks 3 te:ᶦk . tɷk . tɷk, ○∼[1] . te:ᶦks 4 te:k . tɷk, ○ɑ∼[3] . tɷk . te:ks 5 te:k, ○‖∼[1] . tɷk . te:kn . te:ks 6 te:k . tɷk, tək . tək . te:ks 7 te:k . tɷk . te:kn . te:ks

25 O 1 teək . tɷk, ○∼[2] . teəkn . teəks 2 tæk, ○‖tɛɩk[1,3] . tɷk . tækn . tæks 3 te:k . tɷk . tɷk . te:ks 4 te:k, ○∼[1(3x)], ○×∼[1] . tɷk . te:kn, ○tɷk[1,2,4] . te:ks 5 teᶦk, ○te:k[2], ○‖∼[2,3] [te:kəᵗəwe[2] *taker-away n.*] . tɷ̜k . tɷk . teɩks 6 teɩk, ○∼[3] . tɷk . tɷk . teɩks

IX.3.8 CATCH*. CAUGHT† (*3 p.t.sg.*) CAUGHT† (*p.p.*)

Q. Our cat saw a mouse but was too slow to . . . . it.
Our cat saw a mouse and very quickly . . . . it.
Our kitten has seen a few mice but has never actually . . . . one.

Rr. inf.:—CATCH(ED)

3 p.t.s.:—CATCH(ED), CAUGHT

p.p.:—CATCH(ED), CAUGHT

Note 1—The rr. to the three parts of the q. are separated below by full stops.

Note 2—Some ii. used the verb COP, COPPED, COPPED. It has been included below between square brackets untransliterated.

Note 3—Where practicable, superior ◇ denotes a form that is both 3 p.t.s. and p.p. Further, superior ᴅ marks a 3 pr.s., superior ɑ a 1 p.t.s., superior ★ a 3 p.t.pl., and superior ‖ n.d.g.

Note 4—CATCH–HOLE/PIT occurs at I.3.11; CATCH *inf.* at IV.9.10; CATCH *n.* meaning *latch* at V.1.9; and CATCHING meaning *infectious* at VI.12.2.

7 Ch 1 katʃ . katʃt . kɔ:t, ○katʃt ["rare"] 2 kjɛtʃ, ○kɛtʃ[2,4], ○ᴅkjɛtʃɩz[2], ○katʃ[2] *3 pr.pl.*, ○¶əkɛtʃɩn[2] . p. kjɛtʃt [kɒpt] . kɔ:t, s.f. kjɛtʃt, ○∼[2] VI.12.2 3–4 kɛtʃ . ◇kɛtʃt 5 katʃ . ◇kɛtʃt 6 kɛtʃ, ○kɛtʃ[2] . ◇kɛtʃt

8 Db 1 kɛtʃ, ○∼[1] [kɒp "pref."] . ◇kɛtʃt 2 kɛtʃ . ◇kɛtʃt 3 katʃ [kɒp] . ◇kɔ:t 4 kɛtʃ . ◇kɛtʃt 5 kɛtʃ, ○katʃ[1] . ◇kɛtʃt 6–7 kɛtʃ . ◇kɛtʃt

11 Sa 1 kɛtʃ . ◇kɛtʃt 2 kɛtʃ . ◇kɛtʃt, ○∼[2] *p.t.*, ○‖∼[2] 3–4 kɛtʃ . ◇kɛtʃt 5 kɛtʃ, ○∼[2,3], ○∼[2] *2 pr.s.* . ◇kɛtʃt, ○∼[3] *p.t.* 6 kɛtʃ . ◇kɛtʃt 7 kɛtʃ, ○∼[1] . ◇kɛtʃt 8 kɛtʃ . ◇kɛtʃt, ○∼[2] *p.t.* 9 kɛtʃ . ◇kɛtʃt 10 kɛtʃ, ○∼[3], ○ᴅkɛtʃəz[3] . ◇kɛtʃt, ○∼[2] *p.t.* 11 kɛtʃ . ◇kɛtʃt

12 St 1 kɛtʃ, ○‖∼[3]. katʃt, ○kɛtʃt[1]. kɛtʃt 2 kɛtʃ, ○‖∼[2]. ◇kɛtʃt 3 kɛtʃ, ○∼[1], ○∼[2] *2 pr.pl.*, ○‖∼[1,2]. kɛtʃt, ○∼[1] *p.t.* kɛtʃ, ○kɛtʃt[1] 4 kɛ̝tʃ, ○kɛtʃ[2] *1 pr.s.*. ◇kɔ:t 5 kɛtʃ, ○‖∼[1]. kɛtʃt, ○★katʃt[2]. kɛtʃt, ○∼[2] 6 kɛtʃ, ○∼[1], ○‖∼[2(2x)]. kɛtʃt, ○◖∼[1]. kɛtʃt, ○∼[1] 7 kɛtʃ, ○∼[1]. kɛtʃt. kɔ:t, kɛtʃt 8 kɛtʃ, ○∼[1]. kɔ:t, ○★kɛtʃd‿[1] [+V.; kɒpt[1] *3 p.t.s.*]. kɔ̝:t 9 kɛtʃ, ○‖katʃ[2(2x)], ○¶əkatʃɪn[1]. kɛtʃt. kɛtʃt, ○katʃt 10 katʃ. ◇kɔ:t 11 kɛtʃ, ○∼[2(2x)]. kɔ:t. kɔ̣:t

15 He 1 kɛtʃ. ◇kɛtʃt 2 kɛtʃ. ◇kɛtʃt 3 kɛtʃ, ○▷kɛtʃəz[2]. ◇kɛtʃt, ○◖∼[1] 4 kɛtʃ. kɛtʃt, ○∼[2]. kɛtʃt 5 kɛtʃ, ○‖∼[3]. kɛtʃt. kɛtʃt, ○∼[2] 6 kɛtʃ. ◇kɛtʃt 7 katʃ, ○kjatʃ[3], ○▷kɛtʃɪz[1], ○¶katʃɪn[1], ○‖kjæ̝tʃ[2]. ◇kɔ:t, ○‖∼[2]

16 Wo 1 kɛtʃ. kɛtʃt, ○katʃt[1]. kɛtʃt 2 katʃ. ◇katʃt 3 kɛtʃ. kɛtʃt, ○∼[2], ○◖∼[1]. kɛtʃt, ○∼[2,3] 4 kɛtʃ, ○∼[2], ○¶kɛtʃɪn[2]. ◇kɛtʃt 5 kɛtʃ. kɛtʃt. kɛtʃt, ○∼[1] 6 kɛtʃ, ○∼[1], ○‖∼[2,3]. kɛtʃt, ○∼[3]. kɛtʃt 7 n.r., ○kɛtʃ[1,3,4], ○‖∼[1], ○▷kɛtʃɪz[3,4(2x)] [kɛtʃɪz *catches n.*]. p. kɔ:t. kɛtʃt

17 Wa 1 kɛtʃ. kɛtʃt. kɔ:t, kɛtʃt ["prob. older"] 2 katʃt, ○katʃ[1,4], ○∼[1] *3 pr.pl.*, ○‖kætʃ[4], ○‖katʃt [kɔp[4(2x)] *1 pr.s.*]. n.r. [kɔpt]. s.w. katʃt 3 kætʃ, ○∼[1]. ◇katʃt 4 kjatʃ. ◇kjatʃt 5 kɛtʃ, ○kɛtʃɪz[1] *2 pr.s.*. ◇kɛtʃt 6 katʃ. ◇kɛtʃt 7 kɛtʃ. ◇kɛtʃt

23 Mon 1 kɛtʃ. ◇kɛtʃt 2–3 kɛtʃ, ○‖∼[3] *v.* ◇kɛtʃt 4 katʃ. ◇kʰɔ:tʰ, ○◖∼[3], ○★kʰɔ:t[1] 5 kɛ̝tʃ. kɔ:ᵊtʰ. kɔ:tʰ 6 kɛtʃ, ○‖∼[1] *v.* kɛtʃt. kɛtʃ 7 n.a.

24 Gl 1 kɛtʃ. ◇kɛtʃt 2 kɛtʃ, ○∼[1]. ◇kɑʳ:ṭ 3 kɛtʃ, ○¶əkɛtʃɪn[2]. ◇kɛtʃt 4 kɛtʃ, ○∼[3]. ◇kɛtʃt 5–6 kɛtʃ. ◇kɛtʃt 7 kɛtʃ, ○∼[2]. kɒt. kɔ:t

25 O 1 kɛtʃ, ○∼[2]. ◇kɛtʃt 2 kɛtʃ. ◇kɛtʃt, ○‖∼[1] *v.*, ○‖kɑ:t[1] *v.* 3 kɛtʃ. ◇kɛtʃt 4 katʃ, ○∼[1]. ◇kɔ:t 5 katʃ, ○kɛtʃ[2], ○‖∼[1] *v.* ◇kɔ:ʔ 6 kɛtʃ [kɛtʃpɷəst[1] *c.-post n.* IV.3.4]. ◇kɛtʃt

IX.3.9 GROW* (*inf.*). GREW† (*3 p.t.pl.*)

Q. We put potatoes in the ground to make them . . . .
Last year it was astonishing how quickly they . . . .

Rr. inf.:—GROW

3 p.t.pl.:—DID GROW, GREW, GROWED

Note 1—The rr. to the two parts of the q. are separated below by a full stop.

Note 2—In the i.m. below, an attached superior ◇ denotes a 3 pr.s., superior × a 3 pr.pl., and superior ᴅ a p.p.

Note 3—GROWING meaning *waxing* (ref. the moon) occurs at VII.6.5.

7 Ch 1 gɹọ:. gɹọ:d 2 gɹọ:, ○~¹, ○gɹu:¹, ○¶əgɹəɷɪn². dɪd gɹọ:, p. gɹɪü, ○ᴅgɹoɷən² 3 gɹọ:, ○gɹo:². gɹɪʏ: 4 gɹọ:, ○◇gɹo:². gɹọ:d, ○◇gɹo:d², ○ᴅ~² 5 gɹụ:. gɹọ:d 6 gɹo:. gɹo:d

8 Db 1 gɹo:. gɹʏ: 2 gɹɒɷ. gɹɪu: 3 gɹo:. gɹu: 4 gɹo:ᵚ. gɹᵚu: 5 gɹo:ᵚ. gɹo:ᵚd 6 gɹo:ᵚ. gɹo:ᵚd, ○ᴅgɹo:ᵊn¹ 7 gɹo·ɷ. gɹo·ɷd

11 Sa 1–3 gɹo. gɹo:d 4 gɹo:. gɹo:d, ○~² *p.t.* 5 gɹo:. gɹo:d 6 gɹo:. gɹo:d, ○~ *p.t.*, ○ᴅ~ 7 gɹo:. gɹo:d, ○~¹⁽²ˣ⁾ *p.t.*, ○ᴅ~¹⁽²ˣ⁾ 8 gɹo:. gɹo:d 9 gɹo:, ○gɹo:z¹. gɹo:d, ○~¹ *p.t.* 10–11 gɹo:. gɹo:d

12 St 1 gɹoɷ, ○~¹⁽³ˣ⁾. gɹoɷd 2 gɹoɷ. gɹoɷd 3 gɹɛɷ. gɹɛɷd 4 gɹoɷ, ○¶gɹoɷɪn². gɹoɷd 5 gɹoɷ, ○gɹɷ:¹, ○×~², ○~² *pr.t.* gɹü: 6 gɹoɷ. gɹü:, gɹoɷd ["old"], ○◇~¹, ○gɹu:² 7 gɹoɷ, ○¶gɹoɷwɪn¹ [gɹoɷθ¹ *growth n.*]. gɹü: 8 gɹoɷ. gɹü: 9 gɹoɷ. gɹoɷd 10 gɹoɷ. gɹü: 11 gɹọɷ, ○◇gɹoɷz². gɹu:

15 He 1 gɹo:ɷ, ○¶əgɹo:ɪn¹ [ʌndəʳgɹo:θ¹ *undergrowth*]. gɹo:ɷd 2 gɹæɷ. gɹæɷd, ○ᴅ~³ 3 gɹəɷ. gɹəɷd 4 gɹəɷ. gɹæɷd 5 gɹæɷ. gɹæɷd, ○◇gɹu:d² 6 gɹæɷ. gɹæɷd 7 gɹoɷ, ○gɹo·ɷ³. gɹu:

16 Wo 1 gɹɒɷ, ○×gɹoɷ¹. gɹɒɷd, ○◇~² 2 gɹoɷ. gɹoɷd 3 gɹˈu:. gɹˈu:d 4 gɹaɷ. gɹaɷd. ○ᴅ~¹⁽²ˣ⁾, ○ᴅgɹɒɷd¹ 5 gɹəɷ:. gɹəɷ:d 6 gɹɒɷ, ○gɹu:¹. gɹɒɷd 7 gɹəɷ, ○~⁴, ○×~³, ○¶gɹəɷɪn². gɹəɷd, ○◇~³, ○ᴅ~¹,³ [æɷtgɹu:² *outgrew 3 p.t.s.*]

17 Wa 1 gɹoɷ, ○◇gɹọɷz². gɹu: 2 gɹəɷ, ○gɹɑɷ² *1 pr.pl.* p. gɹu:, ○◇~³ *p.t.*, ○ᴅgɹəɷd², ○ᴅgɹɑɷd² 3 gɹọɷ, ○~¹. gɹu: 4 gɹọɷ, ○◇gɹɒɷz². gɹọɷd 5 gɹɒ̣ɷ, ○◇əgɹɒɷz¹. gɹɒ̣ɷd 6 gɹọɷ. gɹü: 7 gɹoɷ. gɹu:

23 Mon 1 gɹʌɷ. gɹʌɷd 2 gɹo:. gɹɪu: 3 gɹo:. dɪd gɹo: 4 gɹọ:. gɹo:d 5 gɹo:, ○gɹou². gɹoud, ○◇~³ 6 gɹo:. gɹo:d 7 n.a.

24 Gl 1 gɹæɷ. gɹæɷd 2 gɹæɷ, ○¶əgɹæɷɪn¹, ○¶gɹæɷɪn³. gɹæɷd 3 gɹɒɷ. gɹɒɷd 4 n.r. [gɷd gɹɒɷd³ *good growed* (i.e. tall)] 5 gɹɑɷ. gɹɑɷd 6 gɹᵚu:. gɹᵚu:d 7 gɹoɷ. gɹu:

25 O 1 gɹoɷ. gɹu: 2 gɹəɷ, ○~¹. gɹü:, gɹəɷd ["older"] 3 gɹọ̈ɷ. gɹọ̈ɷd 4 gɽo:, ○¶gɽo·ɪn². gɽu: 5 gɹoɷ. gɹoɷd 6 gɹoɷ. gɹu:

IX.3.10 RODE† (*1 p.t.sg.*)

Q. As a boy I had a bike but hardly ever . . . . it.

Rr. RID, RODE

7 Ch 1 ɹɪd, °ɹɑɪd *inf.* 2 ɹǫ:d, °¶ɹaɪdɪn³ [dɔŋkɪɹaɪd³ *donkey-ride*] 3–4 ɹɪd 5–6 n.a.

8 Db 1 ɹɪd 2 ɹo:d 3 ɹɪd 4 ɹo:ᵒd, °¶ɹɑɪdɪn³ VI.14.13 5 ɹɪd 6 n.a. 7 ɹo·ɷd

11 Sa 1–3 ɹo:d 4 ɹɪd 5–11 ɹo:d

12 St 1–3 ɹɪd 4–8 ɹoɷd 9 ɹɪd 10–11 ɹoɷd

15 He 1 ɹoɷd 2–7 ɹo:d

16 Wo 1 ɹɒɷd 2–3 ɹoɷd 4–5 ɹo:d 6 ɹoɷd 7 ɹɔɷd, °¶ɹɔɪdɪn⁴, °¶əɹɔɪdɪn⁴

17 Wa 1 ɹǫɷd 2 ɹɔɷd, °¶ɹɔɪdɪn⁴ 3–6 ɹǫɷd 7 ɹoɷd

23 Mon 1 ɹo:ᵒd 2–4 ɹo:d 5 ɹo:ᵊd 6 ɹo:d 7 n.a.

24 Gl 1–3 ɹo:ɷd 4 ɹɒɷd, °ɹəɪd¹ *inf.* 5–7 ɹo:d

25 O 1–3 ɹɪd 4 ɽo:d 5–6 ɹɪd

IX.4.1 I SHALL‡

Q. I like walking. Yesterday I walked to X, this morning I walked to Y and tomorrow I . . . . walk to Z.—April 1955, *I* after *tomorrow* moved to before SHALL and made a key-word.

Rr. I AM GOING (TO), I BE GOING, I'LL, I SALL~SHALL, WILL

Note 1—The f.ws. occ. omitted to rec. the subj. pron., as well as the TO foll. I AM GOING.

Note 2—All i.m. exs. cited below are of unstressed I'LL and I S(H)ALL prec. an inf. Exs. of WE'N, THEY'N and WE SHAN are reproduced in context below between square brackets for their special interest.

Note 3—For additional exs. of I'LL and I S(H)ALL, see VII.5.8, VIII.8.10, IX.4.3 and IX.9.3; and of SHALL and WILL, see IX.4.2.

7 Ch 1 a‿l 2 a‿l, °~¹,²⁽¹²ˣ⁾,³⁽²ˣ⁾,⁴, °ɔ‿l³, °ɔ:‿l¹, °a sl² [wɪ‿n se:³ *we shall say*] 3 a sl 4 a‿l [wɪ ʃən su:n an ðə bakɛnd ᵊ ɪə³ *we shall soon have the back-end of* (the) *year*] 5 a sl [wɪ ʃn bɛɪ ɪn² *we shall be in*] 6 a‿l

8 Db 1 a‿m gʏ:ɩn, °a‿l[1] 2 a‿l, °∼[1] 3 a sl, °∼[1] [wɩ‿s fɛɩd ə[1] *we shall feed her*] 4 a‿l, °∼[2(2x),3] 5 a‿l 6 a‿l, °a:‿l[1] 7 a sl

11 Sa 1 a‿l 2 aɩ‿l [ˈðe:‿n ˈpæɷnd ə ˈkæɷ[1] *they will pound a cow* (i.e. stock a cow's udder)] 3–4 l 5 ʃl, °aɩ‿l[3] 6 l 7 a‿l, °aɩ‿l[1] 8–10 aɩ‿l 11 aɩ‿l, °∼[2(2x)]

12 St 1 ʃal, °a‿l[1] 2 ʃəl [wi:‿n av əz ti:[1] *we shall have our tea*] 3–4 ʃal 5 ʃəl, °a‿l[2] 6 ʃal, °ɒ:‿l[1] 7 ʃal, °a‿l[2] 8 ʃal, °aɩ‿l[2] 9 ʃal, °ɒɩ‿l[2] 10 ʃəl 11 wɩl, °a‿l[2(2x)]

15 He 1 ʃɫ 2 æɩ‿ɫ 3 əɩ‿ɫ, °æɩ‿ɫ[2] 4 əɩ ʃəɫ 5 əɩ‿ɫ 6 əɩ ʃl 7 aɩ‿m gən ə, °ɑɩ‿ə[1] [+ w], °aɩ‿l[4], °aɩ ʃəl[4]

16 Wo 1 ɒɩ‿l, °∼[1] 2 a‿ɫ, °ɒɩ‿l[2] 3 ɒɩ‿l 4 ə‿ɫ, °ɒɩ‿ɫ[2], °ɒɩ sɫ[2] 5 ɒɩ‿ɫ 6 ɒɩ‿l 7 əɩ‿m gɷɩn tə, °əɩ‿l[1(5x),4], °ɔ‿l[3], °a‿l[4], °əɩ ʃl[3], °əɩ ʃəl[4]

17 Wa 1 a‿l, °a‿l[1] 2 a sl, °∼[1], °a ʃəl[1], °əɩ ʃəl[4(2x)], °əɩ‿l[2,3,4], °ɔ‿l[4], °a‿l[4], °∼[4] VI.4.4 3 a‿ɫ[(2x)], °a‿l[1(2x)] 4 əɩ‿m əgu:ɩn tə, p. əɩ‿ɫ 5 əɩ ʃɫ, °əɩ‿l[1(2x)] 6–7 a‿ɫ

23 Mon 1 əɩ‿ɫ 2 əɩᵊ‿l 3 əɩ‿ɫ 4 əi‿l, °∼[3] 5 ʃɫ 6 əɩ‿ɫ, °∼[1(2x)] 7 n.a.

24 Gl 1 əɩᵊ‿ɫ 2 əɩ‿ɫ 3 ʃɫ 4 ʃɫ, °əɩ ʃɫ, °əɩ ɫ[3] 5 ə̈ɩ bɩ go:n 6 ʌɩ bɩ gwæɩn, °a‿l[2] 7 ʌɩm gwȩɩn

25 O 1 ə̈ɩ‿m əgwɷɩn, ə̈i bɩ gɷɩn, °a‿l[1] 2 ə̈ɩ bi gɷɩn, p. a sl, °ə̈ɩ‿l[1] 3 ə̈ʏ bɩ gwe:n[(2x)], °a‿l[2] 2 əɩ‿m gən ə, °əɩ s‿[2] [+ V.], °a‿ɫ[4], °ɑɩ‿ɫ[4,5] 5 ʃə 6 ɫ, ə̈ɩ‿l

IX.4.2 SHALL‡

Q. I'm old-fashioned; I've always done it that way and I think I always . . . .

Rr. SHALL, WILL

Note 1—When rec. in the r., the inf. DO is reproduced below.

Note 2—For additional exs. of SHALL and WILL, see IX.4.1 (and refs.).

7 Ch 1 ʃal 2 s.w. wɩl, s.w. ʃal 3 ʃɒl 4–5 ʃal 6 n.a.

8 Db 1 ʃal· 2 ʃal 3 ʃɒl 4 ʃal 5 ʃɒl 6–7 ʃal

11 Sa 1–4 ʃal 5 ʃɒl dɩu: 6 ʃal 7 ʃæl 8 ʃal 9–10 ʃæl 11 ʃal

12 St 1–2 ʃal 3 ʃal dɛɷ 4 wɩl dü: 5 ʃal dü: 6 ʃal 7 ʃal dü: 8–9 ʃal 10 wɩl, ʃal 11 ʃal

15 He 1 ʃæɬ 2–5 ʃɒɬ 6 ʃæɬ 7 ʃal, ○wɩl [fr. i.'s wife, nat.]

16 Wo 1 ʃal 2 ʃaɬ 3–4 ʃɒɬ 5 ʃɷl 6 ʃæɬ 7 s.w. ʃɑl

17 Wa 1 ʃæɬ 2 s.w. ʃal 3 ʃæl 4 ʃaɬ 5 ʃɒɬ 6–7 ʃæɬ

23 Mon 1–3 ʃæɬ 4 ʃal:, wɩl: 5 ʃal 6 ʃæɬ 7 n.a.

24 Gl 1 ʃæɬ 2 ʃɒɬ 3 ʃæɬ 4 ʃaɬ 5 ʃɑl 6 ʃɛɬ 7 wɷᵊɬ

25 O 1 ʃæɬ 2–3 ʃal 4 ʃaɬ, ○∼[3] 5 wɩᵊɬ, ʃaɬ ["older"] 6 ʃæɬ

IX.4.3 I SHALL‡

Q. To a boy you caught stealing apples in your garden, you might say: Just let me catch you here again and I . . . . beat you.—April 1955, *I* after *and* moved to before SHALL and made a key-word.

Rr. I SHALL/WILL

Note 1—The f.ws. occ. omitted to rec. the subj. pron.
Note 2—For additional exs. of (I) SHALL and WILL, see IX.4.1 (and refs.).

7 Ch 1 a‿l(2x) 2–6 a‿l

8 Db 1–5 a‿l 6 a‿l(2x) 7 a‿l

11 Sa 1 a‿l 2 aɩ‿l 3 a‿l 4 ‿l 5 aɩ‿l 6 ‿l 7–11 aɩ‿l

12 St 1 ʃəl 2–3 ɒɩ‿l 4 aɩ‿l(2x) 5–6 ɒ:ɩ‿l 7 ɒɩ‿l 8 aɩ‿l 9 ɒɩ‿l
10 a:ɩ‿l 11 ʃəl

15 He 1 ɒɩ‿ɬ 2 æɩ‿ɬ 3–5 əɩ‿ɬ 6 əɩ‿l 7 aɩ‿l

16 Wo 1 a‿l 2 aɩ‿ɬ 3–4 ɒɩ‿ɬ 5 ɒɩ ʃɬ 6 ɒɩ‿ɬ 7 əɩ ʃəl

17 Wa 1 a‿ɬ 2 əɩ‿l 3 a‿l 4 əɩ‿ɬ 5 əɩ‿ᵊɬ 6 əɩ ʃɬ 7 əɩ əɬ

23 Mon 1–3 əɩ‿ɬ 4 əi‿l 5 əi‿ɬ 6 əɩ‿ɬ 7 n.a.

24 Gl 1 əɩ ʃəɬ 2 əɩ ʃɬ 3 ə‿ɬ 4 ɬ̩ 5 a‿l 6 a‿ɬ 7 a‿l

25 O 1–2 a‿l 3 ӛʏ ʃl 4 ɑ‿ɬ 5 a‿l 6 ӛɩ‿ɬ

IX.4.4 I SHAN'T‡

Q. You can't have my spade today because I want it, but you can have it tomorrow, because then I . . . . want it.—April 1955, after *then, I* moved to before SHAN'T and made a key-word.

Rr. SHAN'T, WON'T

Note 1—When rec. in the r., the subj. pron. I is reproduced below.

Note 2—In the i.m. below, an attached superior × denotes a form having a 3 sg. subj.; superior ◇ a 1 pl. subj. I.m. SHAN'T used anaphorically is reproduced below between square brackets untransliterated.

Note 3—The i.m. form at 12.11 is app. a double negative.

Note 4—For additional exs. of SHAN'T and WON'T, see IX.4.5; for SHALL, see IX.4.1 (and refs.).

7 Ch 1 ʃanə 2 ʃa:nt, ○◇ʃanə⁴ 3 ʃɒnə⁽²ˣ⁾ 4 ʃanə, ○a ʃanə 5 ʃanə, ○◇ʃɒnə² 6 ʃanə

8 Db 1 a ʃanə 2 ʃa:nt 3 ʃɒnə, ○ʃalnə² 4 ʃɒnə, [◇ʃɒnə¹] 5–7 ʃanə

11 Sa 1–2 ʃanə 3–4 ʃa:nt 5–9 ʃanə 10 ʃænə 11 ʃanə

12 St 1 ʃɒnə 2 ʃanə 3 ʃanə, ○×~² 4–5 ʃanə 6 p. ʃanə 7 ʃanə [ʃanə⁴] 8 ʃɑ:nt 9 ʃanə 10 ʃa:nt 11 ʃɑ̊:nt [ʃɔ:tən², app. a double neg., Edd.]

15 He 1–2 ʃænə 3 ʃɑ:nt, ○ʃɑ:n³ 4 ʃɑ:nt 5–6 ʃænt 7 ʃant

16 Wo 1 ʃɑ:nt 2 ʃanə 3 ɒɩ ʃɑ:nt 4–5 ʃɑ:nt 6 ʃæ:n 7 ɔɩ ʃɑ:nt, ○ʃɔ:nt³, ○ʃɑ:nt⁴

17 Wa 1 ʃa:nt 2 ʃɔ:nt, ○~⁴ [◇ʃɔ:nt⁴, ~⁴] 3 ʃa:nt, s.w. ʃanə [but not used] 4 ʃɔ:nt 5 ʃɔ:nt [ju:l manɪdʒ nɛɷ ʃa:nt jə¹ *you'll manage now, shan't you?* 6–7 ʃa:nt

23 Mon 1–2 ʃænt 3 ʃænt [◇ʃæn¹ (+ «əv» *have*)] 4 ʃa:nt° 5 ʃa:nt 6 ʃænt 7 n.a.

24 Gl 1 ʃæ:nt 2 ʃa:nt 3 ʃæ:n 4 ʃant, ○×ʃa:n³ [rec. in «no:ɷ ɷðəʳ da:g ʃa:n av ŋ̩» *no other dog shan't* (i.e. shall) *have it*] 5 ʃa:nt 6 ʃa:n 7 ʃä:nt

25 O 1 ʃa:nʔ 2 wɷnʔ, ʃa:nʔ 3 ʃa:nt⁽²ˣ⁾ 4 ɑɩ ʃa:nt 5 ʃa:n⁽²ˣ⁾ 6 ʃa:nʔ⁽²ˣ⁾

IX.4.5 WON'T‡

Q. If asked to do something and you don't wish to do it, you say: No, I . . . . do it.

Rr. AIN'T GOING TO, SHAN'T, WON'T

Note 1—In the i.m. below, an attached superior ɑ denotes a 2 pr.s., superior × a 3 pr.s., superior + a 2 pr.pl., and superior ◇ a 3 pr.pl.

Note 2—I.m. exs. of anaphoric WON'T are reproduced below between square brackets untransliterated.

Note 3—For additional exs. of SHAN'T and WON'T, see IX.4.4; for SHALL, see IX.4.1 (and refs.).

7 Ch 1 wɪnə 2 ir.r., ○wɪnə^{3}, ◇wɷnə^{2}, ○×~$^{1(2x)}$, ○×wɷnt$^{1,2(2x)}$, ○×wənə^{2}, ○×wĩnə^{3}, ○+wənt^{3}, ○◇wɪnə^{1}, ○◇wɷnɪ^{1} 3 wɷnə 4 wɷnə, ○×~^{3}, ○×wɷnəɹ^{2} [+ V.] 5 wɷnə 6 wɷnə, ○×~^{2}

8 Db 1 wɪnə$^{(2x)}$, ○×~^{1,4} 2 we:nt, ○~^{1,2,3} 3–4 wɷnə 5 we:nt, wɪnə, ○×we:nt^{1} [◇wɪnə^{4}] 6 wɷnə [◇wɷnə^{1}] 7 wɷnə

11 Sa 1 wɷnə 2 wɷnə, ○◇~$^{1(2x)}$ [wɷnə^{3}] 3 wɷnt, wɷnə ["older"] 4 wɷnə 5 wɷnə, ○×~^{2,3} 6 wɷnə, ○×~^{3}, ○×wo:nt^{1} [ɷnə^{3}] 7 ɷnə, ○×~^{1} [◇wɷnə^{1}] 8 wɷnə [×‿ɷnə^{2} (rec. in «t‿ɷnə» *it won't*)] 9 ɷnə 10 ɷnə [×wo:nt^{3} (rec. in «aɪ daɷt i: wo:nt» *I doubt he won't* {i.e. if he will})] 11 ɷnə

12 St 1 ʃɒnə, ○×wɷnə^{2}, ○+woɷnt^{1} 2 ʃɒnə 3 ʃanə, ○wɷnə, ○×~^{1}, ○◇~^{1} 4 ʃanə 5 ʃanə, ○wɷnə^{3} [n.d.g.], ○woɷnt^{2} [n.d.g., + inf.; ◇wɷnə^{3}] 6 ʃanə ["older"], wɷnə [×wɷnə^{1}] 7 wɷnə [wɷnə^{4}] 8 woɷnt 9 woɷnt, wɷnə, ○×~^{2} 10 woɷnt 11 ʃɑ̊:nt, ○×woɷnt^{2} [+woɷ^{2}]

15 He 1 ɷnə [wɷnə^{3}] 2 ɷnə [wo:nt ɷm^{2} *won't them* (=*they*)] 3 wɷnt, ○◇wɷn^{1} 4 wʌnt, ○◇wɷn^{2} [wo:n əm^{2} *won't them* (=*they*)] 5–6 wo:nt 7 ʃant, ○oɷnt^{3}, ○wənə^{4}, ○×~^{2}, ○×woɷnt^{1}

16 Wo 1 wɒɷnt 2 wɷnə 3 ʃa:nt, ○◇wɷn^{1} 4 wo:nt 5 wɷnt, ○×wɷn^{1} 6 woɷn, ○×wɷn^{2} 7 wənt, ○×wɷnt$^{1,3(2x),4}$, ○◇~^{1}

17 Wa 1 wɷnt$^{(2x)}$, wọɷnt, ○×wɷnə^{1} 2 wɷnt, ɷnt$^{(2x)}$, ○+wɷnt^{4}, ○+wɔ:nt^{4} [×wɷnt^{4}] 3 wọɷnt 4 wɷnt, ○~^{3} 5 wɷnt 6 wɷnt, ○×~^{4} [×wɷnt^{4} (rec. in «ɪt aznt i:łd nəɹ ɪt nɛvəʳ wɷnt» *it hasn't healed nor it never won't* {i.e. and it never will})] 7 wɷnṭ

23 Mon 1 wʌnt, ○×wɷn^{1} 2 ɷnt, ○×o:nt^{2} [ɷnt^{3}, ×o:nt^{1}] 3 o:nt, ○×wo:nt^{2} 4 wọ:n 5 wo:nt, ○×wount^{2} [×wount^{2}] 6 o:nt 7 n.a.

24 Gl 1 wo:ɷnt 2 wɷnt, ○×wɷn^{3}, ○◇~^{3} 3–4 wɷnt 5 wɷnt 6 wənt 7 wə·nt

25 O 1 wɷnt [wo:n əs^{2} *won't us* (=*we*)] 2 wɷnʔ, ○×wʌnʔ^{1} [rec. in «nʌθɪn wʌnʔ ɛt ɪʔ» *nothing won't* (=*will*) *eat it*], ○◇wɷnʔ^{1} 3 ʃa:nt, p. wọnt 4 wo:nt, ○+wo:n^{3} [wɷn ɪt^{4} *won't it*] 5 ɛnt goɪn ə, wɷnʔ, ○×wənt^{2} 6 woɷnʔ [+wɷnʔ^{1}, ◇~^{1}]

IX.4.6 OUGHT TO‡

Q. Children are always expected to help their parents in their old age, but if they don't, other people will say they certainly . . . . help them.

Rr. OUGHT (TO), SHOULD

Note 1—In citing the i.m. below, no regard has been paid to grammatical person or number.

Note 2—When rec. in the r., the anaphoric inf. DO is reproduced below. In the rr. at 12.1(1st r.)/2/3(2nd r.), 24.5 and 25.2, the TO has pres. been absorbed.

Note 3—For additional exs. of OUGHT and SHOULD, see IX.4.7–9.

7 Ch 1 ɛɷt‿^{ʔ} dʏ: 2 ɔ:t tə dü:, s.f. ɛ̈ɷt tə dü: [pref.] 3 ɒɷt‿ʔ d'ʏ: 4 ɔ:t ə, ʃɷd 5 ɔ:t tə 6 ɔ:t ə

8 Db 1 ɒɷt‿^{ʔ} dʏ: 2 ɒɷt tə 3 ɛ̈ɷttə 4 ɛɷt tə, °ɔ:‿^{ʔ}[1] [+ «bɩ» *be*] 5 ɛɷt tə 6 ɛɷt‿ʔ dü: 7 ɛɷt tə dɛɷ

11 Sa 1 ɔ^{ɽ}:ʈ‿ə 2–3 ɔ:t‿ə 4 ɔ^{ɽ}:ʈ ʈu: 5 ɔ:t‿ɩu: 6 ɔ:t‿ə 7 ɔ:t‿ə, °‿ɔ:t tə[1] [rec. in «ə^{ɽ}:ɽ‿ɔ:t tə» *her (=she) ought to*] 8 ɔ:t‿ə 9 ɔ^{ɽ}:ʈ‿ə 10–11 ɔ:t‿ə

12 St 1 aɷt dü:, ʃɷd dü: 2 ɛɷt dɛɷ 3 ʃɷd dɛɷ, ɛɷt dɛɷ 4 ɔ:t tü: 5 ɔ:t tə dü: 6 ɔ:t tü: 7 ɔ:t ə 8 ǫ:t tü: 9 ɔ:t tü: 10 ʃɷd 11 ɔ:t tɷ

15 He 1–2 ɔ:t‿ə 3–6 ɑ:t‿ə 7 ɔ: tɷ

16 Wo 1–2 ɑ:t‿ə 3 ɑ^{ɽ}:ʈ‿u: 4 ɑ:t‿ə^{ɽ} 5 ɑ:t‿ə 6 ɑ^{ɽ}:ʈ‿ə 7 ɔ:t tu:

17 Wa 1 ʃɷ̈d, °ɔ:t tu:[1] 2 s.w. ʃɷd 3 ɔ:^{ə} tu: 4 ʃɷd 5 ɔ:t tɷ, °ɔ:t‿ɷ[1] 6 ɔ:t‿ɷ 7 ʃɷd, ɔ:t‿ə du:

23 Mon 1–2 ɑ:t‿ə 4 ir.r., °ɔ:t^{h} tə 5 ɔ:t˳ t^{h}u· 6 ɑ:t‿ə 7 n.a.

24 Gl 1–2 ɑ:t‿ə 3 ɑ^{ɽ}:ʈ‿ə 4 ɑ:t‿ə 5 ɔ:t 6–7 ɔ:t‿u:

25 O 1 ɔ:t tü: 2 ɔ:ʔ [+ «ɛlp» *help*] 3 ɔ:t‿ɷ: 4 ɔ:t‿u:, °ɔ:t ə[5] 5 ɔ:^{ə}ʔ tu: 6 ɔ:ʔ tɷ

IX.4.7 OUGHT TO HAVE‡

Q. Poor old Smith died penniless, and in misery; don't you think his well-to-do children . . . . helped him?

Rr. OUGHT ({TO}) HAVE), OUGHT TO §DONE, SHOULD/SHOULDN'T HAVE

Note 1—When rec. in the r., the p.ps. HELPED and (A–)LOOKED + AFTER are reproduced below. At 12.3/7/11, 16.3 and 17.2/3, the pronominal obj. HIM is also reproduced.

Note 2—The r. at 16.7 pres. includes an additional negative foll. DON'T of the q.

Note 3—In citing the i.m. below, no regard has been paid to grammatical person or number.

Note 4—For additional exs. of OUGHT and SHOULD, see IX.4.6/8/9.

7 Ch 1 ɛʊt‿tʔ ɛlpt, °ʃʊd ə[4] 2 p. ɛ̈ʊt tʊ əv ɛlpt 3 p. ɒʊt‿tʔ ɛlpt 4 ɔ:t‿ə ə 5 ɔ:t ə ɛlpt 6 ɔ:t‿əv

8 Db 1 ɒʊt ɛlpt 2 ɒʊt ə ɛlpt 3 ɛ̈ʊt tə §dʊn 4 ɛʊt tə ɛlpt 5 ɛʊt tʊ ə 6–7 ɛʊt təɹ ɛlpt

11 Sa 1 əʳ:ţ‿əv 2–3 ɔ:t‿əv 4 əʳ:ţ‿əv 5–8 ɔ:t‿əv 9 əʳ:ţ‿əv 10 ɔ:t‿əv, °ʃʌd əv[1], °ʃʌd ə[2] 11 ɔ:t‿əv

12 St 1 aʊt tə ə ɛlpt 2 ɛʊt təɹ ɛlpt 3 ɛʊt tɛ lɛʊkt aftɹ‿ɪm 4 ɔ:t tü: əv ɛlpt 5 ɔ:t tə ə ɛlpt, °ʃʊd ə[2] 6 ɔ:t tə ə 7 ʃʊd əv ɛlpd‿ɪm, ɔ:t tə ɛlpd‿ɪm 8 ǫ:t tü əv, °ʃʊd ə[4] 9 ɔ:t tü: əv, °ɔ:t t‿[3] [+ «ad» *had*] 10 ɔ:t tü: ə 11 ʃʊd əv ɛlpd‿ɪm, °ʃʊd əv[2]

15 He 1–2 ɔ:t‿əv 3 ɑ:t‿əv 4 ɑ:t‿əv, °ʃʊd ə[2] 5–6 ɑ:t‿əv 7 ɔ:t‿ʊ əv

16 Wo 1–2 ɑ:t‿əv 3 ɑʳ:ţ‿ə lʊkt ætəʳţ‿ɪm 4 ɑ:t‿əʳ 5 ɑ:t‿əv 6 ɑʳ:ţ‿əv 7 ʃʊdn əv ɛlpt, °ʃəd ə[1,2], °ʃʊd ə[1]

17 Wa 1 s.w. ʃʊd əv 2 p. ɔ:t tə əv əlʊkt ɑ:ftəɹ ɪm, °ɔ:t tʊ əv[1(2x)] [i:d ɔ:t tə nəʊ[4] *he'd ought to know* (i.e. ought to have known) VII.5.2] 3 ɔ: tʊ əlʊkt ɑ:ftəɹ ɪm 4 ʃʊd əv 5 ɔ:t tʊ əv 6 ɔ: tʊ əv, °ʃʊd əv[4] 7 ʃʊd əv

23 Mon 1–3 ɑ:t‿əv 4 ɔ:tʰ əv[(2x)], °ʃʊd əv[1] 5 ɔ:t̥ tʰu əv 6 ɑ:t‿əv 7 n.a.

24 Gl 1–2 ɑ:t‿əv 3 ɑʳ:ţ‿əv 4 ɑ:t‿əv 5 ɔ:t‿əv 6 ɔ:t‿ə kɛpt 7 ɔ:t‿ə ɛlpt

25 O 1 ɔ:t əv 2 ɔ:ʔ əv 3 ɔ: tʊ əv ɛlpt 4 p. ʃʊd əv ɛɫp, °ɔ:t əv[4], °ɔ:t tʊ ə[4], °ɔ:t‿ə[4(3x)] 5 ɔ:ᵊ tʊ əv 6 ɔ:ʔ tʊ əv

IX.4.8 SHOULD‡. SHOULDN'T‡

Q. Some children don't do what they . . . .
And others do what they . . . .

Rr. OUGHT (TO), S(H)OULD

DIDN'T/HADN'T OUGHT TO, DON'T OUGHT, OUGHTN'T, OUGHT NOT TO, SHOULD NOT, SHOULDN'T

Note 1—The rr. to the two parts of the q. are separated below by a full stop.

Note 2—When rec. in the r, the inf. DO is reproduced below.

Note 3—In the i.m. below, an attached superior ◇ denotes a form foll. by an inf. I.m. exs. of I SHOULD LIKE/SAY (SO)/THINK are reproduced below between square brackets, untransliterated, after the r. to the first part of the q.

Note 4—In citing the i.m. below, no regard has been paid to grammatical person or number.

Note 5—For additional exs. of OUGHT and SHOULD, see IX.4.6/7/9; of SHOULDN'T, see IX.4.9. SHOULD also occurs at IX.9.3.

7 Ch 1 ʃɷd . ʃɷdnt 2 n.a., °◇ʃəd[3], °◇ʃɷd[4] [ä səd θɪŋk[1], a ʃəd θɪŋk[2]] . ʃɷdnə dü:, °◇ʃɷdnə[1] 3 ʃɷd . ʃɷdnə 4 ʃɷd . ʃɷdnt, ʃɷdnə 5 ɔ:t tʹʏ: . dɪdnt ɔ:t‿ə 6 ɔ:t‿ə . ʃɷdnt, °◇ʃɷdnə[2], °~ n.d.g.

8 Db 1 ʃɷd . ʃɷdnə 2 ʃɷd . ʃɷdnt 3 ɛ̈ɷt, °◇ʃɷd[1] . ʃɷdnt 4 ʃɷd . ʃɷdnə 5 ɛɷt . ʃɷdnə 6 ʃɷd . ʃɷdnə 7 ɛɷt tə, °◇ʃəd[1] . ʃɷdnə

11 Sa 1–3 ʃɷd . ʃɷdnə 4 ʃɷd . ʃɷdnt 5 ʃɷd . ʃɷdnə 6 ʃɷd [aɪ‿ʃt θɪŋk[1,4], aɪ ʃəd θɪŋk[4]] . ʃɷdnə 7 ʃɷd . ʃɷdnə 8 ʃɷd, °◇~[2] [aɪ‿ʃt θɪŋk[1]] . ʃɷdnə, °◇~[2] [rec. in «wi: ʃɷdnə bi: əlaɷd tə dɷn ɪt» *we shouldn't be allowed to done it* (i.e. we shouldn't have been allowed to do it)] 9 ʃɷd . ʃɷdnə 10 ʃɷd [aɪ‿ʃt θɪŋk[3]] . ʃɷdnə 11 ʃʌd, °◇~[2] [aɪ‿ʃt θɪŋk[2], aɪ‿ʃt θɪŋ[2]] . ʃʌdnə

12 St 1 aɷt, ʃɷd . ʃɷdnə, °◇dɷnə aɷt 2 ʃɷd . ʃɷdnə 3 ʃɷd . ʃɷdnə dɛɷ, °◇ʃɷdnə[1] 4 ʃɷd . ʃɷdnə [jəd bɪ pɷmpɪn fə bɹɛθ ʃɷdnt jə *you'd be pumping* (VI.8.1) *for breath, shouldn't* (i.e. wouldn't) *you?*] 5 ʃɷd, °◇~[3] . ʃɷdnə 6 ɔ:t tə du: [ɒ:ɪ ʃɷd si: sɷ:[2]] . ʃɷdnə 7 ʃɷd, °◇~[1]. ʃɷdnt, °◇ʃɷdnə[4] 8 ʃɷd, °◇~[1] . ʃɷdnt, °~[1] 9 ɔ:t, ʃɷd [a ʃɷd si:[1]] . ʃɷdnə, °◇ʃɷdnt[1] [ɒɪ ʃɷdnt lɒɪk[1] *I shouldn't like*] 10 ɔ:t . ʃɷdmt [? error for «ʃɷdnt», Edd.] 11 ʃɷd du: . ʃɷdnt, °◇~[1]

15 He 1–2 ʃɷd . ʃɷdnə 3 ʃɷd, °◇~[2] [æɪ‿ʃd̥ sæɪ[1]] . ʃɷdənt 4 ʃɷd . ʃɷdnt [ʃɷdn ɷm[2]] 5 ʃɷd [əɪ‿ʃt θɪŋk[4]] . ʃɷdnt 6 ʃɷd . ʃɷdnt 7 ʃɷd, °◇ʃəd[1] [aɪ‿ʃ θɪŋk[1], aɪ ʃəd θɪŋk[1]] . dɪdn ɔ:t‿ə du:, °dɪdn ɔ:t‿ə, °dɪdn ɔ:t‿ə

16 Wo 1 ʃɷd . ʃɷdn 2 ʃɷd . ʃɷdnə 3 ʃɷd . ʃɷdn du: 4 ʃɷd . ʃɷdnt 5 ʃɷd . ʃɷdn, °◇~[1] 6 ʃɷd [ɒɪ ʃəd se:ɪ[3]] . ʃɷdn 7 n.a., °◇ʃəd[4] . s.w. ʃɷdnt du:, °◇ɔ:tnt, °◇ʃɷdnt[4] IX.4.12

17 Wa 1 ɔ:t tu . ʃɷdnd̥ 2 n.r. [əɪ ʃəd ləɪk[4]] . ʃɷdnt, adnt ɔ:t‿ə 3–4 ʃɷd . ʃɷdnt 5 ɔ: tu: [əɪ ʃəd sɛɪ[1]; əɪ ʃɷd θɪŋk[1]] . ʃɷdnt 6 ʃɷd . ʃɷdnt 7 ɔ:t‿ə du: . adn ɔ:t‿ə du:

23 Mon 1 ʃʌd. ʃʌdn 2 ʃɷd. ʃɷdnt 3 ʃɷd [əɩ‿ʃt θɩŋk[2]]. ʃɷdnt 4 ʃɷd. ʃɷdn 5 ʃɷd. ʃɷdn‿ɒ̝·t° du· 6 ʃɷd. ʃɷdnt 7 n.a.

24 Gl 1 ʃɷd, °◇~[2]. ʃɷdn du: 2 ʃɷd. ʃɷdnt 3 ʃɷd [ʃɷd əz[3] *should us* (=*we*)*?*]. ʃɷdn 4 ʃɷd [əɩ ʃəd ləɩk[1]]. ʃɷdnt 5 ɔ:t‿u:. ɛdnt ɔ:t 6 ɔ:t‿ə. dɩdn ɔ:t‿ə 7 ɔ:t‿ə du:. ʃɷdnt

25 O 1 ʃɷd, °◇~[3]. ʃɷdnt 2 ʃɷd. ʃɷdnʔ 3 ʃɷ̈d [i: ʃəd lʌʏk[1] *he should* (i.e. would) *like*]. adnt ɔ:t tɷ 4 ɔ: tə du:, °sɒ̣d[5] [əɩ ʃəd se: so:[3]; wi: səd se:[15] *we should say*]. ɔ:t nɒt tə du: 5 ɔ:t‿ə. ɔ:ʔnt 6 ʃɷd, °◇~[1]. ʃɷdnʔ

IX.4.9 SHOULDN'T HAVE‡

Q. I expect you as a boy often did what you . . . . done.

Rr. DIDN'T/HADN'T/SHOULDN'T OUGHT TO (HAVE), /DIDN'T OUGHT TO/NEVER OUGHT TO/OUGHTN'T/OUGHT NOT TO/ SHOULDN'T/ HAVE, §OUGHTN'T, §SHOULDN'T, SHOULDN'T DO

Note 1—When rec. in the r., the inf. DO and the p.p. DONE are reproduced below.

Note 2—It is not clear whether the rr. at 11.2/5/8–11, 15.2/3/6 and 16.2/3 represent SHOULDN'T HAVE DONE, in which HAVE has been absorbed into the prec. syll., or SHOULDN'T HAVE DONE; at 16.5/6, 17.1, 23.2/6 and 24.1 it has been interpreted as SHOULDN'T HAVE.

Note 3—In citing the i.m. below, no regard has been paid to grammatical person or number.

Note 4—For additional exs. of OUGHT, see IX.4.6–8; of expressions for SHOULDN'T see IX.4.8.

7 Ch 1 ʃɷdnt ə 2 æɷtnə ə dɷn[(2x)] [a ʃəd nɛvəɹ ə θɔ:t[3] *I should never have thought*] 3 ʃɷdnəɹ‿ə dɷn 4 ʃɷdnə ə 5 ʃɷnəɹ‿ə 6 dɩdnt ɔ:t‿ɷ ə

8 Db 1 ʃɷdnt‿ə 2 dɩdnt ɒɷt tə du: 3 ʃɷdnt dü: [i. insists] 4 ʃɷdnəɹ‿ə 5 ʃɷdn‿ə 6 ʃɷdn‿ə dɛɷ 7 ʃɷdnəɹ‿ə

11 Sa 1 ʃɷdnə 2 ʃɷdn‿ə dɷn 3 ʃɷdnə əv 4 ʃɷdnt [ə]v dɷn 5 ʃɷdn‿ə dɷn 6 ʃɷdn‿əv [a ʃəd nəvə[ɽ] əv no:d[3] *I should never* (VII.8.19) *have knowed* (= *known*; VI.5.17)] 7 ʃɷdn‿əv 8 ʃɷdn‿ə dɷn 9–10 ʃɷdn‿ə dʌn 11 ʃʌdn‿ə dʌn

12 St 1 ʃɷdnə ə dɷn 2 §ɛɷtnə 3 ʃɷdnəɹ‿ə dɷn 4 ʃɷdnə ə dɷn 5 adnəɹ‿ɔ:t tə dü: 6 adnt ɔ:t tə du:, °ʃɷdnt ə[1] 7 ʃɷdnə əv 8 adnt ɔ̝:t tə dü:, °adnt ɔ:t tü: ə[5] 9 ʃɷdnəɹ‿ə 10 ʃɷdnt ə dɷn 11 ʃɷdnt əv ədɷn

15 He 1 dɪdn ɔ:t‿ə 2–3 ʃɷdn‿ə dɷn 4 ʃɷdnt‿ə dʌn 5 ʃɷdnt‿ə 6 ʃɷdn‿ə dɷn 7 ʃɷdnt əv dʌn

16 Wo 1 ʃɷdn̩ ə dɷn 2 ʃɷdn‿ə dɷn 3 ʃɷdn‿ə 4 ʃɷdnt‿ə dɷn 5–6 ʃɷdn‿ə dɷn 7 adnt ɔ:t tu: ə dɷn, adnt ɔ:t tɷ ə dɷn

17 Wa 1 s.w. ʃɷdn̩ ə dɷn 2 adnt ɔ:t‿ə, ʃɷdnt ɔ:t tɷ, ʃɷdnt ɔ:t tɷ ə, °ʃɷdnt‿ə[4] 3 adnt ɔ:t tu: 4 ʃɷdnt‿ə 5 adnt ɔ:t‿u: 6 adn ɔ:t‿ɷ əv dɷn 7 adn ɔ:t‿ɷ ə dɷn

23 Mon 1 ʃʌdn̩ ə dʌn 2 ʃɷdn‿ə dɷn 3 ʃɷdnt‿ə 4 ʃɷdn̩ ə 5 ʃɷdn̩ əv[(2x)], °ʃɷdn̩ əv[2] 6 ʃɷdn‿ə dʌn 7 n.a.

24 Gl 1 ʃɷdn‿ə dɷ:n 2–3 ʃɷdn̩ ə dɷn 4 ʃɷdnt‿ə 5 ɛdnt ɔ:t 6 dɪdn ɔ:t‿ə du: 7 ɔ:t nɒt t‿əv dən

25 O 1 ʃɷdnt‿ə 2 §ʃɷdnʔ [əɪ ʃɷdn̩ ə θɔ:t[2] *I shouldn't have thought*] 3 adnt ɔ:t tɷ əv 4 ɔ:t nɒt tɷ əv dɷn, °nɛvəɽ ɔ:t‿ə ə dɷn 5 dɪdn ɔ:t ə‿v 6 ʃɷdnʔ ə dʌn

IX.4.10 DON'T CARE

Q. If it means nothing to you whether tomorrow it's wet or fine, you say: I . . . .

Idiom.

If he doesn't use *care/caring*, say: Some people would answer with the word *care*; how would you use it?

Rr. BAIN'T A-BOTHERING ABOUT IT, DON'T BOTHER/CARE/MIND/TROUBLE

Note—I.m. exs. of DON'T *1 pr.s.*, and of CARE are reproduced below between square brackets untransliterated. For additional exs. of DON'T, see IX.5.2. See also I DON'T KNOW at VII.5.2.

7 Ch 1 dɷnə kɛ: 2 p. dɷnə kɛə [dɷnə[3(2x),4]] 3 dɷnə kɛ: [kɛ:[2]] 4 dɷnə kɛ·ə 5 dɷnə kɛ: 6 dɷnə kɛ: [dɷnə[3]]

8 Db 1 dɷnə kɛ:: 2 dɷnə kɛə [dɷnə[2]] 3 dɷnə kɛ: 4 dɷnə kɛ: [dɷnt[1]] 5 dɷnə kɛ·ə [dɷnə[4]] 6 dɷnə kɛ: [dɷnə[1(2x)]] 7 dɷnə kɛ·ə

11 Sa 1 dɷnə kɛəɽ 2 dɷnə ke:əɽ 3 do:n kɛəɽ 4 do:n maɪnd, do:n kɛə 5 dɷnə kɛəɽ: 6 dɷnə kɛəɽ 7 dʌnə ke:əɽ, °do:n ke:əɽ[1] 8 dɷnə ke:əɽ 9 dʌnə ke:əɽ, °dʌnə tɹʌbl[1] 10 dʌnə ke:əɽ [do:n[1], dɔ:[3]] 11 dʌnə ke:əɽ [dɷnə[1], do:n[2]]

12 St 1 dɷnə kɛ: [dɷnə²] 2–4 dɷnə kɛ: 5 dɷnə mɒ:ɪnd, dɷnə kɛ: [doɷnt²] 6 dɷnə kɛ: [dɷnə¹] 7 dɷnə kɛ: [doɷnt²] 8 doɷ kɛ: [doɷnt¹] 9 dɷnə kɛ: [dɷ:nt¹] 10 doɷnt bɒðə, doɷnt kɛə 11 doɷn kɛə [doɷnt²]

15 He 1–2 dɷnə kɛəʵ 3 do:n kɛəʵ 4 do:n kjəʵ: 5 do:nt kɛəʵ 6 do:n kɛəʵ [dɑ:nt¹] 7 doɷn bɒðəɹ, doɷnt bɒðəɹ, doɷn kɛəɹ, doɷnt kɛəɹ

16 Wo 1 dɒɷn ke:ə 2 dɷnə kɛ:əʵ 3 doɷn ke:əʵ 4 do:n kəʵ: 5 do:n kʻe:əʵ, °do:n kəʵ:¹ 6 doɷn ke:əʵ, °doɷn kɪəʵ² 7 beɪnt əbɒðəɹɪn əbæɷt ɪt⁽²ˣ⁾, p. doɷnt kɛəʵ [dəɷnt³, doɷnt³⁽²ˣ⁾]

17 Wa 1 doɷnt kɛ: [dǫɷnt¹] 2 dɷn kɛə, °də:nt məɪnd², °dəɷnt məɪnd² [dəɷnt⁴⁽²ˣ⁾, du:nt⁴⁽²ˣ⁾] 3 dǫɷnt kɛ: 4 doɷn kɛ·ə [doɷnt¹] 5 do:n kɛ·əʵ 6 dɷnt kɛ·əʵ [dǫɷn⁴] 7 doɷn kɛ·əʵ

23 Mon 1 do:ɷn kɛəʵ 2 do:n kɛəʵ 3 do:n kɛə 4 n.a. [do:n³] 5 do:n kɛ: [doun²] 6 do:n ke:əʵ 7 n.a.

24 Gl 1 do:ɷn kjəʵ: [do:ɷn¹] 2 dɷn ke:əʵ 3–4 do:ɷn ke:əʵ 5 do:nt kjəʵ: 6 do:n ke·əʵ 7 do:n kẹəʵ

25 O 1 dɷənt kʻəʵ: [dəɷnt²] 2 dəɷnʔ kɪəʵ, dɷənʔ ["older"] kɪəʵ 3 doɷnt keəʵ, °dɷənt [3 *pr. s.*] kɪəʵ¹ 4 do:n kɛəʵ [do:nt¹] 5 dəɷnt kɪəʵ 6 doɷnʔ kɪəʵ

IX.4.11 MUST

Q. You needn't do that job today if you don't want to, but tomorrow you really . . . . do it.

Rr. (HAVE) GOT TO, MUN, MUST, WILL HAVE TO, §YOU'LL HAVE TO DO

Note 1—In citing the i.m. forms of MUST below, grammatical person and number have been ignored. A superior ★ is attached to MUST where foll. by HAVE + a p.p.

Note 2—I.m. exs. of HAVE (GOT {TO}) and HAVE (FOR) TO, all meaning *must*, are reproduced between square brackets below untransliterated. An attached superior ᴅ marks a 1 pr.s., superior × a 3 pr.s., superior ◇ a 1 pr.pl., superior + a 2 pr.pl., and superior ‖ a 3 pr.pl. If rec. as belonging to the same syllable as HAVE, the subj. pronoun has also been reproduced.

7 Ch 1 mɷn, °mɷst² 2 wɪl av tə, s.w. mɷn, °mən¹⁽³ˣ⁾,²⁽⁵ˣ⁾,³ [×az‿t¹ (+ C.), ×az² (rec. in «ɪt az stəp» *it has* (to) *stop*; ×az fə‿tʔ³; ‖ðɛv gət tə³, ‖av (rec. in «ðeɪ av swɪm» *they have* (to) *swim*)] 3 mɷs 4 mɒn, °~² 5 mɷn, °mən¹ IX.9.3 6 mɒn

8 Db 1 §jəl a‿ˀ dʏ:, p. mɷs [◇an t‿¹ (+ V.)] 2 mɷn, ○mən⁴ 3 mɷn, ○★mɷst¹, ○mən² [ðal av tə dü: ɩt *thou'll have to do it*] 4 §jəl av‿ˀ dᵒü: [pref.], p. mɷn, ○mən² IX.9.3, ○★mɷst³ [‖an tə¹] 5 §jəl ɛɩ tə dɩu:, mɷn, ○mən¹ 6 mɷs, p. mɷn 7 mɷn, ○mən¹

11 Sa 1 mʌn 2 mɷn [◇an tə³] 3 mʌst 4 mʌs 5 mɷn, ○~² 6 mɷn 7 mɷn [×ɩt‿s gɒt‿ə¹] 8 mɷn 9–10 mʌn 11 mʌn, ○mɷst¹

12 St 1 mɷs, ○mən³ 2 mən 3 mɷs, ○~ 4 əv gɒt tü 5 mɷn 6 mɷst, ○~² [ɛv tə¹ (n.d.g.); +gɒt² (rec. in «ju: gɒt kaɹi²» *you got* (to) *carry*] 7 gɒt tə 8 mɷst, ○mɷs¹⁽²ˣ⁾ 9 mɷst, ○mɷs¹, ○mən² [+‿av t‿¹ (+ V.); ×ɩ‿z gɒt³ (rec. in «ɩ‿z gɒt fɛɩd əm» *he's got* (to) *feed them*)] 10–11 mɷst

15 He 1 mʌs 2–3 mɷs 4 mʌst 5 mɷs 6 mɷs [‖əv gɒt tə¹] 7 mʌst, ○~

16 Wo 1–2 mɷst 3 mɷst [◇æ tə²; ᴰɒɩ‿v gɒt ə³; ‖ðe:‿v gɒt‿ə²] 4–5 mɷs 6 mɷs, ○~³ 7 p. mɷst, ○mɷs¹ [ᴰaz tə³, +av tə, ᴰɛ tə³, ◇a tə³,⁴, ‖av tə¹; ◇gət‿ə⁴, +~²; ju:l av tə du: ɩt *you'll have to do it*]

17 Wa 1 mɷst 2 mɷst, ○məs³,⁴ 3–4 mɷs 5 mɷs [‖ə gɒt tə¹] 6–7 mɷs

23 Mon 1 mʌs 2–3 mɷs 4 n.a. 5 mʌ̈st 6 mʌst 7 n.a.

24 Gl 1 mɷs 2 mɷst, ○★~³ 3 mʌst 4 mɷs 5 mɷ̜s 6–7 mɷ̜s

25 O 1 mɷs 2 gɒʔ ə 3 mʌs 4 mɷst, ○~¹, ○məst³ 5–6 mʌs

IX.4.12 MUST NOT‡

Q. To tell her child not to play with the fire, a mother might say: You . . . . play with the fire.

Rr. MAUN'T, MUNNA, MUSTN'T, MUST NOT, §SHOULDN'T

Note—I.m. MUST, when 2 pr.pl., has been marked with a superior ɑ. Otherwise no regard has been paid to either grammatical person or number. An attached superior ★ denotes "used anaphorically".

7 Ch 1 mɷnə 2 mɷsnt, s.w. mɷnə⁽²ˣ⁾, ○mɷsnə¹ 3 mɷsnə⁽²ˣ⁾ 4 mɒnə 5 mɷnə 6 mɒnə

8 Db 1 mɷnə 2 mɷnə, ○★ɑ~⁴ 3–4 mɷnə 5 mɷnə, ○ɑmo:nt¹ 6–7 mɷnə

11 Sa 1 mʌnə 2 mɷnə 3 mʌnə 4 mɷnə 5 mɷnə, ○~³ 6–8 mɷnə 9 mʌnə 10 mɷnə 11 mʌnə

12 St 1 mɷnə 2 n.a., ○mɷnə² 3 mɷsnə 4–5 mɷnə 6 mɷnə, ○★~¹ 7 mɷnə 8 mɷs nɒt, ○★mɷnə¹ 9 mɷsnt, mɷsnə 10–11 mɷsnt

15 He 1 mɷnə 2 mɷsnə 3 mɷsnt 4 mʌsnt 5 mɷsnt 6 mɷsn 7 mʌnə(2x), °mənə[4]

16 Wo 1–2 mɷsnt 3 mɷsn 4–5 mɷsnt 6 mɷsn 7 §ʃɷdnt, s.w. mɷs nɒt

17 Wa 1 mɷ̜nʔ 2 mɷsnt 3 mɷsnt, s.w. mɷnə [obs.] 4–6 mɷsnt 7 mʌsnt

23 Mon 1 mʌsn 2 mɷsn 3 mɷsnt 4 mʌ̤̈s̩n 5 mʌ̤̈s nɒt 6 mʌsn 7 n.a.

24 Gl 1–2 mɷsn 3 mʌsn 4 mɷsn 5 mʌsnt 6–7 məsnt

25 O 1 mɷsnt 2 mɷsn 3 mʌsnt 4 mɷsnt 5 mʌ·nt 6 mʌsnt

IX.4.13 MAY‡

Q. A hungry boy, seeing a lot of nice apples, would ask his mother: . . . . I have one?

Rr. CAN (I HAVE /AN APPLE/IT/ONE/SOME/), §GIVE US ONE, MAY

Note 1—A r. comprising a sentence is reproduced below in full.

Note 2—US at 24.5 seems to have an excrescent [t]; and at 12.11 the indef. art. has evidently been absorbed by the foll. V.

7 Ch 1 kɒn 2 kən a av wən 3 kɒn 4 kan 5 kən, kən a av wɒn 6 kan

8 Db 1 kɒn, kɒn a a wɒn 2 kɷd 3 kɒn 4 kɒn, kɒn əɹ a wɒn 5 kan 6–7 kɒn

11 Sa 1 kan, °~[3] VIII.2.2 2 kan aɩ av wɒn 3–4 kan 5 kɒn 6 kan 7 kæn 8 kan 9–10 kæn 11 kan

12 St 1 kɒn 2 kɒn əɹ av wɒn 3 kɒn ɒ:ɩ av wɒn 4 kɒn ɒɩ av wɒn 5 kan ɒ:ɩ av wən, kɒn ɒ:ɩ av wən 6 kɒn ɒ·ɩ av wɒn 7 kɒn ɒɩ av wɒn 8 kan ɒɩ av wɒn 9 kɒn ɒɩ ɛɩ wɒn 10 §gɩv əz wɒn 11 kan aɩ av apl

15 He 1–2 kæn æɩ æv wʌn 3 kɒn əɩ æv wɷn 4 kən əɩ æv wʌn 5–6 kɒn əɩ æv wɷn 7 kən aɩ av ən apəl

16 Wo 1–2 kan 3–4 kɒn ɒɩ æv wɷn 5 kɒn 6 kɒn ɒɩ æv wɷn 7 kn əɩ av ə əpl

17 Wa 1 kən 2 s.w. kən əɩ ɛv ɩt 3 kan 4 kən, kən əɩ av wɷn 5 kən əɩ a wɷn 6–7 kan

23 Mon 1 kən 2–3 kæn 4 kʰən 5–6 kən 7 n.a.

24 Gl 1 kɒn əɩ æ:v wɷn 2 kən 3 4 kɒn 5 §gɩ‿st wɷn ["pref."], p. kjan, °kən[2] 6 §gɩv əs wən [but i. insists] 7 kən

25 O 1 kan 2 kan ɔ̈ɩ a sɷm 3 kö̈d 4 kan a av wɒn 5 kən 6 meɩ

IX.4.14 MIGHT*

Q. Smith said to you: It didn't rain yesterday, though you thought it would. You said: True, but it very easily . . . . have done.

Rr. COULD, MIGHT

Note—In the i.m. below, an attached superior ◇ denotes a form not foll. by HAVE + p.p.; and superior ★ that the form concerned is used anaphorically without a foll. HAVE. No regard has been paid to grammatical person or number.

7 Ch 1 mɑɪt, ○◇~4 2 s.w. maɪt, p. mɛt, ○◇~2(2x), ○◇mɑɪt1 3 mɛt 4 mɑɪt 5 mɛɪt(2x), ○★mɪt3 6 mɛ̨ɪt

8 Db 1 mɛt, ○mɑɪt1 2 mɑɪt(2x), ○★~2,3 3 mɛt 4 mɑɪt 5 mɑ:t 6 §kɷd, mɑ·ɪt 7 mɛɪt

11 Sa 1 mɛɪt 2 maɪt, ○mɛɪt1 [n.d.g.] 3–4 maɪt 5 mɪd 6–7 maɪt 8 mɒɪt 9–10 maɪt 11 məɪt

12 St 1 mɒɪt, mɪt ["older"] 2 §kɷd [mɛtnə1 *mightn't*] 3 §kɷd, mɛt 4 §kɷd 5 mɒ:ɪt [+ *do*] 6 §kɷd 7 mɒɪt 8 §kɷd 9 mɒɪt, mɪt 10 §kɷd, ma:ɪt, ○◇maɪʔ5 11 mɒɪt [+ *do*]

15 He 1–2 mæɪt 3–6 məɪt 7 maɪt, ○~1, ○◇~1(3x)

16 Wo 1 mɒɪt 2 məɪt 3–4 mɒɪt 5 məɪt 6 mɒɪt 7 p. məɪt, ○◇~, ○◇~4 [məɪtnt3 *mightn't*]

17 Wa 1 mɑ̣ɪt 2 məɪt, ○◇~1,4 3 məɪt, ○◇~2 4–7 məɪt

23 Mon 1–2 məɪt 3 məɪt, ○◇~1 4 məitʰ 5 məit 6 məɪt 7 n.a.

24 Gl 1–3 məɪt 4 məɪt, ○◇~3, ○◇mɒɪt3 5 mə̈ɪt 6–7 mʌɪt

25 O 1–2 mə̈ɪt 3 mʌʏt(2x) 4 məɪt, ○◇~1 5 mʌʏʔ 6 mə̈ɪʔ, ○◇mə̈ɪt3

IX.4.15 USED TO‡

Q. Is there much butter made round here now? No, not now, but there . . . . be.

If need be, suggest *use*.

Rr. DID/WOULD USE TO, §HAS BEEN, (HAD) USED (HAD/WAS) USED TO, §WERE

Note 1—When rec. in the rr. and i.m., THERE is reproduced below. In the i.m. below and the r. at 16.6, an attached superior ᴅ denotes a form prec. by [d] forming one syllable with the subj. n. or pronoun. This may be interpreted as HAD or WOULD.

Note 2—In the i.m. below, an attached superior ◇ denotes an item immediately followed by an inf. beginning with a C.; superior × denotes an item immediately foll. by an inf. beginning with a V.; and superior ★ denotes a form used anaphorically. When the item comprises two or more elements, the diacritic is attached to the first.

Note 3—I.m. exs. of /USED TO/USED/ COULD when meaning *used to be able to*, HADN'T USED (TO), USED TO = *accustomed to*, the full. v. USE and its parts, as well as USE *n.*, are reproduced below between square brackets in that order untransliterated. In citing the i.m., no regard has been paid to grammatical person and number, except in the case of the full v. USE.

Note 4—USED *p.p.* occ. occurs at V.7.21; USED (TO) and USES occur at III.3.7. For USEFUL, see V.1.16/17.

7 Ch 1 ɪʏ:s tə, ○ju:s tə^{2} 2 ðəɹ §az bi:n, ðə §wə·ɹ [+ V.], s.f. ðə ◇jü:st, ○◇ðə ju:st^{1}, ○◇ju:st$^{2(3x),3,4}$, ○~^{1} [+ V.], ○◇jɪüst^{2}, ○×ju:st tə^{4}, ○◇ad ju:s tə^{3}, ○◇ad ju:st tə^{3} 3 ◇jʏ:s, ○◇jʏ:s tə^{1} 4 jụ:s tə [¶ju:zɪn^{2}] 5 ◇jʏ:s tə [ju:zn^{1} *2 pr.pl.*] 6 ju:s tə

8 Db 1 jʏ:st tə, ○ðə jʏ:s tə^{1} [+ p.p.] 2 ju:s tə [◇ju:s tə kəd^{4}; ¶ju:zɪn^{3}; ju:sd̥^{4} *p.p.*] 3 ju:s tə 4 §az bˈi:n ["pref."], p. jɛɷs tə [◇ju:st kɷd^{1}] 5 §ɛz bɛn, s.w. jˈu:s, ○◇ju:s tə^{1} 6 jü:st, ○◇~^{1}, ○×jü:s t‿^{1}, ○×★jü:s tə^{1}, ○◇jüst^{1} [◇adnə jü:st^{1}] 7 jɛɷs

11 Sa 1 ju:s tə 2 ju:s tə, ○×~^{3}, ○★~^{3}, ○★d‿ʒɷs tə^{1} [jᵒu:zd^{1} (n.d.g.)] 3 ju:s tə 4 ju:s tə, ○◇ju:st tə^{2} 5 ðəʳɽ‿ad ju:s tə, ○D×ju:s tə^{2}, ○D◇jᵒu:s tə^{2}, ○◇ðen [?=*they'n*] jᵒu:s tə^{2} [★◇adnt u:s tə^{2}] 6 ju:s tə, ○◇ðɛəʳ wɒz ju:st tə^{3}, ○◇ju:st tə^{4} [wɒt dɪd wi:m jus tə kɔʳ:ɭ ɪt^{3} *what did we'm use to call it?*; ju:st tə^{3}] 7 ju:st, ○×ju:st tə 8 ju:s tə, ○◇~^{2} [ju:s tə^{2}] 9 ju:s tə, ○~^{1}, ○◇ju:st tə^{1} 10 ju:s tə, ○◇~^{3}, ○◇ju:st tə^{1,3}, ○◇wəz ju:s tə^{2}, ○◇wɒz ju:s tə^{3}, ○◇dɪd ju:s tə^{2} 11 ðə wəz ju:s tə, ○D◇ju:s tə^{1}, ○◇~^{1,2}

12 St 1 ad ju:st tə, ○★~^{4}, ○D◇ju:st tə$^{1(2x),2(2x)}$, ○D◇ju:st$^{2(2x)}$, ○D★~^{1} [ðəɹ adnə ju:st tə^{3}; ju:z^{3} *inf.*; ju:zd^{1} *p.p.*] 2 ðə ju:st, ○◇ju:st$^{2(2x)}$, ○D◇ju:s^{1}, ○D★ju:st tə, ○D◇~^{3}, ○◇ad ju:st tə^{5} [wɒt ad ðɪ just kɔ:l ɪt^{1} *what had they used* (to) *call it?*; ju:z^{1} *inf.*; ~^{2,3} (n.d.g.)] 3 ad ju:s, ○ad ju:st, ○◇ə [*sic*] ju:st tə^{1}, ○D×ju:s t‿^{1}, ○D◇ju:st$^{1,2(2x)}$, ○~^{1,2}, ○D◇just^{1}, ○D◇ju:s^{2} [wɒt ɛd wɛɪ ju:st kɔ:l ɪt^{1} *what had we used* (to) *call it?*; ◇adnə ju:st^{1}] 4 jü:st tə, ○◇ju:st tə$^{1(2x),2(2x)}$, ○◇~^{1}, ○◇ad ju:st tə$^{1(2x),3}$ [ju:zd^{3} 1 *p.t.s.*, ~^{1} *p.p.*, jusd̥^{1} *p.p.*] 5 ju:st tə, ○◇~^{2}, ○×ju:st t‿^{2}, ○◇ju:z tə^{3}, ○ju:st tü:^{3} [+ V.], ○◇ad ju:st tə^{1} [◇adnə ju:st tə^{2}; ju:z^{2} *inf.*; ju:s *n.*] 6 ad ju:st tə, ○◇~$^{1(2x)}$, ○D◇ju:st tə$^{1(2x)}$, ○◇~$^{2(4x)}$, ○D◇ju:st^{2}, ○~^{2} [ju:z^{2} *inf.*, ju:zd$^{2(2x)}$ *p.p.*; ju:s^{2} *n.*] 7 ad jü:st tə, ○◇ad ju:st tə^{1}, ○◇ðə ju:st tə^{4}, ○◇ju:st tə^{1}, ○◇~^{4} [rec. in «wi: ju:st tə sɛɪ ɛɪpəθ wi: ad» *we used to say halfpennyworth* (VII.7.1), *we had*] 8 ad ju:st tə, ○◇~^{5}, ○ad ju:st tü:^{1} [+ V.], ○ju:st tü:^{2} [+ V.], ○◇ju:st tə$^{3(2x)}$ [ju:z^{3} *inf.*; ju:s *n.*] 9 ad ju:st tə, ○★ad ju:st^{1}, ○D◇ju:st^{2}, ○◇~^{1}, ○D◇ju:st tə^{2}, ○◇~$^{1(8x),2}$, ○×~^{1}, ○◇ju:s^{1} [◇adnt

ju:st tə²] 10 §az bi:n, ju:st tə, ○◁◇∼⁴,⁶, ○◇ðəɹ ad jü:st tə¹, ○◇ad ü:st tə⁴, ○★a:d jü:st tə⁵ [◇adnt jü:st tə³; jü:sd̥⁵ p.p.] 11 ðəɹ ad ju:st tə, ○◇∼¹, ○◇ad just tə², ○★ad ju:st¹, ○◇ju:st tə²⁽⁴ˣ⁾, ○◇just tə² [◇adnt just tə¹; ju:st tə²; ¶juzɪn²; wɒt ad ðɪ ju:st . . . .¹ *what had they used . . . .?*]

15 He 1 ðəɹ æd jɷs tə, ○◇jɷs tə² 2 ðəɹ jɷs tə, ○★∼³⁽²ˣ⁾ 3 jɷs tə, ○◇∼⁴, ○◇ðəʳ jɷs tə², ○★jɷs tə²,⁴ 4 jɷs tə, ○◇∼¹,³, ○◇jɷs təʳ¹ 5 jɷs tə, ○◇∼¹,³, ○ðəʳ wəz jɷs tə³, ○★ju:s tə³ 6 ju:s tə, ○◇jɷs tə 7 ju:st tə, ○◇∼¹,³⁽²ˣ⁾,⁴⁽²ˣ⁾, ○◇∼³ IX.9.5, ○ju:st tɷ¹ [+ V.], ○★jɷst tə⁴ [ju:zɪz³ *2 pr.pl.*; ju:st tɷ³⁽²ˣ⁾ (+ V.)]

16 Wo 1 ju:s tə, ○◇∼¹,³⁽²ˣ⁾ 2 ju:s tə, ○◇∼², ○◇wəd ju:s tə¹, ○◇a·d ju:s tə², ○ðəɹ a·d ju:s tə² [◇adnt ju:z tə²; ju:zd¹ *1 p.t.s.*] 3 ðə jɷs tə, ○◇∼¹, ○◇wəd ju:s tə¹, ○×ju:s t‿² 4 jɷs tə, ○×∼¹, ○★jɷs təʳ¹, ○★jɷs ə² [ðəʳɽ (=*there*) adnt jɷs tə²] 5 ðə wɷz jɷs tə, ○wɷz jɷs tə¹, ○◇wɷz ju:z tə¹, ○◇wəz ju:s tə¹, ○×ju:s tə 6 ðəʳ:ɖ ju:s tə, ○D◇ju:s tə¹, ○◇∼³ [◇ædn ju:s tə¹⁽²ˣ⁾,³; ju:zd² *p.p.*] 7 ðɛəʳ ad ju:st tə, ○◇əd ju:st tə¹, ○◇ad ju:s tə⁴, ○D◇ju:st tə¹, ○D★ju:st tu:¹, ○D★ju:s tu:¹, ○◇ju:st tə ¹⁽³ˣ⁾,²⁽²ˣ⁾,³, ○×∼³⁽²ˣ⁾, ○∼⁴ [+ *p.p.*], ○ju:st t‿³ [+ V.], ○ju:s t‿³ [+ V.], ○∼¹,³ [+ V. and + *p.p.* resp.]

17 Wa 1 ju:s tə, ○◇∼², ○★ju:s tu:¹ 2 ðə ju:st tə, ○◇∼¹,², ○◇ju:st tə²⁽²ˣ⁾,³, ○∼⁴ [+ V.], ○ju:s t‿² [+ V.], ○◇u:st tə¹,⁴⁽³ˣ⁾, ○◇∼⁴ [rec. in «nɛvə u:st tə seɪ ɪt ad ðɛ» *never* (VII.8.19) *used to say it, had they?*], ○◇u:st⁴, ○◇ad ju:s tə⁴ [◇adnt ju:s tə¹,²,³,⁴, ◇ɛdnt ju:s tə⁴; ju:z¹ *inf.*, ju:sɪz *3 pr.pl.* (IX.9.5), ju:zd¹,³ *p.p.*, ju:sd̥¹ *p.p.*] 3 ju:s tə, ○◇∼¹⁽³ˣ⁾ 4 ju:s tə, ○◇∼¹,² [ju:z¹ *inf.*] 5 ju:s tə [★adnt ju:s tu:¹] 6 ju:s tə, ○◇∼⁴, ○ju:s tɷ² [+ V.] 7 ju:s tə, ○◇∼¹ [ju:zd¹⁽²ˣ⁾ *p.p.*]

23 Mon 1 jʌs tə, ○×∼² [jɷs tə²] 2 jɷs tə, ○◇∼¹ 3 ju:s tə 4 ju:s tʰu·, ○★ju·s̬t̥ tʰu·² 5 ju:st tu· 6 jɷs tə 7 n.a.

24 Gl 1 jɷs tə, ○◇∼¹⁽²ˣ⁾,³, ○◇‿s tə² [rec. in «wi:‿s tə kɑ:ɫ ɪt» *we used to call it*] 2 ðəʳɽ æd jɷs tə, ○×æd jɷs tə³, ○jɷs tə²⁽²ˣ⁾, ○★∼² [★ædnt jɷs tə¹] 3 jɷs tə, ○◇∼¹,⁴ 4 jɷs tə, ○◇∼¹,²,³, ○×∼², ○D★∼² 5 ju:s tə, ○D◇∼² 6 ju:s tə 7 ju:s tə, ○◇ju: [*sic*] tə¹

25 O 1 ju:s tə, ○◇∼², ○★∼²⁽²ˣ⁾, ○×ju:s t‿² 2 ɪu:s tə, ○◇ju:s tə¹,³ 3 jü:st, ○◇ju:s tə¹,², ○★∼² 4 ju:st tə, ○◇∼⁴,⁵, ○×∼¹ [ju:st tɷ⁵ (+ V.)] 5 ju:s tə, ○◇∼², ○×ju:st t‿²,³ 6 ju:s tə, ○◇∼³⁽⁵ˣ⁾

IX.4.16 CAN'T*

Q. Yes, tomorrow I could, but today I . . . .

Rr. CAN'T, §COULDN'T, §SHAN'T BE ABLE TO

Note 1—In the i.m. below, an attached superior ◇ indicates a form foll. by an inf.; and superior × a 2 pr.s. form. No regard has otherwise been paid to grammatical person or number.

Note 2—I.m. exs. of CAN'T *interrog.* are reproduced below between square brackets untransliterated.

Note 3—CAN'T also occurs at VII.5.2.

7 Ch 1 kɒnə, ○◇~[2], ○◇kanə[4] 2 kanə, s.f. kənə [pref.], ○◇~[1(2x),2(5x),3(4x),4(3x)], ○◇kanə[2(2x)], ○kǫnə[2], ○◇ka:nt[1,2] 3 kɒnə, ○◇~[2(2x),3] 4 kɒnə, ○~[2], ○◇~[2] [kɒnə[2] *2 pr.pl.*] 5 kɒnə, ○~[1], ○◇~[1] [kɒnə[2] *2 pr.pl.*, kɒnɩ[2] (*sic*) *3 pr.pl.*, ◇×kɒstnə[1]] 6 kɒnə, ○◇~[1,2(3x),3]

8 Db 1 kɒnə, ○~[1], ○◇~[2,3] 2 kɒnə, ka:nt, ○◇~[3] 3 kɒnə, ○◇~[1], ○◇kanə[1] 4 kɒnə 5 kanə, ○◇~[1] 6 kɒnə, ○◇~[1(5x)] 7 kɒnə [◇kɒnst[2] *2 pr.pl.*]

11 Sa 1 kanə 2 kanə, ○◇~[1(4x)], ○~[3] 3 ka:n, ○◇kanə[2] 4 kaʵ:ɳʈ, ○◇ka·nə[2], ○◇kanə[2], ○◇×~[2] 5 kɒnə, ○◇~[2], ○◇~[2] IX.10.1, ○◇kanə[1,3(3x)] 6 kanə, ○◇~[1] 7 kænə, ○◇kanə[1(2x)] 8 kɒnə, ○◇~[1(2x)], ○◇kɔ:[2] IX.3.2 9 kɒnə 10 kænə, ○◇~[1,2(3x)], ○◇kɔ:[3] 11 kɒnə, ○◇~[1], ○◇kanə[2], ○◇kɔ:[2]

12 St 1 kɒnə, ○~[2], ○◇~[1,2(2x),3,4(3x)], ○kanə[1], ○◇~[1,3], ◇ka:nt[1] [◇×kɒnst[1,3]] 2 kɒnə, ○~[2], ○◇~[2(3x),3] 3 kɒnə, ○~[1], ○◇~[1(8x),2(2x)], ○◇~[2] III.3.7, ○◇kanə[1], ○◇kɒsnə[1,2] 4 kɒnə, ○~[2], ○◇kanə[1,2] 5 kɒnə, ○~[3,4], ○◇~[1(6x),2(4x),3], ○◇kɒnəɹ[1] [+ V.], ○◇kanə[3(2x)] 6 kɒnə, ○~[2(2x)], ○◇~[1(4x),2] 7 kɒnə, ○~[1,4] 8 kɔ:n, ○kanə[1] 9 kɒnə, ○~[2(3x)], ○◇~[1,2,3], ○◇kɒnəɹ[2] [+ V.], ○◇kanə[1(2x)], ○◇ka̱:nt 10 ka:nt, ○◇kənt[5] 11 kȧ:nt, ○◇~[2], ○kɔ:[1]

15 He 1 kɒnə, ○~[3], ○◇~[2], ○◇kænə[1,2] 2 kɒnəʵ, ○◇ka:[2] 3 kɑ:nt, ○◇kɑ:n[1,2], ○◇kɒnə[3] 4 kɑ:nt, ○◇kɑ:n[2,3] 5 kɒnt, ○◇kænt[4] 6 kɒnt, ○◇kɑ:nt[1], ○◇ka:[1] 7 kanə, ○◇~[1,2,4(2x)], ○ka:nt[3(2x)] [◇×kanə[4]]

16 Wo 1 kɑ:nt, ○◇kɑ:[1] 2 kɒnə, ○◇kanə[2], ○◇×kɑ:n[2] [◇×kɒnə[2]] 3 kɑ:nt 4 kɑ:nt, ○◇kɑ:n[2] 5 kɑ:nt, ○◇kɑʵ:ɳʈ[1], ○◇kɑʵ:ɳ[1], ○◇kɑ:n[1(3x)] 6 kɑ:nt, ○kɑ:n[2] 7 §ʃɑ:nt bɩ eɩbl tu:, kɑ:nt, ○~[4], ○◇~[3,4(2x)], ○kɑ·n[1], ○◇ka:nt[2], ○◇kɔ:nt[1(6x),3(2x)], ○~[4]

17 Wa 1 ka:nt 2 ka:nt, ○◇~[1], ○~[1] III.3.7, ○◇kɔ:nt[4(4x)], ○~[4], ○◇kɔ:nd [+ V.] 3 ka:nt 4 ka:nt, ○◇~[3], ○◇ka:nʔ[1] 5 kɔʵ:ɳɖ, ○◇kɔʵ:ɳʈ[1] 6 ka:nt 7 ka:nt [◇ka:nt[2] *2 pr.pl.*]

23 Mon 1 kjænt, ○◇kænt[2] 2 kænt 3 kænt, ○◇~[2], ○◇ka:nt[2(2x)] [kænə[1] *2 pr.pl.*] 4 kʰa:nt, ○~[3], ○◇kʰa:n[1] 5 ka:nt, ○~[2], ○◇~[2], ○◇ka·nt[1], ○◇ka:n[2] 6 kænt 7 n.a.

24 Gl 1 kæ:nt, ○◇kɑ:[1] 2 kɑ:nt, ○◇kɑ:n[3], ○◇kɑ:[3], ○◇kæsn[3] 3 kɑ:nt, ○kæ:n[1], ○◇~[4], ○◇×ka:snt[1], ○◇×kɒsnt[3] 4 kant, ○◇kɑ:n[1] 5 kja:nt 6 ka:nt [◇×kasnt[2]] 7 kja:nt

25 O 1 ka:nt, ○◇~[2], ○◇kant[2] 2 ka:nt 3 ka:nt, ○◇~[2] 4 ka:nt, ○◇~[1,3(2x),4] 5 ka:nʔ, ○◇ka:n[2] 6 §kɷdnt, kanʔ

IX.4.17 DARE† NOT†

Q. Your neighbour would like to go and have a drink of beer, but he is so henpecked that he . . . .

Rr. DARED/DARE(S) NOT, DOES NOT DARE, DURST NOT

Note 1—An attached superior ★ below denotes that the form concerned prec. GO *inf.*

Note 2—I.m. forms of interrog. DAREN'T, as well as of I DARE SAY, are reproduced below between square brackets untransliterated.

7 Ch 1 da:nə 2 ★da:nə 3 da:nə 4 dɒsn 5–6 da:nə

8 Db 1 dɛᵻ·ənə 2 dɛənt 3–4 da:nə 5 dɒsnə 6 da:snə 7 da:nə, ○dɒsnə[1] [dɒsnt[1]]

11 Sa 1 dəʳ:ɳə 2 dɛ:ənt [aɩ də: se:[2]] 3 dəʳ:ʂɳʈ 4 dəʳ:ɖnə [a daʳ: se:[2]] 5 daʳ:ɳə 6 dɛədnə 7 dɛəʳ:ɖnə 8 de:ənə 9 dɛəʳ:ɖnə 10 de:ənə 11 de:ədnə

12 St 1 da:znə 2 da:nə, ○dɛ:snt[1] 3–5 da:nə 6 dɛ:nə, da:nə 7 dɷsnə 8 də:znt 9 da:nə 10 dəsnt 11 də:dnt

15 He 1–2 ★dəʳ:ɳə 3 ★dəʳ:ɳʈ 4 dɛəʳɳʈ 5 dəʳ:ɳʈ 6 dɛ:snt 7 dɛəɹ nɒt, dəɹsənt

16 Wo 1 dɛ:ᵊnt 2 dəʳ:ɳʈ, ○★~[2] 3 ★de:ədnt 4 ★dəʳ:ɳʈ 5 dəʳ:ɳʈ 6 de:ədnt 7 ★dɛədnt

17 Wa 1 dɛ:nt 2 dɛədnt 3 dɛ:nt 4 dɛ̣ədnt 5 dɛ·əʳɖɳʈ 6 dɛ·əʳɳʈ 7 dɷsnt

23 Mon 1 dəʳ:ʂɳʈ 2 dɛədn 3 dɛənt 4–5 dɛ:nt 6 dɛəʳɳʈ 7 n.a.

24 Gl 1 dəʳ:ɳʈ 2 dɷsnt 3 de:ənt 4 dəʳ:ɳʈ 5 dʌsnt 6 daʳ:ɳʈ 7 dəʳ:ʂɳʈ

25 O 1 dəʳ:ɖnḓ, ○★daʳ:ɖɳ 2 dʌsnt 3 dɛəʳɳʈ [ʌʏ dɛə se:[1]] 4 dɛəɽʂɳʈ, ○dɷznt dɛəɽ 5 dəɷnt dɛəʳ tü: 6 dɛəʳɳʔ

IX.4.18 DURST† NOT†

Q. He wanted to go for a drink (of beer), *but he was so henpecked that he . . . .*

Rr. DAREDN'T, DAREN(S)N'T, DIDN'T DARE, DURSTN'T

Note—An attached superior ★ indicates that the form is foll. by an inf.

7 Ch 1 dɒsnt 2 da:nə 3 dɒsnə 4 dɒsn 5 dɒsnə 6 dɔ:snə

8 Db 1 dəᶦsnə 2 dɛənt 3–4 də:snə 5 dɒsnt 6 da:snə 7 da:nə

11 Sa 1 dəʳ:ɳə 2 da:nə 3 dəʳ:ʂɳʈ 4 dəʳ:ʂɳʈ 5 daʳ:ɖɳə 6 dɛədnə,
○★∼[3] 7 dəʳ:ɖɳə 8 de:ədnə 9 dɛəʳ:ɖɳə 10–11 de:ədnə

12 St 1 də:snə 2–3 dɒsnə 4–5 da:nə 6–7 dɷsnə 8 də:znt 9 da:nə
10 də:snt 11 də:ɹdnt, ○★∼[2]

15 He 1–2 ★dəʳ:ɖɳə 3 ★dəʳ:ɖɳʈ 4 dɛəʳɖɳʈ 5 dəʳ:ɖɳʈ 6 dɛ:dnt 7
dəɹsənt

16 Wo 1 dɛ:ədnt 2 dəʳ:ɖɳə 3 ★de:ədnt 4 ★dɛəʳɖɳʈ 5 dəʳ:ɖɳʈ 6 ★de:ədnt
7 p. ★dɛədnt

17 Wa 1 dəsnt, ○★∼ 2 dɛədnt 3 dɛ:nt 4 dɛ̣ədnt 5 dɛ·ədnt 6 dɛ·əʳɳʈ
7 dɛʳ:ɳʈ

23 Mon 1 dəʳ:ʂɳʈ 2 dɛədn 3 dɛədnt 4 dɛ:nt 5 dɛ: nɒ̈·t 6 dɛəʳɖɳʈ
7 n.a.

24 Gl 1 dəʳ:ʂɳʈ 2 dɷsnt 3 de:ədnt 4 dəʳ:ɖɳʈ 5 dʌsnt 6 daʳ:ɳʈ
7 dəʳ:ʂɳʈ

25 O 1 dəsnt 2 dʌsnt 3 dəʳɽʂɳʈ 4 dɛəɽʂɳʈ 5 dɩdnt dɛəʳ 6 dɩdnʔ dɛəʳ

IX.5.1 (I) DO†. (he) DOES†. (we) DO†

Q. You don't care for things like that, but I . . . .

Convert for **he does, we do.**

Rr. (I) DO(ES)

(He) DO(ES)/DONE

(We) DO(ES)/DONE

Note 1—The rr. to the three parts of the q. are separated below by full stops.

Note 2—In the i.m. foll. the r. to the second part of the q., an attached superior ɑ marks a 3 pr.s., foll. IT or SHE. In the i.m. given in square brackets foll. the r. to the third part of the q., an attached superior + denotes a 2 pr.pl., and superior ᴅ a 3 pr.pl.

Note 3—In the i.m. below, an attached superior ◇ marks a form of DO used as a full v., superior ‖ forms of periphrastic DO and superior × DO + inf.

Note 4—For exs. of DOES with a 3 pl. pronominal subj., see VIII.5.1.

7 Ch 1 dɪʏ: . dɷz . dɪʏ: [◇+dʏ:²] 2 dü . dɷz, ◦ᴅ~² . n.r. [ᴅdɷz²,⁴, ᴅdɪü², ᴅdü:², ᴅ‖~³, ×ᴅdɷn⁴] 3 dɪʏ: . dɷz . dɷn 4 dᵒü: . dɷz . dᵒu: 5 dᶦu:, dɛ̝ɷ . dɷz . dᶦʏ: [◇ᴅdɷn¹] 6 dᵒṳ̈: . dɷz . dᵒṳ̈:

8 Db 1 dʏ: . dɷz . dʏ: [ᴅdɷz¹] 2 dᵒu . dɷz . dᵒu: 3 dü: . dɷz . dü: [+dɷn³] 4 dɛɷ . dɷz . dɛɷ, ◦dɷn² [‖ᴅdɷz²] 5 dᶦu: . dɷz . dɛɷ [+ɛ: ◇du:⁴ *how* (do you) *do?*] 6 dɛɷ . dɷz . dɷn [×+dɷn¹, ᴅ~¹] 7 dɛɷ . dɛɷ . dɛɷ, ◦dɷn¹

11 Sa 1 du: . dʌz . du: 2 dʏʉ: . dɷz, ◦ɑ~³ . du: [ᴅdɷn³] 3 dᵒu: . dʌz . dᵒu: 4 dᵒu: . dʌz . dᵒu: 5 dɪu: . dɷn . dɷn 6–7 du: . dʌz . du: 8 du: . dɷz . du: 9 du: . dʌz . du: [ᴅdu:¹] 10 du: . du:, ◦ɑdʌz² . du: [×du:² *2 pr.s.*] 11 du: . dʌz . du:

12 St 1 dü: . dɷz . dü: 2 dɪɷ . dɷz . dɷn 3 dɛɷ . dɷz . dɛɷ 4 dü: . dɷz . dü: [‖+dü:¹, ◇ᴅ~²] 5–6 dü: . dɷz . dü: 7 dü: . dɷz, ◦◇ɑ~¹ III.3.7 . dü: [‖ᴅdü:¹] 8 dü:, ◦×du:¹ . dɷz . dü: 9 du: . dɷz . dɷn 10 dü: . dɷz . dü: 11 dü:, ◦◇du:² . dɷz, ◦◇ɑ~¹ III.3.7, ◦‖ɑ~² . dü: [‖ᴅdü:¹]

15 He 1 du: . du: . du: 2 du: . du:, ◦◇du:z³, ◦‖ɑdu:¹,³ . du: 3 du: . du:, ◦◇ɑdɷz¹ . du: [ᴅdu:²] 4 du:, ◦‖də¹⁽²ˣ⁾,²⁽²ˣ⁾ . du:, ◦◇ɑ~¹⁽²ˣ⁾,² . du:, ◦‖də¹⁽²ˣ⁾, ◦du:z¹ [‖ᴅdə¹] 5 du: . du: . du: [ᴅdu:²] 6 du: . du: . du: [ɑdɷ¹, ~¹] 7 du: . dʌz, s.f. du: [occ.] . du:, ◦◇~⁴ [‖ᴅdə¹⁽³ˣ⁾, ×+du:⁴]

16 Wo 1 du: . dɷz . du: [ᴅdɷn¹, ᴅdɷz³, ‖ᴅdu:¹] 2 du: . dɷz, ◦‖ɑdu:² . du: 3 du: . dɷz . du: 4 du: . du: . du: [ᴅdu:²] 5 dɷz . dɷz . dɷz [‖ᴅdɷz¹] 6 du:, ◦◇~³ . du: . du [ᴅdɷz², ‖ᴅ~³] 7 du: . §du: [+ «lɒɪk əm» *like them*] . du:

17 Wa 1 du: . dɷz . du: 2 du: . du: . ◦×ɑdə⁴ . du:, ◦~⁴ [×ᴅdu:⁴, ᴅ~⁴, ‖ᴅ~⁴] 3 du: . dʌz . du: [◇ᴅdu:¹] 4 dü: . dü: . du: 5 dü:, ◦◇dɷz¹ . dɷz . dü: 6 dü: . dɷz . dü: 7 dᶦü . dᶦü: . dü:

23 Mon 1 dᵒu: . dᵒu:, ◦~¹,² , ◦‖~¹, ◦‖də¹ . dᵒu:, ◦‖də¹⁽²ˣ⁾ [◇ᴅdu:⁴, ◇ᴅdᵒu:², ‖ᴅ~², ‖ᴅdə¹,²,³,⁴⁽²ˣ⁾, ‖+də¹] 2 du:, ◦‖də³ . du:, ◦ɑ~², ◦‖də³, ◦‖ɑ~²,³⁽²ˣ⁾ . du:,

○‖dəˡ⁽²ˣ⁾,³ [‖ᴅdəˡ⁽²ˣ⁾,²⁽²ˣ⁾,³⁽²ˣ⁾, ‖ᴅ∼³ VIII.9.4] 3 du:, ○dəˡ⁽³ˣ⁾,²,³⁽²ˣ⁾, ○∼ˡ VIII.6.2. du:, ○‖dəˡ,², ○‖ɑ∼ˡ⁽²ˣ⁾,², ○∼ˡ VIII.7.5. du:, ○‖dəˡ⁽²ˣ⁾,² [‖ᴅdəˡ⁽³ˣ⁾,³, ᴅdu:ˡ, ‖+∼³] 4 du:. du:, ○‖ɑdə² VI.14.14, ○‖ɑ∼³ IX.3.6. du: [ᴅdu:, ‖ᴅdə², ‖ᴅ∼ˡ VIII.5.2, ᴅdʌ̈zˡ, ‖+dəˡ, ‖+dᵊˡ] 5 du:, ○‖dəˡ⁽²ˣ⁾,². du:, ○‖dʌ̈z², ○‖ɑdə²⁽²ˣ⁾. du: [‖ᴅdəˡ,²⁽⁹ˣ⁾, ‖+∼ˡ⁽²ˣ⁾, ‖du:ˡ, ×∼²] 6 du:, ○‖dəˡ. du:, ○‖dəˡ, ○‖du:², ○‖ɑ∼ˡ. du:, ○‖də² 7 n.a.

24 Gl 1 du:. du:. du: 2 dɷz, ○∼³. dᵊu:. dᵊu: 3 dᵊu:. dᵊu:, ○‖dəˡ,²,³,⁴. dɷu:, ○‖də³,⁴⁽²ˣ⁾ [ᴅdəˡ⁽⁴ˣ⁾,³] 4 dᵊu:, ○‖dəˡ,³⁽⁴ˣ⁾. dᵊu:, ○‖ɑdə²,³. dᵊu:, ○‖dəˡ⁽³ˣ⁾,³ [‖ᴅdəˡ,²,³⁽²ˣ⁾, ‖+∼ˡ⁽²ˣ⁾,²] 5 du:. du:. du: 6 du:. du:, ○də²⁽⁴ˣ⁾, ○‖ɑ∼ˡ, ○‖ɑdɷ²⁽²ˣ⁾ VIII.6.2. du:, ○‖dəˡ, ○‖dˡ [ᴅ+dəˡ] 7 du:, ○‖dəˡ. du:, ○‖ɑ∼ˡ, ○‖ɑdəˡ. du: [‖wɛn ð‿əst lʌɪkˡ *when thou* (do)*st like 2 pr.s.*]

25 O 1 dü:, ○dʌz². dü:. du: 2 dü:. dü:. dü: 3 dy·. dy:, ○ɑ∼ˡ. dy· 4 du:. dɷz, ○◇ɑdu:zˡ, ○‖ɑdu:ˡ. du: 5 dü:. dü:. dü: [◇+du:²] 6 dü:. du:. du:

IX.5.2 (he) DOESN'T†. (they) DON'T†

Q. I do care for it, but he . . . .

Convert for **they don't.**

Rr. (He) DOESN'T, DON'T

(They) DON'T

Note 1—The rr. to the two parts of the q. are separated below by a full stop.

Note 2—In the i.m. foll. the r. to the first part of the q., an attached superior ɑ marks a 3 pr.s. foll. IT or SHE. Exs. of the 2 pr.s. and the imp. follow in square brackets, marked with superior ᴅ and superior × resp. In the i.m. given in square brackets foll. the r. to the second part of the q., an attached superior + marks a 1 pr.pl. and superior ‖ a 2 pr.pl.

Note 3—I.m. exs. of DOESN'T/DON'T used as anaphoric substitute are marked with superior ◇.

Note 4—(HE) DOESN'T also occurs at IX.4.17. For exs. of DON'T *1 pr.s.*, see VII.5.2 and IX.4.10; and of DON'T *2 pr.pl. interrog.*, see VIII.3.7.

7 Ch 1 dɷznt [×dɷnə²]. dɷnə 2 dɷznə, ○ɑdɪ̞nəˡ, ○ɑdɷnəˡ, ○ɑdɷznt² [ᴅdɷznə³, ×dənəˡ, ×dɷnə²]. dɷnə, ○∼ˡ, ○◇dɷ:ntˡ, ○◇dɷznt² [‖dɷnt²] 3 dɷnə [×dɷnə³]. dɷnə, ○∼² [‖dɷnə³] 4 dɷnə, dɷzn, ○dɷznt², ○ɑdɷnə² [ᴅdɷnə², ×∼²]. dɷnə, ○∼² [‖dɷnəˡ,²] 5 dɷnə, ○ɑ∼ˡ⁽²ˣ⁾,³ [×dɷnəˡ]. dɷnə, ○∼ˡ,² [+dɷnəˡ] 6 dɷnə. dɷnə

8 Db 1 dɷznt, ○ɑdɷnə⁴. dɷnə, ○∼ˡ 2 dɷznt, dɷnə, ○ɑdɷznt³ [ᴅdɷznə²]. do:nt 3 dɷznə. dɷnə, ○∼ˡ,³ [◇dɷnəˡ] 4 dɷznə [ᴅdɷnəˡ]. dɷnə 5 dɷnə. dɷnə 6 dɷznə. dɷnə, ○∼ˡ 7 dɷnə, ○ɑ∼ˡ. dɷnə [◇dɷnəˡ]

11 Sa 1 dʌnə. dʌnə [+dɷnə[4]] 2 dɷnə. dɷnə [‖dɷnə[3]] 3 dʌznt, dɷnə ["older"]. do:nt, dɷnə ["older"] 4 dʌznt. do:nt 5 dɷnə [ᴅdɷsnə[1]]. dɷnə [‖dɷnə[1]] 6 dɷnə, ○ᑫdʌznt. dɷnə 7 dʌnə, ○ᑫ~[1]. dʌnə, ○do:nt[1] 8 dɷnə. dɷnə, ○~[2] 9 dʌnə. dʌnə, ○~[1] 10 dɷnə. dɷnə [+dʌnə[3]] 11 dʌnə [×dɷnə[2]]. dʌnə

12 St 1 dɷznə, ○~[4], ○ᑫ~[2], ○ᑫdɷnə[1]. dɒnə, ○dɷnə[2] [+dɷnə[1,3]] 2 dɷnə, ○ᑫ~[2] [ᴅdɷnə[1]]. dɷnə, ○~[2] 3 dɷnə, ○ᑫ~[1]. dɷnə, ○~[1] [+dɷnə[1], ‖~[1]] 4 dɷnə. dɷnə, ○~[2] [‖dɷnə[2(3x)]] 5 dɷnə [×dɷnə[2]] 6 dɷnə, ○~[1,2], ○ᑫ~[1]. dɷnə [+dɷnə[2], ‖~[1(2x)]] 7 doɷnt, ○ᑫ~[1(2x),4]. doɷnt 8 dɷznt, doɷnt. doɷnt, ○dɷnə[2] [+dɒnə[1]] 9 dɷnə, ○◇dɷznt[1], ○ᑫdɷnt[2]. dɷnə 10 dɷznt, doɷnt, ○ᑫ◇~[4]. dọɷnt [+doɷnt[2]] 11 doɷnt, ○ᑫ~[1,2], ○ᑫdɷnt[2]. doɷnt [‖doɷnt[2]]

15 He 1 dɷnə, ○ᑫdo:n[2]. dɷnə, ○~[1] [+dɷnə[1]] 2 dʌnə, ○do:n[2]. dʌnə 3 do:nt, ○ᑫdo:n[2] [ᴅdo:n[2], ×do:nt[1]]. do:nt 4–5 do:nt. do:nt 6 do:nt [ᴅdo:[1]]. do:nt 7 dənə, ○ᑫdoɷnt[1,3(3x),4] [×dənə[4]]. dənə [+doɷnt[1], +do:nt[3], ‖do:ᵒnt[1], ‖doɷn[4], ‖doɷnt[4]]

16 Wo 1 dɒɷn. dɒɷnt, ○doɷnt[1(2x)] 2 dɷnə, ○ᑫ◇doɷnt[2]. doɷnt 3 doɷnt. doɷnt 4 do:nt. do:nt 5 do:nt, ○ᑫʃɷnt[1] [rec. in «ɩt ʃɷnt a:f ə:ʳʈ» *it doesn't half hurt*]. do:nt 6 doɷnt. doɷnt, ○doɷn[3] 7 doɷnt, ○~[3], ○ᑫ~[1,3(2x)], ○dəɷnt[3]. doɷnt, ○~[1,3]

17 Wa 1 dọɷnt. dọɷnt 2 dünt, ○du:nt[4], ○ᑫdɷznt[1], ○ᑫdəɷnt[1(2x),2,3] [×doɷnt[3], ×dɒɷnt[3], ×dəɷnt[3,4]]. du:nt, ○~[4], ○dəɷnt[2], ○də:nt[2,3], ○dəɷʈ[1] [+dəɷnt[4], +du:nt[4]; ◇dəɷnt[2], ◇də:nt[3], ‖dɒɷnt[4]] 3 dọɷnt. dọɷnt 4 dọənt, ○ᑫdoɷnt[1]. dọənt 5 dọɷnt. dọɷnt, ○dɷnt[1] 6 dọɷnt, dɷənt ["older"]. dɷənt 7 doɷnt. doɷnt

23 Mon 1 do:ᵒnt. do:ᵒnt 2 do:nt. do:nt, ○dɷn[1] 3 do:nt, ○do:n[2], ○ᑫ~[1] [‖do:n[2]]. do:nt 4 do:nt. do:nt, ○dount°[1] 5 dount[(2x)], ○ᑫdoun[2]. dount 6 do:nt, ○ᑫdo:n[1]. do:nt 7 n.a. n.a., ○do:nt[1]

24 Gl 1 do:ɷnt, ○do:n[1], ○ᑫ◇du:[1]. do:ɷnt 2 do:ɷnt. do:ɷnt 3 do:ɷnt, ○do:ɷn[1] [×dɷsn[4]]. do:ɷnt 4 do:ɷnt. do:ɷnt 5 do:nt, ○ᑫdo:n[2]. do:nt 6 dwənt, ○ᑫdəznt[1]. n.r., ○dwɷnt[2(2x)] [+dwənt] 7 do·ənt. dʷo·ənt

25 O 1 dɷənt [ᴅdʌsnt[1]]. dɷənt [+doɷnt[2]] 2 dɷənt. dɷənt 3 dəɷnt, dɷənt, ○~[1], ○ᑫdọɷnt[1]. dəɷnt, dɷənt, ○dọɷnt[2] [+dɷənt[1]] 4 dɷznt, s.f. do:nt ["rare"], ○dɷznt[4]. do:nt, ○~[2], ○dõ:nt[5] [+do:n[5]] 5 dəɷnʔ, ○dọɷnt[2], ○ᑫdəɷnt[2(2x)], ○ᑫdəɷn[2], ○ᑫdəɷnʔ[2]. dəɷnʔ 6 doɷnt, ○ᑫdəɷnʔ[2]. doɷnt, ○dəɷnʔ[3]

IX.5.3 DOING†

Q. You see a child very busy with something out there; so you ask: What's that child . . . . there?

Rr. (A-)DOING

Note—DOING also occurs at VIII.8.5.

7 Ch 1 dɪʏ:ɪn 2 s.w. düɪn, °dɷɪn[3(2x)], °dɷ·ɪn[4] VI.1.5 3 dᶦʏ:ɪn 4 dᴼu:ɪn 5 dᶦu:ɪn 6 dᴼü̜:ɪn

8 Db 1 dʏ:ɪn 2 du:ɪn 3 dü:ɪn 4 dɛɷɪn 5 dᶦu:ɪn 6–7 dɛɷɪn

11 Sa 1 duɪn 2 dʏʉ:ɪn 3 dᴼu:ɪn, °dɷɪn[2] 4 duɪn 5 dɪu:ɪn 6 du:ɪn, °duɪn[3] 7 du:ɪn 8 du:ɪn, °~[2] 9–11 du:ɪn

12 St 1 dü:ɪn, °düɪn[1] 2 dɪɷɪn, °dü:ɪn[2], °ədü:ᶦn[2] 3 dɛɷɪn, °~[1] 4 ədü:ɪn 5 dü:ɪn, °~[4] 6 dü:ɪn [dɛɷɪnz[2], ~[2] *doings n. pl.* VII.8.8] 7 dü:ɪn 8 dü:ɪn, °~[2] 9 ədu:ɪn 10 ədü:ɪn 11 ədü:ɪn, °du:ɪn[1]

15 He 1 ədu:ɪn, °~[2], °du:ɪn[2] 2–3 ədu:ɪn 4 ədu:ɪn, °~[1] 5–6 du:ɪn 7 dɷ·ɪn

16 Wo 1 du:ɪn, °ədu:ɪn 2 ədu:ɪn, °~[2], °du:ɪn[2] 3 ədu:ɪn, °~[1] 4 ədu:ɪn, °~[3] 5 əduɪn, °ədu:ɪn[1] 6 ədu:ɪn, °~[3] 7 dɷ·ɪn, °dɷɪn[1(3x)], °ədu·ɪn[3]

17 Wa 1 du:ɪn 2 s.w. du·ɪn, °dɷɪn[4], °ədɷɪn[4] [dɷɪnz[4] *doing n. pl.*] 3 dɛ̈ɷɪn, °duɪn[1], °du:ɪn[2] 4 dü:ɪn 5 du:ɪn 6 du:ɪn, °~[3], °ədu:ɪn[4] 7 du:ɪn

23 Mon 1 ədᴼu:ɪn 2–3 ədu:ɪn 4–5 du-ɪn 6 du:ɪn 7 n.a.

24 Gl 1 ədu:ɪn 2 ədɷu:ɪn, °ədu:ɪn[3] VIII.3.2 3 ədᴼu:ɪn 4 ədᴼu:ən 5 du·ɪn 6 ədu:ɪn 7 du:ɪn

25 O 1 düɪn, °ədu:ɪn[2] [+ «ɒn ɪt» *of it*] 2 du·ɪn, °ədu·ɪn[2] 3 du:ɪn 4 dɷ·ɪn, °~[3] 5 duɪn 6 du:ɪn

IX.5.4 DO YOU†. DOES HE†. DID YOU†

Q. If you want to know how much rent Jack pays for his house, you ask him: Jack, how much rent . . . . pay?

Convert for **does he,** p.t. **did you.**

The corresponding q. in V.4 of the Qr., which was used at 16.7 and 17.2 read: *You want to know how much Jack gave for his car, so later you might ask him: Jack, how much . . . . pay?* Accordingly, at the locs. concerned, the only r. is a form of DID YOU. But i.m. forms of the wanted r. are reproduced in the locs. concerned.

Rr. DO(ES) THOU/YOU, DOST (THOU)
ir.r. DID HE, DO(ES) HE
DID(ST) THOU/YOU, ir.r. DO YOU

Note 1—The rr. to the three parts of the q. are separated below by full stops.

Note 2—In the list above, THOU and YOU subsume THEE and YE resp.

Note 3—At 15.1 no aux. v. was rec. At 17.6 no pron. was rec.

Note 4—In the material below, [‿s] represents DOST forming a syll. with a prec. word.

Note 5—In the i.m. below DOES THEM/WE and DO THEM/YOU are cited between square brackets untransliterated after the r. to the first part of the q.; DOES HER~HOO~SHE and DO HER/IT are cited after the r. to the second part of the q.; and DID/HE/THEM/US after the r. to the third part.

Note 6—Exs. of and expressions for DO YOU also occur at VII.5.1, VII.6.26 VII.8.17/18, VIII.3.7, VIII.8.6 and IX.9.4.

7 Ch 1 dɷz tə, °‿z ðə[2] [rec. in «aɪ mɛnɪ‿z ðə want» *how many* (dost) *thou want?*; dn ðɪ[2]]. ir.r. dɪd ɪ. dɪd ðə 2 dɷst, p. dɷst ðɪ, p. dɷn ju:. p. dɷz u: [dɷz ʃi:; dɷz ə[2]]. n.r., °dɪd jə[2(2x)] 3 dɷst [dɷn ðɪ[3]]. dɷz ɪ. dɪst 4 dɷn ðɪ, °d‿jə[3]. dɷz ɪ. dɪd jə, °~[2] 5 dɷst ðɛɪ, °dɷn jo:[2]. dɷz ɛɪ. dɪst 6 dɷn jə, °~[2]. dɷz ɪ. dɪd jə

8 Db 1 dɷst. dɷz ɪ. dɪd‿ʔ 2 dɷz ðə, °dɷn jə[1]. dɷz ɪ. dɪd tə 3 dɷst, dɷn jə, °dɷn ðɪ[3], °dɷst[2]. dɷz ɪ. dɪdst 4 dɷst, °~[1,2]. dɷz ɪ. dɪdst 5 dɷst, °dɷn jə[2,3(2x)] [wɒt‿s əm kɔ:l ɪt[4] *what does they call it?*]. dɷz ɪ. dɪd ða 6 dɷst. dɷz ɪ. dɪdst 7 dɷn jə, dɷs tə. dɷz ɪ. dɪdst

11 Sa 1 dʌn jə. dʌz ɪ. dɪdst 2 dɷn jə. dɷz ɪ. dɪd jə 3 dʌn jə. dʌz ɪ. dɪd jə 4 dɷ jə. dʌz ɪ. dɪd jə 5 dɷs, °‿s[1] [rec. in «wɒt‿s wɒnt» *what dost want?*]. dɪu: i:. dɪdst ðɪ 6 dɷn i:. dɷn ɪ. dɪd i: 7 dʌst θɪ. dʌn ɪ. dɪd jə 8 dɷs ðɪ, °dɷn jə[1]. dɷn ɪ. dɪds ðɪ 9 dʌst ðə, °‿s tə[1] [rec. in «wɒt‿s tə want» *what dost thou want?*]. dʌn ɪ. dɪdst ðə 10 dɷn jə [du: ðɪ *do thee imp.*]. dɷn ɪ. dɪd jə 11 dʌn jə, °dɷ ju:[1], °dɷn jo:[2]. dʌn ɪ. dɪd ɪ

12 St 1 dɷst, °~[1]. dɷz ɛɪ. dɪdst 2 dɷst, °~[5]. dɷz ɛɪ. dɪdst ðɛɪ 3 dɷst, °~[1(4x)], °dɷst ðɛɪ[1], °dɷn ðɪ[1(2x)]. dɷz ɛɪ. dɪdst, °~[1,2] [dɪd ɪ[1]] 4 dɷst. dɷz ɛɪ. dɪdst 5 dɷn jə. dɷz ɛɪ. dɪd jə 6 dɷn jə, °də ðɪ[1], °dɷst[2]. dɷz ɛɪ. dɪd jə 7 də joɷ, °d‿ʒoɷ[1(2x)]. dɷz ɛɪ. dɪd joɷ 8 də jə. dɷz ɪ. dɪd jə 9 dɷst ða:, °d‿jə[2]. dɷz ɛɪ. dɪd ða: 10 də jə, °d‿ʒə[5]. dɷz ɪ. dɪd‿ʒə 11 dən joɷ, °d‿ʒə[2]. dɷz i:. dɪd jǫɷ

15 He 1 ði: [rec. in «ˈæɷ ˈmʌtʃ ˈɹɛnt ˈði: ˈpe:ɩ» *how much rent* (do) *thee pay?*]. du: ɩ. dɩd‿ʒə 2 dɷs ði:, ○‿s tə³. du: i: [du: əʳ²]. dɷ ðæɩ 3 dɷz jə, ○dɷst³ [du: ɷm²⁽²ˣ⁾]. du: ɩ. dɩd jə 4 də jə [dɷz wi:¹]. dɩd jə 5 dʌs ðɩ, ○‿s jə¹. du: i:. dɩds ðɩ 6 dɷs ðɩ, ○‿s jə¹. du: ɩ. dɩd ðɩ 7 d‿ʒə, ○d‿jə⁴⁽²ˣ⁾. dəz i: [dɷz ʃɩ⁴]. dɩd jə

16 Wo 1 dɷ jə. dɷz ɩ. dɷd jə 2 dɷs ði:, ○dɷz ju:²⁽²ˣ⁾. dɷst i:. dɩds ði: 3 d‿ju:, ○dɷz jə⁵, ○‿s ðɩ² [dɷz əm³]. dɷz i:. dɩd jə 4 dɷs. du: ɩ. dɩds ðɩ 5 dɷs ði:, ○dɷz jɷ¹. dɷz i:. dɩds ði: [dɩd ɷm¹] 6 dɷz ju:, ○~¹, ○d‿ʒə²,³ [du: ɷm²]. dɷz ɩ. dɩd jə 7 n.a., ○dɷs ðə⁴, ○dɷst¹. n.a., ○dəz i:⁴. dɩdst

17 Wa 1 dɷ jə, ○dɩ jə². dɷz ɩ. dɩd jə 2 n.a., ○dɩ jə²,⁴ [du· əm²]. n.a. dɩd jɷ 3 də jə. dɷz ɩ, ○‿z i:³. dɩd jə 4 dɩ jə. du: ɩ. dɩd jə 5 dɷz jə [dɷz ɷm¹]. dɷz ɩ. dɩd‿ʒə 6 də jə. dɷz ɩ. dɩd 7 dɷst ði:. dɷz ɩ. dɩd jə

23 Mon 1 dʌs ðˈi: [dᵚu: əm²]. dᵚu: ɩ, ○~². dɩds ðɩ 2 d‿jə. du: ɩ. dɩd jə 3 də ju: [du: əm³]. du: i:. dɩd jə [dɩd ʌs²] 4 d‿ʒu· [də wi·¹]. du· i·. d‿ju· 5 d‿ju. du·i. dɩd u: 6 d‿jə. du: ɩ, ○~². dɩd jə 7 n.a.

24 Gl 1 dɷs ði: [du: ɷm¹,²]. du: ɩ [du: ɩt¹]. dɩds ði: 2 dɷs ði:, ○dɷst³. dɷz ɩ. dɩds ði: 3 dɷs ðəɷ. dᵚu: ɩm. dɩd‿ʒə [dɩd ə³] 4 dᵚu: ɩ, ○~³, ○dᵚu: ə³, ○d‿ʒə¹ [rec. in «wɒd‿ʒə wɒnt» *what* (do) *you want?*; dᵚu: ɷm¹]. dᵚu: ˈi:. dɩd ɩ 5 dɷst. dɷz. dɩdst 6 dəs ði:. du: i:. dɩdst ði: 7 dəs ði:. du: ə. dɩtst

25 O 1 dɷst ði:. du: i:. dɩd i: 2 du: i:. du: i:. dɩd i: 3 du: i:, ○d‿jə¹. du: i:. n.r. 4 d‿ju:, ○~⁴. dəz i:. d‿jə 5 dɩ ju [du: əm³]. du: i:. dɩd jə 6 du: i:. du: i:. dɩd jə

IX.5.5 DID NOT DO‡

Q. Your wife suddenly says to you: This vase is broken, and you at once say: Well, I can truthfully say I . . . . it.

Rr. DIDN'T §BREAK/DO, §HAVEN'T /BROKEN/DONE/HAD NOTHING TO DO WITH/, NEVER DID/DOED/DONE

Note 1—When rec. in the r., IT is reproduced below.

Note 2—Sometimes the f.w. omitted to rec. the wanted DO.

Note 3—I.m. exs. of DIDN'T, DO *inf.* and DO (*inf.*) IT are reproduced below between square brackets untransliterated.

Note 4—DIDN'T also occurs at IX.4.8/9/18; and DO *inf.* at VII.5.8, VII.8.13, VIII.8.6 and IX.9.5.

7 Ch 1 dɪdnt dɪʏ: ɪt [dʏ:^{2}] 2 §anə dɷn ɪt, s.w. dɪdnə dü: ɪt [dɪdnə^{3}; du:$^{1,2(3x),3,4(5x)}$, dü^{3}, dɪü^{3}] 3 §anə bɹɒkn ɪt, p. dɪdnə dˡʏ: ɪt [dɪdnə^{2}] 4 dɪdnə d^{ɷ}ü: ɪt [d^{ɷ}u:^{2}, du:^{2}] 5 dɪdnə dȩɷ [du:^{1}] 6 nɛvə dɪd, °nɛvə d^{ɷ}ü̧:d ɪt [dü:^{3}]

8 Db 1 dɪdnə dʏ: ɪt [dʏ:^{2,3}] 2 dɪdnt du: [dɪnt^{3}; du:^{3}] 3 §avnə dɷn, °dɪdnə dü: [dɪdnt^{1}] 4 dɪdnə dɛɷ 5 dɪdnə dɛɷ [dɪdnə$^{3,4(2x)}$] 6 §anə bɹɒk ɪt, dɪdnə dɛɷ ɪt [dɪdnə^{1}; dɛɷ^{1}, dü:^{1}] 7 dɪdnə dɛɷ [dɪdnə^{1}]

11 Sa 1 dɪdnə du: 2 dɪdnə dʏʉ: ɪt [dʏʉ:^{1,3}, du:^{2}] 3 dɪdn d^{ɷ}u: 4 dɪdnə du: [dɪnə^{1}, dɪdnə^{2}] 5 dɪdnə dɪu: [dɪu:^{2}] 6 dɪdnə [dɪdnt^{3}] 7 dɪdnə 8 dɪdnə, °dɪdnə du ɪt^{2} [du:^{1,2}; dɷn^{2}] 9 dɪdnə [dɪdnə^{1}; du:$^{1(2x)}$] 10 dɪdnə [du:$^{3(2x)}$] 11 dɪdnə

12 St 1 §anə bɹɒkn ɪt, dɪdnə, °dɪdnə du:^{2} [dɪdnə$^{2,3(2x)}$; du:^{2}, dü:^{3} IX.4.8] 2 dɪdnə §bɹi:k ɪt, §anə bɹɒkn ɪt [dɪdnə^{2}; dü:^{2,5}] 3 §anə bɹɒkn ɪt, dɪdnə dɛɷ ɪt [dɪdnə^{1}, dɪdnt^{1}; dɛɷ^{2}, dü:^{1,2}, du:^{1}] 4 nɛvə dɪd ɪt [dü:^{4}] 5 dɪdnə dü: ɪt [dü$^{2(2x),3(5x)}$] 6 §anə bɹɒkn ɪt, dɪdnə dü: ɪt ["old"; dɪdnə$^{2(2x)}$, dɪnə^{1,2}; dü:$^{1(2x),2}$, du:^{1,2}] 7 dɪdnə dü: ɪt [dɪdnə^{1}; dü:$^{2(2x),4(3x)}$, du:^{1}] 8 dɪdnt dü: ɪt [dü:^{1}, dü^{6}] 9 dɪdnə dü: ɪt [dɪdnə$^{2(2x)}$; dü:$^{1(2x),2(2x)}$] 10 dɪdnt dü: ɪt 11 nɛvə dɪd ɪt, §ɛ:ɪ bɹoɷk ɪt [dɛɪ^{2} rec. in «ʃi: dɛɪ ạ:f skɹat ɪz fɛɪs» *she didn't half scratch his face*; du:$^{1,2(2x)}$, dü:$^{1(2x)}$]

15 He 1 dɪdnə du: ɪt [du:$^{2(3x)}$] 2 dɪdnə du: ɪt [dʒɷnt^{2}, dʒʌnt^{3}; du:^{3}] 3 dɪdn du: [du:$^{1(3x),3}$] 4 dɪdn du: ɪt [du:^{1,3}] 5 dɪn du: ɪt [du:$^{2(2x)}$] 6 dɪdnt du: 7 dɪdn du: ɪt [dɪdnə^{1}, dɪdnt^{1,4}; du:$^{1(3x),2,3,4(6x)}$]

16 Wo 1 §ɛɪnt dɷn ɪt [dɪdnt^{3}] 2 dɪdnə du:, de: du: ɪt [du$^{2(2x)}$] 3 dɪdn §bɹe:ɪk ɪt [du:$^{1(2x)}$] 4 dɪdn du: ɪt 5 dɪdn du: ɪt [du: ɪt^{1}] 6 dɪdn du: ɪt [du:$^{3(2x)}$] 7 dɪdnt §bɹeɪk ɪt [dɪdnt$^{3(2x)}$; du:$^{1,3(3x),4}$]

17 Wa 1 dɪdnt du: [dɪdnt^{1} III.1.7; du: $^{1(3x)}$] 2 §eɪnt ad nɷθɪŋ tə du: wɪð ɪt, p. §eɪnt dɷn, s.w. dɪdn du: ɪt [du:$^{2(2x),4(3x)}$] 3 dɪdnt du: 4 dɪdnt dü: ɪt 5 dɪdn̥ du: ɪt 6 dɪdnt du: [dü:^{1}] 7 dɪdnt du: ɪt

23 Mon 1 dɪdn dɷu: [d^{ɷ}u:$^{1(3x),2(2x)}$, du:^{4}] 2 dɪdn du: ɪt 3 dɪdn du: [du:^{1}] 4 nɛvə dʌ̣n [du·^{1}] 5 dɪdn duw ɪt, °dɪdn du·^{2} [du:$^{2(3x)}$] 6 dɪdn du: ɪt 7 n.a. [dɪdnt^{1}]

24 Gl 1 dɪdn du: 2 dɪdn [du:$^{3(2x)}$] 3 nɛvəʳ dɷn‿t, dɪdn d^{ɷ}u: ɪt [du:^{1}, dɷ^{1}; d^{ɷ}u: ɪt^{3}] 4 dɪdn d^{ɷ}u: 5 dɪdnt du: [dɷ‿t^{1,2}] 6 nɛvə dən‿t 7 dɪdnt dɷ‿t

25 O 1 dɪdnt du: [du:$^{2(2x)}$, dɷ^{2}] 2 dɪdnt dü: [dü:^{1}; dɷ‿t^{1}] 3 nɪvəʳ dʌn ɪt [du:^{1}] 4 dɪdn du: ɪt [du:$^{1,3(4x),4(6x)}$] 5 nɛvəɽ dʌn ɪʔ [du:$^{2(3x),3}$] 6 dɪnʔ du: ɪʔ [du:$^{3(3x)}$]

IX.5.6 DONE†

Q. Tell me then: Who has . . . . it (viz. broken the vase)*?*

Rr. (A)DONE

Note 1—When rec. in the r., the pronominal obj. IT is reproduced below.
Note 2—DONE also occurs at V.7.21, VI.13.8, VIII.8.6 and IX.4.9.

7 Ch 1 dɷn, ○∼[4(2x)] 2 n.a. 3 dɷn‿t, ○dɷn[3] 4 dɷn 5 dɷn, ○∼[1] 6 dɷn

8 Db 1 dɷn 2–5 dɷn 6 dɷn‿t 7 dɷn

11 Sa 1 dʌn 2 dɷn, ○∼[1] VII.3.17 3–4 dʌn 5 dọn 6 dʌn, ○∼[3] 7 dʌn 8 dɷn 9 dʌn, ○∼[1] 10 dɷn 11 dʌn

12 St 1 dɷn, ○∼[2,4] 2 dɷn, ○∼[1(2x),2] 3 dɷn ɪt, ○∼[1,2(3x)], ○∼[1] VIII.1.26 4 dɷn ɪt, ○dɷn[4] 5 dɷn ɪt 6 dɷn, ○∼[1(4x),2(3x)], ○∼[1] VIII.1.26 7–8 dɷn, ○∼[1] 9 dɷn ɪt, ○dɷn[2(2x)] 10 dɷn ɪt, ○dɷn[3,4(3x),5] 11 dọn ɪt

15 He 1 dʌn, ○∼[1] 2 dʌn, ○∼[2] 3 dɷ:n, ○∼[1], ○dɷn[1(2x)] 4 dʌn 5 dɷn 6 dɷn ɪt 7 dʌn ɪt, ○dʌn[2,3,4], ○dɷn[1,2]

16 Wo 1–2 dɷn 3 dɷn ɪt 4 dɷn ɪt [dɷn əwaɪ ɷ *done away with*] 5 dɷn, ○∼[1] 6 ir.r., dɷn ɪt, ○dɷn[3], ○dɷ:n[3] 7 dɷn, ○∼[4(2x)]

17 Wa 1 dɷn, ○∼[1(2x)] 2 dɷn, ○∼[4(2x)] 3 dʌn 4–6 dɷn 7 dɷn ɪt

23 Mon 1 dʌn 2 dɷn, ○∼[3] 3 dʌn, ○∼[2(3x)] 4 dʌ̣̈n, ○∼[1] 5 dʌ̣̈n 6 dʌn 7 n.a.

24 Gl 1 dɷn, ○∼[2] 2 dɷn 3 dʌn, ○∼[4], ○dɷn‿t[1,4] 4 dɷn 5 dọn 6 dən‿t 7 də·n‿t, ○ədən ɪt[1]

25 O 1 dɷn 2 dọn 3 dʌn 4 dɷn ɪt 5–6 dʌn

IX.5.7 GONE†

Q. Your boy has just left the house, so you simply ask your wife: Where has he . . . .

Rr. GONE (TO), WENT

Note—GONE occurs at III.1.9/12 and V.7.21.

7 Ch 1 gɒn, ○∼[2(2x)] 2 gən, ○∼[2,3(4x)] 3 gɒn[(2x)], ○∼[1] 4 gɒn, ○∼[1] III.7.2, ○∼[2] 5 gɒn, ○∼[1(2x)], ○gan[2] 6 gɒn, ○∼[2]

8 Db 1 gɒn· 2 gɒn, ○∼[4] 3 gɒn 4 gɒn, ○∼[1] III.7.2, ○∼[3] 5–7 gɒn

11 Sa 1 gɒn 2 gɒn, ○~[2] 3–4 gɔ:n 5 gɒn, ○~[3] 6 n.r. 7–11 gɔ:n

12 St 1–2 gɒn, ○~[1,2,5] 3 gɒn, ○~[1,2] 4 gɒn, ○~[2(2x)] 5 gɒn, ○~[2,3] 6–7 gɒn 8 gɒn, ○~[4] 9 gɒn, ○~[1,2(3x)] 10 gɒn, ○~[4] 11 gɒn tü:, ○gɒn[1,2]

15 He 1 gɔ:n, ○gɒn[1] 2 gɔ:n, ○~[3] 3 gɑ:n, ○~[1] 4 gɑ:n, ○wɛnt[2] 5 gɑ:n, ○~[1] 6–7 gɒn

16 Wo 1 gɒn 2 gɑ:n, ○gɔ:n[1] 3 gɑ:n, ○gɒn[2] 4 gɑ:n, ○gɒn[1,2] 5 gɑ:n, ○~[1] 6 gɑ:n 7 gən tu:, ○gən[1(2x),3,4], ○wɛnt[1]

17 Wa 1 gɒn, ○~[2] V.6.12 2 gən, ○~[3,4(2x)], ○wɛnt[1(2x),4] 3–4 gɒn 5 gɒn, ○~[1] 6–7 gɒn

23 Mon 1 gɑ:n 2 gɑ:n, ○~[3], ○wɛnt[3] 3 gɑ:n 4–5 gɔ:n 6 gɑ:n, ○~[2] 7 n.a.

24 Gl 1 gɑ:n, ○~[2(2x)] 2 gɑ:n, ○~[2,3] 3 gɑ:n, ○~[4] 4 gɑ:n 5–6 gɒn 7 gɒ·n

25 O 1 gɔ:n, ○gɔ˞:ɳ[2], ○gɒn[2] 2 gɑ:n 3 gɔ·n, ○gɔ:n[1,2] 4 gɒn, ○~[1,4], ○~[1] V.6.12, ○gɔ:n[2], ○wɛnt[3,4] 5 gɔ:n, ○~[2] 6 gɔ:n

IX.5.8 GO AND‡

Q. You hear a noise in the yard and you want your boy to find out what the trouble is, so you say: Johnny, will you [g.] . . . . see what is the matter?

Rr. GO (AND)

Note 1—When rec. in the rr., LOOK and SEE are reproduced below.

Note 2—In citing the i.m. exs. of GO (AND) below, the inf. has not been differentiated from the imp. or the pr.t. The v. foll. i.m. GO (AND) is not included below.

Note 3—For additional exs. of GO, see II.3.5, VIII.5.1, VIII.6.1 and VIII.7.9.

Note 4—SEE also occurs at VI.3.2, VIII.3.2 and IX.5.8; and LOOK at III.13.18 and VIII.1.23.

7 Ch 1 gɷ ən 2 gɷ ən si:, s.w. gɷ si:, ○gɷ· ən[3], ○gɷ: ən[3] 3 gʏ: ən 4 gɷ ən, ○~[3] 5 gʉ̞: ən 6 gɷ ən

8 Db 1 gʏ: ən, ○go· ən[4] 2 gɷ ən, ○~[4] 3 gɷ ən, ○~[1] 4 gᶷü: ən 5 gɷ ən, ○~[1] 6 gɷ ən 7 gᶷü: ən, ○gü: ən[1]

11 Sa 1–2 go:‿n 3–4 go: n̩ 5 go: n̩ sˡi: 6–7 go:‿n 8–9 go: n̩ 10 go:‿n 11 go: n̩

12 St 1 gɷ ən sɛɩ 2 gɷ: sɛɩ 3 gɷ: ən sɛɩ, ○gɷ: ən[2(3x)], ○gɷ ən[2] 4 gɷ ən sɛɩ 5 goɷ ən lɷk 6 gɷ: ən sɛɩ 7 gɷ ən lɷk, ○gɷ ən[4] 8 goɷ ən si: 9 gɷ: ən sɛɩ, ○gɷ: ən[1(2x),3] 10 gɷ ən si: 11 gʉ̞: ən si:

15 He 1 go:ɷ‿n si: 2 go:‿n si: 3–4 gu:‿n si: 5–6 go: n̩ si: 7 goɷ ən si:, °go: ən[3]

16 Wo 1 gɒɷ‿n 2 goɷ‿n 3–4 gu:‿n si: 5 go:‿n si:, °gu:‿n[1] 6 goɷ‿n si: 7 gɷ: ən si:, °gɷ: ən[3]

17 Wa 1 gọɷ ən 2 gu: ən si:, °gɷ ən[1], °gɷ· ən[3,4] 3 gọɷ ən, °go: ən[1] 4 gü: ən s[ə]i: 5 gü: ən, °gọɷ ən[1] 6 gɷ· ən 7 gọɷ ən

23 Mon 1 go:[ɷ] ən 2–3 go: n̩ si: 4 gɷ‿n, °go· ən[3] 5 gọ ən, °go:‿n[2] 6 go: si: 7 n.a.

24 Gl 1 goɷ: n̩ si: 2 go:ɷ n̩ s[ɪ]i: 3–4 go:ɷ n̩ z[ɪ]i: 5 go: ən si: 6–7 gɷ ən

25 O 1 gɷ ən, °~[1] 2–3 gɷ ən 4 go: ən si:, °go: ən[1(2x),3], °gɷ ən[4] 5 gɷ ən, °~[1] 6 goɷ ən

IX.5.9 TO‡

Q. If I asked: Why did you come to X last week? And suppose your reason was a visit to the doctor, you'd say: I came . . . . see the doctor.

Complete the phrase.—(Added April 1953).

Rr. /(FOR) SEE/TO, TO SEE
The foll. are u.rr.:—TO THE DOCTOR, WENT TO /(THE) DOCTOR/VISIT/

Note 1—When rec. in the rr. (THE) DOCTOR is always included below.

Note 2—The non-occurrence of TO is indicated by a superior ◇ attached to the rec. form of SEE. In *Vol. IV ad loc.* it was indicated by *zero*.

Note 3—TO + an inf. also occurs at VIII.3.2 and occ. at III.3.2. For SEE, see VI.3.2, VIII.3.2 and IX.5.8.

7 Ch 1 ◇si:, °fə si:, °fə[4(2x)] 2 n.a., °fə‿t[2], °fə tə[3] 3 ◇sɛɪ‿ð dɒktə 4 tə 5 tə sɛɪ 6 tə

8 Db 1 ‿ʔ si:, °fə‿ʔ[1] III.1.12, °fə‿t[4], °fə‿ʔ[4] 2 tə 3 ‿ʔ si:, fə si: 4 ‿ʔ sɛɪ 5 tə si: 6 ‿ʔ sɛɪ 7 ◇sɛɪ, °◇~

11 Sa 1 tə 2 tə si: ðə dɒktə 3–4 tə 5 tə, tə s[ɪ]i: ðə dɒktə[ɾ] 6–11 tə

12 St 1 tə sɛɪ 2 ◇sɛɪ‿θ dɒktə, °fə[2,3] 3 sɛɪ‿θ dɒktə, °fə‿t[2] 4–5 tə 6 tə sɛɪ 7–8 tə si: 9 tə sɛɪ, °fə tə[1] 10 tə si: 11 tü:, tə

15 He 1 ◇si: ðə dɒktə[ɾ] 2 §tə ðə dɒktə[ɾ] 3 tə si: 4 §wɛnt tə vɪzɪt 5 tɷ 6 §wɛnt tü: dɒktə[ɾ] 7 tə si:

16 Wo 1–2 tɷ 3 ə si: [rec. in «ɒɩ wɛnt ə si: ðə dɒktəʳ *I went to see the doctor*] 4 tə si: ðə dɒktəʳ 5 tɷ sɩ ðə dɒktəʳ 6 tə sɩ ðə dɒktəʳ 7 n.a.

17 Wa 1 tə si: ðə dɒktə 2 n.a. 3–6 tə 7 ‿t si:

23 Mon 1 tə sᶦi: ðə dɒktəʳ 2 tə si: 3 tə si: dɒktə 4 tʰọ̈ 5–6 tə 7 n.a.

24 Gl 1 tə si:, §wɛnt tə ðə dɑ:ktəʳ 2 tə sᶦi:(2x) 3 tə 4 tə zɩi: ðə dɑ:ktəʳ 5 tə sɩ 6 tə 7 ə, ○ə si: [rec. in «a kəm ɩn ə si:» *I came in to see*]

25 O 1 ʔə 2 tə, ʔə 3 tə 4 tə si: ðə dɒktəɽ 5 ʔə 6 ‿t si:

IX.6.1 (I) HAVE†. (he) HAS†

Q. Have you got a match? Yes I . . . .

Convert for **he has.**

Rr. 1 pr.s.:—HAN, HAVE

3 pr.s.:—HAN, HAS, HAVE

Note 1—The rr. to the two parts of the q. are separated below by a full stop.

Note 2—In citing i.m. forms of the 3 pr.s., the gender of the subj. pron. has been ignored.

Note 3—For additional exs. of *1 pr.s.* anaphoric HAVE, see VIII.8.13.

7 Ch 1 av . av 2 n.a., ○av³ . n.a., ○az³ 3–6 av . az

8 Db 1 av . az 2 ɛv . ɛz 3–4 av . az 5 ɛv . ɛz 6–7 av . az

11 Sa 1–2 av . az 3 a·v . a·v 4 a:v . a:z 5 an . an 6 av . an 7 æn . æn 8 an . an 9 æv . æz 10 æn . æn 11 an . an

12 St 1–8 av . az 9 ɛv . ɛz 10 av . az 11 æv, ɑ̇: . æz ɑ̇:

15 He 1–6 æv . æv 7 av . az, av, ○~, ○æv¹

16 Wo 1 av . az 2 a·v . a·v 3 æv . æz 4 æv . æv, ○~² 5 æv . æv, ○~¹ 6 æ:v . æ:v, ○~² 7 av . n.a.

17 Wa 1 av . az 2 av . n.a. 3 av . az 4 av, ○~³ . az 5 av . az 6 æv . æz 7 av . av, ○~¹

23 Mon 1 æv . æv, ○~¹,³ 2 æv . æv 3 æv . æv, ○~¹ 4 av . av 5 av . ir.r. 6 æv . æv 7 n.a.

24 Gl 1 æ:v, ○æ:v¹, ○æz³ . æ:v, ○~³, ○æv³ 2 æv . æv, ○~³ 3 æ:v . æ:v 4 a:v . a:v 5 ɛv . ɛz 6 av . az 7 av . av

25 O 1 av . av, ○~¹, ○az¹ 2 av . av 3 a·v . a·v 4–6 av . av

IX.6.2 (he) HASN'T. (I) HAVEN'T†. (we) HAVEN'T†

Q. I have a match but he . . . .

Convert for **I haven't, we haven't.**

3 pr.s.:—HAINT~HANNA~HANT~HENT, HASNA~HASN'T, HAVEN'T

1 pr.s.:—HAINT~HANNA~HANT~HAVENA~HAVEN'T~HENT

1 pr.pl.:—HAINT~HANNA~HANT~HAVENA~HAVEN'T

Note 1—The rr. to the three parts of the q. are separated below by full stops. An attached superior × means that the form concerned occurs as the r. to all three parts of the q., and superior ◇ that the form concerned occurs as the r. to both the second and the third part.

Note 2—In citing i.m. forms of the 3 pr.s., the gender of the subj. pron. has been ignored.

Note 3—The r. at 12.11 and the 3 pr.s. form at 16.2 pres. represent HAINT.

Note 4—I.m. forms of HAVEN'T *interrog.* are reproduced below between square brackets untransliterated.

7 Ch 1 aznt . ◇avnt 2 n.a., ○ant[4] . ◇n.a. 3–4 ×anə 5 anə . anə, ○~[2] . anə 6 anə . anə . anə [anə[3]]

8 Db 1 aznə . ◇anə 2 ɛznt . ◇ɛvnt 3–4 aznə . avnə . anə 5 ɛznə, eːˈnt . ɛvnt . eːˈnt, ɛvnə 6–7 ×anə

11 Sa 1 anə . avnə . anə 2 ×anə 3 aznt . avnt . avnt [anə[2]] 4 aznt . ◇avnt 5 anə . anə [aːnt[1]] . anə 6 ×anə 7 ×ænə 8 anə . anə, eːnt . anə 9–10 ×ænə 11 ×anə

12 St 1 aznə . avnə . anə 2–4 ×anə 5 anə . anə, ○~[2] . anə 6 anə, ○~[1] [ant[1]] . ◇anə 7 anə [ɛɪnt[1,3]] . ◇anə 8 aznt . ◇avnt 9 ×anə 10 aznt . ◇avnt 11 ×æːt

15 He 1 ænə . ænə . ænə, ○aːnt[2] [+ V.] 2 ×ænə 3–4 ×aːnt 5–6 ×ævnt 7 aːnt, ○anə . ◇anə

16 Wo 1 ɛɪnt . ◇avnt 2 eː . aːnt . avnt 3 ×ɑːnt 4 ɑːnt, ævnt . ɑːnt, ○jænt[1] . ɑːnt 5 ×aːnt 6 ×æːnt 7 n.a.

17 Wa 1 aznt . ◇avnt 2 ɑːnt [ɛnt[4]] . ɛnt . n.a. 3 aznt . ◇avnt 4 ×aːnt 5 ×ɛɪnt 6 aznt, ɛɪnt . ɛɪnt . avnt, ○ɛɪnt 7 aznt . ◇avnt

23 Mon 1 ævnt [æn[1]] . ◇ævnt 2 ævnt [ævn[2]] . ævnt [~[1]] 3 ×ævnt 4 avnt . havnt . avnt 5 avntʰ . avntʰ, ○avnt[2] VIII.8.13 . ɛnt 6 æɪnt, ○~[1] . ◇ævnt 7 n.a.

24 Gl 1 ˣæ:nt 2 a:nt . a:nt, ○aʳ:ɳʈ^{3} . a:nt 3 æ:nt, ○ævnt^{1} . æ:nt, ○~ . æ:nt [æn^{1} (+ V.)] 4 ˣa:nt 5 ˣe:nt 6 a:nt . a:nt, ○~^{1} . a:nt 7 a:nt . a:nt, ○~^{1} . a:nt

25 O 1 aʳ:ɳʈ . aʳ:ɳʈ . aʳ:ɳʈ [a:n^{1} (+ V.)] 2 εɩnʔ . ◇εɩnʔ 3 avnt, a:nt ["older"] . ◇a:nt 4 aznt, s.f. avnt . ◇avnt 5 εᶦnʔ . ◇a:nʔ 6 a:nt . ◇a:nʔ

IX.6.3 (I) HAVEN'T†. (he) HASN'T

Q. I can't tell you what Smith's house is like, because so far I [*i. looking*] . . . . *seen it.*

Convert for **he hasn't.**

Rr. 1 pr.s.:—HA, HAINT, HAM NEVER, HAMT, HANNA, HANT, HAVENA, HAVEN'T, HAVE NEVER/NOT, NEVER (HAVE)

3 pr.s.:—HA, HAINT, HANNA, HANT, HASNA, HASN'T, HAS NEVER/NOT, HAVEN'T, NEVER

Note 1—The rr. to the two parts of the q. are separated below by a full stop.

Note 2—In the rr. below, an attached superior ◇ means that the form concerned occurs as the r. to both parts of the q.

Note 3—In citing i.m. of the 3 pr.s., the gender of the subj. pron. has been ignored. I.m. exs. of aux. HAVE in the negative other than 1 and 3 pr.ss. have been reproduced below between square brackets untransliterated; an attached superior ɑ denotes a 2 pr.s., superior × 1 pr.pl., superior + 2 pr.pl., and superior ǁ 3 pr.pl.

Note 4—The 2nd i.m. form at 15.3 pres. represents HANT.

Note 5—For additional exs. of the negative aux. HAVE, see IX.5.5.

7 Ch 1 avnt . aznt [⁺anə^{4}] 2 n.a., ○anə^{2,3} . n.a., ○aznt^{1}, ○εznt^{1} [ǁanə^{2}, ǁanɩ^{2}] 3 ◇anə 4 anə . anə, ○aznt^{2} [⁺anə^{2}] 5 nεvə, anə . anə, ○~$^{1(2x)}$ [ǁanə^{1}] 6 anə, ○~$^{2(2x),3}$. anə, ○~^{2}

8 Db 1 anə, ○~^{2} . anə, ○~ 2 avnt . εznt 3 ◇anə 4 anə . aznə [ᵅa:snə^{2} *interrog.*] 5 εvnə . εznə 6 anə, ○anəɹ [+ V.] . anə [ᵅastnə^{1}] 7 anə . ‿z nɩvə

11 Sa 1 ◇anə 2 anə, ○~^{2,3} . n.r., ○anə^{2} [ˣanə^{2}] 3 anə 4 avn . azn 5 anə . anə, ○~^{3} 6 anə, ○~^{1,3}, ○avnə^{3} . anə [⁺anə^{3}] 7 ◇ænə 8 anə, ○~^{2} . anə 9 ænə, ○~^{1} . ænə [ǁanə$^{1(2x)}$] 10 ◇ænə 11 anə . anə, ○ant^{2}

12 St 1 anə, °~^{4}, °amt^{1}. aznə, °~^{4} 2 anə. anə, °~$^{5(2x)}$ 3 anə, °~$^{1(2x),2}$. anə [×anə^{1}] 4 ◊anə 5 ◊anə [‖avnt^{2}] 6 anə, °~^{1}. anə, °~^{1} [+avnt^{1}] 7 ◊anə 8 avnt. aznt [+an^{1} *interrog.*] 9 anə, °~^{2}. anə [‖anə^{2}] 10 ‿v nɒt. ‿z nɒt 11 æ:, °a:m nɛvəɹ^{2} [+ V.]. æ:

15 He 1 ænə, °~^{1}. ænə, °~^{1} III.1.7 2 ænə, °~^{2}. ænə, °ævn^{1}, °ævnt^{2} [+ænə^{2}] 3 a:nt, °~^{3}, °a:n^{3}, °ænə^{1,2}, °aʳ:ɳʈ^{1}, °‿v nɛvəʳ$^{1(3x)}$. a:nt [+a:nt *interrog.*] 4 a:nt. a:nt, °~^{2}, °ɑ:nt^{1}, °ævnt [+a:nt *interrog.*] 5 ænt, °nɛvəʳʈ æv^{1}. ænt 6 ænt, °‿v nɛvəʳʈ^{1} [+ V.]. ænt, °ævnt^{1} 7 avn, ɑnə, °ɛnə^{1}, °avn$^{3(2x)}$, °anə$^{4(3x)}$, °ɛnt^{4}. anə, °ant^{4}, °eɪnt^{4}, °‿z nɛvəɹ^{3}, °‿z nɛvə^{3}, °nɛvəɹ^{3} [×ævn^{1}, ×anə^{4}]

16 Wo 1 avnt, °~^{2}, °e:nt^{1}, °nɛvəʳ. ɛɪnt, °e:n^{3} 2 anə, °a:nt^{2}. anə [a:nt^{2} *interrog.*; ‖anə^{2}] 3 ɑ:nt, °~^{4}, °ævnt^{3}. n.r. 4 ◊ɑ:nt 5 a:nt, °~^{1}, °ɑ:nt$^{1(2x)}$. a:nt 6 æ:nt, °ɑ:nt^{2}, °ɑ:n^{2}. æ:nt 7 avnt, ɑ:nt [pref.], °ɑ·nt$^{4(2x)}$, °avnt$^{3(2x)}$. ɑ:nt [◊ɑ:nt^{4}, +~^{1}]

17 Wa 1 avnt. aznt 2 ɛnt, °~^{4}. ɛnt, °~^{2}, °aznt^{1}, °‿s nɛvə^{2} [‖ɛnt^{4}] 3 nɛvə, ɛɪnt. aznt [ɛɪnt^{2} *interrog.*] 4 a:nt. a:nt, °ɛnt^{1} [+nɛvə^{2}; ‖ɛɪnt^{1}] 5 nɛvə, °aɪnt^{1}, °ɛnt$^{1(2x)}$. ‿z nɛvə, °ɛnt^{1}, °aɪnt^{1} [‖ɛnt^{1}] 6 ‿v nɛvə. ‿z nɛvə, °ɛnt, °aznt^{4} 7 avnt. aznt, °ɛznə^{1}

23 Mon 1 ænt, °~^{2}. ænt 2 ævn, °nɛvəʳ. ævn, °ævnt^{3} 3 ænt. ænt, °ævn^{2} 4 ◊avn 5 ant, °‿v nɛvə$^{2(2x)}$. avn, °~ [+avn^{2}; ‖~^{2}] 6 ævnt, °nɛvəʳ^{2}. ævnt, °~^{1} 7 n.a.

24 Gl 1 æ:nt, °aʳ:ɳʈ^{2}. æ:nt, °ævn^{1} [+a:nt^{1}] 2 a:nt. a:nt, °ævn^{2} 3 æ:nt. æ:nt, °~^{4} 4 a:nt, °aʳ:ɳʈ^{3}. a:nt 5 e:nt. e:nt, °jɛnt^{2} V.6.12 [×e:nt^{1,2}] 6 ‿v nɛvə, a:nt, °~^{1}. 7 nɛvə. a:nt

25 O 1 aʳ:ɳʈ, °~^{2,3}. aʳ:ɳʈ 2 ɛɪnʔ, °~. ɛɪnʔ [×ɛnʔ^{3}] 3 a:nt, °aʳ:ɳʈ^{1}. a:nt, °~^{1}, °ɛnt^{2} [‖ɛnt^{2}] 4 avn, °avnt^{4}. p. aznt, s.f. avnt, °‿z nɛvəʈ^{4} [×havn^{3}] 5 a:nʔ, °a:nt^{2}, °nɛvəʳʈ əv^{2}. anʔ$^{(2x)}$, °anə^{2} [+ant^{2} *interrog.*; ×e:nʔ^{2}] 6 a:nʔ, °a:nt^{2}. a:nʔ, °aʳ:ɳʔ^{3}

IX.6.4 (we) HAVE GOT‡

Q. You say to a friend: Shall I give you one of these pups? But he answers: No thanks, we . . . one.

Rr. GOT, HAN (GET{TEN}/GOT{TEN}), HAVE (GETTEN/GOT)

Note 1—When rec. in the rr., the subj. WE and the objs. ONE and SOME are reproduced below.

Note 2—I.m. exs. of pr.t. aux. HAVE other than 1 pr.pls. foll. by forms of GOT p.p. have been reproduced below between square brackets untransliterated. When rec., the subj. pron. is always reproduced below. The form [av] for 1 pr.s. pres. includes the pron. I. An attached superior ᴅ below indicates a 1 pr.s.; superior ɑ, 2 pr.s.; superior ×, 3 pr.s.; superior +, 2 pr.pl., and superior ‖, 3 pr.pl. Superior ◇ attached to a form ending in a voiced C. denotes that it is foll. by a word beginning with a V. The aux. HAVE was freq. n.r. before GOT p.p. and was in these cases evidently not used.

Note 3—Aux. HAVE occurs at III.1.7/11/12, III.4.6, VIII.8.6 and IX.5.5. Aux. HAVE foll. by GOT *p.p.* also occurs at VI.5.8 and VII.5.1/2. GOT *p.p.* also occurs at VII.8.8. For GET, see VI.2.2; and for ONE, see V.7.11 (and refs.) and VII.1.1 (and refs.).

7 Ch 1 wɪn gɛtn wɒn [ᴅav gɒtn^{4}; ×ɪz gɒt$^{4(2x)}$] 2 n.a., ○wɪn gɪtn^{2} [ᴅav gɛtn^{2}; ×ɪz gət^{2}; +jən gɛtn^{2}, +jəv gətn^{2}; ‖ðɛv gət^{3}] 3 wɪn gɛtn wɒn, ○wɪn gɛtn^{1} [×ɪz gɛtn$^{3(2x)}$] 4 wɪn gɒtn wɒn, ○~^{2} [ɑðɪz gɒt^{2}; +jo·v gɒtn^{1}; gɒt^{2}] 5 wɪn [ᴅav gɒt^{2}; ɑðɛɪs gɒt^{1}; +jə gɒtn] 6 an

8 Db 1 an wɒn [gɛtn^{1}] 2 wɪ ɛv wɒn, wɪ an wɒn, ○wɪn gɒt^{2} [gɒt^{3}] 3 an [ᴅa gɛtn^{1}; ×ɪz gɒt^{1}; +jən gɛtn^{1}] 4 wɪn gɛt wɒn [ᴅav gɛt^{3}] 5 ɛv, ○wɪv gɛtn wɒn [ᴅav gɒt^{2}] 6 wɛɪn gɒt [×əz (=*she's*) gɒt^{1}] 7 wɛɪn gɒt

11 Sa 1 wɪ gɒt wʌn 2 wɪ an wɒn, ○wi: an wɒn^{1}, ○wi:n gɒt^{2} [×ɪz gɒt; +ju:m gɒtn^{3}, +ju:n gɒt^{1}; ‖ðɪn gɒt^{1}; gɒt^{2,3}] 3 an [×əʳʐ gɒt^{2}] 4 wɪv gɒt 5 wɪn gɒt wɷn [×ɪi:z gɒt^{1}, ×əʳʐ gɒt^{1}] 6 wi:n gɒt [ᴅaɪ gɒt^{1}; gɒt^{3}] 7 wi: an wɒn [×ɪts gɒt^{1}; +ju:m gɒt^{1}, +jə gɒt^{1}, +ju: gɒt^{1}; ×‿ʐ gɒt^{1}; gɒt^{1}] 8 an [ᴅaɪv . . . . gɒt^{1}; gɒt^{2}] 9 æn wɒn [×i:z gɒt^{1}] 10 wi: æn wɒn [×i:z gɒt$^{2(2x)}$, ×ɪz gɒt^{2}, ×ɪts gɒt^{4}] 11 wɪ an wɒn [ᴅaɪ gɒt^{2}; gɒt^{2}; ×ɪz gɔ:t^{2}, ×əʳ:ʐ gɒt^{2}; +ju:m gɒt^{2} V.7.21; gɒt^{2}]

12 St 1 wɛɪn gɛt wɒn, ○wɛɪn gɒt^{3} [ᴅam gɒtn^{1}; ×ɪts gɒt^{3}; +jəv gɒt^{2}] 2 wɛɪn gɒt wɒn [gɒt^{2}] 3 wɛɪn gɒtn [×ɛɪz gɒt^{2}; +jəv gɒtn^{1}, +jəv gɒt^{2}, +ju:n gɒt^{2}; ‖ðɛɪn gɒt^{1}; gɒt^{1}; gɒtn$^{1(2x),2}$] 4 wi:n gɒt wɒn, ○wi: gɒt^{1} [×ɪ az gɒt^{1}; ‖ðɛɪn gɒt^{2}] 5 wɛɪ gɒt, ○wɛɪn gɒt^{1}, ○wɪn wɷn^{2}, ○wɪv gɒt, ○wɛɪv gɒt^{2} [ᴅav gɒt; ×ɛɪz . . . . gɒt^{2}, ×ə:z gɒt^{2}, ×‿z gɒt^{3}; +jəv gɒt^{2}; gɒt^{2}] 6 wɛɪn gɒt wɒn, ○wɪ gɒt^{2}, ○wɛɪ av gɒt$^{1(2x)}$ [ᴅɒ:z gɒt^{1,2}; ×ɛɪz gɒt$^{1,2(2x)}$, ×ɛɪ gɒt$^{1(2x),2}$; ×‿z gɒt$^{1(2x)}$; +jən gɒt$^{1(2x)}$, +jən gɒt$^{1(2x)}$, +ju: gɒt^{2}; gɒt$^{1(2x)}$] 7 wi:n gɒt sɷm [+joɷn gɒt^{3}] 8 wɪv gɒt wɒn [ᴅaɪm gɒt^{5}; ×ɪz gɒt$^{1(2x),6(2x)}$; gɒt$^{1(2x),2}$] 9 wɛɪn gɒt wɒn, ○wɛɪn gɒt$^{1,2(2x)}$, ○wi:n gɒt^{1} [ᴅɒɪv gɒt^{1}, ᴅɒɪn gɒt$^{1(2x)}$; ×i:z gɒt, ×ɪz gɒt, ×ɛɪz gɒt^{1}, ×əz (=*she's*) gɒt^{1,3}, ×ɪts gɒt^{1}; +ju:n gɒt$^{1,2(3x)}$, +jə gɒt^{1}; ‖ðɛɪn gɒt^{2}] 10 wɪv gɒʔ wɷn [+jəm gɒt^{5}, jɷm gɒɹ (+ V.)] 11 wi:n gɒt wɒn, ○wi:n gɒt^{1} [×ɪz gɒʔ^{2}; ‖‿z gɒʔ^{1}; gɒt^{2}]

15 He 1 wɩ gɒt wʌn, °wɩ gɒt^{2} 2 wɩ æv wʌn [^{d}ði:z gɒt^{2}; +ju: gɒt^{2} *interrog.*; gɒt^{2}] 3 wɩ gɒt wɑ:n [^{d}əɩ gɑ:t^{3}; ×əʵʐ gɒt^{2}] 4 wɩ gɒt wʌn [^{D}əɩ ə gɒt^{1}, ^{D}əɩ gɒt wɒn^{1}; ×ɩm gɒt$^{2(2x)}$; gɒt^{2}] 5 wɩ gɒt wɷn [×ɩm ə gɒt^{2}] 6 wɩ gɒt wɷn [× ‿z əv gɒt^{1}; +jəv gɒt^{1}] 7 wɩ gɒt wɒn, °wɩ gɒt$^{1(2x),3,4}$, °wi:v . . . . gɒt^{4} [^{D}aɩv gɒt^{3}; ^{D}aɩ gɒt$^{3(2x),4(2x)}$; ×i:z gɒt$^{4(2x)}$, ×ɩz gɒt^{3}; ×i: ə gɒt^{4}, ×ʃi: gɒt^{4}, ×ʃɩ gɒt^{4}, ×ɩts gɒt^{4}; +ju:v gɒt^{4}, +ju: gɒt$^{1,4(2x)}$; gɒt$^{1,4(5x)}$]

16 Wo 1 wɩv gɒt wɷn [^{D}ɒɩv gɒt^{3}; gɒt^{1}] 2 wɩv gɒt wɷn [‖ðɛm əz əz gɒt^{1} *them as has got* III.3.7; gɒt^{2}] 3 wɩ gɒt wɷn [^{D}ɒɩv gɒt^{3}, ^{D}ɒɩ gɒt^{1}; ×əʵʐ gɒt^{2}; ‖ðe:v gɒt^{2}, ‖ðe: gɒt^{2}; gɒtən^{4}] 4 wɩ gɒt wɷn [×ɩz gɒt^{2}, ×əʵ:ʐ gɒt^{3}; gɒt^{1}] 5 wɩ əv gɒt wɷn [^{D}ɒɩ gɒt^{1}, ^{D}ɒɩ gɒ^{1} (*sic*)] 6 wɩ gɒt wɷn [×əʵ gɒt^{2}] 7 ir.r., °wɩv gət^{1}, °wi:v gət^{1,2}, °wɩ gət$^{4(2x)}$ [^{D}əɩ gət$^{3(3x),4}$; ×i: gət^{4}, ×ʃi: gət^{4}, ×ə:z (=*she's*) . . . . gət^{1,4}, ×ə:v (= *she have*) gət^{4}, ×ɩts gət^{1}, ×ɩt ə ◇gəd^{4}, × ‿z gət^{1}, × ‿s gət^{4}, ×ə gət^{1}, ×əz gət^{1}, ×əv . . . . gət^{4}; +ju . . . . ə gət^{4}, +ju:v gət^{4}, +ju: gət^{2}; ‖ðɛɩv gət^{3}, ‖ðɛv gət^{4}; gət$^{1(3x),3}$]

17 Wa 1 wɩv gət [×i: az gɒt^{2}] 2 wɩ gɒt [^{D}əɩv gət^{4}, ^{D}əɩ gət$^{4(3x)}$ ^{D}əs gɒt; ×i: gət^{2}, ×ʃɩz gət^{4}, ×ə:z gət^{4}; +jəv gət^{1,3}, +ju: gət$^{4(2x)}$; +jəɷ gət^{4}; ‖ðɛv gət^{4}, ‖ðæɩ ə gət^{4}; ‖ðeɩ gət^{4}; gət$^{1(2x),2,4(3x)}$] 3 wɩv gɒt 4 wi: gɒt wɷn [^{D}əɩ gɒt^{1}; ×ɩz gɒt^{1}; gɒt^{1}] 5 wi: gɒt [^{D}av gɒt^{1}; ×ə gɒt^{1}, ×əz gɒt^{1}; +ju:v gɒt^{1}; gɒt$^{1(3x)}$] 6 wɩv gɒt wɷn [×əʵ:ʐ gɒt^{1}; gɒt$^{4(3x)}$, ~^{4} III.3.7] 7 wi: gɒt wɷn [^{D}əɩ gɒt^{1}]

23 Mon 1 wɩ gɒt wʌn [gɒt^{4}] 2 gɒt wɒn 3 wɩ gɒt wʌn 4 wɪ̞:v gɒ̞˂t wʌ̞̈n [‖ðe̞:ᶦv gɒt^{h}] 5 ‿v gɒ̞˂t^{h} wʌ̞̈n [+u:z (=*you has*) gɒ˂t^{2}] 6 æv wʌn [^{D}æm gɒt^{2}; ×i: gɒt^{1}, ×i: gɑ:t^{1}] 7 n.a.

24 Gl 1 wɩv gɑ:t wɷn [×i: æ:v gɒt^{1}; ‖ðæɩ gɒt^{1}] 2 gɑ:t wɷn [^{D}əɩ gɒt^{3}; gɑ:t^{2}] 3 gɒt wœ:n [×ɩm ə gɑ:t wœ:n^{4}; gɒt$^{1,4,3x)}$] 4 gɒt wɒn [gɒt^{3}] 5 wi ə gɒt wʌn 6 wɩ gɒt wən [gɒt^{1}] 7 wɩ gɒt wən

25 O 1 wi gɒt wɷ̨n [+jə gɒt^{1}] 2 wi: gɒʔ wən [×əʵ:ʐ gɒt^{1}; ◇gɒɹ^{3}] 3 wi: gɒt wən [gɒt$^{1(3x)}$] 4 wɩ gɒt wɒn, °wɩ gɒt^{1}, ◇wi: gɒd^{2} [^{D}əɩ gɒt$^{1(3x),3(2x)}$; ×i:z gɒt^{1}; ×ɩz gɒt$^{2(2x)}$, ×ɩ gɒt^{1}, ×ʃɩz gɒt^{1}; +ju: gɒt^{1,4}; ‖ðɛ gɒt^{3}; gɒt^{3,4}] 5 wi gɒʔ wʌn [gɒʔ^{2}] 6 wi: gɒʔ wən

IX.7.1 AM I†

Q. To find out whether you're right, you ask quite simply: . . . . right?

Rr. AM/ARE/BE~BIN/IS I, ir.r. AIN'T~AMMAD~ANNA/BAINT I

Note 1—At 25.2 the f.w. pres. omitted to rec. the pron.

Note 2—When rec. in the r., RIGHT is reproduced below. For additional exs., see VI.7.13 (and refs.).

7 Ch 1 am ɑɩ ɹɛɩt 2 n.a. 3 am a ɹɛɩt 4 am a ɹi:t 5 ir.r. anəɹ a rɛɩt 6 am aɩ, p. bɩn aɩ

8 Db 1 am a ɹi:t 2–4 am a ɹɛɩt 5–6 am a 7 am a ɹɛɩt

11 Sa 1–2 am aɩ 3 am a 4 bɩn aɩ 5 ir.r. aməd aɩ 6 bɩn aɩ 7 am aɩ 8–9 bɩn aɩ 10 bi: aɩ 11 bɩn aɩ

12 St 1 am a 2 am ə ɹɛɩt, °am ə 3 am a ɹɛɩt 4 am ɒɩ ɹɒɩt, °am ɒɩ 5 am ɒ:ɩ ɹɛɩt 6 am ɒ:ɩ 7 am ɒɩ ɹɒɩt, °~[1], °am ɒɩ 8 am aɩ ɹɒɩt 9 am ɩ ɹɛɩt 10 am a 11 bɩn a:

15 He 1 bi: æɩ 2 æm æɩ 3 bɩ əɩ ɹəɩt 4 bi: əɩ ɹəɩt 5–6 bɩ əɩ 7 am aɩ

16 Wo 1 am ɒɩ 2 bɩn əɩ 3 bi: ɒɩ 4 əm ɒɩ ɹəɩt, °ɑ:ɹ ɒɩ[3] 5 bɩ ɒɩ 6 bi: ɒɩ 7 s.w. bi: əɩ ɹəɩt

17 Wa 1 a:ɹ ɑɩ ɹɑɩt 2 am ɔɩ ɹɔɩt, °əm ɔɩ 3 am a 4 am ɔɩ 5 am ɔɩ ɹɔɩt, p. bɩ ɔɩ ɹɔɩt 6 am ɔɩ, s.w. bi: ɔɩ [rare] 7 am ɔɩ

23 Mon 1 ir.r. ɛnt əɩ 2 bi: əɩ ɹəɩt 3 bi: əɩ 4 bj‿əi 5 am əɩ̥ ɹəɩtʰ 6 æm ə 7 n.a.

24 Gl 1 bɩ əɩ, °bɛn əɩ[1] 2 bi: əɩ 3 bʽi: əɩ 4 bɩ əɩ ɹəɩt 5 bi: ə̈ɩ 6–7 bɩ ʌɩ ɹʌɩt

25 O 1 bi: ə̈ɩ 2 bi: 3 bi: ʌʏ 4 p. am əɩ ɽəɩt 5 bi: ʌʏ ɹʌʏʔ 6 bi: ə̈ɩ

IX.7.1a WRONG*

Q. Am I right or am I . . . . ? (Added November 1952)

R. WRONG

7 Ch 1 ɹɷŋg 2 n.a., °ɹɒŋ[1], °ɹɷŋ[4] 3 ɹɷŋg 4 ɹɒŋg, ɹaŋg [very old] 5–6 ɹɷŋg

8 Db 1 n.a. 2–3 ɹɒŋg 4 ɹɷŋg 5 ɹɒŋg 6–7 ɹɷŋg

11 Sa 1 ɹɒŋ 2 ɹɒŋg 3 ɹɒŋ 4 ɹɔ:ŋ 5 ɹɷŋg 6 n.a. 7–8 ɹɒŋ 9 ɹɔ:ŋ 10–11 ɹɒŋ

12 St 1 ɹɷŋ 2 ɹɷŋg 3 ɹɒŋg 4 ɹɒŋg, °~[2] 5 ɹɷŋg 6–7 ɹɒŋg 8 ɹɷŋg, °~[6], °ɹɒŋg[1] 9 ɹɒŋg 10 n.r. 11 n.r. [əɹɒŋg[2] *a-wrong* (=*wrongly*)]

15 He 1 ɹɒŋg̊ 2 ɹɒŋ 3 ɹɷ:ŋ 4 ɹʌŋ, °ɹɷŋ[1] 5–6 ɹɒŋ 7 n.a.

16 Wo 1–2 ɹɷŋg 3–6 ɹɷŋ 7 n.a., °ɹɷŋ[1]

17 Wa 1 ɹɒŋg 2 ɹɔŋ, ɹɷŋ 3–4 ɹɒŋ 5 ɹɷŋ 6–7 ɹɒŋ

23 Mon 1 ɹʌŋ 2 ɹɒŋ 3 ɹɑ:ŋ 4–5 n.a. 6 ɹɒŋ, °ɹɑ:ŋ[1] 7 n.a.

24 Gl 1 ɹɷ:ŋ, °ɹɒŋ[1] 2 ɹɷŋ, °~[3] 3 ɹɒŋ, °~ 4 ɹɒŋ 5 n.r. 6 ɹɒŋ 7 ɹɒŋ, °~[1]

25 O 1 ɹɒŋ 2 ɹɑŋ 3 ɹɒŋ 4 n.r. 5–6 ɹɒŋ

IX.7.2 ARE YOU† MARRIED? IS SHE†. ARE THEY†

Q. To find out whether I had a wife, you'd ask me: . . . .

If he uses *thou* ask him if he would say the same to a man older than himself. If he doesn't use *thou,* ask him if he ever does and to whom. Convert for **she is, are they.**

Rr. ARE THOU (WED)?, ARE THOU/YOU (MARRIED)?, §AREN YOU WED?, ART THOU MARRIED?, BEEST THOU (MARRIED/WED)?, BE YOU (MARRIED/WED)?, BIN YOU MARRIED?, §HAST THOU GOT A MISSIS?, IS THOU MARRIED?

BEEN HER, BE SHE, IS HE/HER/HOO/SHE

AM/ARE/ART THEY, ARE THEM §TWO, BE /§BOTH OF THEM/THEM/THEY (§TWO)/, BEEN THEM/THEY

Note 1—The rr. to the three parts of the q. are separated below by full stops.

Note 2—In the list of rr. above, THOU subsumes THEE and YOU subsumes YE. Furthermore, acc. to the view taken here, THOU has been freq. absorbed in the prec. ART/BEEST.

Note 3—When the i. stated that THOU/THEE was never used, the r. to the 1st part of the q. has an attached superior D. Other information relating to the use of THOU/THEE is given in square brackets after the r. to the 1st part of the q. or are represented by the foll. diacritics which are attached to the pronoun concerned:—superior ◇ = to an older person; superior ɑ = to anybody; superior × = to younger people; superior s = to one's social superior; superior E = to a social equal or to a friend, and superior F = to strangers.

Note 4—Though the f.ws. were not required by the q. to rec. MARRIED in the rr. to the 2nd and 3rd parts, they often did so. Accordingly, when all three forms are identical, a superior ★ is attached —as in the corresponding articles in *Vols. II* and *IV*, though not in *Vol. I*, where it means "THOU is used to close friends", thus corresponding to superior E in this article—to the form reproduced in the 1st r., the other two being omitted. At 8.2, 23.4 and 25.1/6 the f.w. omitted to rec. MARRIED in any of the rr.

Note 5—For additional exs. of MARRIED, see VIII.1.17 and IX.7.3; and of ARE YOU, see VII.8.18, VIII.2.8 and IX.9.4.

7 Ch 1 a ðə ★maɹɪd̥, ◇a jə. ɪz ʏ:. a ðɪ 2 n.a. 3 at ðɛɪ maɹɪd [*you* to strangers]. ɪz ëɷ. a: ði: 4 a jə maɹɪd, a jə, ɪz ðɪ maɹɪd [old], ɪz ðɪ, bɪn ◇jə maɹɪd, bɪn jə, ○~[2]. ɪz ᵚü[(2x)], bɪn ɔ:[(2x)] [older]. bɪn ðɛm[(2x)] 5 a jə ★maɹɪd. n.r. at ðɛɪ 6 ᴰbɪn jə maɹɪd. ɪz ʃɪ. bɪn ðɪ, bɪn ɷm [older]

8 Db 1 a±:t maɹɪd, ˢa±: jə maɹɪd. n.a. 2 a ðə, ˢa jə. ɪ ʃə, ɪz ᵚu [rare]. a ðɪ 3 ᵅa:t maɹɪd, ○ət[2]. ɪz ü:. a: ðɪ 4 at maɹɪd [*you* to older people, parson and schoolmaster]. ɪz ɔ. a ðɪ 5 a ða wɛd, ○a ðə[2,3]. ɪz ɛ:. a: ðe:[1] 6 §ast ðɛɪ gɒt ə mɪsɪs, a:t maɹɪd, ○ət[1]. ɪz ɔ:. a ðɪ 7 a:t maɹɪd, a: ˢjə. ɪz ɔ. a: ðɪ

11 Sa 1 bɪs ★maɹɪd. ɪz əʳ:. bɪn ðe: 2 ★an jə ★wɛd. ɪz əʳ:. am ðe: 3 ᴰbɪn ɪ ★maɹɪd. bɪn əʳ:. bɪn ðɪ 4 bɪn jə ★ma·ɹɪd. ɪz əʳ:. bɪn ðe: 5 ˣbɪs mɒɹɪd. ɪz əʳ:. bɪn ðe̹: 6 bɪn i: maɹɪd. ɪz əʳ:. bɪn ðɪ 7 bɪs ðɪ maɹɪd. ɪz əʳ. bɪ ðe: 8 bɪs ðɪ maɹɪd. ɪz əʳ. bɪn ðɪ 9 b‿jo: maɹɪd. ɪz əʳ. bɪ ðɛm 10 bɪs ðɪ ★mæɹɪd. ɪz əʳ:. bɪn ðe: 11 bɪs ðɪ maɹɪd. ɪz əʳ. bɪn ðɪ

12 St 1 ᴱɑ:t ★maɹɪd, ɑ: ju:. ɪz aɷ. ɑ: ðɪə 2 ᴱat ★maɹɪd. ɪz ɔ. a ðɪ 3 a:t ★maɹɪd. ɪz ɔ. a: ði: 4 ᴱa:t maɹɪd. ɪz ɔ:. a ðɛɪ 5 a: jə ★maɹɪd [*thou* used very rarely], ○ət[4]. ɪz ɔ. a: ðɪ 6 ᴰa: jə ★maɹɪd. ɪz ɔ:. a: ðɛɪ 7 a joɷ ★maɹɪd [*thou* rare]. ɪz ɔ. bɪ ðɛɪ 8 bi: joɷ maɹɪd. ɪz ɔ maɹɪd. bi: ðɛɪ 9 a:t ★maɹɪd. ɪz ɔ. a: ðɛɪ 10 ᴰa jə ★maɹɪd. ɪz ɔ:. a: ðɛm §tü: 11 bɪn joɷ ★maɹɪd. ɪz ɔ:ɹ. bɪn ðɛɪ

15 He 1 bɪ jə mæɹɪd [«ði:» used occ. to friends], ○bɪs ði:[1]. ɪz əʳ. bɪ ðe:ɪ 2 bɪs ᴱði: mæɹɪd. ɪz əʳ. bɪ ðæɪ 3 bɪ jə mæɹɪd. ɪz əʳ. bɪ ðæɪ 4 bi:s ᵅðɪ mɒɹɪd [obs.]. ɪz əʳ. bɪ ðæɪ 5 bɪs ði: mɒɹɪd. ɪz əʳ. bɪ ðæɪ 6 bɪs ði: mɒɹɪd, ○bɪs ðə[1]. ɪz əʳ. bɪ ðæɪ 7 ə ju: ★maɹɪd, ɑ·ɹ jə. ɪz ʃi:, s.w. ɪz ɔɹ [very rare]. ɔɹ ðeɪ

16 Wo 1 bɪ jə ★maɹɪd. ɪz ɪ [=*she*]. bɪ ðɪ 2 bɪs ðɪ ★maɹɪd, bɪn ◇jə. ɪz əʳ. bɪ ðɛm §tu: 3 bi: ju: mɒɹɪd. ɪz əʳ:. bɪ ðe:ɪ 4 bɪs ðɷ mɒɹɪd. ɪz əʳ. bɪ ðaɪ 5 bɪs ði: mɒɹɪd, ○bɪs ðɪ[1]. ɪz əʳ. bɪ ðaɪ 6 bɪ ju: ★wɛ:d, ○bɪs ðɪ[3]. ɪz əʳ. bɪ ðe:ɪ 7 bɪs ◇ði: ★maɹɪd. ɪz ɔ:, ɪz ɔ. s.w. bi: ðeɪ, bɪ §bɷθ ə ðɛm, ○bi: əm[4]

17 Wa 1 ᴰa: jə maɹɪd. ɪz ʃɪ. a: ðə 2 ɛ jə ★maɹɪd. s.w. ɪz ɔ:. ɑ: ðeɪ 3 ᴰa ju:. ɪz ʃɪ, ɪz ɔ: [rare]. a: ðɛɪ 4 ᴰaʳ: jə maɹɪd. ɪz əʳ:. a: ðɛɪ 5 ᴰbi: jə maɹɪd. ɪz əʳ:. bi: ðɛɪ 6 ᴰə ju: maɹɪd. ɪz ɔ:. a: ðɛɪ 7 ᴰaʳ: jə maɹɪd. ɪz əʳ:. bɪ ðɛɪ

23 Mon 1 bɩs ˣðɩi: mæɹɩd. ɩz əʵ. bɩ ðæɩ 2 bi: jə ★mæɹɩd. ɩz əʵ. bɩ ðɩ 3 ᴰa: jə mæɹɩd. ɩz ʃɩ. a: ðɩ 4 bi· ju·. bi· ʃi·. bi· ðei 5 ə ju· ★maɹi·d. ɩʃ ʃi:. ə ðei 6 a: jə mæɹɩd. ɩz ʃɩ. a: ðɩ 7 n.a.

24 Gl 1 bɩs ◇ði: mɒɹɩd. ɩz əʵ. bɩ ðæɩ, °bi: ɷm[1] 2 bɩs ði: mæɹɩd, °bɩ ᑫði:[3]. ɩz əʵ, °~[3]. bɩ ðæɩ 3 bɩs ᴱðəɷ mærɩd. ɩz əʵ:. bɩ ðæɩ, °bᶥi: ɷm[1] 4 bɩs ðɩ mɒɹɩd [*thee* rare now]. ɩz əʵ. bɩ ðaɩ, °bᶥi: ɷm[3] 5 bɩst maɹɩd, a: ꟳju:. ɩz əʵ:. bɩ ðæɩ(2x) 6 bɩst ᴱðɩ maɹɩd. ɩz əʵ:. bɩ ðæɩ 7 bɩst ★maɹɩd. ɩz əʵ:. bɩ ðɛ̢ɩ §tu:

25 O 1 bɩst ðɩ, aʵ: jə. °bɩst ðə[2]. bɩ ʃɩ. bɩ ðeɩ 2 bɩst ðə wɛd, æ̝: jə. ɩ ʃi:. æ̝: ðɛɩ 3 ᴰbi: ju: maɹɩd. ɩz ʃi:. bi: ðe: 4 ə ju: ★maɽɩd. ɩz ʃi:, s.w. ɩz əɽ. əɽ ðe: 5 a:ɽ jə maɽɩd. ɩ ʃə, ɩz ʃi:. bɩ ðe:, bi: ðɩ, °bi: əm[3] 6 bi: jü:. n.r.

IX.7.3 AREN'T YOU†. ISN'T SHE† AREN'T THEY†

Q. If you saw me wheeling a pram and then gathered from our conversation that I was not married, you might ask me in some surprise: But . . . . married?

Convert for **isn't she, aren't they.**

Rr. AIN'T~AMMA~EN'T/BAIN'T~BEN'T/ISN'T YOU, /ANNA~AREN'T/BINNA~BYUN'T/ THOU~YOU, ARTEN THOU, BEESN'T (THOU), ? ir.r. YOU AIN'T MARRIED

AIN'T~EN'T~YEN'T, YAN'T/YUN'T/AREN'T/BEN'T~BINNA~BYUN'T/INNA(D)~IN'T~ISNA~ISN'T SHE, §SHE'S NOT

AIN'T THEY §TWO, AIN'T~AMMA~EN'T~YAN'T~YEN'T~YUN'T/ANNA~AREN'T~ARTNA/BAIN'T~BEN'T~BINNA~BIN'T~BYUN'T/ THEY, BYEN'T THEY (§TWO)

Note 1—The rr. to the three parts of the q. are separated below by full stops.

Note 2—In the lists of rr. above, THOU subsumes THEE, YOU subsumes YE, SHE subsumes HE/HER/HOO and THEY subsumes THEM.

Note 3—When rec. in the rr., MARRIED/WED is reproduced below. When the same form was rec. in the rr. to all three parts of the q., superior ★ is attached to the form rec. in the r. to the 1st part.

7 Ch 1 anə ðə. ɩznt ʏ:. a:nt ðɩ 2 n.a. 3 a:tnə. ɩnəɹ ëɷ. anə ði: 4 anə ðɩ. ɩzn ᵒu:. bɩnə ðɩ 5 atn ðə. ɩnəɹ ə. ɩnəɹ əm 6 bɩnə jə. ɩnə ʃɩ. bɩnə ðɩ, °~

8 Db 1 a±:tʔ͜nə . ιnˀ ʃι, ιnt ʏ: . a±:nt ðι 2 anə jə wɛd, ιznt jə . n.r. anə ðι 3 a:tnə . ιznəɹ ü: . anə ðι 4 a:tn ðə . ιznəɹ ə: . a:tnə ði: 5 ɛn jə . ιnt ʃι . anə ðι 6 anə jə [more polite], a:tnə . ιnəɹ ə: . anə ðι: 7 a:tnə . ιnəɹ ə . a:nt ði:

11 Sa 1 anə jə . ιnəɹ əʵ: . bιnə ðι 2 amə jə ⋆wɛd . ιznt əʵ: . amə ðe: 3 anə jə . ιnəʵɽ əʵ . bιnəʵ ðι 4 bιnə jə . ιnə əʵ: . bιnə ðι 5 bιsnt ðι . ιnəʳɖ əɽ . bιnə ðe̜: 6 bιnι ðι . bιnəɹ əʵ· . bιnə ðe· 7 bιnə jə . ιnəɹ əʵ . bιnə ðι 8 bιnə ði: . ιnəɹ əʵ . bιnə ðι 9 bιnə jə . ιnəɹ əʵ . bιnə ðι: 10 bιnə jə . ιnəɹ əʵ: . bιnə ðι 11 bιnə jə . ιnəɹ əʵ . bιnə ðe·

12 St 1 ɑ:tnə maɹιd . §aɷz nɒn . ɑ:tnə ðɛι 2 atnə maɹιd . ιnt ə . anə ði: 3 a:nt ðɛι . ιnt ə . a:nt ði: 4 atnə maɹιd . ιnt ə: . anə ðɛι 5 anə jə maɹιd . ιnəɹ ə . anə ðɛι 6 ant ʃə, anə ju: maɹιd . ιnəɹ ə . anə ðι 7 ɛιnt joɷ . ɛιnt ə: . a:nt ðɛι 8 ɑ:nt jə . ɛιnt ə . bɛιnt ðɛι 9 a:nt ðι ⋆maɹιd . ιnt ə . ιnə ðɛι 10 a:nt jə . ɛιnt ə: maɹιd . ɛιnt ðɛm §tü: 11 ir.r. joɷ ɛ:ι maɹιd . ɛ:ι ə: maɹιd . ɛ:ι ðɛ:ι

15 He 1 e:ιnt jə mæɹιd . e:ιnt əʵ . e:ιnt ðe:ι 2 bιsnt ði: mæɹιd . ιnəɹ əʵ . bjɷnt ðæι 3 bjɷnt jə . ɛnt əʵ . bjɷnt ðæι 4 bjʌnt ðι . ɛnt əʵ . ɛnt ðæι 5 bιsnt ði: mɒɹιd . bɛnt əʵ . jɷnt əm 6 bιsnt ðι . jɷnt əʵ . jɷnt ðæι 7 ɑɹnt ju: . ιzn̥t ʃi: . ɑɹnt ðeι

16 Wo 1 bɛιnt jə ⋆maɹιd . ɛιnt ι [=*she*] . ɛιnt ðι 2 bιsnt ði: ⋆maɹιd . ιnəɹ əʳ . bιnə ðι 3 bjɷnt jə . bjɷnt əʵ . bjɷnt ðι 4 bιsn ðι mɒɹιd . ιzn əʵ . bɛnt ðaι 5 bιsn ðι mɒɹιd . jɷnt əʵ . jɷnt ðaι 6 bɛntʃ jə ⋆wɛ:d . ɛnt əʵ . ɛ:nt ðe:ι 7 bιsnt ði: ⋆maɹιd, ○~[4] . jant ə: . s.w. jant ðe̜ι

17 Wa 1 a:nt jə . ιznt ʃι . a:nt ðι 2 ɛnt jə . ɛnt ʃi: . ɛnt ðeι, ○~[4] 3 ɛιnt jə . ιznt ʃι . e̜ιnt ðe̜ι 4 a:nt jə . a:nt əʵ: . a:nt ðe̜ι 5 ɛnt ju: . ɛnt əʵ: . ɛnt ðɛι 6 ɛιnt jə maɹιd . ɛιnt əʵ: . ɛιnt ðɛι 7 aʵ:ɳʈ jə . ιznt əʵ: . jɛnt ɷm

23 Mon 1 bιsnt ðι . ɛnt əʵ . bɛnt ðæι 2–3 ɛnt jə . ɛnt ʃι . ɛnt ðι 4 ɛnt ju· spləist [=*spliced*, i.e. married] . ɛnt˳ ʃi: . ɛnt˔ ðei 5 ɛnt ju· ⋆maɹi·d . ιzn ʃi· . ɛnt˳ ðei 6 a:nt jə . e:nt ʃι . e:nt ðι 7 n.a.

24 Gl 1 bjɷsnt ði: . bjɷnt əʵ . bjɷnt ðæι 2 bιsnt ðι . jɷnt əʵ . bjɷnt ɷm 3 bιsn ðʿi: . jɷnt əʵ: . bjɷnt ðæι 4 bιsnt ðι . ɛnt əʵ . bjɷnt ðι 5 bιsnt maɹιd, ○bιsnt ðι maɹιd[2] . ιznt əʵ: . bjɛnt ðæι §tu: maɹιd 6 bιsnt ði: maɹιd . jɛnt əʵ: . bjɛnʔ ðæι 7 bιsnt ði: maɹιd . jənt ʃi: . bιnt ðe̜ι

25 O 1 bɛnt jə. bɛnt ʃɩ. bɛnt ðɩ 2 ɛnt jə wɛd. ɛnt ʃɩ. ɛnt ðɩ 3 bɛnt i: maɽɩd. n.r. 4 aɽɳʈ ju: maɽɩd. ɛnt ʃi: maɽɩd. bɛnt ðeɩ mäɽɩd 5 ɛnt jə, °~. ɛnt ʃɩ. n.r. 6 bɛnt jə. bɛnt ʃɩ. bɛnʔ ðeɩ

IX.7.4 AREN'T I†

Q. Of a man who has just won a thousand pounds, you would say: Isn't he lucky? And if it was you, you'd say of yourself: .... lucky?

Rr. AIN'T~AMMAD~AM(N)T~EN'T~IN'T~YENT~YUNT/ANNA~AREN'T/BAIN'T~BEN'T~BYEN'T~BYUN'T I, §BE I

Note—At 12.9 the f.w. omitted to rec. a pron.

7 Ch 1 a:nt a 2 n.a. 3 anəɹ ɑɩ 4 anəɹ aɩ 5 anəɹ a 6 bɩnə aɩ

8 Db 1 amt a 2 a:nt a 3 amt aɩ 4 amənt a: 5 anəɹ a, e:ˈnt a 6 amt a: 7 a:nt a

11 Sa 1 bɩnəɹ ə 2 amt aɩ 3 bɩnə aɩ 4 a:ɹnt aɩ 5–7 aməd aɩ 8 e:nt aɩ 9 bɩnəɹ‿aɩ 10 æmᵊd aɩ 11 bɩnəɹ aɩ

12 St 1 ɩnt ɒɩ 2 ant ɒɩ 3 a:nt ɒ:ɩ 4 anə ɒɩ 5 a:nt ɒ:ɩ 6 ant ɒ:ɩ 7 ɛɩnt ɒɩ 8 bɛɩnt aɩ 9 ɛɩnt 10 a:nt a:ɩ 11 §bɛɩ a̱:ɩ

15 He 1 e:ɩnt æɩ 2 be:ɩnt æɩ 3 ɛnt əɩ 4 bjʌnt əɩ 5 jɛnt əɩ 6 jɷnt əɩ 7 ɑɹnt aɩ, eɩnt aɩ

16 Wo 1 ɛɩnt ɒɩ 2 e:nt ɒɩ 3 jɷnt ɒɩ 4 bjɷnt ɒɩ 5 jɷnt ɒɩ 6 ɛnt ɒɩ 7 bjɛnt jə

17 Wa 1 a:nt ɑɩ 2 n.a. 3 a:nt əɩ 4 aʳɳʈ əɩ 5 ɛnt əɩ 6 ɛɩnt əɩ 7 jɷnt əɩ

23 Mon 1–3 ɛnt əɩ 4 ɛn əi 5 ɛntʰ əɩ̥ 6 a:nt əɩ 7 n.a.

24 Gl 1 ɛnt əɩ 2 jɷnt əɩ, °bjɷnt əɩ³ 3–4 bjɷnt əɩ 5 bjɛnt ə̈ɩ 6 bjɛnt ʌɩ 7 bɩn ʌɩ

25 O 1–2 bɛnt ə̈ɩ 3 bɛnt ᴀʏ 4 ent əɩ 5 bɛnʔ ᴀʏ 6 ɛnʔ ə̈ɩ

IX.7.5 ISN'T HE†? AREN'T I†? AREN'T YOU† (*2nd sg.*)? AREN'T THEY†?

Q. You can say: We're all right here, aren't we? Now, speaking of that man over there, you can say: He's all right there, ...

Convert for **aren't I,** (2nd sg.) **aren't you, aren't they.**

Rr. AI(N'T)~EN'T~YAN'T~YUN'T/BEN'T/INNA(T)~IN'T~ISN'T HE

AIN'T~AMMAD~AM'T~EN'T~YUN'T/ANNA~AREN'T/BAI(N'T)~BEN'T~BINNA~BYEN'T~BYUN'T/INNA I, ir.r. AREN'T WE

AIN'T~AMMAD~EN'T~YEN'T/ANNA~AREN'T/BAIN'T~BEN'T~BINNA~BIN'T~BYUN'T YOU, AIN'T~YUN'T/AREN'T/BEN'T~BINNA/BEESNA/INNA THOU, ARTNA, BEESNA~BEESN'T

AIN'T~EN'T~YEN'T~YUN'T/ANNA~ARNA~AREN'T/BAIN'T~BEN('T)~BIN('T)~BINNA~BYEN('T)~BYUN'T/INNA~ISN'T THEY

Note 1—The rr. to the four parts of the q. are separated below by full stops.

Note 2—At 24.4 (1st r.), the f.w. omitted to rec. HE.

Note 3—In the lists of rr. above, THEY subsumes THEM, THOU subsumes THEE, and YOU subsumes YE. ARTNA prob. represents ART THOU NOT. Similarly, BEESNA and BEESN'T both seem to represent BEEST THOU NOT. If so, the foll. THOU at 15.2/5 and 16.3/5 is redundant.

Note 4—The 3rd r. at 8.4 is obscure, but the v. may be a phonetic reduction of AREN'T.

7 Ch 1 ɪzn ɪ. a:nt a. a:nt ðə. anə ðɪ 2 n.a. 3 ɪnt ɪ. amt ɪ. a:tnə. anə ðɪ 4 ɪzn ɪ, ɪnəɹ ɪ. anəɹ aɪ. bɪnə ðɪ. bɪn ðɪ, ○ɪzn ɷm[2] 5 ɪnt ɪ. a:nt ɑɪ. atnə. anə ðɪ 6 ɪnəɹ ɪ. bɪnə aɪ. bɪnə jə. bɪnəɹ ɷm

8 Db 1 ɪnt ɪ. amt a. aʳ:ʈɳə. aʳ:ɳə ðɪ 2 ɪnt ɪ. a:mt a. a:nt ðə. a:nt ðə 3 ɪnəɹ ɪ. a:nt a. a:tnə. anə ðɪ 4 ɪznt ɪ. amt ɪ. a:t ðɪ. a:nt ðɪ 5 ɪnt ɪ[2], e:ˈnt ɪ[3]. e:ˈnt a[2], anəɹ a[3]. a:nt ðə[2,3]. e:ˈnt ðɪ[2], anə ðɪ[3] 6 ɪnt ɪ. amt a. a:tnə. a:nt ðɪ 7 ɪnt ɪ. a:nt a. a:tnə. a:nt ðə

11 Sa 1 ɪnəɹ ɪ. anəɹ aɪ. anə jə. anə ðɪ 2 ɛnt ɪ. a:nt aɪ. a:nt jə. a:nt ðɪ, ○amə ðɪ[2] 3 ɪnəʳɽ ɪ. anəʳɽ aɪ. bɪnə jə. bɪnəʳ ðə 4 ɪzn ɪ. ir.r. aʳ:ɳʈ wɪ. aʳ:ɳʈ jə. aʳ:ɳʈ ðɪ 5 ɪnəɹ ɪ. bɪnəɹ aɪ. bɪsnə. bɪnə ðɪ 6 ɪnəd ɪ. aməd aɪ. amə jə. amə ðɪ 7 ɪnəɹ ɪ. aməd aɪ. anə jə. bɪnə ðɪ 8 ɪnəɹ ɪ. ɪnəɹ ɒɪ. ɪnə ðɪ. ɪnə ðɪ 9 ɪnət ə. bɪnəɹ aɪ. bɪnə ðɪ. bɪnə ðɪ, ○bɪnɪ ðɪ[1] 10 ɪnəɹ i:. æməd aɪ. bɪnə jə. bɪnə ðɪ 11 ɪnəɹ ɪ. bɪnəɹ aɪ. bɪnə ði:. bɪnə ðɪ

12 St 1 ɪnt ɪ. amt ɪ. ɑ:nt ðə. ɑ:nt ðə 2 ɪnt ɪ. ant ə. atnə. ant ðɪ 3 ɪnt ɪ. a:nt ɪ. a:nt ðə. a:nt ðɪ 4 ɪnəɹ ɪ. anəɹ a. ant ʃə. ant ðɪ 5 ɪznt i:, ɪnəɹ i: [old]. anəɹ ɒ:ɪ. a:nt jə. anə ðɪ 6

ɪznt ɪ. ant ɒːɪ. aːnt jə. aːnt ðɪ 7 ɛɪnt ɪ. ɛɪnt ɒɪ. ɛɪnt jə. ɛɪnt ðɛɪ 8 ɛɪnt ɪ. ɛɪnt ɒɪ. ɛɪnt jə. bɛɪnt ðɛɪ 9 ɛɪnt ɪ. aːnt ɒɪ. aːnt ðə. ɛɪnt ðɪ, °ant ðɪ[1] 10 ɛɪnt ɪ. ɛɪnt aɪ. ɛɪnt jə. ɛɪnt ðɛɪ 11 ɛːɪ ɪ. bɛːɪ a̱ːɪ. bɛːɪ jə. bɛːɪ ɷm

15 He 1 ɛnt ɪ. ɛnt æɪ. bɪnt jə. ɛnt ðɪ 2 ɛnt iː. ɛnt æɪ. bɪsnt ə. bɛnt ðæɪ 3 ɛnt ɪ. ɛnt əɪ. ɛnt jəʳ. ɛnt ɷm, °ɛn ɷm[1] 4 ɛnt ɪ. ɛnt əɪ. bjʌntʃ jə. ɛnt əm 5 ɛnt ɪ. ɛnt əɪ. bɪsnt ðɪ. jɷnt əm, °bɛnt ɷm[1,2], °bɛn əm[4], °bɪn ɷm[2], °ɛn ɷm[4] 6 jɷnt ɪ. jɷnt əɪ. jɷnt ðə. jɷnt əm, °bɛn ɷm[1] 7 ɛnt ɪ. ɛnt aɪ. ɛnt jə. ɑɹnt ðeɪ

16 Wo 1 ɛɪnt ɪ. ɛɪnt ɒɪ. ɛɪnt jə. ɛɪnt ðɪ 2 eːnt iː. eːnt ɒɪ. beːnt jə. aʳːɳʈ ðɪ, eːnt ðɪ ["older"] 3 jɷnt ɪ, °jɛn iː[4]. jɷnt ɒɪ. bɪsnt ðɷ. jɷnt ɷm, °eːˈnt ðiː[3] 4 ɛnt ɪ. ɛnt əɪ. ɛnt ðɪ. ɛnt ɷm 5 jɷnt ɪ. jɷnt ɒɪ. bɪsn ðiː. jɷnt ðaɪ, °bjɷn ɷm[1(2x)] 6 jɷnt ɪ. jɷn ɒɪ. bɪsnt ðɪ. bɛnt ɷm, °bjɛn ɷm[3], °ɛnt ðeːɪ[1] 7 jant ə. bjɛnt əɪ. bjɛnt jə. jant əm, °an ə[4]

17 Wa 1 ɪznt ɪ. aːnt a. aːnt jə. aːnt ðɛ̣ɪ 2 ɛnt ɪ. ɛnt əɪ. ɛnt jə. ɛnt ðeɪ 3 ɪznt ɪ. ɛɪnt əɪ. ɛɪnt jə. ɛɪnt ðɛɪ 4 ɪznt ɪ. aːnt əɪ. aːnt jə. aːnt ðɛɪ 5 ɛnt iː. ɛnt əɪ. ɛnt jə. ɛnt ðɛɪ 6 ɛɪnt iː. ɛɪnt əɪ. ɛɪnt jə. ɛɪnt ðɛɪ 7 jɷnt ɪ. ɛnt əɪ. jɛnt jə. ɛnt ðɛɪ

23 Mon 1 ɛnt ɪ. ɛnt əɪ. bɪsn ðɪ. bɛnt ðɪ 2 ɛnt ɪ. ɛnt əɪ. ɛnt jə. ɛnt ðɪ 3 ɛnt ɪ, °ɛn ɪ[1]. ɛnt ə. ɛnt jə. ɛnt ðɪ, °ɛn əm[1] 4 ɛnt i·. ɛnt əi. ɛnt ju·. ɛn ðei 5 ɛntʰ iː. aːntʰ əɪ. aːnt˳ juː. aːnt˳ ðei 6 ɛnt ɪ. ɛnt əɪ. ɛnt jə. ɛnt ðɪ 7 n.a.

24 Gl 1 ɛnt ɪ, °jɛn ɪ[2], °ɛn ɪ[3]. ɛnt əɪ. bɪsnt. ɛnt ɷːm, °ɛn ɷm[3], °bɛn ɷm[3], °bɛnt ɷm[3(3x)] 2 jɷnt ɪ. jɷnt əɪ. bɪsnt ðɪ. bjɷnt ɷm 3 jɷn ə. bjɷn əɪ. bɪsn. bjɷn ɷm 4 jɷnt. bjɷnt əɪ. bɪsnt. bjɷnt ɷm, °aːnt ɷm[2] 5 jɛn ɷ [*sic*]. bjɛn ɪ. bɪsnt. bjɛn ɷm, °jɛn əm[2] 6 jɛn ə. bjɛnt ʌɪ. bɪsnt. bjɛn əm 7 jən ə. bjən ʌɪ. bɪsnt. bjən əm, °bɪn əm[1]

25 O 1 bɛnt ɪ. bjɛn ə̈ɪ. bɪsnt. bjɛn əm 2 bɛnt ə. bɛnt ə̈ɪ. ɛnʔ jə. bɛnt ɷm 3 ɛnt iː. bɛnt ʌʏ. bɛnt iː. bɛnt əm 4 ɛnt ɪ. ɛnt əɪ. ɛnt jə. a·ɽɳʈ ðeɪ, °ɛnt ðeɪ[1] 5 ɛnʔ ɪ. bɛnʔ ʌʏ. bɛnt jɪ. bɛn əm 6 bɛnʔ iː. bɛnt ə̈ɪ. ɛnʔ juː. ɛnʔ ðɪ

IX.7.6 WASN'T I†? WEREN'T YOU†? WASN'T SHE†? WEREN'T THEY†?

Q. We could say: We were late, weren't we? You could say of yourself: I was late . . . . ?

Convert for (2nd sq.) **weren't you, wasn't she, weren't they.**

Rr. WADN~WASN'T/WEREDN'T/WERENA(D)/WEREN'T I,

WASNA~WASNTST~WASTNA/WASN'T/WERENA/WEREN'T THOU, WASN'T/WEREDN'T/WERENA/WEREN'T YOU, WERESNA

WASN'T/WEREDN'T~WERENA~WEREN'T SHE, WASNA~WASN'T/WEREDN'T~WERENA~WEREN'T THEY

Note 1—The rr. to the four parts of the q. are separated below by full stops.

Note 2—The equivalent q. in Version 4 of the Qr., which was asked at 16.7 and 17.2, was similar in substance to the above, except that WASN'T HE was required instead of WASN'T SHE. The r. concerned has been reproduced below.

Note 3—The rr. at 12.11 have been regarded as forms of resp. WEREN'T I, WEREN'T HER and WEREN'T THEM.

Note 4—In the lists above, SHE, THEY, THOU and YOU subsume resp. HOO/HER, THEM, THEE and YE.

7 Ch 1 wɒzn ə. wωzn ðɩ. wωzn ʏ:. wə:n^{ʔ} ðɩ 2 n.a. 3 wɒnəɹ ɩ. wɒnt ɩ. wɒnt ə. wɒsnə 4 wɒnə aɩ, °wɒnəɹ aɩ[2]. wɒnə ðə. wɒnəɹ ^{ω}ü:. wɒnə ðɩ 5 wɒnt a. wɒsn ə. wɒnəɹ ə. wɒnə ðɩ 6 wɒnəɹ aɩ. wɒnə jə. wɒnə ə:. wɒnə ðɩ, wɒnəɹ ωm

8 Db 1 wə^{ɫ}:nt a. wə^{ɫ}:tnə. wə^{ɫ}:nt ʏ:. wə^{ɫ}:nə ðə 2 wə:nt a. wə:nt ðə. wə:nt ʃɩ. wə:nt ðɩ 3 wɒnəɹ ɩ. wəsnə. wə:nt ə. wə:nt ðə 4 wə:nt a:. wɒsnə. wə:nt ə. wə:nt ðɩ 5 wɒnəɹ a, wə:nt a. wə:nt ða. wɒnəɹ ə. wɒnə ðɩ 6 wənt a. wɒstnə. wɒnt ə. wɒnt ðɩ 7 wə:nəɹ a. wə:nə ðə. wə:nt ə. wə:nt ðə

11 Sa 1 wɒnəɹ ə. wɒnə jə. wɒnəɹ ə^{ɽ}. wɒnə ðɩ 2 wɒnə aɩ. wɒnə jə. wɒnə ə^{ɽ}:. wɒnə ðɩ 3 wɒznt a. wɒznt jə. wɒznt ʃɩ. wɒznt ðɩ 4 wɒznt aɩ. wə^{ɽ}:ɳʈ jə. wɒznt ʃɩ. wə^{ɽ}:ɳʈ ðɩ 5 wɒnəɹ aɩ. wɒsnə. wɒnəɹ ə^{ɽ}. wɒnə ðɩ 6 wɒnəd aɩ. wɒnə jə. wɒnəɹ ə^{ɽ}:. wɒnə ðɩ 7 wɒnəɹ aɩ. wɒnə jə. wɒnəɹ ə^{ɽ}. wɒnə ðɩ 8 wɒnt ɒɩ. wɒnə ðɩ. wɒnəɹ ə^{ɽ}. wɒnə ðɩ 9 wɒnəɹ ə. wɒnə jə. wɒnə^{ɽ}ʈ ə^{ɽ}. wɒnə ðɩ· 10 wɒnəɹ aɩ. wɒnə jə. wɒnəɹ ə^{ɽ}. wɒnə ðɩ 11 wɒnəɹ aɩ. wɒnə ði:. wɒnəɹ ə^{ɽ}. wɒnə ðɩ

12 St 1 wɔːnt a . wɔːsnə . wɔːnt ə . wɔːnt ðə 2 wɒnt ə . wɒnt ðɪ . wɒnt ə . wɒnt ðɪ 3 wɔːnt a . wɔːsnə . wɔːnt ə . wɔːnt ðə 4 wɒnt ɒɪ . wɒnt jə . wɒnt ə . wɒnt ðɪ 5 wɒnt ɒɪ[3], wɒznt ɒːɪ[1] . wɔːnt jə . wɒznt ə . wɔːnt ðɛɪ 6 wɒznt ɒːɪ, wɒnt ɒːɪ [older] . wɒnt jə . wɒnt ə . wɒnə ðɪ 7 wɒnt ɒɪ . wɒːnt jə . wɒnəɹ ə . wɔːnt ðɛɪ 8 wɔːnt ɒɪ . wɔːnt joʊ . wɔːnt əː . wɔːnt ðɛɪ 9 wɒnt a . wɒnt ða . wɒnt ə . wɒnt ðɛɪ 10 wɔːnt aɪ . wɔːnt jüː . wɔːnt əː . wɒznt ðɛɪ 11 wɔːt a̱ːɪ . n.r. wɔːt əːɹ . wɔːɹ ʊm

15 He 1 wɔːnt æɪ . wɔːnt jə . wɔːnt ə . wɔːnt ðɪ 2 wɔːnt æɪ . wɔːnt ðɪ . wɔːnt əʳ . wɔːnt ðæɪ 3 wɑːnt əɪ . wəznt jə . wəznt əʳ . wɑːnt ʊm 4 wɒnt əɪ . wɒzntʃ jə . wɒznt əʳ . wɒznt əm 5 wɑːnt əɪ . wɒznt ðɪ . wɑːnt əʳ . wɑːnt əm 6 wəznt əɪ . wəsnt . wəznt əʳ . wəznt ðæɪ 7 wɒznt aɪ . wəɹnt juː, °wɒznt juː[4] . wɒznt ʃɪ, wɒnt əɹ(2x) . wəɹnt ðeɪ

16 Wo 1 wɑːnt ɒɪ . wɑːnt jə . wɑːnt ə . wɑːnt ðɪ 2 wɑːnt ɒɪ . wɑːnt ðɪ . wɑːnt ʃɪ . wɑːnt ðɪ 3 wɑːnt ɒɪ . wɒznst . wɑːnt əʳ . wɑːnt ðɪ 4 wɑːnt əɪ . wɑːnt ðɪ . wɑːnt əʳ . wɑːnt ðɪ 5 wɑːnt ɒɪ . wɑːnt ðɪ . wɑːnt əʳ . wɑːnt ðaɪ 6 wɑːnt ɒɪ . wɒznst . wɑːnt əʳ . wɑːnt ðɪ 7 wɒznt ɪ . wɒznt jə . wʊznt ə [=*he*] . wʊzn əm

17 Wa 1 wɒzənt ɑɪ . wə̟ːnt ju . wɒzənt ʃiː . wə̟ːnt ðɛɪ 2 wɔːnt əɪ . wɔːnt jə . wɔːnt ɪ [=*he*] . wɔːnt ðeɪ 3 wɒznd̥ əɪ . wɒznt jə . wɒznt ʃɪ . wɔːnt ðɛɪ 4 wəʳːɖɳʈ əɪ . wɔːdnt jə . wɔːdnt ə . wɔːdnt ðɛɪ 5 wəʳːɳʈ əɪ . wɔːʳɳʈ jə . wəʳːɳʈ əʳː . wəʳːɳʈ ðɛɪ 6 wəʴːnt əɪ . wəʴːnt jə . wəʴːnt əʴː . wəʴːnt əm 7 wɒznt əɪ . wɒznt ðɪ . wɒznt əʳː . wɒznt ʊm

23 Mon 1 wɒzn əɪ . wɒzn ðɪ . wɒnt əʳ . wɒnt ðɪ 2 wɒznt əɪ . wɒznt jə . wɒznt ə . wɒznt ðɪ 3 wɒdn əɪ . wɒznt jə . wɒznt ʃɪ . wɒznt ðɪ 4 wɒ̈·n əi . wɒ̈·n ju· . wɒ̟·n ʃi· . wɒ̟·n ðei 5 wɒ̟·znt^h əɪ̥ . wɒ̟·znt juː . wɒ̟·znt ʃiː . wɒ̟·znt ðei 6 wɒznt əɪ . wɒznt jə . wɒznt ʃɪ . wɒznt ðɪ 7 n.a.

24 Gl 1 wɑːnt əɪ . wʊznst . wɑːnt əʳ . wɑːnt ðɪ 2 wɑːnt əɪ . wʊznst . wɑːnt əʳ, °wʊn əʳ[3] . wʊznt ʊm 3 wɒzn əɪ . wɒznt . wɒzn əʳ . wɒzn ʊm 4 wɑːnt əɪ . wɒznst . wɑːnt əʳ . wɑːnt ðɪ 5 wɒzn ə̈ɪ . wɒsnt . wɒzn ə . wɒzn ʊm [wɒzn ʌs *wasn't us* (=*we*)] 6 wɒznt ʌɪ . wɒsnt . wɒznə . wɒzn əm 7 wəzn ʌɪ . wəznt . wəznt ʃɪ . wəzn əm

25 O 1 wə̈ʵ:ɳʈ ə̈ɩ . wəzntst . wəzn ə . wəzn əm, ○wɒzn əm[2] [wɒzn ə[2] *wasn't he*] 2 wɒznt ə̈ɩ . wɒznt jə . wɒznt . wɒznt əm 3 wəʵ:ɳʈ ʌʏ . wəʵ:ɳʈ i: . wəʵ:ɳʈ ʃɩ . wəʵ:ɳʈ əm 4 wɒznt əɩ . wəɽɳʈ jə . wɒzn ʃi: . wəɽɳʈ ðe: 5 wəʵ:ɳʔ ʌʏ: . wəʵ:ɳʈ jɩ . wə:nʔ ʃɩ . wə:nʔ əm 6 wəʵ:ɳʔ əɩ . wə:nt jə . wə:nt ʃɩ . wə:nt ðɩ

IX.7.7 I AM†. YOU ARE† (2nd sg.) SHE IS†. THEY ARE†

Q. Which of you is English here? For yourself you could answer . . . .

Convert for (2nd sg.) **you are, she is, they are.**

Rr. I AM/ARE/BE~BIN

THOU ARE/ART/BE(EST), YOU AM/ARE/BE~BIN

SHE BE(EST)/BIN/IS

THEY AM/ARE~AREN/BE(EST)/BIN

Note 1—The rr. to the four parts of the q. are separated below by full stops.

Note 2—In the lists of rr. above, SHE and THOU subsume respectively HOO/HER and THEE.

7 Ch 1 ɑɩ am . ða a: . ʏ: ɩz . ðẹ: a: 2 n.a. 3 ɑɩ am . ðaɩ at . ɛ̈ɷ ɩz . ðɩ a: 4 aɩ bɩn . ðį: bɩst . ᶱu: ɩz . ðį: bɩn 5 ɑɩ am . ðɛɩ at . ə:ɹ ɩz . ði: a: 6 aɩ bɩn . jo: bɩn . ə: bɩn . ðe: bɩn

8 Db 1 aɩ am . ðaɩ aʵ:ʈ . ʏ: ɩz . ðe aʵ: 2 aɩ am . ða a:t . ʃi: ɩz, ᶱu: ɩz . ðɩ a: 3 aɩ am . ðaɩ a:t . ü: ɩz . ðe: a: 4 ɑɩ am . ðɛ: a:t . ə:ɹ ɩz . ði: a: 5 ɑ: am . ðɛ̧: a:t . ɛɷ ɩz . ðe: a: 6 a:ɹ am . ðɛ: a:t . ɛ̈ɷ ɩz . ði: a: 7 a: am . ðɛ: a:t . ə:ɹ ɩz . ðe:ɩ a:n

11 Sa 1 aɩ bɩn . jo: bɩn . əʵ: bɩn . ðe: bɩn 2 aɩ am . ju: am . əʵ: ɩz . ðe: am 3 aɩ am . ju: bɩn . əʵ bɩn . ðe: bɩn 4 aɩ a:m . ju: bɩn . əʵ: bɩn . ðe: bɩn 5 aɩ bɩn . ðˡi: bɩst . əʵɽ ɩz . ðẹ: bɩn 6 aɩ bɩn . θaɷ bɩst . əʵ: bɩn . ðe: bɩn 7 aɩ æm . jo: bɩn . əʵ: bɩn . ðe: bɩn 8 ɒɩ bɩn . ði: bɩst . əʵ bɩn . ðe: bɩn 9 aɩ bɩn . jo: bɩn . əʵ bɩn . ðe: bɩn 10 aɩ bɩn . jo: bɩn . əʵ: bɩn . ðe: bɩn 11 aɩ bɩn . θi: bɩst . əʵ bɩn . ðe: bɩn

12 St 1 ɒɩ am . ðaɷ ɑ:t . aɷ ɩz . ði: ɑ̊: 2 ɒɩ am . ð‿ɛɩt [*sic*] . ə:ɹ ɩz . ðɛɩ at [*sic*] 3 ɒ:ɩ am . ðɛɩ a:t . ə:ɹ ɩz . ði: a: 4 ɒɩ am . ju: a: . ə:ɹ ɩz . ðɛɩ a: 5 ɒ:ɩ am . ju: a: . ə:ɹ ɩz . ðɛɩ a: 6 ɒ:ɩ am . ju: a: .

ɔ:ɹ ɪz . ðɛɪ a: 7 ɒɪ am . joɷ a: . ɔ:ɹ ɪz . ðɛɪ a: 8 ɒɪ bi: . joɷ bi: . əʳ: bi: . ðɛɪ bi: 9 ɒɪ am . ða:ɷ a:t . ɔ:ɹ ɪz . ðɛɪ a: 10 a:ɪ am . ju: a: . ɔ:ɹ ɪz . ðɛɪ am 11 a̱:ɪ bɪn . joɷ bɪn . ɔ:ɹ ɪz . ðɛ:ɪ bɪn

15 He 1 æɪ bi: . ði: bɪst . əʳ:ɽ ɪz . ðe:ɪ bi: 2 æɪ bi: . ði: bɪst . əʳ:ɽ ɪz . ðæɪ bi: 3 əɪ bi: . ju: bi: . əʳɽ ɪz . ðæɪ bi: 4 əɪ bi: . ði: bi: . əʳɽ ɪz . ðæɪ bi: 5 əɪ bi: . ði: bɪst . əʳɽ ɪz . ðæɪ bi: 6 əɪ bi: . ði: bɪst . əʳɽ ɪz . ðæɪ bi: 7 ɑɪ am . ju: ɑ·ɹ . ʃi: ɪz . ðeɪ äɹ, s.f. ðeɪ bi:

16 Wo 1 ɒɪ ɑ: . ju: am . əʳ: ɪz . ðe: am 2 ɒɪ bi: . ði: bɪst . əʳ: bɪn . ðe: bɪn 3 ɒɪ bi: . ði̥: bɪst . əʳɽ ɪz . ðeɪ bi: 4 ɒɪ bi: . ðɪ bɪst . əʳɽ ɪz . ðaɪ bi: 5 ɒɪ bi: . ði: bɪst . əʳ: bɪst . ðaɪ bɪst 6 ɒɪ bi: . ði: bɪst . əʳɽ ɪz . ðe:ɪ bi: 7 n.a.

17 Wa 1 ɑɪ am . ju: a: . ʃi: ɪz . ðɛɪ a: 2 n.a. 3 əɪ am . ju: a: . ʃi: ɪz . ðɛɪ a: 4 əɪ a:, əɪ bi: . ju: a:, ju: bi: . ə: bi:, əʳ: ɪz . ðɛɪ bi:, ðɛɪ a: 5 əɪ bi: . ju: bi: . əʳ: ɪz . ðɛɪ bi: 6 əɪ am . ju: a: . əʳ: ɪz . ðɛɪ bi: 7 əɪ bɪ, əɪ am . ju: bi: . əʳ: ɪz . ðɛɪ bi:

23 Mon 1 əɪ bɪi: . ðɪi: bɪst . əʳɽ ɪz . ðæɪ bɪi: 2 əɪ bi: . ju: bi: . əʳɽ ɪz . ðe: bi: 3 əɪ bi: . ju: bi: . ʃi: ɪz . ðe: bi: 4 əi bi: . ju· bi· . ʃi· bi· . ðei bi· 5 əi am . ju: a: . ʃi: ɪz . ðei a: 6 əɪ a:m . ju: a: . ʃi: ɪz . ðe: a: 7 n.a.

24 Gl 1 əɪ bi: . ði: bɪst . əʳ: bi: . ðæɪ bi: 2 əɪ bi: . ði: bɪst . əʳɽ ɪz . ðæɪ bi: 3 əɪ bˡi: . ðˡi: bɪst . əʳɽ ɪz . ðæɪ bˡi: 4 əɪ bɪi: . ðˡi: bɪst . əʳ:ɽ ɪz . ðaɪ bɪi: 5 ə̈ɪ bi: . ði: bɪst . əʳ: bi: . ðæɪ bi: 6 ʌɪ bi: . ði: bɪst . əʳ:ɽ ɪz . ðæɪ bi: 7 ʌɪ bi: . ði: bɪst . əʳ: ɪz . ðɛ̧ɪ bi:

25 O 1 ə̈ɪ bɪ . ði: bɪst . əʳ: ɪz . ðeɪ bi: 2 ə̈ɪ bi: . ju: bi: . ʃi: bi: . ðɛɪ bi: 3 ʌʏ bi: . ju: bi: . ʃi: bi: . ðe: bi: 4 əɪ am . ju: aɽ . ʃi: ɪz . ðe: aɽ 5 ʌʏ bi: . ju: bi: . ʃi: ɪz . ðe: bi: 6 ə̈ɪ bi: . ju: bi: . ʃi: bi: . ðeɪ bi:

IX.7.8 (we) WERE‡. (I) WERE‡. (she) WERE‡

Q. Talking about being well-off, we could say: We'd all buy lots of things if we . . . . rich.

Convert for **I were, she were.**

Rr. WAS, WERE(N)
WAS, WERE(N)
WAS, WERE(N)

Note 1—The rr. to the three parts of the q. are separated below by full stops.

Note 2—When rec. in the rr., the subj. prons. have been reproduced below. US was occ. rec. meaning *we*.

7 Ch 1 wɩ wə. a wə. ʏ: wəz 2 n.a. 3 wən. wə. wə 4 wəz. wəz. wəz 5 wɩ wən. a wəz. ə: wəz 6 wən. wəz. ə: wəz

8 Db 1 wə. wə. wə 2 wɩ wə. a wə. ʃɩ wə 3 wɩ wə. a wə. ü: wə 4 wɛɩ wə. a wə. ɛɷ wə 5 wɩ wə. a wə. ə wə 6 wɛɩ wə. a wə. ɛ̈ɷ wə 7 wɩ wə. a: wə. ə: wə

11 Sa 1 wə. wəz. wəz 2 wɩ wə. a wə. əᶉ wə 3 wə. wəz. wəz 4 wə. wə. wə 5 wən. ə wən. əᶉ wən 6–7 wə. wə. wə 8 wɩ wə. a wə. əᶉ wə 9 wɩ wə. aɩ wə. əᶉ wə 10 wɩ wə. aɩ wə. əᶉ: wə 11 wə. wə. wə

12 St 1 wə. wə. wə 2 wɛɩ wə. ɒɩ wəz. ə: wə 3 wɩ wəz. ɒ:ɩ wə. ə: wə 4 wə. wə. wəz 5 wɒz. ɒ:ɩ wəz. ə: wəz 6 wɩ wəz. ɒ:ɩ wə. ə: wə, ° ə wəɹ[1] [+V.] 7 wɩ wəz. ɒɩ wəz. ə: wəz 8 wə:. wɒz. wəz 9 wəz. wəz. wəz 10 wə:. a:ɩ wə. ə: wə 11 wəz. wəz. wəz

15 He 1 wɩ wə. æɩ wəz. əᶉ wəz 2 wɩ wə. æɩ wə. əᶉ wə 3 wəz. əɩ wəz. əᶉ wəz 4 wɩ wə. əɩ wə. əᶉ wə 5 wə. əɩ wə. əᶉ wə 6 wəz. əɩ wəz. əᶉ wəz 7 wi: wəz. ɑɩ wəz. ʃi: wəz, əɹ wəz [fr. i.'s son]

16 Wo 1 wɩ wə. ɒɩ wə. əᶉ: wə 2 wɩ wə. a wə. əᶉ wə 3–4 wɩ wə. ɒɩ wəz. əᶉ wəz 5 wɷz. ɒɩ wɷz. əᶉ: wɷz 6 wi: wəz. ɒɩ wəz. əᶉ wəz 7 n.a.

17 Wa 1 wə. wəz. wəz 2 wi: wəz. əɩ wəz. n.a. 3 wəz. wəz. wəz 4 wɩ wə. əɩ wə. əᶉ: wə 5 wəz. wəz, °əɩ wəz[1]. wəz 6 wəz. wəz. wəz 7 wɩ wə. əɩ wə. əᶉ: wə

23 Mon 1 wə. əɩ wə. əᶉ wə 2 wə. əɩ wəz. əᶉ wəz 3 wə. əɩ wə. ʃɩ wə 4 wi· wəz. əi wəz. ʃi wəz 5 wi· wɒ. əi wʌ̤̈z. ʃi· wʌ̤̈z. 6 wəz. əɩ wəz. ʃi: wəz 7 n.a.

24 Gl 1–3 wəz. əɩ wəz. əᶉ wəz 4 wə. əɩ wə. əᶉ wə 5 wi wəz. ə̈ɩ wəz. əᶉ: wəz 6 wəz. wəz. wəz 7 wi wəz. ʌɩ wəz. əᶉ: wəz

25 O 1 wɩ wəz. ə̈ɩ wəz. ʃi: wəz 2 wəz. wəz. wəz 3 ʌs wəz. wəz. ẘəz 4 wi: wəʐ, °wi: wəz[1]. əɩ wəz. ʃi: wəz 5 wəz. wəz. wəz, °ʃɩ wəz[2] 6 wəz. wəz. wəz

IX.7.9 WE ARE†. I AM†. YOU ARE†. SHE IS†

Q. *If I say: You people aren't English, you can contradict and say: Oh yes . . . .*

Convert for I am, you are, she is.

Rr. US BE, WE AM/ARE~AREN/BE~BIN

I AM/ARE/BE~BIN

THEE BEEST, THOU ARE/ART, YOU AM/ARE/BE~BIN

HER AM/BE(EST)/BIN/IS, HOO/SHE IS

Note 1—The rr. to the four parts of the q. are separated below by full stops.
Note 2—At 25.6 the f.w. omitted to rec. the wanted prons.

7 Ch 1 wɩ a: . a: am . ða a: . ʏ: ɩz 2 n.a. 3 wɩ a: . ɑɩ am . s.f. ða a:t . ɛ̈ɷ ɩz 4 wɩ an . a bɩn . jo: bɩn . °u: ɩz 5 wɩ a: . a: am . ðɛɩ a:t . əɹ ɩz 6 wi: am . aɩ bɩn . jo: bɩn . ə: bɩn

8 Db 1 wɩ a±: . aɩ am . ðaɩ a±:t . ʏ: ɩz 2 wɩ a: . a: am . ðaɷ a:t . °u: ɩz 3 wɩ a: . aɩ am . ða a:t . ü: ɩz, ɛ̈ɷ ɩz 4 wɛɩ a: . ɑɩ am . ða a:t . ə:ɹ ɩz 5 wɩ a:ɹ . a: am . ðɛ: a:t . ɛɷ ɩz 6 wɩ a: . a:ɹ am . ðɛ: a:t . ɛɷ ɩz 7 wɛɩ a: . a:ɹ am . ðɛɩ a:t . ə:ɹ ɩz

11 Sa 1 wɩ am . aɩ am . ju: a: . ə˞: bɩn 2 wi: am . aɩ am . ju am . ə˞: am 3 wi: bɩn . aɩ bɩn . ju: bɩn . ə˞: bɩn 4 wɩi: a˞: . aɩ a:m . ju: a˞: . ʃɩi: ɩz 5 wɩ bɩn . aɩ bɩn . ðɩi: bɩst . ə˞:ɽ ɩz 6 wɩ bɩn . aɩ bɩn . jo: bɩn . ə˞: bɩn 7 wi: a˞: . aɩ am . jo: bɩn . ə˞: bɩn 8 wɩ bɩn . aɩ bɩn . ði: bɩst . ə˞ bɩn 9 wi: bɩn . aɩ æm . jo: bɩn . ə˞: ɩz 10 wi: æm . aɩ bɩn . jo: bɩn . ə˞: bɩn 11 wi: bɩn . aɩ bɩn . θi: bɩst . ə˞: bɩn

12 St 1 wɛɩ ɑ̇: . ɒɩ am . ðạ: ɑ̇:t . aɷ ɩz 2 wɛɩ a: . ɒɩ am . ðɛɩ at . ə:ɹ ɩz 3 wɛɩ a: . ɒ:ɩ am . ðɛɩ a:t, ju: a: . ə:ɹ ɩz 4 wi· a: . ɒɩ am . ju: a: . ə:ɹ ɩz 5 wɛɩ a: . ɒ:ɩ am . ə:ɹ ɩz . ju: a: 6 wɛɩ a: . ɒ:ɩ am . ju: a: . ə:ɹ ɩz 7 wi: ɑ̇: . ɒɩ ạm . joɷ ɑ̇: . ə:ɹ ɩz 8 wi: bɩn . aɩ am . joɷ bi:, °joɷ ɑ:[2] . ə:ɹ ɩz 9 wɛɩ a̱: . ɒɩ ɑ̇: . joɷ ɑ̇: . ə:ɹ ɩz 10 wi: a: . a:ɩ am . jü: a: . ə:ɹ ɩz 11 wi: bɩn . a̱:ɩ bɩn . jọɷ bɩn . ə:ɹ ɩz

15 He 1 wi: bi: . æɩ bi: . ju: bi: . ə˞: bi: 2 wi: bi: . æɩ bi: . ju: bi: . ə˞:ɽ ɩz 3 wi: bi: . əɩ bi: . ju· bi: . ə˞:ɽ ɩz 4 wi: bi: . əɩ bi: . ju: bi: . ə˞:ɽ ɩz 5 wi: bi: . əɩ bi: . ju: bi:, ○~[4] . ə˞ɽ ɩz 6 wi: bi: . əɩ bi: . ju: bi: . ə˞:ɽ ɩz 7 wɩ ä·ɹ . ɑɩ am . ju ä·ɹ . ʃi: ɩz

16 Wo 1 wɩ am . ɒɩ am . ju: am . ə^{r}: ɩz 2 wi: am . ɒɩ am . ju: am . ə^{r}:ɽ ɩz 3 wi: bi: . ɒɩ bi: . ju: bi: . ə^{r}: bi: 4 wi: bi: . ɒɩ bi: . ði: bi: . ə^{r}: bi: 5 wɩ bi: . ɒɩ bi: . ði: bɩst . ə^{r}: bɩst 6 wi: bi: . ɒɩ æ:m . ju: bi: . ə^{r}:ɽ ɩz 7 n.a.

17 Wa 1 wɩ a: . ɑɩ a: . n.a. ʃi: ɩz$^{(2x)}$ 2 n.a. n.a. ju: a: . n.a. 3 wɩ a: . əɩ am . ju a: . ʃi: ɩz 4 wɩ a: . əɩ bi: . ju: a: . ə^{r}:ɽ ɩz 5 wi: bi: . əɩ bi: . ju: bi: . ə^{r}: ɩz 6 wi: a^{r}:, p . wi: bi: ["very old-fashioned"] . əɩ bi: . ju: am . ə^{r}: ɩz 7 wi: bi: . əɩ am . ju: bi: . ə^{r}: ɩz

23 Mon 1 wɩ bɩi: . əɩ b^{ɩ}i: . ð^{ɩ}i: bɩst . ə^{r}ɽ ɩz 2 wi: a: . əɩ a:m . ju: a: . ə^{r}:ɽ ɩz 3 wi: bi: . əɩ bi: . ju: bi: . ʃi: ɩz 4 wi· bi: . əi bi: . ju· bi: . ʃi· bi: 5 wi: a: . əɩ̣ am . ju· a: . ʃi· ɩz 6 wi: a: . əɩ a:m . ju: a: . ʃi: ɩz 7 n.a.

24 Gl 1 wi: bi: . əɩ bi: . ði: bɩst . ə^{r}: bi: 2 w^{ɩ}i: b^{ɩ}i: . ə^{ɩ} b^{ɩ}i: . ð^{ɩ}i: bɩst . ə^{r}ɽ ɩz 3 w^{ɩ}i: b^{ɩ}i: . əɩ b^{ɩ}i: . ð^{ɩ}i: bɩst . ə^{r}:ɽ ɩz 4 w^{ɩ}i: b^{ɩ}i: . əɩ b^{ɩ}i: . ð^{ɩ}i: bɩst . ə^{r}:ɽ ɩz 5 wi: bi: . ə̈ɩ bi: . ði: bɩst . ə^{r}: ɩz 6 wi: bi: . ʌɩ bi: . ði: bɩst . ə^{r}:ɽ ɩz 7 wi: bi . ʌɩ bi: . ði: bɩst . ə^{r}: ɩz

25 O 1 wi: bi: . ə̈ɩ bi: . ði: bɩst . ʃi: bi: 2 wi: bi: . ə̈ɩ bi: . ju: bi: . p . ʃi: bi:, ʃi: ɩz 3 ʌs bi: . ʌʏ bi: . ju: bi: . ʃi: bi: 4 wɩ a·ɽ . əɩ am . ju: a·r . ʃi: ɩz 5 wɩ bi: . ʌʏ bi: . ju: bi: . ʃi: bi: 6 a^{r}: . bi: . a^{r}: . ɩz, bi:

IX.7.10 I'M NOT†. SHE ISN'T†. THEY AREN'T†

Q. If I said to you: You're drunk, you would answer: Oh no, ...

Convert for **she isn't, they aren't.**

Rr. I AIN'T~(Y)EN'T~YUN'T/AMMA~AMNA/ANNA BAIN'T~B(Y)EN'T~BINNA~BYUNT/BEESN'T, I'M NONE/NOT

SHE AIN'T~EN'T~IN'T~YEN'T~YUN'T/INNA~ISNA~ISN'T/ BAIN'T~BINNA

THEY AIN'T/EN'T~YUN'T/AMMA/ANNA~AREN'T/ BEN'T~BINNA~BYUN'T/INNA, THEY'M NOT

Note 1—The rr. to the three parts of the q. are separated below by full stops.

Note 2—In the lists of rr. above, SHE subsumes HOO/HER.

Note 3—At 11.1 (1st r.), 11.11 (1st and 3rd rr.), 15.4 (1st r.) and 17.3 (2nd r.), the f.w. did not rec. the subj. pron. At 11.1 (1st r.), the subj. pron. may have been absorbed in the v. The vv. at 12.11 are here regarded as forms of BAIN'T, AIN'T and BAIN'T resp.

Note 4—I.m. exs. of emphatic forms foll. a pron. other than I, SHE and THEY are included between square brackets after the r. to the 3rd part of the q. I.m. forms without context in the r.bb. have been regarded as prob. emphatic anaphoric forms, and have therefore been included here with an attached superior ×.

7 Ch 1 am nɒt. ʏ: ɪznt. ðe:ᵊ nɒt 2 n.a. [×ɪt ɪnə¹ *it inna* (=*isn't*)] 3 ɑɪ anə. ɛ̈ɷ ɪnə. ði: anə 4 aɪ anə, aɪ bɪnə [older]. ᵒu: ɪnə. ðɪ anə, ðɪ bɪnə 5 ɑɪ anə, a bɪnə. əɹ ɪnə. ðɪ anə 6 aɪ bɪnə. ə:ɹ ɪnə. ðe: bɪnə, ðe: amə [×ðəɹ ɪnə² *there inna* (=*isn't*)]

8 Db 1 aɪ amnə. ʏ: ɪznə. ðe: aʳ:ɳʈ 2 am nɒt. ʃɪ ɪnt. ðə nɒt 3 am nɒn. ü: ɪznə. ðɪ a:nə 4 am nɒt, ᵒa amnə³. ɛɷ ɪznə. ðɪ nɒt [ɛɪ ɪznə² *he isna*] 5 ɑɪ e·ˈnt, ɑɪ amnə. ɛɷ ɪznə. ðe:ˈ ɪnə [×ɪt ɪznə¹ *it isna*] 6 a: amnə. ɛ̈ɷ ɪznə. ði: a:nə 7 a: amnə. əɹ ɪnə. ðe·ɪ a:nə

11 Sa 1 amə. əʳ: ɪna. ðɪ bɪnə 2 aɪ amə. əʳ: ɪnə. ðe: anə 3 aɪm nɒt. əʳ: bɪna. ðe: bɪnə 4 a bɪnə. ʃɪi: ɪnə. ðe: a:ɹnt 5 aɪ bɪnə. əʳ:ɽ ɪnə. ðe̜: bɪnə [×tɪnə³ *t'inna* (=*t'isn't*)] 6 aɪ amə. əʳ:ɽ‿ɪnə. ðɪ bɪnə 7 aɪ anə. əʳɽ ɪnə. ðe: bɪnə 8 aɪ bɪnə. əʳ bɪnə. ðɪ bɪnə 9 aɪ bɪnə. əʳɽ ɪnə. ðe: bɪnə [×tɪnə¹ *t'inna*] 10 aɪ ænə. əʳ:ɽ ɪnə. ðe: bɪnə 11 be:ənt. əʳ jənt. bɪnə

12 St 1 ɒɪ amnə. aɷ ɪznə. ði: ɑ̈:nə 2 ɒɪm nɒn. ə:ɹ ɪnə. ðɛɪ anə 3 ɒ:ɪ amnə. ə:ɹ ɪnə. ði: a:nə̧ 4 ɒɪ anə. ə:ɹ ɪnə. ðɛɪ anə 5 ɒ:ɪm nɒt. ə:ɹ ɪnə. ðɛɪ anə [ɪt ɪznt² *it isn't*] 6 ɒ:ɪ anə. ə:ɹ ɪnə. ðɛɪ anə, ᵒ×ðɪ anə¹ 7 ɒɪ ɛɪnt. ə:ɹ ɛɪnt, ᵒʃɪ ɪznt¹. ðɛɪ a:nt 8 ɒɪ bɛɪnt. ə:ɹ ɛɪnt. ðɛɪ ɛɪnt 9 ɒɪ anə, ᵒɒɪ ɛɪnt². ə:ɹ ɪnə. ðɛɪ anə [×ɪt ɛɪnt² *it ain't*] 10 aɪ eɪnt. ʃi: ɛɪnt. ðɛɪ ɛɪnt 11 a̱: bɛ:ɪ. ə:ɹ ɛ:ɪ. ðɛɪ bɛ:ɪ

15 He 1 æɪ bɪnə. əʳ:ɽ ɛnt. ðe:ɪ bɪnə [×i: ɪnə³ *he inna*; tɛnt¹, ×∼¹ *t'en't*] 2 æɪ e:ɪnt. əʳ:ɽ ɪnə. ðæɪ be:ɪnt 3 əɪ jɷnt. əʳɽ ɛnt. ðæɪ jɷnt 4 bjʌnt. əʳ: jʌnt. ðɪ jʌnt 5 əɪ bɛnt. əʳɽ ɛnt. ðɪ ɛnt 6 əɪ bjɷnt. əʳ jɷnt. ðæɪ bjɷnt [×tjɷnt¹ *t'yunt* (=*it isn't*)] 7 əɪ ɛnt. ʃi ɛnt. ðeɪ aɹnt

16 Wo 1 əm nɒt. əʳɽ ɪnt. ðɪ nɒt 2 ɒɪ be:nt. əʳ:ɽ‿ɛnt. ðe: be:nt 3 ɒɪ jɷnt. əʳ jɷnt. ðe:ɪ bjɷnt 4 ɒɪ bɪnə, ᵒɒɪ ɛnt³, ᵒ×∼³. əʳɽ‿ɛnt. ðaɪ bɪnə 5 ɒɪ bɪsnt. əʳ: jɷnt, ᵒ×əʳ:ɽ jɷnt¹. ðaɪ jɷnt [×ju: bjɷnə¹ *you byunna* (=*aren't*); ×ɪt ʃɷnt¹ *it yun't* (=*isn't*)] 6 ɒɪm nɒt. əʳ jɷnt. ðe:m nɒt [×ɪ jɛnt¹ *he yen't* (=*isn't*)] 7 n.a.

17 Wa 1 ɑɪm not. ʃɪ ɪznt. ðɛ: nɒt 2 n.a. 3 ɑɪm nɒt. ɪznt. ðɛɪə nɒt 4 əɪ ɛnt. əʳ:ɽ ɛnt. ðe̜ɪ ɛnt 5 əɪ ɛɪnt, əɪ ɛnt [pref.]. əʳ: ɛɪnt, əʳ: ɛnt. ðɛɪ ɛnt 6 əɪ bɪənt. əʳ: ɛɪnt. ðɛɪ bɪənt 7 əɪ ɛnt, əɪ bjɷnt. əʳ: jɷnt, əʳ: ɛnt. ðɛɪ ɛnt, ðɛɪ bjɷnt

23 Mon 1 əɪ bɛnt, ○×∼[2]. əʳɽ ɛnt. ðæɪ bɛnt   2 əɪ ɛnt. əʳɽ ɛnt. ðɪ nɒt   3 əɪm nɒt. ʃɪ ɛnt. ðɪ ɛnt [×ɪt ɛnt[1] *it en't*, ×tɛnt[3] *t'ent*]   4 əi ɛnt. ʃi ɛnt. ði ɛnt   5 əɪ̣m nɒ̣·tʰ. ʃi:z nɒ̣·tʰ. ðei ɛntʰ   6 əɪ ɛnt. ʃɪ ɛnt. ðɪ ɛnt [×ɪt ɛnt[1] *it en't*]   7 n.a.

24 Gl 1 əɪ bjɷnt. əʳɽ ɛnt. ðæɪ ɛnt [×tʃɷnt[2] *t'yun't (=t'isn't)*]   2 əɪ bjɷnt. əɽ jɷnt, ○×∼[3]. ðæɪ jɷnt   3 əɪ bjɷnt. əʳ: jɷnt. ðæɪ bjɷnt, ○×ðə bɛnt[1] [×ɪ bjɷn[3] *he byun't*]   4 bjɷnt. əʳ: jɷnt. ðaɪ bjɷnt   5 ə̈ɪ bjɷnt. əʳ: jɷnt. ðæɪ bjɷnt   6 ʌɪ bjɛnt. əʳ: jɛnt. ðə bjɛnt [×tʃɷnt[2] *t'yun't* (=*t'isn't*)]   7 ʌɪ bjənt. ʃi: ənt. ðə bjənt

25 O 1 ə̈ɪ bɛnt. ʃi: bɛnt, ○×ʃɪ ɛnt[2]. ðeɪ bɛnt   2 ə̈ɪm nɑt, əɪ bɛnt. ʃi bɛnt. ðeɪ bɛnt [×ɪt ɛnʔ[2] *it en't*]   3 ʌʏ bɛnt. ʃi ɛnt. ðe: bɛnt   4 əɪ bɛnt. ʃi: ɛnt. ðe: ɛnt   5 ʌʏ ɛnʔ, ○× ʌʏ amnʔ[3]. ʃi: ɛnʔ. ðe: ɛnʔ   6 ə̈ɪ eɪnʔ. ʃi: eɪnʔ. ðeɪ eɪnʔ

IX.7.11 NOT

Q. If you were angry about what I said, you might say: Get away, I'm . . . . drunk.

R. NONE/NOT

The foll., since they do not contain the str. form of NOT, are strictly speaking u.rr., though the ii.' comments would suggest that they are the usual expressions:— AMMA, (I) ANNA/BYUN'T/EN'T, I AIN'T∼YUNT/BEN'T∼BINNA∼BYENT/INNA

Note—NOT also occurs at III.1.8, V.7.8 and IX.7.10.

7 Ch 1 nɒd̥   2 n.a.   3 §anə ["pref."]   4 §aɪ anə [i. insists], §aɪ bɪnə ["older"; i. insists]   5 §aɪ anə ["pref."], p. nɒt   6 §aɪ bɪnə

8 Db 1 nɒn   2 nɒn, no·ən   3–4 nɒn   5 nɒn, ○∼[2,3,4]   6 nɒn   7 nɒn, ○∼[2]

11 Sa 1–3 nɒt   4 nɒt, §amə ["usu."]   5 nɒt   6 nɒt, ○∼[3]   7 nɒt, ○∼[1]   8 nɒt, ○∼[2]   9 nɔ:t, ○nɒt[1(2x)]   10 nɒt, ○∼[2(2x)]   11 nɒt

12 St 1–3 nɒn   4–5 nɒt   6 nɒn[(2x)]   7–10 nɒt   11 §a̱:ɪ ɛ:ɪ, §a̱:ɪ ɪnə ["older"]

15 He 1–2 nɒt   3 §əɪ jənt, ○nɒt[4]   4 §bjʌnt, ○nɒt[3]   5 nɒt, ○∼[4]   6 nɒt, ○∼[1]   7 nɒt

16 Wo 1–2 nɒt   3 nɒt, ○∼[1]   4 nɒt   5 nɒt, ○∼[1]   6 nɒt, ○nɑ:t[3]   7 n.a., ○nət[2,4]

17 Wa 1 nɒt, °~¹ 2 n.a. 3 nɒt, °~²⁽²ˣ⁾ 4 ɔɩ §ɛnt ["pref."] 5 nɒt 6 nɒt, ɔɩ §bɩɷnt [pref.] 7 p. nɒt, §ɛnt [pref.], §bjɷnt [pref.]

23 Mon 1 nɒt 2 nɒt, °~² 3 nɒt, °~¹ 4 nɒt, §ɛnt [pref.] 5 nɒ̞·tᵊ, °nɒ̞·t¹,², °nɒt¹, °nɒ̈t², °nɒ̞·ʔ² 6 nɒt 7 n.a., °nɒt¹⁽²ˣ⁾ VI.13.1 [ɔ· nou¹ *or no* (="*or not*")]

24 Gl 1 nɑ:t 2 nɒt, °~² 3 nɑ:t 4 nɒt, °ɑ~³ 5 ɔ̈ɩ §bjɷnt, °nɒt² 6 ʌɩ §bjɛnt 7 ʌɩ §bjənt

25 O 1–2 ɔ̈ɩ bɛnt 3 nət 4 nɒt, °~⁴ 5 nɒʔ, °~¹,² 6 nɒt

IX.7.12 SURE*

Q. If asked whether the postman had been, and you were somewhat doubtful, you'd say [using his own words (as given in his response to IX.7.11)]: *I'm not . . . .*

Rr. CERTAIN, SURE

7 Ch 1 sa:tɩn 2 n.a., °ʃɩüə² 3 ʃᶦʏ:ə 4 ʃṳ̈ə⁽²ˣ⁾ 5 ʃᶦʏ:ə⁽²ˣ⁾ 6 ʃuə

8 Db 1 ʃʏ:əᶦ· 2 ʃu·ə 3 ʃü:ə 4 ʃᶱu·ə 5 ʃu·ə 6 ʃiü:ə⁽²ˣ⁾ 7 ʃᶱü:ə

11 Sa 1 ʃɩuəʳ 2 ʃʏʉ:əʳ 3 ʃɩuəʳ 4 ʃɩɷəʳ 5 ʃu:əʳ 6 ʃɷəʳ [sjuəlɩ⁴ *surely*] 7 ʃu:əʳ 8 ʃu:əʳ, °ʃuəʳ² 9 ʃɩu:əʳ 10 ʃɷəʳ, °ʃu:əʳ 11 ʃɩuəʳ

12 St 1 ʃu:ə 2 ʃɷə, °ʃu:ə⁵ 3 ʃju:ə 4–5 ʃu:ə 6 ʃɷ:ə 7 n.a. 8 ʃü:ə 9 ʃu:ə 10 sjü:ə 11 ʃu:ə

15 He 1–3 ʃɷəʳ 4 ʃu:əʳ 5 ʃɷəʳ, °əm [=*am*] ʒɷəʳ⁴ 6 ʒɷəʳ, °ʃu:əʳ¹, °ʃɷəʳ¹ 7 ʃɷəɹ

16 Wo 1 ʃɷə 2 ʃɷəʳ 3–4 ʃu:əʳ 5 ʃɷəʳ 6 ʃu:əʳ 7 n.a.

17 Wa 1 ʃu:ᶱə 2 n.a. 3 ʃọə 4 ʃü:ə 5 ʃu·əʳ 6 ʃu:ə 7 ʃu·əʳ

23 Mon 1 ʃᶱu:əʳ 2 ʃu:əʳ 3 ʃɷə, °ʃu:əʳ³ 4 ʃu·ə 5 ʃuə 6 ʃu:əʳ, °ʃɷəʳ¹ 7 n.a.

24 Gl 1 ʃu:əʳ 2 ʃɷəʳ 3–4 ʃᶱu:əʳ 5 ʃuəʳ 6 ʒu·əʳ 7 səʳ:tɩn, ʃu·əʳ

25 O 1 ʃɷəʳ· 2 ʃɷəᶦ 3 ʃuəʳ 4 ʃɷəɽ⁽²ˣ⁾ 5 ʃuə: 6 ʃuəʳ

IX.8.1 US

Q. You hear voices upstairs and call out: Who's there? Your children up there answer back: It's only . . . .

Rr. US, WE

Note—I.m. exs. of US as the subj. of a sentence are reproduced below between square brackets untransliterated. Additional exs. occur at VII.2.14. Unstr. exs. of US meaning *me* occur at IX.8.2–4.

7 Ch 1 ɷz 2 n.a. 3–4 ɷz 5 ɷs 6 ʌs, wi: [rare]

8 Db 1–7 ɷz

11 Sa 1 ʌs 2 ɷs 3 ʌs 4 ʌs [ʌs²] 5 ɷs 6–7 ʌs 8–9 wi: 10 ʌs 11 wi:

12 St 1–3 ɷz 4 ɷs 5–7 ɷz 8 ɷs 9 wɛɩ 10 ɷz 11 ɷs, wi:

15 He 1 wi: [ʌs²] 2–6 wi: 7 ʌs

16 Wo 1 wi: 2 wi: [ɷz²] 3–5 wi: 6 wi: [ɷz¹] 7 s.w. wi: [əz¹,²]

17 Wa 1 ɷs 2 ɷs [ɷz⁴⁽³ˣ⁾] 3 ɷs 4 ɷs [ʌ̣s²] 5–6 ɷs 7 ɷs [ʌs¹]

23 Mon 1 wɩi: [ɷs², ʌz⁴, ʌs²] 2 wi: [ɷs²] 3 wi: [ʌs¹,²⁽²ˣ⁾] 4 ʌ̣̈s 5 ʌ̣̈s [ʌ̣̈s²]
6 ʌs 7 n.a.

24 Gl 1 wi: [ɷs³] 2 wˡi: 3 wˡi: [ɷz¹, ɷs¹] 4 wˡi: 5 wi: [ʌs] 6 wi: [əs²]
7 wi:

25 O 1 ʌs [əs¹,²⁽²ˣ⁾, ʌz²] 2 ɷs 3 ʌs [ʌs¹⁽³ˣ⁾, ~³ IX.7.9, ʌz ¹⁽²ˣ⁾, ɷs ¹⁽²ˣ⁾, əs¹⁽²ˣ⁾]
4 ɷs 5–6 ʌs

IX.8.2 GIVE* IT† ME†

Q. Jack wants to have Tommy's ball and says to him, not: Keep it! but [g.] . . . !

Rr. GIVE IT/§HERE/(TO) ME/, GIVE ME IT (HERE)
GIVE ME §THAT/§THE/§YOUR BALL

Note 1—In the list of rr. above, IT subsumes EN and ME subsumes I (=*me*) and US (=*me*).

Note 2—In the i.m. exs. of GIVE reproduced below between square brackets, an attached superior ◇ denotes an inf., superior × an imp., superior ‖ 3 pr.s., superior + 1 p.t.s., and superior ★ 3 p.t.s. Superior ᴅ denotes an ex. foll. by a word beginning with a V., and superior ɑ denotes an ex. foll. by a word beginning with a C. Exs. of GIVE *imp.* + ME or US (=*me*) are included here untransliterated. GIVE US occ. occurs at IX.4.13.

Note 3—GIVE and its parts also occur at III.5.1/2, VII.6.15, VIII.8.10 and IX.9.3. For the p.p., see IX.8.3. For additional exs. of EN and IT after a C., see V.7.7 (and refs.); and of EN and IT after a V., see I.7.1 (and refs.). For ME and US (=*me*), see IX.8.3/4 (and refs.).

7 Ch 1 gɪv ɪt ɷz [◇gɪv^{4}; gɪvn^{2} *3 pr.pl.*; ¶gɪvɪn^{1} III.1.12] 2 n.a. [◇gɪv; ×~^{3}; ‖gɪvz^{1,3}, ‖gɪz^{3}; +gɪv^{3}; ~^{1} *1 p.t.pl.*; gɛn^{1} *2 p.t.pl.*; ~^{1} *3 p.t.pl.*; gɪv$^{1,4(2x)}$ *v.*] 3 gɪv ɪt mɪ [¶gɪvɪn^{3}] 4 gɪn ɪt mɪ 5 gɪv ɪt əs 6 gɪv ɪt ʌs [gɪv mɪ^{3}]

8 Db 1 gɪv ɪt əz 2 gɪ ɪt mɪ [‖gɪz^{2}; +gɪd^{2}; ◇gɪ^{3}; ᴰgi:^{2} *v.*] 3 gɪv ɪt əz [◇gɪv^{1}] 4 gɪ‿t mɪ [◇gɪ^{2}; ◇gɪv] 5 gɪ ɪt mɪ [gɪ^{4} *v.*] 6 gi:‿t mɛɪ 7 gɪ‿t mɪ [ᵈgɪn^{1} *1 pr.pl.*]

11 Sa 1 gɪv ɪt ʌs 2 gɪv ɪt əs [ᵈgɪn^{2} *3 p.t. pl.*] 3 gɪv ɪt ʌs 4 gɪv ɪt əs 5 gɪ‿z ɪt ɪəʳ [×ᵈgɪz^{2}] 6 gɪv ɪt əs [ᵈgɪv^{3} *1 pr.pl.*] 7 gɪv ɪt ʌs 8 gɪv ɪt mi: [ᵈgɪv^{1} *3 pr.pl.*] 9 gɪv ɪt əs 10 gɪv ɪt əs 11 gɪv ɪt əs [◇ᵈgɪv^{1}; ◇ᴰ~^{2}; ¶gɪvɪn^{2}]

12 St 1 gɪv mɛ̝ɪ §ðat baɷ, gɪv ɪt mɛ̝ɪ [◇gɪ^{1}; gɪv^{2} *v.*] 2 gɪv ɪt mɪ 3 gɪv ɪt mɪ [gɪv^{2} *v.*] 4 gɪv ɪt mi: [×gɪv^{4}; +gɛn^{2}] 5 gɪv ɪt mɛɪ [◇gɪv^{2}] 6 gɪ ɪt tə mɛɪ [◇gɪ^{1}] 7 gɪv ɪt §ɪə [gɛv^{2} *3 p.t. pl.*] 8 gɪv ɪt ɷz [◇gɪv^{1}] 9 gɪ‿z ɪt ɪə [×gɪv^{2}; +gɛn$^{1(2x)}$; ~$^{1(2x)}$ *p.p.*; gɪ^{3} *v.* III.13.12; ×gɪ‿z^{2}] 10 gi ɪt mɪ [◇gɪv^{4}] 11 gɪ əz ɪʔ, gɪ‿z ɪʔ [‖gɪz^{1}; gi:^{1,2} *v.*]

15 He 1 gɪv əz ɪt 2 gɪv əs ɪt [‖gɪvz^{3}] 3 gɪv ɪt əs [◇gɪv^{2}; ★~^{1}] 4 gɪv ɪt mə 5 gɪv ɪt mɪ 6 gɪv ɪt əɪ 7 gɪv ɪt ʌs, gɪv əz̥ §ðə bɔ:l [◇gɪv$^{1(2x)}$; ×gɪv^{4}; gɪ‿s^{4}]

16 Wo 1 gɪv ɪt mɪ [◇gɪv^{2}] 2–3 gɪv ɪt mi: 4 gɪ ɪt mɷ 5 gɪv ɷz ɪt [×gɪv^{1}; ×gɪ^{1}; ★gɪn$^{1(2x)}$] 6 gɪv ɪt ə mi: [★gɛn^{2}; gjɛn^{2} *2 p.t.s.*] 7 gɪv mi: §jəɹ bɔ:, gɪv mi: §jəɹ bɔ:l [◇gɪv$^{1,3(2x)}$; ◇gɪv^{1} VII.5.8; gɪz^{3} *1 pr.pl.*; +gɪv^{4}; ★gɛn$^{1(2x)}$; gɪ^{2}, gɪv^{4} *v.*, ~^{3} *v.* III.3.2; ◇gi:^{4}]

17 Wa 1 gɪv ɪt· mᵉɪ: [◇gɪv^{2}; ‖gɪvz; ¶gɪvɪn^{1}] 2 gi: əs §ðat bɔ: [◇gɪ^{4}, ◇gɪv^{3,4}; ×gɪv^{1,3}, ×gi·^{4}; +gɪn^{2}; ★gɪv^{3}; ~^{3} *v.*, gɪ^{4} *v.*] 3 gɪv ɪt mɪ 4 gɪv ɪt ɷs 5 gɪv əs ɪt 6 gɪ‿t mᶦi: 7 gɪ‿t mɪ [◇gɪv^{2}]

23 Mon 1 gɪv əs ɪt [gɪv^{2} *3 pr.pl.*; ¶gɪvɪn^{2} III.1.12] 2 gɪv əz ɪt 3 gɪv ɪt mi: 4 gɪv ɪt° mi: 5 gɪv ɪt° mi: [◇gɪv^{2}; ~$^{1(2x)}$ *v.*] 6 gɪv ɪt əs [◇gɪv^{1}] 7 n.a.

24 Gl 1 gɪ ɪt tə mi: [gɛn$^{2(2x)}$ *p.t.*] 2 gɪ:‿s ɪt 3 gɪv n̩ əs [◇ᵈgɪ^{3}] 4 gɪv əs n̩ 5 gɪ‿s n̩ 6 gɪv ɪt ʌɪ [◇ᵈgɪ^{2}; ◇ᵈ~^{2} VII.5.1] 7 gɪ‿t ʌɪ

25 O 1 gɪv ɪt mɪ [★gɪ^{3}] 2 gɪv ɪʔ tə mi:, gɪv ɪt əs ["older"; ×gɪv^{3}] 3 gɪv ʌs ɪt [◇gɪv^{2}] 3 s.f. gɪv əs ɪt [◇gɪv^{1,4}; ×gɪ^{4}; ★gɪv^{4}; ~^{2} *1 p.t. pl.*; ~^{1}] 5 gɪv əs ɪʔ [¶gɪvɪn^{2} VII.5.9] 6 gɪv ɪʔ ðɪ [+gɪv^{3}]

IX.8.3 GIVEN† (it me)

Q. Jack might say: I have waited a long time for him to give it me, and at last he has .... it me.

Rr. GAVE (IT I/ME), GEN/GIVEN (IT ME/US), GEN HIM I/ME, GEN IT, GIED (EN TO ME), GIED IT I/ME, GIVE (IT{ME}), GIVED/GIVEN IT

Note 1—Any phrase rec. in the r. is reproduced below in full.
Note 2—For GIVE, see IX.8.2 (and refs.).

7 Ch 1 gɛn ɩt ɷz 2 n.a., °gɛn[1(2x)], °gɩvən[1] 3 gɛn ɩt mɩ 4 gɩn ɩt mɩ 5 gɛn ɩt əs 6 gɩn ɩt ʌs

8 Db 1 gɛn, °gɩn[3] 2 gɩn ɩt mɩ 3 gɩn ɩt mɩ, °gɩvn[1] 4 gɛn 5 gɛn ɩt mɩ, °gɩn[1] 6 gɛn‿t mɩ 7 gɩn ɩt mɩ

11 Sa 1 gɩn 2–3 gɩv 4 gɩvn 5 gɩn 6–8 gɩd 9 gɩd, °ge:v[1] 10–11 gɩd

12 St 1–3 gɛn ɩt mɩ 4–5 gɩn ɩt mɩ 6 gɛn ɩt mɩ, °gɛn[1] 7–8 gɩv ɩt mɩ 9 gɩn ɩt mɩ 10 gɩvd ɩt 11 gɩd ɩt mɩ

15 He 1 gɩd ɩt mɩ 2 gɩd ɩt mə 3 gɩv ɩt mɩ, °gɩv[1] 4 gɩv ɩt mə 5 gæɩv ɩt mɩ 6 gɛv ɩt əɩ 7 gɩvn ɩt mɩ, s.w. gɩvn ɩt ʌs

16 Wo 1–2 gɩv 3 gɩn ɩt mi:, °gɩn[2] 4–5 gɩv ɩt mɷ 6 gɩv ɩt mi:, °gɛn[2] 7 gɩv ɩt mi:

17 Wa 1 gɩv ɩt mᵉɩ: 2 gɩn ɩt mɩ, °gɩn[4], °gɩvən[3] 3 gɩvn ɩt 4 gɩv ɩt mɩ 5 gɛn ɩt ɷs 6 gɛn ɩt mᶦi: 7 gɛn ɩt mə

23 Mon 1 gɩd, °ge:ˈv[2] 2 gɩv 3 gɩd 4 gɩv 5 gɩvn 6 gɩd ɩt mə 7 n.a.

24 Gl 1 gɛn 2 gɩn ɩm mɷ, °gɩv[3] 3 gɩd 4 gɩv 5 gɩn ɩm ɑ̈ɩ 6 gɩd ɩt ʌɩ 7 gɩd n̩ tɷ mɩ

25 O 1 gɛn ɩt 2 gæn ɩt 3 gɩn ɩt mi: 4 gɩvn ɩt mi: 5 gɛn 6 gɩv ɩʔ

IX.8.4 WITH ME‡

Q. You want your friend to accompany you somewhere, so you ask him: Will you come .... ?

Rr. LONG WITH I/ME, (ALONG) WITH I/ME/US

Note 1—I.m. exs. of (A)LONG WITH and WITH + C. are reproduced below between square brackets untransliterated.

Note 2—WITH + C. also occurs at III.7.9, IV.8.6, V.7.7, VIII.7.9 and VIII.8.12. For WITH + V., see VI.3.3 (and refs.). Exs. of ME and I/US all meaning *me* also occur at VII.5.1/8, VIII.2.2 and IX.8.2/3.

7 Ch 1 wɪð ɷz [wɪ^{3}, wɪð^{2}] 2 n.a. [wɪ$^{1(2x),2(3x),3(2x)}$, wɪð$^{2,3(2x),4}$, wɪθ$^{1(2x)}$; wɪt‿θ^{1} *w. the*] 3 wɪ mɪ [wɪ^{3}, wɪθ^{2}] 4 wɪ mɪ [wɪ^{1}] 5 wɪ mɛɪ 6 wɪð mɪ

8 Db 1 wɪ mə 2 wɪð əz, wɪ əz [pref.; wɪ^{2}] 3 wɪ mɪ [wɪ^{2}] 4–5 wɪ mɪ 6 wɪ mɛɪ [wɪ^{1}] 7 wɛɪ mɪ

11 Sa 1 wɪð əs [wɪ^{4}] 2 wɪ mi: [wɪ$^{1,2(2x)}$] 3 wɪð mi: 4 wɪð əs 5 lɷŋg ə mɪi: 6 wɪð mɪ [wɪð$^{3(2x)}$] 7 wɪð ʌs [wɪð$^{1(2x)}$] 8 wɪð mɪ [wɪ^{2}] 9 wɪ mi: [wɷð$^{1(2x)}$] 10 wɪð əs [wɪð$^{3(2x)}$, ə^{1}] 11 əlɒŋ ə mi:, °lɒŋ ə mi:^{2} [wɪð$^{2(2x)}$, ə^{2}]

12 St 1 wɛɪ mɪ [wɪ^{2}, wɪð^{1}] 2 wɪð mɪ 3 wɛɪ mɪ, °~ [wɪ$^{1(6x),2(2x)}$, wɪð$^{1(2x)}$] 4 wɪ ɷz [wɪ^{1}, wɪð^{1}] 5 wɪð mɛɪ [wɪð$^{1(3x)}$, wɪ$^{2(3x),3}$] 6 wɪ mɛɪ [wɪ$^{1(5x),2(2x)}$] 7 wɪð mɪ [wɪð^{1}, wɪ^{1,2,4}] 8 wɪð mɛɪ [wɪð^{1,3,6}] 9 wɪ əz [wɪ$^{1(2x)}$, wɪð^{3}] 10 wɪ mi: [wɪ^{5}, ə^{2}] 11 wɪ mi: [wɪð$^{2(3x),3(3x)}$]

15 He 1 əlɒŋ ə mi: 2 əlɒŋ əð əs [əð^{2}, ɷð^{2}, ə^{1,2}] 3 əlɷŋ ə mi: [ə^{2,3}, wɪð$^{2(2x),3}$] 4 əlɷŋ ə mi: [əlɷŋ ə^{2}; əð^{3}, əv^{2}] 5 əlɒŋ ə mi: [əv^{2}] 6 əlɒŋ ə əɪ [wɪð^{1}] 7 əlɒŋ ə mi: [əlɒŋ ə^{4}, lɒŋ ə$^{1(2x)}$; wɪ^{1,2}, wɪð^{1,2,3}]

16 Wo 1 wɪð mɪ [wɪð^{1}, wɪd^{3}] 2 wɪð mɪ [ɷð^{1}] 3 əlɷŋ ə mi: [əlɷŋ ə^{1}; ə^{1,4}] 4 əlɷŋ ə mɷ 5 əlɷŋ əv ɷz 6 əlɷŋ ə mi: [ə$^{3(3x)}$, əv$^{1(2x)}$, ɷð^{2}] 7 əlɒŋ ə mi:, p. wɪð mɪ [ə$^{1(4x),2,3(2x),4}$]

17 Wa 1 wɪð mˈɪ [wɪ^{1}] 2 wɪð əz [wɪð$^{3(2x)}$, wɪθ^{1,3}, wɪ$^{2,3,4(2x)}$] 3 wɪð mɪ [wɪð^{2}] 4 wɪ mɪ 5 wɪð mɪ [ə^{1}] 6 wɪð mˈi:, wɪ mɪ [pref.; wɪ^{2}] 7 wɪ mɪ [wɪ^{1}]

23 Mon 1 lʌŋ ə mˈi: [əv^{1}, əð^{3}] 2 əlɒŋ ə mi: [wɪð^{2} V.7.21] 3 əlɒŋ ə mi: 4 wɪ mi: 5 wɪð mi: [wɪð$^{1,2(2x)}$, wɪ^{2}] 6 lɒŋ ə mi: [ə^{1}, əv^{1}] 7 n.a. [wɪ^{1}]

24 Gl 1 lɷŋ ə mi:, °wɪð mɷ^{1} [ə^{3}, əv^{2}] 2 lɷŋ əv əɪ [ə$^{3(2x)}$] 3 əlɒŋ ə mɪi: [ᵈwˈi^{3}] 4 əlɒŋ əv əɪ [wɪð^{3}, wˈi:^{1}] 5 wɪ ɔ̈ɪ, °~^{2} [wɪ^{2}] 6 n.r. [wɪ^{2}] 7 wɪ ʌɪ [wɪ (rec. in «wɪ‿n» *with en* {=*him*})]

25 O 1 wɪ mə [wɪ^{2}, ~^{2} VIII.3.1, wɪð^{1}] 2 wɪ mɪ [wɪ^{1}, wɪð^{3} V.7.21] 3 wɪ mɪ· [wɪ^{1}, wɪð^{1}] 4 wɪð mi:, s.f. wɪ mɪ [wɪ^{1,4}, wɪð$^{1(8x),3(2x),4}$, wɪθ^{4}] 5 əlɔŋ ə mi: 6 wɪð ɔ̈ɪ

IX.8.5 YOURS† (sg.). MINE†. HIS†. HERS†. OURS†. YOURS† (pl.). THEIRS†

Q. I have my troubles and you have ....

Convert for **mine, his, hers, ours, yours, theirs.**

Rr. THINE, YOURN, YOURS
MINE
HIS(N)
HERN, HERS
OURN(S), OURS
YOURN, YOURS
THEIRN, THEIRS

Note—The rr. to the seven parts of the q. are separated below by full stops.

7 Ch 1 ðɑɩn. mɑɩn. ɩz. əʴ:z. a:z. jɩəz, ○~. n.r. 2 n.a. 3 ðɑɩn. mɑɩn. ɩz. əʴ:z. a:z. jọ:əz. ðɛ:z 4 juəz, ðɑɩn. mɑɩn. ɩz. ə:z. aωəz. juəz. ðɛ:z 5 ðɑɩn. mɑɩn. ɩz. ə:z. a:z. juəz. ðɛ:z 6 joəz. maɩn. ɩz. əʴ̣:z. aωəz. joəz. ðɛəz

8 Db 1 ðaɩn. maɩn. ɩz. əʴ̣:z. ɛʴ̣:z. jo·əʴ̣z. ðɛʴ̣:z 2 ðɑɩn. mɑɩn. ɩz. ə:z. a:z. jo·əz. ðɛ:əz 3 ðaɩn. maɩn. ɩz. ə:z. ɛ̈ωəz. jo·əz. ðɛ:z 4 ðɑɩn. mɑɩn. ɩz. ə:z. a:z. jo:z. ðɛ:z 5 ðɑɩn. mɑ·ɩn. ɩzn. ɛ:n. a:n. jo·ən. ðɛ:ᵊn 6 ðɑ̃·ɩ̃n. mɑ̃ɩ̃n. ɩzn. ə:z. n.r. jo·ən. ðə:n 7 ðɑ̃·ɩ̃n. mɑ̃·ɩ̃n. ɩzn. ə:n. a:z. jo·ən. ðɛ·ən

11 Sa 1 jəʵ:ɳ. mɛɩn. ɩz. əʵ:ʐ. aωᵊn. jəʵ:ɳ. ðəʵ:ɳ 2 jωəz. maɩn. ɩz. əʵ:ʐ. æωəz. jωəz. ðɛ:əz 3 jo:əʵʐ. maɩn. ɩz. əʵ:ʐ. aωəʵ:ʐ. jo:əʵ:ʐ. ðəʵ:ʐ 4 jɔ:əz. mɛɩn. hɩz. əʵ:ʐ. aωəʵ:ʐ. jɔ:əz. ðɛəʵ:ʐ 5 ðaɩn. maɩn. ɩzn. əʵ:ɳ. ɛωəʵɳ. jo:əʵɳ. ðɛəʵɳ 6 jωəʵ:ʐ. maɩn. ɩz. əʵ:ʐ. aωəʵ:ʐ. jωəʵ:ʐ. ðɛəʵ:ʐ 7 jo:əʵʐ. maɩn. ɩz. əʵ:ʐ. aωəʵ:ʐ. jo:əʵʐ. ðe:əʵʐ 8 ðɒɩn. mɒɩn. ɩz. əʵʐ. aωəʵɳ. jo:əʵɳ. ðe:əʵʐ 9 jo:əʵ:ʐ. maɩn. ɩz. əʵ:ʐ. aωəʵ:ʐ. jo:əʵ:ʐ. ðɛəʵ:ʐ 10 jo:əʵʐ. maɩn. ɩz. əʵ:ʐ. aωəʵʐ. jo:əʵʐ. ðe:əʵʐ 11 ðaɩn. maɩn. ɩz. əʵʐ. aωəʵɳ. jo:əʵɳ. ðe:əʵʐ

12 St 1 joɷəz, ðɒɩn. mɒɩn. ɩz. ə:z. aɷə. joɷəz. ðɩə [*sic*] 2 joɷəz. mɒɩn. ɩz. ə:z. a:z. joɷəz. ðɛ:z 3 ðɒ:ɩn. mɒ:ɩn. ɩzn. ə:z. a:n. jɷ:ən. ðɛ:n 4 jə:n. mɒɩn. ɩz. ə:z. aɷəz. jə:n. ðɛ:z 5 jə:n. mɒ:ɩn. ɩzn. ə:zn. a:zn. jə:n. ðɛ:z 6 jə:n. mɒ:ɩn. ɩz. ə:n. a:n. jə:n. ðɛ:n 7 jə:n. mɒɩn. ɩzn. ə:zn. a:n. jə:n. ðɛ:n 8 jə:z. mɒɩn. ɩz. əʴ:z. aɷəz. joɷəz. ðɛ:n 9 jə:n. mɒɩn. ɩz. ə:n. a:n. ðɒɩn. ðɩəz 10 jɷəz. maɩn. ɩz. ə:z. aɷəz. jɷəz. ðɛəz 11 joɷən. mɒ:ɩn. ɩzn. ə:ɹn. aɷən. joɷən. ðɛɩən

15 He 1 jə:əʴʐ. mæɩn. ɩz. n.r. æɷəʴʐ. jə:əʴʐ. ðɛəʴ:ʐ 2 ðæɩn. mæɩn. ɩzn. əʴɳ. æɷəʴɳ. jɷəʴɳ. ðɛəʴɳ 3 jɷəʴɳ. məɩᵊn. ɩzn. əʴ:ɳ. əɷəʴɳ. jɷəʴɳ. ðɛəʴɳ 4 ðəɩn. məɩn. ɩzn. əʴ:ɳ. əwəʴɳ. jo:əʴɳ. ðɛəʴ:ɳ 5 ðəɩn. məɩn. ɩzn. əʴɳ. ʌɷəʴɳ. jɷəʴɳ. ðæɩəʴɳ 6 jɷəʴɳ. məɩn. ɩz. əʴʐ. əwəʴɳ. ðəɩn. ðæɩəʴɳ 7 jɷəɹz. maɩn. ɩz, s.f. ɩzn. əɹz. aɷəɹz, s.f. aɷəɹn. jɷəɹz, s.f. jə·ɹn. ðɛəɹn, s.f. ðɛəɹn

16 Wo 1 jɷən. mɒɩn. ɩzn. əʴ:ɳ. ɛɷən. jɷən. ðɛ:ən 2 ðəɩn. məɩn. ɩz. əʴ:ʐ. ɛɷəʴɳ. jo:əʴɳ. ðɛ:əʴɳ 3 joɷəʴʐ. mɒɩən. ɩzn. əʴ:ɳ. ɛu:əʴɳ. joɷəʴɳ. ðe:ɩəʴɳ 4 ðəɩn. məɩn. ɩzn. əʴ:ɳ. əɷ:əʴɳ, ○ạ̈ɷəʴɳ[1]. jɷəʴɳ. ðəʴ:ɳ 5 ðəɩᵊn. məɩᵊn, ○~[1]. ɩzn. əʴ:ɳ. əɷ:əʴɳ. jɷəʴɳ. ðaɩəʴɳ 6 ðɒɩn. mɒɩn. ɩzn. əʴ:ɳ. ɛu:əʴɳ, ○ɛu:əns[2]. joɷəʴɳ. ðe:əʴɳ 7 jɷəʴʐ. n.r. ɩz, s.f. ɩzn. əʴɳ. æɷəʴɳ. jɷəʴɳ. ðɛən, ðɛ̧ɩəʴɳ

17 Wa 1 jə:z. maɩn. ɩz. ə̧:z. ɛ̈ɷəz. jə:z. ðɛ:z 2 ju·əz, jəɷən [pref.]. n.r. ɩzn. ə:n. æɷən. jəɷən. ðæɩən, ○~ 3 jə:z. məɩən. ɩz. ə:z. ɛ̈ɷəz. jə:ᵊz. ðɛ:əz 4 ju·əʴ·ɳ. məɩn. ɩzn. əʴ:ɳ. ɛɷəʴ·ɳ. ju·ən. ðɛ̧ɩəʴɳ 5 ju·əʴɳ. məɩn. ɩzn. əʴ:ɳ. ɛɷəʴɳ. ju·əʴɳ. ðɛ̧·əʴɳ 6 ju·əʴɳ. məɩn. ɩzn. əʴ:ɳ, ɛɷəʴɳ. ju·ən. ðɛɩəʴɳ 7 ju·əʴɳ. məɩn. ɩzn. əʴ:ɳ. ɛɷəʴɳ. ju·əʴɳ. ðɛ·əʴɳ

23 Mon 1 ðəɩn. məɩn. ɩzn. əʴɳ. ʌɷəʴɳ. jᵚu:əʴɳ. ðæɩəʴɳ 2 jɷəz. məɩn. ɩz. əʴ:ʐ. ʌɷəz. jɷəz. ðɛəz 3 ju:ən. məɩn. ɩzn. əʴ:ɳ. əɷən. ju:ən. ðɛən 4 ju-ən. məin. ɩz. œ:n. əu-əz. ju·ən. ðɛ:n 5 juəz. məin. ɩz. œ̧̈:z. əuəz. juəz. ðeiᵊz 6 ju:əʴɳ. məɩn. ɩzn. əʴ:ɳ. əɷəʴɳ. ju:əʴ·ɳ. ðɛəʴ:ɳ 7 n.a.

24 Gl 1 ðəɪ^{ə}n . məɪ^{ə}n . ɪzn . ə^{r}ɳ . əɷ:^{ər}ɳ . ju:ə^{r}ɳ . ðæɪə^{r}ɳ 2–3 ðəɪn . məɪn . ɪzn . ə^{r}:ɳ . əɷə^{r}ɳ . jɷə^{r}ɳ . ðæɪə^{r}ɳ 4 ðəɪ^{ə}n . məɪ^{ə}n . ɪzn . ə^{r}:ɳ . əɷə^{r}ɳ . jɷə^{r}ɳ . ðaɪə^{r}ɳ 5 ðə̈ɪn . mə̈ɪn . ɪzn . ə^{r}:ɳ . ʌɷə^{r}ɳ . jo·ən . ðæɪə^{r}ɳ 6 ðʌɪn . mʌɪn . ɪzn . ə^{r}:ɳ . ^{ɷ}u:ə^{r}ɳ . ju·ə^{r}ɳ . ðæɪə^{r}ɳ 7 ðʌɪn . mʌɪn . i:z . ə^{r}:ʐ . ^{ɷ}u:ə^{r}ɳ . joə^{r}ɳ . ðɛ̜ɪə^{r}ɳ

25 O 1 ðə̈ɪn . mə̈ɪn . ɪzn . ə^{r}:ɳ . ɛ̈ɷə^{r}ɳ . jɷə^{r}ɳ . ðɛə^{r}ɳ 2 jɷə̠n . mə̈ɪn . ɪzn . ə̠:n . æɷə̠n . jɷə̠n . ðɛə̠n 3 juə^{r}ɳ . mʌʏn . ɪzn . ə^{r}:ɳ . ɛɷə^{r}ɳ . juə^{r}ɳ . ðeə^{r}ɳ 4 jɷ·əɽʐ . məɪn . ɪz . əɽʐ . æɷəɽʐ . jɷ·əɽɳ . ðɛəɽɳ 5 joə^{r}ɳ . mʌʏn . ɪzn . ə^{r}:ɳ . ɛ̈ɷə^{r}ɳ . joə^{r}ɳ . ðɛə^{r}ɳ 6 jɷə^{r}ɳ . mə̈ɪn . ɪzn . ə^{r}:ɳ . ɛ̈ɷə^{r}ɳ . jɷə^{r}ɳ . ðɛə^{r}ɳ

IX.8.6 FATHER'S† BOOTS

Q. If these boots belong to your father, then you could say: These are my . . . .

Rr. DAD'S BOOTS/SHOES, FATHER'S (BOOTS/SHOES)

Note 1—At 25.5 the f.w. omitted to rec. BOOTS.

Note 2—In the i.m. below, cross-refs. have been supplied only when the phrase concerned also appears in some other article and is not covered by the list of cross-refs. in Notes 3 and 4 below.

Note 3—Compare COW'S LEGS at IX.8.7. For exs. of FATHER, see VIII.1.1 (and ref.); and of BOOTS, see VI.14.23.

Note 4—For additional exs. of possessive nouns, see I.6.5, III.6.1, III.1.18 and VIII.1.1/8.

7 Ch 1 fẹ:ðəz bʏ:ts 2 n.a. [kjɑ:vz ne:vəl[1] *calf's navel*; kɒks tɹɛdɪn[2(2x)] *cock's treading* IV.6.9; kɒbl̩əz waks[2] *cobbler's wax*; ɔ:sɪz fɷt[2] *horse's foot* IV.3.10; ɔ:sɪz fi:t[1] *horse's feet*; ɔ:sɪz ü:y̥[1] *horse's hoof*; nakəz kja:t[1] *knacker's cart*; mɷðəz apənstɹɪŋz[3] *mother's apron-strings*; pa:sənz ɪə[3] *parson's ear*; ʃaŋksɪz pɷ:nɪ[3] *shanks's pony*] 3 fe:ðəz bʏ:ts 4 fẹ:ðəz b^{ɷ}ü:ts 5 fe:ðəz b^{ɪ}ʏ:ts 6 fe:ðəz b^{ɷ}ü:ts

8 Db 1 fe:ðə̠z bʏ:ts [stɛpmɷðəz blɛsɪnz[3] *stepmother's blessings* VI.7.11] 2 faðəz b^{ɷ}u:ts [dʒɒn daŋk aɷs[4] *John Dank*('s) *house*] 3 fe:ðəz ʃü:z 4 fe:ðəz b^{ɷ}üts 5 fe:ðəz b^{ɪ}u:ts 6 fe:ˈðəz bɛɷts 7 fe·ɪðəz bɛɷts

11 Sa 1 fa:ðəz bu:ts 2 fe:ðəz bʏʉ:ts 3 fa:ðə^{r}:ʐ b^{ɷ}u:ts 4 fa^{r}:ðə^{r}:ʐ bu:ts 5 fẹ:ðə^{r}ʐ bɪu:ts 6 fa:ðə^{r}:ʐ bu:ts 7 fe:ðə^{r}:ʐ bu:ts 8 fe:ðə^{r}ʐ bu:ts 9 fe:ðə^{r}:ʐ bu:ts 10 fe:ðə^{r}:ʐ bu:ts [klɒgə^{r}:ʐ wɷd[2] *clogger's wood*] 11 fe:ðə^{r}:ʐ bu:ts

12 St 1 fɛɩðəz bu:ts 2 fɛɩðəz bɛɷts [gɹanfɛɩðəz klɒk[1] *grandfather's clock* (n.d.) 3 fɛɩðəz bɛɷts [fɛɩðəz æɷd wi:[2] *father's old way*; gɒndəz nɛk[2] *gander's neck*; ʃaŋksɩz poɷnɩ[1] *shanks's pony*] 4 fɛɩðəz bü:ts [bə:dz nɛsɩs[1] *birds' nests*; wɩks ɒlɩdɩ[3] *week's holiday*] 5 fɛɩðəz bü:ts [ka:vz stɷmək[3] calf's *stomach*; fa:məz joɷgl[3] *farmer's yokel*] 6 fɛɩðəz bü:ts [foɷksɩz fɛɩt[1] *folks's feet*] 7 dadz bü:ts [tü: ɩəz gɹoɷθ[1] *two years' growth*] 8 dadz bü:ts [wɩks ɒlɩdɩ[1] *week's holiday*] 9 fɛɩðəz bü:ts [sənt klɛmɩnsɩz[1] *Saint Clement's*; sənt klɛmɩnsɩz dɛɩ[1] *St. Clement's Day*; dʒɛɩkəbz ladə[2] *Jacob's ladder*; ʃanksɩz poɷnɩ[2] *shanks's pony*] 10 fɛɩðəz bü:ts [bɛɩkəz dɷzn[2] *baker's dozen*] 11 fɛɩðəz bu:ts [bɛɩkəz dɷzn[2] *baker's dozen*]

15 He 1 faðəʳz̜ bu:ts 2 fe:ðəʳz̜ bu:ts [ʃɩps jʌd[1] *sheep's head*] 3–4 fe:ðəʳz̜ bu:ts 5 fɛ:ðəʳz̜ bu:ts 6 fe:ðəʳz̜ bu:ts 7 fa:ðəɹz bu:ts, dadz bu:ts [faɹməɹz glo:ɹɩ[1] *farmer's glory* (i.e. binder-twine) I.7.3; ɛnz bɩl[2] *hen's bill*; mɩstəɹ adɩsɩz fæ̯:ðəɹ[3] *Mr. Addis's father*]

16 Wo 1 fe:ðəz bu:ts 2 fɑ:ðəʳ:z̜ bu:ts 3 fɛ:əðəʳz̜ bu:ts 4 fɛəʳðəʳz̜ bu:ts 5 fe:ðəʳz̜ bu:ts [ʃɩps jɷd[1] *sheep's head*] 6 fe:əðəʳz̜ bu:ts [ɒsɩz fɩtməʳ:ks[2] *horse's feet-marks* IV.3.10] 7 dadz ʃu:z, fa:ðəz bu:ts [babɩz napɩ[3] *baby's nappy*; bɔɩz meɩts[4] *boy's mates*; tʃaps sɷn[4] *chap's son*; tʃaps ɷŋkl[4] *chap's uncle*; ɔ:sɩz tɹæɷt[1] *horse's trough*; mɩsɩzɩz da·d[1] *missis' dad*; mɩsɩzɩz fɑ:ðə[3] *m. father*; sæɷz bɹɩsəłz[4] *sow's bristles*; stɛpfa:ðəʳz̜ ʃɩəʳz̜[4] *step-father's shears*]

17 Wa 1 fa:ðəz bu:ts 2 fe:ðəz bu:ts [babɩz bənɩt[4] *baby's bonnet*; bɩlz dad[1] *Bill's dad*; fa:məz glɔ:ɹɩ[1] *farmer's glory* (i.e. binder-twine) I.7.3; gɹanɩ bɹɷðə[4] *granny's brother*; kɩdz klatə[4] *kid's clatter*; ɷvənz mæɷθ[3] *oven's mouth*; pɩgz tʃɩklɩnz[3] *pig's chicklings* (=*chitterlings*); pɩgz fɹɔɩ[3] *pig's fry*; pɩgz gɷts[3] *pig's guts*; pɩgz mɛlt[3] *pig's melt*; ʃɩps mɷðə[3] *sheep's mother*; ʃɩps plɷk[3] *sheep's pluck*; sɷməz fɔlə[2] *summer's fallow*; wɔɩfs pɩnmɷnɩ[1] *wife's pin-money*; wə:ldz wɔə[4] *world's war*] 3 fa:ðəz 4 fa:ðəz bü:ts 5 fe·əðəʳz̜ bu:ts [dɒŋkɩz ɩəʳz̜[1] *donkey's years*; fɩləʳz̜ tak[1] *filler's tack* (i.e. gear for shaft-horse); ɹabɩtspɛlt *rabbit's-pelt* III.11.8] 6 fe·əðəz ^△^bu:t 7 fɛəðəʳz̜ bu:ts

23 Mon 1 fe:ɩðəʳz̜ bᵚu:ts 2–4 fa:ðəz bu:ts 5 fa:ðəz bu:tᵊs 6 fa:ðəʳz̜ bu:ts 7 n.a.

24 Gl 1 fe:ðəʳz̜ bu:ts 2 fe:ðəʳz̜ bɷu:ts 3 ve:ˈðəʳz̜ bᵚu:ts 4 fjɛðəʳz̜ bᵚu:ts 5 fa:ðəʳ·z̜ bu:ts [mɑʳ:ɳɩnz ɷd[2] *morning's wood* V.4.2] 6 fjaðəʳz̜ bu:ts 7 fa:ðəʳz̜ bu:ts [ʃaŋksɩz po:nɩ[1] *shanks's pony*]

25 O 1 feəðeʳʐ bu:ts 2 feəðə̠z bɷts 3 fa:ðəʳʐ bu:ts 4 fɑ:ðəɽʐ bu:ts [be:bɪz stɷmək[3(2x)] *baby's stomach*; fɽɛd ɛdwədzɪz sɷn[3] *Fred Edward's son*; fɑɽməɽʐ ɽɔɪt[2] *farmer's right*; mɷŋks płe:s[1] *monk's place*; mɷðəz tɛt[3] *mother's teat*] 5 faðəʳʐ 6 fæðəʳʐ bu:ts

IX.8.7 COW'S† LEGS

Q. ☐ *These are the legs of this cow. So you can say, in a shorter way: These are this . . . .*

Rr. BEAST'S/COW'S LEGS

Note 1—Compare FATHER'S BOOTS at IX.8.6.

Note 2—In the i.m. below, cross-refs. have been supplied only when the phrase concerned also appears in some other article.

Note 3—For exs. of COW, see III.1.1 (and refs.); -LEGGED occurs at III.3.3 and VI.9.6.

7 Ch 1 kaɷz lɛgz 2 n.a. [kja:z paps[1] *cow's paps*] 3 kaɪz lɛgz [kaɪz ɔ:nz[3] *cow's horns*] 4 kaɷz lɛgz, °kɛɪz lɛgz [older] 5–6 kaɷz lɛgz

8 Db 1 kɛ̞ɷz lɛgz 2 kaɷz lɛgz 3 kɛ̈ɷz lɛgz 4 kɛ:z lɛgz 5 kɛ̞:ᵊz lɛgz 6–7 kɛ:z lɛgz

11 Sa 1 kaɷz lɛgz 2 kæɷz lɛgz 3 kaɷz lɛgz 4 kɛu:z lɛgz 5 kɛɷz lɛgz 6–7 kaɷz lɛgz 8 kɛɷz lɛgz 9–11 kaɷz lɛgz

12 St 1 ka:z lɛgz 2 kaɪz lɛgz 3 kjaɷz lɛgz 4 kæɷz lɛgz [kaɷz ü:st *cow's hoast*] 5 kaɷz lɛgz 6 kæ:z lɛgz 7 kæɷz lɛgz 8 bi:sts lɛgz 9 ka:z lɛgz 10 ka:ɷz lɛgz 11 kæ:ɷz lɛgz

15 He 1–2 kæɷz lɛgz 3–4 kəɷz lɛgz 5 kʌɷz lɛgz 6 kəɷz lɛgz 7 kɑ̆ɷz lɛgz [kɑ̆ɷz ɷfs[2] *cow's hoofs*]

16 Wo 1–2 kɛɷz lɛgz 3 kɛu:z lɛgz 4 kəɷ:z lɛgz [kəɷ:z mɪłk[2] *cow's milk*] 5 kəɷ:z lɛgz 6 kɛu:z lɛgz 7 kæɷz lɛgz [kæɷz ɔɪd[4] *cow's hide* III.11.7]

17 Wa 1 kɛ̈ɷz lɛgz 2 kæɷz lɛgz [kæɷz bu:zɪ[3] *cows' boosy* (i.e. manger); kæɷz ɔɪd[3] *cow's hide* III.11.7; kæɷz klɛɪ *cow's clee* (i.e. hoof)] 3–4 kɛɷz lɛgz 5 kɛɷz △lɛg 6–7 kɛɷz lɛgz

23 Mon 1–2 kʌɷz lɛgz 3 kəɷz łɛgz 4 kʰəuz lɛgz 5 kəuz lɛgz 6 kəɷz łɛgz 7 n.a.

24 Gl 1 kəɷ:ᵊz lɛgz 2 kəɷ:z lɛgz 3–4 kəɷz lɛgz 5 kʌɷz lɛgz 6–7 kᵒu:z lɛgz

25 O 1 kɛ̈ɷz lɛgz 2 kạɷz lɛgz 3 kɛɷz lɛgz 4 kạɷz łɛgz 5–6 kɛ̈ɷz lɛgz

IX.8.8 ONE†. THE† OTHER*

Q. You cut an apple in half, and to your little girl you give [*g.*] . . . . *half.*

And to your boy you give [*g.*] . . . .

Rr. ONE (HALF/PIECE), THE ONE (HALF),
/THE OTHER/TOTHER/ HALF, THE OTHER, (THE) TOTHER

Note 1—The rr. to the two parts of the q. are separated below by a full stop.

Note 2—I.m. exs. of ONE used adjectivally are reproduced below untransliterated between square brackets foll. the r. to the 1st part of the q.

Note 3—I.m. exs. of THE OTHER (ONE) are cited after the r. to the 2nd part of the q.

Note 4—Untransliterated i.m. exs. of ANOTHER, OTHER and TOTHER are cited between square brackets below immediately foll. the r. to the 2nd part of the q. An attached superior ◇ denotes "used pronominally" and attached superior × denotes "used adjectivally".

Note 5—For additional exs. of ONE, see VII.1.1 (and refs.). For EACH OTHER('S) and ONE ANOTHER('S), see III.2.10, III.13.16 and VI.2.8. (T)OTHER and (T)OTHER'S also occur at IX.10.3/6. For HALF, see VII.5.4 (and refs.).

7 Ch 1 wɒn . tωðə 2 n.a. n.a., ○tωðə[1,2(2x),3], ○θ‿ωðə[1] [×ənωðə[3,4]; ×ωðə[3(2x)]; ×tωðə[1]] 3 wɒn . tωðə, ○ð‿ωðə[1,3] [□ωðəz[2]] 4 wɒn ẹ:f . ð‿ωðə 5 wɒn . ðə ωðə 6 wɒn . ð‿ωðə [□◇ωðəz[3] IX.10.5]

8 Db 1 wɒn . tωðə 2 wɒn e:f [wɒn[2]] . tωðə [×ωðə[4]; ◇tωðə[2]] 3 wɒn . tωðə, ○ʔ tωðə[3] 4 wɒn e:f . tωðəɹ e:f [◇ωðə III.3.7] 5 wɒn e:ˡf . tωðə [◇ωðə[1]] 6 wɒn [wωn[1]] . tωðə 7 wɒn e·ɩf . tωðəɹ e·ɩf

11 Sa 1 wʌn . ðə ʌðəɽ 2 wɒn e:f . ðə ωðəɽ 3 wɒn e:f . ðə ɒðəɽ 4 wɒn [wɒn[2]] . ðɩ ʌðəɽ 5 ðə wωn ẹ:f [wɒn[1]] . ðə tωðəɽ [×ənωðəɽ[3(2x)]] 6 wɒn, wɒn e:f . ðə ʌðəɽ, ○ðə ʌðəɽ· 7 wɒn . ðə ʌðəɽ, ○ðə ʌ·ðəɽ[1], ○ðɩ ʌðəɽ[1] [□◇ʌðəɽ:ʐ[1]] 8 wɒn e:f [wɒn[1,2]] . ðə tωðəɽ, ○~[2] [×ənωðəɽ[2]] 9 wɒn . ðə ʌðəɽ 10 wɒn e:f . ðə ʌðəɽ, ○~[3(2x)] [×ʌðəɽ[2]] 11 wɒn . ðə ʌðəɽ

12 St 1 wωn ɛɩf . tωðəɹ ɛɩf, ○tωðə[1], ð‿ωðə[3] [□◇ð‿ωðəz[2]] 2 wɒn ɛɩf . ð‿ωðə, ○‿θ tωðə[3] 3 wωn ɛɩf [wɒn[2]] . tωðəɹ ɛɩf [×ənωðə[1], ◇~[2]; ×ωðə[2]] 4 wɒn ɛɩf [wωn[2]] . tωðə [×ənωðə[3]] 5 wɒn pɛɩs . tωðə [◇ənωðə[1]] 6 wɒn pɛɩs . ðɩ ωðə, ○ðə tωðə[1] 7 wɒn ạ:f [wɒn[1(5x)], wωn[4]] . ðɩ ωðə, ○ð‿ωðə[1] [×ənωðə[3], ◇~[1]] 8 wɒn ɑ:f [wɒn[1(4x)]] . tωðə 9 wɒn ɛɩf . tωðə [◇ənωðə[1]; ×tωðəɹ] 10 wωn a:f . ðə tωðə, ○tωðə [□◇tωðəz[5]] 11 wɒn [wɒn[1], wɒ̣n[2] IX.1.3, wωn[1]] . ðə tωðə, ○ð‿ωðə[1(2x)] [×ənωðə[2]; ◇ωðə[2]]

15 He 1 ðə wʌn. ðə ʌðəᵗ, ᵒ~¹ 2 ðə wʌn i:f. ðə tʌðəᵗ, ᵒðə ʌðəᵗ² [◇ənʌðəᵗ², ◇ʌðəᵗ¹] 3 wɷn. ðə ɷðəᵗ [◇ɷðəᵗ¹] 4 wʌn. ðə tʌðəᵗ, ᵒ~², ᵒðə tɷðəᵗ² 5 wɷn. ðə ɷðə, ᵒ~⁴, ᵒðə ʌðəᵗ¹ [□◇ɷðəᵗz̧⁴] 6 wɷn. ðə tɷðəᵗ 7 wɒn a:f [wɒn³⁽²ˣ⁾]. tʌðəɹ a:f, ᵒð‿ʌðəɹ²,³, ᵒð‿ɷðəɹ², ᵒðɩ ɷðəɹ⁴, ᵒðɩ ɷðə⁴ [ˣnʌðəɹ¹; ˣʌðəɹ³]

16 Wo 1 ðə wɷn ɑ:f, ᵒðə wɒn¹. ðə tɷðə [□◇tɷðəᵗz̧¹] 2 wɷn. ðə tɷðəᵗ [□◇tɷðəᵗz̧¹] 3 wɷn ɑ:f [wɷn¹]. ðə ɷðəᵗ 4 ðə wɷn, ᵒ~². ðə ɷðəᵗ, ᵒ~¹,², ᵒðə tɷðəᵗ³ [ˣɷðəᵗ¹] 5 wɷn. ðə tɷðəᵗ, ᵒ~¹⁽²ˣ⁾ 6 wɷn. ðə ɷðəᵗ, ᵒtɷðəᵗɽ² [+ V.; ◇ənɷðəᵗ¹] 7 wɷn a:f [wɷn¹⁽⁴ˣ⁾,³,⁴⁽³ˣ⁾, wən¹,⁴]. ðɩ ɷðəɹ a:f, ᵒðɩ ɷðə¹, ᵒð‿ɷðəᵗ¹ [ˣənɷðə¹, ◇~²; ˣɷðə¹,³,⁴, ◇ɷðə³,⁴⁽²ˣ⁾]

17 Wa 1 wɒn a:f. ðɩ ɷðəɹ a:f 2 wən a:f [wən¹,², ~⁴ VI.3.6, wɷn³]. ð‿ɷðə, ᵒ~¹, ᵒ~⁴ VI.3.6, ᵒtɷðə²,⁴ [ˣənɷðə³⁽²ˣ⁾; ˣɷðə¹] 3 wɒn [wɒn³]. ðə ɷ̜ðə 4 wɷn. ðə tɷðə, ᵒ~¹,² 5 wɷn [wɷn¹⁽³ˣ⁾, ~¹ III.2.7]. ðə tɷðəᵗ, ᵒ~¹⁽²ˣ⁾, ᵒðə tɷðəɹ¹, ᵒðə tɷðə¹, ᵒðə tʌðə¹ 6 wɷn [wɷn³]. ðə tɷðəᵗ [◇ənɷðə²] 7 wɷn [wənʃɩə³ *one-shear* III.6.4]. ðə tʌðəᵗ

23 Mon 1 wʌn. tʌðəᵗ [◇ənʌðəᵗ¹] 2 wɷn. ðə ɷðəᵗ 3 wʌn. tʌðə, ᵒðə ʌðə¹ [◇ʌðə¹] 4 ðə wʌ̤̈n [wʌ̤̈n¹]. ði· ʌ̤̈ðʌ̤̈ 5 ðə wʌ̤̈n. ðᵊ ʌ̤̈ðə, ᵒði ʌ̤̈ðə² 6 wʌn. tʌðəᵗ 7 n.a. [wʌ̤n¹]. n.a., ᵒðə ʌ̤ðə¹ V.2.5

24 Gl 1 wɷ:n [wʌn³]. ðə tɷðəᵗ, ᵒ~²⁽²ˣ⁾, ᵒðə tʌðəᵗ¹, ᵒtɷðəᵗ³ 2 wɷn [wɷn³]. ðə tɷðəᵗ 3 wœ:n [wʌn³]. ðə tɷðəᵗ, ᵒðə tʌðəᵗ³ 4 wɒn. ðə tɷðəᵗ, ᵒtɷðəᵗ¹ [ˣɷðəᵗ³] 5 wɷ̜n a:f [wən¹ VII.5.8]. ðə tʌðə, ᵒ~², ᵒðə tɷðə² 6–7 wən. təðəᵗ

25 O 1 wɷn [wən²]. tʌðəᵗ 2 wən [wən¹]. tʌðəᵗ, ᵒðə tɒðəᵗ¹ [◇ənʌðə¹; □◇ð‿ʌðəᵗz̧²] 3 wən. tʌðə 4 wɒn a:f [wɒn¹, wɷn¹,²,⁵]. ð‿ɷðəᵗ, tɷðəɽ a:f, ᵒð‿ɷðəɽ¹⁽²ˣ⁾ [ˣənɷðəɽ¹; ◇ɷðəᵗ⁵] 5 wʌn [wʌnsö̈ɩd² *one-side* (i.e. askew) *adj.* IX.1.3] tʌðəᵗ [◇ənʌðəᵗ²; ˣʌðə²] 6 wən. ðə tɒðəᵗ, ᵒð‿ʌðəᵗ²

IX.9.1 WHO*

Q. Your wife comes back after answering the door, and you, being curious, might ask her: . . . . was it?

R. WHO

Note—For additional exs. of WHO *interrog.*, see IX.9.3/4; and for exs. of WHO *rel.*, see III.3.7 and IX.9.5.

7 Ch 1 ʏ: 2 n.a., ᵒu:⁴ 3 ü: 4 ᵒu:, ᵒu:² 5 ṳ̈: 6 ᵒṳ̈:

8 Db 1 ʏ:, ○~ 2 ʘu: 3 ü: 4 ʘü: 5 u: 6 ü: 7 ʘü:

11 Sa 1–4 u: 5 ʘu: 6 u:, ○~[3] 7 u: 8 u:, ○~[1,2] 9–11 u:

12 St 1–5 u: 6 ü [*sic*] 7–8 u: 9–10 ü: 11 u:

15 He 1–2 u: 3 u:, ○~[1] 4–6 u: 7 u:, ○~[1,4]

16 Wo 1–2 u: 3 u:, ○~[2] 4–5 u: 6 u:, ○~[3(2x)] 7 u:, ○~[4]

17 Wa 1–2 u: 3 u:, ○~ 4–5 u: 6 ü:, ○u: 7 u:

23 Mon 1 ʘu: 2–3 u: 4 u:, ○hu:[1] 5–6 u: 7 n.a.

24 Gl 1 u: 2–4 ʘu: 5 u:, ○~ 6 u:, ○~[2] 7 u:, ○~[1]

25 O 1 ü: 2–3 u: 4 u:, ○~[4] 5 u: 6 ü:

IX.9.2 WHOSE IT IS‡

Q. You see a dog chasing your sheep, and you know it's not yours, so you wonder . . . .

Rr. WHO IT BELONGS, WHOSE /HE BE/HER IS/IS IT/THAT IS/'TIS/, WHOSE IT BE/IS/§WAS, WHOSEN /IT IS/'TIS/, WHOSES IT IS

Note 1—At 8.1/2 and 17.3/7 the f.w. omitted to rec. the wanted IT IS.

Note 2—For additional exs. of WHOSE, see IX.9.6.

7 Ch 1 ʏ:z ɪʔ ɪz 2 n.a. 3 ü:z tɪz 4 ʘu:z ɪt ɪz 5 ˈʏ:z ɪt ɪz 6 ʘṳ̈:z ɪt ɪz

8 Db 1 ʏ:z 2 ʘu:z 3 ü: ɪt bɪlɒŋz [pref.], p. ü:z ɪt ɪz 4 ʘü:z ɪt ɪz 5 u:z ɪt ɪz 6 ü:z əɹ ɪz 7 ʘü:z ɪt ɪz

11 Sa 1–4 u:z ɪt ɪz 5 ʘu:z ɪt ɪz 6–11 u:z ɪt ɪz

12 St 1 ü:z ɪt ɪz 2 u:z ɪt ɪz 3 u:z tɪ̞z 4 u:z ɪt ɪz 5 u:z ɪt §wɒz 6 u:zɪz ɪt ɪz 7 ü:z ɪt ɪz 8 u:z ɪt ɪz 9–10 ü:z ɪt ɪz 11 u:zn ɪt ɪz

15 He 1–5 u:z ɪt ɪz 6 u:z ɪt §wəz 7 u:z ɪt ɪz [u:z[4] *whose*]

16 Wo 1 u:z ɪt ɪz 2 u:z ɪt bi: 3 u:z ɪt §wɷz 4 u:z ɪ bi: 5 u:z ɪt ɪz [u:z ðɛm bi:[1] *whose them be* (i.e. whose they are)] 6 u:zn ɪt ɪz 7 u:z ɪt ɪz

17 Wa 1–2 u:z ɪt ɪz 3 ü:z 4 ü:z ɪt ɪz 5–6 u:z ɪt ɪz 7 ɷz

23 Mon 1 ʘu:z ɪt §wʌz 2 u:z ɪt bi: 3 u:z ɪt ɪz 4 u:z ɪz ɪt 5 u:z ɪtʰ ɪz 6 u:z ɪt ɪz 7 n.a.

24 Gl 1 u:z ɩt ˢwɑ:z 2 ᵒu:z ɩt ɩz 3–4 ᵒu:z ɩt bˡi: 5 ɷzn‿ʔt ɩz 6 u:z ðat ɩz 7 u:z tɩz

25 O 1 u:z ɩt ɩz 2 u:z tɩz 3 u:z ɩt ɩz 4 u:z tɩz 5 ɷzn tɩz 6 ü:z ɩʔ ɩz

IX.9.3 TO WHOM‡

Q. You have something to give away and before deciding on the person to be given it, you might ask yourself: I wonder .... I shall give it?

Rr. /WHICH I SHALL/WHO TO/ GIVE IT TO, WHO I /BETTER/ COULD/MUN/SHALL (HAVE TO)/SHOULD/ GIVE IT TO, WHO (SHALL~SHOULD I) GIVE IT TO, WHO /I'D BETTER/ I'LL/I SHALL~SHOULD/TO/ GIVE THIS TO, WHO I'LL GIVE IT (TO), WHO (.... TO)

Note 1—A r. consisting of a phrase or sentence is reproduced below in full.

Note 2—Though they do not actually include TO, the rr. at 11.1/3/5–11, 15.6, 16.1/2/5, 23.1–3/6 and 24/1–4 are clearly idiomatic and relevant. Unfortunately, at 7.4, 17.3 and 25.5, the f.w. omitted the central part of the r.

Note 3—For additional exs. of GIVE, see IX.8.2 (and refs.); of WHO *rel. pron.*, see IX.9.5 (and ref.); and of WHO *interrog. pron.*, see IX.9.1.

7 Ch 1 ʏ: ʃʏd a gɩv ɩt tʏ: 2 n.a. 3 ü:‿t gɩv tʏ̈: 4 ᵒu: .... tɷ 5 ˡʏ: a mʌn gɩv ɩt tˡʏ: 6 ᵒṳ̈: a ʃᵊd gɩv ɩt tᵒṳ̈:

8 Db 1 ʏ:‿tʔ gɩv ɩt tʏ: 2 ᵒu: a ʃl av tə gɩ ɩt tᵒu: 3 ü:‿t gɩv ɩt tü: 4 ᵒu: a mən gɩ‿t tᵒü: 5 u: a kəd gɩv ɩt tu: 6 ü:‿t gi:‿t tɛ̈ɷ 7 ᵒu: a sl gɩ ɩt tɛɷ

11 Sa 1 u: 2 wɩtʃ aɩ ʃl gɩv ɩt tu: 3 u: 4 u: aɩl gɩv ɩt tu: 5–11 u:

12 St 1 u:‿t gɩv ɩt tü: 2 u: gɩv ɩt tɩɷ 3 u:‿t gɩv ɩt tɛɷ 4 u: ʃəl a gɩv ɩt tü: 5 u: a kɷd gɩv ɩt tü: 6 u: a ʃəl gi: ɩt tü· 7 ü: ɒɩ ʃəl gɩv ɩt tü: 8 u: al gɩv ðɩs tu: 9 ü: ɒɩl gi ɩt tü: 10 ü: a ʃəl gɩv ɩt tü: 11 u: a:ɩ ʃəl gi: ɩt tü:

15 He 1 u: tə gɩv ɩt tu: 2 u: əɫ gɩv ɩt tu: 3 u: ɫ̩ gɩv ɩt tu: 4–5 u: əɫ gɩv ɩt tu: 6 u: 7 u: aɩl gɩv ɩt tu:

16 Wo 1–2 u: 3 u: ɒɩl gɩv ɩt 4 u: tə gɩv ɩt tu: 5 u: 6 u: ɒɩɫ gɩv ɩt 7 s.w. u: a ʃəl gɩv ɩt tu:

17 Wa 1 u: tə gɩv ɩt tu: 2 u:l [? error for «u:», Edd.] ɔɩd bɛtə gɩ ðɩs tu: 3 ü: .... tɷ 4 u: tə gɩ ðɩs tu: 5 u: ɔɩd bɛtə gɩ ðɩs tu: 6 ü: tə gɩv ɩt tü: 7 u: tə gɩv ɩt tu:

23 Mon 1 ᵒu: 2–3 u: 4 u: əil gɩv ɩt tʰu· 5 u: əɭ ʃɫ gɩv ɩt˳ tʰu: 6 u: 7 n.a.

24 Gl 1–2 u: 3–4 ᵒu: 5 u: ðɩ ʃʌd gɩ ðɩs tu: 6 u: ʌɩ ʃəl gɩ ðɩs tu: 7 u: ʌɩ bɛtə gɩ‿t tu:

25 O 1 u: ðɩ ʃʌd gɩv ɩt tu: 2 u: ðɩ ʃəd gɩv ɩt tü: 3 u: ʌʏ ʃəd gɩv ɩt tʏ: 4 u: tə gɩv ɩt tu: 5 u: . . . . tü: 6 ü: ðɩ ʃəd gɩv ɩʔ tü:

IX.9.4 WHO ARE YOUR PARENTS?

Q. A little boy comes up and talks to you in the street, and you are not sure you know him, so you say: Tell me, ...

Rr. /§TELL ME/WHAT'S/ YOUR NAME, WHERE DO (YOU) COME FROM?, WHO ARE YOU (WHEN YOU'RE AT HOME)?, WHO DO YOU BELONG TO?, WHO'S YOUR DAD/FATHER?, WHOSE /BOY/(LITTLE) LAD/YOUNG ONE/ ARE YOU?

Note 1—In the list above, ARE YOU subsumes ARE/ART/BE/BEEST THOU and AM/AREN/BE/BEEN YOU. DO YOU subsumes DOST THOU and D'YOU; YOU subsumes THOU and THEE; and YOUR subsumes THY.

Note 2—At 7.3, 8.1/3/4/7 and 12.2, THOU has been absorbed by the v.

Note 3—The 1st r. at 25.6 does not suit the context and has therefore been designated u.r. below.

Note 4—For additional exs. of WHO, see IX.9.1 (and refs.); of WHOSE, see IX.9.2/6; of ARE YOU, see IX.7.2; and of FATHER(–), see VIII.1.1 and IX.8.6.

7 Ch 1 ʏ:z lad ə ðẹ: 2 n.a. 3 ü:z lad at 4 wɒts juə nẹ:m 5 n.a. 6 ᵒu:z jə fe:ðə

8 Db 1 ʏ: a꞉t' 2 ᵒu:z lɩtl lad a jə, p. ᵒu:z lɩtl lad a ðə 3 ü:z lɩtl lad a:t 4 ᵒü:z lɩtl lad a:t 5 u: a:t ə 6 ü:z lad ət ðɛɩ 7 ᵒü:z lad a:t

11 Sa 1 u:z lad bɩn jo: 2 u:z lɩtl lad ə ju: 3 u:z jə fa:ðəʳ, u:z lad a ju: 4 u:z jɔ:əʳ da:d 5 ᵒu: bɩst ðʲi: 6 u:z bɒɩ am jo: 7 u:z læd bɩn jo: 8 u:z lad bɩ ði: 9 u:z bɷi: bɩ jo: 10 u:z bɷɩ bɩn jo: 11 u: bɩn jo:

12 St 1 u: ət ðɛɩ, ᵒwɒts ðɩ nɛɩm, ᵒwɛ: dɷst kɷm fɹɒm 2 u: at 3 wɒts ðɩ nɛɩm 4 wɩə‿st ðɛɩ kɷm fɹɒm 5 u: ə ju: 6 wɒts jə nɛɩm 7 wɛ: joɷ kɷm fɹɒm 8 wɒts jɔ: nɛɩm 9 wɒts ðɩ nɛɩm 10 ü: ə jü: 11 u: bɩn jaɷ, u:‿n jaɷ

15 He 1 u: djə bɩlɒŋ tu: 2–3 u:z bwɒɩ bɩ ju: 4 u:z ðɩ fe:ðəʳ 5 u: bɩ ju: 6 u:z bwɒɩ bɩ ju: 7 u:z lɩtl bəɩ əɹ ju:, u: ɑ·ɹ jə [fr. i.'s son]

16 Wo 1 u:z lad əm ju: 2 u: dɷ ju: bɩlɷŋ tu: 3 u:z lɩtl bwɒɩ bɩ ju: 4 u:z ðɩ fɛəʳðəʳ 5 u:z læd bɩ ju: 6 u: bɩ ju: ðɛ:n [=*then*] 7 u:z lɩtl bəɩ bi: ju: ðɛn [=*then*]

17 Wa 1 u:z lɩtl bɒɩ a: jə 2 u: ə ju: 3 u:z lɩtł bɒɩ ə ju: 4 wɒts jọə nɛɩm, ᴼu: ə ju: wɛn jəɹ ət ɷm 5 u: bi: jə 6 u: də ju: bɩlɒŋ tu: 7 u:z lɩtł bɒɩ ə ju:

23 Mon 1 ᴼu:z jəʳ fe:ɹðəʳ 2 u:z bɒɩ bɩ jə 3 u: də ju: bɩłɒŋ tu: 4 n.a. 5 wɒ̣·ts juə nẹ:m 6 u:z bɒɩ ə ju: 7 n.a.

24 Gl 1 u: bɩst ði: 2 u: bɩs ð'i: 3 ɷu:z bwɒɩ bɩst 4 ᴼu:z bwɒɩ bɩs ð'i: 5 wɒts ðɔ̈ɩ ne:m, u:z ðɩ fa:ðə 6 u:z ðɩ fjaðəʳ 7 u:z lɩtl bwɒɩ bɩ ju:

25 O 1 u:z bʷəɩ bɩst ði: 2 u:z jʌŋ ən bɩ jü: 3 u: bɩ jü: 4 wɒs jɷəɽ ne:m 5 wɔˀs juəʳ ne:m 6 §tɛl mɩ jə nɩəm, wəts jə nɩəm ["older"]

IX.9.5 WHO‡

Q. The woman next door says: The work in this garden is getting me down. You say: Well, get some help in. I know a man . . . . will do it for you.

Look out for the omission of the relative.

Rr. A CHAP /AS WILL/WHICH WILL HELP YOU/WHO'D/WHO'LL DO IT/WHO'D (COME)/, A FELLOW WILL, A MAN AS /WILL~WOULD DO IT FOR YOU/WOULD COME/WOULD DO IT/, A MAN WHAT WOULD DO IT, AN OLD YOUTHER AS WOULD HELP YOU, AS (WILL/WOULD), AS CAN/WILL DO IT, AS WILL COME AND /DO IT (FOR THEE)/GIVE YOU A DAY/, AS WILL GIVE YOU SOME HELP, AS WOULD COME (/AND GIVE THEE A HAND/AND HELP YE/), AS WOULD /DO IT FOR THEE/HELP YOU/, WHAT (WILL/WOULD), WHAT WILL /DO/HELP YOU/, WHICH, WHO'D HELP YOU, WHO('LL), WHO'LL /COME/DO IT/, WHO WANTS A JOB, (THAT) WILL DO IT

Note 1—A r. consisting of a phrase or sentence is reproduced below in full.

Note 2—Acc. the view taken here, the verbal el. at 7.3 and 8.4 is WILL, while that at 7.1, 2nd r., and 25.5 is WOULD.

Note 3—I.m. exs. of phrase with a zero rel. pron. are included below between square brackets. For additional exs. of the defining rel. pron., see III.3.7. WHO *interrog.* occurs at IX.9.1.

Note 4—The i.m. has not been provided with cross-refs. The inclusion of a word here does not, therefore, preclude its appearance elsewhere.

7 Ch 1 əz ɭ, ə tʃap əd dʏ: ɩt 2 n.a. [ðəz ə spɛɷt kɷmz ðɛə³ *there's a spout* (which) *comes there*] 3 ə fɛləɹ əl 4 əz əd, ᴼə mɒn əz əd kɷm 5 əz əd, ən ɛɷd jaɷθəɹ əz əd ɛlp jə 6 əz

8 Db 1 əz ɭ 2 wɒt əd 3 ə tʃap ü:d 4 ət ʃapp‿əl dɛɷ ɩt, ᵒü:l dɛɷ ɩt 5 əz ɭ 6 tʃap əz ɭ 7 əz, əz ɭ dɛɷ ɩt

11 Sa 1 əz ɭ 2 əz ɭ du: ɩt 3 az ɭ 4–8 əz 9 u: 10–11 əz

12 St 1 əz əd daɷ ɩt fɔ: ðɩ 2 u:l 3 ə mɒn əz ɭ dɛɷ ɩt fɔ: jə 4 əz ɭ 5 əz kən du: ɩt 6 u:d ɛlp jə, əz ɭ dü: ɩt ["old"] 7 wɒt ɭ ɛlp jə 8 əz əl kɷm ən gɩv j‿ə dɛɩ 9 u:l kɷm, əz əd kɷm 10 ɭ dü: ɩt, p. ðət ɭ dü: ɩt 11 ə man əz əd dü: ɩt fɒ jə

15 He 1 əz ɬ du: ɩt 2 əz ɬ [ðə wʌn ə wəʳ:k əð[2] *the one* (whom) *I work with*] 3 əz ɬ 4–6 əz 7 u: wɒnts ə dʒɒb, s.w. əz əl du: ɩt [ə man ju:st tə goɷ[3] *a man* (who) *used to go*; tu: pi:pl spi:ks ðə seɩm[3] *two people* (who) *speak the same*]

16 Wo 1–2 əz 3 əz ɬ 4 əz ɬ du: ɩt [wɒn ɒɩz ɩəʳ:ɖ[2] *one* (which) *I've heard*] 5 əz ɬ 6 əz ɬ du: ɩt 7 əz əl gi: jə sɷm ɛɬp

17 Wa 1 wɒt 2 ə mɒn əz əd du: ɩt [ðəz ə gɷd mɛnɩ ju:sɩz əm[2] *there's a good many* (who) *use them*; ð‿ɔ:nlɩ wɒn ɛvəɹ ɔɩ si:n[1] *the only one* (that) *ever I saw*] 3 wɒt ɬ 4 əz ɬ 5 wɒt, ə mɒn wɒt əd du: ɩt 6 ɷz əd 7 əz əd

23 Mon 1–3 əz 4 ạ̈l 5 əz [also zero form] 6 əz 7 n.a.

24 Gl 1 wɩtʃ, ə tʃæp wɩtʃ ɬ ɛɬp jə 2 əz 3 əz ɬ 4 əz 5 əz ɭ, əz ɭ kọm ən dɷ‿t fəʳ: ðə 6 əz əd kəm ən ɛlp ɩ[(2x)] 7 əz, ᵒəz ɭ kɷm ən dɷ‿t

25 O 1–2 əz ɬ 3 əz əd 4 əz əd kɷm ən gɩ ðɩ ə ünd 5 ə tʃap əd kʌm [ɩəʳẓ wʌn ɩəʳ wɔ:nts fʌɣv mɩnɩʔs[2] *here's one here* (which) *wants five minutes*] 6 wɒʔ ɭ du:

IX.9.6 WHOSE UNCLE WAS DROWNED‡

Q. That man's uncle was drowned last week. In other words you might say, that's the chap . . . .

Rr. AS /HAD HIS UNCLE/HIS NUNC WAS/ DROWNED, AS HIS UNCLE GOT/WAS DROWNED, AS HIS UNCLE DROWNED HIMSELF, AS LOST HIS UNCLE, WHAT HIS UNCLE WAS DROWNED, WHAT'S UNCLE GOT DROWNED, WHOSE (N)UNCLE WAS DROWNED, WHOSE UNCLE /GOT/HAS BEEN/ DROWNED

Note—For additional exs. of WHOSE, see IX.9.2; and of UNCLE, see VIII.1.12.

7 Ch 1 ʏ:z ɷŋkl wəz dɹɑɪnd 2 n.a. 3 əz ɪz ɷŋkl wə dɹaɪnt 4 əz ɪz nɷŋk wəz dɹaɷnd 5 əz ɪz ɷŋkl wəz dɹaɪndɪd 6 ᶷʉ̜:z ɷŋkl wəz dɹaɷnd, °əz lɔ:st ɪz ɷŋkl

8 Db 1 ʏ:z ɷŋkl wəz dɹɛ̧ɷnd 2 wɒt ɪz ɷŋkl wə dɹaɷnd 3 əz ɪz ɷŋkl gɛt dɹɛ̈ɷnd 4 ᶷu:z ɷŋkl gɛt dɹɛ:nd, wɒts ɷŋkl gɛt dɹɛ:nd [pref.] 5 əz ɪz ɷŋkl wə dɹɛ̧:nd 6–7 əz ɪz ɷŋkl gɒt dɹɛ:nd

11 Sa 1 u:z ʌŋkl wəz dɹaɷnd 2 u:z ɷŋkl wəz dɹæɷnd 3 u:z ʌŋkl wəz dɹaɷnd 4 u:z ʌŋkl wəz dɹɛund 5 ᶷu:z nɷŋkl wəz dɹɛɷnt 6 u:z ɷŋkl wəz dɹaɷnd 7 u:z ʌŋkl wəz dɹaɷnd 8 u:z ɷŋkl wəz dɹɛɷnt 9–11 u:z ʌŋkl wəz dɹaɷnd

12 St 1 əz ɪz ɷŋkl gɛt dɹa:ɷnd 2 əz ɪz ɷŋkl gɒt dɹaɪnd 3 əz ɪz ɷŋkl wə dɹaɪnd 4 u:z ɷŋkl wəz dɹæɷnd 5 əz ɪz ɷŋkl wəz dɹæɷnd 6 əz ɪz ɷŋkl dɹæ:ndɪd ɪzsɛn 7 əz lɒst ɪz ɷŋkl 8 u:z ɷŋkl‿z bɪn dɹæɷnd 9 əz ɪz ɷŋkl wəz dɹa:nd 10 ü:z ɷŋkl wəz dɹa:nd 11 az ɪz ɷŋkl gɒt dɹæɷnd

15 He 1 u:z ɷŋkɫ wəz dɹæɷnd 2 u:z ʌŋkɫ wə dɹæɷnt 3 u:z ɷŋkɫ wəz dɹəɷnt 4 u:z ʌŋkɫ wəz dɹəɷnt 5 u:z ɷŋkl wəz dɹʌɷnt 6 u:z ɷŋkl wəz dɹəɷnt 7 u:z ʌŋkl wəz dɹɑ̆ɷndɪd

16 Wo 1 u:z ɷŋkl wəz dɹɛɷnd 2 u:z ɷŋkɫ wəz dɹɛɷnd 3 u:z ɷŋkɫ wɷz dɹɛu:nd 4–5 u:z ɷŋkɫ wɷz dɹəɷ:nt 6 u:z ɷŋkɫ wɷz dɹɛu:nt 7 s.w. u:z ɷŋkl wəz dɹæɷnd

17 Wa 1 u:z ɷŋkl wəz dɹɛ̈ɷnd 2 əz ɪz ɷŋkl dɹæɷndɪd ɪzsɛlf 3 ü:z ɷŋkɫ wə dɹɛ̈ɷn 4 əz ɪz ɷŋkɫ gɒt dɹɛɷnd 5 u:z ɷŋkɫ wəz dɹɛɷnd 6 əz ɪz ɷŋkɫ wəz dɹɛ̈ɷnd 7 u:z ɷŋkɫ wəz dɹɛɷnd

23 Mon 1 ᶷu:z ʌŋkɫ wəz dɹʌɷnd 2 u:z ɷŋkɫ wəz dɹʌɷnt 3 u:z ɷŋkɫ wəz dɹəɷnt 4 u·z ʌ̣̈ŋkl wəz dɹəundɪd 5 u:z ʌ̣̈ŋkɫ wəz dɹə̨und 6 u:z ʌŋkɫ wəz dɹəɷnd 7 n.a.

24 Gl 1 u:z ɷŋkɫ wəz dɹəɷnt 2–4 ᶷu:z ɷŋkɫ wəz dɹəɷnt 5 əz ɪz ʌŋkl wəz dɹʌɷndɪd 6 əz ɪz əŋkɫ wəz dɹᶷu:ndɪd 7 əz ad ɪz əŋkl dɹᶷu:nd

25 O 1 əz ɪz ʌŋkɫ wə dɹɛ̈ɷndɪd 2 əz ɪz ʌŋkɫ wəz dɹæ̣ɷndɪd 3 əz ɪz ʌŋkl wəz dɹɛɷnd 4 u:z ɷŋkɫ wəz dɽaɷnd 5 u:z ʌŋkl wəz dɹɛ̈ɷnd 6 u:z ʌŋkl wəz dɹɛ̈ɷndɪd

IX.9.7 WHERE*

Q. Your friend says: Look at that cuckoo over there. You can't see the bird and so you ask: . . . . is it?

Rr. WHERE(ABOUTS)?, WHERE DID YOU SEE HIM?, WHERE IS (HE/HER~HOO/IT)?, WHERE–TO IS IT?

Note 1—Rr. comprising a phrase or sentence are reproduced below in full.

Note 2—In the i.m. below, an attached superior ◇ denotes "foll. by a word beginning with a V." and superior × "foll. by a word beginning with a C." I.m. exs. of WHERE'S are reproduced below between square brackets untransliterated.

Note 3—WHERE also occurs at VII.6.26 and IX.9.4. For ANYWHERE(S), see VII.3.16; for EVERYWHERE, see VII.8.14; and for SOMEWHERE, see V.8.4.

7 Ch 1 wɪəɹəbaɪts, ○×wɪə^{2} 2 n.a., ○wɪə$^{1,2(2x),3(3x),4(2x)}$, ○×wɛə^{2,3}, ○◇wɪəɹ^{3} [wɪəz$^{2(2x)}$] 3 wɪəɹ ɪs‿t [wɪəz^{3}] 4 wɪə, ○~^{2}, ○×~$^{1,2(2x)}$ [wɪ‿n ðɪ dlʊvz^{2} "*where are thy gloves*"?] 5–6 wɪə

8 Db 1 wɪə꞉ 2 wɪəɹ ɪz ɪt 3 wɪə, ○◇wɪəɹ^{2,3} 4 wɪə, ○×~^{3} 5 wɪəɹ ɪz ɪt, ○×wɪə$^{1(2x),3}$ [wɪəz^{1}] 6–7 wɪəɹ

11 Sa 1 wɛəʴ 2 wɛəʴ, ○wɪə$^{2(2x)}$ 3 wɛəʴ 4 wəʴ: 5 wɪəʴ [no:wɪəʴɽ ɪls^{1} *nowhere else*] 6 wɛəʴ· [wɛəʴ:ʐ^{3}] 7 wəʴ: 8 we:əʴ 9 wɛəʴ· 10 we:əʴ 11 we:əʴ

12 St 1 wɛ:əɹ ɪz ɪt, ○wa:^{1} 2 wɪə, ○◇wɪəɹ^{5}, ○×wɛ:^{1,3}, ○×wə:^{1} 3 wɪə, ○×~^{1,2}, ○wɪ^{1} [rec. in «wɪ‿st» *where hast*], ○×wiə^{1}, ○◇~$^{1(2x)}$, ○×wɛ:^{2} 4 wɛ:ɹ ɪz ɪt, ○×wɛ:^{1} 5 wɪəɹ ɪz, ○wiə^{2,3} 6 wɪəɹ ɪz ɪt, ○×wɪə$^{2(2x)}$, ○×wɛ:^{2} 7 wɛ:ɹ ɪz ɪt, ○×wɛ:$^{1(2x)}$ 8 wɛ:ɹ ɪz i:, ○wɛ:^{1,3} 9 wɪə 10 wəɹ ɪz ɪt 11 wiə, ○×wʊə^{2} [*sic*; wiəz$^{2(2x)}$]

15 He 1 wəʴ:ɽ ɪz i: 2 wəʴ: 3 wəʴɽ ɪz i: 4 wəʴ:ɽ ɪz ə, ○×wəɽ^{1} 5 wəʴ 6 wəʴ, ○~ 7 wə:ɹ ɪz ɪt, ○×wɛəɹ^{1,3}, ○×wə·ɹ^{4}, ○×wɛə^{1,2,4} [wɛəɹz^{4}]

16 Wo 1 wɛ:ə, ○×wɪə^{2}, ○×wɪəʴ^{2}, ○◇wɪəɹ^{1,2} 2 wəʴ: [ɛvɹɪwəʴ:^{2} *everywhere*; ×wɛ:əʴʐ^{2}] 3 wəʴ: ɪz əʴ:, ○×we:əʴ^{1}, ○◇wɛ:əɹ^{5} 4 wəʴɽ ɪz ɪ, ○wəʴ:^{1,2}, ○◇wəʴɽ^{3} 5 wəʴ:, ○×~$^{1(3x)}$, ○◇~^{1}, ○◇wəʴ:ɽ^{1} 6 wɪəʴ, ○×wəʴ:^{3}, ○◇wɛəʴ^{3} 7 wəʴ dɪd jə si: ɪm, ○◇wə·ʴ^{1}, ○◇wɛəɹ$^{1(2x),4}$, ○×wɛəʴ^{1,4}, ○×wɛə$^{1,4(3x)}$ [wɛəz^{4}]

17 Wa 1 wɛ:ɹ ɪz ɪt 2 wɪəɹ ɪz ɪt, ○wɪəɹ$^{1,2,4(2x)}$, ○×wɪə$^{1(2x)}$, ○×wə:^{1,3} [wɪəz^{3,4}] 3 wɛ:ɹ ɪz ɪt, ○×wɪə^{1} [wɪəz^{3}] 4 wɪə 5 wɪəʴ, ○×~$^{1(2x)}$ 6 wɪəʴ 7 wɪəʴ, ○×~^{1,2}

23 Mon 1 wəʴ: 2–3 wɛə 4 wɛ·tʰu: ɪz ɪt 5 wɛ: 6 wəʴ:, ○◇wəʴɽ^{2} 7 n.a.

24 Gl 1 wəʳ: [wəʳ:ʐ[2]] 2 wəʳ: 3 wəʳ:, ○×~[1] 4 wəʳ: 5 wəʳ: ɩz ɷ 6 wəʳ: ɩz ə 7 wəʳ:ɽ ɩz ə

25 O 1 wəʳ:, ○×~[1], ○×wɛəɽ[2] [nɔɷwəʳ: ɛls[2] *nowhere else*] 2 wɩ̞əʳ, ○◇wɩəʳ[2], ○×~[1], ○×wəʳ:[2] 3 wɩəʳ, ○◇wɩəɹ[1] 4 wə·ɽ ɩz ɩt, ○×wə·ɽ[4], ○×wəɽ[5], ○×wɛəɽ[2], ○×wɛə[1,3(2x),4] [wɛəɽʐ[4]] 5 wəɽ 6 wəʳ:

IX.10.1 THAT

Q. Here are two coins [put one close to him and the other a little further away]. Say which you'll have. You'll have [p.] . . . .

Rr. THAT (ONE {OVER THERE}), THICK (ONE)

Note 1—The 2nd r. at 7.6 is pres. a form of THAT ONE. At 7.1, 15.5/6, 16.4, 23.1–3/6 and 24.2, the f.w. evidently asked IX.10.2 before IX.10.1. The requisite adjustments have been made in the rr. below.

Note 2—For additional exs. of THAT *pron.*, see VIII.8.6 and IX.10.2/3/7; of THAT ONE, see V.7.11 and IX.10.2/3. THAT *rel. pron.* occurs at III.3.7. For additional exs. of unstr. ONE, see V.7.11 (and refs.). THICK ONE(S) also occurs at IX.10.3/4/6.

7 Ch 1 ðat 2 n.a. 3 ðat n̩ 4–5 ðat 6 ðat, s.w. ða‿n[(2x)] ["rare"]

8 Db 1–4 ðat 5–6 ðat n̩ 7 ðat

11 Sa 1 ðat n̩ 2 ðat, ○~[1(2x),2(4x)] 3–4 ða·t 5 ðat n̩, ○ðat[2,3] [ɩ kɒnə dɩu: ɩt əðatəns[2] *he can't do it athatans* (i.e. in that way)] 6 ðat, ○~[1(5x),2,3(2x),4(2x)], ○~[3] VIII.3.2, ○ða·t[4], ○ða:t[4] 7 ðæt 8 ðat 9–10 ðæt 11 ðat

12 St 1 ðat 2–4 ðat n̩ 5–6 ðat 7–9 ðat n̩ 10 ðat wɷn ɷɷvə ðɛ: 11 ðaʔ n̩

15 He 1–4 ðæt n̩ 5–6 ðæt ən 7 ðat, ○ðɩk[1]

16 Wo 1–2 ðat n̩ 3–6 ðæt ɷn 7 ðat n̩

17 Wa 1 ðat 2 ðat n̩ 3 ðat 4 ðat n̩ 5 ðat 6–7 ðat n̩

23 Mon 1–3 ðæt n̩ 4 n.a. 5 ðatʰ 6 ðæt n̩ 7 n.a.

24 Gl 1 ðæ:t ɷn 2 ðæt ɷn 3 ðæt n̩ 4 ðat n̩ 5 ðat ɷn 6–7 ðək ən

25 O 1–2 ðat n̩ 3 ðat ən 4 ðӓt 5–6 ðaʔ

IX.10.2 THIS

Q. (Here are two coins [put one close to him and the other a little further away]. Say which you'll have. You'll have that.) *Not* [*p.*] . . . .

Rr. THAT/THIS (ONE), THICK ONE

Note 1—It is clear that at 7.1, 15.5/6, 16.4, 23.1–3/6 and 24.2–4 the f.w. asked IX.10.1 and IX.10.2 in reverse order. The appropriate adjustments have been made in the rr. concerned.

Note 2—THIS *pron.* also occurs at V.7.21 and IX.10.7. For THICK (ONE), see IX.10.1 (and refs.). Additional exs. of unstr. ONE occur at V.7.11 (and refs.).

7 Ch 1 ðɩs °~[4] 2 n.a. 3 ðɩs n̩ 4–6 ðɩs

8 Db 1–4 ðɩs 5–6 ðɩs n̩ 7 ðɩs

11 Sa 1 ðɩs n̩ 2–4 ðɩs 5 ðɩs n̩, °ðɩs[2] 6–11 ðɩs

12 St 1 ðɩs 2–4 ðɩs n̩ 5–6 ðɩs 7–9 ðɩs n̩ 10 ðɩs 11 ðɩs n̩

15 He 1–4 ðɩs n̩ 5–6 ðɩk ən 7 ðɩs

16 Wo 1–2 ðɩs n̩ 3 ðæt ɷn 4–6 ðɩs ɷn 7 ðɩs n̩

17 Wa 1 ðɩs 2 ðɩs n̩ 3 ðɩs 4 ðɩs n̩ 5 ðɩs 6–7 ðɩs n̩

23 Mon 1–3 ðɩs n̩ 4 n.a. 5 ðɩs 6 ðɩs n̩ 7 n.a.

24 Gl 1–2 ðɩs ɷn 3–4 ðɩs n̩ 5 ðɩs ɷn 6–7 ðɩs ən

25 O 1–2 ðɩs n̩ 3 ðɩs ən 4–6 ðɩs

IX.10.3 THAT OVER THERE

Q. Now look! We have three coins [put the third some distance from him]. Now you will choose, not [p.] this, nor [p.] that, but [p.] . . . .

Rr. FARTHEST, THAT (/FARTHERMOST/THERE/OTHER {ONE}/ {OVER} YONDER/), THAT ONE ({OVER} THERE/YONDER), /THAT/THE TOTHER/THICK ONE/ OVER THERE, THAT TOTHER (THERE), THE /FAR~OTHER ONE/(T)OTHER/, THICK ONE THERE/YONDER), (THICK) TOTHER, YON(D), YONS

Note—For additional exs. of THAT *pron.*, see IX.10.1 (and refs.); and of OVER, see V.6.8.

7 Ch 1 ðat ðɩə 2 n.a. 3 ð‿ɷðə 4 ðat ɷðə 5–6 ðə tɷðə

8 Db 1 jɒnd 2 jɒnd, °jɒn[3] 3 jɒn 4 jɒnz 5 tɷðə 6 ðat n̩ o·ə ðɩə 7 ðat ðɩə

11 Sa 1 ðat n̩ 2 ðə fəʳ:ɽ ən 3 ða·t 4 ða:t wən 5 ðat n̩ jɒndəʳ [jandəʳ[2] *yonder*] 6 ðat ðɛəʳ· 7 ðæt 8 ðə ɷðəʳ 9 ðæt n̩ 10 ðæt 11 ðə tʌðəʳ

12 St 1 ðat tɷðə 2 fəːðɩst 3 ðat tɷðə ðɩə 4–5 tɷðə 6 tɷðə wɒn 7 ð‿ɷðə 8 ðə fəːɹ ən 9 tɷðə 10 ðat wɷn 11 ðə tɷðə

15 He 1–2 ðæt n̩ ðəʳː 3 ðæt n̩ oːvəʳ ðəʳː 4 ðæt n̩ jændəʳ 5 ðɩk ən jɒndəʳ 6 ðɩk ən ðəʳ [jɒndəʳ¹ *yonder*] 7 ðat oɷvəɹ ðɛəɹ

16 Wo 1 ðat n̩ jɒndə 2 ðat n̩ ðɩəʳ 3 ðæt ɷðəʳɽ ɷn 4 ðæt ɷn ðɩəʳ 5 ðæt ɷðəʳɽ ɷn 6 ðæt ɷn ðɩəʳ 7 ðat n̩ oɷvə jəndə

17 Wa 1 ðat wɷn 2 ðat n̩ əɷvə jəndə 3 ðɩ ɷ̜ðə 4 ðat n̩ o̜ɷvə ðɩə 5 ðat fəʳːðəmɷst 6 ðat n̩ o̜ɷvə ðɩəʳ 7 ðə tɷðəʳ, ðat ɷðəʳ [pref.]

23 Mon 1 ðɩk n̩ 2 ðæt n̩ jɒndəʳ 3 ðæt n̩ jɒndə 4 n.a. 5 ðatʰ 6 ðæt n̩ jɒndəʳ 7 n.a.

24 Gl 1 ðæːt n̩ ðəʳː 2 ðæt ɷn ðəʳː 3 ðɩk tɷðəʳ 4 ðɩk n̩ 5 ðə tɷðəʳ 6 ðə təðəɽ oːvəʳ ðəʳː 7 ðək ən oːvə ðəʳː

25 O 1 ðat jɒndəʳ, p. ðat n̩ jɒndəʳ ["older"] 2 ðaʔ n̩ jɒndəʳ̩, ðaʔ n̩ jandəʳ̩ ["older"] 3 tʌðəɽ wən 4 ðät oːvəɽ ðɛəɽ 5 ðaʔ oɷvəʳ ðɛəʳ 6 ðaʔ oɷvəʳ jɒndəʳ

IX.10.4 THOSE

Q. Now (of two coins placed at each of three places) *you can choose* [*p.*] . . . .

This and the following q. were designed to elicit the general differences in meaning and usage between the pronouns THOSE and THESE, or their synonyms. The rr. referring specifically to the context of the two coins must be differentiated from those used with a wider application. Accordingly, the rr. THEM TWO and THE SECOND LOT are here regarded as u.rr. and are so designated below.

Rr. §THE /MIDDLE ONE/SECOND LOT/, THEM/THOSE ONES, THEM §TWO, THEY, THOSEUN

Note 1—At 11.5, 12.1, 15.5/6, 16.4, 23.1–3/6, and 24.2–4/7 the f.w. evidently asked IX.10.5 before IX.10.4. The requisite adjustments have been made in the rr. below.

Note 2—For additional exs. of THOSE, see IX.10.6.

7 Ch 1 ðɛm 2 n.a. 3–6 ðɛm

8 Db 1–7 ðɛm

11 Sa 1–4 ðoːz 5 ðoːzn ["no *s*"] 6–11 ðoːz

12 St 1–2 ðɛm 3 ðɛm §tɛɷ 4–7 ðɛm 8 §ðə mɩdl wɒn 9–10 ðoɷz 11 §ðə sɛknd lɒt

15 He 1 ðo:ɷz 2 ðɛm ənz 3 ðɛm n̩z 4 ðo:z 5 ðo:z ənz 6 ðo:z 7 ðoɷz, °ðɛm

16 Wo 1 ðɒɷz n̩z 2 ðoɷz n̩z 3 ðoɷz ɷnz 4–5 ðo:z ɷnz 6 ðoɷz ɷnz 7 ðɛm

17 Wa 1–2 ðɛm 3 ðǫɷz 4–7 ðɛm

23 Mon 1 ðo:ɷz n̩z 2–3 ðo:z n̩z 4 n.a. 5 ðo:z 6 ðo:z n̩z 7 n.a.

24 Gl 1 ðo:ɷz n̩z 2 ðɛm 3 ðæɩ 4 ðɒɷz n̩z 5 ðæɩ 6 ðək ənz 7 ðɛ̞ɩ

25 O 1–2 ðɛm 3 ðɛm ənz 4 ðɛm §tu: 5–6 ðɛm

IX.10.5 THESE

Q. *Or* (of two coins placed at each of three places, you can choose) [*p*.] . . . .

This and the previous q. were designated to elicit the general differences in meaning and use between the pronouns THESE and THOSE, or their synonyms. The rr. referring specifically to the context of the two coins must be differentiated from those used with a wider application. Accordingly, the rr. THE FIRST TWO and THESE TWO are here regarded as u.rr. and are so designated below.

Rr. §THE /FIRST TWO/NEAR ONE/, THESE/THICK (ONES), THESE §TWO, THESEUN

Note—At 11.5, 12.1, 15.5/6, 16.4, 23.1–3/6 and 24.2–4/7 the f.w. evidently asked IX.10.4 and IX.10.5 in reverse order. The appropriate adjustments have been made in the rr. concerned.

7 Ch 1 ðe:z, °~4 2 n.a. 3 ðɛɩz 4 ð[ə]ɩəz 5 ðɛɩz 6 ði:z

8 Db 1–5 ði:z 6–7 ðɛɩz

11 Sa 1–4 ði:z 5 ð'i:zn ["no *s*"] 6–11 ði:z

12 St 1 ði:z 2 ðɛɩz 3 ðɛɩz §tɛɷ 4 ði:z 5–6 ðɛɩz 7 ði:z 8 §ðə nɩə wɒn 9 ðɛɩz 10 ði:z 11 §ðə fɷst tü:

15 He 1 ði:z 2 ði:z ənz 3 ði:z n̩z 4 ði:z 5–6 ðɩk ənz 7 ði:z

16 Wo 1–2 ði:z n̩z 3 ðe:ɪz ɷnz 4–5 ði:z ɷnz 6 ðoɷz ɷnz 7 ði:z

17 Wa 1–7 ði:z

23 Mon 1 ðˈi:z n̩z 2–3 ði:z n̩z 4 n.a. 5 ði:z 6 ði:z n̩z 7 n.a.

24 Gl 1 ðe:z n̩z 2 ðˈi:z 3 ðɪk 4 ðe:z n̩z 5 ðe:z 6 ðɪz ənz 7 ðɨ:z

25 O 1–2 ði:z 3 ði:z ənz 4 ði:z §tu: 5–6 ði:z

IX.10.6 THOSE OVER THERE

Q. *Or* (of two coins placed at each of three places, you can choose) [*p.*]....

Rr. THE /FARMOST/FAR §ONE/FARTHEST/, §THE /(T)OTHERS/ OTHER ONES/THIRD/, THEM /FARTHERMOST/(T)OTHERS/ TOTHER §TWO/, THEM (ONES/OVER) THERE~YONDER, THEY OVER THERE, THICK /ONES (YONDER)/(ONES) THERE/, THOSE (/ONES YONDER/OTHER ONES/OVER YONDER/ {ONES} THERE/), THOSEUN (YONDER), TOTHER ONES, TOTHERS, YON(S), YOND (FAR ONES), YONDER

7 Ch 1 ðɛm ðɪə 2 n.a. 3 ðᵊ fɔ:məst 4 ðɛm ɷðəz 5 ðə tɷðəz 6 ðɛm ɷðəz

8 Db 1 jɒnd 2 jɒnd fa:ɹ ənz 3 jɒn, jɒndə, ○~¹ 4 jɒns 5 tɷðəz 6 ðɛm o·ə ðɪə 7 ðɛm ðɪə ðɪə

11 Sa 1 ðo:z 2 ðɛm ðɛ:əʳ 3–4 ðo:z 5 ðo:zn ["no *s*"] jɒndəʳ 6 ðo:z ðɛəʳ 7 ðo:z 8 ðɛm o:vəʳ ðɪəʳ 9–11 ðo:z

12 St 1 ðɛm tɷðə §tü: 2 fɔ:ðɪst 3 ðɛm tɷðə §tɛɷ 4 ðɛm ɷðəz 5 ðɛm tɷðəz 6–7 ðoɷz 8 ðə fɑ: §wɒn 9 tɷðəz 10 ðɛm 11 §ðə θə:ɹd

15 He 1 ðo:ɷz n̩z ðəʳ: 2 ðɛm ənz ðəʳ: 3 ðɛm n̩z ðəʳ 4 ðɛm jændəʳ 5 ðɪk ənz jɒndəʳ 6 ðɪk ənz ðəʳ 7 ðo:z o:vəɹ jɒndəɹ, ○ðɛm o:vəɹ jɒndəɹ

16 Wo 1 ðɒɷz n̩z jɒndə 2 ðoɷz n̩z ðɪəʳ 3 ðɛm oɷvəʳ ðəʳ: 4 ðo:z ɷnz ðɪəʳ 5 ðo:z ɷðəʳɽ ɷnz 6 ðoɷz ɷnz ðɪəʳ 7 ðɛm oɷvə jəndə

17 Wa 1 ðǫɷz 2 ðɛm ɔɷvə jəndə 3 ðɛm 4 ðɛm ǫɷvə ðɪə 5 ðɛm fəʳ:ðəmɷst 6 ðɛm ðɪəʳ 7 ðɛm ɷðəʳʐ

23 Mon 1 ðɪk n̩z 2 ðo:z n̩z jɒndəʳ 3 ðo:z n̩z jɒndə 4 n.a. 5 ðɛm 6 ðɛm n̩z jɒndəʳ 7 n.a.

24 Gl 1 ðo:ɷz ŋ̣z ðəʳ: 2 ðɛm ɷnz ðəʳ: 3 ðɪk ðæɪəʳ 4 ðɪk ŋ̣z 5 ðɛm o:vəʳ ðəʳ: 6 ðæɪ o:vəʳ ðəʳ: 7 ðɛ̣ɪ o:və ðəʳ:

25 O 1 ðɛm jɒndəʳ 2 ðɛm jɑndəɹ 3 tʌðəɹ ənz 4 ðɛm o:vəɽ ðɛəɽ 5 ðɛm əɷvəʳ ðɛəʳ 6 ðɛm oɷvəʳ jɒndəʳ

IX.10.7 IN THIS WAY

Q. If I asked how you fold your arms, you'd probably show me and say: Well, I just do it . . . .

Rr. ATHISEN(S), LIKE THAT/THIS, SO, THAT WAY, THIS ROAD/WAY

Note 1—At 17.4 the f.w. omitted to complete the phrase.

Note 2—I.m. exs. of WAY are reproduced below between square brackets untransliterated.

Note 3—(-)WAY(S) also occurs at I.3.7, VII.6.26 and IX.1.8. Cf. the exs. of AWAY at VIII.7.9 (and refs.).

7 Ch 1 lɑɪk ðɪs, ðɪs ɹọ:d 2 n.a. [we:²] 3 əðɪsn 4 lɑɪk ðɪs 5 lɑ:k ðɪs 6 n.a.

8 Db 1 ðɪs we:, laɪk ðɪs 2 lɑɪk ðɪs 3 laɪk ðɪs 4 lɑ:k ðɪs 5 lɑɪk ðɪs, ðɪs ɹo:ᵊd 6 lɑ:k ðat 7 lɑɪk ðɪs

11 Sa 1 ðɪs we: 2 laɪk ðat 3 laɪk ðɪs 4 lɛɪk ðɪs 5 əðɪsns [wẹ:²] 6 laɪk ðɪs [we:³] 7 laɪk ðɪs 8 lɒɪk ðɪs [we:¹] 9–10 laɪk ðɪs 11 laɪk ðɪs [gɪvɪn we:² *giving way* VII.6.15]

12 St 1 lɒɪk ðɪs 2 əðɪsn, ðɪs ɹoɷd 3 lɒ:ɪk ðɪs [wi:¹,²] 4 ðɪs ɹoɷd 5 ðɪs wi: [wi:², we:³] 6 lɒ:ɪk ðɪz [gi:-ɪn wi:² *giving way* VII.6.15] 7 lɒɪk ðɪz 8 ðɪs wɛɪ 9 soɷ, lɒɪk ðɪs [wẹɪ¹, wɛɪ¹, wi:¹] 10 la:ɪʔ aʔ 11 ðɪs ɹoɷd [wɛɪ², ᵔwɛɪz²; tɛɪk bad wɛɪz² *take bad ways* (i.e. fester) VI.11.8]

15 He 1 ləɪk ðɪs 2 læɪk ðɪs [wæɪ³] 3 ləɪk ðɪs [wɛɪ²; gɪv wæɪ¹ *give way* III.1.12] 4 ləɪk ðɪs 5 ləɪk ðɪs [wæɪ¹,²] 6 n.a. [wæɪ¹; fɛɹɪwæɪ¹ *ferry-way* IV.1.3] 7 laɪk ðɪs, s.w. ðɪs ɹo:ᵊd [weɪ³, we:ɪ⁴]

16 Wo 1 lɒɪk ðɪs 2 ləɪk ðɪs 3 lɒɪk ðɪs [we:ɪ⁵] 4 ləɪk ðɪs [waɪ¹,², ᵔwaɪz¹] 5 ləɪk ðɪs [waɪ¹⁽²ˣ⁾] 6 lɒɪk ðɪs [skʲu:wæɪz³ *skew-ways* IX.1.3] 7 ləɪk ðɪs, p. ðɪs ɹoɷd [weɪ¹,⁴⁽²ˣ⁾, wẹɪ¹, wɛɪ³]

17 Wa 1 ðat wẹɪ, °lɒɪk ðat² [a:fwɛɪ¹ *half-way*] 2 ləɪk ðɪs [wẹɪ⁴] 3 ləɪk ðɪs 4 ləɪk [wẹɪ¹, wɛɪ²] 5–7 ləɪk ðɪs

23 Mon 1 ləɩk ðɩs 2 ðɩs we: 3 ləɩk ðɩs 4 n.a. 5 ləɩ̢k ðat^{h} 6 so: [wɑ^{r}:ʈə^{r}we:^{1} *water-way*] 7 n.a.

24 Gl 1 ləɩk ðɩs [we:^{3}, wæɩ^{1}] 2 ləɩk ðɩs 3 ð'i:z ɹo:ɷd 4 ləɩk ðɩs [waɩ^{3}] 5 ðɩs wæɩ [wæɩ^{2}] 6 ðɩs wæɩ [wæɩ^{2}] 7 lʌɩk ðɩs [wɛ̢ɩ^{1}]

25 O 1 lə̈ɩk ðɩs [□wæɩz^{2}; gaŋwæɩ^{1} *gangway* I.3.18] 2 lə̈ɩk ðɩs [skju:wɛɩ^{1} *skew-way* IX.1.3] 3 lʌʏk ðɩs [we:^{1}] 4 p. ðɩs we:, ɫəɩk ðɩs [we:^{4}, weɩ^{1}; də·əʈwe:^{4} *door-way* V.1.8] 5 ðɩs we$^{\iota}$ [we:^{2}; aknɩ we:^{2} *Icknield Way* (pl.n.)] 6 lə̈ɩk ðɩs

IX.11.1 WASH MYSELF‡

Q. *If you don't want to feel dirty, one of the first things you do after getting up in the morning is to . . . .*

If the reflexive form does not emerge, ascertain the existence of wash **me/myself.**

Rr. §HAVE A /(GOOD) SWILL/WASH/, WASH (/ME/§MY FACE/ MYSELF~MYSELL~MYSEN/§YOURSELF~§YOURSEN/)

Note 1—At 11.11 and 12.10 the f.w. omitted to rec. the wanted WASH. A superior × attached to a r. denotes that the inf. stated the reflex. pron. was not used.

Note 2—I.m. exs. of MYSELF, and also of OURSELVES, THYSELF and YOURSELF used reflexively, are reproduced below between square brackets untransliterated. But i.m. exs. of pronouns in –SELF/SELVES that are n.d.g. are marked with an attached superior ◇. I.m. exs. of other prons. used reflex. are also cited between square brackets, but are transliterated.

Note 3—For additional exs. of reflex. prons., see V.8.13, VIII.3.3/6 and IX.11.2–4. For additional exs. of WASH, see V.9.5 and VI.5.3.

7 Ch 1 wɛʃ mɩsɛl [ðɩsɛl^{4}] 2 n.a. [◇a:sɛnz^{3}; ðɩsɛl^{3}; mɩ^{2} *me*] 3 §av ə wɛʃ [◇jəsɛl^{2}; ◇əzsɛl^{3} *herself*] 4 wɛʃ mɩ 5 wɛʃ mɩsɛl [◇mɩsɛl^{2}] 6 wɛʃ mɩsɛɫf

8 Db 1 wɛɩʃ mɩ 2 wɛʃ mɩ [◇ðɩsɛl^{4}] 3 wɛʃ mɩ 4 §av ə wɛʃ, wɛʃ mɩsɛl 5 wɛʃ mɩssɛn [ðɩsɛn^{3}; jəsɛn^{1}] 6 wɛʃ mɩ [ðəsɛnz^{1} *theirselves* III.2.10] 7 wɛʃ §jəsɛn [◇mɩsɛn]

11 Sa 1–2 wɒʃ mɩsɛlf 3 wɒʃ mɩsɛl [jəsɛl^{2}] 4 wɒʃ mɩsɛlf 5 wɛʃ mɩsɛlf [ðɩsɛlf^{1}] 6–7 wɒʃ mɩsɛlf 8 wɛʃ mɩsɛlf [av (*2 pr.pl.*) ə wɛʃ *have a wash*] 9 wæʃ mɩsɛlf [aɷəsɛlvz^{1}] 10 wɒʃ mɩsɛlf 11 mɩsɛlf

12 St 1 wɛʃ mɩ, §av ə wɛʃ 2 wɛʃ mɩsɛl [◇mɩsɛl^{2}; ðisɛl^{1}; ◇ðɩsɛl^{5}] 3 §av ə wɛʃ, wɛʃ mɩsɛn 4 wɛʃ mɩsɛl, ○wɒʃ mɩ^{2} 5 §av ə wɛʃ, wɛʃ mɩsɛlf [jəsɛlf^{2}] 6 p. wɛʃ mɩsɛn, §av ə swɩl 7 wɒʃ mɩsɛlf 8 §av ə wɒʃ 9 wɛʃ mɩsɛn [◇mɩsɛn^{3}; ◇əsɛlz^{1}] 10 §av ə wɒʃ, §av ə swɩl, mɩsɛlf 11 waʃ mɩsɛn, §av ə waʃ

15 He 1 §æv ə wɛʃ 2 wɛʃ mɪsɛɫf 3 §æv ə wɛʃ, wɛʃ mɪsɛɫf 4 wɛʃ mɪsɛɫf 5 wɛʃ mɪsɛɫf, §æv ə wɛʃ [◇mɪsɛɫf[4]] 6 wɛʃ mɪsɛɫf 7 §av ə wɒʃ, p. wɒʃ mɪsɛf, §a̱v ə gʊd swɪl

16 Wo 1 wɒʃ mɪ [mɪsɛlf[3]] 2 wɒʃ mɪsɛɫf 3 waʃ mɪsɛɫf 4 §æv ə wɛʃ, wɛʃ mɪsɛɫ 5 wɒʃ mɪsɛlf 6 wɛʃ mɪsɛɫf 7 ir.r. [æz (*1 pr.s.*) ə swɪɫ *has a swill*; əʳ:ʂɛlf[1] *herself*]

17 Wa 1 wɒʃ mɪ 2 p. wəʃ mɪsɛlf 3 §av ə wæʃ 4 ×§av ə wɒʃ 5 §av ə wɒʃ [əzɛɫz[1]] 6–7 ×wɒʃ

23 Mon 1–2 wɒʃ mɪsɛɫf 3 wɛʃ §jəsɛɫf 4 wɒ̣·ʃ məisɛlf 5 wɒ̣·ʃ mɪ̈sɛlf 6 wɒʃ mɪsɛɫf [◇mɪsɛlf[1]; jəsɛɫf[1]] 7 n.a.

24 Gl 1 wɒʃ mɪsɛɫf 2 §æv ə wɛʃ ["usu."], wɛʃ mɪsɛɫf [◇mɪsɛlf[2]] 3 wɛʃ mɪzɛɫf [mɪsɛɫf[4]] 4 wɛʃ mɪzɛɫf 5 ×§ɛv ə wɒʃ 6 waʃ mɪsɛlf 7 §av ə wɔ·ʃ, ×wɒʃ §mɪ fe:s

25 O 1 ×wæ:ʃ 2 ×wɒʃ 3 wəʃ, wəʃ mɪsaɫf [◇mɪsaɫf[1]] 4 §av ə wəʃ, p. wɒʃ mɪsɛɫf 5 §av ə wɔ:ʃ 6 ×wɔ:ʃ

IX.11.2 HIMSELF†. HERSELF†

Q. Some people might say: He committed suicide, but you can say, in a much simpler way: He killed . . . .

Convert for **herself.**

Rr. HIMSELF~HIMSELL~HIMSEN~HISSELF, HISSELL~HISSEN

HERSELF~HERSELL~HERSEN

Note 1—The rr. to the two parts of the q. are separated below by a full stop.

Note 2—I.m. exs. of the reflex. prons. ITSELF and THEMSELVES are reproduced below, untransliterated, between square brackets following the r. to the second part of the q. Superior ◇ marks a form that is n.d.g.

Note 3—For additional exs. of –SELF see IX.11.1 (and refs.).

7 Ch 1 ɪzsɛl . əsɛl 2 n.a., ᵒɪ̞zsɛn², ᵒɪzsɛlf² VI.13.15 3 ɪzsɛl . əsɛl [ᵒðəsɛlz³] 4 ɪmsɛl . əːsɛl 5 ɪzsɛl, ᵒᵒɪzsɛl . əsɛl, ᵒ~² 6 ɪmsɛɫf . əːsɛɫf

8 Db 1 ɪzsɛl . əˑ̵sɛl 2 ɪzsɛn, ɪzsɛl . əːsɛn, əːsɛl 3 ɪzsɛl . əsɛl 4 ɪzsɛl . əsɛl, ᵒ~¹ III.1.12 5–7 ɪzsɛn . əsɛn

11 Sa 1 ɪzsɛlf . n.r. 2 ɪmsɛlf . əʳːʂɛlf 3 ɪzsɛl . əʳʂɛl [ðəmsɛlvz²] 4 hɪzsɛlf . əsɛlf 5 ɪsɛlf . əʳʂɛlf 6 ɪzsɛlf . əʳːʂɛlf 7 ɪzsɛlf . əʳʂɛlf 8 ɪzsɛlf . əʳːʂɛlf 9 ɪmsɛlf . əʳːʂɛlf 10 ɪzsɛlf . əʳːʂɛlf 11 ɪzsɛlf . əʳʂɛlf

12 St 1 ɪzsɛn, ᵒɪzsɛl⁴ . əːsɛl [ᵒðəsɛlvz¹] 2 ɪzsɛl . əːsɛl 3 ɪzsɛn . əːsɛn 4 ɪzsɛlf, ᵒɪmsɛlf³ . əːsɛlf 5 ɪzsɛlf . əːsɛlf 6 ɪzsɛn . əːsɛn 7 ɪmsɛn . əːsɛn 8 ɪmsɛlf . əːsɛn 9 ɪzsɛn . əːsɛn [ɪtsɛlf⁴] 10 ɪzsɛlf . əːsɛn [əmsɛlvz⁵ III.13.6] 11 ɪmsɛlf, ɪzsɛlf . əːɹsɛlf, əːɹsɛn

15 He 1 ɪzsɛɫf . əʳʂɛɫf 2 ɪsɛɫf . əʳːʂɛɫf 3 ɪzsɛɫf . əʳʂɛɫf 4–5 ɪzsɛɫf . əʳʂɛɫf 6 ɪzsɛɫf, ᵒ~¹ . əʳʂɛɫf 7 ɪmsɛlf, ᵒɪzsɛlf² . əɹsɛɫf

16 Wo 1 ɪzsɛlf . n.a. 2 ɪzsɛlf . əʳʂɛɫf 3–4 ɪzsɛɫf . əʳːʂɛɫf 5 ɪzsɛɫf . əʳʂɛɫf 6 ɪzsɛɫ . n.a. 7 ɪzsɛlf . əˑʳʂɛlf [ðəsɛlvz⁴]

17 Wa 1 ɪzsɛɫf . ə̣ːsɛɫf 2 ɪzsɛlf, ᵒ~⁴⁽³ˣ⁾, ᵒᵒɪzsɛl⁴, ᵒɪmsɛlf⁴ . əːsɛlf [ðəsɛlz⁴; ᵒðəsɛlvz⁴] 3 ɪzsɛɫf . əːsɛɫf 4 ɪzsɛɫf . əʳːʂɛɫf 5 ɪzsɛɫf . əʳːʂɛɫf [ðəsɛɫf¹] 6 ɪzsɛɫf . əʳːʂɛɫf 7 ɪzsɛɫf . əʳʂɛɫf

23 Mon 1–2 ɪzsɛɫf . əʳʂɛɫf 3 ɪzsɛɫf, ᵒᵒɪzsɛɫ² . əsɛɫf 4 ɪʂ̞ɛɫf . əʂ̞ɛlf 5 ɪz̥sɛlf, ɪmsɛlf . əsɛlf, ᵒᵒ~² 6 ɪzsɛɫf . əʳʂɛɫf [ðɛəʳʂɛɫvz²] 7 n.a.

24 Gl 1 ɪzsɛɫf, ᵒᵒəsɛɫf [*sic*] . əʳʂɛɫf 2 ɪzsɛɫf . əʳʂɛɫf 3 ɪzɛɫf . əʳːʐ̨ɛɫf 4 ɪmsɛɫf . əʳʐ̨ɛɫf [ðəʳʐ̨ɛɫvz¹ III.13.6] 5 ɪzsɛɫf . əʳːʂɛɫf 6–7 ɪzsɛɫf . əʳːʐ̨ɛɫf

25 O 1 ɪzsɛlf . əʳːʂɛlf 2 ɪzsæɫf . əˑ̵sæɫf 3 ɪzsaɫf . əʳʂaɫf [ᵒðəsɑlvz²] 4 ɪzsɛɫf . əɽʂɛɫf 5 ɪzsɛɫf . əʳɽʂɛɫf 6 ɪzsɛɫf . əʳːʂɛɫf

IX.11.3 BY MYSELF

Q. If you had done something without the help of anybody else, you could say: I did it all . . . .

Rr. §ALONE, (BY) MYSELF~MYSELL~MYSEN, §ON MY OWN

Note 1—I.m. exs. of prons. ending in –SELF/SELVES are reproduced below between square brackets untransliterated, except when not readily recognisable. All of them follow prons.

Note 2—For additional exs. of –SELF/SELVES, see IX.11.1 and refs.

7 Ch 1 bɩ mɩsɛl 2 n.a. [əzsɛn[3]; əzsɛn[3] *ourselves;* ðəmsɛlvz[1] III.13.6] 3–5 mɩsɛl 6 mɩsɛɫf

8 Db 1 mɩsɛl [ðəsɛl[1] *themselves*] 2 mɩsɛn, mɩsɛl, °bɩ mɩsɛn[4] [ɩzsɛn[2]] 3–4 mɩsɛl 5–6 bɩ mɩsɛn 7 mɩsɛn

11 Sa 1 mɩsɛlf 2 baɩ mɩsɛlf 3 mɩsɛl 4 mɩsɛlf 5 baɩ mɩsɛlf 6 mɩsɛlf 7 baɩ mɩsɛlf [ɩmsɛlf[1]] 8 mɩsɛlf 9 baɩ mɩsɛlf [ðɛmsɛlvz[1]] 10 baɩ mɩsɛlf 11 mɩsɛlf

12 St 1 mɩsɛn 2 mɩsɛl [ɷzsɛlvz[2]] 3 mɩsɛn 4 bɩ mɩsɛlf 5 mɩsɛlf 6–7 mɩsɛn 8 bɑ: mi:sɛlf 9 mɩsɛn 10–11 mɩsɛlf

15 He 1–3 mɩsɛɫf 4 n.a. 5 mɩsɛɫf 6 baɩ mɩsɛɫf 7 mɩsɛlf [ðəmsɛlf[4]]

16 Wo 1 mɩsɛlf 2–6 mɩsɛɫf 7 §ɒn mɩ ɑɷn, p. mɩsɛlf

17 Wa 1 bɩ mɩsɛɫf 2 mɩsɛlf 3 mɩsɛɫf 4–6 bɩ mɩsɛɫf 7 mɩsɛɫf

23 Mon 1 bəɩ mɩsɛlf 2 mɩsɛɫf 3 bəɩ mɩsɛɫf 4 n.a. 5 bəɩ̞ mïsɛlf 6 məsɛɫf 7 n.a. [əusɛlvz[1]]

24 Gl 1 məɩsɛlf 2 bəɩ mɩsɛlf [ðəɩsɛlf[1]] 3 mɩsɛɫf 4 bəɩ mɩsɛɫf 5 mɩsɛɫf 6 bʌɩ mɩzɛɫf 7 mɩzɛɫf

25 O 1 mɩsɛɫf 2 mɩsæɫf 3 bɩ mɩsaɫf 4 mɩsɛɫf, §əɫo:n, §ɒn mɩ o:n 5 mʌʏsæɫf 6 mɩsɛɫf

IX.11.4 HIMSELF†. THEMSELVES†

Q. I know he wants to sell his house, because he told me . . . .

Convert for **themselves†**.

Rr. HIMSELF~HIMSELL~HIMSEN~HISSELF~HISSELL~HISSEN

(TH)EMSELVES~(TH)EIRSELF~THEIRSELL(S)~THEIRSELVES THEIRSEN(S)~THEMSENS~THEMSELVES

Note 1—The rr. to the two parts of the q. are separated below by a full stop.

Note 2—I.m. exs. of HERSELF, ITSELF, MYSELF and OURSELVES when used for emphasis are reproduced below between square brackets after a full stop foll. the r. to the 2nd part of the q.

Note 3—For additional exs. of –SELF/SELVES, see IX.11.1 (and refs.).

7 Ch 1 ɪzsɛl . ðəsɛl . [əsɛl[2] *herself*] 2 n.a. [ɪtsɛɫf[1] *itself*] 3 ɪmsɛl . ðəsɛl 4 ɪmsɛl . ðəsɛl(2x) 5 ɪzsɛl . ðəsɛlz 6 ɪmsɛɫf . ðəsɛɫvz

8 Db 1 ɪzsɛl . ðəsɛlz 2 ɪzsɛn, ɪzsɛl . ðəsɛn, ðəsɛl 3–4 ɪzsɛl . ðəsɛl 5 ɪzsɛn . ðəsɛnz 6 ɪzsən . ðəsɛnz 7 ɪzsɛn . ðəsɛnz

11 Sa 1–2 ɪmsɛlf . ðəmsɛlvz 3 ɪmsɛl . ðəmsɛlvz 4 ɪmsɛlf . ðɛəʳsɛlvz 5 ɪzsɛlf . ðəʳʂɛlf 6–7 ɪzsɛlf . ðəmsɛlvz 8 ɪzsɛlf . ðəsɛlvz 9 ɪmsɛlf . ðəmsɛlvz 10 ɪzsɛlf . ðəsɛlvz, ◦~[3] 11 ɪzsɛlf . ðe:əsɛlvz

12 St 1 ɪzsɛn . ðəsɛn 2 ɪzsɛl . ðɪsɛl, ◦ðɪsɛlvz[3] 3 ɪmsɛn . ðɪsɛnz 4–5 ɪzsɛlf . ðɛmsɛlvz 6 ɪmsɛn . ðəmsɛnz 7 ɪzsɛn . ðɪmsɛnz 8 ɪmsɛlf . ðəmsɛlvz 9 ɪzsɛn . ðəmsɛns [*sic*] 10 ɪmsɛlf . ðəsɛlvz 11 hɪzsɛlf . ðəsɛlvz

15 He 1 ɪzsɛɫf . ðəʳʂɛɫf 2 ɪzsɛɫf . ðəmsɛɫvz 3 ɪzsɛɫf . ðəʳʂɛɫvz 4 ɪzsɛɫf . ðəmsɛɫvz . [əʳʂɛɫvz[1] *ourselves*] 5 ɪzsɛɫf . ðəʳʂɛɫf 6 ɪzsɛɫf . ðəsɛɫvz 7 ɪmsɛlf . ðəsɛlvz . [mɪsɛlf[4] *myself*]

16 Wo 1 ɪzsɛlf . ðəsɛlvz 2 ɪzsɛɫf . ðəʳʂɛɫvz, ◦ðəmsɛlvz[1] 3 ɪmsɛɫf . ðəʳʂɛ̧lf 4 ɪzsɛɫf . ðəʳ:ʂɛɫvz 5 ɪzsɛɫf . ɷmsɛɫvz 6 ɪmsɛlf . ðe:əʳʂɛɫvz 7 ɪzsɛlf . ðəsɛlvz

17 Wa 1 ɪzsɛɫf . ðəsɛɫvz 2 ɪzsɛlf . ðəsɛlvz 3–4 ɪzsɛɫf . ðəsɛɫvz 5 ɪzsɛɫf . ðəʳʂɛɫvz 6 ɪzsɛɫf . ðəsɛɫvz 7 ɪmsɛɫf . ðəsɛɫvz

23 Mon 1–3 ɪzsɛɫf . əmsɛɫvz 4 ɪʂɛlf . ðɛ·sɛlvz 5 ɪmsɛlf [pref.], ɪẓsɛlf . ðɛ:sɛlvz 6 ɪmsɛɫf . ðɛəʳʂɛɫvz 7 n.a.

24 Gl 1–2 ɪzsɛɫf . ðəʳ:ʂɛɫvz 3 əsɛɫf . ðəʳʂɛɫf 4 ɪmsɛɫf . ðɛɪəʳʂɛlvz 5 ɪzsɛɫf . ðəsɛɫvz 6 ɪzzɛɫf . ðəʳẓɛɫvz 7 ɪzsɛɫf . ðəzɛɫf

25 O 1 ɪzsɛɫf . ðəʳʂɛɫvz 2 ɪzsæɫf . ðəsæɫvz 3 ɪzsaɫf . əʳsaɫf 4 ɪmsɛɫf . ðəɽʂɛɫf [mɪsɛɫf[3]] 5 ɪzsæɫf . ðəʳʂæɫf 6 ɪzsɛɫf . ðəʳ:ʂɛɫf

IX.11.5 ENOUGH

Q. If you are fed up with all these questions, you might say to me: Stop, I've had . . . .

R. ENOUGH

Note 1—When rec. in the r., ON (=*of*) IT is reproduced below.
Note 2—For ENOUGH *adj.* and *adv.*, see III.8.4a (and refs.).

7 Ch 1 ənʊf 2 n.a. 3–5 ənʊf 6 ənʊf, ○ənᵒü:[3], ○~[3] [n.d.g.]

8 Db 1–2 ɪnʊf 3 ənʊf 4 ɪnʊf 5 ənʊf 6 ənʊf, ○~[1] 7 ənʊf

11 Sa 1 ənəf 2 ɪnʊf 3–4 ənʌf 5 ənʊf 6 ənʌf 7 ɪnʌf 8 ɪnʊf 9 ənʌf 10 ɪnʌf 11 ənʌf

12 St 1 ənʊf, ○~[1] 2 ənʊf 3 ənʊf ɒn‿t 4 ɪnʊf 5–6 ənʊf 7 ɛnʊf ɒn ɪt 8–9 ənʊf 10 ɛnʊf, ○ɪnʊf[3] 11 ɪnʊf

15 He 1–2 ənʌf 3 ənɑ:f 4 ənʌf 5 ənʊf, ○ɪnʌf[2] [n.d.g.] 6 ənʊf 7 ənʌf, ○~[1]

16 Wo 1 ɪnʊf, ○ənʊf[1] [n.d.g.] 2 i:nʊf 3–6 ənʊf 7 ənʊf, ○~[3,4], ○ənɑ:f[3]

17 Wa 1 ənʊf 2 ənʊf, ○nʊf[1] 3 ɪnʊf 4 ənʊf 5 ɪnʊf 6 ənʊf 7 ənʊf, ənɛʊ [used by i's grandfather, nat.]

23 Mon 1 ənʌf 2 ənəf, ○ənʊf[3] [n.d.g.] 3 ɪnʌf, ○~[1] [n.d.g.] 4 ənʌ̣̈f 5 ɪ̈nʌ̣̈f 6 ənʌf 7 n.a.

24 Gl 1–2 ənʊf 3 ənʌf 4 ənʊf 5 ənọf 6 ənəf, ○ɪnəf[2] [n.d.g.] 7 ənəf

25 O 1 ənʌf 2 ənʌf, ○~[3], ○ənʊf[2] [n.d.g.] 3 ənʌf ən ɪt 4 ənʊf, ○~ 5 ənʌf, nʌf 6 ənʌf

ERRATA AND ADDENDA

Volume II, Part I

p. 31 7 Lyonshall *For* June, 1962 *read* June, 1952
I.1.8 24.5 *Add* 6–7 k^{ɷ}u:-^{ɷ}u:s
I.3.13 24.5 *For* fɒɷəgɹaɪn^{2} *read* °fɒɷəgɹaɪn^{2}
I.4.1 17.4 *Add* 5–7 ɹak

Volume II, Part II

p. 344 line 4 f.b. *After* word *add* foɪ
p. 717 line 5 *For* III.10.7, 25.5 *read* III.10.7, 23.5

560 00324 2